A COLLECTION OF UPPER SOUTH CAROLINA

GENEALOGICAL and FAMILY RECORDS

Volume I

Editor:
   James E. Wooley

Please direct all correspondence and orders to:

www.southernhistoricalpress.com
or
SOUTHERN HISTORICAL PRESS, Inc.
PO BOX 1267
375 West Broad Street
Greenville, SC   29601
southernhistoricalpress@gmail.com

ISBN #0-89308-157-4

Printed in the United States of America

PREFACE

This is the first volume in a proposed series of titles on
Upper South Carolina genealogical and family records and it is
hoped that they will provide considerable source material for
those people who's research efforts have been stymied in that
area of Upper S.C. formerly known as Old 96 District.

These records are taken from the vast files of the late Pauline
Young of Liberty, S.C. , probably the most well-known genealogist
in Upper South Carolina. Her most widely known book "Abstracts of
Old Ninety-Six and Abbeville District, S.C." is still the "bible"
for people doing research in this area.

The files from which this volume is taken were given to the
Publisher in 1968 and they were loose sheets that filled some three
file cabinet drawers. At the same time an equal number, if not a
larger number, of similiar typed papers were sold to the Ladson
Library in Vidalia, Georgia. This private library has now been
given to the city of Vidalia and is probably the largest genealogical library in Georgia with the exception of the Georgia State
Department of Archives and History. Mr. John E. Ladson, Jr.'s
private collection of books numbering over 40,000 volumes.

Mr. James E. Wooley of Asheville, N.C. and his wife Vivian have
been doing personal genealogical research for thirty or more years
and in recent years came to be good friends with the Publisher.
As a result of the Publisher mentioning these records to Mr.
Wooley and asking if he would be interested in working on these
miscellaneous family papers from Miss Young's files, Mr. Wooley
agreed to see what he might do to make them available to the
public in book form.

Originally, we had hoped that we might be able to abstract and
condense these papers down from their original length. However,
the more involved he became the more Mr. Wooley realised that Miss
Young had already condensed them from the originals, so that in
effect there was little that could be done to shorten them.

In order to try and present as balanced a set of data and
records as possible, it was decided to provide more data on those
letters of the alphabet from which more surnames began,i.e., A,B,
C, J. M, S, W,etc. and for those letters like I, Q, O, Z, etc. to
include families beginning in letters similiar to these in another
volume. Hence, for instance, in this Volume I, the reader will
note that there are no headings for Surnames beginning with "I"
"Q" etc. and such names beginning in these and other letters will
appear in future volumes. Volume II will be out in mid-1980.

At some future date these private family files belonging to the
Publisher will be given to a repository for cataloging and for use
by the public. At this point it is not definite which Library will
benefit from these records, but most likely the new Ladson Memorial
Library in Vidalia, Georgia, so that the complete Pauline Young
collection can be available in one place.

October 1979
The Rev.Silas Emmett Lucas,Jr.
Publisher

ABBETTMETER

Deed from Mrs. Dorcas Abbettmeyer to F. Abbettmeyer her husband. Dated 30 Dec. 1856. For the sum of one dollar for 236 acres on negro fork of Coneross Creek. Adj. Joseph Gresham line, Joel Kelley land, Daniel Johnson line. Mrs. Dorcas Abbettmeyer was a Watkins before marriage. Wit: I. H. Ostendorff, Sr., N. Sullivan. Signed Dorcas Abbettmeyer seal. Attested before John H. Ostendorff, Mag. J.P. by I. H. Ostendorff, Sr. on 26 June 1857. Recorded 20 Oct. 1857. Ref. Vol. H-I, page 399. Pickens Co., S. C.

ABBOTT

Will of Solomon Abbott. Dated 24 Apr. 1854. Spartanburg Co., S.C. Item 1 Just debts be paid... 2. Son John has his share and to get no more... 3. Daughter Cyntha Dermet has had her share and gets no more... 4. Daughter Louisa Abbott wife of Norman Abbott and Raymoth Bishop wife of Alberry Bishop, and my clubfuted grand child of my daughter Cynthia by the name of Van. Each to get fifty dollars. 5. My faithful servant Prov who has been kind and faithful to me through life, she and her children are to be taken care of. 6. Other six children to share alike, Elizabeth wife of Sampson Soesbee, William Abbott, Agnes wife of Joseph Bankstone, the children of Eli Abbott, the children of Telletha Odem, Sarah wife of James Spencre. Executors, John Potter, James Turner, Wit: Geo. W. H. Legg, R. E. Cleveland, J. B. Archer. Signed Solomon X Abbott Seal. Solomon died in 1857 at age of 96 years, no probate given.

Will of John Abbott. Box 40. #448. Probate Judge Office, Pickens, S. C. Sell Eliza & Joaner two negro girls on a note to Jacob Scrodr for 500 dollars, and one mare, one yoke of oxen, one waggon and all other things not given by deed of gift to wife Sarah and Willier and Oliver Abbott. Rest of estate to be sold and divided between my children of the first wife, named are, Betsey An Dickerson, Polly An Gillison, William Abbott, Jane Hull, Lucenda Jenkins, Arey Phillips. Sons Simpson, John and G. W. are to get no more than I have given them. Make George Phillips Executor and to hold this will till I die... Wit: N. F. Perry, L. W. Allen, J. W. Earle, Signed John X Abbott.. seal. No probate date given. In 1858 Mary An Gillison is mentioned as the wife of Elijah Gillison.

Estate of William Abbott. Box 48. #527. Probate Judge Office. Pickens, S. C... Est. Admr. by James Abbott, J. B. McGufin, Alexander Bryce, Sr. who are bound unto W. J. Parson, Ord. in the sum of $400.00 5 July 1858. Heirs are: Julia the widow, John Mason & wife Elizabeth, Bird Abbott, Lewis Eaton & wife Mary, Jacob Abbott, Jr., Alexander Graham & wife Temperance, Mary M. Fountain, James Fountain, Willey Fountain, Willis W. Abbott, Jephthamg Abbott, L. Madison Crenshaw & wife Martha, L. Franklin Graham & wife Mary M., Lula Abbott, John & Sarah Dowis. Recd. shares 7 Aug. 1866 Arvilla Eveline Fountain of Walhalla, S. C. recd share. Julia the widow owned 150 acres adj. land of Foster Perry, Nathaniel Hull, Simpson Abbott, 7 others... 11 Aug. 1862 Noah Abbott of Cherokee Co., Ga. appointed George T. Broughs of Milton Co., Ga. as attorney to receive his share from his father William Abbott estate.

Capt. George W. Abbott. Box 32 #369. Probate Judge Office, Pickens, S. C. Est. Admr. 9 Oct. 1854 by William Dickson, John Gillison who are bound unto W. J. Parson, Ord. in the sum of $1200.00. On 4 Jan. 1858 paid widow Sarah C. Abbott gdn. of John S. Abbott & others $58.00.

Estate of Jacob D. Abbott. Box 36 $415. Probate Judge Office. Pickens, S. C. Est. Admr. 2 Feb. 1855 by Mary Abbott, John Adair who are bound unto Wm. J. Parson, Ord. in the sum of $2,000.00.

Jacob D. Abbott. Box 2 #52 Pickens Co., S. C. On 2 June 1856 Mary
Abbott and Leonard Towers were bound unto W. J. Parson Ordinary of
Pickens Co. in the sum of $65.00 Mary Abbott appointed guardian of
Jacob D. Abbott a minor under 21 years.

Solomon Abbott. Pension records, #17806. Bounty land warrent 15188-
160-55. Solomon Abbott to militia duty in Roebucks Reg. before and
after the fall of Charleston L22-0-0/L 32.11.5. On the 1 Oct. 1835
personally appeared Solomon Abbott a resident of Spartanburg Dist.,
S. C. age 74 last March. and states he entered service in Spt. Dist.
a few weeks after the battle at Kings Mountain as a private, he was in
several tures against the tories. He was born in North Carolina but
not certain what county. Have no record of his age, there was one in
possession of my brother who does not live near me. Again in 1835
on 27 April in Sptg. Dist. he applied this time he was 94 years old.

Willis W. Abbott, deed from Isaac Baldwin. Dated 17 Nov. 1853 in the
sum of 81 dollars paid by Willis Washington Abbott of Pickens Co. to
Isaac Baldwin of same county for 27 acres on middle fork of Martins
Creek and waters of Seneca River. Wit: D. A. Ledbetter, G. W. Dodd.
Signed Isaac (X) Baldwin seal. Attested before Wm. S. Woolbright
Mag. P.D. by D. A. Ledbetter on 7 Jan. 1854. Also on same date
Drucilla Baldwin wife of Isaac Baldwin renounse her dower to the land.
Recorded 25 May 1854.

Willis Abbott, deed to M. R. Hunnicut. Dated 18 Jan. 1854 for the sum
of 101 dollars paid by the said Milton R. Hunnicut for 27 acres on
Martins Creek and waters of Sececa River. Wit: G. W. Dodd, Tyre B.
Mauldin. Signed Willis Abbott, seal. Attested before Tyre B. Mauldin,
N.P. by G. W. Dodd dated 18 Jan. 1854. Same date Marie E. Abbott wife
of Willis Abbott relinquish her dower before Tyre B. Mauldin, N.P.
Recorded 23 May 1854.

Mathew Abbott to Temperance Abbott & Clementine Abbott. Dated 20 June
1851 for love and good will I do bear to my daughters for 171 acres
on the waters of Tamassa Creek of Little River. The land whereon I
now live. Wit: Wm. Rowland, I. D. Hembree. Signed Mathew Abbott seal.
Attested before John Knox, Mag. P.D. by William Rowland on 21 June 1851.

William Abbott deed from A. W. Sullivan Admnr. of the estate of William
Sullivan of the state of Georgia county of DeKalb. Dated 17 June 1828.
for the sum of 150 dollars paid unto Augustin W. Sullivan by William
Abbott for 140 acres on the West side of the North fork of Conaross
waters of Keowee River. Wit: Bird Abbott, Noah Abbott, Jacob (X)
Abbott. Signed Augustin W. Sullivan, seal. Attested before W. L.
Keith, C.C. by Jacob D. Abbott Dated 19 Oct. 1841. Recorded same date.

John Abbett to Sarah Abbett, Wilburn Abbett and Oliver Abbett. Dated
24 March 1856. For love affection I have for Sarah Abbett my wife and
Wilburn and Oliver Abbett my two sons, I give, grant convey the plantation and track of land I now live on, one negro named Hester, horses,
colts, cattle, hoggs and household furniture to have and hold the
said property and no more. The balance to be sold and devided between
my first wife children. Wit: G. W. Phillips, Lucinda Jenkins. Signed
John (X) Abbett, Senr. Attested before E. Hughs, M.P.D. by G. W.
Phillips on 19 Nov. 1856. Recorded 24 Nov. 1856.

Mary Abbett deed from J. A. Ballenger. Dated 25 March 1856. The sum of
260 dollars paid by Mary Abbett for all that track of land sold by
William Watson to John O. Grisham and from him to G. W. Phillips. Adj.
John Adair, J. O. Lewis, James McGriffin did live, containing 150 acres.
Wit. Simpson, J. O. L. Abbott. Signed James A. Ballinger, seal.
Attested before John Adair, M.P.D. by Simpson Abbett on 25 March 1856.
On same date Marie E. Ballinger the wife of James Ballinger renounce
and release her dower before John Adair, M.P.D.

Ida M. Abbott deed from Aaron Boggs, dated 30 June 1894. For the sum of
90 dollars paid by Ida M. Abbott for lots #15 & 16, also one hundred
feet square of land North of A. J. Boggs barn. Wit: J. W. Smith,

A. J. Boggs. Signed Aaron Boggs, seal. Attested before A. J. Boggs, N.P.S.C. Dated 30 June 1894. On same date Elmira L. Boggs wife of Aaron Boggs renounce and release her dower to the said land. Signed: A. J. Boggs, N.P.S.C. Recorded 2 July 1894.

Rev. Wilburn Abbett, born 1847 on bear swamp creek. Oconee Co. Died 1931 at his home near Coneross Church on the Westminister and Walhalla highway, Oconee Co. Buried at Coneross Church. The son of Capt. John Abbett and wife Sarah Doyle. Rev. Wilburn Abbott married Louiza Alexander who was born in 1851 and died in 1922. She was the daughter of James Alexander who died in Virginia during the war. She is buried in Conneross Church Cemetery. Their children are (1) James Sloan Abbett born 9 June 1871 married Mary Josephine Julian the daughter of Jerry M. Julian who was born 16 April 1842, died Nov. 1929 and his wife Martha A. Traynham who was born 30 Jan. 1847 and died 23 Jan. 1933. They lived in Dacusville, now in Pickens Co. Mary Josephine Julian Abbett was born 25 Oct. 1869. (2) John Wilburn Abbott, born 1873. Died Jan. 1953. Married Carry Wingo. (3) Simeon Doyle Abbett, born 1875, died 1904. (4) Lilly Burt Abbett born 1878, died 1904. Buried at Conneross Church. (5) Puumer Simpson Abbett, born 1880, buried at Seneca, S. C. Married Ethelfhen Cannon. (6) Sallie Abbott born 1882, married Ed. Cox. (7) Haskell Thomas Abbett born 1884. (8) Roy Marcus Abbett born 1886, lived at Seneca, S. C. (9) Annie Abbett, lived in Seneca, S.C. (10) Jay Milton Abbett lived at Liberty, S.C. (11) Burt Benjamin Abbett, married Londene Burgess. (12) Mertie a twin to Burt Benjamin. She married Sam Isbell.

William Abbott, inquest of his death. Pack 109 #1, Clerk of Court Pickens County, S.C. An inquest was held the 11 May 1858, concerning the dead body of William Abbott. Mr. N. J. F. Perry and Mr. James McGuffin stated to the jurors who had come to his tanyard on the 10th of May Instant were the first persons that saw the old man after the accident occurred. That as Mr. McGuffin started home he walked out with him some 2 or 3 hundred steps from the yard they saw the old man lying there but had no thought of him being dead untill they got up to him and that he was lying on his back with his walking stick in one hand and a hickory or riding switch in the other that there was no appearance or sign of his moving hand or feet, after he fell they saw some sign that the horse made as tho he had sprung forward for a jump or two that the little sack of cotton seed that the old man was riding on which he had been after to G. W. Phillips was lying some 15 or 20 steps from him. This was between 10 and 12 o'clock a.m. on the 10 Inst... The jury brought it out that William Abbott came to his death by the misfortune of falling off his horse, by which means the back part of the skull was fractured which caused his immediate death. The same occurred near the tanyard of N. J. F. Perry in Pickens Co., S.C. on the 10th Inst. between the hours of 10 and 12 a.m.

John Abbott will. Will book H, page 120-121, Probate Judge Office, Columbia, S.C. Dated 29 Jan. 1825. Wife Hannah my land and plantation during widowhood, also one mare and saddle, bed furniture and one cow. My three sons to get the land after death of wife or widowhood. Also furniture and cow, and horse or ox. Daughters Rachel bed furniture and cow., daughter Polley one bed, furniture and one cow, daughter Zely bed, furniture and one cow, daughter Hannah bed and furniture and one cow. Make my wife as sole Executrix and son Isaac to assist his mother. The sons are: Isaac, John and Jonathan. Wit: Obdiah (X) Wilson, James Thornhill, Isaac Abbott. Signed John (X) Abbott, seal. Filed 29 March 1825.

ABERCROMBIE

Clarinda Abercrombie, widow. An application under act of 1919 Class C #3 Post Office, Ceder Rock, Pickens County. States that she is the widow of Haynes Abercrombie who enlisted in Company C 1st. S.C. rifels, Captain Hamilton Boggs, on the 1st day of October 1861, and served in the command until captured Oct. 28, 1863 and in prison at

Indianpolis Feb. 1864 when he died. Clarinda Abercrombie states that
she was born 10th May 1838 and was married to Haynes Abercrombie the
10th May 1860. She resides at Deder Rock in Pickens Co. R. A. Bowen
of Company E Regiment 2 Rifels and W. T. Bowen of Company E 2 Rifels
states that the said Abercrombie was a private in Co., E Reg 2 S.C.
Rifels and that his wife has resided in the state all her life. That
she is 82 years of age. Sworn to before J. B. Newberry. Probate
Judge the 29 Sept. 1919. County Pension Board - Elias Day, Sr.,
S. H. Brown, B. J. Johnston.

ABNEY

Paul Abney, will. Box 2 Pack 33. Probate Judge Office, Edgefield,
S. C. I give to my son John Abney five negros namely, Juda, Sarah,
Mary, Ben and Sam. He is to pay his sisters 100 dollars each in twelve
months after receiving the negroes. Daughter Jane Barnes an equal
part, also one horse value at $80.00. Daughter Martha Patterson an
equal part, also her son Paul Abney Peterson to get one half of the track
of land on West end of the land I now live on. His parents to have use
of land until he is twenty one years old. Daughter Mary Baber?, equal
part. Daughter Tabitha Hicks an equal part, also one track of land on
the head of Tarsity Creek. Daughter Elizabeth Black, an equal part,
also the other half of the land I gave to Paul Abney Patterson. Make
John Chapman and John Abney Executors. Dated 24 Oct. 1819. Signed
Paul Abney, seal. Wit: John Chapman, Agatha Abney and Sophia Chapman.
Recorded Jan. 20, 1821.

John Abney in Equity 78 Edgefield County, S. C. filed 8 June 1819.
Heirs Dr. Charles O'Neal & wife Charlotte, Arthur Dillard & wife
Polly, Nathaniel Townsend & wife Eliza., Jacob P. Abney, Sarah, J. M.
Abney, Ann Abney, Susannah Spearman & Edmund Spearman, Joseph Reardin
& Nancy his wife, John Abney owned about two thousand acres of land.
Persons complaining aforesaid and Lark Abney, Henry M. Abney, Jonathan
Abney, Ira Abney. Land on Saluda River bordering on the lands of Zach
L. Brooks, Jno. Inlow, Azariah Abney, Sarah Carson, Crawford Perry.

John Abney, in Equity 155. Edgefield Co., S.C. dated 6 Sept. 1819.
Dr. Chas. O'Neal and wife Charlotte late Abney that Jno. Abney decd.
devised to Lark Abney and Arthur Dillard his Exors. in trust for Char.
O'Neal a track of land on which Dr. O'Neal then lived containing 319
acres on Saluda River. Bounded by land of Wm. Abney, decd. and Jas.
Summers on West by Urban Nicholasons and Wm. Abney land.

Martha Abney in Equity 273. Edgefield Co., S. C. Dated 16 May 1825.
Jno. Chapman & wife Sophia, Wm. Griffin and wife Polly, that the mother
of your oratirx Sophia and Polly, Martha Abney, formerly Martha Willy?
at the time of her intermarriage with their father Jno. Abney, she
owned 300 acres of land she inherited from her father Mathew Wells or
Wills? Martha Abney died in 1817 leaving a husband Jno. Abney and children, Sophia wife of Jno. Chapman, Polly wife of Wm. Griffin, Nancy
Abney, Ellen Abney, Mathew Abney and Daniel Abney. Nancy and Wm. Died
after Martha under 21 years. After her death Jno. Abney married
Martha Griffin by whom he had two children Joseph and John Abney.

Maston Abney Estate. Adm. Feb. 5, 1838 by Wm. Abney No 1-18 Edgefield
Co. Ordered that Simon Abney Adr. of Maston Abney dec'd. do sell at
the house of Wm. Abney on Fri 27th inst. the estate of said decd. sale
made 27 Feb. 1835. Buyers are Jas. Maynard, Lewis Sample, Simeon Abney,
Benj. Nicholason, David Payn, Wm. Abney, W. T. Abney, Wm. Scurry,
Jesseeh Laney, Edw. Clark, Sampson Cristy, Hazle Culbreath, Jno. Brown,
Samul Scum, Cadaway Clark, Thos. Christian, Saml. Deloach, Walter W.
Brown, Sineondean, Benj. Grigsby, Larkin Carter, Jno. H. Allen, Benj.
Broadaway, Wm. Harman. Sophia S. Abney the wife of Simeon Abney the
Adm. Est adr. Nov. 9, 1836 by Wm. Abney, Calbe H. Lindsey Anwd. Burnham
in the sum of $3,512.00.

Simeon Abney, Est. adr. Mar. 15, 1837 by And. Burnham, Abdalom T. Abney, Thos. Scurry, Jr. 10 Dec. 1836 pd. Hiram Abney acct. for W. T. Abney $9.25. Jno. Jones married the widow. Ment. Nov. 12, 1839 on Jan. 7, 1839 Pd. Peter Black for Sophia Jones $100.00 cit. pub. at Sister Springs Church Feb. 20, 1836, also cit. pub. before a congregation at Chestnut Bridge Mar. 11, 1837.

ACKER

Peter Acker. A petition for the administration of the estate of Peter Acker in box 1 no. 10 Anderson County, S.C. The petition was signed on 5 March 1821 by Susanna & Halbert Acker before John Harris, O.P.D. Said petition was given on 27 March 1821. The estate was appraised by William Harper, Aaron Broyles, Wm. Smith, the estate was appraised for $6,922.75. A sale was to be held on 15 Aug. 1821. In pack 575 Probate Judge of Greenville, S.C. Estate of Peter Acker, Heirs, to Susannah Acker (widow) Holbert Acker, Alexander Acker, William Mattison and Elizabeth his wife, Joel M. Townsend and Mary his wife, Allen McDavid and Teresa his wife, Jesse McGee and Lucinda his wife, Peter Acker, Joel M. Acker, Joshua S. Acker and the heirs at law of Frances Hammond decd. legal heirs and representatives of Peter Acker decd. who died intestate.

ADAMS

David Adams. A deed from David Adams to James Tuttle, Jr. Book A, page 124 Elbert Co., Ga. Dated 13 Jan. 1793, recd. 31 Jan. 1793. For ten pds. sterling for 36 acres of land on the North fork of Broad River, adj. Dudley line and Tuttle line. Wit: John Fergus. Signed David Adams. Seal.

James Adams. A deed from Archer Bentson and James Adams, Admr. of the estate of David Adams decd. to George Grissell all of Elbert Co., Ga. Dated 5 Oct. 1801. For $220 a track of land of 100 acres on Waihatchie Creek. Adj. Benjamin Cook, Thomas Benton and H. Moore. Wit: Adam Gaer, Nathl. P. Black, D. Hudson, J.P. Signed: Arche Benton and James Adams. seals. Reg. 5 Oct. 1801.

Jasper Adams. Box 11, No. 149 Probate Judge Office, Pickens Co., estate admr. Sept. 19, 1843 by Placidia F. M. Adams and Samuel Magrant who are bound unto James H. Dendy Ord. of Pickens Co. in the sum of $25,000. Citation published at St. Paul, at Pendleton. Placidia Adams is the widow. Expend: Expences of Ann R. Adams for 1846. Cash paid by Mrs. Benthan to her while in Charleston for clothing, pocket money 7 music teacher and hire of piano while in Charleston. Pd. Mrs. Benthan acct. $42.50. Elizabeth, Caroline, Joseph M., Fanny Adams were also mentioned.

Jasper Adams minors children, Box L, #1 Probate Judge office, Pickens Co. On Jan. 18, 1847 Placidia Adams, Samuel Magrant, F. M. Adams were bound unto Miles M. Norton Commissioner in Equity in the sum of $6,000. Whereas in Dec. 1846 Placidia Adams was appointed guardian of her children, Ann R. Adams, Elizabeth A. P. Adams, Carolina C. W. Adams minors under 21 years of Pickins Co. Also appointed guardian of Joseph A. Adams, Fanny C., B. Adams minors under 14 years. they were the children of Jasper Adams decd.

Jeter Adams. Pack 59 Equity, Clerk of Court Office, Pickens Co. (Basement) To the honors the Chancellors of said state. Humbly complaining your orator Frances M. Adams sheweth unto your honors that his father the late Jasper Adams departed this life intestate in Oct. 1841 being at the time of his death seized and possessed of certain estate real and personal subject to distribution amongst his heirs at law to wit, the widow of said decd. Mrs. Placidia Adams being entitled to one third part thereof and six children, your orator being one son

of a former marriage and the remaining five being children of the
latter marriage and all minors to wit: Ann R. Adams, Elizabeth A. P.
Adams, Carolina C. W. Adams, Joseph A. Adams and Fanny C. B. Adams
the last named two being under the age of 12 years and the former over
that age. That the real estate consists of a tract of land situated
in Pickens Dist. on waters of 18 miles Creek containing 215 acres more
or less being the place known as "The Woodlandd" whereon the said decd
resided at the time of his death and formerly owned by William Carter.
That the said tract of land is manifestly incapable of being distributed
by assigning to each their share its principal value consistion in the
costly buildings erected and used as a manison house and the apperten-
ances. Your orator further shews that the personality consists mainly
of choses in action being invested in stock, bonds for money at interest and cash in the hands of a factor. That there was however other
personal estate consisting of a few slaves, household and other furniture, with plantation implements, carriages & stock of horses, etc.
That sometime after the death of said Jasper Adams letter of Admr. were
granted to the said Placidia Adams who has since taken upon herself the
burden of Admr. The slaves Gabriel and Betsy were conveyed by deed of
Trust for the separate use of Pacidia Adams by one Samuel Magrant
Filed 22 May 1844. (This letter to Col. Miles M. Norton. Pickens
Courthouse The plantation called "Woodland" was near Pendleton, S. C.
There is another letter to Mr. M. M. Norton from Placidia Adams with
regard to the guardianship to her children.)

Jacob Adams. Inquest of Jacob Adams, Pack 109 #2, Clerk of Court
office, Pickens Co., S.C. On March 24, 1841 Nathan Boon Coroner of
Pickens Dist. was called to the home of the widow Adams to view the
dead body of Jacob Adams who stated that Jacob Adams on 23 Mar. 1841 was
found dead on the road in Pickens Dist. and that he had no marks of
violence upon him and the jury brought it out that he died by the visitation of God in a natural way. James Oliver stated that he was
walking down the road and saw Jacob Adams lying by the side of the
road and thought something was wrong with him and he went and told Mr.
McKee. Thomas J. McKee said that Mr. Oliver told him he had better
go and help Jacob Adams to the house. He went with Mary Adams to the
place and found Mr. Adams lying dead. He said he was well in the
morning of March the 23 the same day that he was found dead and that
he ate his breakfast. Mary Adams stated that she went with Mr. McKee
and that Mr. Adams was lying dead, that he was not very well and that
he had the Palsey.

Priestly Adams. Inquest of Priestly Adams, Pack 109 #3, Clerk of Court
Pickens Co. An inquest was held at the house of Claibourn P. Pools in
Pickens Dist. on the 16th Aug. 1855 before E. Hughes a Magistrate
acting as a coronor for said Dist. to view the body of Priestly Adams
of Habersham Co., Ga. who came to his death on the 15th Aug. of this
Inst. On the highway near C. P. Pools in Pickens Dist. by an act of
Providence by a stroke of lighting.

J. J. Adams. Confederate pension records of J. J. Adams of Murphey,
Pickens County, S. C. States that he enlisted in Company D 1st Reg.
of State troops under Capt. Grice, on the 14th Sept. 1864 and served
in that command until 15th Apr. 1865. I was discharged from the ser-
vice at Spartanburg on 15th Apr. 1865 and was at that time a member of
Company D 1st Reg. of S. C. Rifles. I was born on the 17th Feb. 1849.
I reside at Murphey in Pickens Co. I recd no bodily injury while in
service. Sworn to before J. B. Newberry, Probate Judge. 22 Jan. 1921.
R. E. Parrott of Company D. Reg. of S. C. Troops and W. P. Davis of
Company D. Reg. S. C. Troops states that they know the said J. J. Adams.

Sarah A. Adams. Application of Sarah A. Adams widow, Easley, Rt. 2,
Pickens Co., S. C. That she is the widow of P. L. Adams who enlisted
in Company F. Reg. of 24 S.C. Battalion of Inft. Under Capt. B. F.
Hill in the year 1862. He was discharged from the service at Murphys-
boro, N. C. in 1865 and was at that time a member of Company F Reg. of
24 S. C. Battalion of Inft. under Capt. Hill. I was born 7 July 1843
and was married to P. L. Adams the 14th Sept. 1870. My husband died
on the 25th June 1906. Sworn to before John J. Prince, N.P.S.C. the

8 Oct. 1919. J. O. McAdams of Company F. Reg. 24 S. C. Inft. and
A. W. McKee of Company F. Reg. 24 S. C. Inft. states that they knew
the said P. L. Adams.

John Adams. A deed from James Hughey to John Adams, Pack 381 Titles for
land Clerk of Court Office, Abbeville, S. C. Dated ⌐ Sept. 1835. In
the sum of $300 dollars paid by John Adams for 105 3/4 acres lying on
a branch of Norrises Creek and waters of Long Cain. Adj. Isaac Miller,
Hugh Armstrong. Being part of a tract purchased from John Stewart and
Christian Barnes. Wit: Luke Mathis, Saml. L. Hill. Signed James
Hughey, seal. Attested by Saml. L. Hill, before Jas. Forster, J.P.
9 Oct. 1838. Recorded 26 June 1839.

John Adams. A deed from Emry Vann to John Adams, Pack 381 Deeds, Clerk
of Court Office, Abbeville, S.C. Dated 22 Jan. 1841. In the sum of
$100 for 26 acres lying on a branch of Norrises Creek waters of Long
Cane. Adj. Emry Vann and Adams own land. Wit: Alex Stevenson, Thos.
Hinton. Signed Emry Vann, seal. Attested to by Thos. Hinton before
Saml. L. Hill, J.Q. Dated 22 Jan. 1841. no recorded date.

John Adams. Estate of John Adams, Pack 267, Clerk of Court Office,
Abbeville, S. C. In Equity to the Honorable the Chancellors of the
State. That on the third day of August 1858, John Adams departed this
life intestate seized and possessed at the time of his death with two
tracts of land lying and being in the Dist of Abbeville to wit, the
Long Cane tract containing two hundred acres more or less, bounded by
land of Robert H. Wardlaw, James M. Perrin and Dr. W. W. Marshall. The
other tract where the said John Adams lived containing twelve or thirteen hundred acres both on waters of Long Cane Creek. The large
tract bounded by land of Thomas E. Owen, The Estate of Charles Dendy,
Absaloem L. Gray, Enoch Nelson and others. That the said John Adams
leaving children and grandchildren to wit: Susan the wife of Hughey,
Edney the wife of John Hinten, Elizabeth the wife of Thomas Kirkpatrick, John J. Adams, Samuel Adams, Edward Adams and Franklin Adams,
Saml. S. Tolbert a minor of about five years old the only child of Sarah
Ann Tolbert the wife of Franklin Tolbert who died before her father and
William Adams who died after the death of his father leaving three
children Samuel Adams, Annie Adams, Masen Adams. All of whom were
minor of tender age. The administration of the goods and chattels was
granted by William Hill ordinary of Abbeville District on the ___ day
of Aug. 1858 to William Adams and James H. Cobb of whom James H. Cobb
is the surviving administrator. The personal estate has been sold as
the court so ordered, with the notes due the estate amounted to more
than thirty thousand dollars, the indebtedness is very small and
inconsiderable. "Your orator Samuel Adams sheweth unto your Honors
that Thomas Kirkpatrick, the husband of your orators sister the said
Elizabeth Kirkpatrick is adicted to the unfortunate habit of intem-
perance that he is a very bad manger. That the property of a former
wife and all of his own was sold for the payment of his debts. Your
orator therefore, desires and prays this Honorable Court to order a
settlement of the distributive share of his sister Elizabeth Kirkpatrick in her fathers estate real and personal, to be separated and
sold use of his sister during her life and at her death to be equally
divided amongest her children by a former marriage. She having no
children and no prospect of any by her present husband the said
Thomas Kirkpatrick. And as in duty bound your orators and oratrixes
will ever pray. etc. etc. Filed 1 Dec. 1859." In the pack John Adams
is said to reside in Proidence P. O. Columbia Co. Florida. In Oct.
1858 Samuel Adams resides in Greenville, S. C. Edward Adams lives in
Oadville, Texas.

Stephens Adams. A deed from Stephens Adams to Allen Keith. Pack 405
#5 Clerk of Court office, Pickens Co. We Stephens Adams & Patience
Adams his wife both of Pendleton Dist. Dated 25 Nov. 1823. Sum of
$900.00 for 300 acres on Adams Creek and Reighleys line, Wm. Hood line,
land being part of two grants, one to John Adams Sen. the other to
James Jett. Wit: Wm. L. Keith, William Sadler. Signed Stephen Adams
& Patience (X) Adams, Seals. Attested to by Wm. L. Keith before
James Southerland, J.Q.P.D. on 25 Oct. 1824.

Lydia Adamson. The Will and Estate of Lydia Adamson. Box 3, pack 48
Probate Judge Office, Abbeville Dist., S. C. I Lydia Adamson afflicted
in body but sound mind and memory etc. etc. Pay my just debts and
funeral expense. I will to my daughter Peggy the wife of John Argo
two dollars. I will to my other three children viz. Jonathan Adamson,
Sally Adamson and Harriet Adamson, the remaining of my property whatsoever. If they can't agree on the division they are to get three others
and make the division and divide imparshally. Lastly I do appoint my
beloved son Jonathan to be executor. Witness my hand and seal 6 June
1819. Wits: Saml. Perrin & James Thompson. Signed Lydia Adamson,
seal. Probated Abbeville Dist. by Moses Taggart, Ord. Personally
came Samuam Perrin, Esq. and swore he saw Lydia Adamson, decd. sign,
seal and execute the within will, also saw James Thompson sign the
same before me Moses Taggart, OAD. this 5 Feb. 1827. The estate was
appraised on 26 Feb. 1827 a list is hwon about half way through the
list is the "The following is considered the property belonging to the
estate of James Adamson, decd. The other list is shown. Signed W. M.
Chiles, Jas. Wiley, Thos. W. Chilse.

James Adams. Will and probate of James Adams estate, Box 105, Pack
2565 Probate Judge office, Abbeville, S. C. (Ninety Six Dist.) I
James Adams being in perfect mind and memory. Pay all just debts,
give unto loving wife Sarah during her natural life the use of all my
estate. Sons Thoms. and Drury to divide the land on Horns Creek. To
son Littlebury all that land between Rambo's and the first branch on the
East side and one negro named Rogers. Son Benjamin to land on West
side of Rambo's also one negro named Isaac. Daughters Sarah, Elizabeth
and Rachel to get one negro each. The children and grandchildren of
James dec. John, Mary, Thomas, Drury and Rebecka are to get two
negroes. Make son Drury, executor and wife Sarah exectrick. As
witness my hand and seal 14 Oct. 1781. Wits: John Herndon, John
Goldin, Benjamin (X) Moseley, Hannah (X) Moseley. Signed: James (X)
Adams. Benjamin Moseley made oath that he saw James Adams sign, seal
and execute his last will before John Ewing Calhoun Esq. Ord. 26 Apr.
1782. John E. Calhoun, Esq. Ord. Ninety Six Dist. appointed Nichael
Burkhalter, John Martin, Lewis Tilman as appraiser of James Adams
estate. 26 Apr. 1782. Same was returned on 14 May 1782. Total amount
₺ 3708-15-0.

Benjamin Adams. Will and Estate of Benjamin Adams. Box 1 Pack 2
Probate Judge Office, Abbeville, S. C. I Benjamin Adams being in sound
mind and perfect memory etc. I give to my beloved wife Mary Adams
four negroes, one choice horse, one bed and furniture. I give unto my
daughter Lusy Wilson four negroes, named. I give my son Benjamin
Adams two negroes, named. "I consider I have given to my children by
my first wife as much property in cash, as I have for the maintainance
and schooling the five children by my last wife Mary and to give them
an equal share with those by my first wife." The five sons are:
James Adams, Hezekiahiah Adams, Gideon Adams, Nathaniel Adams, Irmsey
Adams. The sons are to get twenty three negroes, named. All land,
crops, stock, tools, household and kitchen furniture to be divided
between them and wife Mary. She is to get support with the children
until they are twenty one or that she marries, then her share to be
cut off. Make friend Patrick Noble and Alexder Hamilton Esqrs.
Executors and wife Mary Executrix. I set my hand and seal this 10 Jan.
1826. Wit: E. Lomax & Amos Edwards. Signed Benjn. Adams. This will
was probated on 17 Feb. 1826. John D. Adams, James Weems, Donald
Douglass, David Thomas, Morris P. Holloway and Mary Adams who are
bounded unto Moses Taggart, Ord. Abbeville Dist. in the sum of
$50,000.00. On May 8, 1828 Henry Gray was bound also with the others.
On May 8, 1828 John D. Adams made an account of money received by the
estate (date and amount omitted) John Wright, Francis Cooper, John
McCcely, John Thompson, Michael Peaster, Samuel Thompson, Andrew
Davidson, Timothy Hughs, John Downy, George B. Judd, Robert C. Willson,
James Cethea, James Stephenson, Peter Lomax, John Youngblood, Hunter
Simpson, Alexander Simpson, William Lomax, Nathaniel Lanear, Wilkins
Holloway, Stephens Williams, Michael Peast, Joseph Norrell, Lewis
Lomax, Mathew Burt, Malon Morgan and John Wright. Cash paid out as
James Lomax Co., James Wardlaw, Watt & Bowie, John H. Williams, Henry

Gray, David Brackenridge and William Lomax. On 6 Sept. 1830 Judge
Moses Taggart cited Jessee Adams, John D. Adams, Joseph Norrell and
Mary his wife and Robert C. Wilson to appear on Sept. 16, 1830 to show
why the estate couldn't be settled.

ADAIR

John Adair. Estate of John Adair decd. Box 2 Pack 30 Probate Judge
Office, Abbeville, S. C. Sarah Adair, James Adair, Joseph Adair and
James Montgomery are bound unto John Thomas, Esq. Ord. Ninety Six Dist.
in the sum of one thousand pds. sterling as admr. of John Adair estate.
Judge Thomas appointed Thomas Ewing, James Gragg, Benjamin Adair as
appraisers of the estate on the 9 June 1784. Sale held on 30 July
1782. Those who bought were: Sarah Adair, Thomas Hues, John Adair,
Benjamin Adair, James Dillard, John McCreary, John Jones, John McDowel,
Samuel Ewing, William Price, James Miller.

ADDIS

William Addis. Box 30 #356 Probate Judge Office, Pickens Co., S. C.
June 1, 1849 William Addis owned 100 acres more or less on Beaverdam
Creek Adj. land of C. Hunt, William Grant & other. Widow Mary Addis,
John Sanders was Guardian of Sarah Elizabeth Addis and Lydia Adaline
Addis, minors under 12 years. David Addis a minor over 14 years and
William Madison Addis under the age of 14 years. Heirs: Samuel Addis,
Pinckney Mason and Elizabeth his wife, John Thomas and Sarah his wife,
Thomas Smith and Nancy C. his wife, William Addis, Mary Addis, George
W. Fuller and Jane his wife are out of State and the children of James
Addis decd. Real Estate Book A, page 108 Probate Judge Office,
Pickens Co. Samuel Addis Petition to W. D. Steel, O.P.D. for sale or
division of the real estate of William Addis decd. Alexander Bryce and
Robt. Fullerton were to appraise the land by 2 Apr. 1849. The sheriff
is to sell the land on first Monday in July next to the high bidder.

Samuel Addis. The will of Samuel Addix, Box 53 #586 Probate Judge
Office, Pickens, S. C. I Samuel Addis being in feeble health but sound
mind etc. First i appoint H. R. Gaston to be my sole executor.
Second to my son William John Addis a tract of land West of my land
of 150 acres more or less adj. G. W. Phillips, Robert Stuckey and
others, also one good horse, saddle and bridle. Third the balance of
my personal and real estate to my beloved wife Eunice Addis for her
natural life or widowhood. Then to be divided between Eliza Addis,
Susan Addis, Anne T. Addis and my son William each to have one bed, one
cow and calf, one spinning wheel and cards, one chest and one hog.
The other things to be sold and divided between my other children
Miriam Milford, Lucinda Clinkscales, Hester E. Cole, Harrett M. Brown.
Wit. E. L. Ballinger, W. D. Ballenger and N. Brown. Signed: Samuel
Addis, seal. Will proven Apr. 27, 1860. Recorded Will book #1, page
277-278.

AGNEW

Anadrew Agnew. Estate of Anadrew Agnew, Box 1 Pack 9 Probate Judge
Office, Abbeville. The estate of Andrew Agnew was probated 6 Nov. 1837
by Samuel Agnew, Senr. James B. Richey and John Miller who are bound
unto Moses Taggart, Ord. Abbeville Dist. in the sum of $10,000.00.
The same day three appraisors named they are James Turner, R. C. Sharp,
and James Burton. There is about two pages of the sale that was held
on Nov. 28, 1838. The last returns made Samuel Agnew Admr. was on
Nov. 7, 1842. Paid William Agnew $187.26 and Jaoeph Agnew $187.26.
signed Samuel Agnew.

Dr. Enoch Agnew. Deed of Dr. Enoch Agnew from Jno. T. Johnson, dated
20 Dec. 1860. Sum of one thousand four hundred ten dollars and 63 cents

for a parcel of land containing forty one acres adj. Marshall Sharp,
H. Y. Gilliam and G. B. Riley. Wit: Maeshal Sharp, Wesley Robertson,
Signed Jno. T. Johnson, seal.

Dr. Enoch Agnew. Estate of Dr. Enoch Agnew, No. 17 Clerk of Court
Office, Abbeville. To the Honorable the Chancellors of said State.
Your Honors your oratrix Ellie H. Agnew, that her husband Dr. Enoch
Agnew departed this life on the day of __ in the year of our Lord 1863,
with a tract of land on New Bridge Road, bounded by Marshal Sharp,
Green Riley and others. Containing 41 acres having been the residence
of the deceased who died intestate and leaving as his heirs and distributees your oratrix his widow and his children. Mary Ann Agnew,
Jennie Agnew, James Beauford Agnew and Ada Elisa Agnew, all of whom
are minors. Your oratrix desirix partition of the above real estate
and her share thereof be assigned to her according to the practice of
this Court. Filed 10 Oct. 1863.

ALBERTSON

Samuel Albertson Sr. Box 89 #940 Pickens Co., S. C. On May 7, 1866
Samuel owned 120 acres on Fidlers Creek waters of Little River, adj.
A. B. Grant, Wm. Whitmire and others, also 160 acres on Little River
adj. Wm. Whitmire, Philip Sneed. Heirs: Cyntha Albertson widow.
Heirs of Elizabeth Cox decd. J. C. Albertson & Saml. Cox. Julia A.
Stephens, Elias F. Albertson, F. M. Durham and wife Sarah C. Elizabeth
E. Albertson, heirs of J. D. Albertson decd. his widow Catherine &
children viz. Lucinda J., Rachel M., Sarah E. and Mary Albertson.
Joel R. Buckheister and wife Nancy. J. B. Smith and wife Malinda.
Saml. Albertson out of State.

Jacob Albertson. Pack 174 #4, Clerk Office, Pickens Co., S. C. In
Jan. 1874 Jacob Albertson did rape Sally Graham in Pickens Co. Sarah
Graham sworn saus. On Wednesday morning Jan. 14, last she went out
of the house towards the brick yard and when she got there, she found
Jacob Albertson there and he told her that he wanted her to go with
him and he would take her to see her folks and that her brother James
was there waiting for her, she refused to go, but Jacob told her she
must go, for her brother was there waiting for her. When she got to
where he said her brother was and did not find him, she then tried to
go back, but Jacob would not let her go, he then carried her thru a
large field, he asked her to ly down for him, she refused then he took
hold of her and threw her down, pulled up her clothes, held her fast
with one hand and did commit a rape upon her. He then let her up and
went about 200 yards then he threw her down the second time and
ravished her again. They went a few miles together, Jacob making her
walk before him. He quarreled with her all the time because she would
not give her consent for him to be with her again. He then left her
and said she had better not tell on him, she told him that her pap
would make him pay, for what he was doing to her and Jacob said he was
going to Anderson. Sallie Graham was the daughter of Charles Graham.

ALDRIDGE - AULDRIG

Benjamin Aldridge. Estate of Benjamin Aldridge, Box 1 #9 Probate
Judge Office Anderson, We Rebekah Auldrig, Jonathan Vandivor and
Hollansworth Vandivor are bound unto John Harris Esq. Ord. in the sum
of $1,000. Rebekah Auldrig is administratrix of the estate of Benja-
min Auldrig decd. She is to make a true and perfect inventory of all
goods, chattels and credits and exhibit it unto said Court. This
bond and obligation was made 5 July 1800. The inventory was made by
Wm. Miller, Leonard Saylors, John Shirly. No given here.

ALEXANDER

John Alexander. Wil of John Alexander. Vol. 1, page 12. Probate Judge Office, Charleston, S. C. (As written) In ye name of God I John Alexander of ye province of Carolina Mercht. Considering of ye certainty of death and ye uncertainty of ye time of my death do make this my last will and testament. first I commend my Soul to ye Mercy of God ye gave it and my body I commit to ye Earth to be buried in such place and with such charges as my Execut. shall think fit and for ye wordly estate which God hath blessed me with I dispose of ye same in manner and form following vizt. Imp. I do give and bequeath to ye ministery of ye Church at Charles Town commonly called ye Presbyterian Church ye sum of fifty pounds to be delivered unto and left at ye discretion and management of John Jones gunsmity and robert ffenwick Item I give and bequeath unto Avid Adams liveing in Charles Town widdo. Then pounds sterling Item I give and bequeath unto ye rt honable Joseph Blake and George Logan Esq. Executrs ten pounds each to buy them selves Mourning Item I do give, grant, devise and bequeath to my beloved wife Ann Alexander one full moiety or half part of all and singular my real and personal estate whatsoever not already by this will bequeathed have and to hold ye sd full moiety and half part of my sd real and personal estate in whatsoever part of ye world ye same is or shall be unto my sd wife Ann Alexander her heirs and assignes for ever Item I do give grant devise and bequeath to my beloved daughter Ann Alexander ye other full moiety or half part of all and singular my real and personal estate whosoever not already by this will bequeathed to have and to hold ye said other full moiety or half part of my sd real and personal estate in whatsoever part of ye wordly ye same is or shall be unto my sd daughter Ann Alexander her heirs and assignes for ever. Item my will is yt in case my sd daughter Ann should happen to dye before she come of age yn I give, grant, devise and bequeath, ye moiety or half part of my real and personal estate, by this will bequeathed unto my sd Ann unto my beloved wife Ann Alexander. Item also my will is yt in case my beloved wife Ann Alexander should happen to dye now yt yn I give, grant, devise and bequeath my whole estate real and personal by this will bequeathed unto my sd wife Ann Alexander and daughter Ann Alexander unto my loveing brother Robert Alexander hie heirs and assignes for ever Lastly I do make and ordain my sd wife Ann and friends yert honoable Joseph Blake and George Logan to be Executrs of this my last will and testamt. requireing my sd executrix and Executors to see ye same performed and I utterly revoke all former wills and tastamts. by me heretofore made and declared in witness whereof I have hereunto sett my hand and seal this twentieth and sixt day of September in ye year of our Lord one thousand Six hundred Ninety and Nine. Signed Sealed and declared in the presence of us. Abraham Eve, John Cock Senior, William Sadler, John Cock Junior. John Alexander (Seal) Proven Jan. 15, 1699.

James Alexander. Will of James Alexander. Apt 1 File 16 Probate Judge Office, Greenville, S. C. I James Alexander being in sound mind and memory, ect. ect. Item 1, I give and bequeath to my beloved wife Mary or Polly Alexander, the tract of land I now live on, beginning at the mouth of Spring Branch, right fork to Henry Ceeley's line, to John Watson land, and thence to William C. Gunnels' land to Jabez Terry's land. Also one negro man named Tom and two negroes women named Kate and Fanny. Also farming utensils household and kitchen furniture. Item 2, I give and bequeath unto my daughter Racheal one negro named Matilda, one horse with saddle and bridle, three cows and calves with other household and kitchen furniture. Item 3, I give and bequeath to my four daughters viz: Rachael, Nancy Anderson, Harriet Baker and Jane Caroline Ceeley four negroes named ect. ect. Item 4, I give and bequeath unto my son Robert two children viz; Matilda Johnson and George Alexander two hundred dollars each. Item 5, I give and bequeath to my son James Alexander the tract of land he now lives on. Item 6, I give and bequeath to my son-in-law Alexander Thompson and his six children Viz; Joseph, James, Jane M. Peden, John, Mary and William Thompson. Six hundred dollars to be devided between them and ten acres of land. Item 7 and 8 is how his wife property is to be devided after her death. Item 9, Sell the tract of land on the North

side of Spring Branch at public sale to pay all expences and devide as
I have directed. Item 10 I do hereby appoint my son-in-laws John W.
Baker and John Anderson to be my executors. Dated 17 April 1839.
Wit; Jabez Terry, James Adams, James Dunbar. Signed James Alexander,
seal. (Probated July 12, 1839)

Daniel Alexander. Will. Box 31 #361 Pickens Co., S.C. I Daniel D.
Alexander of Cheohee, Pickens Co. being in sound mind and memory ect.
ect. The wife is to keep the estate and sell only enough to pay all
lawfull debts. Her to send my minor children to school as much as the
older ones. There are four minor boys, Jacob, Jourdan, Elias Franklin,
James. There are three girls named, Artia Malissa, Elizabeth,
Nancy Ann. If wife should marry or die the boys is to devide the land
and the girls the personal property. I appoint my son Isaac and my
wife my Executors and executrix. Dated 11 June 1853. Signed D. D.
Alexander. Wit: L. N. Robins, Nathan Lusk and William Whitmire.

    Codicil on Daniel Alexander Will. Same date as will 11 June 1853,
son Micajah to get one hundred dollars, sons David and Isaac has their
share already in the price they paid for their land. Wit: L. J.
Robins, L. J. Johnson, Micajah Alexander. Signed D. D. Alexander.
(Proven 5 Dec. 1853)

Thomas Alexander. Box 39 #438 Pickens Co. On Dec. 7, 1857 James S.
Alexander an heir of Thomas Alexander decd. petition the court to sell
the real estate of Thomas Alexander decd. lying on Conneross Creek
adj. land of Wm. Adair, N. F. J. Perry, and others containing 290
acres. Heirs are, Jane Alexander, Widow, Wm. Deaton and wife Eleanor,
Andrew Alexander, James S. Alexander, Memory Alexander, Elijah Deaton
and wife Mary, John H. Alexander, Alfred Adair and wife Loocy, Isaac N.
Alexander, Martha and Joseph Alexander.

Susan Alexander. Box 41 #460 Pickens Co. Estate Admr. 24 July 1856 by
Miles M. Norton, Joseph J. Norton, Levena & E. E. Alexander. On 15
July 1861 paid S. P. Bruce, James T. Steel, P. M. Alexander, Julia A.
Alexander, Vinetta J. Alexander, Mrs. L. Alexander each recd $111.28.

Thomas Alexander. Will, Box 41 #462 Pickens Co. Being in sound mind
but weak in body ect.ect. First, I give and bequeath to my wife the
Wm. Murphree place, she is to pay the balance from my estate, when she
dies the part I paid is to be my children. 2rd. She is to have her
support from my place for one year only, 3rd to take all with her she
fetch with her as here one and is not to have any part of my estate
that I had before I mared her Mary Murphree. 4th. I give to my daughter
Deanah Alexander the place I now live on, to have full power and if
she mared or die its to be sold and devided between my lawfull children
ect. ect. I appoint Daniel Alexander, Joshua Holden, and William Hurd
my executors. Dated 29 Sept. 1856. Wit: Robert Sterwrt Esq., W. G.
Grant, Wm. P. Riggins. Signed Tho. Alexander, seal. Proven 10 Oct.
1856. Heirs in 1860. Carter Durham, G. W. Gaines, Jordan Rice,
Eliz. Durham, Elijah Gibson.

Mary Alexander, and James M. Murphree, Executor and Executrix of the
last will of William Murphree decd. Pickens Co. Pack (96) Clerk of
Court Office. Dated 23 July 1856. Sum of $137.50 for 110 acres to
James Cass being part of a survey and grant to Hamilton Reid the 3 Aug.
1791. Wit: James M. Stewart, William Stweart. Signed James M.
Murphree and Mary Alexander, Seals. On 23 July 1856 William Stewart
appeared before W. J. Parson, O.P.D. that he saw James Murphree and
Mary Alexander sign their name.

Thomas Alexander. decd. of 12 mile creek owned 2 tracts of land in
Pickens Co. 345 acres on 12 mile creek and Keowee River adj. Wesley
Grannt, Jenkins Adams, the other tract of 50 acres on Keowee River
adj. William Alexander, John Owens. Heirs in this state are, George
Gibson and wife Nancy, Elijah Gibson and wife Polly, Jordan Rice and
wife Emila, Joshua Holden and wife Keziah, Carter Durham and wife
Hannah, Joseph Durham and wife Elizabeth. George James and wife
Dianah William Herd and wife Letty. Out of state are, James Alexander,

William Durham and wife Malinda, Sally Boatner formerly Alexander.
Book A, page 222 Probate Judge Office, Pickens Co.

Mary Alexander, wife of Thomas Alexander died in 1891 in Pickens Co.
Owned land that formerly belonged to William Murphree decd. Thomas
Alexander died in the fall of 1856. Her first husband was Wm. Murphree
who died in 1846. Clerks Office Pack 647 #7 Pickens Co.

Elisha Alexander decd. owned land on Big Crow Creek in June 1861 land
adj. Wm. Alexander, Watson Collins. Heirs: Widow Mary A., William J.,
Elisha Marion Alexander, Wm. Alexander Guardian of Mary A. Alexander
a minor. Book B, page 58. Probate Judge Office. Pickens, S. C.

Prior Alexander, owned 125 acres of land on Keowee River, adj. Mrs.
Powers Prior Alexander and others, Widow Victoria Alexander, two minor
children Josephine and Richard Alexander. Dated Dec. 1, 1869. Book B
page 166 Pickens Co. Probate Judge Office.

Isaac Alexander, Will, Box 86 #906 Pickens Co. I Isaac Alexander
being of sound mind and memory ect. ect. I give and bequeath to my
wife Charlotte a child part of all personal and real property. The
residue to be equally devided between my lawfull heirs. Likewise
Charlotte Alexander to be Executrix. Dated 21 April 1865. Wit: John
Owens, Samuel Capehart, Martha J. Whitmire. Signed Isaac Alexander
Esal. Rec. 3 Feb. 1866.

Micajah Alexander. Deed from John Nix to Micajah Alexander Junr. Box
96 #1012 Pickens Co. Dated 29 Sept. 1849. Sum of $180.00 for more than
300 acres that John Nix bought from Wm. Nix on 13 Aug. 1845. Land on
Dyers Mill Creek. Wit: Micajah Alexander, Wyat Hudson. Signed John
Nix. Micajah Alexander made oath he saw John Nix sign sd. deed and
Wyatt Hudson witnessed same on the 15 Dec. 1854. Before T. J. Keith,
Dep. Clerk.

Micajah Alexander, states Micajah Alexander Junr. died intestate,
leaving neither wife or children, he owned more than 300 acres of land
on Little Eastatoe Creek adj. J. J. Parrott, Mrs. Winchester and
others. The said real estate to be devided between the next of kin.
viz. Your petr. the father of said decd. and his brothers and sisters
and their representives are: 1 Micajah Alexander Sr., 2 Elisha Alexander
3 John Alexander, 4 Elizabeth Murphree, 5 Jerry J. Parrott and wife
Milly, 6 Ephraim Gilstrap and wife Louisa, 7 The heirs of Mary Cantrell
decd. viz. John Cantrell, Staten Cantrell, Bailus Stephen and wife
Louisa, Micajah Cantrell, heirs of Wm. Cantrell decd. 8 Heirs of Anna
Roberts decd. name and number unknown. 9 Heirs of Melvina Roberts
decd. viz Jeremiah Roberts, Lena Roberts, Louisa Rhodes and husband
Pickney Rhodes, Milla Ann who married (name not given) and Malissa
Roberts who resides in Greenville, S. C. the other three are out of the
state. 10 Heirs of David Alexander decd. name and number unknown, out
of state, 11 Heirs of Isaac Alexander decd. Jacob, Jordan, Elias
Alexander who lives in Oconee Co., S. C. Nancy Madden wife of Thomas
E. Madden. Heirs of Elizabeth Watson decd. Daula, James and Elizabeth
H. Watson, 12 Heirs of Melissa Parrott decd. viz; David, Elizabeth,
Levina J. Parrott. Dated July 13, 1869.

Prier Alexander, Jr. Box 97 #1018 Pickens Co., S. C. On Dec. 1, 1869
Prier Alexander owned 125 acres of land lying on Keowee River, adj.
Mrs. Powers, Prier Alexander and others. Heirs: Victoria Alexander
the widow and two children Richard N. and Josephine Alexander.

Prier Alexander Sr. Box 98 #1031. April 3, 1871 E. B. Alexander
states that Prier Sr. died in 1870. Heirs: Minerva the wife of W. M.
Billingsley who resides in Ala., E. B. Alexander, Thomas P. Alexander,
Elizabeth Billingsley resides in Georgia., Elmina Bell wife of John H.
Bell, Amanda wife of Wm. H. Billingsley, Carolina Alexander wife of
Irvin Alexander, Richard and Josephine minor heirs of Prier Alexander
Jr. Prier Sr. owned 130 acres of land on Four mile Creek waters of
Keowee River. land adj. John OBryant and others. Est admr. Sept. 5,
1870 by Elisha Alexander, Thos. P. Alexander and Arthur R. Craig.

David Alexander. Box 70 #752 Pickens Co., S. C. Estate Admrs. 10 June 1870 by Sarah A. Alexander, Robert Craig are bound unto W. E. Holcombe ord. in the sum of $6,000.00.

Terrell Alexander. Box 100 #1046 Pickens Co., S. C. On Aug. 15, 1870 the petition of Mary C. E., Addison A. Francis P. and Sussndor E. Alexander minors children of David A. Alexander and Sarah A. their gdn. and wife of David A. Alexander shews that their father owned 350 acres on both sides of Crow Creek waters of Keowee River adj. land of Lemuel Thomas and others. It being the same tract of land deeded to said David A. and Terrell Milton Alexander by Fountain Alexander on the 6 Oct. 1856 and that your petrs. are the rightful owners of one half and T. M. Alexander who resides on the place the other half.

Fountain Alexander. Box 47 #516 Pickens Co., S. C. A letter of Admr. was granted on Dec. 19, 1856 to David A. and T. M. Alexander. Susan Alexander a daughter of said decd. on 1 July 1873 states that David Alexander the admr. has since died. An account of estate Susannah, Freeman, Addison, Mary, W. N. Craig and wife Elizabeth, Naomi, Nammer Alexander.

Capt. Elisha Alexander. Box 56 #615 Pickens Co. Est. admr. 26 Nov. 1860 by William and Prier Alexander, bound unto W. E. Holcombe Ord. in the sum of $800.00 Mary Alexander widow recd $145.01 as her dower of the real estate. Elisha was the son of William Alexander.

Elisha Alexander. Box 60 #646 Pickens Co., S. C. Mary A. Alexander the widow owned 142 acres on Big Crow Creek adj. land of Wm. Alexander, Watson Collins and others. Heirs: Mary A. widow, William J., Sela A., George W., Nancy Ann, Elisha Marion Alexander. Dated 21 June 1861. Wm. Alexander was the guardian of the minors.

Daniel Alexander Sr. Box 22 #264 Pickens Co., S. C. Est admr. 27 Dec. 1850 by Micajah Alexander, W. L. Keith they are bound unto Wm. D. Steel Ord. in the sum of $2,000.00. Settlement, paid, James Nix, F. Mills Fields, Tyry Boon, Margaret Hudson, Wm. Littleton their share, paid Thomas Alexander his acct. $60.00, Letty Nix $25.00, E. Alexander $2.93.

Pleasant Alexander. Pack 232 #3, Clerks of Court Office, Pickens Co. Mr. R. A. Thompson Esq. Comr. in Equity. Please pay Miles M. Norton Admr. of the Estate of P. Alexander dec. $242.84 out of our share of the Real Estate of said decd. Signed: S. P. Bruce and Emma Bruce. On Jan. 1, 1864 Lucretia Lawrence recd. $620.00 her share of as. estate. On Jan. 1, 1864 James T. Steel and Laura A. Steel recd. $620.00 their share of said estate. Rec. of Robt. A. Thompson Esq. C.E.P.D. $2170.29 in full of our share of the home tract and town lots N. 53 and 54 sold by him for partition amongst the legal heirs of Pleasant Alexander decd. and purchased and held by the Admr. of the estate of his family and to which by the order of sd. admr. the commissioner afore said is to or has executed titles to Mrs. L. Alexander for life with remainder in fee to Joseph N. Lawrence, Sydney P. Bruce, James Steele, Pleasant McD. Alexander, Julia A. Alexander and Venetta J. Alexander. Witness our hands and seals this 15 July 1861 (all signed)

Tate Alexander. Book 1 page 34, dated 29 Aug. 1837. Heirs John Pulliam in right of wife, Robert Alexander, Wm. Alexander, Robert Ballew, John Alexander, Joseph Rust, Jonathan Williams, Joseph Alexander, Saml. Alexander. Owned 500 acres on Longnose Creek water of Tugaloo River, adj. land of Christopher Whisenant, Major David Humphreys and others.

Robert Alexander. on 29 Jan. 1840 in Gilmore County, Ga. appointed John P. Alexander of the same county his Atty to receive his part from the estate of Tate Alexander decd.

William Alexander, of Burke Co., N. C. on 18 June 1839 appointed Robert Ballew, Jr. of Pickens Co., S. C. his atty. to collect of John Pulliam Admr. of Tate Alexander decd. late of Habersham Co., Ga. his part as a heir.

Caroline Alexander. Box 5 #2 Equity. Pickens Co. On 2 June 1864
Prier Alexander sheweth that Caroline Alexander is a minor under 12
yrs. and daughter of Sargent Alexander decd... Prier Alexander, her
grandfather.

Richard Alexander. Box #1051 Pickens Co., S. C. Est Amdr. 7 Jan. 1871
by Joseph C. Alexander. Left widow Sarah and two minor children, Frank
M. and Margaret G. Alexander. In March 1872 Frank M. was 3 yrs old and
Margaret G. Alexander was 1 1/2 years old.

Tate Alexander. Real Estate Book A, page 34 Probate Judge Office
Pickens Co., S. C. August 1837, to the Ordinary of Pickens Dist.
The undersign beg leave to represent to you that he has an interest in
a certain tract of land lying in Pickens Co. On the Tugaloo River of
about 500 acres as to why if any the tract of land should not be
divided as the law of 1824 hath made provision for. Signed John
Pulliam in right of his wife. Defendants are: Robert Alexander,
William Alexander, Robert Ballew, John Alexander, Joseph Rust, Jonathan
Williams, Joseph Alexander and Samuel Alexander. The land was sold
on 6 Nov. 1837.

Fountain Alexander to David A. and Terrel M. Alexander a deed of gift
Estate papers Pack 86 Clerk of Court Office, Pickens Co., S. C. Dated
6 Oct. 1856. Sum of five dollars to me paid in hand by my loving sons
David A. and Terrel M. Alexander for 350 acres on both sides of Crow
Creek, adj. Holdens land, Lemuel Thomas land. First granted unto
Barney Glenn and Robert Craven. Wit: D. M. Alexander, T. W. Alexander.
Signed F. Alexander seal, recorded 8 June 1857.

Fountain Alexander to Henson Alexander a deed of gift. Clerk of
Court Office, Pickens Co., S. C. Dated 6 Oct. 1856. Sum of five
dollars paid by my loving son Henson Alexander all that tract of land
I now live on. Adj. Watson Stewart, Robert Stewart, William Newton,
Robert Morgan. Wit: D. M. Alexander, William K. Alexander. Signed
F. Alexander, seal. Recorded 8 June 1857. (Fountain Alexander died
in the month of Oct. in the year 1856.)

Fountain Alexander. Estate of Fountain Alexander was in equity in 1859
as recorded in pack 86 Clerk of Court Office, Pickens Co., S. C.
Thomas Keith brought suit for the widow, she being Mariah C. the widow.
Sons David A., Terrel M., Henson. Daughters Susan B. Ovarra T. and
Elizabeth who has intermarried with William N. Craig. Henson, Ovarra
and Susan are minors under the age of twenty one. Filed 12 Dec. 1859.

Mrs. Ruthey X Alexander applies under the act of 1919 for the widow
of the war between the states. She is the widow of E. B. Alexander
of the Company B 2 Reg. of Rifles Battl. of Capt. R. A. Thompson. He
enlisted on the 21 day March 1862. Was discharged at Appomattox, Va.
the 9 Apr. 1865. They were married the 10 Sept. 1858. He died the
9 Dec. 1868. All her income and property does not exceed $500.00. She
was 78 years old and resided at Central Rt. 2 Pickens Co., S. C. since
she was married in 1858. Robert Stewart and R. A. Bowen swore they
knew the both of them, and her statement was true. Signed Ruthey X
Alexander.

Thomas Alexander. A note to Thomas Alexander from John Owens, pack 382
#18 Clerk of Court Office, Pickens Co., S. C. Note dated Feb. 1855 in
the sum of three hundred with interest from date, secured by two
tracts of land, one lying on Keowee River known as the Wm. Capehart
tract, adj. W. N. Craig, and J. Grosham, the other 260 acres I purchased from the said Alexander. No witnesses.

Pleasant Alexander, from Capt. Alexander Harris. Rec. in book D,
page 420 Clerk of Court Office, Pickens Co., S. C. Pleasant Alexander
paid $375.00 for lot #10 and house in the town of Pickens. Dated 29
Nov. 1841. The same where W. D. Sloan did live. Wit: by Elijah E.
Alexander, W. L. Keith. Signed: Alexander Harris, seal. Cyntha
Harris did this day release renounce and for ever relinquish her
interest in the said land. It is stated that she is the wife of

Capt. Alexander Harris. Signed W. L. Keith, C.C. & Ex off. Recorded 17 Dec. 1841.

Elisha Alexander. Wil of Elisha Alexander, Box 3 #31 Pickens Co., S.C. Dated 8 Aug. 1832 I Elisha Alexander being of sound mind and memory. 1. My beloved sons Elijah Thomas and Daniel that part of my tract of land situated on Crow Creek above the still house branch, joining the land of Daniel Alexander Sr. 2. To my beloved son George Washington and Elisha the balance of said land lying below Crow Creek and joining Pryior Alexander on which my dwelling house stands. 3. Elisha to get a negro boy named Bob. 4. Wife Nancy to get negro Milly for her life time. Then her things to be divided between all my children. Take one fifth for my son in law Henry Grogen. The rest to be sold and applied to my lawful and just debts. Wit: Charles M. Reese, Elijah Alexander, John F. Hers, seals. Signed Elisha X Alexander, seal. Will proved on oath of Elijah Alexander and John Herd on Sept. 10, 1832. J. H. Dendy, O.P.

Deed from William Alexander to Pleasant Alexander Pack 69 Clerk of Court Office Pickens Co. Dated 20 Oct. 1838. Sum of twelve hundred dollars for 237 acres on Keowee River about two miles from Pickens Court House. Originally granted unto James Jett, being the same William Alexander purchased from Tarleton Lewis and the same Lewis purchased from Richard Holden. Wit: W. L. Keith, Arthur Craig. Signed William X Alexander, seal. Deed attested before W. L. Keith, C.C. by Arthur Craig on the 10 Dec. 1835. On 22 Oct. 1839 Ann Alexander renounce and release her rights and claim of dower before W. L. Keith, C.C. & Ex Off. Recorded 26 Oct. 1839.

William Alexander. Will of William Alexander Box 13 #175 Pickens Co., S. C. I William Alexander being of sound mind and memory ect.ect. I will to my wife Anny all my land and property to raise my children, when they go to themselves to have a portion as may think proper. Sons named, Jacob, Daniel, James John, Thomas, William and Harrison. Make wife Anny, Jacob Alexander and brother Thomas Alexander my Executors. Dated 20 Feb. 1845. Wit: Jordon Rice, Thomas Alexander. Signed William Alexander. Proved June 6, 1845.

ALLEN

Thomas Allen. The estate of Thomas Allen. Real Estate Book A, page 16, Probate Judge Office, Pickens Co., S. C. Elizabeth Allen applicant viz William H. and Jane T. Allen, defendants for division of a tract of land of 150 acres lying opposite Parises Ford. Adj. land of John Gossett. (no date) On 27 Apr. 1835 Col. B. Hagood made his oath that the land lying on Paris's Ford on Saluda River that was sold by the Sheriff to Nathaniel Dacus and sold to Thomas Brackenridge who sold to the Thomas Allen decd. The said land cannot be worth one thousand dollars. Robert B. Duncan and Saml. Mauldin made oath that they was acquainted with the said land and that it would be advantage to sell the land divide the proceeds. Dated 13 Apr. 1835.

Elizabeth Allen and her two minor children are living in Greenville Dist. and they are the heirs of Thomas Allen decd. Dated 23 Mar. 1835.

George Allen of Greenville Dist. made his will June 17, 1803. Will proved Feb. 14, 1804. Execr. Archabald Taylor, George Solmon, William Nelson. Wit: John Taylor, Hannah Lovlady. The land he now lives on to go to sons Jesse and David Allen. $200.00 to son George. $200.00 to son Dueke. $100.00 to daughter Nancy Dill's first child. $200.00 to his daughter Rebeccah. $200.00 to daughter Sally. On March 7, 1804 Henry Prince, David Jackson and Duncan Wilkison were to appraise the estate. Debts due the estate of George Allen are: Smallwood Middleton. George Russell, William Middleton, John Lucas, William Bullion, Arch. C. Taylor, William Jackson, Angus McAllister, James West, Massey Aerasmith, Richard Dill, Jonas Dauson, Jacob Swafford, John Stanford, William Nelson, John Dill, William Dill, David Rogers,

John Stewart, George Allen's property was sold 8 Mar. 1804 those who
bought were: George Allen Junr., William Stewart, William Dill, John
Lucas, William Nelson, William Tubb, Solomon Forrest, Jessee Allen,
Aaron Swafford, James Nicoll, Reuben Barrett, Esq., James Ponder,
Thomas Smith, Richard Wallen, William D. Thomas, John Crawford, William
Middleton, Portman Howard, William Loftis, John Burns, Richard Forrest,
Richard Dill, Isaac Ward, Harden Roberts, James Barnhill, John Tucker,
Benjamin Boswell, Robert Ross, Abraham Goodman. In the settlement the
estate was to be divided between 5 1/2 legatee's. No names given. I
another place Isaac Praytor was the husband of one of the legatees.

Charles Allen who lived in Pickens Co. Wife was Sarah Clayton, ref.
Real Estate Book, page 113, Probate Judge Office Pickens Co., S. C.

William Allen estate was admr. 21 July 1834 by John Allen, Cornelious
Keith, William L. Keith, James Madison Keith. Who are bound unto James
H. Dendy Ord. in the sum of $1,000. One paper mentions 10 heirs but
gives no names. In Estate papers of William Allen Box 5 Pack 52
Probate Judge Office, Pickens Co., S. C. these are to appear on 6 Oct.
1835 before the Ord. for a division of William Estate; Abner Chastain,
James Allen, Wm. Robertson, John Allen, Hugh Allen, Cornelious Keith.
heirs of Eliza Reid, heirs of Milly Castle, heirs of Sarah Powell.
Another paper; "On Dec. 7, 1839 Simeon Youngblood of Benton County,
Ala. wanted Mr. Dendy the Ord. to send by Barton Griffin his wife part
of the estate of William Allen decd. late of Pickens Co. My wife is
the daughter of John Castle. Wyley Ann we were married by Joseph Reid
Esq. on 11 Sept. 1839. Mr. Dendy please pay William Castle $3.25 out
of my wife estate of William Allen. Signed Simeon Youngblood.

James Allen. Estate of James Allen, Box 56 #611 Probate Judge Office
Pickens Co. On 12 Sept. 1860 the estate was Admr. by David S. Strib-
ling, William H. Stribling, James E. Hagood who are bound unto W. E.
Holcombe Ord. 11 heirs are, Mary King, Sarah Cristian, Jinna Holland,
Vinas Sisk, decd., Nancy Blackstock decd., Meka Ivans, Elizabeth
Holland, William Allen, Holland Allen, Fany Johnston decd. John Allen.

William Allen. Estate of William Allen Apt. 15 #126. Probate Judge
Office Pickens Co. On 10 Apr. 1901 Jack Sitton states that one William
Allen died some years ago leaving a will. That he named as one of his
legatees Lidie Sitton the daughter of Jack Sitton who is now 15 years
old. William Allen was the grandfather of Lidie Sitton. 21 Apr. 1896.
William Allen the son of William Allen Sr. and was over 14 years old.
His guardian was W. M. Hagood, William Allen was over 21 on 6 Jan. 1901.

Charles Allen. Will of Charles Allen, Apt. 1 file 4 Greenville, S.C.
Dated 13 Nov. 1820 I Charles Allen of Greenville Dist. being in sound
mind and memory ect.ect. First I give all land and personal property
to my beloved wife Sara. Sons, Thomas, Recy, William, daughters
Betsy, Anny, Grandchildren named. Isaac, Polly and Carlina Allan.
Appoint wife Sara and son Thomas as Executrix and Executor. Wit: Wm.
E. Wickliffe, Solomon Hawkins, Z. Goodlett. Signed Charles Allen.
Proved by Zion Goodlett before Spartan Goodlett Ord. on the 27 Jan.
1821. The first year return of the estate amount paid out and nothing
received. paid to J. Cleveland, Catharine Hawkins, John Brown, Alexander
Vickers, Benjamin Bridges, George Ivens, Daniel Timmons, Sloan and
Crayton, Col. Dunham Thos. West, Jesse Hawkins, Stephens F. Philips.
Doct. John Robbinson, Jermiah Cleaveland.

Charles Allen. Estate of Charles Allen, Box 1 Pack 18 Probate Judge
Office, Abbeville, Ninety Six Dist. Appraisement by John Thomas Junr.,
Esq. Ord. To Robert Ross, Nehemiah Franks, Marshall Franks, Robert
Cooper. All or any three of you shall be directed unto Lucy Allen
Administratrix of the estate of Charles Allen decd. To make a true
and perfect inventory and appraisement and cause same to be returned
to me within sixty days. Dated 29 Apr. 1785. The inventory was made
21 March 1787. In the same pack was another inventory dated for 30
Dec. 1777. This inventory was almost the same as the other except
memo. 4 young negroes born since the decd. dyed. Ł 150 for each when
div. with Chas. Allen sons to the 21 June 1783.

Josiah Allen. Estate of Josiah Allen, Box 1 Pack 20 Probate Judge
Office, Abbeville, Ninety Six Dist., Administrator bond. We James
Allin, Enoch Grigsby, Fredrick Sisson are bound unto John Ewing Calhoun
Esq. Ord. In the sum of 14,000 pds. current money of this State, being
equal in value to two thousand pds. sterling money of Great Britian.
The obligation is such that if the James Allin the administrator of
the estate of Josiah Allen, shall well and truly administer all etc.
etc. Signed at Long Cane on 20 Aug. 1782. Wit: James Caldwell. In
the Citation James Allin is from Richland Creek and is the next of kin
to Josiah Allen. The citition was read at my company, 14 Aug. 1782.
Capt. Wm. Butler. In another bond for the appraisers Josiah Allen is
listed as a Senr. and the appraisers are William Sisson, Enoch Grigsbe,
Russell Wilson, John Davis. It was held on 13 Sept. 1782.

Lewis Allen. Will of Lewis Allen, Box 3 Pack 41, Probate Judge Office
Abbeville, S. C. I Lewis Allen being of sound mind and memory etc.etc.
I give to my niece Anna Craig Gray two hundred dollars. 2. I give to
Mary Gray Weed daughter of Major Andrew Weed the sum of one hundred
dollars. 3. I give to my sister Hannah Gray all the rest of my estate
both real and personal. Appoint my brother in law John Gray executor.
Dated 26 June 1816. Wit: B. H. Saxon, John McGaw, Robert Wadel.
Signed: Lewis Allen. Will proved by B. H. Saxon before Tato. Livingston O.A.D. on the 13 July 1816. Appraisers named the same day, they
are. Joseph Hutton, Andw. Weed, John Weed, W. M. Gray, James Gray or
any three of you. Estate closed out on 13 Apr. 1819 by John Gray Exor.

John Allen. Estate of John Allen, Box 1 Pack 3 Probate Judge Office,
Abbeville, S. C. The estate was admr. 8 Nov. 1838 by Jane L. Allen.
Dr. John F. Livingston and David Lesley. Sale of household and farm
tools, with no date given or heirs listed.

Elizabeth Allen recd. on Apr. 3, 1841 from Canady Creek Church, N.
Carolina Henderson Co. Rec by letter. Ref. Church records of Oolenoy
Church, Pickens Co., S. C.

                              ALLGOOD

Barnett Allgood. Will of Barnett Allgood, Box 59 #637 Probate Judge
Office Pickens Co. I Barnett Allgood being in sound mind and memory
etc.etc. First I will and bequeath unto my daughters Polly Miller wife
of Isaac Miller, Jane Murphy wife of Ellis Murphy, Amelia Miller wife
of George Miller, Patsey Ellis wife of Stephen Ellis, Nancy Ellis wife
of Jeremiah Ellis, Fanny Kennemore widow of Benson Kennemore the sum
of one hundred dollars each, and to the children of my daughter
Cassandra Major decd. one hundred dollars equally divided between them.
Secondly, as soon after my death as convenient to sell upon such terms
as they think proper all my property except my negroes. Thirdly, I
wish my several negroes each for him or hersely individually to be
permitted to choose his or her master or mistress ect.ect. Fourthly,
after the sale of my property pay my living daughters and make an equal
division between my beloved wife Elizabeth Allgood, my sons Bannister,
Alexander, Deforrest, Alvin Allgood, and my sons in law Isaac Miller,
Ellis Murphy, George Miller, Stephen Ellis, Jeremiah Ellis and my
widowed daughter Fanny Kennemore, and the children of Cassandra Major
decd. Wit: A. M. Folger, A. T. Clayton, A. Hester, signed Barnett
Allgood, Seal. Will proved by A. T. Clayton before W. E. Holcombe,
O.P.D. on 6 Sept. 1861. (The above will was made 8 July 1861.)
Allgood real estate was one tract on Rices Creek waters of 12 mile
River adj. Jessee Miller, A. Hester Estate, A. T. Clayton and others.
The estate was appraised on the 30 Sept. 1861. by Wm. Hunter, Reese
Bowen, A. Hester, J. B. Clayton.

ALLISON

James Allison. Will of James Allison of the settlement of Enoree, Box 2 Pack 29 Probate Judge Office, Abbeville, S. C. Being in perfect mind and memory ect.ect. Make my trusty and well beloved friends, Capt. William Berrey and Mr. Robert Templeton my sole executors and admr. of this my last will and Test. I leave my son Joseph Allison 150 acres on the upper end of my tract. If my son Joseph never returns, then the property to be his brother Robert Allison, son Joseph to get other household and farm items. I give to my son Robert the land I now live on, with other household and farm items. I leave to my daughter Margret the sum of five shillings. I leave to my daughter Jean the sum of five shillings. I leave to my daughter Isable one cow and a looking glass. I leave to my daughter Elizabeth one young heifer. Grand children named for items are James Linch Senr., James Linch Junr. and Joseph Linch, James Casey and Joseph Casey. Also Jean Linch daughter of Edward Linch and Jean Linch the daughter of Aaron Linch, Jean Casey daughter of William Casey. I give to Elizabeth Stone a four gal. pot. Dated 10 Aug. 1778. Wit: William Berrey, Petr. Brookes, Hugh X Smith. Signed: James Allison. Will proved by Peter Brookes before John Thomas Junr. Ord. Ninety Six Dist. 23 Aug. 1784.

AMBLER

James Ambler. Estate, Pack 224 Equity Clerk of Court Office, Pickens Co. James Ambler Sr. died 26 June 1849, shortly after his father's death he James H. Ambler the defendant became the Admr. of the estate. His father and mother became feeble and unable to care for themselves. In Dec. 1845 his mother died and he bought land and removed to it, carring his father with him and all his personal property with him. His father died on 26 June 1849. The defendant is the only son and the youngest child. The suit is over two slaves who their grandfather had let James and Susan have. Susan was before marriage Susan Hagood. The other heirs in this suit is Charlotte wife John Burdine, Adaline wife of Benjamin the Complainant, and Ann wife of Elihu Griffin. The deed from James Amber Sr. to James Amber, dated 5 Mar. 1849, James Amber gives all his stock, cattle, hoggs, household goods, and farm tools ect.ect. Wit: S. D. Keith, Joseph Masingill. Signed James X Amber. Deed attested to by S. D. Keith before O. E. Barton, M.P.D. Dated 16 Mar. 1849.

AMORY

Jonathan Amory. Will of Jonathan Amory, Vol. 1 Page 5, Probate Judge Office, Charleston, S. C. Will dated 3 Nov. 1697. I Jonathan Amory Merch. of ye Province of Carolina. being weak in body but in perfect mind and memory. ect.ect. I give and bequeath unto my son Joseph Croskeys all ye pieces of land to ye tract of land next to my dwelling house which I gave to my daughter also my best silver headed cane. Item, I give to Sarah Rhett daughter to Capt. Willm Rhett, ten pds., Item I give to Doctr Atkin Williamson ten pds. I give to Doctr Todd ten pds. Item I give to the poor of Charleston fifteen pds. Item I give to Thomas Noble twenty pds. Item I give unto my loving wife Martha my dwelling house in Charleston, for her natural life and at her death to go to sons Thomas and Robert. Item I give to daughter Sarah Armory and my daughter Ann both three hundred pds. I appoint my sons Thomas and Robert my Executor and wife as Executrix. Wit: Geo. Logan, Fra. Fidling, Joane Hearne. Signed Jonathan Amory, seal. Recorded 17 Oct. 1699.

Martha Amory. Will of Martha Amory, Vol. 1 page 7, Probate Judge Office, Charleston, S. C. I Martha Amory of Charleston widow. Being weak in body but sound mind and perfect memory, ect.ect. Item I give unto my dear friend Sarah Rhett my gold watch, my horse and horse

to be hole and sole executors. Dated 18 May 1782. Wit: Thomas
Entriken, James Middleton, Ansorth Middleton. Signed James X Anderson.
seal. Will proved by James Middleton before J. Hunter, J.P. on the
6 May 1783.

Robert Anderson. The Estate of Robert Anderson, Box 2, Pack 33 Probate
Judge Office, Abbeville, S. C. the estate was admr. 17 Feb. 1816 by
William Reynolds, Joseph Eakin, Bartholomew Jordan, William Reynolds
are bound unto Taliaferro Livington Ord. in the sum of ten thousand
dollars. Only the money recd. to the estate is recroded. There is one
paid rec. that is to Nancy Anderson for one dollar and seventy five
cents. The final settlement was 15 Apr. 1821.

Robert Anderson. The estate of Robert Anderson, #28 in Equity, Clerk
of Court Office, Pickens Co. An answer of Maria Anderson to a bill of
Samuel B. Pickens and wife. The defendants are Maria widow and four
minor children of the late Robert Anderson decd. Maria with son
Robert and George T. Anderson as admr. After selling the personal
property the indebtness of the decd. which may exceed the assets.
Edmund, Caroline A., John and Edward wanted their mother Maria to be
their guardian. This was in 1836. The land sale was held on the first
Monday in Oct. next. Robert and George T. Anderson purchased most of
the land.

Mary Anderson. Power of Attorney of Mary Anderson to Edward Noble,
Pack 47 Clerk of Court Office, Abbeville, S. C. I Mary Anderson wife
of Robert Anderson of Pendleton, S. C. the daughter of the late Ezekiel
Pickens. Do constitute and appoint Edward Noble of Abbeville Dist. my
true and lawful attorney to receive the legacy of two thousand dollars
bequeathed to me by the last will of the late James E. Boisseau of
the city and state of New York.
      To give full receipts and discharges therefore to the Executors
of the Estate of the late James E. Boisseau ect.ect. I have set my
hand and seal the 31 July 1852. Wit: Allen Vance, Jas. H. Riley.
Signed Mary B. Anderson and Robert Anderson. Attested to by Allen
Vance before D. L. Wardlaw, Judge. 2 Aug. 1852. Abbeville, S. C.

Denny Anderson. Will of Denny Anderson, Senr. Box 7 #83 Probate
Judge Office, Pickens, S. C. The last will of Denny Anderson of Spartanburg Dist. Item 1 I direct that all my debts be paid as soon after
my deceased. 2. The tract of land that I now live on and also the
river tract, for the use of my beloved wife Elizabeth Anderson for her
life time. Also all my negroes, horses, stock of every kind and household items, ect.ect. 3. After the death of my wife, my will that the
tract of land where I now live and the one adjoining it shall belong to
my son John Anderson provided he will relinquish his titles to a tract
of land I formerly gave him and will remove to this place and manage
and provide for my wife her lifetime. The other tract of land adj.
Denny Anderson Junr. and the other title from William Leonard. After
the death of my wife the River tract to be divided with Hiram Bennetts
the Western direction to the river, and the Southern division to son
James Anderson. 5. I give my son in law Henry Anderson three hundred
dollars. 6. I give to son Thomas Leonard three hundred dollars. 7. I
give to my daughter in law Mary Anderson widow of Samuel Anderson decd
five dollars. 8. I give to son in law John S. Bennett a bed and furniture. I give to my granddaughter Mary Elizabeth Anderson daughter of
Samuel decd. three hundred dollars after the death of my wife. 10. I
give to William O. Bennett son of my daughter Martha decd. the sum of
four hundred dollars after the death of my wife. I do hereby appoint
and make my sons John and James Anderson my Executors. Dated 27 Nov.
1832. Wit: Z. F. Westmoreland, Staphen Marchbanks, William X Henderson
Sen. Proven Dec. 31, 1832.

John Anderson. Pack 106 in Equity Pickens Co., S. C. John Anderson
died in Feb. 1840. Letter of admr. was granted to William Nimmons.
After his death Isaac Anderson a son took possession of the negroes
slaves viz: Andrew about 26 years old, Juda about 35 years old and her
children Henry and Hiram. The heirs of John Anderson are, James
Stephens and Drucilla his wife, John Brock and Sally his wife, Rachel

Reece, Moses Stephens, Thomas Turner and Polly his wife, John Anderson, son of Abram Anderson decd. and James Anderson and other linial descendants of John Anderson decd. Isaac Anderson states that his father gave him the slaves by a deed of gift. (There are about ten statements that John Anderson decd was about 80 years old and heard deft and that he was incapable of transacting any business...no date given.)

James W. Anderson. A deed from James W. Anderson to Caswell Anderson (no ref. given) I James W. Anderson contracted and sold to my brother Caswell Anderson my entire interest in the estate of my Grand Father the late John Anderson of Pickens Dist. Dated 19 June 1845. Wit: J. N. Whitner, J. W. Anderson seal.

A. J. Anderson. Nancy Holland dtr. of Weyman Holland decd. of Pickens Co. in 1842 as being the wife of A. J. Anderson. Ref. Probate Judge Office, Pickens Co. Box 2 #49.

John Anderson. Will of John Anderson (only the last part of will is found, the county is not named). It seems that all is to be sold at public sale, wife Mary Anderson to get one third her natural life, but if she marry again, then she is to get only a child part. The balance to be divided amongst my ten children viz: daughter Ann G. Chapman and her husband Hewelet Chapman. My sons, James, William, Thomas, Erven, John, George, Robert. Anderson and daughter Mary Jane Anderson and my son David G. Anderson. I do appoint my brothers James and William Anderson and my two sons James and William Anderson, executors. Dated 7 May 1837. Wit: Tully Bolling, Isaac Davenport, Micajah Berry. Signed: John Anderson, seal. Will probated 11 Dec. 1837. No other inf.

Henry Anderson. Box 7 #83, Probate Judge Office, Pickens Co., S. C. Power of Atty. from Elizabeth Anderson, James Anderson Jr. and William Leonard of Spartanburg Dist. appointed Denny Anderson of the same state and Dist. to act as our lawfull attorney in adjust, settle the estate of Henry H. Anderson decd. late of Pickens Dist. Dated 29 Mar. 1837.

J. T. Anderson. Box 116 #13 Probate Judge Office, Pickens, S. C. Est. Admr. Nov. 30, 1888 by Ida Anderson, W. J. Ponders who are bound to J. B. Newberry Ord. in the sum of $300.00 Ida was the widow. He died in Oct.

Jacob Anderson. Estate of Jacob Anderson, Box 3 Pack 43, Probate Judge Office, Abbeville, Estate was Admr. 16 Dec. 1823 by Elizabeth Anderson, Perry F. Anderson and William A. Huggins. A sale was held on 9 Jan. 1824. Elizabeth the widow bought most of the household items, the stock was bought by viz: Perry F. Anderson, James Scott, David Cunningham, Wesley Brooks, Robert Cheatham, Malkiyah Abney, Joseph Wardlaw, John Kary, Charles T. Connerly, Albert Waller, Wm. B. Lewis, Barzilla Jay, Jahu Roden, Thomas Stallsworth Senr., Jackson Holliday, Charles S. Patterson, John L. Gaines, Thomas Stallsworth Junr., James Pert, James Stallsworth, Maxmillion Hutcheson, Thomas Goodman, Jessee Henderson, Martin Hackett, Wm. A. Adams. In the receipts for the year 1827 Stephen Ross is listed as Admr. in right of his wife. In pack 3230 Clerks of Court Office, Abbeville, S. C. in Equity. Jacob Anderson died some years ago intestate and at the time of death had a tract of land containing 330 acres adj. Thomas Cheatham, John Partlow, Peter McKeller and others leaving the widow and six children, William H., Benjamin F., Nathan, Martha, Elizabeth and Jacob Anderson of these Benjamin F., Martha and Elizabeth are dead under twenty on years of age and unmarried, the surviving children, except Jacob who is still a minor, are attained legal age. The widow Elizabeth has intermarried with Stephen Ross. William H. and Nathan deeded their part to their mother, but now says they are entitled to a partition of the land. William H. Anderson lived in Pike County, Georgia at this time and Nathan lived in Montgomery County, Alabama.

Robert Anderson. Estate of Robert Anderson decd. Box 2 Pack 40 Abbeville, S. C. Probate Judge Office, Abbeville, S. C. Dated 17 Feb.

1816. William Anderson and Joseph Eakins, Admr. Money paid receipts
only info in pack. Paid 1817. Samuel Spence for Huey Dixon three
dollars, paid Thomas Atkins 178 dollars on note, paid Thomas Herren
for Alen Glover thirty three and eight seven one half cents paid
William Runnolds in part of his share of said estate forty two and four
cents, paid Barthoimey Jordon one hundred eighty seven dollars and
fifty six cents, paid William Motes twenty two dollars and fifty seven
cents, paid Joseph Foster one hundred seventy eight dollars, William
Motes one hundred forty nine dollars and seventy five cents, paid
William Runnels one hundred thirty dollars and ninety six cents, William
Anderson eighty three dollars in part of his share estate, paid Mary
Anderson one thousand two hundred seventeen dollars and seventy nine
cents, paid Isbel Marshall seventy five cents, paid Abenezer Foster
eight dollars for schooling, paid John Boyd two dollars, paid Edward
Forbee one dollar and fifty cents. In the year 1818, paid John Anderson
three hundred dollars of his share, paid William Glover sixty two and
one half cents, paid William Anderson one hundred dollars, paid Lewis
Grant one dollar and fifty cents for schooling, paid William Motes
being advanced by the intested in his lifetime one hundred twenty two
dollars, Bartholimey Jurdon being advanced by the intested in his lifetime one hundred twenty two dollars, Joseph Foster being advanced by
the intested in his lifetime one hundred twenty two dollars, William
Anderson being advanced by the intested in his lifetime eighty seven
dollars, paid Meary Anderson three hundred forty eight dollars and
ninety four cents for Nancy J. Anderson her share in full.

William Anderson. Estate of William Anderson decd. Box 2 Pack 40
Probate Judge Office, Abbeville, S. C. The estate admr. 12 Oct. 1816
by William Anderson Senr. William Anderson Junr., Thomas Herron, David
Taggart, William Brownlee, Samuel Pruet, who are bound to Tal. Livings-
ton Esq. Ord. in the sum of ten thousands dollars. On a petition of
Wm. Anderson Senr. one of the Admr. for a citation calling on William
Anderson Junr. as acting Admr. to come forward and show cause why he
had not made a regular return for the estate. Dated 4 Mar. 1821.
Cash paid 1822. Paid William Anderson Senr. $200.00, 1823 paid the
Admr. of the estate of James Anderson decd. $268.00... in 1825 paid
Thomas Anderson Senr. in full $268.00... Paid C. Anderson in full
$244.00, paid S. Austin and Mary Austin in full $125.34... To John
Anderson on acct. $11.81 1/4 in the year 1819, paid David Anderson in
his part $273.00, paid C. Anderson widow, in part $357.43 3/4, paid
Mary Anderson in part $53.00.

James Anderson. Estate of James Anderson decd. Box 3 Pack 46, Probate
Judge Office, Abbeville, S. C. Estate Admr. 21 Oct. 1820 by William
Mattison, John Anderson, William Collins, John Mattison who are bound
unto Moses Taggart Ord. in the sum of $3,000.00 The sale was held 24
Nov. 1820, no heirs are named.

Moses Anderson. Estate of Moses Anderson, Box 1 #4, Probate Judge
Office, Anderson, S. C. Pendleton Dist. We Mary Anderson, Wm. Welch,
Alexander Orr are bound unto the Judge of the County Court. This 26
Jan. 1796. Mary Anderson was administratrix of the goods and chattles
and was to make a perfect inventory of all. A very small inventory
taken.

William Anderson. Estate of William Anderson decd. Box 1 #7, Probate
Judge Office, Anderson, S. C. Pendleton Dist. We Thomas Green and
William Anderson are bound unto John Harris, Ord. in the sum of $100.00
bond dated 3 Feb. 1823 to make a true and perfect inventory and Admr.
the goods and chattles of the decd. The sale was held 25 Mar. 1823.
It was very small.

John Anderson. Estate of John Anderson decd. Box 1 #8, Probate Judge
Office, Anderson, S. C. An inventory is all of this estate, no will
or bond in file. No date on the inventory.

Bayley Anderson. Deed from Bayley Anderson to James Walker. Deed
Book D, page 225 Greenville, S. C. This indenture made between Bayley
Anderson of Pendleton Dist. and James Walker of Greenville Co., S. C.

Dated 6 May 1795, in the sum of seventy five pds. sterling for 106 and
1/2 acres lying on both sides of Cheeharoah River waters of Saluda
River. Being one half of a grant given unto Robert Anderson of 213
acres on the 21 Feb. 1785. Wit: Mathew Caldwell, Andrew Walker.
Signed: Bayley Anderson, seal. Deed attested to by Mathew Caldwell
before Vincent Anderson Esq. on the 16 Apr. 1796.

Vincent Anderson. Deed from Vincent Anderson to James Walker both of
Greenville Co., ref. Book D, page 226. Greenville Co., S. C. This
indenture made 23 Feb. 1795. In the sum of 100 pds sterling for 160
acres on the West side of the North side of Saluda River. Originally
granted unto Thomas Farrar dated 16 July 1784 and conveyed to Stephen
Swillevan, who conveyed to Joseph Reed, who conveyed to Vincent
Anderson. Wit: George Salmon, Alexander Anderson, Andrew Walker.
Signed: Vincent Anderson, seal. Proved by Alexander Anderson before
William Anderson Esq. and recorded 17 Apr. 1796.

Henry Anderson. Estate of Henry Anderson Decd. Box 7 #83 Probate Judge
Office, Pickens Co., S. C. We Susan Anderson and Frances Knox are
bound unto James H. Dendy Esq. Ord. in the sum of three thousand dollars.
Bond dated 1 Mar. 1836 to Admr. the goods and chattles of Henry H.
Anderson decd. to make a true and perfect inventory of all. Inv. made
18 Mar. 1836. (A power of attorney in this estate is on page 24.) In
the year 1837, Susan Anderson in account current with the estate of
H. H. Anderson:

Sale amount of personal property	$1,618.81
Cash on hand at deceased death	14.00
Amount paid out in 1 & 2 years	88.03
Widow claim on the estate of Denny Anderson Senr. Decd.	150.00 as per will
Widow Susan Anderson half	697.39
Legatees (not named) $87.17 each	

The above estate and dividend was made and declared on the belief that
the widow has an interest derived under the will of Danny Anderson decd
the father of Henry H. Anderson but to what amount we cannot say not
having yet recd a copy of sd will. It is therefore subject to correc-
tion whenever the facts of the case are ascertained Ordinaries office
the 17 Apr. 1837... In the real estate book A, page 27, Probate Judge
Office, Anderson, S. C. Susan Anderson (widow) applicant, vizt:
Elizabeth Anderson (mother of decd.)
Hiram Bennett in right of his wife
Denny Anderson   Wm. Leonard
James Anderson Junr.
Thomas Leonard in right of wife
Heirs of Samuel Anderson decd. and John Anderson defendants

George Anderson. Estate of George Anderson, Cox 1 #2, Probate Judge
Office, Anderson, S. C. Pendleton Dist. I George Anderson make this
my last will and testament. I give to my loving wife Molley Anderson
the plantation I now live on containing 125 acres, all household
furniture working tools, also to leave her some negroes during her
natural life to work for and school my children. To my son David L.
Anderson to have what he now has... To my daughter Margrat Burnsides
what she now has.. to son James Anderson to have what he now has ..
also my son William Anderson to have what he now has. Also Judey
Weiar to have the balance of the land. I give to John Anderson the
land lying down the creek known to this plantation also a negro named
Harry.T daughter Polly Anderson a negro named Anckey and a mare and
half of the Meeting house tract of land. Daughter Salley a negro named
Silvy when she comes of age and a horse and saddle. To son Serson
Anderson (torn place) a negro named Gilbort and two hundred and fifty
dollars to school him... Make wife Molley Anderson son Anderson and my
brother Lewis Anderson my lawfull executors. Dated 18 July 1807.
Wit: Lewis Sherrill, John Dickson, James Dickson. Signed Geo. Anderson, seal. No recording date given, an inventory was made 18 July
1808. Sale held on 21 Oct. 1808.

APPLING

<u>John Appling</u>. Will of John Appling, Will book 1., page 5, Amelia Co.,
Va. I John Appling of Parish of Nottoway and County of Amelia, Va.
being in full health and perfect memory ect.ect... I give to my son
John Appling one negro boy named Ben and one girl named Diley, one
feather bed and furniture. I give to my son Daniel Appling one negro
boy named Charles and one negro girl named Muryear, one feather bed and
furniture... I give to my son William Appling one negro boy named Will
and one negro girl named Pink, one feather bed and furniture... I
give to my daughter Elizabeth Appling one negro woman named Lyd and
one negro boy named Peter, one feather bed and furniture... I give to
my daughter Lucy Appling one negro man called great Charles and one
negro girl called little Hannah, one feather bed and furniture... I give
to my daughter Pattey Appling one negro boy called little George and
one negro girl named Darcus and one feather bed and furniture... Item I
give to my well beloved wife Martha Appling the use and profits of all
my land, stock, household furniture and personal estate whatsoever
during her natural life and widowhood, ect.ect. Wit: Charles Jackson,
Phillip Jackson, Mary X Jackson. Signed John Appling, seal.

<u>John Appling</u>. Virginia Sur. at a court held for the County of Amelia
the twenty third of Nov. 1775... The last will and testament of John
Appling deceased of which the writing hereunto annexed is a true copy
was proved by the oaths of Charles Jackson and Mary Jackson and
Phillip Jackson. The witnesses and ordered to be recorded. Test.
Thomas Griffin Peachy, Ad. Cmr. State of Georgia Richmd Cty; Personally
appeared before me Martha Appling the named Executrix to the last will
and testament of John Appling decd. and qualified as such. Given under
my hand this ___ day of Nov. and in the year of our Lord 1777. Wm.
Jackson, R.P. (The other Executors are Charles Connally and William
Cryer.)

APPLETON

<u>Thomas Appleton</u>. Estate of Thomas Appleton, Box 2 Pack 31, Probate
Judge Office, Abbeville, S. C. Admr. Bond, Ninety Six Dist. We
Joachim Bulow, William Shinholser and Davi Zubly are bound unto John
Ewing Calhoun, Esq. Ord. in the sum of fourteen thousand pds. Signed
at Long Cane the 13 Sept. 1782. in the presence of John Lockridge.
The citation to Joachim Bulow of Beach Island in the said Dist. listed
as the next of kin. William Dunbar and John Murry Esqr. are to qualify
the appraisers. The appraisers are David Zubly, Daniel Shaw, Casper
Nail, this 17 Sept. 1782. The appraisement was held the same day.

ARMSTRONG

<u>Benjamin Armstrong</u>. Will of Benjamin Armstrong, Box 3 #35 Probate
Judge Office, Pickens S. C. I Benjamin Armstrong of Pickens Dist.
being in low health, but sound disposing mind and understanding. First
I give to my son Abner Crosby Armstrong 240 acres layed off by Thomas
Lamar the 28 Apr. 1830 being that part I now live on. Also negro boy
named Hardy, one mare and two colts. Second.. I give to my daughter
Nancy Gainer, Rebackah, McWhorter, Gillam Wooten and Syntha Armstrong.
The tract of land layed off for each of them by Thomas Lamar, as I
afore gave them in a separate deed. Also I give to Abner Crosby
Armstrong and my daughter Syntha all the household and kitchen furniture to be equally divided. I do hereby appoint Abner Crosby Armstrong and Ezekiel McWhorter Executors. Dated 12 Oct. 1831. Wit:
James H. Dendy, Benjamin D. Dupre, William Perkinson. Signed Benj. X.
Armstrong, seal. There is a letter from Tunnel Hill Ga. Dated 7th
1875 from Mrs. Charlotte Wooten to the Ord. for Pickens County, S.C.
that her husband was Benjamin C. Wooten and that Benjamin Armstrong
was his grandfather and that he left some money to him in a will. If

this be so how could she get same as she needed it very badly. Letter
signed by L. B. Hambright. On Aug. 6, 1859 Margaret Armstrong and
L. D. Boling were bound unto Robert A. Thompson, Comm. in equity as
guardian of Turner Armstrong her minor so under 12 years, son of
Abner Armstrong decd., Benjamin Armstrong will proved 13 Dec. 1832.

Hughey Armstrong. Deed of Hughey Armstrong from Isaac Miller, Pack
260 Clerk of Court Office, Abbeville, S. C. Dated 23 Feb. 1837. In
the sum of $100.00 for fifty acres on the waters of Long Cain Creek
bound on North by Hugh Armstrong and East and South by Jesse Miller.
Wit: John H. Armstrong, Lewis J. Miller. No recording date given.

Margaret Armstrong. in Equity Pickens County #2. To the Honourable
the Chancellors of the State. Abner Armstrong her late husband died
intestate on the __ day of 1850. Possessed in fee simple of considerable real estate and personal property, which was sufficient to pay
the indebtness of the estate. She wishes a writ of partition for the
three plats of land viz. Tract #1 140 acres adj. Matthew Crenshaw,
Alexander Bryce, Wallace Miller. Tract #2 of 250 acres adj. E. P.
Verner, Mary McWhorter, Alexander Bryce and Zachariah Powers. Tract
#3 of 190 acres adj. Lafayette Allen, Daniel Hull and others. The
partition is to be made between herself and the six children of Abner
Armstrong decd. Viz: William Armstrong who is over 21 years. and
resides in Georgia, Alexander B., James, Andrew, Turner and Crosby
Armstrong. The last five are minors. Dated 1 Apr. 1858. Alexander
Bryce Senr. appointed guardian of the minors. A power of attorney
from Margaret Armstrong widow of Abner Armstrong decd. do appoint
Jacob P. Reed and Samuel Wilkes residing at Anderson Courthouse, S. C.
My true and lawful attorney Ect.ect. Dated 31 Mar. 1858. Margaret
Armstrong.

ARNOLD - ARNDELL

Readick Arndell. Will of Readick Arndell, Box 1 Pack 11, Probate Judge
Office, Spartanburg, S. C. I Readick Arndel of Spartanburg Dist. being
afflicted in body but in sound mind and memory. I give to my beloved
wife Rhoda the land whereon I now live during her natural life or
widowhood. Also one negro woman named Eliza and one negro boy named
Wylie. I bequeath to my daughter Elizabeth Barram the sum of six
dollars. To Nancy Daffern thirty six dollars, Rebeckah Paskell thirty
six dollars, Margaret Adams thirty six dollars, Mary Gelmon thirty
six dollars, William Arndel twenty six dollars, Silas Gelman twenty
four dollars, and if any is remaining it is to be divided between
Daniel Gelman, Anthony Gelman, John Arndel, James Arndel, Delila
Buchannan and Mary Reppy. It is my wish that at the death or marriage
of my wife the land is to be divided between my son Richard and
daughter Delitha, ect.ect. Wife Rhoda Arndel Executrix and Elijah
Turner Executor. Dated 1 Aug. 1826. Wit: John Sarratt Senr. John
Sarratt Junr., Robert Byars. Signed Readick Arndell, seal. Recorded
1 Sept. 1834. (This will was recorded as the will of Reddick Arnlod.)

Benjamin Arnold. Estate of Benjamin Arnold, Box 1 Pack 5 Probate
Judge Office, Abbeville, S. C. We Rebeca Arnold, George Taylor, Samuel
Serratt, are bound unto John Thomas Junr. Esq. Ord. Ninety six Dist.
in the sum of two thousand pds. sterling on the Admr. bond, dated 1
Oct. 1784. Same day Daniel McClaran, Nathaniel Robertson, Samuel
Sarratt three freeholders are to appraise the goods and chattels of
Benjamin Arnold decd. In another place it states that the widow
Rebeckah and John Arnold the eldest son and a majority of the heirs, do
agree to the said appraisers. Dated 11 Nov. 1784. No others heirs
given.

Benjamin Arnold. Will and Estate of Benjamin Arnold, Will Book C,
page 48, Greenville, S. C. I Benjamin Arnold being in perfect health
of body, mind and memory, ect. 1. I give to William Arnold decd. my
eldest son, two negroes James and Hannah, and cows, beds and to his
sons Anderson and William the tract of land in Bedford County, Va.
whereon he lived at his decd. The two sons is to get twenty shillings

after the decease of my wife. 2. I give to my son Edward Arnold two
negroes and the sum of twenty five pds. to be paid by my youngest son
Benjamin Arnold also twenty five shillings at the decease of my wife.
3. I give to my son Hendrick Arnold decd. one negro and her increase
which is Humphrey, Sarah, Phebe and Thelma and to his son William
twenty five shillings at the decease of my wife. 4. I give to my son
John Arnold, two negroes Lucy and Jack and the tract of land where he
now lives of 199 acres. Also twenty shillings at the decease of my
wife. 5. I give to my son Thomas Arnold the following negroes viz:
Milly, Omy, Joseph, Young, Dick and the tract of land there he now
live and twenty shillings at the decease of my wife. 6. I give to my
son Benjamin Arnold, seven negroes, named, and to get twenty shillings
at the decease of my wife. 7. I give to my daughter Charity Martin,
four negroes, named, and twenty shillings at the decease of my wife.
8. I give to my daughter Temperance Hamilton, four negroes, named,
and twenty shillings at the decease of my wife. 9. I give to my
beloved wife Ann Arnold, four negroes, household furniture and stock
of all kinds, during her natural life or widowhood. Thomas and Benjamin
Arnold as Executors. Dated 30 Jan. 1796. Wit: Hu.m Cobb, James
Chastain, George Grace. Signed Benjamin X Arnold. The appraisers
are John McElroy, Hewlett Sullivant, Joseph Dunklin. Dated 10 Oct.
1794. (Note will was dated 1796.)

William D. Arnold Senr.   Box 32 #368 Probate Judge Office, Pickens Co.,
S. C. I William Arnold Senr. being in sound mind and memory, ect.ect.
I will and bequeath unto my beloved wife during her natural life or
widowhood all my estate both real and personal. After the death of
wife executors to sell all personal property and give each a equal
share with my departed daughter Nancy D. Power one share to her child
or children. I will to my two sons William A. and Silas Arnold all
my land. Two daughters Frances and Catharine are to share equal with
the others. Make sons James N. and Reuben Arnold executors. Dated 6
Aug. 1849. Wit: Reuben Gaines, Robt. C. Scott, Balias Gaines. Signed
Wm. D. Arnold. Proven 24 July 1854. In 1868 there were 10 heirs viz:
S. N. Miller, H. E. Campbell, E. G. Mullinax, G. B. Smith, J. W. and
Joana Power, J. L. Mullinax, heirs of Albert Arnold, J. N. Arnold,
Reuben Arnold.

William A. Arnold. Estate of William A. Arnold, Box 35 #397. Probate
Judge Office, Pickens, S. C. Estate admr. 8 Dec. 1854 by Bryan
Boroughs and A. B. Sargent are bound to W. J. Parson Esq. Ord. in the
sum of $1,200.00. Left a widow and two children. Bought at sale
Newton Arnold. Reuben Arnold, Elizabeth Arnold.

Silas Arnold. Estate of Silas Arnold, Box 73 #782, Probate Judge
Office, Pickens, S. C. Estate Admr. 17 Feb. 1864 by Sarah E. C. Arnold
widow, Samuel Parsons, Barnett S. Gaines who are bound to W. E. Holcombe, Ord. in the sum of $4,000.00. He left four heirs names not
given.

William & Mary Elizabeth Arnold. Box 8 #13, Probate Judge Office,
Pickens, S. C. On 29 July 1870 John C. Watkins, Jacob H. Boroughs,
Joab Mauldin are bound unto Irvin H. Philpot, Ord. in the sum of $380.00
John C. Watkins was made guardian of Mary E. and William A. Arnold
minors of William A. Arnold decd. who are minors over 14 years. In
March 1876 Mary E. Smith and William A. Arnold received their full share.

Hendrick T. Arnold. Estate of Hendrick T. Arnold, Box 102 #1074, Probate Judge Office, Pickens Co., S. C. Estate Admr. 17 Oct. 1872 by
Jane L. Arnold, A. S. Briggs, H. C. Briggs who are bound unto I. H.
Philpot, Ord. in the sum of $1,200.00. Also Hendrick T. died 7 Apr.
1872 Non Compas Mentis. The widow was Jane L. Arnold.

Jane L. Arnold. Estate of Jane L. Arnold, Box 92 #978, Probate Judge
Office, Pickens, S. C. Mrs. Jane Arnold died July 15, 1875. Heirs at
law were viz: her sons Alexander S. Briggs, Henry C. Briggs and her
daughters Elizabeth Watson, Myra L. Watson and the children of her pre-
decd. daughter Harriet Grisham to wit. Joseph Grisham, Fannie Grisham,
Agnes Grisham, Lizzie M. Grisham a minor above the age of 14 and the

following great grandchildren of Jane Leatherbury, a pre-decd. daughter
of the said Mrs. Harriet Grisham to wit Harriet G. Leatherbury, age 20
years, Sarah W. Leatherbury age 18 years, George S. Leatherbury, age
13 years, Katie W. Leatherbury age 11 years, Joseph G. Leatherbury,
age 7 years. Children and grandchildren of Mrs. Harriet Grisham decd.
being a citizen of the state of Mississippi, dated 12 Feb. 1879. Jane
Arnold owned 297 acres more or less on Georges Creek, known as the Jane
Arnold Homestead. Jane Elizabeth Watson of Edgefield Co. sold for the
sum of $800.00 to M. W. Watson her entire interest in the land owned
by my mother Mrs. Jane L. Arnold. Dated 5 Feb. 1876.

<u>B. V. Arnold</u>. Estate of B. V. Arnold, Box 113 #1095 Probate Judge
Office, Pickens, S. C. Estate Admr. 13 Aug. 1882 by Silas O. Arnold
and James S. Hall who are bound to O. L. Durant Ord. in the sum of
$700.00. He died 22 May 1882.

<u>Marcus M. Arnold</u>. Estate of Marcus M. Arnold, Box 107 #1020, Probate
Judge Office, Pickens Co., S. C. Estate Admr. 13 Oct. 1874 by Louisa
M. Arnold, Nathaniel M. Madden, Frederick L. Garvin who are bound to
I. H. Philpot Ord. in the sum of $100.00. Louisa M. Arnold later
married a Alexnader.

<u>James N. Arnold</u>. Will of James N. Arnold, Box 108 #1036, Probate Judge
Office, Pickens, S. C. I James N. Arnold being in sound mind and
memory, ect.ect. Sell enough of the estate to pay all debts and the
remainder of my estate both real and personal be kept till my youngest
son Reuben H. Arnold arrive at the age of twenty one. Under the control and management of my son Frederick N. Arnold. When Reuben arrives
at the age of twenty one, my Executors to sell both real and personal
property. Reuben to get one hundred dollars as a special legacy, my
two grandchildren John A. and Elias W. Madden fifty dollars as a
special legacy. Daughter Elizabeth to get twenty dollars in lieu of
a cow. The remainder to be equally divided between my wife Sarah C.
and my nine children. I appoint my sons Thomas B. and Frederrick N.
Arnold as sole Executors. Dated 6 Aug. 1875. Wit: W. E. Holcombe,
E. H. Nash, G. W. Boroughs. Signed J. N. Arnold. Filed 7 Oct. 1875.

<u>Arnold Minors Children</u>. Estate of the Arnold minors children. Box 11
#178 Probate Judge Office, Pickens, S. C. Joana A. Arnold was made
guardian of Lilly Lee, Minnie Bell, and William Capers Arnold minors
under 21 years. Joana A. Arnold is their mother. They the children of
John T. Arnold decd. On 12 Nov. 1883, recd. $46.16 from the estate of
Silas Arnold.

<u>Arnold and Briggs</u> data. Pack 238 Equity, Clerk of Court Office,
Pickens Jane Arnold late widow of Robert H. Briggs decd. and her
present husband.. Arnold and Elizabeth Watson, daughter of Robert H.
Briggs and over 21 years and Elijah Watson her husband.. and Harriet T.
Grisham daughter of Robert H. Briggs and John O. Grisham her husband
and A. S. Briggs son of the said Robert H. Briggs. Died some years
since intestate ect.ect. Jane Arnold and William Holcombe took out
the letter of admr. That the said Robert H. Briggs left at his death
children who are minors viz: Henry C. Briggs, Myra L. Briggs, A. S.
Briggs, Elizabeth Watson and Harriet Grisham. Filed 18 Feb. 1840.
Briggs owned five tracts of land, tract #2 and 3 sold to Revd. H. T.
Arnold. #4 sold to William Holcombe, #5 to Elijah Watson, #6 to Readin
Freeman.

ARTER

<u>James Arter</u>. Box 26 #309, Probate Judge Office, Pickens, S. C. Estate
Admr. 29 Jan. 1852 by Reese Bowen who is bound unto W. D. Steel Ord.
in the sum of $600.00. Wm. Arter, Bet Arter bought at the sale. Paid
Jack Arter for Solomon Arter on note $5.61. Paid George Arter for
driving and attending to horses $8.00.

Jackson Arter. Apt. 111 #1056. Probate Judge Office, Pickens Co., S. C. I Jackson Arter in sound mind and memory and in enjoyment of Common health, ect.ect. 1. Pay all debts and funeral expenses. 2. I desire immediately after my death that my beloved illegitimate son Baylis Ladd most commonly known as Baylis Arter have all my property both real and personal provided he never marrys then I desire that my illegitmate grandson Buncombe Ladd now known as Buncombe Arter has the above named property of my estate but if my above named son should marry and have children of his own body then I will and desire that my grandson as before mention only becomes equal heirs in my estate with the bodily heirs of my beloved son Baylis... Lastly I appoint my friend and neighbor W. E. Welborn my Executor. Dated 24 May 1876. Test: E. J. Elrod, J. M. Welborn and Happy Welborn. Signed Jackson X Arter. Proven 1 Feb. 1877.

ASHLEY

Joshua Ashley. Ref. Equity records of Cador Gantt, Pack 345, Clerk of Court Office, Abbeville, S. C. Joshua Ashley married Mary Burton a daughter of Josiah and Mary Burton of Abbeville Dist. She had the following brothers and sisters viz: Caleb Burton of Abbeville Dist., John Burton living in Alabama, Peter Burton who was also living out of state. Dated 1850.

ASHWORTH

Joseph Ashworth. Deed from Joseph Ashworth to David Trainam, Deed Book C, page 261, Mesne Conveyance Office, Greenville, S. C. This indenture made between Joseph Ashworth to David Trainam both of Greenville County. Dated 7 July 1792. For 100 pds sterling for 160 acres on Horse Creek of Reedy River. Part of a tract originally granted to Thomas Lewis on 16 July 1784. Lewis conveyed to John Thomas on 6 March 1790. Thomas conveyed to Vincent Davis and from Davis to Joseph Ashworth the 10 Mar. 1791. Wit: Thos. Camp, Hustings Diel, Robt X Thompson. Signed Joseph Ashworth, seal. Deed proved in May Court before John Alexander Esq. and recorded 6 June 1793.

ATKINS

Francis Atkins. Will of Francis Atkins, Pack 3 Equity, Clerk of Court Office, Abbeville, S. C. Francis Atkins made his will 1 Sept. 1855. Francis died in March 1856. Named son Robert Atkins as Executor, others heirs are daughter Margaret Dale, sons Ravenna and James now minors and wife Elizabeth. All is to share and share alike. With Robert as Executor, trustee and overseer and supervisorship over all. Wits: R. W. Lites, J. C. Lites, J. W. Lites. Signed Francis Atkins. Will proved 18 March 1856 by R. W. Lites, before W. Hill O.A.D. By Nov. 1856 it is stated that Margaret Dale former husband was dead and she had married Dr. C. C. Porter. Also in Nov. 1856 the widow was in the Court of Equity for her share and the interest as stated in the will... In 1860 R. W. Lites was guardian of Ravenna and James Atkins, minors of Francis Atkins decd.

Henry Atkins. Deed of Henry Atkins to John Adams. Pack 451 #5 Clerk of Court Office Abbeville, S. C. This indenture made between Henry Atkins and John Adams both of Abbeville Co. Dated 13 Nov. 1857. In the sum of one thousand dollars for 120 acres on the waters of Long Cane Creek. Wit: John A. Wier, M. McDonald. Signed: Henry Atkins, seal. On the same day Mrs. Sarah Atkins the wife of Henry and renounce her dower before Matthew McDonald C.C. Also on the same day John A. Wier attested to the deed before M. McDonald, C.C.

ATKINSON

Timothy Atkinson. Estate of Timothy Atkinson, Box 3 Pack 47, Probate
Judge Office, Abbeville, S. C. We Nathaniel Howell, Casper Nail Senr.,
John Meyer are bound unto John Thomas Junr. Ord. of Ninety Six Dist.
in the sum of five hundred pds. The condition that Nathaniel Howell
truly Admr. the goods and chattles of Timothy Atkinson decd. Dated 7
Jan. 1786. The appraise are John Meyer, Jonathan Meter, Casper Nail
Junr. to view, appraise and make a perfect inventory of the goods and
chattel of Timothy Atkinson decd. Dated 7 Jan. 1786. The sale was
held but no date given. Those who bought were, Jean Atkinson, Nathl.
Howell, Benjamin Harris, Samuel Burriss, Joe Hix, John Savage, John
Clark.

Amos Atkinson. Estate of Amos Atkinson, Box 1 #11, Probate Judge Office
Anderson, S. C. The estate was Admr. 4 June 1810 by John Williams and
George Head who are bound unto John Harris Ord. of Pendleton Dist. in
the sum of fifteen hundred dollars. This citation was read 13 May
1810 at the Rev. Robt. Orr's meeting house. John Williams was Admr.
of the estate. Those who bought at sale were, Elizabeth Atkinson, John
Williams, Polley Atkinson, Robert Granger, George Head, William Sutton,
Those who received from the estate, 2 July 1821, James H. Atkinson
in full sixty six dollars, 9 Sept. 1817 Elizabeth Atkinson in full
sixty six dollars, 2 July 1821 Bill G. Dilworth in full sixty six
dollars, 12 May 1815 John E. Norris (Mary Norris may be the wife?)
sixty six dollars two cents and one mill in full.

ATTAWAY

Mary Ann Attaway wife of H. B. Attaway of Burke Co., Ga. Recd property
from the will in 1861 of a Lemuel Robinson of Barnwell Co., S. C.
(Will #19)?

AUGUSTE

Seasor Auguste. Will of Seasor Auguste, Box 1 #5, Probate Judge Office,
Anderson, S. C. I Seasor Auguste being weak in body but sound mind.
Pay my just debts then I bequeath unto my beloved wife Holley the land
I now live on with all stock, household furniture and farming utensils
as long as she remains a widow, if she marry the hole to be sold and
equally divided between my children named John, Patcey, Peggay, Januy.
Son John to get my gun and shottage and shumakers tools. Sell the
tract of land Adj. John Cochran and use to the advantageous of my
children. Wit: Joab Lewis, Joseph X Woods, James X Hughes. Signed
Seasor X Auguste, seal.
    Also its my will that my beloved wife Holley be appointed Execu-
trix and John Cochran Executor. Signed and sealed this 5 Dec. 1804.
Seal. On 11 March 1805 Joel Lewis and Joseph Woods after being sworn
that they saw Seasor Auguste sign, seal and declare this his last will
and Test. And that they beleave that the above naming Executrix and
Executor was not intentional but through neglect. Inventory made Dec.
1805.

AUSTIN

James M. Austin. Estate of James M. Austin, Apt. 11, file 123, Probate
Judge Office, Greenville, S. C. To John Watson, Ord. we Nancy Austin
and William Goldsmith, sheweth that James M. Austin died lately intestate. Your petitioners pray that a letter of Admr. be granted to said
William Goldsmith. Dated 27 Oct. 1848. Signed Nancy Austin and
William Goldsmith. On 13 Nov. 1848 William Goldsmith Admr. pray for a
sale of the personal property of decd. as he left a widow and family of

young children. Sale granted and held 13 Dec. 1848. Final settlement
was made Jan. 2, 1850. Viz: paid J. Watson, Ord. fee for final sett.
$4.50, paid William Goldsmith commission at 5% $217.28, paid Nancy
Austin (widow) Bal. her share $79.79, paid the share of Mary Jane,
William Thomas, John P., Margaret H. and Sarah Ellen Austin all minors
for whom I am guardian, each $511.91 1/2 for a total of $2,559.58 1/2.
Total $4,345.64.

Nancy Austin. Deed from Nancy Austin to Wm. T. Austin. Deed Book AA,
page 501. This deed made 18 Sept. 1867. For three hundred dollars for
all my interest, title and claim in the plantation on which I now live,
it being one third of her decd. husband land. On the waters of
Raburns Creek. adj. land of Wm. Cox, J. T. Bennett, J. R. and K. Stone
and others. Wit: E. Ed. Bozeman, Thomas Goldsmith. Signed: Nancy
Austin, seal. Recorded 20 Sept. 1867.

Nancy Austin. Deed from Nancy Austin to Wm. Goldsmith, Deed Book CC,
page 63, Greenville, S. C. Deed dated 18 Dec. 1868. For fourteen
hundred dollars paid by Wm. Goldsmith, Nancy sell a tract of land
known as the home place of Tho. Goldsmith, Sr. decd. containing 490
acres, adj. James Lock, decd. Isaac Cox and T. L. Bozeman and Thomas
Goldsmith, Bennett and Thomason. Wit: Jas. W. Goldsmith and W. T.
Austin. Signed: Nancy Austin. Proved and recorded 14 March 1870.

Nancy Austin. Deed from Nancy Austin et al to Wm. Goldsmith. Deed
Book CC, page 62. This indenture made between the heirs of Thomas
Goldsmith Senr. decd. and William Goldsmith, dated 18 Dec. 1868,
Thomas Goldsmith did direct his Admr. or agent to sell a tract of land.
This was done and William Goldsmith was the highest and last bidder.
For the sum of $255.00 for 124 acres on Horsepen Creek. Wit: W. T.
Austin and T. B. Goldsmith. Signed by the heirs or their agents.
The deed was proved 14 March 1870. and recorded the same day. The
heirs who signed the deed are: Nancy Austin, Thomas Goldsmith, James
W. Goldsmith, Thomas L. Woodsides and wife Sarah Woodsides, Barksdale
Charles and wife Mary Charles and Thomas Goldsmith Attorney or agent
for A. B. Fall and his wife Peremila G. Fall of Davis County, Missis-
sippi and William Goldsmith, all of Greenville Co. but the Falls.

Walter Austin. Estate of Walter Austin, Apt. 11 File 90. Probate
Judge Office, Greenville, S. C. I Walter Austin of Greenville Dist.
being in perfect mind and memory, ect.ect. First pay just debts,
second, I leave and bequeath to my wife Elender the land where on I
now live, with all tools, household and kitchen furniture. Two horses,
two cows and calves of her own choosing from my stock with three
negroes of her own choosing. After the death of my wife the land to
be divided between my sons William M. and Nathaniel Austin also I
give to my daughter Jane McCew forty acres tract where John Austin
formerly lived, adj. land of Carter Johnson, James Gault, let John
Austin spring branch be the dividing line. The balance to be sold and
equal divided betwixt my lawful heirs. viz: Nancy Glenn, Elizabeth
Jones, Martha Clark, John P. Austin, James Austin, Jane McCew, Walter
Austin, Rebecca Glenn, Wiley Thomason who is an heir, Rutha Simpson
decd. William M. and Nathaniel Austin.

BAGBY

John Bagby. Power of Attorney from John Bagby to Robert Jackson. Pack
485, Probate Judge Office, Anderson, S. C. Gwinnett County, Ga. I
John Bagby of said County do niminate and appoint Robert Jackson of the
County of Campbell in the said State my true and lawful attorney to
use, ask, demand and recover from the Executor or any other person in
South Carolina Anderson Dist. all sum of money belonging to the estate
of Samuel McCuller that is due me in right of my wife Ellender McCuller.
Dated 4 Oct. 1834. Wit: Daniel Sanford, G. W. F. Lamkins. Signed
John Bagby, seal. Rec. on this power. $42.21 from John Harris, Ord.
29 Oct. 1834. Wit: J. E. Reese, proved before George E. W. Foster,
N.P.

BAILEY

Charles A. Bailey, late of Kershaw County the grandfather of Elliott H. Bowen, Eva H. Bowen, Earle H. Bowen, Eunice H. Bowen minor children in Jan. 1898. Their guardians were A. H. Bowen and M. A. Bowen. (File 36)

BAKER

William R. Baker. Pack 251 #3, Clerk of Court Office, Pickens Co., S. C. On 24 July 1860 William R. Baker gave to James E. Hagood two thousand dollars in a trust for the use of Harriet M. Martin and Laura Toccoa Baker and any other children of Harriet M. Baker. That the trust has become burdensome to the plaintiff and Thomas C. Martin the husband of Harriet M. is willing to except the trust and is a fit person. That the defendant has intermarried with Thomas C. Martin and has issue viz: Benjamin F. & Oscar B. Martin. That they with Laura Toccoa Baker are minors under 14 years and reside with Thomas C. Martin. Thomas C. Martin the stepfather of Laura Toccoa Baker. Dated 25 March 1873.

BALDWIN

Samuel Baldwin. #20 in Equity, Clerk of Court Office, Pickens Co. Your Oratrix Peggy Baldwin of the State and Dist. aforesaid, That her late husband Samuel Baldwin departed this life intestate on the 7 Oct. 1862, leaving your Oratrix his widow and eight children, Nancy who married Antony Minton, Elsy C. who married Obediah Minton, Mary E. who married Thomas Adair, Levi G. Baldwin, all of this Dist. and Thos. H. Baldwin of Anderson, S. C. George W. Baldwin in the State of Georgia and there died. Leaving a widow without children... Sarah who married David Linah, residence unknown, Margaret who married William Hembree who took out a letter of Admr. upon the estate of the Saml. Baldwin decd. and are now out of the state, Margaret sold the personal property, and Nancy had a deed of trust made on the land and left the widow and other children bare. The land was for 122 acres on the waters of Seneca River and a branch of Martin Creek. Adj. land of Wm. Hunnicutt, John B. Earle, Berry Phillips, George Fredricks.

Samuel Baldwin, Estate. Box 68 #733 Probate Judge Office, Pickens, S. C. Estate Admr. 13 Feb. 1863 by Margaret Baldwin widow, Stephen Baldwin and Wm. Hembree who are bound unto W. E. Holcombe Ord. in the sum of $500.00. Wm. Hembree is her son in law.

Elizabeth Baldwin. Clerk of Court Office, Pack 644 #1, Pickens, S. C. An inquest was held at Dempsey Yows place in Pickens Co. Nov. 30, 1859 upon the body of an infant child found in Martin Creek. Mrs. Yow called upon Mrs. Nancy Cox and Mrs. Margaret Baldwin to show them the body. Thought it had been in the creek about three weeks and that the baby was a full grown baby when born. Believes the mother of the baby is Miss Elizabeth Baldwin living near Martin Creek. Mrs. Drucilla Baldwin mother of Elizabeth Baldwin states that her daughter has not been in a family way that she knows of. That her daughter was suspected of being pregnant and that about three weeks ago she was quite sick with her monthly menstruation. Her daughter was 23 years old. Elisa Ann Baldwin sworn also, she was a sister to Elizabeth.

BALL

Peter Ball. Estate of Peter Ball, Box 8 Pack 151. Probate Judge Office, Abbeville, S. C. (Will) I Peter Ball do make and ordain this my last will and Test. To keep all my estate together till the death of my wife Elizabeth Ball. I give to my son Jeremier Ball all that

tract of land lying on Saluda River adj. John and Zachary Pullom of
150 acres. At the death of my wife I give to all my children one
horse of equal value, Pollay, Lucay, Nancy, Jeremier, Jinsay, Elizabeth.
I leave my brother Lewis Ball, George Ball and Henry Hitt as Executors.
Dated 25 Feb. 1816. Wit: Zachy Meriwether, John Hatter, Polly Whitlow.
Signed Pet Ball. Will proved by John Hatter before Talo. Livington,
O.A.D. 12 Mar. 1816. The sale of Ball's estate was held 29 March 1816.
The buyers at the sale are, Elizabeth Ball, Plesent Right, Damuel Lucas
Doctr. Zecheriah Merawether, Robert Cheatham, David Stots, George Ball,
Lewis Ball, Nathan Lipscomb, John Foshee, Charles Maxwell, William
Sample, John Lewis, Philip Day, Robert Turner, Nancy Ball, John
McKeller, Richard Golding, John Sadler, Samuel Whitlow, Benjamin Bell,
John Boyd, James Turner, Henry Hitt, David Stwert.

BALENTINE

Richard Balentine. Estate of Richard Balentine, Box 68-97 #730-1017.
Probate Judge Office, Pickens Co., S. C. Estate was Admr. 2 Feb. 1863
by Mrs. Nancy Balentine, James Ellison, Osborn Mauldin are bound unto
W. E. Holcomb, Ord. in the sum of $3,000.00. He left a widow and five
children viz: Nancy, Albert C., Andrew E., James A., William C., Mary
A. Balentine, Mary A. married D. W. T. Johnston and rec. $25.36
19 Nov. 1870. Richard owned 30 acres of land on Brushy Creek adj.
land of H. C. Briggs & B. Day.

William C. Balentine. Estate of William C. Balentine, Box 73-8-104.
#783-132-1094, Probate Judge Office, Pickens Co., S. C. William Estate
admr. 17 Feb. 1864 by Lucinda A. Balentine, widow, Henry L. Russell,
Saml. Parson who are bound unto W. E. Holcombe in the sum of $1,000.00.
William C. left the wife Lucinda and one child, also named William A.
He recd his father share in his grandfather, Richard Balentine Estate.

BANKHEAD

James Bankhead. Will of James Bankhead, Will Book, page 93, Probate
Judge Office, Union Co., S. C. I James Bankhead being in sound mind
and memory ect.ect. I give to my wife Elizabeth the plantation that
I now live on to raise my children. I give to my son John Bankhead
five shillings, to daughter Hannah five shillings, I give my girls one
bed when they marry and one horse and saddle. I give to the boys a
horse and saddle if they stay with their mother till the age of twenty
one years. I appoint my wife & Henry Good to be Executors. Dated
27 Oct. 1805. Wit: John Jackson, Jas. Davidson, James McCane. Signed
James X Bankhead, seal. Will proved by John Jackson before William
Rice, Esq. Ord. 18 March 1806.

James Bankhead. Will of James Bankhead, Apt. 4 file 68. Probate Judge
Office, Chester Co. I James Bankhead being weak in body but sound in
mind and memory, ect.ect. I give to my son Robt. Bankhead who has
rec. his part one dollar. Also my son Samuel Bankhead who lives with
me I give him fifty dollars. Also Mary Blair who has recd. her part
one dollar. Likewise Jane Stewart one dollar. To my daughter Margaret
Harper I give to her twenty dollars. To daughter Elizabeth Sloan I
leave her one hundred dollars. I give to my grandson Samuel Stewart
twenty dollars, to grandson James Blair twenty dollars, to grandson
James Bankhead Junr. twenty dollars. To grandson Robt. Moore Sloan
twenty dollars. Make my son Thomas Bankhead and Robert Stewart
Executors. Dated 4 Jan. 1821. Wits: Thos. Bankhead, Elizabeth X
Sloan, Wm. Strong. Signed Jas. X Bankhead. Probated 5 Feb. 1821.

BANKS

Joab Banks. Estate of Joab Banks, Box 40 #450, Probate Judge Office,
Pickens Co., S. C. Estate Admr. 1 Feb. 1856 by Warren T. Banks,
Alexander Bryce, who are bound unto W. J. Parsons Ord. Pickens Co. in
the sum of $1,000.00. He left seven children, names not given. In
the expend acct. On 20 Aug. 1861, paid James A. or M. Banks in full
$5.06, paid Wm. H. Banks, John Gilliland, W. M. Banks, W. T. Banks,
Thomas G. Porter, W. A. or M. Cantrell each in full $5.06. Buyers at
sale Sarah Banks, etc.

Rachel Banks. Estate of Rachel Banks, Box 46 #512, Probate Judge
Office, Pickens Co., Est. Admr. 10 Aug. 1857 by Milly Merk, E. E.
Alexander, Samuel Chepman who are bound unto W. J. Parson Ord. in the
sum of $300.00 (Letter of Admr. Milly Merck was written Emilia Merck.)

Banks, Minors Children Guardian, Box 2 #41, Probate Judge Office,
Pickens Co., S. C. 3 Mar. 1854 Emelia Merck, James George are bound
to W. J. Parson Ord. in the sum of $500.00. Emelia Merck gdn. of
Daniel Lively Merck, Rachel Jane Banks minors under twenty one.

Emily Banks. Estate of Emily Banks, Box 111 #1064. Probate Judge
Office, Pickens, S. C. Emily Banks states that on 3 Oct. 1872. Wm.
Banks by deed of gift gave to her, George, John, Baylis Banks, 254
acres on branches of Golden and Rice Creeks, water of 12 mile River,
Known as James Taylor tract. All of age except Baylis a minor.

Emily Banks. Deed from Emily Banks to Baylus Banks, Book D Page 435
Pickens Co., S. C. I Emily Banks of Pickens Co. for and in consideration of natural love i Have for my son Baylus Banks and for the further
consideration that the said Baylus Banks agrees to take care of me and
furnish me a comfortable support during the term of my natural life
and the sum of five dollars. To have all my one fourth interest in a
tract of land known as the Robinson tract, containing two hundred
acres on the South side of Golden Creek. Also my part in the other
tract known as the Chumpey Seiglor tract, adj. land of J. B. Clayton,
Ed Phair, Cato Johnson and others. Dated 14 March 1882. Wit:
J. L. O. Thompson, W. H. Amber. Signed Emily X Banks, seal. Attested
the same date. Recorded 7 Sept. 1883

G. W. Banks. Will of G. W. Banks, Box 135 #5, Probate Judge Office,
Pickens Co., S. C. I G. W. Banks being in sound mind and memory ect.
ect. I give to my wife Mary C. Banks and daughter Frances Banks all
that tract of land I had surveyed off of my home tract. Adj. James
Barrett, H. E. Mull and all the remainder of my home tract containing
seventy five acres for and during their natural life. And as much
fire wood as may be necessary. At the death of both Mary C. and
Frances I give and bequeath unto Abram Banks the son of Frances Banks
a one half interest in fee simple in the said seventy five acres, and
the other half to be divided between my other children viz: Nancy
Turner, John Henry Banks, Ranson Allen Banks, Roswell Banks, Sallie
Capps and Elizabeth Byers to share and share alike. I give and
bequeath unto my wife all my personal property and make her Mary C.
Banks my Executrix. Wit: John Julien, E. G. Jones, J. L. Looper.
Dated Oct. __ 1895. Signed: G. W. (X) Banks. Filed 7 May 1900.

M. M. Banks. Land Warrant of M. M. Banks, Pack 407 #10 Clerk of Court
Office, Pickens, S. C. To J. B. Clayton or some other lawful deputy
surveyer for the said county. You are hereby authorized and required
with proper attention to lay off and locate unto M. M. Banks a tract
of vacant land within the said county, ect.ect. Given under my hand
and seal of office at Pickens Court House. 12 Jan. 1869. R. A. Bowen,
C.C.P. G.S.

Henry Banks. Petition of Henry Banks, Pack 178 #1, Clerk of Court
Office, Pickens, S. C. To the Honorable County Supervisor and County
Commissioners of Pickens Co. Whereas Henry Banks has an invalid
mother who is 84 years old and an invalid sister who is about 60 years

of age, and is afflicted with a cancer. The said Henry Banks is their sole support except Nancy Gillam gets $20.00 pension. Also Henry Banks has a wife and five small children to support and that he is a very poor man and needs assistance to keep his mother and sister from the poor house. Therefore we petition your Humble Body to help them. We your petitioners ever pray. Dated 13 Feb. 1909. Signed R. T. Hallum, C.S.C. Also signed: T. H. McWhorter, F. R. McClanahan, S. Roper, Jno. L. Gravely, J. B. Newberry.

BARKER

James Barker, Senr. Will of James Barker, Senr. Box 5 #51. Probate Judge Office, Pickens, S. C. I James Barker Senr. being weak in body but sound mind and memory. 1. Pay my just debts, 2. My will that the rest and residue and remainder for the benefit of my present wife and my beloved children. 3. To wife Charlotte the land on the south-side of Little River where I now live containing about 300 acres, it being part of the tract I purchased from Sol Palmour, at the death or widowhood to be divided between all my children by my present wife, viz: Josiah, Martha, Eli, Joshua, Elizabeth and Peggy Barker to share and share alike, but give Eli two shares. Also my Executors to pay my daughter Rebecca Davis twenty five dollars 1 Feb. 1835. James Barker Junr. to get twelve dollars a year just to carry out my will. When the youngest is of age then divide all with my present wife and her children. All my children by my first wife have left me and are capable of gaining a living, I leave them nothing more except my prayers for their prosperity and happiness. Make wife Charlotte Executrix and James Barker, Junr. Executor. Dated 1 Dec. 1833. Wit: Joseph Grisham, John Swaford, Joseph Burnett. Signed James X Barker. Will proved 11 Mar. 1834. Rec. Book 1, page 30-31.

James Barker. Estate of James Barker, Probate Judge Office, Pickens Co., S. C. On Aug. 24, 1855. James H. Johnson applied for letter of Admr. No other papers.

Josiah Barker. Land Warrant of Josiah Barker, Clerk of Court Office, Pickens Co., S. C. By W. L. Keith, Clerk of the Court, to any lawful surveyor you are authorized to lay out unto Josiah Barker a tract of land not exceeding one thousand acres and make a true plat of same within two months. Executed of the within, 329 acres on the 23 Oct. 1850. Tyre B. Mauldin, Dep. Sur.

BARKSDALE

Henry Barksdale. Estate of Henry Barksdale was appraised 17 Jan. 1818. by Vincent McElhhenney, James Hutcheson, Joseph C. Mathews. The estate paid for schooling for Steth Barksdale and schooling for Delia Ann Barksdale in the years 1818, 1819, 1820. This is from Abbeville Court House, Abbeville, S. C.

Higgason Barksdale, Junr. of Ninety Six Dist. Being in perfect mind and memory ect.ect. 1. My just debts be paid, 2. My beloved wife Fanney to have one third of my estate during her lifetime. At her death that my brother to have it. 3. I will to my sister Fanney Mathersons children a tract of land containing 228 acres joining land called Shankiss Place and rented to John Baily. I will all the rest of my estate to my brother Richard Barksdale except two negroes Mary and ___ they to be freed at my death. Make wife Fanney Executrix and Richard Executor. Wit: Bartlett Thompson, James McCelvey, Jno. Middleton. Signed: H. Barksdale, seal. Dated 17 Nov. 1798. Will proved by John Middleton on 2 May 1800. By August, Mrs. Patty Sharp a sister of the said deceased was in court to have the estate settled. In the same package there is an inventory and appraisement of the estate of Thomas Barksdale of Ninety Six Dist. dated 4 Aug. 1784. Appraisors: Danied Ramsey, John Harris, George Whitefield.

Sherod Barksdale. Estate of Sherod Barksdale, Abbeville, S. C.
Sherod Barksdale died intestate in May 1859 in Abbeville Dist. and
William Truitt was made Admr. Barksdale left a widow and four children
viz: William W. Barksdale now twenty eight years of age of Elyton, Ala.
James T. Barksdale of the same place age twenty four years, George T.
Barksdale now thirty years of age, last heard from in Edgefield Dist.,
S. C. and John Lewis Barksdale, now dead. Said Truitt the Admr. sold
two houses land and personal property, we or our mother who lives near
us have received our share, ect. Dated 23 March 1869.

BARNES

Christian Barnes. Deed to Christian Barnes from John and Ann Stewart,
Pack 260 Clerk of Court Office, Abbeville, S. C. Deed dated 7 May
1832. In the sum of 500 dollars paid by Christian Barnes for all that
plantation or tract of land lying on Fraszers Creek a branch of Norrises
Creek, waters of Long Cane. adj. land of Isaac Miller, Jessee Miller,
and James Caldwell. The land in two tracts, one granted to Wm. Covey,
the other to Gean Turk. Wit: Jesse Miller, Lewis J. Miller. Signed
John Stewart and Ann X Stewart. Deed proved on 8 May 1832 by Jesse
Miller. before Hamilton Hill, J.P. Recorded 4 June 1832.

John N. Barnes. Estate of John N. Barnes, Box 65 #700, Probate Judge
Office, Abbeville Co., S. C. Est. Admr. 10 Oct. 1862 by James T.
Barnes, Thaddeus S. Miller who are bound to W. E. Holcombe Ord. Pickens
Dist. in the sum of $400.00 James T. Barnes a brother was of Lowndes-
ville, Abbeville Dist.

BARRETT

Reubin Barrett. Will of Reubin Barrett, Apt. 1 File 44. Probate Judge
Office, Greenville Co., S. C. I Reubin Barrett of Greenville Dist.
being weak in body but in sound mind and memory, ect.ect. 1. I give
to my daughter Peggy her bed and furniture and her saddle two cows and
calves in the presence of my son Reuben. 2. I give to my son Reuben
one horse colt named Phillip and saddle. I give to my daughter Hannah
her bed and furniture one cow and calf and a fourteen dollar saddle to
be bought for her. The balance of my estate to be keep to pay debts
and support my two young sons Arthur and William and Prudence Plumley
and Betsey Willson my two young daughters and their education. When
Betsey the youngest comes of age, the estate is to be divided thus,
the four youngest to get fifty dollars more than sons Joseph, John,
David and Ruebin Barrett. The older daughters are, Mary Jackson, Peggy
Barrett, Nancy Sulur, Hannah Barrett. Make brother Aurther and son
Admr. Dated 5 Apr. 1812. Wit: Arthur Barrett, Coswell Barrett,
Rebekah X Barrett. Signed Reubin Barrett. Probated 17 March 1814.

Rebecca Barrett. Sept. 25, 1823 Rebecca Barrett an heir of Thomas
Barton decd. of Greenville Dist. (Ref. Probate Judge Office, Greenville
S. C. Apt. 1 file 41.)

Caswell Barrett. Estate of Caswell Barrett, Apt. 1 file 19, Probate
Judge Office, Greenville Dist., S. C. On 14 Feb. 1831 Joseph Barrett
applied for Admr. on the estate of Caswell Barrett decd. On 27 Feb.
1846 Joseph Barrett states that the children of Caswell Barrett are now
nearly of age. He left a widow Nancy Barrett and children Kinian,
Arthur I. or J.?, Polly B., Elizabeth Barrett.

Martin Barrett. On 11 July 1834 Martin Barrett granted unto Mathew
Mansell 158 acres lying on Wolf Creek.

Frances Barrett. On 28 Sept. 1846 Frances Barrett was deeded 150
acres on Wolf Creek by Matthew Mansell. (Both Ref. Pro. Jud. Office,
Pickens, S. C. Box 76 #811.)

William Barrett. Will of William Barrett, Box 50 #555, Probate Judge
Office, County (not given). I William Barrett being in sound mind and
memory, ect.ect. 1. Pay my just debts. 2. To my beloved wife Mary
the land I now live on it being on a prong of George's Creek water of
Saluda River. adj. land of Mrs. Melinda Archer, William T. King, and
others, of about 100 acres one bay mare, five head cattle, eight head
hoggs, ect.ect. Household furniture, farm tools, account book, notes,
ect.ect. My three younger daughters to have a bed, and a cow. They
are Mary A., Sarah Jane and Melinda P. Barrett, my two older daughters
are Lucretia Caroline McMahan, Rebeccah Eveline McCoy. In 1869 the
heirs are viz: Jesse McMahan and wife Caroline, John Barrett, Sarah
Jane Hamilton, Wm. J. King and wife Melinda. The heirs of James and
Evaline McCoy they are, William, Alice, Laurence, Annie McCoy, John C.
Powers and wife Mary resides in Spartanburg Co. and the heirs of
Benjamin Barrett decd. viz: Wm. Milton, David and Benjamin Barrett who
resides in Georgia. (In this paper William Barrett died on 12 June
1859.) ... The will was wit: by Wm. T. King, R. F. King, Joshua
Jameson. Signed: William Barrett. Will dated 2 June 1859. Filed
4 July 1859.

Arthur and Mary Barrett. Power of Attorney from Arthur and Mary
Barrett, Pack 228 #14, Clerk of Court Office, Pickens Co., S. C.
State of Mississippi Neshoba Co. We Arthur Barrett and Mary Barrett
his wife do this day appoint William Holland of Pickens Co., S. C. our
lawful Attorney in fact for us. To sue our name and receive any
moneys which may come to us from the portion of Margaret Webster share
of the estate of Thomas Caradine decd. Dated 4 May 1861.

Martin Barrett. Will of Martin Barrett, Box 106 #1112, Probate Judge
Office, Pickens, S. C. I Martin Barrett, being in sound mind and disposing memory, ect. I give to my loving wife Jane Barrett, all my
property, both personal and real during her life time and after her
death of my wife, all my property should be equally divided between
Benjamin Franklin Kennemore and Margaret F. Prince to share and share
alike. I appoint my friend James E. Hagood, Executor. Dated 25 June
1872. Wit: Wm. Freeman, R. K. Pace, A. E. Kelley. Signed Martin
Barrett, Seal. Filed 21 April 1874.

Martin Barrett. Pack 271 #7, Clerk of Court Office, Pickens Co., S.C.
On 12 May 1854 Martin Barrett made oath that John A. Satterfield of
Pickens Dist. did on May 11, 1854 commit an assault upon his wife Jane
Barrett by cursing and abusing her at her own residence.

BASKIN

Thomas Baskin. Guardian bond, Box 108, Pack 2938. Probate Judge
Office, Abbeville, S. C. Thomas Baskin with Saml. Crawford, Wm.
Crawford are bound unto Andrew Hamilton Esq. Ord. all of Abbeville
Dist. in the sum often thousand dollars. Dated 29 Jan. 1807. The court
of ordinary of said dist. did appoint Thos. Baskin guardian of person
and personal estate of Nancy M. Long, Martha L. Long and John Long.
With full power to collect and receive the same he giving security for
what he shall collect and receive. To provide for homage, with necessary meat, drink, washing, lodging, apparrel and learning according
to their degree. Signed before Al. Hamilton, Ord. A.D.

John G. Baskin. Estate of John G. Baskin, Pack 328, Clerk of Court
Office, Abbeville, S. C. In the year 1863 John G. Baskin departed
this life unmarried and intestate with James T. Baskin Admr. with W. S.
Baskin and S. F. Gibert as executed bondsman. The heirs of John G.
Baskin are, James H. Baskin, father, William Stuart Baskin, brother,
and Elizabeth the wife of James Gibert, Carrie the wife of S. F. Gibert,
Margaret G. Williams the widow of Adolphus A. Williams decd. your ora-
trix pray that John T. Baskin was indebted into Adolhus A. Williams,
Baskin left no estate to pay his debts but when a lot and house on
depot street in this city was sold by the sheriff of this dist.
Honr. Joseph T. Moore, John T. Baskin become the purchaser in the sum

of three thousand and fifteen dollars, The said sheriff made no deed
to Baskin for the property. The lot and house has been taken over by
one Dennis O'Neall unknown to your oratrix. Now the Honr. Joseph T.
Moore has died and Henry S. Carson is the successor. Your oratrix
will ever pray and so forth... Dated 26 April 1867.

BATES

John Bates. Will of John Bates, Apt. 1 File 47 Probate Judge Office,
Greenville, S. C. I John Bates of Greenville Dist. being weak in body
but in sound mind and memory, ect.ect. I lend to my wife Susannah
Bates during her natural life the land I now live on, this is the
tract I purchased from Robert Prince, also two negroes named Fanny and
Daniel. With farm tools, household furniture. I give to my daughter
Polly Bates one small negro girl named Juliet. I give to my daughter
Nancy Bates on negro named Eliza. I give my son one negro named Luke,
and a tract of land I purchased of Earle. Sell all other real and
personal property and divide in this manner. The children of my daugh-
ter Elizabeth Shelton decd. five dollars each. To my son Moses Bates
one hundred dollars. To daughter Tyrza Bates two hundred dollars.
The balance to be equally divided between my sons Isaac Bates, John
Bates, William Bates, Daughter Polly Bates, daughter Sally Greene,
Nancy Bates. Make son in law Leroy Greene and son John Bates Executors.
Wit: Jos. Otis, Geo. Salmon, Thos. Wynne. Signed John Bates, seal.
Probated 12 Nov. 1821.

Joseph Bates. Tavern license. Pack 181 #13, Clerk of Court Office,
Pickens, S. C. To the undersigned most respectfully peition your board
for a license to retail spiritous liquors at his hotel at Table Rock
for the term of three months commencing on the 18 day of July 1870.
Dated 4 July 1870.

Enley H. Bates. Will, Box 120 #12, Probate Judge Office, Pickens, S.C.
I Enley Bates being in sound mind and memory, ect.ect. I will that my
wife Elizabeth F. Bates have my interest in my present place, lying
in George's Creek during her life time, then equally divided between
my two daughters Ida Caroline Green and Fannie Hula Green. I give to
my two daughters Iola Fields and Etta Gertrude Bates to have two
hundred dollars. I give to my beloved grandson Esley Bates Green my
watch and shot gun. Make W. W. F. Bright and son in law B. A. Green
my Executors. Dated 20 May 1892. Wit: W. F. Smith, John Roper, S. M.
Banks. Bates died 3 July 1892. Will filed 18 July 1892.

BEACH

Ann Beach and Labon G. Beach. Deed from Ann Beach and Labon G. Beach,
Rec. in Clerks Office Mesme Conveyance Book F, page 128, Pickens Co.,
S. C. We Ann Beach and Labon G. Beach widow and an heir of Abraham
Beach decd. For and in consideration... we have fully received our
share or portion of the real estate of Abraham Beach decd. Do grant,
bargain, sell and release unto Philip Young all that real estate lying
on both sides of Little Eastatoee Creek, waters of Keowee River, it
being the same where Philip Young now lives. Containing 867 acres.
Adj. land of Bright Gilstrap, Joseph Winchester, Joseph Gravley, John
Gravley, and Labon G. Beach. Dated 2 Feb. 1843. Wit: Wm. H. Gillaspie,
Jeptha J. Jones. Signed Ann X Beach and Labon G. Beach.

BEAL - BELL

Benjamin Beal. Estate of Benjamin Beal, Box 7 Pack 115, Probate Judge
Office, Pickens. I Benjamin Beal being sick and low condition but of
sound mind, ect.ect. I will and bequeath all my negroes to Lucinday
Gray to her and her heirs forever. And to Mourning Roberts, I will and

bequeath the balance of my estate both real and personal. Cash on hand,
notes, book accounts, horses, stock and the tract of land I am entitled
to and on which my father lived. Mourning Roberts share is to be
turned into cash and put on interest and paid to her annually. I
appoint James Calhoun as trustee and Executor. Dated 15 Aug. 1827.
Wit: Moses W. Houston, James L. Brough, Rebeckah Calhoun. An inventory of the goods and chattels was held on the 4 Dec. 1827. A letter
dated 5 March 1849 "I send to you by my nephew Benj. Roberts for my
money according to a statement sent me by you some years ago I am
entitled to one hundred and seventy five dollars after your commissions
were taken out but last you only sent me one hundred and sixty five,
I wish you to see to this and send me all I am entitled to which I
know you will do. Dated 5 March 1849. Wit: J. H. LeRoy. Signed
Mourning X Roberts.

Benjamin Bell. Estate of Benjamin Bell, Box 7 Pack 116. Probate
Judge Office, Abbeville, S. C. We Littleton Myrick, Eli S. Davis and
C. Daniel all of this Dist. are bound unto Moses Taggart Esq. Ord. in
the sum of three hundred dollars. Dated 10 Feb. 1824. This bond and
citation was read at Rockey Creek Meeting House. Littleton Myrick as
the Admr. he to make a true and perfect inventory ect.ect. Wit: A. C.
Hamilton. The inventory was held on 16 Feb. 1824. Sale was held 16
April 1825.

BEATY

John Beaty, Sr. Estate of John Beaty Sr. Box 2 #51, Probate Judge
Office, Anderson, S. C. I John Beaty Senr. of the Dist. of Pendleton,
being in low state of health and weak in body. ect.ect. I give unto
my son William Beaty one negro named Lett and fifty dollars. I give
unto my son John Beaty fifty dollars, I give unto my daughter Margaret
B. Beaty fifty dollars, also one black mare, two cows and calves with
all the sheep, I give unto my son Samuel W. Beaty fifty dollars, two
cows and calves with all the hogs and all the farm tools, I give unto
my daughter Mary McCarley one negro girl named Kate. Daughter Margaret
to get negro girl named Sinthy. Samuel to get negro named Harry,
I ordain my brothers William and Thomas Beaty and my son Samuel W.
Beaty as Executors. Wit: John Reid, William Beaty Senr. Thomas Beaty,
signed John Beaty, seal. Dated 29 Jan. 1816. Was appraised on the
10 Oct. 1816 by John Reid, John Milford, Wm. Staphenson, Wm. McKay,
appraisers.

BECK

Benneford Beck. Probate Judge Office, Box 11 #138. Pickens Co., S.C.
Wenneford Beck was probably a dtr. of Jesse Nevill of Pickens Dist.
In his will for 1842 he left her $1.00.

BEE

William C. Bee. Will of William C. Bee, Box 113 #1090. Charleston, S.C.
I William Bee of the city of Charleston declare this my last will and
testament. I give to my dear daughter Valeria North Chisolm my house
and lot on Meeting Street #33. And all household furniture, beding,
linen, pictures, library, ect.ect. To my step daughter Susan E.
Chisolm the sum of fifteen thousand dollars. To my step daughter Jane
C. Crawford wife of John A. Crawford, ten thousand dollars. To my
step son John M. Chisolm the sum of one thousand dollars. To my grand
children, the children of my decd. daughter Ann Alicia Ravenal wife of
W. Parker Revenal, namely; Henry Revenal five thousand dollars, to
William B. Ravenal, Jane N. or V. Ravenal, Ann Alicia Ravenal ten
thousand dollars each. To my sister Mrs. Rosa A. Gelzer and Mrs. Ellen
Williman the wife of Christopher Williman three thousand each. I give

to Mrs. Rosa A. Gelzer the sum of three thousand dollars in a trust
for my sister Mrs. Ann L. Guerard, this with interest for her maintenance during her natural life. To Mrs. Eliza Chisolm wife of my
step son, Mr. Alfred Chisolm one thousand dollars. To each of my
sisters in law Mrs. Anna H. Stock and Mrs. Margaret A. Dawson one thousand dollars each. To each of my neices namely Rebecca wife of Rev.
B. B. Sains, Jane wife of Mr. Francis A. Mitchell, Fanny wife of Mr.
Glenn E. Davis. Margaret Charlotte Beckie and Patsy the four daughters
of Mrs. Margaret A. Dawson, I give one thousand dollars each to my
God daughter Rebecca North daughter of the late Dr. North. To my God
son Wm. B. North I give one thousand dollars. The rest and residue
both real and personal to be divided into two equal shares. One to my
daughter Valeria A. North Chisolm. The other share to my grand sons
William B. Ravenal and Elias Prioleau Revenal, and my granddaughter
Jane N. Ravenal the children of my decd. daughter. I appoint Mr.
Theodore D. Jervey, Col. Edward McCrady Junr. and my step son Mr.
Alfred Chisolm, Executors. Dated 30 July 1880. Signed sealed declared
before C. A. Chisolm, Lewis S. Jervey, Wm. B. Chisolm, Probated 19
Feb. 1881, before Judge of Probate.

BELCHER

Mary E. Martin Belcher. No 23 Clerk of Court Office, Abbeville, S.C.
1856 John F. Livington was guardian of Mary E. Martin a minor. Rec.
from B. Y. Martin Admr. and Mary A. Martin Admrx. of the estate of
Jobual Martin decd. $8648.32. In 1857 sellement and that Mary A.
Martin has intermarried with William W. Belcher.

William W. Belcher. Estate of William W. Belcher, Pack 269, Clerk of
Court Office, Abbeville, S. C. Abbeville Dist. in Equity, Your Honors
your orator Robert J. White and your Oratrix Sarah J. his wife.
William W. Belcher the uncle of your oratrix departed this life on the
20 Nov. 1859 intestate and never been married and left neither father
or mother, brother or sister surviving him. His only heirs are the
children of his two decd. brothers viz; brother, Robert E. Belcher
decd. children are, Warren P., William W., Williamston H. Belcher who
are over twenty one years of age. John H., Henry Clay, James N.,
Mary and Rebecca Belcher, all of whom are minors. Brother James
Belcher decd. children are viz: Your oratrix who married Robert J.
White and is now of age, William W., James C., Mary H., Preston, and
Robert Edmund Belcher, who are minors. The Admr. was granted unto
Warren P. and William W. Belcher. The intestate died with a large
personal estate, believe to be over one thousand dollars and two large
tracts of land. One tract of one thousand and fifty acres, adj. land
of Thomas Thomson, Esq. Dr. John S. Reid, Moses Oliver McCaslan and
Samuel Link. The other of three hundred and sixty five acres, adj.
land of Mrs. Margaret Wideman, A. Boak Kennedy, Edmund Cowan. Your
orator and Oratrix for ever pray. Filed 19 Dec. 1859.

BELLOTTE

A. D. Bellotte. Estate of A. D. Bellotte, Box 117 #3 and 15. Probate
Judge Office, Pickens, S. C. Estate Admr. 7 June 1889 by Kate R.
Bellotte, widow and B. J. Johnston are bound unto J. B. Newberry Ord.
in the sum of $800.00. He died 11 Dec. 1886. On 3 Apr. 1890 Kate R.
Chatham, J. H. Rowland, E. G. Rowland of Greenville Co. are bound unto
J. B. Newberry Ord. in the sum of $666.60 Kate R. Chatham made gdn. of
Clarence Dupree Bellotte a minor under 21 years residing in Central,
Pickens Co. Kate Chatham nee Kate Bellotte. grd. also of Carrie
Irene Bellotte, On Mar. 19, 1890. Kate states that Clarence D. was
7 years old, Carrie Irene Bellotte 5 years old and the children of
A. D. Bellotte decd. of Central, S.C.

John E. Bellotte. Will of John E. Bellotte, Box 116 #16, Probate
Judge Office, Pickens, S. C. I John E. Bellotte being in ill health

but in sound mind and memory, ect.ect. 1. First pay my just debts
and funeral expenses. 2. Having provided for my beloved wife Susannah
C. Bellotte by an insuring my life in the Knights of the Golden rule
in the sum of $2,000.00 in lieu of her dower. 3. It is my desire that
my interest in the store of J. E. Bellotte shall be sold and at Pickens
or Central. 4. One tenth of said sale to go to my son Thomas A.
Bellotte and the remainder to be divided into four equal parts, one
part of my son Samuel A. Bellotte, one part to my son William E.
Bellotte, the other part equally divided between my three grand children
viz: Oswald M. Breazeale, Ada Breazeale, and Mollie M. Breazeale and
one part to be divided between my two grand children viz: Clarence
Bellotte and Irene Bellotte. I appoint John E. Breazeale my executor.
Dated 12 Feb. 1889. Wit: J. D. Warnock, J. R. Williams, L. T. Shirley.
Signed J. E. Bellotte. Filed 14 May 1889.

BENISON

William Benison. Estate of William Benison, Box 11 Pack 224. Probate
Judge Office, Abbeville, S. C. I William Benison of Abbeville Dist.
being weak in body but in sound mind and memory, ect.ect. I give to
my daughter Faney Wallace one dollar, I give to my son John Benison one
dollar, I give to my daughter Margaret Bell one dollar, I give to my
daughter Maryan McWhertor one dollar, I give to my daughter Batsey Step
one dollar. I give to my daughter Jean Step one dollar. I request
that my property to be appraised in the month of October next and after
paying debts the ballance to remain with my wife Margret Benison for
her life time. After her death to be divided between my sons William
and James Benison. I appoint John McAdams and James Richey Senr. the
sole Executors. Dated 30 Apr. 1817. Wit: John Shirley, John McAdams
Junr., William Bennison. Signed William Benison, seal. Will proved
by John McAdams before the Ordinary of said Dist. on 2 Feb. 1818.
An appraisement was made 14 Feb. 1818. By James Brownlee, John Kay,
Benjamin Smith.

Henry Bently. Deed from Henry Bently to John F. Pelot, Pack 76.
Clerk of Court Office, Abbeville, S. C. This deed made 10 Feb. 1838
between Henry Bently and John F. Pelott both of Abbeville Dist. In the
sum of $500.00 paid by John F. Pelott trustee for Jane Houston and
heir, that is to say, heirs of her body. For 190 acres lying on Little
River, adj. land of John A. Mars. Covin and King, and Mary Scott and
others. Known as the Tulloses place. Wit: John A. Mars, Philip
LeRoy. Signed Henry X Bently, seal. Isabella Bently did renounce
and release her dower and all interest in the said land. Dated 6 July
1838. Before Alexander Houston, J.Q. for sd. Dist.

BENNETT

Elisha Bennett. Estate of Elisha Bennett, Pack 18 Probate Judge
Office, Anderson, S. C. I Elisha Bennett Senr. being in a low state
of health but in perfect mind and memory, ect.ect. I give unto my son
John two hundred and fifty dollars to make him equal with the others
that have left me. I my son Archibald a negro named Nathan, a sorrel
horse that he now has, a good bed and furniture to make him equal with
the others. Then an equal distribution of all my property to all my
children. The part that shall fall to Jenney shall be for her and her
lawful increase of her body alone. My sons Stephen or Adam shall have
the disposition thereof. The negro family of Sam and Lucy with all
their children except Nathan shall be valued and taken by my children,
and that Sam and wife be not separated at a distance from each other.
Make William Magee and my son Archibald my Executors, Dated 17 Sept.
1833. Wit: James Major, John Vandiver, Robert Brown. Signed Elisha
Bennett, seal. Will proved by James Major before John Harris Esq. on
30 Oct. 1833.

A. T. Bennett. Power of Attorney from A. T. Bennett. Pack 18 Anderson Co., S. C. Dated 29 Nov. 1834, Rev. W. Magee, I hereby authorize and request you to pay to John T. Bennett all the money coming to me and Jenny Dowdle of my father estate and this shall be your receipt for the same by so doing you will oblige your sincere friend. Signed A. T. Bennett.

Elisha Bennett. Power of Attorney from Tabitha Mayfield, Pack 18, Anderson, S. C. State of Alabama Tuscaloosa County. Know now ye that I Tabitha Mayfield of State and County above. Have made J. T. Bennett my true and lawfull attorney to ask, demand, receive of and from the estate of Elisha Bennett decd. Dated 19 Nov. 1833. Wit: George Cobb, J.P. Signed Tabitha Bennett. An inventory of Elisha Bennett estate was held on 12 Nov. 1833.

James Bennett. An inquest of James Bennett, Pack 17 (no county given, may be Pickens Co., S. C.) An inquest was taken at the residence of James Bennett alias James Martin the 28 Dec. 1860 to view the dead body of said James Bennett. The jury brought it out that the decd. came to his death by gunshot wounds at his own house on 27 Dec. 1860 early in the morning, by a revolver in the hands of Joel Buckhuster in the discharge of his duty as an officer. Miles Galloway, Rhoda Bennett, Mary Jane Martin, Ben Martin and J. E. Coffee all testified.

BENSON

Prue Benson. Estate of Prue Benson, Apt. 1, file 46. Probate Judge Office, Greenville, S. C. Prue Benson died intestate before the 9 Feb. 1792, for on this date a letter from Samuel Earle, Clerk of Greenville Co. granted unto Enoch Benson as admr. of his father estate. By 14 Feb. 1799 a warrant of appraisement was issued to Robert McAfee, John Tubb, Isaac Green, Moses Kemp. They were to repair to all places as directed by Benjamin and Joshua Benson the admr. of the estate of Prue Benson decd. This was done on the 12 March 1799. The sale held with no date given. The purchasers name and his or her securities name are given.

Purchasers	Securities
Elizabeth Benson, Junr.	Elizabeth Benson, Senr.
Jeremiah Smith	William Armstrong
Jonathan Nesbett	Michael Miller
Robert McAfee	Isaac Green
Isaac West	Samuel Walker
James Taylor	Joseph McAfee
William Tubb	James Tubb
William Fauguson	Richard Simmons
Henry Benson	Enoch Benson
Charles Benson	Ben Benson
Gibson Suthern	Joseph McAfee
John Wood	James McAfee
Elizabeth Benson widow	
Isaac Green paid in money	
George Sanders paid in money	
James Stigler	Wm. Brown

Prue Benson. The heirs of Prue Benson by 1809 were: Thomison Henry, Benjamin Benson, Henry Benson, Sarah Humes, Enoch Benson, Frances Benson, William Benson, Robert Benson, Zachariah Benson, George Benson, Joshua Benson, Walker Benson, Jemima Henry, Mary Stigler, full amt. from ancestor Clary James also full amt. from Elizabeth Benson the widow.

Elizabeth Benson. Estate of Elizabeth Benson, Apt. 1 File 35. Probate Judge Office, Greenville, S. C. I Elizabeth Benson being sick but in my sences. I bequeath unto my son Henry Benson one feather bed, one chest, one pewter pot. I bequeath unto my son Robert Benson one pair of springs, one big Bible, I bequeath to my daughter Walker my bed,

two pieces of cloath, all my cloathing three puwter bason, three
plates, all my tin ware. To Enoch Benson all my property, ect.ect.
Wit: Benjamin Brewton, James X Parks, Jacob Wilson. Signed:
Elizabeth X Benson. Dated 11 Feb. 1812. Will proved by James Parks
and Jacob Wilson before David Goodlett Esq. Ord. on 16 July 1813.
On same date Enoch Benson was made Admr. estate was appraised on
8 Aug. 1814. No heirs given. Will probated 16 July 1813.

Joseph Benson. Will of Joseph Benson, Apt. 1 File 33. Probate Judge
Office, Greenville, S. C. I Joseph Benson of Greenville Co. make and
ordain this my last will and testament. I lend to Henry Hopson Senr.
as long as he lives two negroes called Sam and Billy, one feather bed,
one beast and saddle. I give to my wife Jane Benson all the rest
and residue of my estate, both real and personal. After the death of
said Hopson the estate I lent to him shall be returned to my wife and
her heirs for ever. I appoint my wife Jane Benson Executrix. Dated
30 Nov. 1799. Wit: Nancy Benson, Merry Hall. Signed Joseph Benson,
seal. Will probated 25 July 1802.

Prue Benson. Will of Prue Benson, Apt. 1 File 18. Probate Judge
Office, Greenville, S. C. I Prue Benson being in sound mind and memory
ect.ect. I give to my son in law John Gowen, four negroes named.
My half of the mill built between J. Gowen and myself. I give to my
son William B. Benson five negroes, named. And my tract of land where
the Regimental Mustres are held also my still, bed and furniture. I
give unto my daughter Jean Benson five negroes named, one bed and
furniture, one horse beast, the rest of the estate to be sold and
divided between the named heirs. Make John Gowen and William B. Benson
Executors. Wit: Thos. Benson, Henry Hall, Evaline Benson. Signed:
P. Benson, seal. Probated 1 Oct. 1821.

Charles Benson. Will of Charles Benson, Apt. 1 File 50. Probate Judge
Office, Greenville, S. C. I give to my wife Frances Benson two negroes
and all my land except where my son John now lives. She is to have all
tools, household furniture, grain of all kinds for her natural life,
then it is to go to Elizabeth Benson, Clary Benson, Henrietta Benson,
Mary Ann three children viz; Elisaan Winn, Joseph Winn, James Berry
Winn, Lizza Cunningham. Be it understood that Clement Winn is to have
two dollars only from the estate, the property is to go to Jane Winn
children. Prue Benson is to have the land he now lives on. John
Benson is to have where he now lives. I leave to Blue Benson wife
Mary M. Benson one dollar. It is my desire that Balis Benson two
children viz: Susan Frances Benson and Mander Benson shall have an
equal division of the lot of negroes and they are to stay with the
Executors until they are twenty one years of age. I appoint my wife
Frances my Executrix and Williss Benson my Executors. Dated 5 Apr.
1839. Wit: Delilah Bradley, Susanna Bradley, Tidence Bradley. Signed
Charles Benson, seal. Will probated 15 July 1839.

William P. Benson. Deed from William P. Benson and Samuel A. Easley
both of Pickens Co. Recd. Deed book F-1, page 524, Clerk of Court
Office, Pickens, S. C. In the sum of $542.00. I do sell unto Samuel
A. Easley a tract of land containing 52 & 1/4 acres on the North side
of the South prong of Georges Creek of Saluda River. adj. land of
Griffin Hamilton the heirs of Samuel Crayton decd. Dated 25 Jan. 1851.
Wit: John Bowen, Wm. R. Bowen, Signed W. P. Benson, seal. Attested to
by Wm. R. Bowen before John Bowen, N.P. Dated 25 Jan. 1851.

Charles Benson. Land plat of Charles Benson, Greenville, Apt. 1 File
50, Probate Judge Office. At the request of Willis Benson Esq. I have
surveyed and laid off 57 acres which belongs to James Winn when the
dividing line shall be decided on by the parties. Have laid off 50
acres for James Winn which shall be the line between the two as per
Charles Benson decd. will. Situate about eight miles North West of
the town of Greenville on the East side of the White Horse road so
called. Surveyed 16 Dec. 1858. John C. Hoyt, D.S.

William P. Benson. Estate Admr. 14 Nov. 1853. The letter of Admr. was
granted unto Nancy G. Benson, widow, and J. G. Hamilton both of Pickens

Co. He left the widow and four children viz: Louisa RoHanna the wife
of Henry S. Walker, Thornton Oscar Benson, Jefferson Franklin Benson,
Mary Catherine Benson all of whom are minors and the latter three of
whom resides beyond the limits of this State. In the year 1861 the
widow married one Hugh Dickson. The estate was in Equity by 1862
Ref. No. 34 Clerk of Court, Pickens Co. Also in Equity Pack 245.
Clerk of Court, Pickens Co. By 1864 Thomas Jefferson Benson, Box 74
#793. He and Robt. A. Thompson were bound to W. E. Holcombe in the sum
of $3,000.00 He was late of Fulton Co., Ga. and the son of Wm. P.
Benson, decd.

BENISON

William Benison. A vendue list of William Benison decd. personal
estate sold on the 17 Feb. 1818. There were 61 items and about the
same purchasers. Signed by John McAdams, Senr. no other inf.

BERROUM

Peterson Berroum. A deed from Peterson Berroum to Cary G. Snelgrove.
Deed book 44, page 313, Edgefield Co., S. C. Peterson Berreum and
Ellender Leflers to Cary G. Snelgrove both of Edgefield Co. Dated 30
Dec. 1829. In the sum of 350 dollars we do sell grant and release
298 & 1/2 acres. Beginning on a hickory on the River to the mouth of
the creek. (No names given.) Wit: John Holly, David Richardson.
Signed: Ellender X Leflore, Peterson Berroum. Deed proved by David
Richardson in Newberry Co. Before Benjamin Lindsey, J.Q. the 27 May
1830.

BICKLEY

Joseph Bickley. Will of Joseph Bickley, Box 7 Pack 128. Probate
Judge Office, Abbeville, S. C. I Joseph Bickley being in sound mind
and memory ect.ect. Joseph had a daughter named Caroline Covington
the wife of Richard Covington, and they had one infant daughter "as
dear as its mother that is gone" Caroline had received five negroes,
and land worth about three thousand dollars. Wife Frances and the
other two children Mary Ann and William are to be equally divided
between them, only that William is to continue in pursuite of his
education. If my wife shall die before my two children are of age,
I appoint my brothers John and Waller O. Bickley as guardians. I
also appoint my wife Frances and Waller O. Bickley as Executors. Wit:
Geo. Whiteside, James W. Speed, Wm. Bradshaw. Signed Joseph Bickley.
No other inf.

BIDDELL

Ann Biddell. Will of Ann Biddell, Recd. in original Will Book 1711-
1718. Charleston, S. C. I Ann Biddell being weak in body but in sound
mind and perfect memory, ect.ect. I give to my loving daughter
Hipeibauth diddell(?) all my real and personal estate, excepting these
legasys hereafter named. That in case my daughter dye before she
arrives to the age of one and twenty years or the day of marriage that
then my whole estate be equally divided between the children of Samuel
West, as Mary Isabell Sarah and Samuel, and as a legacy of love and
friendship I give one negro woman named Rachell to Sarah the daughter
of Samuel West. I give to Samuel West and wife Sarah each a mourning
ring as a token of my love and friendship. Also to my respectfull
friend John Pendarvis one other mourning ring. My will and pleasure
that Samuel West be Executor. Dated 8 Feb. 1713/4. Wit: Richard
Butler and John Pendarvis. Signed: Ann Biddell, seal. Will proved

10 March 1713/4 by Governor Richard Butler.

BIDDLE

Nicholas Biddle. Will of Nicholas Biddle, Recd. Will Book 1774-1779, page 696. Charleston, S. C. I Nicholas Biddle declare this my last will and testament. I give to Elizabeth Elliott Baker daughter of Richard Bohum Baker of the state of S. C. Esq. the sum of twenty five thousand pounds lawful money of this state. The remainder unto my mother Mary Biddle of the state of Pennsylvania. But if she dies without a will I desire that such sums of money or property shall be equally divided between my brothers James, Edward and my sister Lydia McFunner and Mary Biddle of the state of Penn. I do appoint Thomas Furr, Joshua Ward, Esq. as Executors. Dated 12 Jan. 1778. Wit: Wm. Graham, David Werhamll, William Binnie. Signed Nicholas Biddle, seal. No other inf.

BIGBEA

Archibald Bigea. Estate of Archibald Bigea, Box 10 Pack 191. Abbe-ville Dist., S. C. We Daniel F. Lucius, Wm. Bigbea, Abner Nash, Andrew Richey, are bound unto Talf. Livington Esq. Ord. in the sum of ten thousand dollars. The conditions are to make or cause to be made a true and perfect inventory of all goods and chattels, ect.ect. Wit: by James Sweeny.

William Bigbea. Daniel Lucius and William Bigbea hath made suit to me to grant them a letter of Admr. of the estate of Archibald Bigbea, late 2nd Lieutenantt in the 43 Regiment of the United States Infantry as next of kin. Dated 11 Sept. 1815. Wit: Reuben Nash, Lieut. Col. Signed: Talo. Livingston, seal, seal. The Appraisement of the estate was held on 16 Sept. 1815. With Abner Nash, Reuben Nash, Andrew Richey, Conrad Hackleman, and Jno. Cullins or any three or four of you. Talo. Livingston, Ord. Only military items were given.

BIGBY

James Bigby. Statement of James Bigby, Pack 268 #7, Clerk of Court Office, Pickens Co., S. C. On Jan. 5, 1858 James Bigby of tunnel hill in Pickens Co. says that on the night of Jan. 26, 1858 while he was coming home from the Poplar Gap, David Williams and J. F. Lathem attempted to kill him by knocking him down with rocks and beating him with sticks and striking him with a knife which cut his hand badly.

William A and Alcipia E. Bigby. Petition of Guardian, Pack 108, Clerk of Court Office, Pickens Dist., S. C. Your Petitioners William A and Alcipia E. Bigby Sheweth that they are minor children of Rev. George Bigby decd, the former about seventeen years of age and the latter about fifteen. They are entitled to a portion of the estate of their father, owing to their minority they cannot manage for themselves. Therefore, they pray that their mother Mary A. Bigby may be appointed their guardian. They are in school and cannot be present in court. Dated 17 Nov. 1855.

BIRDSONG

John Birdsong. Will of John Birdsong of Union Co., S. C. No other ref. Being in perfect and sound mind and memory, ect.ect. I give to my son Batte Birdsong one negro named Oliver, also I confirm to him the legasy that he received in Virginia which John Birdsong my father gave to me to the use of my son Batte. I give to my son John Birdsong one negro

named Dick and confirm to him the other things he has already received.
I give to my son William Birdsong one negro named Dilee and confirm to
him the things he has already received and one rifle gun and my silver
watch. I give to my son Henry Birdsong one negro named Davy and after
the death of my wife another negro named Tom also one smooth bore gun.
I lend to my beloved wife Mary Birdsong four negroes and one half of
the land I now live on. With all tools, cattle, hoggs, sheep and
household items as she may require. I give to my son Jesse Birdsong
the other half of the land or 200 acres, he to possess it at the age
of eighteen years of age and one rifle gun. I give to my daughter Lucy
Waddell one negro named Moses. I give to my daughter Sarah Ramsey one
negro named Jane. I give to my daughter Mary Drake one negro named
Daniel. I give to my daughter Rebekah Minter one negro named Jacob and
all the money her husband is due me on bond, for ever. I give to my
daughter Elizabeth Howard one negro named Peggy, with an order to John
Minter for a feather bed and a cow and calf. I give to my daughter
Nancy Birdsong one negro named Hannah, bed and furniture, mare colt
named Peg. and twenty pounds. I give to my daughter Lidia Birdsong one
negro named Patience, bed and furniture, one mare colt, and twenty five
pounds. After the death of wife there is another division. Make sons
William and Henry Birdsong Executors. Dated 21 Sept. 1790. Wit:
Joseph West, Richard Davis, Rinsoy West. Signed John Birdsong, seal.
Recorded 27 Sept. 1790.

BLACK

Jacob Black. Estate of Jacob Black decd. Apt. 1 File 63, Probate
Judge Office, Greenville, S. C. The petition of Brasher Henderson and
James Cox Admr. of Jacob Black crave an order of sale for the whole
of the personal and real estate. Dated 30 Sept. 1839. The date of
Black death is not given, he had one tract of land containing two
hundred acres on Reedy River, adj. land of Thos. Long, Wm. T. Dacus
and others, first granted to Samuel Pyle. The other tract of one
hundred acres on branches of Fall Creek on the waters of North fork of
Saluda River, adj. the State place on the turnpike road above Col.
Hodges, First granted to John Yandle. There is a petition from the
heirs to have the estate sold and divided and all heirs are of age.
The sale was held on 11 Oct. 1839 for the personal effects, with about
forty bought at the sale. By the year 1842 the final settlement was
made. The heirs are viz: James Cox and wife Dianah, Hance Black,
Jeremiah Hide and Sarah his wife, Elizabeth Hide decd. heirs are:
Jacob Hide, Jeremiah Hide, Charles Hide, Reuben Hide, Parker Bottoms
and wife Polly, Anthony Fowler and wife Sarah, Thomas Sanford and wife
Elizabeth, Thomas Weaver and wife Nancy, all of Pickens Co., S. C.
George Owens and wife Nancy of Haywood Co., N. C. Jacob Black of west
Tenn, Carroll Co. Wm. Askew and wife Polly, Carroll Co., Tenn. James
Kelly and wife Susannah of Elbert Co., Ga.

John T. Black. Estate of John T. Black, Pack 84 In Equity, Clerk of
Court, Pickens Co. Your orator John H. Black and your oratrix Nancy
Black both of Pickens Dist. That John T. Black the father of your
orator and husband of your oratrix died year 1857, intestate. With
considerable real estate, one tract of 500 acres called "Home place"
on the head waters of Wold Creek, adj. land of Elizabeth Fields,
Roswell Hill and others. The said land is subject to distribution
among the heirs at law of John T. Black. viz: a widow, your oratrix and
ten children, John H. Black, Rosanna Rice wife of Isaac Rice, Amanda
Brazeals wife of James Brazeals, Margaret Hudson wife of Wyatt Hudson.
Sarah Freeman wife of J. G. Freeman, Malinda Alexander wife of Jasper
Alexander, Martha Black, Jane Black a minor about the age of eighteen,
and Arminda A. Black a minor about the age of sixteen and Margaret
Crane, Harper Crane, Mary Crane, Davis Crane, Addison Perry Crane,
Lawrence Orr Crane minors of Elizabeth Crane decd. daughter of John T.
Black who died before her father and resided in the state of Georgia
where also resides the said James J. Black. Filed 24 March 1859.

William Pickens Black. Petition of guardianship of minor children of
William Pickens Black decd. Pack 97 Clerk of Court Office, Abbeville,
S. C. The humble petition of Eleanor Black, widow, sheweth that her
two minor children Anna Elizabeth Black about four years old and
Harriet R. E. P. Black about two years old, are entitled to an estate
of about fifteen hundred dollars as the heirs of their father, and are
unable on account of their minority to receive and manage same. Your
petitioner ask the court to appoint her the said guardian of her minor
children, etc.ect. Dated 25 Nov. 1857.

Estate of Allen Black, Box 41 #463, Probate Judge Office, Pickens Co.
Estate Admr. 21 Oct. 1856 by Edward Hughs Esq., J. R. Hunnicut, F. N.
Garvin, Thomas N. Stribling, who are bound unto W. J. Parson, Ord. in
the sum of $3,000.00. Expended; 24 Jan. 1859 paid the widow Jane Black
$424.59, paid James M. Black, Zachariah Johns and wife Nicey, D. A.
Liles for wife Jane, Sarah Ann Black, William Black, John R. Black,
D. W. Black, Robert Powell and wife Polly Ann, Rebecca Black each
$94.33. In another paper states that Martha J. Black and John Black
left 9 children. In another paper in Dec. 1857, Zachariah Johns and
wife Nicey and Robert Powell and wife Polly Ann and J. J. Brown lived
out of State. Allan Black owned 148 acres on Long Nose Creek waters
of Tugaloo River adj. land of J. H. Leroy and 271 acres on Little
Toxaway Creek waters of Tugaloo River, adj. land of R. A. Gilmore and
others.

BLACKBURN

Thomas Blackburn. Estate of Thomas Blackburn, Real estate Book A,
page 12. Probate Judge Office, Pickens, S. C. A Petition of Lyda
Hughey one of the heirs of Blackburn decd. for a sale and distribution
to the heirs of the real estate of said decd. Dated 27 Jan. 1834.
Wit: Wm. D. Sloan. Signed by Lyda X Hughey, B. W. F. Capehart,
Ambrose Reid, William Adair, and heirs of Silvy William Blackburn. On
another paper, Matilda Malinda, and George W. Blackburn, Minors and
William L. Keith, Guardian ad Litem. After advertizing in the
Pendleton Messenger on the 4th Monday in Dec. and no objection made the
sale is ordered. The land was on Keowee River and some on Little
River known as White Oak Cove. (In the book Marriage and Death Notices
from Pendleton Messenger by Holcombe, Thomas Blackburn died 12 Aug. 1833.

BLACKSTOCK

James Blackstock. Estate of James Blackstock, real estate book A, page
21. Probate Judge Office, Pickens, S. C. Lavina Blackstock, applicant, vizt: Sarah and Nehemiah Blackstock, John Evans in right of his
wife Milly, John and Richard Blackstock, defendants: a bill for division
or sale of the real estate of James Blackstock decd. Land on Tugaloo
River, adj. land of William Barton Esq. and Thomas Collins and others.
Petition dated 8 Feb. 1836. Sale ordered on 2 May 1836.

BLAIN

William Blain. Estate, 1 July 1849 Recd. of Mary Blain Extrx. of Wm.
Blain, decd. By the hand of Wm. P. Martin acting for her $523.27 in
full of all the personal property sold by her of the will of Wm. Blain
to her for life and in full of all matters (except) her life estate
or what she reserved in the covenant and we fully concure in the settlement. Signed Samuel Smith and Jane Smith. Another dated 10 July 1849
signed by Wm. P. Martin and Mahala Martin. Tombstone inscriptions
taken from "Old Greenville Church" about 3 or 4 miles from Donalds
to Hodges, S. C. Sacred to the memory of William Blain who departed
this life on the 23 March 1829, aged 60 years. In memory of Mary Blain
Concort of Wm. Blain decd. born Aug. 15, 1775 departed this life

47

May 17, 1857 in the 82 year of her age.

BLAIR

James Blair. Deed from James Blair to John Dyle, Pack 383 #3, Clerk
of Court Office, Pickens, S. C. This indenture made between James
Blair, Senr. of Habersham Co., Ga. and John Dyall of Pickens Co., S.C.
Dated 10 Nov. 1834. in the sum of $100.00 for 100 acres on the East
side of Conneross Creek, deeded to Blair by Jessey Coffey. Wit:
Hyram X McCracken, Powell Blair, J.P. Signed James Blair.

BLASSINGAME

John Blassingame. On Feb. 16, 1824 Gen. John Blassingame of Greenville
Dist. deeded land to the following children in his life time viz:
Enoch B. Benson, Joseph Cleveland, William E. Blassingame, Dr. John
Robinson, Wm. E. Wickliff, Thomas M. Sloan, John W. M. Blassingame.
On Jan. 9, 1824 all the children were of age except one. Had one child
in Pendleton Dist. one in Laurens and one in Spartanburg. Elizabeth
Blassingame was the widow. Ref. Probate Judge Office, Greenville,
S. C. Apt. 1 File 27.

B. Blassingame. Aged 67 years and Elizabeth Blassingame aged 60 years
were living in the poor house of Pickens Dist. on 20 Oct. 1863. Ref.
Clerk of Court Office, Pack 645 #3.

John Blassingame. Sarah M. Soan wife of John Blassingame decd and
dtr. of David Sloan of Pickens Dist. who died in 1834 and his widow
Nancy Sloan. Ref. Clerk of Court Office, Pickens, S. C. Pack 642 #7.

Ann Blassingame. of Pickens Dist. made oath that on July 31, 1867
she delivered of a female bastard child with black hair and black eyes
and that Charles Rosemond a colored farmer of said Dist. did get her
with said child. Ref. Clerk of Court Office, Pickens, S. C. Pack 641
$4.

BOATNER

Sally Boatner, formerly Alexander was an heir of a Thomas S. Alexander
decd. of 12 mile River, Pickens Co. On June 21, 1858 listed as being
out of state. Ref. Book A, page 222. Probate Judge Office, Pickens
Co., S. C.

BOATRIGHT

William Boatright. Will of William Boatright, Box 30 #358, Pickens Co.
I desire to be decently buried and my just debts paid. I give and
bequeath to my son Abner Boatright a portion of my land during my wife
life time, all the lower part from a cross fence including the house I
now live in. He is to rent the other to support my wife, and he is to
repairs to the house to make her comfortable and the house George
Lowery lives in. Wife Elizable to have all use to household furniture.
After the death of wife sell her things and equally divide amongst all
my children viz: Nancy Moss, Ruthy Sherly, Abner Boatright, Charity
Ellard, Anny Clinton, Drusilla Davidson, Mary Crow, William Boatright,
Francis Lowery, Elizabeth Quinn or Gwinn, Sarah Vandiver. I appoint
my son Abner Boatright and Marcus T. Trimmier Executors. Dated 27
Oct. 1850. Wit: F. H. Hall, John Weaver, M. T. Trimmier. Signed
Wm X Boatright. Will proved 21 Feb. 1851. No other info.

Aaron Boggs. Estate of Aaron Boggs, Admr. 12 Jan. 1835 by Martin Boggs,
Pleasant Alexander, Carter Clayton who are bound unto Jas. H. Dendy,
Ord. in the sum of $2,000.00 sale on 26 Jan. 1835, Buyers, Joseph G.,
Wm. David H., Thos., A. M. Boggs, Jonathan Lee, Absalom Mullinax, Wm.
Odell, Henry Sargeant.

David H. Boggs. Estate of David H. Boggs, Box 15 #198 Pickens Co.
Est. Admr. by Wm. Boggs, Major John Ariail, W. L. Keith, who are bound
unto W. D. Steel, Ord. in the sum of $2,400.00. Martha Boggs the widow
and eight children, viz: Joseph G., John R., Aaron, A. M., J. N.,
Thos., Eliz. Nally, the heirs.

William Boggs. Estate of William Boggs, Box 46 #513. Pickens Co.,
S.C. Est. Admr. 30 Oct. 1857 by G. W. B. Boggs, C. M. Lay, James E.
Haggood, Miles M. Norton. who are bound to W. J. Parson in the sum of
$10,000.00. Est. Admr. again 9 Dec. 1864 by Aaron Boggs, James E.
Hagood, Elizabeth Lay are bound unto W. E. Holcombe, Ord. in the sum
of $10,000.00. Aaron Boggs was also Admr. of Lettice Boggs decd. wid.
who died Nov. 1864. Letter of Admr. granted to AAron Boggs of Georgia,
was ordered to appear in Walhalla, S. C. Dated 1 Feb. 1872. Expend:
9 Jan. 1865 paid Elizabeth Boggs #396.55. G. W. Taylor recd. his share
of estate... left four heirs viz: C. M. Lay, G. W. B. Boggs, G. W.
Taylor, Aaron Boggs.

Aaron Boggs. Estate of Aaron Boggs, Box 105 #1101. Pickens Co., S.C.
I Aaron Boggs Senr. being advanced in life and frail in body, but of
sound mind and memory, ect.ect. I give to my beloved wife Matilda
Boggs for her natural life my home place containing 345 acres, adj.
land of E. B. Calhoun, Nathaniel Madden and others. I give to wife
Matilda all household items, my library and all property in my dwelling
house at the time of my death. I give to my son William B. Boggs the
control and management of the place during Matilda life time. At the
death or marriage of Matilda, Wm. B. is to have the place in fee
simple. I give to my grand son Aaron M. Boggs Smith he being the
oldest son of my daughter Martha M. Brock. I have to say having given
to the children of my first wife their full share except Martha M.
Brock, the fifty dollars will fill it out. I appoint my son William B.
Boggs Executor. Dated 29 Aug. 1871. Wit: William J. Gantt, Reuben
Arnold, John F. Arnold. Signed: Aaron Boggs, Senr., seal. Will
proved 19 Aug. 1874.

E. K. Boggs. Estate of E. K. Boggs, Box 114 #1105. Pickens Co., S.C.
Est. Admr. 11 Jan. 1887 by J. E. Boggs, E. E. Mauldin, T. C. Robinson
are bound unto J. B. New Berr, Ord. in the sum of $800.00. He died
5 Mar. 1886. J. E. Boggs was a son

J. N. Boggs. Estate of J. N. Boggs, Box 118 #15. Pickens Co., S.C.
Est. Admr. 28 Mar. 1891 by T. G. Boggs, A. M. Boggs, Thos. E. Willard,
are bound to James B. Newberry Ord. in the sum of $300.00. He died
18 Dec. 1890. T. G. Boggs was a son.

Boggs Minors. Box 153 #10. Pickens Co., S. C. On 8 May 1875 Eliza.
K. Boggs was bound to J. H. Philpot Ord. in the sum of $4,305.64. Made
gdn. of John B., Thos. and Josie Boggs minors over 14 years of age.
Children of G. W. B. Boggs decd. All of age in 1882. Josie married
a Horton.

Isaac Boggs. An inquest of Isaac Boggs dec. Pack 405 #3, Pickens Co.,
S.C. An inquest was held at the house of John M. Hendricks in Pickens
Dist. 19 Jan. 1871 upon the dead body of Isaac Boggs, P.C. The jury
brought it out that he came to his death accidently by a discharge of
blast. Geo Walker sworn says that he and Isaac were down in the well
at John M. Hendricks on 18 Jan. 1871 about one o'clock when by tamper-
ing the blast it went off. I think we ran it to hard. I said to
Isaac that I thought it were ran hard enough. When he said hit 2 more
I did and then that will do. I struck the 2nd lick the blast went off

blowing myself and Isaac Boggs with it. Mat Hamilton said that he was
at work near Hendricks house when he heard the report of a blast from
the well in Hendricks yard. Found Joseph Walker drawn out of the well,
went down into the well and found Boggs mashed down and head hung down,
found his leg smashed all to pieces, right leg lying under the left
leg both broken. Isaac Boggs said Uncle Mat am I hurt? He raised up
his head and I said yes Isaac you are torn all to pieces. Tied him into
the well bucket to get him out of the well. After being carried into
the house he lived some three or four hours.

James A. Boggs to Marinda J. Boggs. Pack 650 #3, Clerk of Court Office
Pickens, S. C. James A. Boggs to Marinda J. Boggs, dated 3 May 1876.
In the sum of $600.00 for 100 acres on the west side of eighteen mile
Creek, it being part of a grant to Henry Parson. Wit: Josiah N.
Boggs, Catherine J. X. Boggs. Signed Jas. A. Boggs, seal. Attested
by J. N. Boggs, before J. J. Garvin, N.P. 21 Aug. 1876. Certified
15 Nov. 1877.

Martha Boggs. Estate of Martha Boggs, Box 59 #641. Pickens Co., S.C.
Est. Admr. 5 Dec. 1861 by Mary J. McDow, Robert Craig, Jr., are bound
unto W. E. Holcombe Ord. in the sum of $300.00. No other info.

G. W. B. Boggs. Will of G. W. B. Boggs, Box 61 #660. Pickens Co., S.C.
I G. W. B. Boggs being in sound mind and memory, ect.ect. I give to
my beloved wife Eliza K. Boggs, all land, servants, stock, farming
tools, and the children to have a good education. The other part of
will is how a division is to be made if wife remarry or dies. I appoint
C. M. Lay Executor. Dated 27 May 1861. The witnesses signed their
names and place of residence T. G. Boggs, Pickens County, Robert
McWhorter, Golens Creek Place, Pickens Dist., Thos. H. Boggs, Pleasant
Hill, Pickens Dist. Signed G. W. B. Boggs, Proved 2 June 1862. He
died 4 May 1862. Owned 598 acres adj. land of Benjamin Boggs, Abner
O'Dell, Wm. O'Dell, Thos. Parkins. and others. The mill place of 11
acres adj. land of Wm. O'Dell, Samuel McCracken and the home place.
The mountain place of 252 acres adj. land of Ira Smith, Abner O'Dell,
Cynthia Hollingsworth, Hester Richardson, Abner Mullinix and others.
Heirs; Eliza K., widow, Milinda who married Thos. Smith and resides in
Anderson, S. C., Julius E. Boggs, John B. Boggs, Thos. H. Boggs, Josy
Boggs. The last three are minors on 12 Aug. 1874.

Thomas H. Boggs. Estate Admr. Box 62 #674. Pickens Co. Est Admr.
22 Aug. 1862 by Martha A. Boggs, Thos. H. McCann, Joseph Addison are
bound to W. E. Holcombe Ord. in the sum of $12,000.00 Joseph A. and
Marth A. bought at the sale...

Martha Boggs, Guardianship, Box 3 #89 (Equity) Pickens Co., S. C.
12 June 1849 Aaron Boggs, Josiah N. Boggs are bound to Miles M. Norton,
Ord. in the sum of $200.00 Aaron Boggs guardian of this daughter
Martha M. Boggs. She over 12 yrs. entitled to an interest in the
estate of her grandfather Henry Garner, A. M. Boggs a minor over 14
years has an interest in same estate in right of his decd. mother
Sylvana Boggs.

Essie Boggs. Divorce. Case #3988, Dist. Court, Anderson Co., Texas.
Apr. Term 1890. Essie Boggs vs. Wm. Boggs. This 26 day of Apr. 1890.
The defd. was called and came not. ect.ect. It is therefore ordered
adjudged and decreed by the Court that the bonds of matrimony heretofore existing between the plaintiff Essie Boggs and the Defendant Wm.
Boggs be dissolved. ect.ect. Pack 404 #2. Pickens Dist. They married
17 Jan. 1886.

Thomas H. Boggs. Estate of Thomas H. Boggs. (In Equity) Clerk of
Court Office, Pickens Co. Thomas H. Boggs, died 6 July 1862. Martha
A. appointed admr. At his death Thomas had 454 acres on 18 mile Creek
adj. land of Cynthia Hollingsworth, Wm. S. Williams and others. Having
looeing her slaves by emancipation the estate is now insolvent.
Martha A. widow, heirs: J. Edward, Marcus A., Wallace H., minors over
14 years, Charles J., minor under 14 years... Dated 9 Apr. 1867.

Joseph Boggs. Estate of Joseph Boggs, Box 72 #773. Pickens Co., S.C. Este. Admr. by Saml. A. Gary, James L. Boggs, Jas. E. Hagood, Wm. N. Craig are bound to W. E. Holcombe Ord. in the sum of $40,000.00 Heirs: Andrew Boggs, Heirs of Josiah Boggs decd. number and names unknown. Heirs of Nancy Alexander decd. Number and names unknown out of state. The widow Sarah Boggs, E. P. Cason and wife Jane, Joseph Prather and wife Elizabeth, Sarah Obriant, B. F. Boggs, Heirs of Harrison Boggs decd. viz: Sarah Williams, Martha and Oscar Boggs and one of the heirs of Josiah Boggs decd. Viz: Eliza Ann.

Joseph Harrison Boggs. Box 80 #850. Pickens Co., S. C. Est. Admr. by Robert A. Thompson C.E.P.D. bound unto W. E. Holcombe, Ord. in the sum of $1,000.00. Died 9 Dec. 1863. In 1870 Minors were: Sarah L., Wm. E., Martha J., James O., Chas. H. Boggs. Owned 112 acres on Golden Creek adj. land of Benj. Boggs, Robt. McWhorter, where the minors now lives, Dilly Boggs states that their mother was intermarried with one James A. Thomas who is the minors guardian.

H. G. Boggs. Estate, Box 72 #772. Pickens Co., S. C. Est. Admr. Robert A. Thompson, Comm. in Equ. bound to W. E. Holcombe, Ord. in the sum of $800.00. Widow Sarah C. Boggs. Sale 13 Jan. 1864, buyers Sarah Dodson, Rosa Boggs, Susan Cothran, Sarah C. Boggs, ect.ect.

David H. Boggs. Book 1, page 97. (Rel Est) Pickens Co., S.C. May 1, 1848. Boggs owned 165 acres lying on branches of Rice and Golden Creeks, adj. land of Robt. McWhorters, Elihu Griffin and others. Joseph G. Boggs was applicant vs. Martha Boggs widow, Wm. Boggs, Aaron Boggs heirs of J. N. Boggs, John R. Boggs in right of wife Jane, Martin Boggs, heirs of Thos. Boggs, heirs of Elizabeth Nally. some of the heirs reside out of state.

A. Madison Boggs. Box 121 #5. Pickens Co., S. C. I A. Madison Boggs being in sound mind and memory, ect.ect. I will to my son J. Frank Boggs shall have the home place with two mules and two horses and farm tools. I will that my beloved wife Eliza A. shall have support as long as she lives given by son J. Frank. Also my daughter Georgia and her child Eathel shall have support and a home if she remains single. I give to my daughter Margret A. Hamelton my watch and chain and one hundred in cash at her and her husband death the watch to be given to daughter Georgia or her child. Sons John E. and William M. to divide the Banks land between them. Make J. Frank Boggs and son in law C. Earl Hamelton Executors. Dated 25 Jan. 1893. Wit: T. F. Taylor, T. G. Boggs, T. N. Hunter. Signed A. M. Boggs, seal. Filed 23 Feb. 1893.

Milton R. Boggs. Will of Milton R. Boggs Box 130 #10. Pickens Co., S.C. I M. R. Boggs being in sound mind, I do make this my last will and testament. ect.ect I will and bequeath to my dear wife Julia all my personal property and all real property North of the WAW branch to have and hold till her death. Then to be equally divided between all my legal heirs. The real estate South of the WAW branch my executors to sell, rent, lease or what ever they think best for my creditors and if any surplus is to be given to my wife for her use. I appoint my wife Julia and Jefferson D. Boggs, Executors, and if they demise or can't act then I appoint as alternates my son Samuel C. Boggs and nephew A. John Boggs. Dated 18 June 1898. Wit: J. E. Anderson, R. M. Martin, Aaron Boggs. Signed Milton Reese X Boggs, seal. Proven 19 Sept. 1891.

Boggs Minors. Box 1 #25. (Equity) Pickens Co., S.C. Oct. 6, 1856 Joseph A. Boggs, Thos. H. Boggs, W. S. Williams bound to Robt. A. Thompson C & E in the sum of $600.00. Whereas on 30 June 1856 Josepha. Boggs made gdn. of John Thos. and George L. Boggs minor under 21 years.

Matilda Boggs, was a daughter of James and Nancy Gainer of Pickens Dist. Her father will proved in 1841. Probably wife of Aaron Boggs the Exeor. Ref. Probate Judge Office, Pickens Co., S. C. Box 25 #298.

Rebecca S. Boggs, was a maternal aunt of Sephaniah A. Hendricks, Wm. C. Hendrick, John Hendricks who were minors in 1881 in Pickens Co. Ref. Judge Probate Office, Pickens Co.

Sarah Boggs, wife of J. Addison Boggs residing in Georgia was a daughter of Hundley E. Campbell who died in 1859 in Pickens Dist. Dated 13 May 1867. Ref. Clerk of Court Office, Equity, rec. of Hundley Evatt. 649

J. N. Boggs, states that he is almost 63 years old on March 25, 1882, also James A. Boggs stated he was 61 on the same date, both of Pickens Dist. ref. Clerk of Court Office, Pack 651, #4.

Marinder C. Boggs, was the daughter of William G. and Philadelphia Mullenix of Pickens Dist. Aaron Boggs witnessed her father will on 9 Aug. 1858 and will was proven 7 Jan. 1861. Her father willed her property valued at $40.00. Ref. Wm. G. Mullinix's will. Box 57 #617. Pickens Dist.

Julia Boggs, Box 137. #2. Pickens, S. C. I Julia Boggs being in sound mind do make and declare this my last will and testament. I give to my son Samuel Cherry Boggs my home place with 40 acres and may buy 20 more if he so elects, with all personal property, household furniture, horses mules, etc,etc. The balance of my real estate to be sold and equal division among the balance of my children. Samuel to pay all debts and erect tombstones to mine and his father grave. I appoint Samuel and J. C. Boggs and in case of death of either or both, I appoint my son J. D. Boggs and T. L. Watkins executors. Dated 18 Feb. 1901. Wit: L. G. Clayton, Alice Cochran, Jane Prince. Filed 5 Apr. 1901. Paid Expend: Dec. 5, 1902. Paid, John C., J. D., W. C., Wade H. Boggs, Julia Watkins each $52.55. Paid heirs of W. R. Boggs decd. viz: Bula, Ed, Rufus, Coyl, Civiteus, Clayton Boggs $52.55. Paid heirs of R. L. Boggs, decd. viz: Emmett, R. L. Boggs $52.55...

Martin Boggs, will of.. Box 138 #2. Pickens Co., S. C. I, Martin Boggs, the love and affection I have for my brothers and sisters. My sister Mary E. McWorter wife of Robert McWorter one mare mule and fifty acres of land where Edgar Shirley now lives. To my brother Aaron J. Boggs mules and fifty acres of land. To my brother Samuel T. Boggs one hundred acres where Griffin Mauldin now lives adj. land of Cherry McWorter to my sister Mrs. Hariet L. Sims five dollars, and two hogs. To my nephew Pinkney L. Boggs fifty acres land on South East Adj. land of Gil Fowler, to my brother Same L. Boggs five dollars, to John C. Boggs five dollars. To my sister Ida E. Marchbanks five dollars. My sister Liddie A. Freeman, to my sister Martha J. Wright five dollars. Dated 12 July 1901. Witt: N. S. Reeves, T. F. Taylor, W. M. Boggs. Signed Martin Boggs, seal. Proved 1 Aug. 1901.. (No executors given)

BOLT

Oliver S. Bolt. Box 90 #954. Pickens, S. C. On Oct. 29, 1883 J. J. Lewis states that the said decd. died intestate more than 6 months ago. No Admr. took place...

Bolt. Minors, Box 129 #2. Pickens Co., S. C. April 17, 1897, J. J. Morgam, R. A. Bowen, J. A. Robinson are bound to J. B. Newberry Ord. in the sum of $354.58, J. J. Morgan made gdn. of Mary Florine & Ollie Bolt minors under 21 yrs... Jan. 18, 1897, J. J. Morgan stated that Oliver S. Bolt was born Sept. 1883 now of this county a minor child of O. S. and Mary Bolt decd... Mary Florine Bolt entitled to a share of estate of B. F. Morgan decd... 10 Aug. 1901 paid Florine Bolt Norris share $83.09...

BOLTER

Henry Bolter. Box 119 #16. Pickens Co., S. C. Estate Admr. 14 May
1891 by Georgia Bolter, widow, Henry Laurence, Richard Rosemond are
bound to J. B. Newberry, Ord. in the sum of $600.00 Was of Central,
S. C. Henry died 11 March 1891.

BOMAR

George W. Bomar. Married Emily C. Sloan a daughter of David Sloan of
Pickens Co., S. C. Who died in 1834 and his widow was Nancy Sloan. Ref.
Clerk of Court Office, Piack 642 #7, Pickens Co., S. C.

BOND

Robert Bond. Estate of Robert Bond, Box 5 Pack 85. Probate Judge
Office, Abbeville, S. C. Will of Robert Bond, being in a low state of
health but in sound mind and memory, ect.ect. I give to my loving wife
a living from my plantation while she liveth and one third of the
movable property... "I give this plantation I now live on to my son
Roberts oldest son and to Robert I give all the plantation tools and the
third of all moveable property. Thirdly I give to my daughter Mary the
third of all moveable property that is in my possession at this time and
all other land that I possess I leave to my son Robert but he shall pay
James Campbell fifty pds. sterling in cash out of these lands that I
possess." Witt: William Pickens, James Carlile. Signed: Robert Bond.
"And I leave for my executors my loving wife for one and James Carlile
for the other" Will dated 5 Feb. 1791. Admr. 5 April 1791 by Mary
Bond, James Carlile, Richard Ross, James Ponder. In the sum of one
thousand dollars... Debts collected from Viz: Adam Garr, Edward McGary,
Wm. Stevenson, Wm. Graves, Samuel Post, Peter Thomson, David Miller.
Dated 12 Sept. 1792. Debts paid by the Estate viz: James Ponder, Aaron
Steel, Robert McGowen, John Waggon, William G. Pickens, William Mcune,
Wm. Baskin, Admon Shakleford, Rev. Mr. McMullan, John McKinzie,
Abraham Pickens, Joseph Carmichail, Wm. Norris, Joseph Turnbull,
Alexander Eliott, John Pickens, Andrew Hamilton, Mr. Stinchcomb. Dated
14 Sept. 1792.

BOON

Ratliff Boon, Estate of. Box 2 #52. Probate Judge Office, Anderson,
S. C. On 15 Sept. 1815 Nancy Boon, Tyre Boon, James McKinney, Elisha
Alexander are bound unto John Harris, Ord. in the sum of two thousand
dollars. Nancy the widow and Tyre Boon are Admr. Witt: Cader Boon.
On 23 Sept. 1815 a true inventory was taken and the heirs received a
part of the estate before the sale. The heirs are Cader Boon, Thomas
Harben, John Palmer, Zachariah Candler, Joseph Boon, Tyre Boon, Nancy
the widow is not listed as taking a part... By 1832 the estate was not
settled and at this time Nancy Boon was then Nancy Hooper and was
living outside of this state.

Thomas Boon. A Deed to Thomas Boon from Maaman Curtis, Book A-1, Page
14, Clerk of Court Office, Pickens Co., S. C. A deed from Naaman Curtis
to Thomas Boon both of Pickens Dist. Dated 12 Feb. 1824 in the sum of
two hundred dollars for thirty three acres on the west side of Keowee
River originally granted to Rev. John Harris. Adj. land of Nathan Boon,
Naaman Curtis and Thomas Robertson line. Witt: John Curtis, John
Donaldson. Signed Naaman Curtis, seal. On 8 Jan. 1828 Milly Curtis
wife of Naaman Curtis did forever relinquish her dower. Before Nathan
Boon, J.P.

Nathan Boon. Estate of Nathan Boon, Esq. Box 16 #209. Est Admr. 30
Oct. 1848 by Mrs. Sarah Curtis, W. L. Keith, S. R. McFall. Are bound
to Wm. D. Steel, Ord. Pickens Dist. in the sum of $6,000.00. Left five
heirs viz. Sarah Curtis, Wm. Curtis, Amry Alexander, Elijah S. Foster,
Thos. Boon. 13 May 1850 paid Thos. Alexander #396.98 3/4. Sarah Curtis
and Mary Alexander were daughters of decd. Elijah S. Foster and wife
recd. property.

Thomas Boon. Deed from Thomas Boon to S. Reid & P. Alexander. Pack
69 Clerk of Court Office, Pickens Dist. Thomas Boon to S. Reid & P.
Alexander all of the same Dist. Dated 24 Sept. 1834. In the sum of
three hundred dollars paid by Samuel Reid & Pleasant Alexander for a
tract of land of thirty three acres on the west side of Keowee River.
Originally granted to the Rev. John Harrin. Land between Nathan Boon
and Naman Curtis and Thomas Robinsons line. Witt: Robert Knox, Elijah
Alexander. Signed Thomas Boon, Margaret Boon the wife of Thomas and
renounce, released, her interest, and dower in the said land before
William L. Keith, C. C. and Off Qm. seal. Dated 1 Oct. 1835.

BOSTICK

Willis Bostick. Estate of Willis Bostick, Box 7 Pack 114. Probate
Judge Office, Abbeville, S. C. Est. Admr. 5 March 1827 by Henry
Pirtchard, James Patterson, George Pressly who are bound unto Moses
Taggart Ord. in the sum of $3,000.00. The Est. was Admr. again 7 Aug.
___ by James A. Ward, Charles Neely, John A. Adams who are bound to
Moses Taggart, Ord. in the sum of $2,000.00. Citation was published at
Siloam Church July 16, 1826. Sale was held on 25 July 1826. No heirs
given.

BOSWELL

Benjamin Boswell. Will of Benjamin Boswell, Apt. 1 File 25. Probate
Judge Office. Greenville, S. C. I Benjamin Boswell of Greenville Dist.
being in sound mind and memory, ect.ect. I give to my loving wife
Frances Boswell two negroes named Brister and Reuben with all my stock
horse, cattle, hoggs, household furniture during her life time, also
impower her to sell barter or convey the whole or part of my property
and make a good titles to same. Heirs are John Boswell, Martha P.
Pool, Lemuel Boswell, Frances, widow, grandson Benjamin Boswell, other
part of will, how to be divided among the three children after the
death of wife. Exectutor John P. Pool, Lemuel Boswell. Dated 16 Jan.
1825. Signed Benjamin Boswell, seal. Witt: Washington Nicoll,.
Wm. Barton. Probated 6 Feb. 1826. On 9 Apr. 1858 Boswell decd. heirs
are: son John living in Alabama, heirs of Martha Pool decd. J. W. P.
Pool, T. P. Pool, Hiram Cox and wife Frances, Benjamin Landreth and
wife Elizabeth and the heirs of children of Polly Edwards decd. on
1 Apr. 1859 the heirs of Polly Edwards decd. are in Texas. Heirs mentioned also on another paper. S. B. Hutching, M. Hutching, James M.
Bailey, Nancy McKinney, Caroline Bailey, Benjamin Boswell, Alderd Pool,
Lucretia Talley.

Lemuel Boswell. Estate of Lemuel Boswell, Apt. 1 File 38. Probate
Judge Office, Greenville, S. C. On 15 Sept. 1838 Nancy Boswell as Admr.
of her husband estate viz. Lemuel Boswell, decd. of Greenville Dist.
he left three children. Advancement were made to Benjamin Boswell,
John and Mary Edwards... on 2 May Nancy McKinney late Nancy Boswell...

BOTTOMS

David Bottoms. Warrant of David Bottoms for land. Pack 630 #33, Clerk
of Court Office, Pickens Co., S. C. By James E. Hagood, Clerk to any
lawful surveyor you are authorized to lay off unto David Bottoms a

tract of land and make a true plat in two months. Dated 10 Dec.1857..
Bottoms received 368 acres 15 Dec. 1857. Tyre B. Mauldin, Dept. Suvr.

BOWEN

George Bowen. Estate of George Bowen decd. Citation was published at
Swift Creek Chr. Ann Downs of Camden Dist. applied for Admr. on 1 Sept.
1786. (Ref. File 36)

Bowens, Minors. 5 Sept. 1870 Green Bowen about 5 years. Henry Bowen
about 2 years, Philip P. Bowen their father. Their grandfather was
John Ross, of Camden Dist. on 8 Mar. 1877 Burwell Abbert was their
guardian (File 36)

Burwell A. Bowen. Age 36 years, born and raised in Kershaw County. A
farmer. A Methodist. Son of Charles P. & Catharine Bowen. His wife
was Sallie C. Kinard a nurse at the state Asylum. Brother in law
W. L. Kinard also a nurse. A lunatic in Sept. 22, 1902. Jan. 28, 1898
A. H. Bowen, M. A. Bowen, were guardian of Elliott H. Bowen, Eva H.
Bowen, Earle H. Bowen, Eunice H. Bowen minors... Charles A. Bailey late
of Kershaw Co. their grandfather. (File 36).

John Bowen, Sr. Estate of John Bowen Sr., decd. of Camden Dist. estate
Admr. 18 Sept. 1826 by his widow, Anna Bowen and Frederick Bowen. (File
36).

Zacharaih Bowen. Estate of Zacharaih Bowen decd of Camden Dist. Admr.
27 Apr. 1849 by John Bowen, Charles Bailey. (File 36)

John A. Bowen. Will of John A. Bowen of Kershaw Dist. recorded 22
May 1857. Wife Mary A. Bowen, children, Anderson H. Bowen, Sarah A.
Bowen. (File 37)

John Bowen. Will of John Bowen of Charleston, S. C. Probate Judge
Office, Vol. 32, page 506. I John Bowen of St. James, Goose Creek,
being with a sore and grevious malady but of sound mind and memory,
ect.ect. I give to my beloved wife the place or farm whereon I now live,
also the place which I cultivate on Goose Creek in St. James Parish. I
give to my daughter Mary Withers my two places on Goose Creek called
Morris Hill, and Sambo Hill. To my son John Withers Bowen I leave in
fee simple the two places in which his mother (my beloved wife) has
during her natural life. My son during his minority shall be maintained
and educated from the estate left him and his mother. The slaves (not
named) to be made into three equal lots, with my wife first choice of
house servants. Sell my sloop for the benefit of all. I appoint my
wife Rebecca Executrix, and my son in law John Withers Junr. with
Theodre A. Z. Smith Executors. Dated 2 Dec. 1811. Witt: Frances
Baker, Ann E. Smith, Charlotte. Signed John Bowen, seal. Proved
3 Jan. 1812.

William Bowen, Senr. Will of William Bowen, Senr. Vol. 21, page 629.
Charleston, S. C. I William Bowen, Senr. of the Parish of St. George's
Dorchester being sick and weak in body, but in perfect mind and memory,
ect.ect. I give unto my Nephew Mathew Bowen, my brother Ryley Bowen
son all my tract of land lying in Ninety Six Dist. on Durbin's Creek, of
one hundred acres. I give unto my niece Rebecah Crow daughter of my
sister Mary Crow, one feather bed and furniture. I give unto my nephew
Isaac Bowen son of my brother John Bowen decd. one horse colt, now
suckling it mother.. Sell my large black mare and the money ariseing
shall be put with what is left after paying my debts to the schooling
my three nephews, Jacob, Isaac, and James Bowen sons of brother John
Bowen decd. I appoint my nephew William Bowen, Junr. and friend
Edward Pue with my sister in law Hannah Bowen my Executors. Dated
17 Aug. 1784. Witt: William Lord, Samuel Postell. Signed William
Bowen, seal. Proved 7 March 1785.

Margaret Watson Bowen. Will of Margaret Watson Bowen, Vol. 49, page 1019. Charleston, S. C. I, Margaret Watson Bowen, widow, make this my last will and testament. It is my will that my Executor hereinafter named be the trustee of all my property. Trustee is to sell all and invest the money on interest. Make three equal division among my three daughters, viz: Anna H. wife of John Y. Stock, Isabella Catherine wife of Joseph W. Faber, Susan wife of Charles Linning, Esqs. Condition of will and trust are given. I nominate my friend John F. Blacklock Executor and Trustee. Dated 19 Dec. 1857. Witt: J. L. Petigru, C. E. Powell, James Lowndes. Signed. Marg. W. Bowen, seal. Ex: G. B. Probated before George Buist, O.C.D. 9 Sept. 1862. On the 25 May 1863, Qualified Charles Linning, Administrator Will annexed durante absentia Executoris..

John A. Bowen. Will of John A. Bowen of Kershaw Dist. Will book A, page 288, Camden, S. C. I John A. Bowen, being in a sound mind and memory, ect.ect. After all just debts are paid, I give in the following manner. I give unto my wife Mary A. Bowen and by my unmarried children during her life or widowhood, my plantation whereon I now live and two negroes named Joe and Agnis. All stock, farm tools, household furniture, ect. If my wife ceases to be my widow either by death or marriage, then the plantation shall belong to my son Anderson H. Bowen. In this case the plantation to be appraised and my son to give my daughter Sarah A. Bowen one half of the value for her share. The negroes George Henry, Aaron, Douglass, Rebecca, Warren, Mary, Frank, Lucy, Norah, and Martha to be divided between my children, with the money I may have at death till my son is twenty one years of age. If any other children are born after the making of this will, then it is to share alike. Sell the tract of land on twenty five mile Creek on Beaver Dam known as Nonden and Cherry tracts supposed to be four hundred acres, I give unto my wife to dispose as she thinks proper. I appoint my wife Mary A. Bowen sole Executrix. Dated 14 June 1853. Wit: William Nelson, W. B. Hackabee and Jno. X. Worrin. Signed J. A. Bowen. Recorded 22 May 1857 by J. R. Joy, Ord. KD.

Zachariah Bowen. Will of Zachariah Bowen, No. 250 Kershaw Dist., Camden, S. C. I Zachariah Bowen of Kershaw Dist. being in health of body and sound mind and memory, ect.ect. I will to my sons Isaac and John by my beloved wife, together with my sons James, Archibald and Daniel by Mrs. Priscilla Robinson, all my land to be divided among them share and share alike... To my daughter Aurena by Priscilla Robinson I give six negroes named, viz: Clare and her two children, Ed & Binn, Lucy and her infant child and a boy twelve years old named Billy. The said negroes not be subject to daughter Aurena husband debts or contracts. If Aurena dies without issue, the said negroes to be divided between my five sons. I give to my son Isaac a negro named Nat, about seventeen years of age, and a negro woman named Ann also seventeen years of age, also a boy named Black Henry about nine years of age. I give to my son John, one negro man named George and a negro girl named Eliza both seventeen years of age. I give to my son James one negro boy named Simon, about fifteen years of age, and one negro boy named Yellow Henry about seven years of age. I give to my son Archibald on negro named Colonal about twenty years of age, and one negro boy named Ben five years of age. I give to my son Daniel one negro woman named Sally about twenty five years old and her child three years old. Sell all crops, stock, household furniture, farm tools, to pay my debts and if not enough the five boys are to equally divide the amount and pay themselves. I appoint my son Isaac, my brother Fredrick Bowen and friend John J. Blair, Executors. Dated 18 July 1831. Witt: Additon Boykin, Saml. S. Taylor and D. Schrock. Signed Zachariah X Bowen, seal. (This will was revoked.)

John A. Bowen. Estate admr. 27 Apr. 1849 by John A. Bowen, Charles Bailey, T. D. Murry, and E. M. Bonney who are bound unto John R. Joy, Ord. in the sum of $20,000.00. On 14 Feb. 1853 paid Mary Bowen the widow her share $248.80 1/2. Paid Frederick Bowen guardian for minors Victoria, Benjamin, and Preston Bowen their share $298.56.

Bowen, Minors Children. Box 8 #246. Kershaw Dist., Camden, S. C.
Burwell Abbett, Wiley Albert are bound to J. F. Sutherland Ord. in the
sum of $300.00 Dated 8 March 1877. Burwell Abbett guardian of Henry
and Green Bowen minors. On 5 Sept. 1870 Green Bowen about 5 years old
and Henry Bowen about two years old. Philip P. Bowen their father sheweth that by the death of their grandfather John Ross late of Camden
Dist. who died about 5 Jan. last they became entitled to an estate.
Dated 5 Sept. 1870.

Robert Bowen. Estate of Robert Bowen, Box 15 #195. Pickens Dist.
Estate Admr. on 16 Feb. 1846 by Reese Bowen, John Bowen, Franklin
Blassingame who are bound unto W. D. Steel Ord. in the sum of $1,000.00
John Bowen was gdn. for the heirs of Robert Bowen decd. no names
given.

Anna Bowen. Estate of Anna Bowen, Box 16 #202. Pickens Dist., Pickens,
S. C. Estate Admr. 23 Mar. 1847 by Jane Barton, Pleasant?, Wm., Elijah,
Danl. M. Alexander bound to Wm. D. Steele Ord. Pickens Dist. sum of
$8,000.00 Est Admr. agin 18 Nov. 1846 by Bailey Barton, Daniel Durham,
Fountain Alexander, Jas. Dean bound unto Wm. D. Steele, Ord. in the sum
of $5,000.00 Expend: Feb. 5, 1849 paid Reece Bowen $401.84. 19 Jan.
1850 paid Bowen gdn. for children $1252.24.

William Bowen. Will of William Bowen, Box 46 #510. Pickens Dist.,
Pickens, S. C. I William Bowen being in sound mind and memory, ect.
ect. I will unto my beloved wife Sarah Bowen one eighth part of my
real and personal estate in liue of all dower. I will to my daughter
Elizabeth Benson, wife of Thornton Benson one eighth part of my real
and personal estate. I will unto the children of my daughter Nancy
Blassingame decd. former wife of Robert Blessingame one eighth part of
my real and personal estate. I will to my daughter Mary Blessingame decd
childrens one eighth part of my real and personal estate. I will to my
daughter Rebecca Dillard five dollars in full as her portion, as I have
already given her a tract of land whereon she now lives. I give to my
son Robert Bowen one eighth part of my real and personal estate. I will
to my son Thomas Bowen one eighth part of my real and personal estate.
I will to my son William Bowen one eighth part of my real and personal
estate. I will to my son John Bowen one eighth part of my real and
personal estate. I give to my daughter Martha Welborn wife of Joel E.
Welborn five dollars as her full share of my estate, as I have given
her husband a considerable amount. I appoint my son Robert Bowen and
my esteemed friend John Bowen my Executors. Dated 2 Sept. 1856. Witt:
Davis W. Hodges, J. T. McDaniel and D. Hoke. Signed Wm. Bowen. Proven
21 Dec. 1857.

Darcus L. Bowen. Guardian bond, Box 171 #11 Pickens Dist. Pickens,
S. C. Jan. 9, 1882, W. R. Bowen, R. E. Bowen, Wm. McMahan are bound to
Olin L. Durant, Ord. in the sum of $400.00... W. R. Bowen made gdn. of
Darcus L. Bowen a minor under 21 years. Dtr. of John G. Bowen decd.

Bowen. (Equity) Box 1 #22, Pickens Dist., Pickens, S. C. Jan. 1, 1848
John Bowen trustee of Mary Durham paid her share of est. of Elijah
Barnett decd. $209.00. Gdn. of O. E. Bowen, Lucy A. Bowen, Dorcas J.
Bowen.

W. R. Bowen. Box 128 #12, Pickens, S. C. Est. Admr. 2 Oct. 1896 by
J. M. Stewart, J. T. Looper, T. R. Price are bound unto J. B. Newberry
Ord. in the sum of $300.00. 4 Oct. 1898 paid Martha A. Bowen her share
$435.09. Paid her as gdn. for J. C. and W. R., Lillie A. and Hugh G.
Bowen minors each $435.08.

W. Walter Bowen. Estate, Box 139 #3, Pickens, S. C. Estate Admr.
21 Nov. 1901 by T. J. Bowen, A. R. Hamilton, Wm. Ellis who are bound
to J. B. Newberry, Ord. in the sum of $10,000.00. Died 22 Oct. 1901.
March 9, 1903 paid T. J., H. B., J. T., Lidie, R. E., Saml. Bowen
each $1046.92. Paid Netty Tate $1046.92. Lived in Easley, S. C.

Samuel Bowen. Guardian, Box 143 #5, Pickens, S. C. On 9 Apr. 1903
T. J. Bowen, H. B. Bowen, A. R. Hamilton are bound unto J. B. Newberry

Ord in the $2100.00. T. J. Bowen gdn. of Saml. W. Bowen minor under
21 years. 4 March 1903 Sam Bowen state she was son of T. J. Bowen and
a minor under 17 years. Brother to W. Walter Bowen.

Reese Bowen. Estate of Reese Bowen, Box 140 #2, Pickens, S. C. Estate
Admr. by R. A. Bowen, Reese Bowen, W. T. Bowen who are bound unto J. B.
Newberry Ord. in the sum of $5,000.00. Reese died 6 July 1900. Ref.
Box 140 #4 Reese Bowen widow Elizabeth Bowen died 7 April 1902. They
owned 222 acres adj. land of W. T. Field, Reese Bowen, Jr. and McDuffie
Farmer and others. Heirs are: John Y. Bowen, Lawrence O. Bowen,
Pickens Bowen, W. T. Bowen, G. W. Bowen, Martin H. Bowen, Martha E.
Nimmons, Nancy E. Nimmons, Rebecca A. Allgood. There is a power of
attorney from L. O. Bowen of Holbrook, Navajo Co., Arizona appointed
W. T. Bowen of Pickens Co. his Att. to receive his part of the estate.
Dated 12 June 1902.

J. H. Bowen. Box 141 #1, Pickens, S. C. Estate Admr. 12 Feb. 1903 by
L. E. Hunt, R. G. Hunt, R. E. Bowen who are bound unto J. B. Newberry
in the sum of $600.00. He died 15 Jan. 1903.

Cynthia Bowen. Will, Box 142 #1, Pickens Dist. I Cyntha Bowen being
of sound mind and memory, ect.ect. I give to my husband Samuel Bowen
ten dollars from my personal estate. I give to my son Augustus Bowen
ten dollars from my personal estate. I give to my son Frank Bowen ten
dollars from my personal estate. I give, devise to my grand son
Washington Bowen two thirds of all my real estate also two beds ticks,
one bed stead and four quilts. I give to my beloved daughters Emma
Bowen and Anna Blassingame the other one third of my real property.
I will that the remainder shall be divided between my beloved husband
Samuel, sons Augustus and Frank Bowen. I appoint Augustus Clark and
Anderson Langston to be Executors. Dated 7 Aug. 1903. Witt: J. M.
Jameson, Della Blassingame, Ed. Murphy. Signed Syntha X Bowen. Filed
19 Feb. 1903.

John Bowen. Estate, Box 102 #1067. Estate Admr. 11 Oct. 1871 by
Col. Robert E., Thos. J., Robt. A.Bowen and W. E. Holcombe who are
bound unto J. H. Philpot, Ord. Pickens Co. in the sum of $2,000.00.
Expend; in the years, 1876, 1878, 1879. Paid; Wm. R. Bowen $50.00.
Reece Bowen $64.73, Tenanna Bowen $39.00, Mrs. Fieldin Gossett $175.00,
Mrs. E. Bowen $443.00, M. D. L. Bowen $233.52, Elizabeth Berry $208.33,
Mrs. S. A. McMahan $16.05, Mrs. D. J. Dalton $225.00, Elvira Bowen
$39.00, Saml. Bowen $230.00, Thos. Bowen $288.83, J. H. Bowen $85.10.

Bowen. Equity Papers Box 1 #9 (Mixed) Pickens Co., June 25, 1847.
John, Reece, Thos. H. Bowen are bound to M. M. Norton C.E. in the sum of
$2,000.00. John Bowen made gdn. of Eliza Ann P. Bowen minor under 21
years. Bailey Barton decd her grandfather. John Bowen gdn. also for
Bailey A., John C., O. E., Bowen Minors under 14 years and Dorcas J.,
Louisa A., Martha Ann minors under 12 years. Eliza Ann Bowen mother
Annah F. was a decd. daughter of Bailey Barton and wife of Robert Bowen
decd. John Bowen her uncle. Nov. 10, 1848 Reece, John, Thos. H. Bowen
are bound to Miles M. Norton C in E sum of $9,000.00. Reece Bowen made
gdn. of Wm. T. Field minor under 14 years son of Joseph A. Fields decd.
Mother Elizabeth Field. Reece Bowen his uncle.

John G.Bowen. Box 92 #973. Pickens Co. Estate Admr. 17 Aug. 1880 by
Wm. R. Bowen, R. E. Bowen, T. J. Bowen who are bound to Olin L. Durant,
Ord. in the sum of $400.00. Oct. 10, 1881 paid Wm. R. Bowen gdn. for
Darcus Lacretia Bowen $135.00.. left four heirs viz; J. S. Bowen, Robt.
G. Bowen, W. R. Bowen, Darcus Lucretia Bowen.

John Bowen. (Land) Box 106 #1110. Pickens Co. On 24 Aug. 1874
R. E., T. J. Bowen states that John Bowen died 4 June 1871. Owned tract
#1 One half interest in the mill tract of 26 acres, adj. land of
Bennett Freeman, L. T. Addington. Tract #2, 215 acres known as the
power mill tract, adj. land of F. N. Garvin, Green Stephens. Tract #3,
259 acres known as the Major & Morgan tract, adj. land of L. Hughes,
A. T. Clayton. Tract #4, known as the Corban tract adj. land of
W. Manning Jones. Tract #5 known as the Sutherland tract adj. land of

Joseph Bates, Stephens D. Keith. Heirs viz; R. E. Bowen, T. J. Bowen,
W. R. Bowen, John H. Bowen, Saml. H. Bowen, M. D. L. Bowen, the heirs of
Malinda Taylor decd. to wit: Flora, John, Ella, Ida Taylor. Elvira
Holcombe wife of R. E. Holcombe, Dorcus J. wife of L. R. Dalton, M. E.
wife of Lawrence Berry and M. T. Bowen and W. R. Bowen in Missouri.
John H. Bowen in Georgia. S. H. in Texas. Flora, John Ella, Ida Taylor
heir of Malinda Taylor are all minors. Alfred Taylor gdn. of minors.

John Bowen. Deed to John Bowen from James Major, Pickens Co., no other
ref. Dated 4 Dec. 1851 between James Major to John Bowen both of
Pickens Co. in the sum of 154 dollars for 77 acres on Golden Creek waters
of 12 mile River. Adj. land of John Bowen, the widder Smiths heirs and
George Taylor and myself. Land first granted unto George Miller the
5 Nov. 1792. Witt: John W. Major, Stephen A. Major. Signed: James
Major.

John Bowen. Will of John Bowen, Box 6 #79. (County not given)... I
John Bowen of Pendleton Dist. being weak in body but sound mind, ect.
ect. I give to my beloved wife Patsay Bowen the whole of my estate both
real and personal with full power and authority to make a division as
she thinks equitable when they marry or leave her. If my wife do marry
again I give her two negroes Dinar and Caty during her life and at her
death to return to my children. My ounger children to be schooled from
my estate. At wife death or children all of age an equal share to all.
Witt: Abramham Burdine, James Lathem, Bird Stegall. Make wife and son
John overseer Executors. Signed: John Bowen. Dated 13 Aug. 1820.
Proven 3 Dec. 1832.

Charles Caldwell. Estate of Charles Caldwell, Box 15 Pack 317.
Probate Judge Office, Abbeville, S. C. We Abigail Caldwell, Hugh Morrah,
Hugh Dickson are bound unto Taliaferro Livington, Ord. for Abbeville
Dist. in the sum of ten thousand pds. lawfull money of this state.
Dated 4 March 1816. Witt: Wm. Cochran. There is a petition of Louisa
W. Cochran, dated 14 Jan. 1827 or 1829 (Not plain) In her petition
Louisa Cochran states that she was a child of Charles Caldwell decd. and
that a letter of Admr. was granted to Abigail his wife and Hugh Morrow
That Abigail had lately died intestate and the surviving Admr. refused
to act. An inventory was made 29 March 1816. The only reference made
to another heir is dated 12 Feb. 1817. "Paid Wm. Morrow in part of his
wife legacy due from her uncle John Coldwell decd. Paid $20.00.

Abigail Caldwell. Estate of Abigail Caldwell, Box 15 Pack 318, Probate
Judge Office, Abbeville, S. C. We Robert Wilson, W. Wilson, George
W. Hodges are bound unto Moses Taggart, Ord. in the sum of three thousand
dollars lawful money to make a true inventory and a report each year.
Etc. etc. Witt: G. W. O. Catlin. Admr. Robert Wilson had a sale of
Abigail Caldwell personal estate 10 May 1828. On 11 Apr. 1830
Dr. Samuel L. Watt, applied for a letter of Admr. of Abigail estate
(Robert W. Wilson, decd.) The only family or heirs given are viz:
"Expate Levinda & Sophia Caldwell pet. for guardn. Shoes for daughter
Elizabeth.

Curtis Caldwell. Estate of Curtis Caldwell, Box 20 Pack 455. Probate
Judge Office, Abbeville, S. C. We Sarah Caldwell, John Fondren, James
Wilkinson. Are bound unto John Thomas Junr. Ord. of 96 Dist. in the
sum of two thousand pds. Dated 5 June 1784. The inventory was taken,
but no date given, and it was "certified to us in Virginia money."
The sale was held on 27 Aug. 1784. (At the sale the name Caldwell was
spelled Kelwelld) Those who bought at the were viz; Sarah Kalwelld,
slaves Chana, Jain, Sam, Hannah. Nethan Lankford, Emye.. William Jordon,
Rachel, Robert Hobs, Filies, Mathew Kelwelld, John Jonsome, Robert
Hodges, No heirs given.

Edna Caldwell. Will of Edna Caldwell, Pack 387. Clerk of Court Office,
Abbeville, S. C. I Edna Caldwell being in perfect mind and memory,
etc. etc. 1. It is my will, I give to my son George R. Caldwell in
trust for my daughter Anne Webber the following slaves. viz; one negro
woman named Elizer and her four children, Solomon, Jack, Daniel and
Ellen, also one boy named Smith, one girl named Lizzy. To be used to

support my daughter during her natural life. 2. I give to my son
George R. Caldwell one negro named Harriet and her two sons named,
Peter, Gains. also man named Hampton. With household items, farm tools
etc. Also the tract of land known as the home place. 3. I give to my
daughter Margaret R. Caldwell one negro woman named Rachel and her five
children viz; Joe, Westley, Willis, Dave, Della. Also one girl named
Caroline with other household items. 4. I give to my granddaughter
Virginia Pickens Maynard, one negro boy named Jeff, with other household
items... Sell all other property not named in this will except $200.00
it to be put on interest and said interest to support Mount Moriah Church
I appoint Stanmore Brooks and my son George R. Caldwell Executors.
Dated 1 Feb. 1855. Witt: John Cothran, C. W. Sproull, W. C. Hunter.
Signed Edna Caldwell. A petition of George Caldwell Webber by Matthew
McDonald his next friend. (In equity) George Webber mother received
the slaves per Edna Caldwell will. Ann E. Webber died 2 July 1858
leaving a husband Theodore Webber and your orator and his two sisters
namely George about eight years old. Sarah C. about six years old,
Edna B. about four years old. Your orator thinks that his father has
declared to leave the state and he prays that a guardian be set up for
he and his sisters.

George F. Caldwell. Estate of George F. Caldwell, Box 14 Pack 303.
Probate Judge Office. Abbeville, S. C. We Stanmore Brooks, William B.
Brooks and Samuel Perryman are bound unto Moses Taggart Ord. in the sum
of twenty thousand dollars, etc,etc, In the settlement of the estate
14 Feb. 1837. Its states that George F. Caldwell died 12 March 1834,
leaving a widow and five children. The appraisement was held 9 Dec.
1834 by Samuel Caldwell, James Carson, Samuel Perryman. With the sale
held on Dec. 10 1834. Most of the items was bought by Edna Caldwell
and Saml. Perryman. Its doesn't say that these are heirs, but in the
final settlement. Edna, Ann, Rebecca, George and James Caldwell are
paid some money.

James Caldwell. Estate of James Caldwell, Box 23, Pack 523. Probate
Judge Office, Abbeville, S. C. We William H. Harris, John G. Caldwell
and William H. Caldwell. Are bound unto David Lesly, Ord. in the sum
of twenty four thousand dollars to make a true and perfect inventory,
etc,etc. Dated 28 Nov. 1842. In the petition for the Admr. bond
William H. Harris states that he was a son in law of James Caldwell decd.
That he left a widow and nine children, some of whom are minors. In
another place it states that Caldwell died in July 1842. In a statement
of Nathaniel J. Davis Admr. of the estate of Jane Y. Caldwell dated
Jan. 1, 1844 that he found a note for $38,000.00 signed by Jane Y. and
W. H. Caldwell, this note was given to W. H. Harris on 14 Dec. 1850.
In the 1846 report of the estate advancements was made to viz; W. H.
Harris and wife, J. J. Caldwell, Saml. T. Caldwell, D. O. Mecklin and
wife. These may be heirs. At the sale of the slaves viz; Wm. H. Harris
bought June, Amy, Ester, Jackson, Lucy Ann, Gilbert, Lucinda, Milley,
Mariah and two children, Lucy and child, John Baskin bought Jack and
Lucy, John A. Speer bought John, Williamson Norwood bought Sigh., Wm.
Caldwell Junr. bought Nelson, Joseph Baker bought Isabel and two children
and Jack, Wm. C. Cozby bought Jerry, Maj. L. Harper bought Anderson,
Stephen Jones bought Sam, J. J. Caldwell bought Agnes, Eleven, Martha.

James H. Caldwell. Estate of James H. Caldwell, Box 24, Pack 553.
Probate Judge Office. Abbeville, S. C. We N. Jefferson Davis, John C.
Red, McKinney Thomas. are bound unto David Lesly, Ord. in the sum of
two thousand dollars, to make a true and perfect inventory of the goods
and chattels of James H. Caldwell decd. Dated 2 Dec. 1844. Witt:
William Gainers. In Davis petition he states that Caldwell died
leaving a widow and one child. The widow was Jude Caldwell. On 8 Dec.
1846 Vachael Hughey? acknowledge from N. J. Davis Admr. of James H.
Caldwell estate that $842. 23 being my wife part and my ward Jas. H.
Caldwell, minor. (Juda, the widow must have married Michael Hughey.)

Charlotte S. & Ann Elizabeth Caldwell. Guardianship of Charlotte S. &
Ann Elizabeth Caldwell, Box 22 Pack 504 Probate Judge Office, Abbe-
ville, S. C. We Dr. Samuel Perryman, Stanmore B. Brooks & William B.
Brooks are bound unto Moses Taggart Ord. in the sum of three thousand

dollars bond dated 14 Feb. 1837.. Another guardian bond was signed
12 Apr. 1841 by Edna Caldwell, John P. Barrett and James H. Cobb who are
bound unto the Ord. in the sum of two thousand dollars. This bond is
for Ann Elizabeth Caldwell only. On 14 Feb. 1837, recd. of Stanmare
Brooks Admr. of the Estate of George Caldwell decd. $880.17 also, May
23, Recd of commission of Newberry Dist. the 1st and 2nd installment
of share of land of estate of Jas. Caldwell $55.45, Also Abbeville Dist.
"Personally came Dr. John P. Barrett Exor. of the estate of Dr. Saml.
Perryman decd. and made oath that the above is such a return as he could
make from the papers of the decd. and he believes it is correct and true.
Dated 3 Jan. 1839. Signed John P. Barrett." also signed Moses Taggart,
Ord. Abb. Dist.

Sarah Caldwell. Guardianship of Sarah Caldwell, Box 22 Pack 495.
Probate Judge Office. Abbeville, S. C. We Peggy Stewart, John Logan and
Jessee Beazle are bound unto Moses Taggart Ord. in the sum of four thousand dollars, bond dated 16 July 1833. It seems that a Dr. John Logan
was guardian of this child before this date. Abbeville Dist. "Personally came Doctor John Logan guardian of the person and personal estate
of Sarah Caldwell a minor and made oath that the above return of receipts
and expenditures is just and true as there stated. Dated 8 May 1832.
Signed John Logan. Moses Taggart, O.A.D. Her share was $1122.64.
Parents not given here.

Joseph Caldwell. Estate of Joseph Caldwell, Box 20 Pack 425. Probate
Judge Office, Abbeville, S. C. We Charles Caldwell, Henry Caldwell,
William Hamilton, James Kyle are bound unto Andrew Hamilton, Ord. in
the sum of five thousand dollars. This bond dated 8 Jan. 1803. The
condition they make a true and perfect inventory of the goods and
chattels of Joseph Caldwell decd. The Inv. made 15 Jan. 1801, with the
sale on the twentieth day of Jan. 1803. Those who bought viz; Charles
and Henry Caldwell, Samuel Weems, John Sanders, Alexr. Foster, Jos.
Sanders, James Johnston, John Wardlaw. No heirs given.

John Caldwell. Will of John Caldwell, Box 19 Pack 394, Probate Judge
Office, Abbeville, S. C. I John Caldwell of Abbeville County, S. C.
(Carpenter) being in sound mind and memory, etc, etc. I will to my
beloved wife Nancey Caldwell all my household, kitchen furniture, my
bay mare, colt, cows the choice of my stock, I will my brother Henry my
carpenters tools. It is my will that my cross cut saw and steelyards
be keep in the family and not vested in any particular one. The rest of
my property expose to public sale with the house and lot in Pickensville to be sold. I will a title to the tract of land I let Hugh Morrow
have, with my heirs having no claim on him. Make a title to Josiah
Chambers for the land I bought from him, and he will refund the money.
Put all money on interest and support my wife during widowhood, but if
she marry, then only one third to her, and the rest to my brothers,
Charles, James, Joseph, Henry Caldwell. I appoint Charles, James
Caldwell, John Ravling Executors. Dated 25 Oct. 1797. "Before
signing I think it proper to alter the same, I will to my four brothers
my wearing apparel to divid as they may find most convenient. I will
to John Caldwell (son of brother James Caldwell) my silver watch. Also
I will out of the money mentioned, Jenny Reid and James Caldwell Reid
son and daughter of Capt. Saml. Reid five pds. sterling. Witt:
Betsey X Ravling, Jenny X Revling, Jas. Wardlaw. Signed John Caldwell.
Recorded 28 March 1798.

John Caldwell. Estate of John Caldwell, Box 19 Pack 400, Probate
Judge Office, Abbeville, S. C. We William Caldwell, James Caldwell,
Richard Griffin, Bartlett Saterwhite free holders of Ninety Six Dist.
are bound unto John Ewing Calhoun, Esq. Ord. in the sum of fourteen
thousand Pds. Signed, sealed at Pages Creek this 21 Jan. 1783. Witt:
Robt. Gillam, Danel X Megin. The estate was first inventory on 27
Dec. 1779. Slaves named was, Mindo and Child, Abram, Tom. The inv.
taken by Wm. Houseal, David Glyn, Sims Brown. At the end of the notes
it's states that the law was not complyed with, as one Charles Tower had
a writing in possession to comply with the law but fled to the north-
ward since that time there has not been an opportunity of acting in
respect concerning the said writing as the law directs. Signed:

Coll. John Thomas, Esq. Dated 24 May 1783.

John Caldwell, Senr. Will of John Caldwell, Senr. Box 19 Pack 404.
Probate Judge Office, Abbeville, S. C. I John Caldwell being low in
body but sound judgement and perfect memory, etc.etc. I will to my
beloved wife Elizabeth Caldwell my negroes Gill & Dob. During her widowhood, if she marry they are to be disposed of in the best manner to
support my youngest son and daughter Andrew and Jane Caldwell. I give
to my oldest son William Caldwell the land I bought from George Huston
with the fifty acres he now lives on. I will to my son David Caldwell
one hundred and fifty acres, taken off the west side of the land bought
from Black. The remainder of my land to be divided my sons James and
Andrew Caldwell, allowing my wife to live off the land. I give to my
daughters Ann Kilb and Isebel Pickens ten shillings and to daughter
Mary Black two cows. I ordain John Caldwell Junr. and Joseph Black my
Executors. If my negro woman be with child, it to be the property of
Isebel Pickens.. Dated 21 June 1795. Witt: Ma. Linton, Matthew Wilson,
William Caldwell. Signed John Caldwell. Recorded 10 Nov. 1795.

John Caldwell. Estate of John Caldwell, Box 16 Pack 336. Probate Judge
Office, Abbeville, S. C. Margaret Caldwell and Jesse Beasley made suit
to me for a letter of Admr. of the estate of John Caldwell decd. Dated
8 June 1818. The bond for (Peggy) Caldwell, Thomas Brightman, Jesse
Beasley & Jno. Sample who are bound unto Taliaferro Livington, Ord.
Conditions to make a true and perfect inventory of the goods and
chattels, etc.etc. Dated 8 July 1818. Slaves named, Man Jack, Boy
Washington, Girl Ann, Boy Ditte, Girl Queen, Boy Dick, 2 Girls Harriatt
and Mariah, Mother Hannah and child Mary, Inv. made 23 July 1818 with
part of the sale. 28 Sept. 1818. Heirs are not named, but William
Caldwell, paid 480.12 on Feb. 19, 1820. Same day Alex. Caldwell paid
$451.76. Paid Drewry Wilson $461.79. These may be heirs. Paid
Edmund Beasley guardian, $1443.29 for minors Edmund, James, John, Jesse,
Polly. This estate has 24 pages.

Samuel Caldwell. Estate of Samuel Caldwell, Box 14 Pack 300. Probate
Judge Office, Abbeville, S. C. The petition of John Cothran, J. L.
Pearson, Anthony Caldwell has made suit to me for a letter of Admr. of
the estate of Samuel Caldwell decd. dated 1 Feb. 1837. Bond was
issued with Wade S. Cothran and Lewis Perrin as Sec. in the sum of
Twenty thousand dollars. Bond date 1 March 1837. Conditions to make a
true and perfect inventory, etc.etc. The inventory was had on 9 March
1837. Slaves named viz; Woman Lucy, Woman Harriet, Boy Jack, Man Sam,
old man and Woman Bob & Juda, Woman Rachel, Woman Jinney, one Woman
Hannah and $ children Frank, Charles, Harry, Cyrus, Sank, Leah,
Leander, Burrel.

James Caldwell. Old Records, Book "B" Abbeville, S. C. Probate Judge
Office, James Caldwell 115 acres on waters of little River the N. W.
fork of Long Cane. Surveyed by William Lesly D.S. on the 19 Apr. 1783
and recorded 23 Aug. 1785. Page 152.

David Caldwell. Same book, David Caldwell, 300 acres on the North
fork of Sawney Creek a branch of Great Rockey Creek. Sur.by Wm.
Lesly, D.S. 21 July 1785 and recorded 23 Aug. 1786. Page 152.

James Caldwell. Same Book, James Caldwell, 200 acres on branches of
Currtail and Reedy Fork on branch of Long Cane. Sur. by Wm. Lesly
D.S. 16 Sept. 1786 and recorded 30 Oct. 1786. Page 167.

David Caldwell. Same Book, David Caldwell, 47 acres above the line
on Great Rockey Creek sur. by Wm. Lesly D.S. 7 March 1786. Recorded
15 Apr. 1786. Page 117.

John Caldwell. Same Book, John Caldwell, 190 acres above the line
on a branch of Great Rockey Creek called Governors Creek. Sur. by
Wm. Lesly D.S. 16 Apr. 1785. Recorded 19 Apr. 1786. Page 122.

John Caldwell. Same Book, 792 acres above the line on Wilson's Creek
a branch of Great Rockey Creek. surv. by William Lesly D.S. on the

15 Nov. 1786. Recorded 21 Apr. 1786. Page 126.

Paul Caldwell. Same Book, 97 acres on the road leading to Mr. Barks-
dale ferry on Savannah River. Land adj. Richard Hutchins, John
Delwood, William McCrones, first surveyed for Joseph Reid by Patt.
Calhoun D.S. 6 Aug. 1785. Recorded 18 Oct. 1785. Page 73.

Henry Caldwell Junr. Will of Henry Caldwell Junr. Vol. 28 page 189.
Probate Judge Office. Charleston, S. C. I Henry Caldwell grocer in
the city of Charleston, S. C. being in sound mind and memory, etc.etc.
First pay my just debts from cash on hand, if not sufficient sell
some personal property. Have a general sale of all personal estate
when it can be made with decency and in order. The money put on
interest or bank stock with the approval of my wife Sarah Caldwell
and remain there till youngest child Sarah Calwell arrives at full
age of twenty one. My real property to be rented out and money to
support my wife and children. If wife marry again she forfit all claim
both to share of annual interest and other real property. The children
are to share and share alike viz; Eliza, Sarah, Mary and Henry
Calwell. I appoint my friends Philip Moser, Seth Yates, Samuel Rivers
as Executors. Dated 14 Sept. 1801. Wit: Daniel Brown, Sebbe Sebben,
Signed Henry Calwell. seal.
     A codicil was added to the above will giving his wife Sarah
Calwell all household and kitchen furniture. Codicil added 19 Sept.
1801. Will proved 2 Oct. 1801 at the same time Executors examined.

William Caldwell. Will of William Caldwell, Vol. 31, page 381. Probate
Judge Office, City of Charleston, S. C. I William Caldwell being weak
in body but sound mind and memory, etc, etc. I give and bequeath unto
Andrew Simmons of Charleston, S. C. a lot of land lying in the city
of Natchez, Mississippi adj. the large spring under the bluff which I
purchased from Isaiah Packard on 29 Dec. 1807. I do hereby give to
Andrew Simmons all the rest, and remainder of my estate. I appoint
Andrew Simmons my Executor. No date on body of will. Witt: Edmond
Jacobs, Rich. Fairweather, John Smith. Signed Wm. Caldwell, seal.
Proved 8 Aug. 1810.

                              CANE - CAIN

Mary Cane. Will of Mary Cane, Box 21 Pack 471. Probate Judge Office,
Abbeville, S. C. I Mary Cane being very sick in body, but in perfect
mind and memory, etc.etc. First I make, ordain my friend James Lomax
and my son James Cane my sole executors. I give to my oldest daughter
Sarah Cane four dollars, all my body clothes. I give to my youngest
daughter Elizabeth Bradly two cows and three calves. All spun thread,
yarn and cloth, except her brother James winter clothing and four
dollars. I give to my son James Cane all real estate, one negro boy
named Jesse, all cash, bonds and bills. Dated __ Oct. 1795. Witt:
Hugh Porter, Jenny X Watters, Jane X Lomax. Signed Mary X Cane.
Recorded 27 March 1798. An inventory was made 11 May 1798 by George
Conner, William Hairston, William Bell. In the inventory there is a
negro woman named Nance.

Michael Cain. Estate of Michael Cain, Box 21 Pack 456. Probate Judge
Office, Abbeville, S. C. We Mary Cane, Jesse Kennedy, Robert Black
and James Pringle are bound unto Andrew Hamilton, Ord. in the sum of
five thousand dollars. Dated 7 Feb. 1803. Conditions are to make a
true and perfect inventory, etc.etc. Witt: Andrew X Defoor. An
inventory was made 21 Feb. 1803. William Black, Wm. Brownlee, Robert
Black Appraisers. Sale held 31 March 1803. Those bought are: Mary
Cain, Bala Hardin, Mathew Russel, Robert Black, Francis Drinkard,
Joseph Bell, Alexander McCoy, Edmond Monday, Moses Parnel, Wilson
Kanady, Mathew Fox, James Able, John Dilwood, Danel Manier, Henry
Buckhanon, Wm. Brightman, Huston McNeir, Daniel McNeir, Thomas Rusel,
James Caldwell. Debts due by the estate. Due Wm. Richards, Estate of
Robt. Boggs, Tos. Russel, Sm. Savage, Wm. Hamilton, David Wardlaw,

Donald Fraser, Thos. Shanklin, Wm. Dunlap, Thos Black, Francis Hodg, Sm. Black decd., Edward Sharp, Widow Gorge, Jos. or Jas. Kenedy.

Jonathan Cane. Estate of Jonathan Cane, Box 20 Pack 445. Probate Judge Office, Abbeville, S. C. We John Cane, John Pearson, Robert Burns are bound unto John Thomas Junr. Ord. of 96 Dist. in the sum of two thousand pds. Sterling, to make a true and perfect inventory of goods and chattels of Jonathan Cane decd. Dated 30 Nov. 1784. The Petition for the above bond was made 31 Aug. 1784. An Inventory and appraised value in sterling was made 6 Dec. 1784. Slaves was one woman and four children. Signed Abel Pearson. John Clarke, David Smith. No heirs given.

William Cain. Estate of William Cain, Box 21 Pack 460. Probate Judge Office. Abbeville, S. C. We Mary Cain, Isaac Morgne and John Chasteen are bound unto Taliaferro Livington Esq. Ord. in the sum of five thousand dollars. Condition that they make a perfect and true inventory of the goods and chattels, of Wm. Cain decd. etc.etc. Dated 20 March 1817. Witt: John W. Wilson, Estate was appraisers were Drury Breazeale, John Morgne, Peter Smith, Joshua Hill and made same 12 April 1817. Negroes named in the inventory: Watt, Sam, Dick, Sally, Dennis, Mary, Charles, Henry, Jane Milly and a baby, Rachel, Betty, Isham, Lucy. In the petition for Admr. Mary Cain is called Mrs. Mary Cain, Administratrix. No other heirs named.

Thomas Cain. Estate of Thomas Cain, Box 23 Pack 521. Probate Judge Office, Abbeville, S. C. To D. Lesly, Ord. "The petition of Michael Hackett, sheweth that Thomas Cain departed this life intestate leaving a widow in the state of Alabama. That the estate is somewhat indebted Your petr. is desirous as the friend of the deceased to administer thereon and pray that he be appointed on the usual terms." Dated 8 March 1842. Sale was held on 5 July 1842, sold one horse for $10.00 on credit till 1 Jan. 1843.

Mary Cain. Estate of Mary Cain, Box 114 Pack 3363. Probate Judge Office, Abbeville, S. C. Will of Mary Cain. I Mary Cain being of sound mind and perfect memory, etc.etc. I will to my granddaughter Mary E. Davis and her issue one negro girl named Phebe. I will to my granddaughter Mary E. Middleton and her issue a negro girl named Martha. I will to my grandson John E. Cain a negro boy named Wilson. I desire that after my death the remainder of my negroes be divided between my daughters Barsheba A. Harris, Margaret B. Morgne and my son Sampson V. Cain. I will to my son Randolph P. Cain the sum of three hundred and fifty dollars to be paid by Isaac Moragne and Dr. N. Harris. Said sum to be vested in a negro for the use and support of Randolph and at his death to be divided between his children. My son William Cain having relinquished his claim for a consideration, I desire that his children may not come in for any portion of my estate. Lastly I desire that my old and faithful negro woman, Ginny, may have a home and maintainance among any of my children whom she may select and be regarded as free. Dated 7 Apr. 1845. Signed Mary Cain, seal. Witt: Catherine B. Moragne, N. Harris, I. M. Moragne. Will probated 6 Sept. 1847. Negroes named in the inventory are, Mary Ann and child (Robt), John, Margaret, Amelia, Francis, Amanda, Mary. Appraisers were: W. Tennant, Benj. McKittrick, William P. Noble.

Jesse Cain. Bond of Jesse Cain, Box not given. From Anderson Co., S.C. I Jesse Cain am held unto Benjamin Smith in the sum of $800.00. Dated 7 Feb. 1806. Conditions that he make a good and lawful deed unto Benjamin Smith for the tract of land he bought from Elisha Floyd he bind his heirs, assigns forever, etc.etc. Signed Jesse Cain, seal. Wit: Robt Keth, Nathan Boon. Recorded 26 Dec. 1806.

CALHOUN

John E. Calhoun. #25, In Equity, Clerk of Court's Office, Pickens, S.C. Your oratrixes Martha M. Calhoun Senior. Sheweth that John E.

Calhoun departed this life, ___ day of ___ 1847, leaving a widow and four
children viz; Martha M. Calhoun Junior, William R., Henry D., Edward B.
Calhoun. The two last being minors. The widow being entitled to one
third part, and the children the other two thirds. The widow was made
Admr. and the estate was in debt, and desires to sell some of the real
estate, before the personal property. The land for sales was on 12
mile Creek and in excess of six thousand acres. If she can keep the
negroes and the home place she can it in production and support the
family. Also she desire a guardian appointed for the minors. James
Louis Petigru was the guardian of Henry David age 10, and Edward
Bisseau Calhoun age 8, and their sister Martha Maria Calhoun age not
given. Dated 15 May 1849. A letter on the back of this paper."
West Point, New York. Sept. 30, 1848. I herewith give my consent to
the sale of a portion of the land belonging to my father estate.
Signed: W. Ransom Calhoun." William Ransom was 21 years of age on the
22 July 1848.

William Ransom Calhoun. Estate of William Ransom Calhoun, Box 71 #763.
Pickens Co., S. C. Est. Admr. 15 Sept. 1863 by Henry D. and Edward B.
Calhoun and John H. Holmes, who are bound unto W. E. Holcombe, Ord. in
the sum of $100,000.00. Est. Admr. again 1 Sept. 1866 by Edward B.
Calhoun, Armistead Burt, John H. Holmes, who are bound to same Ord. in
the sum $4,000.00. He left no parents, wife or children, Edward B.
Was a brother. A letter in file "To W. E. Holcombe, Ord. dated 21 Apr.
1866. Dear Sir: Will you be kind enough to say whether the oath
taken by Capt. Calhoun yesterday will be sufficient and whether the
administration bonds executed in presence of a witness will be accepted
by you. The estate of Col. John E. Calhoun was never divided between
his widow and children and after the death of his widow the estate of
the children were never divided but held in common all the children
except Capt. E. B. Calhoun departed this life intestate, childless and
unmarried. Capt. E. B. Calhoun is consequently the survivor and
entitled to the whole estate real and personal. All the objects of
an Administration will be accomplished by the payment of the debts of
W. Ransom Calhoun and Henry D. Calhoun, the debts of Col. John E.
Calhoun and of Mrs. M. M. Calhoun having already been paid. Upon the
payment of the debts of Col. W. Ransom Calhoun and of Henry D. Calhoun
the entire estate real and personal will rest in Capt. E. B. Calhoun.
Your Serv. Signed Armistead Burt, Atty. at law."

Martha Maria Calhoun. Estate of Martha Maria Calhoun, Box 32 #372.
Pickens Co., S. C. Est. Admr. 30 June 1854 by W. R. Calhoun, P. Alex-
ander who are bound unto W. J. Parsons Esq. Ord. in the sum of $1300.00.
Est. Admr. again 5 Apr. 1867 by Edward B. Calhoun, Armistead Burt and
John H. Holmes who are bound unto W. E. Holcombe, Ord. in the sum of
$1,000.00.

Henry D. Calhoun. Estate of Henry D. Calhoun, Box 88 #929. Pickens Co.,
S. C. Est. Admr. 12 Sept. 1866 by Edward B. Calhoun, Armistead Burt,
John H. Holmes who are bound unto W. E. Holcombe, Ord. in the sum of
$4,000.00. Edward B. Calhoun states that his brother Henry C. Calhoun
died 27 March 1866. He left no parents, wife or child. Inv. made 16
March 1867 of the personal belonging to W. R. Calhoun, H. D. Calhoun.
E. B. Calhoun found on the plantation known as Keowee, a letter to
General Garvin. "My dear General; As I am anxious to get well and am
now improving I have concluded to act prudently and not go to Pickens
Co., S. C. tomorrow myself but to accept your very kind offer to go
for me. Mother desires to file a letter applying to be appointed
administratrix and I Administrator in the estate of my father. Mother
full name is Margaret Maria Calhoun and mine John Caldwell Calhoun. We
both fully authorize you to sign our names to the necessary papers.
Please have the land drawn up and bring it with you so that I can have
the securities in it by the time the letter of Administration are
issued. Urge Mr. Holcombe to let us have the letter of Administration
as soon as he possibly can for I have much business to attend to
connected with the estate before I leave home. You had also better
have the board of appraisers appointed tomorrow. I have seen none of
the gentlemen but have no doubt they will act viz; yourself - Dr. Miller,
Dr. Wm. Jenkins and if more are necessary Mr. Carver Randal and

Mr. Snellgrove. I am really Genl. very much obliged to your for your
kind offer to go to Pickens for me. Yours very truly, John C. Calhoun..
N.B. We have just heard through the Newberry paper that "Duff" was
wounded in the knee in a fight near Smithfield, N. C. on the 16th the
very day father died. J.C.C. No date on this letter.

John Ewing Calhoun. Estate of John Ewing Calhoun, Box 16 #208. Pickens
Co., S. C. Est. Admr. 13 May 1854 by W. R. and Andw. P. Calhoun, John
T. Sloan who are bound unto M. J. Parson, Ord. in the sum of $200,000.00.
Est. Admr. again by Edw. B. Calhoun, Armistead Burt, John H. Holmes who
are bound unto W. E. Holcombe, Ord. in the sum of $2,000.00. Est. Admr.
again 10 Dec. 1847 by Martha M. Calhoun, W. L. Keith, F. Burt, who are
bound unto Wm. D. Steel Ord. in the sum of $50,000.00 inv.ment. that
he owned 77 slaves.

Hon. J. C. Calhoun. Estate of Hon. J. C. Calhoun, Box 25 #292. Pickens
Co., S. C. Est. Admr. 7 Apr. 1851 by Florida Calhoun, J. E. Cornelia,
W. L. Calhoun, R. A. Maxwell who are bound unto Wm. D. Steel, Ord. in
the sum of $50,000.00 A letter found in the file states that Andrew
Calhoun applied for a letter of Admr. stating that he was the eldest
son and at the request of the family and that two of his brothers are
of full age and will join him in the bond.

Andrew P. Calhoun. Estate of Andrew P. Calhoun, Box 82 #875. Pickens
Co., S. C. Est. Admr. 10 Apr. 1865 by Margaret M. Calhoun, John C.
Calhoun, D. G. Calhoun, B. T. Sloan, H. C. Miller who are bound unto
W. E. Holcombe, Ord. in the sum of $500,000.00. Est. Admr. again 27
Nov. 1865 by John C.Calhoun, D. G. Calhoun, S. P. Ravenel, A. R. Taylor
who are bound unto W. E. Holcombe, Ord. in the sum of $36,000.00.

Martha M. Jr. Estate of Martha M. Jr. Box 92 #967. Pickens Co., S. C.
Est. Admr. 5 Apr. 1867 by Edward B. Calhoun, Armistead Burt, John H.
Holmes who are bound unto W. E. Holcombe in the sum of $800.00.

James Edward Calhoun. Will of James Edward Calhoun, Box 117 #10.
Abbeville Co., S. C. I James Edward Calhoun of Millwood being of sound
mind and memory etc. I will and direct my executors to cut off by
metes one hundred and fifty acres of land in Elbert Co., Georgia at
such place they think best and convey by deed to my faithful servant
Caroline Calhoun to be hers for life then her children to share and
share alike. I will and direct my executors to cutt off 150 acres in
Georgia or Abbeville Co., S. C. at a place they think best and make a
deed to Edward Kiser to be held by Kiser in fee simpel. I will and
direct that the rest of my land, rights and hereditaments in the county
of Abbeville, S. C. and Elbert County, Ga. to be divided between the
following persons to wit; Edward B. Calhoun of Abbeville, John C.
Calhoun of Palatka, Fla., Benjamin Putman Calhoun also of Palatka, Fla.
John C. Calhoun of New York City. Margaret Maria Calhoun of Atlanta,
Ga. daughter of my nephew A. P. Calhoun, Patrick Calhoun of Atlanta,
Ga. and Andrew P. Calhoun son of Duff G. Calhoun decd. of Atlanta, Ga.
My Executors to divide my land in the counties of Oconee and Pickens
between the following persons to wit: Edward B. Calhoun of Abbeville,
Co., S. C. John C. Calhoun of Palatka, Fla. also Benjamin Putman
Calhoun of Palatka, Fla. John C. Calhoun of New York City. Margaret
Maria Calhoun of Atlanta, Ga. daughter of A. P. Calhoun, Patrick Calhoun
of Atlanta, Ga. Isabella Lee of the state of New York. Maria Butler
niece of my lamented wife. I will that the interest bequeathed to
Andrew Pickens Calhoun be held until he is twenty one years of age. I
appoint my nephew Patrick Calhoun of Atlanta, Ga. my sole executor. I
will that the bequeath to my nephew Edward B. Calhoun shall be kept
by my executor in trust for the sole use of his wife and children and
not liable for the debts or obligations of Edward B. Calhoun. He was
to get only the annual interest from the money. Dated 19 Oct. 1889.
Wit: M. C. Butler, Marcus Woodard, James M. Green. Proven 27 Dec. 1889.

Rebecca Calhoun. In equity, Box 1. No county given. June 1860
Rebecca J. Calhoun late Todd by her next friend Elizabeth Todd, is
entitled to a share of her father John Todd decd. of a tract of land
adj. Saml. McCall, Wm. Todd and others. John Todd died 1 April 1860

leaving a wife and 6 children. Rebecca married Jas. Calhoun in 1850.

Thomas W. Calhoun. Pack 220 #1, Clerk of Court Office, Pickens Co.,
S. C. Rebecca Jackson took out a peace warrant against Thomas W.
Calhoun and his wife Lucinda Calhoun. Dated 5 Apr. 1859.

Will of William Calhoun Senr. Box 17 Pack 344 Probate Judge Office.
Abbeville, S. C. I William Calhoun being in sound mind and memory. etc.
The real and personal property to remain in the possession of my beloved
wife to assist in the maintainance and schooling of my younger children.
I give to my wife Rebecah my negro man Enock and Grace and her child
Stephen. I give to my daughter Rachel one negro man named Prince in
fee simple, with a cow and calf and household furn. if wife can spare it.
I give to my daughter Rebecha Catherine one negro named Jacob in fee
simple. With other property as Rachel has. I give to my daughter Mary
Elizabeth one negro named Isaac in fee simple and other property as her
sisters has. I give to my son Leroy one negro named Jack in fee simple,
it is also my will that when my son Joseph arrives at the age of twenty
one, put the plantation on sale and my wife to get one third and the
other two thirds divided between my sons Ezekiel, Leroy, William,
James and Joseph--equally after deducting from Ezekiel share $800 I
advanced in his education. I appoint my son Ezekiel Noble Calhoun
Executor and my wife Executrix. Dated 5 Dec. 1821. Witt: Jos. Hutton,
J. Houston, A. Calhoun. Signed Wm. Calhoun. Proved by Alex. Calhoun
on the 6 Aug.1827. Est. appraised by James, Joseph Senr. Joseph
Calhoun Junr. and James Taggart. Dated 26 Oct. 1827.

CALLAHAN

Elizabeth Callahan. Box 83 #874. Probate Judge Office. Pickens Co.,
S. C. Elizabeth Callahan was an heir of Henry Hendricks decd. whose
will was proved 27 March 1865. In Pickens Co. (probably a daughter).

Basil Callahan. Box 9 #147. Probate Judge Office, Pickens Co., S. C.
Basil Callahan who was the guardian of Lawrence A. Hendrix was probably
the husband of Eliza Callahan.

Martha Adeline Calaham. Box 53 #579. Probate Judge Office, Pickens
Co., S. C. Martha Adeline Calaham a daughter of Thomas Hallum decd.
whose will was proven 17 Feb. 1860 in Pickens Dist. was the wife of
John W. Kalaham.

John W. Callahan. Box 85 #899. Probate Judge Office, Pickens Dist.
Est. Admr. 12 Dec. 1865 by Martha Callahan, John Williamson, Mary Ann
Hallum who are bound unto W. E. Holcombe, Ord. in the sum of $1,000.00
He left a widow and three children.

Callahan Minors Children. Box 117 #7. Probate Judge Office, Pickens,
S. C. Martha A. Callahan, Julia A. Smith, Wm. J. Smith are bound unto
W. E. Holcombe Ord. in the sum of $764.12. Martha A. Callahan guardian
for Carrie J., Baswellh, Julia S. Callahan minors under 21 yrs. children
of John W. Callahan decd. and Martha A. Callahan.

Charles Calaham. Deed of Charles Calaham to Temperance P. Pool (In
Equity) record of Stone and Howard. #26, Pickens, S. C. I Charles
Callaham of Green Co., Ala. for the sum of $212.00 to me paid by
Benjamin P. Pool, I have granted, sell and release unto Temperance P.
Pool (the wife of Seth P. Pool) of the Dist. of Pickens, S. C. to her
bodily heirs forever all the plantation of land lying in the Dist. of
Pickens, S. C. on both sides of Six mile Creek and waters of Keokee
River. Containing 446 acres. First granted to Wm. Swift. Dated
16 May 1835. Witt: William Young, John Franks. Signed Charles
Calaham, seal.

Gersham Calihan. Will of Gersham Calihan, Apt. 2 file 90. Probate
Judge Office, Greenville, S. C. I Gersham Calihan of Greenville Dist.
being low in health, but in sound mind and memory, etc.etc. I will to

my beloved wife and children all of my estate to be equally divided
when the youngest child become of age and in case my wife Belveriddy
Calihan remains my widow she is to have a child part. I wish that as
much as possible my place be kept together to raise the younger children.
I appoint my friend Jno. W. Hodges my sole Executor. Dated 2 June
1836. Witt: Wm. W. Robertson, Charles X Gotherlin, Robert Compton.
Signed Gersham X Callahan, seal. Probated 13 Aug. 1836. Expenditures:
Paid to each viz. Belinda Callahan, Milford Howard and his wife.
Atlantic Howard and his wife, Franklin Barton and Melinda his wife,
James Pittman and Sarah his wife Caroline Callahan, Claiborne P.
Trammell and Martha Jane his wife, Joab Callahan. Out of state were,
John F. Callahan, Belverida Callahan the widow. (Note on most of the
notes the name is spelled Callahan-m)

B. H. Callaham. Deed of B. H. Callaham to J. S. Wilson. #5 Pack 655.
Clerk of Court Office, Pickens Co., S. C. I B. H. Callaham for in
consideration of seven thousand eight hundred and nine dollars paid to
me by J. S. Wilson. I grant sell, release unto said Wilson that certain
tract of land in the township of Liberty on Eighteen mile Creek,
containing 132 1/2 acres. This tract is known as tract #2 of Thomas
Hallums land. Except about one acre which is a family cemetery, and is
not conveyed in this deed. Also another tract of land in Liberty
township containing 130 3/4 acres. Land adj. J. S. Wilson, Sam.
Robinson, Mrs. O. H. Lancaster and others. Dated 23 Jan. 1915. Witt:
J. P. Carey, J. S. Wilson Jr. Signed B. H. Callaham. Recorded 27 Apr.
1915.

CAMPBELL

Alexander Campbell. Will of Alexander Campbell, Richland County, S. C.
no file no. given. I Alexander Campbell being of sound mind and
memory, etc.etc. I give to my wife Sarah Campbell (in lieu of her
dower) the home place and all appurtenances thereon, with two cows and
calves, during her natural life, and after her death to my daughter
Elizabeth and Margaret Campbell. Also I give to my wife Sarah in trust
the tract of land on Robin Branch and Gills Creek, the same to be used
as the family burial ground, after her death to my daughters Elizabeth
and Margaret upon the same conditions. I give the rest and remainder
of my stock of all kinds to my son Matthew and daughter Sarah Daniels
and daughter Martha wife of Jacob Brazel, and granddaughter Sarah
wife of James Campbell and grandson James Beauregard Campbell to be
equally divided between them. I appoint my son Matthew and Jacob
Brazel as Executors. Dated 17 Dec. 1880. Witt: E. S. Percival,
N. N. Percival, W. T. Davis, James McPherson. Filed 10 Aug. 1885.
before John H. Pearson, Judge of Probate.

David Campbell. Will of David Campbell, Vol. 24 page 820. Probate
Judge Office, Charleston, S. C. I David Campbell being of sound mind
and perfect memory, but weak in body, etc.etc. I give to Jacob Meeks
an orphan boy now living with me four cows and calves, to be keep in
care of my Executors till he becomes of full age, then they with their
increase to be given him. I will that both real and personal property
be sold to the best advantage. I give the Methodist College at a
bigdom? in Maryland called Docksbury College the sum of twenty pds.
Pay all just debts. I give to my beloved wife Abigail the whole of my
estate for her use and support, and after her decd. divide into four
equal parts between my sisters and or their heirs to wit; Sarah Conger
or her heirs, sister Martha Thomokins or her heirs, sister Alles Allen
or her heirs, sister Ter Uiah's children she being decd. I appoint
my friend David Rump son of Peter and Joseph Koger my Executors. Dated
29 May 1790. Witt: Edward Smith, Adam Bridge, William Pendarvis.
Signed David Campbell, seal. Proven before Charles Lining Esq. O.C.T.D.
25 Feb. 1791.

Mary Campbell. Will of Mary Campbell, Vol. 50 page 229. Probate Judge
Office, Charleston, S. C. I Mary Campbell being in sound mind and
memory, etc.etc. First pay all funeral expenses and lawful debts.

Second, I give and devise two thirds of my estate to my Executors in
trust for my two daughters each to have an equal portion. They are
viz; Mrs. Catherine Woodside the wife of James Woodside and Mrs.
Margaret Doogan the wife of James Doogan. Each to have an equal share
in their life time and equal divided after death. The remaining one
third to my nephew Henry Campbell, Executors to complete the house now
in the course of errection. etc.etc. I appoint the Revd. Dr. Lynch
the Executor. Dated 23 Sept. 1844. Witt: James Kenny, James Kennedy,
Alexander A. Allemong. Signed Mary X Campbell. Probated before George
Buist, O.C.D. 13 May 1864. On 2 March 1867 filed a renunciation of
executorship by the Rt. Rev. P. N. Lynch.

George Campbell. Will of George Campbell (no file info) Spartanburg
Dist. I George Campbell being weak and low in body but of sound mind
and perfect memory etc.etc. I desire that all my debts be paid. I
desire that my wife Margret Campbell shall have all my land and the rest
of my property as long as she lives, and then to be equally divided
between my children. I appoint my wife and my son Samuel Executors.
Dated 19 March 1808. Witt: John Owens, Joseph Jones. Signed George
X Campbell. Proved 7 Nov. 1808 on oath of John Owens.

Hugh Campbell. Will of Hugh Campbell, Vol. 5 page 147. Probate Judge
Office, Charleston, S. C. I Hugh Campbell of Johns Island in the
parish of St. Johns Colleton County, being very sick on body but of
perfect mind and memory. etc.etc. It is my will and desire that all
my book debts, notes and bonds be called in and the crop on the ground
be sold. First pay all debts. I give to my beloved wife Jane Campbell
one negro man named Jack and one negro woman named Dinah and her child
named Jenney, two horses, two mares and all household furniture. I
give to my daughter Elizabeth Campbell one negro named Will, a young
mare, on James Island branded R, one red cow and calf. I give to my
son Timothy one negro named Tom, a mare colt, one cow with a white spot
and her calf. I give to my daughter Ann one negro named Friday and a
young negro girl called Kate one cow and calf. I appoint my wife Jane
and my daughter Elizabeth Campbell Executrixes with Mr. Robert Cole
Executor. Dated 10 Oct. 1741. Witt: Joseph Phipps, Saml. Shaddock
Junr. James Witter. Signed Hu. Campbell, seal. Will proved before his
Honr. the Lt. Governor the fourth of November 1742 who at the same time
qualified the widow as Executrix.

Hugh Campbell. Will of Hugh Campbell, Vol. 5 page 269. Probate Judge
Office, Charleston, S. C. I Hugh Campbell of Colleton County being
weak in body but sound and perfect mind and memory, etc.etc. I give to
my wife Ann Campbell one negro named Jenny for ever, one riding horse
and saddle, bed and furniture, also the work and labor of three negroes
named Coffey, Isaac, Dafeney. At the death of my wife the three named
negroes to be divided between my four children. I give all the land
being 570 acres to be equally divided between my three sons. Daniel,
Hugh and John Campbell. Share and share alike. All the rest of my
estate to be divided between the four children, male and female to
share and share alike. I appoint my wife Ann Campbell Executrix and
my brother in law Joseph Andrew, Major Lawrence Sanders and Doctor James
Skirving as Executors. Dated 14 Jan. 1742. Witt: John Burnham, David
Jefferyes, Benjamin Cox. Signed Hugh Campbell. Proved the __ Feb.
1743 before Charles Waight Esq.

James Campbell. Will of James Campbell, Book A, page 348. Probate
Judge Office, York Co., S. C. I James Campbell make this my last will
etc.etc. I allow my daughter Frances Dinwordy one blanket from my bed
as her dower. I will to my son Samuel Campbell my large house Bible as
his dower. I will to my son Andrew Campbell all my wearing apparel at
my decd. as his share. I give to my daughter Jennet Campbell all my
household furniture, except that I allow to Samuel agreeable to a
former contract we made. I allow my son John and daughter Jennet
Executors. Dated 31 Jan. 1805. John Campbell, Samuel Campbell, John
Feares. Signed Jas. Campbell, seal. Probated 5 Feb. 1805.

James Campbell. Will of James Campbell, Box 3 page 139. Probate Judge
Office, York Co., S. C. I James Campbell being weak in body but sound

mind and memory I will to my son Thomas Campbell the plantation whereon
he now lives. I will to my son Robert Campbell my plantation whereon
I reside, also my negro boy named Aaron, my waggon my sorrel horse,
farming and blacksmith tools. I will to my sons Elias and James and to
my daughter Sutton each twenty dollars and to my granddaughter Elizabeth
Campbell fifty dollars. I will to my daughter Jane my negro boy
Stephen and that she have her maintenance from the plantation I willed
to Robert. The rest of my property to be equally divided between my
son Robert and my daughter Jane. I appoint my sons Thomas and Robert
as Executor. Dated 20 May 1841. Witt: John S. Moore, H. F. Adickes,
S. R. Moore, Signed James Campbell, seal.

James Campbell Senr. Estate of James Campbell, Senr. (no file given)
Abbeville, S. C. The estate was Admr. by James Campbell Junr. the
appraisers were Benjamin Michael, John Long, Robert Sample. Appraise-
ment dated 18 Aug. 1803. Date of sale not given some who bought;
Daniel Mitchell, Joel Edins, Wm. Stevens, Fielding Stevens, Stephen
Busby, Basil Hallum, Jas. Colhoun, Jas. Campbell, Micajah Stevens,
Alexander Stuart, David Steel,

Jane Campbell. Will of Jane Campbell, case #41, File #1759. York Co.,
S. C. I Jane Campbell being in sound mind, etc.etc. I allow to my
niece Jane Jenkins one hundred dollars if living, if not then to her
daughters. I allow to my niece Jane McCully (the) trunk and all that
is in it also I allow her the note I hold on her. I allow to Mary,
Rebecca and Jane McCully twenty five dollars each. I allow Emilia
Barnett twenty dollars. I allow Jane C. Craig my bureau, also twenty
five dollars to be paid to her father for her use only. I allow to
Martha E. Campbell, Elizabeth P. Parkson and Eliza A. Campbell twenty
five collars to be paid to their father for their use only. I allow
E. A. Campbell my wheels and one small table. I allow Sam Campbell to
have his note I hold on him, also my arm chair and large Bible. I
allow my friend Elizabeth Campbell thirty dollars. I allow to Wm.
Campbell my railroad stock also one bed and cloth belonging to it.
I allow Ann Barnett the bed I have left in with the clothes that belongs
to it. The remainder of my money to pay debts and be equally divided
between my friend Elizabeth Campbell and her children. I appoint my
friend A. P. Campbell and Myles Smith to execute this my will. Witt:
Robert Smith, John Smith, Myles Smith. Signed Jane X Campbell. Dated
6 Apr. 1854. Probated 15 March 1860.

John Campbell. Estate of John Campbell, Box 13 #548, York County, S.C.
Est. was Admr. 11 Feb. 1825 by Hugh Kerr, Joseph Wallace, Duncan
McCollum who are bound unto Benj. Chambers Ord. in the sum of $1,000.00
he lived on Allison Creek. On 5 Dec. 1836 Hugh Kerr, Susannah Campbell
settled the estate. no heirs given.

Thomas Campbell. Estate of Thomas Campbell, Box 13 #560. York County,
S. C. Est. Admr. by Robert Campbell, George Ross and Wm. Campbell who
are bound unto Benj. Chambers Ord. in the sum of $2,000.00. Dated
20 Oct. 1823.

John Campbell. Estate of John Campbell, Box 6 #160. York Co., S. C.
Est. Admr. by Charles L. Clawson, Wm. J. Clawson who are bound unto
J. M. Ross Ord. in the sum of $300.00. Left 2 or 3 brothers and sisters
who resides out of state. Paid James Campbell note $54.34. 1 June
1849.

John Campbell. Estate of John Campbell, Box 18 Pack 370. Probate
Judge Office, Abbeville, S. C. Henry Johnston, John Morrow and Patrick
Johnston are the Executors of the estate of John Campbell late of
said dist. decd. (no will or Admr. bond in file) the appraisement
warrent was dated 15 Apr. 1823. Appraisers are Alexander Hamilton,
Robert H. Lesly, William Lesly, William Yarbrough and William McAlister.
Negroes named in the inventory are man Abin, Lewis, Cloe and child,
Booker, boy Phil, woman Grace, boy Edmund, boy Ceser, boy Jack, girl
Cloe, man Esquire, girl Molly, boy Washington, woman Beck and child,
woman Sarah and child, woman Susan and child, girl Jane, girl Darcus
(on the back of one paper) Patrick Johnston and John Morrow surviving

Executors and Ishal Edwards and Thomas Simmons two of the persons who in right of their wives are residuary legatees and John Campbell who in his own right and as sole heir and distributee of his mother Arabella Martin, and as sole heir, distributee and Administrator of his father Thomas P. Martin, is entitled to the other third of the residue, etc.etc. This is dated 30 Oct. 1828.

James Campbell. Will of James Campbell, Bundle 92 Pack __. Probate Judge Office, Barnwell, S. C. I James Campbell make this my last will and test. etc.etc. I will and bequeath to my beloved wife Sarah Campbell all property after paying my lawful debts. And at the death of my wife, the estate to be divided between my children viz; Martha, Jane, Nancy, John Rowland, Elizabeth, George. Dated 6 March 1847. Witt: Calvin Dunn, Job Hair, Jr., Edwin Stansell. Signed James X. Campbell, Filed 17 March 1847.

Frances Campbell. Estate of Frances Campbell, Bundle 56 Pack 4. Probate Judge Office. Barnwell, S. C. Est. Admr. by Jabez G. Brown, Nathaniel Badger, John Rickenbaker, Charles H. Colding who are bound unto O. D. Allen, Ord. of Barnwell Dist. in the sum of $3,000.00. Citation published at swallow Savannah Church 13 Nov. 1831. Admr. bond dated 18 Nov. 1831.

William Campbell. Estate of William Campbell, Bundle 41 Pack 9 Probate Judge Office. Barnwell, S. C. Est. Admr. 6 Oct. 1823 by Mrs. Mary Fullerton, Nathaniel Badger and John Murphey who are bound unto O. D. Allen, Ord. in the sum of $6,000.00. Citation published at Kirkland Meeting house 7 Sept. 1823. O. D. Allen, Ord states that Mary Fullerton (who afterwards intermarried with Cornelius Taylor and who has since departed this life). This was dated 4 Mar. 1826. William Campbell decd. was father of Mary Fullerton.

William Campbell. Estate of William Campbell, Bundle 58 Pack 2. Probate Judge Office. Barnwell, S. C. Est. Admr. 30 March 1832 by Richard C. Roberts, Wm. McMillian, Richard R. Barker who are bound unto O. D. Allen, Ord. in the sum of $1,000.00. Citation published at Swallow Savannah Meeting House 25 March 1832. 11 Dec. 1832 paid Mildred Bryan her share of estate $513.16. Catherine Campbell, Cornelius Mays, Mary Owens, John Owens bought at sale.

Thomas Jefferson Campbell. Will of Thomas Jefferson Campbell, Box 52 #19 Probate Judge Office. Greenville, S. C. I Thomas Jefferson Campbell being in sound mind but afflicted in body etc.etc. I desire that my Executrix pay to my son T. T. Campbell twenty dollars, to my daughter Mary Elizabeth Edwards five dollars, to my daughter Jemima Ann Lucinda Edwards five dollars. All the rest of my estate of whatsoever kind, my horses, cows, hogs, tools, household furniture, etc.etc. let it consist of what I give to my wife during her natural life. At the death of my wife Elizabeth whatsoever I gave her to be my sons Andrew Jeffe Campbell for taking care of her during her widowhood. I appoint my wife Elizabeth Campbell as Executrix. Dated 6 Aug. 1888. Wit: J. F. Chastain, P. C. X. Carter. Signed T. J. Campbell, seal. Filed 18 Sept. 1888.

Thomas A. Campbell. Estate of Thomas A. Campbell, Box 36 #43 Probate Judge Office, Greenville, S. C. Thomas A. Campbell died 14 Aug. 1874. on 12 Nov. 1874 M. T. Campbell made suit for a letter of Admr. Jemima Campbell, Thomas J. Campbell, Missouri Turner and Andrew M. Campbell were ordered to appear at the court house on the 3 March 1785 to show cause why a final settlement of the estate should not be made. Andrew M. Campbell a minor. Heirs Jamima Campbell, Thomas J. Campbell, Missouri Turner, M. T. Campbell, Andrew M. Campbell, Rebecca Dunlap and Roubert G. Campbell. The latter two lives out of state.

Robert Campbell. Will of Robert Campbell, Will book 11, page 68-69. Probate Judge Office, Darlington Dist. I Robert Campbell being in sound mind and memory etc.etc. I will that my negroes and other personal estate be keep together on the plantation to support my wife and daughter until she is twenty one years old.. I give to my wife

Martha during her life time or widowhood all the plantation south of
the Middle swamp and the Darlington main road. Also six negroes viz;
Prince, Harry, Mariah, Martha, Ben, Lydia. Also farm tools household
furniture, etc.etc. I give to my daughter Francis T. C. all that
tract of land West of the Darlington road. Also I give to my daughter
Francis T. C. four negroes; Laura, Sam, Dorcas, Jane. If my daughter
Francis T. C. die without heirs her share is to go to Wm. Lockhart
children to share and share alike. The children of the first wife to
share with the children of the second wife. I give to James Campbell
Lockhart, Robert Owen Lockhart, William Lockhart Jr. all that tract of
land on the South side of Middle swamp, bound on North side by the main
Road. East by Batson Jordan, and Wm. Lockhart and William Anderson, I
give to the children of my daughter Elizabeth eight negroes, when they
become of age. I give to my granddaughter Elizabeth Lockhart one bed
and furniture. Dated 1 Nov. 1860. Witt: W. B. Pruitt, M. L. Gatlin,
J. G. Gatlin. Signed R. Campbell, seal. Will proved by Margaret L.
Galton on 25 Nov. 1861 before John O. Rupell, Ord. D.D.

CANN

Frances P. Cann. Frances P. Cann, Box 25 #298 Probate Judge Office,
Pickens Dist., S. C. Frances P. Cann was a daughter of James and Mary
Gaines of Pickens Dist. Her father will proved in 1841.

CANNON

Ransome Cannon. Estate of Ransome Cannon, Box 2 #20. Probate Judge
Office, Pickens Co., Est. Admr. 1 March 1830 by Elijah, Malinda A.
Cannon, Absalom Reece, Jeremiah Fields who are bound unto Jas. H.
Dendy, Ord. in the sum of $3,000.00. Expend; 7 March 1831. It is
therefore ordered that Mary Smith formerly widow Boyd shall receive
from the Admr. Elijah Cannon one third of $397.00 and that John H.
Boyd a minor under 14 years be paid the rest. Moses Smith was guardian
of said child. Malinda Ann Cannon was the widow. Jane Cannon was the
mother of decd. and was paid $33.00 on a proven account.

James Cannon. Estate of James Cannon, Box 33 #380. Probate Judge
Office, Pickens Dist., S. C. Est. Admr. 6 Aug. 1855 by John R. Cannon,
Thos. D. Morgan, J. W. L. Carey who are bound unto W. J. Parson Ord.
in the sum of $6,000.00. Owned 200 acres of land on Crooked Creek
waters of Little River adj. land of R. F. Morgan, John R. Cannon and
others. Heirs viz; widow Mary Cannon, James Morgan and wife Nancy,
Joseph Barton and wife Mourning, Thomas D. Morgan and wife Ruth, John
R. Cannon, Maliciah Perry and wife Polly, Jacob Cannon, R. F. Morgan
and wife Melisey.

Russell Cannon. Will of Russell Cannon, Box 35, #405. Probate Judge
Office, Anderson Dist., S. C. Whereas Russell Cannon of Pendleton Dist.
being poorly in health but of sound mind and memory, etc.etc. I give
to my wife Jean Cannon negroes Simon, Rose, Willie, Cate. Also her
choice of two horses, ten head cattle, hogs, likewise all my personal
property. I give to my daughter Harriet Duke negro Ann. All the other
property to be sold and equally divided amongst my children. I appoint
my wife Jean and my son Elijah Cannon to act and see the accomplish-
ment of this my last will. Dated 10 July 1824. Witt: James Hunter,
James E. Hart. Signed Russell X Cannon. Will probated 6 Sept. 1824.
Same day qualified Elijah Cannon as Executor. On 13 July 1855 Harriet
Duke and Ransom Duke made suit for letter of Admr. as there were no
Exors to said will. Russell Cannon owned 207 acres of land on Rices
Creek adj. John Araial, Jas. Mansell. 5 Nov. 1844 Elijah Cannon appli-
cant viz. Abraham Duke, in right of Josiah Marchbanks in right of
wife, Ann Cannon decd. Judy Kendricks, James Cannon and heirs of Wm.
Cannon defendant of the est. of Russell Cannon. Last five legatee are
out of the limits of the state.

James & Mary Cannon. Power of Attorney. Pack 218 #6. Clerk of Court Office, Pickens, S. C. We James and Mary Cannon of Walker County in the state of Alabama have constitute and appoint Zachary C. Pulliam of Pickens Dist., S. C. to be our true and lawful attorney for us and in our name and stead to ask, demand, sue, recover and receive all such money, debts, etc.etc. Especially all such sums of money owing payable or belonging to us from the estate real and personal of Russell Cannon decd. late of Pickens Dist., S. C. etc.etc. Dated 3 July 1858. Signed James Cannon, Mary Cannon. Witt: Delmeda Beachhamp and Zelabe Beach-hamp. The witnesses signature was attested before Thomas M. Gabbert, Judge of Probate. W. C.

Carter Cannon. Power of Attorney. Pack 218 #6. Clerk of Court Office Pickens, S. C. I Carter Cannon of the State of Texas County of Tarrant, and child and heir of Russell Cannon decd. and of Jane Cannon his widow decd. Having this day made constituted and appointed A. G. Fowler of Pickens Co., S. C. my lawful attorney and to receive, to obtain any monies, property, land or other effects, that I am or may be entitled to as heir of Russell Cannon and as heir of Ransom Cannon decd. and the heir of Jane Cannon decd. the widow of Russell Cannon, all of Pickens Co., S. C. etc.etc. Dated 27 Feb. 1857. No witt; signed C. Cannon, seal. State of Texas Tarrant County. Before me the undersigned authority, personally appeared C. Cannon to me well known, as the maker and signer of the within power of attorney,etc.etc. Same date as above. G. Nance C.C.C.T.C. Thos. M. Mathews Deputy.

Virgil M. Cannon. Etc. Pack 218 #6. Clerk of Court Office. Pickens, S. C. State of Mississippi, Kemper County. We Virgil M. Cannon, Harriet Cannon, Adaliza Cannon, Bailes E. Cannon, Darcus D. Dozier and wife Elizabeth Dozier and James Cannon of Kemper Co., Miss. have constituted and appointed Zachary C. Pulliam of Pickens Co., S. C. our true and lawful attorney for us and in our name and stead, may ask, demand, sue, receive recover all money, debts, dues and accounts whatsoever. From the estate both real and personal of Russell Cannon decd. As the legal representatives of William Cannon decd. of Kemper County, Miss. etc.etc. Dated 28 June 1858. Wit: Meredith Roberts, T. S. Campbell. Signed; V. M. Cannon, Harriet Cannon, Adaliza Cannon, Bailis E. Cannon, D. D. Dozier, Elizabeth C. Dozier, James Cannon. Seals.

Cale Cannon. Estate of Cale Cannon, Box 113 #1085. No county given. Cale Cannon died 27 Nov. 1879. On 24 Dec. 1879 Clinton Cannon, Thos. Duke, Jack Cannon, Geo. Cannon, Mary Cannon, Thos. Cannon objected to Toney Ferguson being the Admr. because he is not the nearest of kin. 9 Jan. 1880 Admr. was granted to J. J. Lewis C.C.P.

Starling Cannon. Assault. Pack 230 #1, Clerk of Court Office, Pickens S. C. On 23 May 1894 Starling Cannon did attempt to kill one George W. Cannon of Pickens Dist. George Cannon sworn, on May 23 I went to my dinner at Clinton Cannon in Pickens, S. C. Starling Cannon came in and said George Cannon I mean to kill you. He drew his knife and as I got up he struck me with his knife, Clint ran in between and told me to out, he ran out. I sat the dogs on him, before this he had picked up the ditching shovel and struck me with it on the arm and hurt me bad, threw rocks at me but did not hit, he went off then. I don't know what he was cursing me about. He had been to Georgia. I was in the cook room in the corner by the fireplace. I told his mother that she must keep Starling off my premises. Nancy Arthur sworn says, Starling came and knocked at the door, he spoke to me and Clint. George was sitting by the chimney asleep and I was talking to Starling. Starling is a nephew to Clint and George. I am a sister to George and Clint.

James Cannon. Estate of James Cannon, Book A, page 176. Probate Judge Office, Pickens, S. C. To W. J. Parson Ord. the under signed heirs at law of James Cannon decd. petition your court for an order to sell or divide the real estate lying on Crooked Creek waters of Little River adj. land of R. F. Morgan, John R. Cannon. Containing 200 hundred acres. Signed Mary Cannon the widow. James Morgan and wife Nancy, Joseph Barton and wife Mourning, Thomas D. Morgan and wife Ruth,

John R. Cannon, Jacob Cannon, Maliciah Perry and wife Polly, R. F.
Morgan and wife Melissy. Dated 6 Aug. 1855.

CAPEHART

Leonard Capehart. Will of Leonard Capehart, Pack 85 in Equity. Clerk
of Court Office. Pickens, S. C. I Leonard Capehart of Pickens Dist.
being in usual health and of sound mind and memory, etc.etc. I will and
and bequeath unto my wife Sarah all her wearing apparel, the bed and
furniture which she had when I married her. I will after my death all
my property of every description be sold at public or private slae. Pay
my just debts and the remainder, if any as follows viz; I will to my
beloved wife Sarah one third part, for her support during her natural
life, at her death to be given to my daughter Elizabeth Eveline Capehart.
I will the other two thirds to be equally divided between my sons.
Harvey one fifth part.. The lawful heirs of son John one fifth part.
To my son Samuel one fifth part. The children of my daughter Nancy who
married James Rogers and is dead, viz; Leonard, James, Diver, John,
and Nathan Rogers one fifth part. To my daughter-in-law Mary Ann Capehart (widow of my son B. W. F. Capehart) and her son Hamilton Brevard
the remaining fifth part. I appoint my friend Col. Jephtha Norton,
Capt. Levi N. Rogers and Miles M. Norton my Executors. Dated 3 July
1848. Witt: E. Alexander, W. S. Grisham, W. J. Nevill. Signed
Leonard X Capehart. seal. Probated 22 March 1866. By W. E. Holcombe,
O.P.D. In Equity. Elizabeth E. is still an infant about the age of 19
years who married Waddy T. Hester who is now dead, his son Henry who is
now dead and whose heirs names and number unknown and the place of
their residence is unknown to Sarah Capehart, the heirs of his son John
Capehart who died before his father, name and number and residence
unknown, except Hamilton A. H. Gibson a son of the said John Capehart
who had his name changed from Capehart to Gibson by order of the court,
Samuel Capehart of this state, the children of his daughter Nancy who
married James Rogers and is now dead to wit, Leonard Rogers and John
Rogers who resides in Pickens Dist. Nathan Rogers who died before his
grandfather and left no family, James Rogers who died after the testator
and left the following heirs in this state, Emily C. Rogers widow,
Sarah A. Rogers, Nathan Rogers who are infants under 21 years and upon
whose estate the said Leonard Rogers took out letter of administration.

Leonard Capehart. Land Warrants. Pack 114 Clerk of Court Office,
Pickens, S. C. To any surveyor you are authorized to lay out and
admeasure unto Leonard Capehart a tract of land not exceeding ten
thousand acres. etc. Leonard received 772 acres on Little River. Dated
2 Sept. 1844. On another paper it states that Leonard Capehart died 30
Aug. 1862.

John Capehart. Land Warrant. Pack 114, Clerk of Court Office, Pickens,
S. C. To any lawful surveyor you are hereby commanded to admeasure and
lay out unto John Capehart land, etc. He received 638 acres, no water
course given, dated 11 Feb. 1850.

Harvey Capehart. Assault, #6, Clerk of Court Office, Pickens, S. C.
On 7 Nov. 1842 Harvey Capehart appeared before me Nathan Boon M.P.D.
and made oath that on the 4 Nov. 1842 Jacob Capehart of Pickens Dist.
did at his own premises commit an assault and battery on him, by
drawing his knife and cutting him on the arm etc.(about five or six
gashes) also hit on the head with a stick. William W. and George W.
Gassaway were mentel witnesses in behalf of the state. On the 1st
Monday after the 4th Monday in Oct. 1843 Jacob Capehart was tried and
convicted of an assault and battery and was sentenced to pay a fine of
$10.00 and pay the costs of the prosecution amounting to $29.90.

CARPENTER

Monroe Carpenter. Estate of Monroe Carpenter, Box 54 #590. Probate Judge Office, Pickens, Dist. Est. Admr. 30 July 1860 by Andrew C. Hughes, Jacob A. Carpenter, Robert A. Thompson, L. Coatsworth Craig who are bound unto W. E. Holcombe, Ord. of Pickens Dist. in the sum of $1,000.00. A. C. Hughes states that the notes given at sale by M. A. Carpenter for $172.00 he had on hand and said he the said Carpenter has not been heard of since the war.

CARROLL

Daniel Carroll. Citizenship of Daniel Carroll. Clerk of Court Office, Chester Co., S. C. Daniel Carroll age 20 years, from the county of Tiperary in Ireland. That he arrived in New York City in the month of June 1836. That he stayed about one year in the state of Virginia and has been in South Carolina for the past three years. This petition was dated 2 Apr. 1841. He appeared before Hon. A. P. Butler, Judge. John Kennedy and Chelsea Robins appeared and certified that they are acquainted with the said Daniel Carroll. That they believe and are satisfied that he has been residing with in the state for four or more years, and that he is of good moral character, etc. Dated 11 Apr. 1844. He takes the oath before J. Rosborough, Clerk of Court. Dated 12 Apr. 1844.

CARADINE

Bird Caradine. Guardina, Box 7 #112, Probate Judge Office, Pickens Co., S. C. Bird Caradine was guardian of Elizabeth E. Hester a minor about 19 years and a daughter of Leonard Capehart decd. Bird was her uncle. (Leonard Capehart wife Sarah was a Caradine before marriage.)

Thomas Caradine. Will of Thomas Caradine, Box 1 #28 Clerk of Court Office, Anderson, S. C. In Equity. I Thomas Caradine of Pendleton Dist. being in sound mind and memory etc.etc. I give to my beloved wife Elizabeth one negro girl named Charlotte to her and for her use forever. I leave the whole of my estate, land, negroes, stock of all kinds and household furniture to my wife for life or widowhood. I give to my son Joberry one negro boy named Joe. I give to my daughter Avalina one negro girl named Nancy. I give to my daughter Patsey one negro girl named Arrena. I give to my son Thomas one negro boy named Billey. A negro named Peter I allow him privilege of choosing his own master or mistress among my children. My desire is that none of my black family be sold. I appoint my son William and my wife Elizabeth as Executor and Executrix. Dated 26 April 1820. Witt: Thos. Lamar, Hiram P. Caradine, Elizabeth Caradine, Jane X Wright. Signed Thomas Caradine (Will proved in the year 1820, per Equity papers in Pickens Dist. Pack #228 and that Elizabeth remained a widow till death which took place 20 March 1849. Therefore the estate of Thomas was not settled until after her death. Thomas Caradine was married twice, had five children by the first wife, name not given, and eleven by the second wife. He lived on Martin Creek waters of Keowee River, owning 1253 acres of land. Children by first wife viz; Andrew, died since father, left widow Sally. Jane Miller, a widow still living. Margaret Webster and husband John both still living. Catherine Hull and husband Danial Hull both still living. Nancy Reid decd. husband Hugh Reid still living. Children by second wife fiz; William G. in Mississippi; Bird, still living in Pickens Co.; Hiram, still living in Alabama; Mary Barrett and husband Arthur still living in Miss.; Elizabeth Thomson and husband Fleming still living in Ala.; James F. living in Pickens, S. C.; Sarah Capehart and husband Leonard still living in Pickens, S. C.; Thomas G. in Mississippi; Martha Young and husband James in S. C.; Petunia Avaline in S. C.; Joberry Caradine in S.C.. In a power of Attorney from State of Miss. Chickasaw County, William G. Caradine states that Andrew

Caradine married Sarah Tankersley who is also dead, and his children
are; Andrew, William, Nancy Tidwell, Pernicy Ingram and Elizabeth
Tidwell. Dated 6 July 1858. Another power of attorney from Jane
Miller of Chickasaw Co., Miss. appoint her brother William G. as her
attorney in fact. Dated 19 Oct. 1854. Hiram Caradine of Walker Co.,
Ala. appoint his brother William Caradine his attorney in fact. Dated
25 Oct. 1853. James F. Caradine of Neshoba County, Miss. appoint
William Holland of Pickens County, S.C. as his attorney in fact. Bird
Caradine of Chickasaw Co., Miss. appoint William G. Caradine of the same
county as his attorney in fact. Dated 12 Oct. 1854.

CASON

Elizabeth Cason. Estate of Elizabeth Cason, Box 3 #95. Probate Judge
Office, Anderson, S. C. Est. Admr. 18 Sept. 1812 by Daniel Chamblin
and James Simpson who are bound unto John Harris, Esq. Ord. of Pendleton
Dist. in the sum of $500.00. Citation was published at Mount Pizgah
Meeting house in the vicinity of the decd. on 13 Sept. 1812. Sale was
held on 10 Oct. 1812.

CASSELL

John Cassell. Will of John Cassell, Box 58 #634. Probate Judge Office.
Pickens Dist. I John Cassell being infirm in body but disposing mind
and memory, etc.etc. I give to my beloved wife Fanny Wilson Cassell
the following property. One negro girl about twenty years old, named
Jinny and Beck about eighteen years of age. All household furniture
with all stock, horses, sheep and hogs. I give to my daughter Rosey
Ann Jane one negro named Cesia about six years of age. I give to my
son Ephraim one negro boy named Isham about seventeen years of age, also
my rifle gun. I give to my daughter Louisey one negro girl named Agga
about three years of age. I give to my son Nathaniel Anderson one
negro boy named Dick about seven years of age, also my shot gun. I give
to my son Francis Marion one negro boy named Bob about one year of age.
I desire that my executors sell to the highest bidder all the balance
of my property and divide the proceeds among my first children viz;
William, Meley, John, Temperance, Nancy, Catharine and Sarah. I appoint
Baily Barton, James Alexander my executors. Dated 12 Jan. 1843. Witt:
W. L. Keith, Levi N. Robin, E. Martin. Signed John X Cassell. Filed
16 Aug. 1861.

John Cassell. Estate of John Cassell. Box 75 #803. Probate Judge
Office, Pickens, S. C. John owned about 1,000 acres of land on Davisses
Creek waters of Oolenoy River adj. land of Edward Chastain, Nathaniel
Lynch and others. Heirs; widow Fanny Cassell, Thos. Masters and wife
Nancy, Wm. Masters and wife Tempy, Lemuel A. Howard and wife Catharine,
Robert McJunkin and wife Rosa, Saml. E. Roper and wife Louisa, Ephraim
Cassell, Nathaniel Cassell, Marion Cassell, Hamilton Cassell, Zelia
A. Cassell, Mary Cassell, John Cassell, Ransom Henderson and wife.
The ones out of state are; John Cassell, Ransom Henderson, Simeon Young-
blood and wife Milly and heirs of Wm. Cassell decd.

CAUDLE

Richard Caudle. Estate of Richard Caudle, Box 20 Pack 423. Probate
Judge Office, Abbeville, S. C. We Elijah Baker and wife Barsheba
Baker, Ewal Hill and Lazeras Benten who are bound unto the Justices of
Abbeville County Court in the sum of one thousand pds. sterling. Dated
6 Jan. 1789. Elijah and Barsheba Caudle as the next of kin are to make
or have made a true inventory and list of appraisement of the goods
and chattels of Richard Caudle decd. Witt: W. Shaw. The inventory or
appraisers report not given, except one negro named Sylvia, value 50
pds. signed Gabriel Smithers, Jno. Wilson, Wm. Huggin.

CHAMBERS

Benjamin Chambers. Estate of Benjamin Chambers, Box 17 Pack 347.
Probate Judge Office. Abbeville, S. C. I Benjamin Chambers of Abbeville Dist. being sick and weak in body but of sound mind and memory
etc.etc. First I appoint my friend Thomas Ruffin of Hillsborough,
N.C. my sole Executor of this my last will and testament. It is my
desire that my faithful servent Dick be taken to N.C. and set free. If
this cannot be accomplished then I wish he be sold to some good man near
his family. I loan to my daughter Arabella Crawford a yellow girl about
fourteen years of age, named Harriet at the death of my daughter, then
I give her to my granddaughter Mary Crawford now an infant, hers forever. Having on hand a negro girl named Pricilla belonging to the firm
of Ruffin and Chambers, have her sold and money divided as other part
of the capital of the firm. It is my wish as soon as can be, all my
concern in the firm and my private affairs settled turn all over to my
daughter Arabella Crawford. Dated 28 Nov. 1826. Witt: A. B. Arnold,
George Miller, John H. Miller. Signed Benj. Chambers, seal. I Thomas
Ruffin of the town of Hillsborrogh in N. C. the person appointed in
the foregoing Testament of Benjamin Chambers. Do hereby renounce the
office of the said Executorship. Given under my hand and seal this
18 June 1827. Thomas Ruffin, Will proved by Doctor A. B. Arnold and
George A. Miller before Moses Taggart, Ord. of Abbeville Dist. and
published at Upper Long Cane Church. 24 June 1827 by Wm. H. Barr,
Dr. Alex. B. Arnold was made Admr. of the estate. Sale of personal
property was held 6 Aug. 1827 viz; one negro man Dick sold to Jno. C.
Martin. One negro woman Harriet sold to W. M. Crawford, some other
items. Two negroes belonging to the firm of Ruffin and Chambers, one
negro woman Mark and two children, one negro woman Priscilla and one
child. Wm. M. Crawford bought Mark and her two children. James Huston
bought Priscilla and her child. Estate final settlement 27 May 1830.

William Chambers. Estate of William Chambers, Box 106 Pack 2710. Probate Judge Office. Abbeville, S. C. We Stephen Chambers, John Hearst,
James Edwards, Pat Gibson Junr. of Abbeville Dist. are bound unto the
Judges of Abbeville County Court in the sum of five hundred pds.
sterling. Dated 27 March 1792. The obligation is that Stephen Chambers
will make a true and perfect inventory of all goods and chattels etc.etc.

James Chambers. Estate of James Chambers, Box 106 Pack 2710. Probate
Judge Office, Abbeville, S. C. We Staphen Chambers, John Hearse, Josiah
Chambers, Pat. Gibson are bound unto any Judge of Abbeville Dist. in
the sum of five hundred pds. etc.etc. dated 27 March 1792. The obligation is such that Stephen Chambers will make a true and perfect inventory of the goods and chattels of Jas. Chambers decd. (Both bonds
are in same pack with Jas. Wardlaw as Witt. No more papers in this
package.)

Stephen Chambers. Estate of Stephen Cahmbers, Box 21 Pack 465. Probate
Judge Office. Abbeville, S. C. The estate was Admr. 15 Apr. 1809
by John Sanders, John Brannon and Joseph Sanders all of Abbeville Dist.
and are bound unto Andrew Hamilton Ord. in the sum of five thousand
dollars. Joseph Chambers, John Branna, Robt. Henderson meet to appraise
the estate of Stephen Chambers, decd. Dated 4 May 1809.

Adam Chambers. Estate of Adam Chambers, #7 In Equity. Clerk of Court
Office, Laurens, S. C. To the Honr. Hugh Rutledge, William James and
Waddy Thompson Esqs. Your petition of Samuel Cahmbers of Newberry
Dist. sheweth that Adam Chambers decd. was seized and possessed with
tract of land in fee simple living and being on Hunting fork of Indian
Creek in Newberry Dist. containing one hundred acres or more. That
sometime in the year 1801 Adam Chambers died intestate, leaving a widow
Martha and ten children viz; James who is dead, never married; Ruth who
married Robert Dogan; Samuel; Jane; Margaret; Alexander the last three
named are minors above the age of fourteen; Polly; William; Rachel;
Maxfield infants under the age of fourteen, all of Newberry Dist.
The petitioner Samuel desires his share of said land etc. Martha is
appointed guardian of the children under fourteen and the minors over

fourteen choose their mother as their guardian. The petition is for a
sale of the land, giving the widow one third share and divide the
balance between the living children. The land was bounded by John
Hatton, Peter Brazelman, Samuel Chambers.

Philip Chambers. Land Warrant of Philip Chambers. #32 Pickens Co.,
S. C. By Wm. L. Keith, Clerk of the Court. To any lawful surveyor
you are hereby authorized to lay out unto Philip Chambers a tract of
land etc. This was executed 16 April 1850 for 453 acres by Tyre B.
Mauldin D.S.

CHAPMAN

Chapman, Minors. Box 3 #61. Probate Judge Office, Pickens, S. C.
6 April 1857 J. W. L. Cary, Robt. Craig, M. T. Michelle are bound to
W. J. Parson, Ord. in the sum of $134.45. J. W. L. Cary guardian of
Mary Ann M. Chapman, Jas. A. Chapman, Susan C. Chapman minors under 21
years. In 1870 Mary Ann had married a Jones, Jas. A. Chapman has since
died leaving no wife or child. John W. L. Cary has died leaving his
wife Martha M. Cary Exor. Saml. Chapman, Admr. of John Chapman
decd. Caroline M. Chapman their mother. Susan married John S. Camerly.
14 Mar. 1862 W. C. Jones recd. $5.00 for board and tuition.

Joshua Chapman. Estate of Joshua Chapman, Book 1 page 216. Probate
Judge Office, Pickens Dist. (Rel. Est.) 19 Feb. 1858. Owned 192 acres
on Shoal Creek adj. land of Carter Clayton, Saml. Chapman and others.
Heirs of J. Merck and wife Susannah, Thos. McKinney and wife Mary,
Joel Chapman, heirs of Giles Chapman decd., Jacob Chapman, Rachael
Chapman, Isaac A. Chapman, Margaret Chapman, Isreal Chapman, O or C J.
Wigington and wife Ruth, Saml. Chapman, David Garrett and wife Elizabeth.
Thos. McKinney, Joel Chapman, C. J. Wigington and Isreal Chapman
lives out of state.

John F. Chapman. Estate of John F. Chapman, Box 95 #998. Probate
Judge Office, Pickens, S. C. Est. Admr. 10 Aug. 1868 by Robt. A.
Thompson is bound to W. E. Holcombe Ord. in the sum of $100.00. 10
Aug. 1868 Recd. of Saml. Chapman Admr. of Joshua Chapman $14.42.

Enoch Chapman. Estate of Enoch Chapman, Box 104 #1089. Probate Judge
Office, Pickens, S.C. Est. Admr. 24 March 1873 by Cyrus Chapman, Jas.
E. Hagood, W. A. Hunnicut who are bound unto J. H. Philpot, Ord. in the
sum of $200.00. Cyrus Chapman son of decd.

George J. Chapman. Estate of George J. Chapman, Box 98 #1025. Probate
Judge Office. Pickens, S.C. Est. Admr. 14 May 1870 by Matilda Chapman,
Gideon Ellis, Joab Mauldin who are bound unto J. H. Philpot, Ord. in
the sum of $800.00.

Cyntha J. Chapman. Estate of Cyntha J. Chapman, Box 118 #7. Probate
Judge Office, Pickens, S. C. 10 April 1868. George J. Chapman,
J. C. C. Parson, Wm. S. Williams are bound unto W. E. Holcombe, Ord. in
the sum of $400.00. Geo. J. Chapman Gdn. for Cynthia Jane Chapman
a minor under 21 years. Sarah Chapman decd. was her grandmother.

Chapman Minors. Box 133 #9. Probate Judge Office, Pickens, S. C.
13 Jan. 1872, W. T. Bowen, W. G. Field, Reese Bowen are bound unto
J. H. Philpot, Ord. in the sum of $700.00. W. T. Bowen gdn. for Geo. E.
Chapman minor under 21 years. Gdn. of Saml. Davis Chapman, Wm. J. B.
Chapman sons of Saml. Chapman decd. 13 Jan. 1872 Elizabeth Singleton
the widow of Saml. Chapman decd. Harleston Chapman son of Saml.
Chapman decd.

Chapman Minors. Box 169 #11. Probate Judge Office, Pickens, S. C.
25 Nov. 1879 M. N. Wakelin, G. W. Russell, P. H. Boggs, are bound
unto Olin L. Durant, Ord. in the sum of $191.58. Matilda Wakelin gdn.
for Anna, Julius, Esther Chapman minors under 21 years. Mother of said
Chn...

Green E. Chapman. Estate of Green E. Chapman, Box 91 #958. Probate
Judge Office, Pickens, S. C. Est. Admr. 15 Oct. 1866 by Geo. J.
Chapman, Jas. C. C. Parson, Wm. J. Smith who are bound to W. E.
Holcombe, Ord. in the sum of $800.00. Left 9 heirs, Cynthia Hinton,
dtr.; Thos H. Chapman decd.; Catherine; Benjamin; Ida Chapman Chn. of
John W. Chapman decd; Anna; Julia; Essey Chapman chn. of Geo J. Chapman
decd.; Benj. P. Chapman; Martha Fennell; Rebecca Thomas; the chn. of
Ruth Jones of Alabama names unknown. Amelia Mauldin, Eliza Smith and
that the chn. of Wm. A. Chapman decd. (who was born out of wedlock) are
not legal heirs. Brothers and sisters Rutha Fennell married Harvey
Jones. Amelia Chapman married W. A. Mauldin. Eliza Chapman married
Thos. Smith. Cynthia married J. McHinton. W. A. Chapman chn. viz;
Nancy S. wife of John Gary, Martha E. wife of Patrick H. Boggs, Mary J.
Chapman widow Thos. D. Chapman. Julius Chapman a minor 20 years of
age, Rosaline Chapman a minor 18 years, W. A. Chapman was born about
6 mos. before marriage of his parents and who died before Green J.
Chapman his ward. John E. Chapman died before G. E. Chapman left 3
chn. Catherine about 20 years, Benjamin about 18 years, Ida about 16
years, Geo. J. Chapman died before G. E. Chapman left 3 chn., Anna
about 18 years, Julius about 14 years, Essey Chapman about 11 years,
Benj. P. Chapman now living in Texas. Amelia Mauldin in Georgia.
Dated 8 Apr. 1879. Nancy Chapman widow of John W. Chapman now 23 years.
Wm. B. Chapman will be 21 years. June 15, 1879, Ida Chapman 19 years.
Jan. 21, 1880.

John W. Chapman. Estate of John W. Chapman, Box 95 #999. Probate
Judge Office. Pickens, S. C. Est. Admr. 2 Jan. 1869 by Nancy Chapman,
J. C. Watkins, J. N. Boggs who are bound unto J. H. Philpot, Ord. in
the sum of $550.00.

Racheal Chapman. Will of Racheal Chapman, Box 126 #10. Probate Judge
Office, Pickens, S. C. I Racheal Chapman being of sound mind and
memory etc.etc. First pay all just debts and funeral expenses. I give
to my son J. Harvey Chapman all my money, notes and other amounts due
me from any and all sources. The money I loaned him and he put into
the land where he now lives, I give unto him the amount as he been at
considerable expense in the sickness of my late husband Dr. Jacob
Chapman in paying bills, also care for me in my old age. I desire
whatever personal property I may have at my death equally divide
between my children. I appoint my son J. Harvey Chapman Executor.
Dated 30 April 1895. Witt: C. L. Hollingsworth, R. B. Lumkin. J. T.
Youngblood, J. M. Stewart. Signed Racheal X Chapman. Probated 28 May
1896. Heirs were viz Eliza Mauldin, Milly A. Mann, Mary M. Hawkins,
Martha J. Merck, Jacob Chapman, J. Harvey Chapman, John F. Chapman,
the heirs of Saml. Chapman decd. viz; Luke, Saml. Boro Chapman.

Mary Jane Chapman. Estate of Mary Jane Chapman, Box 130 #7 Probate
Judge Office, Pickens, S. C. Est. Admr. 19 Mar. 1898 by Sarah M. King,
E. B. Webb, W. T. Grubbs who are bound unto J. B. Newberry, Ord. in
the sum of $200.00. She died 19 Feb. 1898. Sarah M. King a daughter
of Fair Play, S. C. Heirs viz; Sallie M. King, Mack, Bluford B. Odell,
John W., M. T. Chapman, W. B. Odell.

Julia Chapman. Estate of Julia Chapman, Box 132 #8. Probate Judge
Office, Pickens, S. C. Est. Admr. 6 Mar. 1899 by Pleasant Whitten,
B. J. Johnston, L. G. Phillips who are bound unto J. B. Newberry, Ord.
in the sum of $579.52. She died 22 Dec. 1898. John B. Chapman her
husband. In 1900 J. B. Chapman was of Cooper, Delta Co., Texas. Also
Roy Chapman was a minor under 14 years, 16 Feb. 1909 James A. Whitten,
Martha Whitten, Lola Whitten was bound unto J. B. Newberry, Ord. in the
sum of $200.00. James A. Whitten gdn. for Walter and Arthur Thos. Mize
minors. P. Whitten who died on or about 27 April 1908 was the former
gdn. of James A. Whitten his son. (A letter in the file from
Cedartown, Ga. Dated 19 Feb. 1907 to Miss Lola Whitten... From "I am
as ever your Aunt" signed Ida C. Terrell.)

James Chapman, Benjamin Chapman. Deed from James Chapman to Benjamin
Chapman. Pack 52 #4. Clerk of Court Office, Pendleton Dist. I James
Chapman for the sum of $600 do sell grant unto Benjamin Chapman 100 acres

of land on 18 mile Creek. First granted unto Bazl. Hallum and Robert McCann in 1785 and 1791. Dated __ 1825. Witt: Regneil Odell, Thomas Odell. Signed James Chapman, seal. On the 19 day Sept. 1825 Rebeckah X Chapman relinquish her rights and all claim of dower before James Osborn J.Q.

CHAPPELL

Rebecca Chappell. Will of Rebecca Chappell, Vol. 24 page 1099. Probate Judge Office. Charleston, S. C. I Rebecca Chappell of the parish of St. Stephens, Marion Co., S. C. being weak in body but in perfect mind and memory etc.etc. It is my will and desire that my property at my death be sold at public outcry and my just debts be paid first. The residue and remainder of my estate be equally divided between my daughters Amelia Munro and Jane Chappell share and share alike. I hereby appoint my son in law Barnabus Munro Executor. Dated 18 Aug. 1785. Witt: Philip Will, John Burckhard. Proved 1 Sept. 1792.

Jesse Chappell. Will of Jesse Chappell, Box 4 #131. Probate Judge Office, Anderson, S. C. I Jesse Chappell of Pendleton Dist. being weak in body but of sound mind and memory etc.etc. I will that all my just debts be paid. I give to my wife Martha Chappell all my estate both real and personal during her life time or widowhood and should she intermarry then my will is that she shall have a certain negro boy named Washington, her choice of a bed and furniture and her horse and saddle. The rest of my property be sold on twelve months credit and the proceeds divided between my heirs; viz; Sarah Thomas, John Chappell, Robert Chappell, Ann Morris (or Norris) Thomas Chappell, Humphris Chappell, Caleb Chappell and Maryan Chappell. Giving Humphris one hundred dollars mare than the rest of the legatees. My wife be made Executrix and John Chappell and Charles Webb Executors. Dated 6 Apr. 1810. Witt: F. Stribling, Charles Webb, Thos X Chappell. Signed Jesse Chappell, seal. Proved on oath of Charles Webb the 18 April 1810 before John Harris Ord. Estate settled 19 March 1813 nameing the same legatees as per the will. Those who bought at sale: John Chappell, Josiah McClure, Robert Chappell, John Timmons, Thomas Thomas, Alexander Calhoun, Thomas Chappell, Lewis Prichard, Stephen Strange, Joseph Gipson, Kincheon Sears, John McCollum, Humphrus Chappell, Mathew Clark.

Henry Chappell. Estate of Henry Chappell, no file number. Probate Judge Office. Edgefield, S. C. I Henry Chappell of Edgefield Dist. being weak in body yet by the nercy of God of sound memory, etc.etc. I give to my wife Mary Chappell one negro woman named Hannah, one negro man named Big Jacob, also one negro boy named Mody and Old Phillis to be her own wright, not to be removed from the plantation until all debts are paid, also the child of Hannah called Flora for use during her life time. I also give to my wife a tract of land lying inside of the old road running until it intersects with the Spring Branch, also the use of the spring. All on the left side of the road to John Towls line. All the property to be keep together until all debts are paid. Then divided between my beloved children viz; Martha, Caroline, Samuel M. and Elizabeth Frances Chappell my children are to be decently educated at the discretion of my Executors. I will that my Executor give Charly Chappell five hundred dollars on his making a little to my children of his claim in my brother William Chappell decd. I will unto Capt. Phill Hazle my saddle and stiff bitted bridle to be his property forever. I appoint John Culbreth, Ralph Scurry, John Chappell and Charles Chappell my Executors. Dated 6 Sept. 1820. Witt: Peter Moore, Edmund Payne, Jesse Culbreth. Signed Henry Chappell. Proved on oath of Jesse Culbreth 23 Oct. 1820. Same time qualified John Chappell as Executor. In the inventory on 28 Oct. 1820. The negroes were viz: man Jake, man Moses, woman Hanner and child, woman Fillis, man Cafe, man Tom, girl Clarresy, girl Mariah, boy Jacob, boy Jack, boy Fed, boy Jerry, girl Jane, woman Matilda and child, boy Peter. The estate last return made 26 April 1838, with no final settlement.

Samuel Chappell. Estate of Samuel Chappell, Box 54 #2275. Probate
Judge Office. Edgefield, S. C. There is no bond or will for the estate.
On the back of the second sheet is: Edgefield Co., S. C. To John Hill,
Esq. Ord. The humble petition of the undersign sheweth that Samuel
Chappell departed this life on the twenty third of June last leaving
a wife and one child. Your petitioner therefor prays you will cause
a citation to be issued in his name so as to be enable him to obtain
letter of administration on said estate. Dated 5 July 1847. The
inventory and appraisement was held 29 July 1847. By Willes Mars,
William Adams, James Adams. Returned to the Ord. Office by O. Towles,
Admr. 2 Aug. 1847. Negroes named in the inv. are Lue, Lewis, Andrew,
Lucinda and two children viz: Bill and Alfred, Jeff, Joe O., Amey and
child Emley, Jane and three children To, Harret and Rhody, Tilda. The
only names that could be heirs are... Paid 25 Sept. 1848 James Clark
in part of his wifes distributive share of Jesse and Ellen Graham
Estate $1274.27. 16 Nov. 1848 Paid James Clark in full of his wife
share of the estate of Jesse and Ellen Graham decd. $1304.27.

DALRYMPLE

Sarah Dalrymple. Estate of Sarah Dalrymple, Box 5 #168. Probate Judge
Office, Anderson, S. C. I Sarah Dalrymple being of sound mind and
memory etc.etc. I give to my trusty friend Herbert Hammond as trustee
for Rosannah Lewis and for their use and benefit of the said Rosannah
during her life time the plantation or tract of land on which Elisha
Lewis and Rosannah Lewis now resides, containing one hundred and sixty
acres together with all improvements. To have said premises without
molestation or hendrence during her natural life and then to descend
to the children of said Elisha and Rosannah Lewis in equal share.
Dated 26 Jan. 1837. Wit: Lewis Sherrill, James M. Lewis. Signed
Sarah X Dalrymple, seal. Probated 20 Feb. 1837.

DANIEL

Robert Daniel. Will of Robert Daniel, Box 3 #33. Probate Judge Office.
Spartanburg, S. C. I Robert Daniel give to my wife Mary Eliza Daniel
to her and her heirs forever all my property and estate of every kind
whatsoever except as herein excepted. I relinquish to my Mother and
brother Andrew I. Daniel all my rights title and interest in the mill
and machine we have in common. I give to my two nephews Robert and
Wilds V. Hunt to them and their heirs one hundred and thirty acres of
land on Beaver Dam Creek which I purchased from David McCorley. I
appoint Jas. J. Vernon, H. I. Dean, J. E. Henry and Andrew I. Daniel
Executors. Dated 4 March 1840. Witt: Jas Ed. Henry, Jas. J. Vernon,
H. I. Dean. Signed R. M. Daniel, seal. Recorded 23 March 1840.

Andrew J. Daniel. Box 51 #33. Probate Judge Office. Spartanburg,
S. C. Andrew J. Daniel died 8 Jan. 1878 and his wife Nancy died 6 Feb.
1895. Had daughter Lou C. Brewton, sons Edgar C. Daniel, Saml. J.
Daniel, Robert J. Daniel, Andrew C. Daniel. no other inf.

Frances Daniel. Book I, page 96. Probate Judge Office. Spartanburg,
S. C. Will dated 4 Oct. 1842. Recorded 24 April 1845. Executor son
Andrew J. Daniel. Witt: Hiram Mitchell, W. W. Harris, Jehu Weels.
Names son James Daniel. Gr.dtr. Frances dtr. of Lucy Snoddy, Grdtr.
Altimic dtr of Lucy Snoddy, grdtr. Lucy Rebeca dtr. of Lucy Snoddy,
Grson Richard son of Lucy Snoddy. Grdtr. Mary and Adaline Hunt, grsons
Robert and Wilds V. Hunt. Grdtr. Armillio and Emeline Smithwick. Son
Andrew J. Daniel, daughter Aseneta Hunt wife of Wm. Hunt.

John Daniels. Estate of John Daniels Box 8 #18. Probate Judge Office.
Spartanburg Dist. Est. Admr. 28 Jan. 1833 by Robt. M. Daniel, Ephraim
Lewis, Henry Turner who are bound unto Christopher Johnson, Ord. in the
sum of $1,000.00. Citation published at the Lower Buck Creek Meeting
House, 19 Sept. 1807.

Richard Daniel. Estate of Richard Daniel, Box 9 #5. Probate Judge
Office. Spartanburg, S. C. I give to my son Robert A. Daniel my
plantation of three hundred acres which land joins Anthony Foster Junr.
on Fare Forest Creek and the tract on which the late Reuben Daniel did
live, also I give to my son Robert two negroes named George and Alleck.
I give to my wife Frances all the remainder of my property, either real
or personal to have and hold or dispose of among our children as she
may think proper. I appoint my sons Robert A. and Andrew J. Daniels
Executors. Dated 29 Nov. 1832. Witt: R. A. Young, Alexander Thompson.
Signed Richard Daniel, seal. Expends; of J. M. Daniel. To boarding and
teaching sons Robt. and Andw. in Spartanburg $196.00. To boarding and
teaching Andw. in Columbia in 1829 $237.00. J. T. Carter an heir of
Richard Daniel recd. $762.08 in property Mar. 5, 1833. Paid J. W. Anon
and wife Sarah recd. property also.

Reuben Daniel. Estate of Reuben Daniel, Box 9 #2. Probate Judge Office.
Spartanburg Co., S. C. I Reuben Daniel of Spartanburg Dist. taking
into consideration the uncertainty of human life from the many accidents
to which it is daily exposed. etc.etc. I give unto my beloved wife
Elizabeth one negro girl named Drucey and also one third part of the
residue of my estate, real and personal. I give to my daughter Sophia
a negro named Milly and her five children, viz; James Hannahm, David,
Peter, and Kaye. With one gray horse, two beds, two cows and calves,
one walnut chest. To my daughter Jincy Wells, I have heretofore given
her one negro named Doll, one mare, two cows and calves, two beds, and
furniture and one bureau, all this to account on her share. I give to
my son Richard the five hundred acres of land, one iron gray horse, one
negro boy named Dave and two cows and calves, and one bed and furniture.
I have given to my son Jesse in the aggregate the sum of one thousand
three hundred and seventy dollars. To my daughter Elizabeth Underwood
I have given one negro boy named Jim, two beds and furniture, two
cows and calves, one horse and a bureau, one negro boy named Kit and two
hundred dollars. I have given to my daughter Nancy High one negro
named Kitty, two beds and furniture. I now give to my daughter Nancy
Wells one negro named Henry. The rest and residue of my estate after
deducting one third share for my dear wife Elizabeth to be divided
each to have an equal share, etc.etc. I appoint John Wells, Enoch
Jones Underwood and my son Richard Daniel executors. Dated 12 Aug.
1825. Witt: W. T. Nuckolls, Ja. Hunt, E. Bomar. Signed Reuben Daniel.
proved 23 Apr. 1827. Citation was published at Bethleham Church 15
Apr. 1827.

Elizabeth Daniel. Will of Elizabeth Daniel, Box 9 #4. Probate Judge
Office. Spartanburg Dist., S. C. I Elizabeth Daniel being in bad
health but of sound mind and memory, etc.etc. I give to my daughter
Patsey Daniel my gray horse. I give to my daughter Sally Liles and
Nancy High all my stock of hogs, cattle to be equally divided between
them. I give to my grand daughter Sarah E. High one hundred dollars.
I give to my daughter Sarah Liles five of the best sheep I may own. I
give to my son Jesse Daniels my waggon and harness. I give to my
daughter Sophia Smith one feather bed and furniture. The balance of my
estate to be divided agreeable to the will of my husband. I appoint
Jehu Wells as Executor. Dated 27 May 1828. Witt: Tho. Tinsley, Thos.
Tinsley, Junr. Signed Elizabeth X Daniel. Recorded 11 Jan. 1832.

DARNAL

James Darnal. Will of James Darnal, Case 16, file 664. Probate Judge
Office, York Co. I James Darnal of the Dist. of York being in allow
and declining state of health but of sound mind and disposing memory,
etc.etc. I give to my daughter Susan Sturgis one negro girl she now
has possession of, with the other property she has received. I give to
my son William my mare named Kiney this I allow as his full share. To
my daughter Hanah I give one negro boy named Joe and one bed and
covering. To my daughter Cinthy, I give one negro named Hariet. To
my daughter Elizabeth, I give one negro boy named Si and my negro woman
Ann. My stock, of every kind, furniture, plantation tools and whatever

else I may die with be sold and out of the money I allow my just debts
to be paid to my son Franklin. I allow one third of the price of the
land to be given to my son John. I allow the other two thirds to be
paid to my three youngest children. viz: Senthy, John and Elizabeth.
(This is all of the Darnal will in the files.)

DARRACOTT

Garland M. Darracott. Estate of Garland M. Darracott, Box 28 Pack 654
Probate Judge Office, Abbeville, S. C. I Garland Darracott of Wilkes
County, Ga. being of sound mind and disposing memory, etc.etc. First
I request that my just debts be paid. Secondly, I give to my wife
Maryann Darracott one bed, one pair sheets and coverled. Thirdly I
give to my two children, both real and personal property, land, money,
negroes (not named) stock, household furniture, to be taken by my
executors after my death and by them managed by them to the best interest
of my two children, namely Francis and Rebecca Darracott. When they
become of age to share and share alike. I do appoint Thomas Jones of
Elbert Co., Ga. and Herbert Darricott of South Carolina, James Wingfield
and Thomas Terrell of this County my Executors. Dated 1 Nov. 1821.
Witt: Thomas Terrell, Edwd. Ballard, Signed G. M. Darracott. Will
attested in Wilkes Co., Ga. Before Lewis T. Brown and William C.
Allison J.P.s by Thomas Terrell, Jas. Wingfield on the 16 June 1829.
Inventory made 4 Aug. 1829 by Joseph Calhoun, Jas. C. Mathews, William
Walker all of Abbeville Dist. Recd. of Herbert Darracott Executor of
Garland Darracott twenty one hundred and inety two dollars and 93 cents.
100 in full for my proportion of said estate. Dated 14 Feb. 1843.
Test. W. G. Darracott. Signed by F. M. Darracott.

DARROUGH

Peggy Darrough. Will of Peggy Darrough, Apt. 2 File 132. Probate Judge
Office. Greenville, S. C. I Peggy Darrough of Greenville Dist. being
in perfect mind and memory etc.etc. I give to my sister Esther Darrough
all my part of the land we now live on to be hers during her life
together with whatever money, stock, cattle, hogs and beds cloaths,
household furniture I may possess at my death. At the death of my
sister Esther, I allow Anna Logan Moore my during her natural life and
at her decease it shall go to her two oldest sons James Wilson Moore
and Hugh Dickson Moore to be theirs forever. I appoint Anthony Savage
and Robt. W. Peden sole Executors. Dated 24 July 1827. Witt: Anthony
Savage, James Ashmore, John Moon. Signed Peggy X Darrough seal.
Probated 3 Sept. 1832, same day Garland Moore applied for letter of
Admr. on the estate.

DAVIS

John F. H. Davis. Estate of John F. H. Davis in Equity. Clerk of Court
Office. Abbeville, S. C. Your orator Henry Riley sheweth that John
F. H. Davis died __ day __ 1864 intestate in the succeeding year a
letter of Admr. was granted to your orator. On 18 Nov. 1865 your orator
sold the personal property, which was small, on credit and the debts
are numerous and pressing. Your orator is informed and believes that
the intestate was a partner with John G. Booser in the merchandise
business in the town of Greenwood, this partnership has never been
settled and that a settlement is necessary to the final estate settlement. At the time of death the intestate he was possessed with a tract
of land of about one hundred and fifty acres in the said Dist. adj. land
of James Strawhorn and others, also a lot in the village of Greenwood
of about two acres. The heirs of John Davis are viz; Mary J. Davis
widow, chn. James, John, Nancy, William, Joseph, Jefferson and George
all are infants under sixteen years of age. Filed 16 Sept. 1867. The
lot in Greenwood was near the G. & C.R.R. depot.

<u>Vann Davis</u>. Estate of Vann Davis. Box 5 #179. Probate Judge Office.
Anderson, S. C. I Vann Davis Senr. being weak in body but of perfect
mind and memory. First as for my twelve children, they have all left
me and have received their full portion viz Hezekiah, Abijah decd.,
Nathan, Jessee, Eliphaz and Vann, my six sons, Martha, Rachel, Hannah,
Melia, Jean, Rhoda my daughters therefore I give to each and every one
of the above mentioned, or either of their heirs one dollar fifty
cents to be paid out of my estate, one year after my death. As touching
my grandson John Davis, I had given him something considerable in my
will of the eleventh of Dec. last, but he proved disobedient and has
left me. I give him nothing more than the sorrel mare and saddle which
property he now has in possession. I give to my beloved wife Lucy
Davis all the remainder of my estate, the land containing 130 acres to
have and hold hers for ever, one negro named Beck, all my stock, farm
tools, household furniture, in a word, all my real estate, goods and
chattles, for her use and disposal. I ordain my wife Lucy as Executrix.
Dated 14 Apr. 1810. Witt: James Hembree Senr. Mark X Pitts, Susannah
Pitts. Signed Vann X Davis, Senr., seal. Proved by Revd. James
Hembree before John Harris, Esq. Ord. Dated 23 Nov. 1810. On 22 Feb.
1812 Thomas Burresas recd. $1.50 in full due his wife. 26 Feb. 1812
David Tate recd. $1.50 in full due his wife. 26 Feb. 1812 Joseph Hall
recd $1.50 in full due his wife. 26 Feb. 1814 Amariah Felten recd.
$1.50 in full due his wife.

<u>Zerah Davis</u>. Estate of Zerah Davis. Apt. 2 File 119. Probate Judge
Office. Greenville, S. C. I Zerah Davis being weak in body but of
sound mind and memory. "1st. It is my will and desire that Jesse
Hammett and his wife Nancy shall take my three children Mary E. Davis,
Susan E. Davis and William H. Davis and raise them until they become
of age." It is my will that my negro woman Dolly go with my three
children to aid and assist in raising and attending to them. He gives
each girl one bedstead bed and furniture and one trunk. The boy
received one bedstead bed and furniture. I give to my brother H. H.
Davis my wearing apparel. All land and other property of every kind to
be sold and put on interest for the three children. There are eleven
lsaves to be sold and how the sale was to be held. Slaves named viz;
Mary, Frank, Reuben, Bob, Ben, Nott, Dice, Jane, Edmund, Eliza, Moses,
I appoint my brother H. H. Davis and William Thurston as Executors.
Dated 9 Feb. 1838. Witt: C. Stroud, Nathan Davis, William Wheeler.
Signed Zerah Davis, seal. Will proved 6 March 1838. The final
Settlement was made 29 Aug. 1842 with $1431.96 for distribution. Signed
Jno. Watson, Ord.

DAWSON

<u>Thomas Dawson</u>. Estate of Thomas Dawson. Box 28 Pack 653. Probate
Judge Office, Abbeville, S. C. Inventory made 16 July 1783 by Wm.
Hutchison, Thos Harbirt. Bill of sale made July 1783 named Elizabeth
Dawkins, John Dawkins, Wm. Dawkins, Thos. Dawkins Junr. and Robt.
Retherfort, Elizabeth Dawkins was the Admr. and there were 7 children.

<u>Joseph Dawson</u>. Citizenship, Clerk of Court Office, Pickens Co., S.C.
Court of General Sessions and Common Pleas. I W. L. Keith, Clerk,
present the Hon. Edward Frost one of the Judges in the said Court on
the __ day of Nov. 1851 came Joseph Dawson a native of Lynne Regis
Dorselshire England by occupation a farmer appeared in open Court and
made application to be made a citizen of the U.S. etc.etc. His age is
55 years.

<u>Samuel Baker Dawson</u>. Citizenship, Clerk of Court Office, Pickens Co.,
S. C. To the Hon. Edward Frost, one of the Judges in the Court of
Common Pleas and General Sessions. The petition of Samuel Baker Dawson
aged thirty two years, occupation Farmer, he was born in Maidstone
Kent England and arrived in the U.S. 2 Feb. 1846. And has lived in
Pickens Dist. since. We the subscribers citizens do hereby certify
that we have know the petitioner Samuel Baker Dawson for five or more
years, and that is is of good moral character. Signed Anderson Burnes,

Joseph ___, W. G. Caradine, O. H. P. Fant, E. E. Alexander, P. Alexander, Allen R. Elliott, James Lawrence, James Young, T. C. McGee. Oath taken 4 Nov. 1851.

DEATON

Burrel Deaton - William Deaton. Deed of Burrel to William Deaton, Book M Page 448. Anderson Co., S. C. Moore County, N.C. I Burrel Deaton of the county and state aforesaid in consideration of $50.00 paid by the said William Deaton of the aforesaid county do sell and release unto William Deaton a tract of land of 105 acres in Pendleton County, S. C. on the waters of Coneross. Dated 30 Nov. 1804. Test Elijah Deaton, Jeremi Williams. Signed Burrel X Deaton. Attested before Jas. Starritt, J.P. by Elijah Deaton on the 24 Oct. 1805. Recorded 4 Dec. 1815.

Elijah Deaton. Deed from Elijah Deaton to Joseph Grisham. Book E-1 page 120. Clerk of Court Office. Pickens, S. C. From Elijah Deaton of Pickens Dist. to Joseph Grisham of West Union in the same Dist. For the sum of $200.00 for 185 acres. Dated 13 Nov. 1843. Land resurveyed by John O. Grisham the 3 March 1842. Lying on both sides of Negro Fork of Coneross Creek. Adj. land of William D. Deaton, Kelly Sullivan, Richards, William Wadkins. Witt: Lewis Fendley, Wm. H. Leather, W. S. Sullivan. Signed Elijah Deaton. Elizabeth Deaton the wife of Elijah Deaton renounce, release her dower before Edw. Hughs, Mag. 6 Apr. 1844. Deed attested before John Adair, M. P. D. by W. S. Grisham, dated 8 Apr. 1844. Recorded 12 Apr. 1844.

Elijah Deaton Sr. - Jackson Deaton. Deed from Elijah Deaton Sr. to Jackson Deaton Book G page 542. Clerk of Court Office. Pickens, S. C. I Elijah Deaton Sr. for the sum of $80.00 from Jackson Deaton for a tract of land of 100 acres lying on the head waters of a branch of Chauga Creek. Beginning at the Burnt School house down the branch to the road from C. Pool to Holly Spring Church. Dated 29 Oct. 1852. Wit: Wm. R. Pitts, Elijah Deaton, Jr. Signed Elijah Deaton Sr., seal. Deed attested before John Adair, M.P.D. by Elijah Deaton, Jr. Recorded 30 Dec. 1854.

DEBRUHL

Stephen C. Debruhl. Estate of Stephen C. Debruhl. In Equity, Clerk of Court Office, Abbeville, S. C. To the Honr: Your oratrix Susan E. DeBruhl that in Nov. 1855 her late husband died possessed with a tract of land lying in Abbeville Dist. Containing about 460 acres bounded by land of John Jacob Martin, Mrs. Cleckley, Jonathan Johnson, Benjamin E. Huger. Leaving the widow and the following named children; Susan C., Stephen C., Marion F., Marshall P. Debruhl and his grandchild William F. D. Barkaloo, the son of a decd. daughter who married William Barkaloo. The Admr. of Stephen Debruhl estate was J. Foster Marshall. Filed 24 Nov. 1855 on this date Stephen C. was 20 years of age. Marion F. was 7 years of age. Marshall P. was 5 years of age. William F. D. Barkaloo was 3 years of age.

DEVENPORT

William Devenport. Will of William Devenport. Apt 9 File 628. Probate Judge Office. Greenville, S. C. I William Devenport being of a sound mind and disposing memory etc.etc. I give to my wife Phebe Devenport during her natural life the plantation I now live on, also as much household furniture, farm tools, stock of every kind as she thinks fit. I give to her negroes Gloster, Jude, Silver, Hannah and Joe during her natural life. After his death the negroes that was with him and those he loaned to his children be divided into five equal lots. One lot to son Isaac, one lot to Susannah McDavid, one lot to Sicily Vance, one lot to Temperance Chandler and one lot to son Francis Devenport. These negroes was given to his children during their natural life and no longer. He had a plat made by Col. Hampton Shumate of his plantation and divided it into five parts for the five children during their natural life and no longer. In another place in the will be bequeath to his children heirs, and their heirs forever. I ordain and constitute Isaac Devenport and Micijah Berry as Executors. Witt: B. F. Perry, William A. Cauble, Alexander McBee. Signed William Devenport, seal. Dated 15 Jan. 1840

A Codicil added, that he purchased a tract of land from John Kirby and his children was to divide said land equal among themselves. Witt: Lewis H. Shumate, Nimrod Donaldson, Willie Chandler. Another codicil added 14 July 1842. Here he names the negroes each child to get viz: son Isaac, I give Dick, Rhoda, Silva, Louisa, Austin and Rebecca. To Francis Devenport, I give viz; Peter, Sarah, Caroline, Harriet. To Temperance Chandler, I give viz; Lula, Sarah, Nancy, Joseph, Robert. To Susannah McDavid, I give viz; Gloster, Jude, Mariah, Isaac, Ann, Bathsheba, Martha. To Sicily Vance, I give viz; Ned, Linda, John Hannah, Amanda, Luch and Margaret. Witt: to this codicil were; Benjamin Arnold, Tully Bolling, David McCullough. Signed William Devenport, seal. Probated 7 Nov. 1842.

DILL

John Dill, Sr. Will of John Dill, Sr. Box 2 #135. Probate Judge Office. Greenville, S. C. I John Dill of Greenville Dist. being old and frail in body but of a perfect mind and memory etc.etc. I give to my grand-daughter Peggey Randolph one feather bed and furniture and one two years old heffer. I give to my well beloved wife Mary Ann Dill all the balance of my estate while a widow or at her death or marriage to be equally divided among all my children. I do ordain and appoint my son Reynolds Dill and George Mitchel Executors. Dated 7 March 1807. Wit: Reuben Barrett, David Barrett. Signed John X Dill Senr., seal. Probated 30 Sept. 1809 on oath of Reuben Barrett before David Goodlet, Esq. Ord. and qualified the Executors at the same time.

Mary Dill. Will of Mary Dill, Apt. 16 File 15. Probate Judge Office. Greenville, S. C. I Mary Dill being at this time of sound mind and disposing memory, I will unto my son Benjamin F. Dill and George W. Dill my negro man named Moses to them during their joint lives and at the death of either the property to be kept by the survivor in the district of Greenville. If either should removed from the district, the property is to be kept by the remaining one in the district. If both removed from the district or die then the said Moses is to be the property of the youngest grandchild as may remain in the district, absolutely and forever. After paying my just debts and funeral expenses whatever remains is to be divided amongst my children living in the district. I appoint my sons Benjamin F. and George W. Dill as Executor. Dated __ July 1849. Witt: William Mitchell, Elliott D. Mitchell, Thomas J. Mitchell, Signed Mary X Dill, seal.

Codicil added. I give to my sons Benjamin F. and George W. Dill the negro Mineta under the same conditions as I have disposed of negro Moses. Dated __ July 1849. Witt: same as will. Signed Mary X Dill. Will was proved on oath of William and Thomas J. Mitchell. Before Robt. McKay Ord. G.D. dated 9 Jan. 1857.

Jesse Dill. Estate of Jesse Dill, Box 2 #133. Probate Judge Office. Greenville, S. C. 12 Oct. 1830 Sarah Dill applied for letter of Admr. on the estate of Jesse Dill decd. Admr. bond missing. He left a widow and one minor child, name not given.

Stephen Dill. Estate of Stephen Dill. Box 2 #123. Probate Judge Office. Greenville, S. C. 17 April 1837 Mary Dill and Elijah Dill applied for letter of Admr. Advancements made by Stephen Dill in his life time (loans) viz; Elijah Dill $150.00, John Dill $150.00, William Dill $150.00, Stephen Dill $60.00, Charles S. Dill $50.00, Ezias Dill

$25.00, Thomas J. Dill $50.00, Frances Henson wife of Richard Henson $50.00, Polly Henson wife of Ebenezer Henson $50.00. Owned 160 acres on Fortenberrys Beaver Dam Creek of Middle Tyger River adj. land of Edward Stewart, Milton Ponder and others. Other heirs mentioned Elias Dill, George W. Dill, Jefferson Dill, Benjamin F. Dill, James Dill.

Elijah Dill. Will of Elijah Dill, No county or Reference given. I Elijah Dill being infirm and ill in body but of sound mind disposing memory etc.etc. I will to my loving wife Elizabeth during her widow-hood my plantation with all houses, household and kitchen furniture, also a negro girl named Faney, also Martha, Mary and a boy called Rube with all stock, cattle, hogs, and sheep and a plenty corn for one year. I give to my son Street T. Dill a tract of land that he now lives on, of about 75 acres bounded by Chandler and Shell and Alewine. I give to my son Lemuel C. Dill a tract of land (amount not given) bounded by Madison Dill line to Alewine line, also one negro girl called Faney. I give my daughter Francis Powell one negro girl named Martha, also one half of the piece of land that I have not willed. I give to my grand-daughter Lewezar Dill one negro girl called Mary, also one horse and saddle, one cow and calf and one bed. I give to my son Uriar Dill one hundred dollars and one negro boy named Rubin to be valid at my wife's death. I appoint my sons Madison and Street T. Dill my Executor. Dated 15 Oct. 1855. Witt: G. M. Stewart, I. Fowler, Robert Stewart. Signed: Elijah Dill.

Sarah Dill. Estate of Sarah Dill, Box 14 #182. Probate Judge Office, Greenville, S. C. 22 May 1854 a letter of Admr. were granted to Anny Henson, Sarah Dill the widow of Elijah Dill and mother of Anny Henson. Owned 150 acres on Blessingame Mill Creek on waters of Middle Tyger River. Heirs were as of 21 Aug. 1854, Rebecca Henson, Sidney Butler, Anny Henson, John Dill, Matthew Garret and wife, Sarah out of state, James Henson son of Rebecca Henson.

Solomon Dill. Estate of Solomon Dill. Box 14 #211. Probate Judge Office. Greenville, S. C. 8 Aug. 1854 John Dill mentioned as the Admr. Owned 149 acres on waters of Middle Tyger River adj. land of Milton Underwood, Elizabeth Jackson and others. Lydia Dill the widow of said decd. Heirs were George Dill, John Dill, Elizabeth Jackson.

Reynolds Dill. Estate of Reynolds Dill. Box 10 #9. Probate Judge Office. Greenville, S. C. 11 Nov. 1844 John Odom applied for letter of Admr. Left a widow and 8 children. 7 April 1845 Theron E. Dill a minor heir of said decd. under 14 years. wanted James Odom to be her guardian. Other names mentioned were Eveline Dill, Stephen Dill, Mary Dill.

Lemuel C. Dill. Will of Lemuel C. Dill, Box 25 #19. Probate Judge Office, Greenville, S. C. I Lemual C. Dill being in sound mind and memory etc.etc. I give to my wife Juda Dill during her life time and then divided between my two children. I give to my oldest daughter Frances Aner Dill the negro woman named Fane. I give to my wife all household and kitchen furniture, also all stock, hogs, cattle to her life time then to my youngest daughter Elizabeth Alice Dill. I appoint my wife Executrix. Dated 7 Apr. 1842. Witt: Jesse Stewart, A. C. Wilson, I. M. Langley. Signed L. C. Dill.

William Dill. Will of William Dill. No ref. Probate Judge Office. Greenville, S. C. I William Dill being of sound mind and memory, etc. He will every thing to his wife both real and personal, goods and chattels during her life or widowhood, wife not named. Then to be equally divided between my children share and share alike, they not named. I appoint T. I. Mitchell as Executor. Dated 28 Nov. 1489. Witt Shadrick Crain, John P. Moon, Lloyd Henson. Signed William X. Dill. No probate date given.

Elias and John M. Dill. Estate of Elias and John M. Dill. Box 8 #584. Probate Judge Office. Greenville, S. C. 5 Oct. 1840 the petition of Elias Dill and John A. Dill minor children of Polly Dill sheweth that they have a small amount of money willed to them by

George Mitchell decd. say about $48.00 and they crave that their
father William Dill may be appointed their guardian.

Elias Dill. Will of Elias Dill. No Ref. Spartanburg County, S. C.
I Elias Dill of Spartanburg County being of sound mind and memory, etc.
First pay just debts and funeral expenses. I give to my daughter
Susanah O'Shields all the land I own East side of James Creek adj. land
of the estate of O'Shields also all the land I own West side of the
Greenville and Rutherford road adj. land of A. Dill and Young O'Shields
I give to my daughter Frances A Cooksey all the land I own South East
of Greenville and Rutherford road. Jameson Creek being the dividing
line including my dwelling house adj. land of T. J.Earle, M. L. Williams
and others. I give to my daughter Susanah all my personal property to
make her equal with Frances. I have given my son A. Dill his portion
of my estate in land, I made him a deed for three hundred dollars, but
he never paid me for the land and I desire him to have no more of my
estate. I appoint E. H. O'Shields my Executor. Dated 4 Aug. 1881.
Witt: W. L. Williams, Jas. J. Clarke, Bill Ellis. Signed Elias Dill,
seal. No record of when proved.

Joseph Dill. Will of Joseph Dill, Book 1740-1747, page 274. Probate
Judge Office. Charleston, S. C. I Joseph Dill of James Island Berkley
County, S. C. a Master Mariner intending to take a trip to England,
being in perfect health and sound mind, etc.etc. I will demise and
bequeath to my well beloved wife Eliza. Dill my negro girl Grace and
her issue for ever, also she be permitted to live on my plantation in
the dwelling house during her natural life by paying one peper corn
yearly is same is demanded. I will to my son Joseph Dill all my land
in Burmuda, reserving to my self the power to cut the timber, I do
hereby impower John Dorril Esq. to make sale of the same. I will to
my son John Dill all my land on James Island. The remainder to be
dept for the daughters namely Elizabeth Mary and Ann Dill. Dated 19
May 1731. Witt: Samuel Rivers, Joseph Atwell, Nicholas Smith. Signed
Joseph Dill, seal. Will probated 2 Jan. 1745. Eliza Dill was Executrix

John Dill. Will of John Dill, Vol. 22 Probate Judge Office, Charleston,
S. C. I John Dill of James Island, St. Andrew Parish, being sick and
weak in body but of sound disposing mind and memory, etc.etc. I give
to my wife Sarah Dill my negro named Marian and her children: Dick,
Mary Amey, Toney. Also to my wife the use of the plantation on Stono
River, also the plantation on Dill's Bluff and the one on Dickson's
Island for her use during her widowhood and at her death the Dill's
Bluff place to go to nephew John Dill. With son-in-law Thomas Taylor
to get the place on Dickson's Island. One half of the place on Stono
River be sold and money divided between Jane Eliz Taylor and Thomas
Taylor to share and share alike. Nephew John Dill to have negroes:
Abraham, Berry, Tom, Grace, Joe, Young, Nat. Wife to have use of negroes
during her life. My old negro named Sarah shall be maintained and fed
and not be turned off or in any wise ill treated during her life. I
appoint my wife as Executrix and brother Joseph Dill with friends John
Witter, William Croskey as Executors. Dated 25 Oct. 1780. Witt:
Robert Smith, Thomas Rivers, Junr., Jonah Rivers. Signed John Dill.
Will proved 23 Dec. 1788. On Jan. 27, 1789. Sarah Dill was qualified
as Executrix.

Joseph Dill Senr. Will of Joseph Dill Senr. of Charleston, S. C.
Vol. 26 Probate Judge Office. I Joseph Dill being of sound mind and
memory etc.etc. I give to my beloved wife Susanna Dill during her
natural life and no longer the use of lotts, dwelling house, with
household furniture of her choice. I give to my son Joseph Dill during
his natural life the free use of all the land on James Island known as
Dill's Bluff, which I bought of my son John, also son Joseph to get
land in St. Paul's parish in Colleton County near the Congareas called
"The Ridge." I give to my daughter Elizabeth Dill my negro girl
named Lydia. I do hereby give to my grand children forty pds. sterling:
Susanna Mason Skrine, Margaret Skrine, Tacitus Gaillard Skrine, Eliza
Skrine and Elinor Skrine. Make Susanna Dill Executrix and son Joseph
Dill, and William Royall Executors. Dated 26 Dec. 1794. Proved 22
March 1796. Same time qualified Susanna Dill and Joseph Dill as Execr.

Sarah Dill. Will of Sarah Dill, Vol. 29, Probate Judge Office,
Charleston, S. C. I Sarah Dill of St. Andrew Parish being of sound
mind and memory. I give to my daughter Jane Elizabeth Dill my negro man
named Paul, and woman named Marian and their children Marchm, Mary,
Amey, Frank, Will, Dick and Moses. I give all the rest and residue of
my real and personal estate, also that part I may be entitled from my
son Thomas Taylor decd. and that I derived from my late husband John
Dill's to my grandchildren viz; John Dill Rivers, Mary Stiles Rivers,
Joseph Mason Dill and Sarah Dill and any children as my daughter Jane
Eliza. may have born in lawful wedlock. Make Elizabeth Dill, Execu-
trix. Dated 18 Feb. 1800. Witt: William Hayward, Jacob Ford,
William Lowndes. Signed Sarah Dill, seal. Proved 21 Dec. 1803 and
Jane Elizabeth Dill Executrix.

Hugh Dobbin. Will of Hugh Dobbin, Book 1771-1774. Probate Judge
Office, Charleston, S.C. I Hugh Dobbin of Edistoe Island, S. C. Being
sick and weak in body but of sound mind and perfect memory, etc. My
will is and I do leave my wench Affee and all her children hereafter
named their freedom. Rose, Isaac, Pegg, Jacob and Sam to act as they
please as free people. I leave the residue of my estate real and
personal to be sold at public out cry to the high bidder and the money
after paying all lawful debts the remainder to be equally divided
between the above named children. Rose, Isaac, Pegg, Jacob and Sam.
I appoint Mr. Joseph Seabrook and Mr. Isaac Rippon, my Executors.
Dated 20 Feb. 1772. Witt: John Adams, Daniel Evans, Joseph Parmenter.
Signed: Hugh Dobbin, seal. Proved 6 Mar. 1772.

James Dobbins. Estate of James Dobbins. Ref. not given. Probate
Judge Office. Anderson, S. C. I James Dobbins of Pendleton Dist. being
in disposed in body but of perfect mind and memory, etc. I will to my
beloved wife Elizabeth Dobbins the land where on I now live with all
other real and personal estate I may possess. During her natural life
or widowhood. At her death or marriage. I will this plantation to my
son James Dobbins Jr. With other items as household and kitchen
furniture, horses, cattle, hogs, waggons and geers. The balance of my
land lying and joining Wm. Hennery, and John Dobbins with all other
property put at public sale, with notes and bills collected to be put
in seven equal shares. I will one full share to my son Robert B.
Dobbins. I will one full share to my son John Dobbins, Also one full
share to my daughter Mary Morris. Also one full share to my daughter
Elizabeth Hillhouse. Also one full share to my daughter Sarah Calaham.
Also one full share to my daughter Jean Liddle. Also one full share to
my son James Dobbins Jr. I appoint my son James Dobbins, Jr. and my
wife Elizabeth as Exectr. Dated 11 March ___. Witt: John Bryce,
Abraham Barron, Willia Hillhouse. Signed James Dobbins, seal.
Proved by William Hillhouse before John Bryce, J.P. the 26 July 1817.
A power of attorney from Sarah Calaham of dekalb County, Alabama.
Dated 20 Oct. 1838 appointed Hugh Caraham her attorney. He was from
the same county and state, must be her husband. A power of attorney
from Robert B. Dobbins of Fulton County, Illinois. Appoint Rev. William
Carlile of Anderson, S. C. his attorney. Dated 22 Oct. 1838. A power
of attorney from Elizabeth Hillhouse appoint James Gainer her attorney
in fact. She was from Giles County, Tenn. in the town of Pulaske.
Dated 19 Sept. 1840.

Carrie A. Dobbins. Estate of Carrie A. Dobbins, Box 119 #3. Probate
Judge Office. Pickens, S. C. I Carrie A. Dobbins being of sound
mind and memory, etc.etc. I give to my three daughters Mattie E.,
Lettie Mand, Jessie C. Dobbins my entire estate, both real and personal
to be equally divided between them. It is my desire that my executor
shall take what ever means necessary to properly educate and care for
my children during their minority. I do nominate and appoint my
brother James F. Lay to be the Executor. Witt: William H. Hester,
F. V. Clayton, W. V. Clayton. Signed Carrie A. Dobbins, seal. Dated
13 July 1891. Filed 7 Dec. 1891.

Jesse C. Dobbins. Estate of Jesse C. Dobbins, Box 100 #1060. Probate
Judge Office. Pickens, S. C. Est. Admr. 4 Nov. 1886 by Carrie A.
Dobbins, Jas. F. Lay, J. E. Boggs who are bound unto J. H. Newton Ord.

in the sum of $800.00. He died 3 Aug. 1886. Carrie A. Dobbins his wife.

Carrie A. Dobbins. Estate of Carrie A. Dobbins, Box 126 #12. Probate Judge Office. Pickens, S. C. Est. Admr. 25 June 1896 by H. J. Martin, Savilla Lay, F. V. Clayton who are bound unto J. B. Newberry, Ord. in the sum of $6,000.00. Heirs. Mattie Dobbins, Lettie Dobbins, Jessie Dobbins. 5 Apr. 1900 recd. of the est. of J. F. Lay $1461.60.

Dobbins, Minors. Box 141 #9 Probate Judge Office, Pickens, S. C. Oct. 7, 1902 N. T. Martin states that Miss Jessie Dobbins a minor was boarding with him in Greenville, S. C. 8 Oct. 1901 W. P. Jacobs, Pres. of Thornwell Orphange at Clinton, S. C. recd. $36.00 for Mattit and Lettie Dobbins, minors from 8 July to Oct. 8, 1901. In 1904 Lettie was in Charlotte, N.C.

DODSON

George Dodson. Will of George Dodson, Box 74 #788. Probate Judge Office. Pickens, S. C. I George Dodson being of sound mind and memory, being on the eve of returning to the army, and it may be never to return and desiring to provide for my family as best as I can. Pay my just debts as soon as possible. Having five head of cattle, 8 hogs, 13 head of sheep and household and kitchen furniture and 100 bushels of corn, in short all my property of every kind so ever to my wife and children to have for their use. Sell my mule and other items not needed to support my family. I appoint my friend Levi N. Robin to be my Executor. Dated 24 Oct. 1862. Witt: Samuel Youngblood, R. E. Steel, M. J. Robin. Signed George W. Dodson, seal. Proven 7 Dec. 1863. The widow Druann Dodson, Mary Dodson, Nelly Dodson bought at the sale.

DONALD

Alexander Donald. Estate of Alexander Donald. Box 106 #1775. Probate Judge Office, Abbeville, S. C. I Alexander Donald of Abbeville Dist. revoking all others appoint this my last will and testament. I give to my three grandsons West Donald, James Donald Junr., Andrew Donald that tract of land of 150 acres in Chester Co., S. C. which my son had in possession when he deceased after their mother decease or marry, and to my grandson George Donald I give the note of hand I have of his in my possession. I give to my son John Donald one tract of land lying on Sandy River in Chester Co. of 172 acres, and one negro woman named Jenne and one negro man named Essick and the tract of land in Richmond County of 120 acres, only that part of said land that Jeremiah Jaggers has paid for and one mare, one still, and my part of the cotton mascheen. I lend to my daughter Mary Gray and Andrew Gray her husband for their life a negro man called Josky and one woman called Anneky and her increase and one negro woman called Linda and one feather bed and furniture. I lend to my daughter Nancy Gray and her husband Robert Gray, one negro called Peter and one negro man called Little Frank and one negro woman called Sary with her increase, and one feather bed and furniture. I give to my son Hezekia Donald one tract of land where he now lives containing 150 acres and one negro man called Charles and one negro woman called Susa and all her children and my smiths tools. I give to my son Archibald Douglass one negro man called Isack and one half of that tract of land lying on the waters of Beaver Dam Creek in Fairfield County conveyed to me by Frd. Hopkins. I give to my great grandson Donald Douglass the other part of my land lying in Fairfield Co. on Beaver Dam Creek and one negro boy called Harry and one feather bed and furniture. I lend to my daughter Mary Gray and Andrew Gray her husband one negro called Ann. Also the estate of my son James Donald decd. to have their equal share of my property. I give to my son Hezekia a negro called Absolem. I appoint John Donald and Andrew Gray my Executors. Dated 5 July 1803. Wit: William Norris, Deborah Norise, James Edmiston. Signed Alexander Donald, seal. Recorded 2 March 1806.

John Donald. Estate of John Donald. Box 26 Pack 603. Probate Judge
Office. Abbeville, S. C. We John A. Donald, Joel Lipford and Dewi
Lipford are bound unto Moses Taggart, Esq. Ord. In the sum of six
thousand dollars. Bond dated 17 June 1831. The latter of Admr. was
granted to John A. Daonald as next of kin dated 3 June 1831. With the
citation read aloud in the public congregation at Asbery Chappel 12
June 1831. The inventory was taken 6 Dec. 1831. The negroes named:
Mary, man Voluntina, man Essick, man George, girl Esther, girl Soos,
girl Tildy, boy Jerr. No heirs give.

West Donald. Estate of West Donald. Box 26 Pack 597. Probate Judge
Office. Abbeville, S. C. John A. Donald made suit to me to grant him
a letter of Adme. of the estate of West Donald decd. he as the next of
kin. Dated 8 Dec. 1834. Citation was published at Asbury Chapel 14
Dec. 1834... by William Lyon. The inventory was held 7 Jan. 1835 by
Charles Sproull, Thos. Lyon, Dewey E. Lipford. With the sale held 10
Jan. 1835... (three full pages of sale). Margaret Donald bought most
of the household items.

John A. Donald. Estate of John A. Donald. Box 30 Pack 664. Probate
Judge Office. Abbeville, S. C. We A. R. Ramey, J. A. Ramey and John
W. Ramey are bound unto David Lesly Ord. in the sum of one thousand
dollars. Dated 20 Dec. 1844. In his petition for the letter of Admr.
Asberry R. Ramey states that John A. Donald died intestate leaving a
widow and two infant chn. as his only heirs. The petition was dated 6
Dec. 1844. A sale of the personal estate was held 8 Jan. 1845. No
heirs given, there is a Mrs. Donald who bought at the sale. There was
one negro for sale, not named.

Alexander Donald. Estate of Alexander Donald. Box 124 Pack 3643
Probate Judge Office, Abbeville, S. C. Petition for the letter of
Admr. of the estate of Alex. Donald decd. was from Bartholomew Jordan.
Dated 16 Nov. 1850. Dond was issued to Bartholomew Jordan, Jonathan
Jordan, A. L. Gray are bound unto F. W. Selleck Esq. Ord. in the sum of
$1200.00. Bond dated 2 Dec. 1850. Most of the household and kitchen
furniture was bought by Martha Donald.

                              DOUGLASS

William A. Douglass. Estate of William A. Douglass, Box 106 Pack 2777.
Probate Judge Office. Abbeville, S. C. I William A. Douglass of
Abbeville Dist. being very weak and low but in perfect senses. First
I give to my wife one half of my estate after paying my just debts. The
other half to be kept in the hands of my Executors to take care of my
mother during her life time, at her death to be equal amongst all
Robert Meriwethers children, that he may have by my sister Barbara.
I appoint my friend John Meriwether and James Gouedy my executors.
Dated 13 Jan. 1807. Witt: Zachary Meriwether Junr., Larkin Whitton,
Esther McGehee. Signed Wm. A. Douglass, seal. Recorded Jan. 29, 1807.
Warrant of appraisement by Andrew Hamilton Ord. to Col. Jno. Logan,
Nichs. Meriwether, Benjamin Hatter, Jos. Meriwether and Jos. Foster.
All or any three of you to view and appraise and make a true inventory
as directed by John Meriwether Admr.

                              DRENAN

David Drennan. Estate of David Drennan, Box 8 #177. Probate Judge
Office, Anderson, S. C. I David Drennan being weak in body but of sound
mind and perfect memory. I give to my wife Mary Weems Drennan the
whole of my estate both real and personal, during her widowhood in
order to assist her in maintaining my children. When my two sons
becomes the age of twenty one the land is to be divided between them.
Sons are James Wilson Drennan and Billy Gilliland Drennan and the
remainder to be divided between my wife and the whole of my children.
I appoint James Anderson as Executor and Mary Weems Drennan as

Executrix. Dated 9 Apr. 1809. Wit: Nathan Lusk, Arthur Meadow, Abner A. Steel. Signed David Drennan, seal. Proven on oath of Nathan Lusk, Abner Steel, Arthur McAdow..before John Harris, Ord. Dated 8 July 1809. Mary Drennan qualified as Executrix 27 July 1809... The appraisement and inventory was made by Alexr. White, Oliver Woods, Patrick White, Andw. Miller, no date.

<u>Samuel Drennan, Sr.</u> Estate of Samuel Drenna, Sr. Box 5 #177. Probate Judge Office, Anderson, S. C. Est. Admr. 27 Oct. 1818 by Thomas Drennan, William Drennan and Benjamin Dickson who are bound unto John Harris, Ord. in the sum of $1,000.00. The citation was published 17 Oct. 1818 at the house of John Anderson. The estate was Admr. again 16 Feb. 1820 by Thomas Drennan, Miles Glasgow, and James Norrell, with the same bond. Miss Mariah Drennan is in school no other heir named. One paper mentioned four children but not named.

<u>Thomas Drennan.</u> Estate of Thomas Drenna. Box 5 #184. Probate Judge Office, Anderson, S. C. Est. Admr. 15 Feb. 1836 by Alexander Moorehead and Elijah Webb. The inventory was held 18 Feb. 1836. Sale held 5 March 1836. No heirs named.

DUFF

<u>Mary Duff.</u> Will of Mary Duff. Probate Judge Office. Pickens, S. C. I Mary Duff being weak in body but of sound mind and memory, etc.etc. I give to my daughter Naomi L. Duff one negro boy named Eli and one girl named Sarah. I give to my granddaughter Mary Telford one feather bed and furniture. I give to my daughter Naomi L. Duff the remainder of the household and kitchen furniture. I direct and require my Executors to sell the remainder of the property, except the plantation where I now live at public sale and out of proceeds pay all just debts and funeral charges. After the sale I give to my daughter Merab Telford the sum of two hundred dollars. I give to my son two hundred dollars. I give to my other children viz: Margaret B. Hallum, Mary P. Barton, Adaline L. Lewis and William R. Duff the sum of one hundred dollars each. Out of the sale money I give to my granddaughter Malinda D. Cox the sum of ten dollars. The tract of land whereon I now live being the joint property of the heirs of my late husband James Duff is left to their disposal as they shall see cause. I appoint Barnet Algood, Esq. and Allen Fuller my Executors. Dated 30 Aug. 1841. Wit: James Parsons, Jas. Taylor, Allen Fuller. Signed Mary X. Duff. Proven 25 Oct. 1841.

DUNN

<u>Nehemiah Dunn.</u> Land Warrent. #115. Clerk of Court. Pickens Co., S. C. By W. L. Keith Clerk of Court. To any lawful surveyor you are hereby authorized to lay out and admeasure unto Mehemiah Dunn a tract of land, etc. And make a true plat and return to my office within two months. from the date hereof. Dated 18 Dec. 1849. Executed for 465 acres signed Tyre B. Mauldin D.S. certified 2 Jan. 1850.

DURHAM

<u>Charles Durham.</u> Estate of Charles Durham. Box 5 #56. Probate Judge Office. Pickens, S. C. I Charles Durham being of sound mind and memory, etc.etc. I give to my beloved wife Mary Durham one bed and furniture, on chest, two chairs, one set plates and one duch oven. I give to Polley Durham one bed, one cotten wheel and cards, one duch oven, one heffer two years old, one set of knives and forkes. I give to my son Jeremiah Durham one tract of land of one hundred acres joining land of Daniel Durham, James Langston. I also will to my son Joseph Durham, Benjamin Durham, Charles Durham Junr. all that tract of land whereon I

now live to be equally divided between them three, allowing my wife to live on the land during her life. Also the rest of my children Lucy Morton, Elizabeth Morton, Patsey Gillstrap, Deliah Gillstrap, Nancy Cantral and Rhoda Hendricks. The last named daughters I have given them their property. The rest of my property to go to my wife Mary and daughter Polly and I will my large Bible and the hymn book to my wife Marey Durham. I appoint my brother Daniel Durham Gidian Ellis, Barnett H. Allgood as Executors. Dated 4 Jan. 1834. Witt: Thomas Moore, Readin Freeman, James Langston. Signed Charles X Durham, seal. Will proved by James Langston before James H. Dendy Ord. Dated 13 Jan. 1834. Bond made the same day for Daniel Durham Admr. The inventory made 18 Jan. 1834. (Mr. Durham may have been a preacher in his books, 3 preacher's manuels, one pocket bible and one sketch on sermons, three books portrait of St. Paul Grace and Truth, two vol. of Westleys, Bensons Sermons, one medical book...).

Daniel Durham. Estate of Daniel Durham. Box 100 #1041. Probate Judge Office. Pickens, S. C. I Daniel Durham being of sound mind but of feeble in body. I give to my wife Gizeal Durham during her life all my real and personal property, she may sell some personal property if she needs. At her death all property to be sold and money divided between my heirs. Wit: Reddin Freeman, George Miller and Martha Looper. Dated 28 June 1868. Signed Daniel X. Durham. Proven 28 Feb. 1871. Est. Admr. 26 May 1871 by Gizeal Durham who was bound unto Irvin H. Philpot, Ord. in the sum of $500.00. 21 Mar. 1888. Mrs. Betsey Durham widow of Stephen Durham decd. a son of Daniel Durham decd. appeared before J. H. Alexander a notary public of Tarrant Co., Texas. Betsey Durham and her sons, W. D. Durham, J. W. Durham, Joseph Durham appointed J. H. Newton of Pickens Co., S. C. as their attorney. Left 16 heirs. 10 Mar. 1875 pd. Carter Durham, Elizabeth Stewart, Eliza Griffin, Gizeal Durham each $18.75. pd. the 9 heirs of Wm. Durham in full. Sale held 10 Dec. 1872 byers. Robt. Stewart, Elisar Durham, Carter Durham, and Daniel Durham, etc.

Gazille Durham. Estate of Gazille Durham Box 103 #1081. Probate Judge Office. Pickens, Co., S. C. Est. Admr. 27 Oct. 1872 by Carter Durham, John W. Major, John C. ___, who are bound unto J. H. Philpot, Ord. in the sum of $200.00. 25 June 1873 to amt. recd. from Pension Office at Washington due Gazille Durham $135.07 pd. Thos. Durham taxes $8.25. Eliza Durham, Gazille Durham, Jane Alexander, Elizabeth Stewart, Carter Durham recd. a share. There were 16 shares in all but only these given.

Mary Durham. Estate of Mary Durham, Box 2 #36 In Equity, Clerk of Court Office. Pickens, Co., S. C. I Mary Durham knowing the certainty of death and being in sound mind and memory etc.etc. Pay my just debts, I will and bequeath to my brother Jeremiah Durham all my cattle, all bedding clothes, all household and cooking vessels, all money that is due me. My wearing apparel I desire that my niece Sarah H. Durham have my new bonnet and my niece Rhoda Ann to have my large new wollen shawl and the rest of my apparel to be divided between my brothers and sisters children. I appoint my brother Jeremiah Durham my Executor. Dated 17 March 1857. Wit: Daniel X Durham, Wm. Hunter, Sarah Cantrel. Signed Mary X Durham. (In 1846 Mary Durham by her next friend John Bowen that she is the dtr. of Elijah Barnet. she must be the widow of Charles Durham, who made will 4 Jan. 1843.)

Wm. O. Durham. Estate of Wm. O. Durham Box 64 #687 and Box 107 #1021. Probate Judge Office. Pickens Co., S. C. Est. Admr. first 3 Oct. 1862. By Madison F. Mitchell, John W. L. Cary, Daniel Hughes who are bound unto W. E. Holcombe, Ord. in the sum of $400.00. Owned 50 acres on Mile Creek waters of Keowee River, adj. land of W. S. Woolbright, Saml. Maverick and others. Heirs: A. Lucinda Durham the widow who died soon after he and left no issue. Berry Durham his father. The following brothers and sisters of whole blood, John Durham, Isaac Durham, Mary Ann who married Chas. Durham who resides in Anderson, S.C. Rebecca who married Wm. Smith, Narcissa Kelly the widow of ___ Kelly, Ellen Durham a minor and David James the father of Lucinda Durham the widow.

W. Riley Durham. Estate of W. Riley Durham, Box 90 #955. Probate
Judge Office. Pickens, S. C. Est. Admr. 17 Sept. 1866 by Robt. A.
Thompson who are bound to W. E. Holcombe, Ord. in the sum of $250.00.
1 Sept. 1866 Elizabeth Durham the widow made suit for letter of admr.

Berry Durham. Will of Berry Durham. Box 106 #1113. Probate Judge
Office. Pickens, S. C. I Berry Durham of Pickens Dist. a soldier of
the army of the Confederate States being in good bodily health and of
sound mind and disposing memory, etc.etc. I give to my wife Nancy
Durham all my household and kitchen furniture, all live stock, all
plantation tools, crop or crops for hers during her natural life. His
land adj. James McKee, Thomas Roe, John Dodson and Marevick. At my
wife marriage or death all my estate both real and personal shall be
equally divided between my sons and daughters; Ailmisa Narcissa Jane
Durham, Mary Ann Durham, Rebecca Caroline Durham, Sarah Ellender Durham,
John Alliston and Isaac Anderson Durham. I appoint Mr. Thomas Roe my
friend and neighbor my Executor. Dated 5 Dec. 1863. Wit; J. M.
Field (John), J. P. Lesley, W.W. Lathem. Signed Berry X Durham.
Filed 2 Nov. 1874.

Gazile Durham. Will of Gazile Durham. Box 127 #1. Probate Judge
Office. Pickens, S. C. I Gazille Durham being of sound mind and
memory etc.etc. I give to my son Allen Durham all my personal property
of every kind and nature, also all my interest in any land that I may
hold or have at my death. I appoint my son Allen Durham my executor.
Dated 17 Aug. 1889. Wit: J. B. Newberry, W. A. Lesley, Jr., Mary
Freeman Gillespie. Signed Gazille X Durham. He died Dec. 1896. Filed
Jan. 5, 1897.

Daniel Durham. Estate of Daniel Durham. Box 107 #1018. Probate
Judge Office. Pickens, S. C. A deed from Andrew Durham et al to Eliza R.
and Gazille Durham. State of Alabama county of Ettawah. We Andrew J.
Durham, James Thompson and wife Sarah Thompson, Milly Crump, the heirs
of Joel Durham decd. to wit: Sarah, Nelly, S. B., Litaha M. Durham,
Sarah E. Durham, Lena Crump, J. W. Durham, Elizar Durham, Jane Cornelius
and Eveline Durham are desirous of conveying our interest in the real
estate of Daniel Durham decd. late of Pickens, S. C. to Eliza R. Durham
and Gazille Durham of the same state and county. For the natural love
and affection which we have for Eliza R. and Gazille Durham and for the
many valuable services rendered by them to the said Daniel Durham
during his life and the sum of five dollars to us in hand paid by
Eliza and Gazille Durham for a tract of land which Daniel Durham lived
at the time of death, lying on Town Creek waters of 12 mile River, adj.
land of E. H. Griffin, Readin Freeman, John B. Clardy, and others,
containing 90 acres. Dated 22 Aug. 1870. Wit: J. D. Thomas, A. J.
Durham. There are thirteen signatures to the deed.

Daniel Durham. Power of Attorney to the Estate of Daniel Durham. State
of Alabama, Jackson Co. We Perry Durham, Ervin Durham and Albert P.
Durham, and Judson N. Owens of the State of Alabama legal heirs of
Daniel Durham decd. late of Pickens Co., S. C. have appointed C. E.
Robinson of Pickens Co., S.C. our true attorney etc.etc. Dated 31 Oct.
1887 at Scottsboro, Ala. We B. C. Durham, M. A. Durham, W. M. Durham,
J. A. Morton, W. P. Morton and W. P. Garrett gdn. of Etta Foster,
J. F. Foster, Willie Foster, Lawson Foster, Sallie Foster, Chn. of
M. A. Morton widow of L. E. Foster decd. Heirs of Daniel Durham decd.
Appoint Chas. E. Robinson of Pickens Co., S.C. their attorney. Dated
5 Oct. 1888 at Athens, Henderson Co., Texas. On 25 Oct. 1888 David
C. Durham, Mary A. Durham, A. P. Durham, states that they were children
of W. K. Durham a son of Daniel Durham decd. and that A. P. Durham died
in 1871 at 17 years. On 25 Sept. 1880 Sarah Ann Stewart, Jas.
Alexander, Nancy A. Martin, Louiza Jane Rice, Mary E. Forester of
Pickens Dist. heirs of Jane Alexander decd. signed away their right
to Eliza Robison Griffin, Gizeal Durham of the estate of Daniel Durham
decd. of Pickens Dist. On 2 Sept. 1881 Malinda Durham, John Durham,
Lenard Durham, Sarah Durham, Carter Durham, Fanny Durham, Mary Durham
of Lincoln Co., Tenn. appoint Wm. Durham their attorney to receive the
money due them from the estate of Daniel Durham decd.

Carter Durham. Estate of Carter Durham Box 138 #4. Probate Judge
Office. Pickens, S. C. Est. Admr. 20 June 1901 by Thos. Durham,
J. A. Durham, J. A. Hubbicut, D. Adams who are bound unto J. B. Newberry, Ord. in the sum of $600.00. Paid 4 March 1904 Daniel Durham,
Thos. Durham, Jackson Durham, Wm. Durham, Carter Durham, Augustus
Durham, Malinda Alexander 7 minors, Nancy Ann Durham recd. a share.
18 May 1907 Daily Jones recd. share. 2Aug. 1904 Alice George recd.
share. 2 Sept. 1909 Backsie Swaney recd. share. Arther Alexander recd.
share.

Charles Durham. Affidavit of Charles Durham. Pack 225 #1. Clerk of
Court Office. Pickens S. C. Personally appeared before me Charles
Durham who upon being duly sworn that he is the father of Julius Durham
against whom a bill of indictment has been found for the killing of
Richard M. Hughes. His son was only 17 years of age and in the condition of intoxication. That he sent his son Lorenzo to Walhalla to see
Mr. Reid and Mr. Keith the counsels he desired. That he has another
son Harrison who left the state a short time before the occurence and
that he has written him to return. Dated 25 Nov. 1872.

William R. Durham. Affidavit of William R. Durham. Pack 268 #8.
Clerk of Court Office. Pickens, S. C. On 15 Jan. 1858 William R.
Durham made oath that Nathan H. Newton did on Monday the 25 Jan. 1858
in Pickens Dist. Assault him by raising a rock and threatening to
strick and burst him head open.

Emaly Durham. Warrant of Emaly Durham. Pack 214 #5. Clerk of Court
Office. Pickens, S. C. On Nov. 3, 1856 Emaly Durham took out a warrant
for Robert Davis for assault and battery that he did on 29 Oct. last
commit an assault on her at her house in Pickens Dist.

Nancy Ellen Durham. Warrant of Nancy Ellen Durham. Pack 220 #10.
Clerk of Court Office. Pickens Dist., S. C. On 28 June 1859 Nancy
Ellen Durham took out a peace warrant for Jane Elizabeth Durham, Berry
Durham, Clary Durham, Jesse Durham.

Durham Family. Book A, Page 222. Probate Judge Office. Pickens, S.C.
On 21 June 1858 Carter Durham and wife Hannah, William Durham and his
wife Malinda were heirs of Thomas Alexander decd. of Pickens Dist.

Durham Family. Book B, Page 99. Probate Judge Office. Pickens Dist.
On 7 May 1866 F. M. Durham and wife Sarah C. were heirs of Samuel
Albertson Senr. decd. and his widow Cynthia Albertson of Pickens Dist.

Durham Family. On 30 Aug. 1843 Benjamin Durham was appointed a constable of Pickens Dist. Clerk of Court Office. Pack 634 #156.

DYASS

Moses Dyass. Will of Moses Dyass of the Parish of Saint Pauls in the
Colony of Ga. (Richmond Co.) Book Page 1. I Moses Dyass being weak in
body but of perfect mind and memory. I give to my son Moses Dyass
the plantation whereon I now live and nine negroes viz; Will, Bob, Dick,
Bristo, Tom, Sam and Hagar, Betty, Mary and two parts of my stock. I
give to my son in law Thomas Grubbs and his wife Ann two negroes
Phillis and Flora, and one third of meat cattle. I give to my son
John Dyass a plantation lying on the Euchee Creek in the Dist. of
Augusta, I will to my well beloved wife Ann Dyass the use and benefit
of the plantation during her life time and after her deceased the above
mentioned bequeath to be enjoyed. Make wife Ann executrix. Date 20
Apr. 1767. Wit: John Gordon, Peter Farris, Sarah C. X Foster.
Signed Moses Dyass, seal. Will proved by John Gordon and Peter Farris
before William Jackson Esq. the 16 Aug. 1777.

EAKINS

Joseph Eakins, Sr. Box 115 Pack 3403. Probate Judge Office. Abbeville,
S. C. I Joseph Eakins being at this time in the enjoyment of my mental
faculties and ordinary health. I will and devise to my beloved wife
Sarah, one half of the plantation whereon I now reside also the following negroes viz: Osborn, Ben, and Letty and her child Frances, and
their increase, also one third of the animals, all money and notes found
to be put on interest for her use and benefit. But be it understood
that at my wife's death the ngroes, stock, money and notes to be
equally divided amongst my sons and daughters, viz: Thos., William,
Samuel and Benjamin, Elizabeth, Sally, Mary and the children of my son
Joseph decd. "I will and bequeath and devise the remaining half of
said plantation to my son Benjamin and also at the death of his mother,
I will bequeath and devise the portion of land above devised to her
during her natural life to my son Benjamin, to him and his heirs forever and I enjoin it on Benjamin as my request and hope that he will be
careful and attentive to his mothers comfort and welfare, during the
short time that she may sojurn with him, and the reflection of so
doing will amply recompense for such care and attention bestowed on
his aged parent." I will the following negroes to my son Benjamin
viz: Jacob, William, Eliza and her child, also one third of the
animals. I will to my daughter Sarah the following negroes viz:
Aleck, Tom, Hulda, Lucy and the remaining one third of the animals.
"In consideration of the peculiar situation of my beloved daughter
Sarah, I hereby appoint my sons Thomas and Benjamin as her guardians
to manage her interest, and watch over her welfare." I appoint my sons
Thomas, Benjamin and son in law George Nickle as Executors. Dated 15
May 1845. Wit: Henry B. Nickle, Henry W. Sharp, William C. Nickle.
Signed: Joseph Eakin. Will proved on oath of Henry Nickle before
D. Lesly O.A.D. on the 11 May 1847. Executors qualified same date.
Power of Attorney from Samuel Akins of Rankin County, Miss. to William
Eakin of Kemper County, Miss. to be his attorney to ask, deman, and
receive his share from the Joseph Eakin estate. Another power of
attorney from Elizabeth Stewart of Kemper County, Miss. appoint William
Eakin also of Kemper Co., Miss. as her attorney to ask, demand, and
receive her share of the estate of Joseph Eakin of Pickens Co., S.C.
The estate was appraised 22 May 1847 by David Keller, L. I. White, W.B.
Bowie, Wm. Morrison. Sale held 15 Dec. 1847.

EARLE

Samuel Earle. Will of Samuel Earle. Box 4 #37. Probate Judge Office.
Pickens Co., S. C. Taking into consideration the uncertainty of life
and having a large family I thought proper to divide my property.. In
addition to the land, stock and other property I have given to my son
Baylis John Earle, I now give him a negro man named Joe and a negro
woman called Sidney and their three oldest children, and all the property
claimed in his life time by his brother Andrew Pickens Earle whose
grave in Ashville, Alabama I enjoin it to him to have enclosed in a
strong stone wall. In addition to the money heretofor advanced to my
son Morgan Priestly Earle to set him up in business, I now give him
all my land and lots in Andersonville, including the one I bought
from McFarland. I give to my son Elias Theron Earle all that on
North Fork Saluda River whereon Reuben McKenzie now lives composed of
part of different tracts amounting to 812 acres, and the family of
negroes on it viz: Harry and his wife Phebe and their six children and
their future increase, all stock and farm tools, To my son Samuel
Maxey Earle and Edward Hampton Earle I give as joint tenants the
whole of my land in the fork of Saluda where on James Harrison Earle
composed of different tracts amounting in whole of 1500 acres or more
including a small piece Jas. in this life time bought of one Keith
also 300 acres in Pickens Dist. opposite where James lived. Purchased
by me from John Wheeler and John Hanks, whereon Edward Hooper now
lives. The negroes hired by Mr. Terry are returned with all stock,
grain and farm tools shall be equal divided by Baylis John Earle, Mr.

Abalom Blythe, Mr. Robert S. C. Foster, Mr. David Terry, Mr. Benj.
Hagood or any three of them. I request Baylis John Earle himself to
superintend the property for the children until they can take charge
of it themselves, or they arrive at the age of twenty one years of age.
I give to my daughter Damaris Meriam Earle two tracts of land on Conorose
one purchased from Abner Crosby the other from Wm. Deal the two agreeable to a survey made by Mr. Kilpatrick for 400 acres, also a tract on
the Col'N Fork got of my father but granted to Peter Gray. Also a
tract on Miers Mill Creek where Eli Vanefort lives containing seven
hundred seven six acres. I give to my daughters Sarah Marie Earle and
Harriet Earle the whole of the tract of land I now live on, to be
divided between them by Beaverdam Creek, from my line crosses it near
James Wrights to the mouth of Middle Fork to Ward line. Maria to have
the Jacksons place next to Toogooloo and Harrett all on the side next
to Seneca including fifty acres purchased from Henry Mires. Also the
tract purchased of Samuel Misser adj. Old Abner Honea. To my granddaughter Harriet, daughter of John Maxwell, I give a negro woman
Betty and her son Marlow now in possession of John Maxwell and my granddaughter Harriet, daughter of Robert Maxwell, I give a negro man Mark
now in possession of John Maxwell. To the children of John Lumpkin
Gill of Alabama I give a tract of land on Long Nose conveyed them some
time ago. Also three lots in Andersonville the papers to be found in
my papers. I have two thousand acres of land on and near Benson's
Turn Pike at Douthet's Gap. I give to Elias Samuel and Edward as joint
tenants to be divided when they think how and proper. I appoint Wm.
Choice, Esq. of Greenville, Jesse P. Lewis of Pendleton Village, John
Maxwell, Baylis J. Earle, Elias T. Earle as soon as he is of age.
Dated 15 Nov. 1831. Wit: Philip Smith, William Smith, Silas Smith.
Signed Samuel Earle, seal. Proven 10 Mar. 1834.

Baylis John Earle. Baylis John Earle from James Hogood. Pack 223 #11.
Clerk of Court Office. Pickens, S. C. Baylis John Earle of Greenville
Dist. bought from James Hagood of Pendleton Dist. for the sum of
$1500.00 all that tract of land lying in Pendleton on the South fork
of Saluda River whereon the said James Hagood has heretofore lived and
now lives. Containing 256 acres, bounded on East and North by land of
John Hagood and Samuel Earle, on South by land of James Hagood, on
West by land of George W. Earle decd. Dated 1 April 1826. Wit:
J. H. Earle, Asaph Hill. Signed James Hagood, seal.

Baylis J. Earle. Deed from Baylis J. Earle to Aaron Roper. Pack 178
#4. Clerk of Court Office, Pickens, S.C. Baylis John Earle of Green-
ville Dist. to Aaron Roper of Pickens Dist. for the sum of $1250.00
all that tract of land on the South side of South Fork of Saluda
River whereon James Hagood formerly lived. Amount of land not given.
Bounded on the East and S.E. by land of Roper and Earle, on the North
by land of Jas. Robinson and West by land of William L. Keith. Dated
3 March 1836. Wit: Joseph Dunn, Tilmon Roper. Signed B. J. Earle.
Deed attested before Joseph B. Reid J.Q. by Tilmon Roper on the 9 March
1836.

George Earle. Estate of George Earle. Box 140 #3 Probate Judge
Office. Pickens, S.C. I George W. Earle realizing the uncertainty
of this life, do make this my last will and testament. Pay all just
debts and funeral expenses. Having fully provided for my beloved wife
by deed I will and direct that she be excluded from receiving any
portion. I will and direct that my executor divided and distribute
among my children equally, share and share alike all my real and
personal property. If any of my children die without issue its share
shall be divided amongst the ones alive, or those who had children.
I appoint C. E. Robinson, J. E. Boggs my Executors. Dated 8 Oct. 1890.
Wit: J. J. Lewis, J. M. Stewart, J. K. Kirksey. Signed G. W. Earle,
seal. Filed 26 Jan. 1903. paid 22 Jan. 1906. Essie Earle gdn. for
Cecil Earle, Eve Earle, Lucius L. Earle, Edwin Earle each red. $48.21.

George W. Earle. On 15 Aug. 1883 George W. Earle did sell to William
M. Ferguson without licenses a certain intoxicating liquor called
Giner Tonic of which spiritous liquors formed an ingredient. Ref. Pack
402. Clerk of Court.

EASLEY

Robert Easley. Will of Robert Easley. Roll Bo. 196. Probate Judge
Office. Anderson, S.C. I Robert Easley of Pendleton Dist. being in my
perfect sense and memory, on the thirty first day of March 1806. First
pay my just debts. I give to my daughter Elizabeth Blassingame the
wife of John Blassingame one negro man named Great Ned. I give to my
granddaughter Mary Blassingame daughter of Elizabeth Blassingame one
negro girl or woman near her age to be purchased of my stock and lands.
I leave Ben, Floro, Jo, Abram, Sam, Rose, Alcy, Morning and James. to
be equally divided between my sons Samuel Easley, John Easley and my
daughter Nancy Blassingame wife of Thomas Blassingame. I give to my
son John Easley two negro men to wit, Little Ned and Daniel. I give to
my beloved wife Catherine her choice of a horse and saddle and bridle
her choice of one bed and furniture and two cows and calves. I lend
unto my wife Catherine during the life time of her father Enoch Benson
my negro woman called Suck and at the death of the said Enoch Benson, I
give my negro woman called Suck to my daughter Nancy Blassingame and at
the death of Nancy the said negro and her increase I give to my granddaughter Polly Blassingame, Nancy's daughter. If my sons or either of
them die without issue the negroes I gave to either are to be given
to my daughter Nancy Blassingame children. It is my wish and desire
that no desputes arise between my children after my death and with
everything to appear fair and easy to be understood, sell the three
tracts of land on Saulda River and Georges Creek and divide between my
sons Samuel and John Easley. I appoint Major John Blassingame and
William Easley of Greenville Dist. as Executors. Dated 31 Mar. 1806.
Wit: Thos. Lorton, John Dyres, Samuel Townes. Signed Robert Easley,
seal. Recorded and proved 9 Dec. 1806.

Samuel A. Easley. Deed of Samuel A. Easley to Doctor John Robinson.
Pack 75. Clerk of Court Office. Pickens, S. C. Samuel A. Easley to
Doct. John Robinson both of Pendleton Dist. For the sum of six thousand dollars paid by sd. Robinson all the plantation or tracts of land
to wit: The Pickensville Tract granted to Charles C. Pikney containing
eight hundred and ten acres. The Saml. Edmondson tract of one hundred
and seventeen acres. Another tract conveyed by Drucilla Thomas and
John Edmondson to John Archer of one hundred and twenty acres and the
David Henderson tract of one hundred, Robert Wilson Tract containing
one hundred and twenty nine acres, The William Henderson tract containing one hundred and thirty five acres, in the whole fourteen hundred
and eleven acres. Dated 1 Feb. 1823. Wit: Henry H. Townes, John
Archor. Signed Saml. A. Easley, seal. Pendleton Dist. Mary Easley the
wife of Saml. Easley appear before J. Douthit, J.Q. this day 22 July
1823 and renounce, release and for ever relinquish, all her interest and
estate, also all her right and claim of dower, etc. Recorded 23 July
1823 in Book Q Page 197, Pendleton Dist.

Col. John Easley. Deed to Col. John Easley from Elizabeth Sloan and
others. Book C-1 Page 558. Clerk of Court Office. Pickens, S.C.
We Elizabeth D. Sloan, Robert B. Duncan, Jno. M. Roberts and Mary Jane
Roberts of Greenville Dist. to John Easley of Pickens Dist. for in
consideration of fifteen hundred dollars and twenty eight dollars, do
sell unto John Easley a certain tract of land in Pickens Dist. lying
on waters of Big George Creek of Saluda River. Containing three
hundred and eighty two acres, bounded by land of John Easley, Anit
Underwood, John Gossett, John Bowen and William Bowen. Dated 30 Dec.
1837. Wit: B. F. Mauldin, C. B. Roberts. Signed Elizabeth D. Sloan,
R. B. Duncan, Jno. M. Roberts, Mary J. Roberts. Recd. 28 June 1838
and examined by me W. L. Keith. C.C. & R.M.C.

Samuel A. Easley. Deed to Samuel A. Easley from William P. Benson.
Book F-1 Page 524. Clerk of Court Office. Pickens, S.C. Samuel A.
Easley from William P. Benson both of Pickens Dist. for the sum of
five hundred and forty two dollars for fifty two and 1/4 acres on the
North side of the South prong of George Creek of Saluda River. Bounded
on land of Griffin Hamilton, the heirs of Samuel Clayton decd. Dated
25 Jan. 1851. Wit: John Bowen, Wm. R. Bowen. Signed W. P. Benson,
seal. Recorded 5 May 1851 by W. L. Keith, C.C. & R.M.C.

James Easter. Will of James Easter. Recd. Records 1791-1803. Page
13-17. Ordinary's Office, Elbert Co., Ga. I James Easter of Elbert
Co., Ga. being in a low state of health and weak in body but perfect
mind and memory, etc.etc. My will and desire is that my just debts
be paid first. I lend to my beloved wife Sarah all that tract of land
whereon I now live as low down as to the mouth of the double branches.
Thence up the near fork of the said branches to the back line, during
her natural life, Likewise four negroes to wit: Frank, Jacob, Sam &
Hanner to be hers forever. likewise I lend to my said wife four
negroes to wit; Hall, Lucy, Tom, Betty untill my son Champin shall come
of age. I give to my daughter Mary Ann one horse bridle and saddle
and no more of my estate. I give to my daughter Elizabeth five
shillings and no more of my estate. I give to my daughter Dolly five
shillings and no more of my estate. I give to my son William Thompson
Easter the tract of land whereon he now lives containing three hundred
acres likewise one negro boy named Simon to him forever. I give to
my son Booker Burton Easter one tract of land lying on the head of
Long Creek in Wilkes Co. containing two hundred and fifty acres. Also
one negro boy named Charles to him forever likewise two cows and calves
and one feather bed. I give to my daughter Patty Aycock and William
Aycock the tract of land whereon they now live. Agreeable to the
division made between him and Thomas Napier when the tract was divided.
Likewise one negro wench named Cruse with her increase forever. I
give to my daughter Tabby Napier and Thomas Napier a tract of land
adjoining of William Aycock agreeable to a division made between them.
likewise one negro girl named Nancy and her increase forever. I give
to my daughter Lotty one negro girl named Silvia with her increase, one
feather bed and furniture. One horse, birdle and saddle and one cow
and calf forever. I give to my sons Lewis and Champion all that
tract of land whereon I now live, which is not lent to my wife. The
land that is lent to my wife is to be divided between my sons Lewis
and Champion at the death of my wife. I give to my son Lewis one negro
named Caleb forever. I give to my son Champion one negro boy named
Pope, likewise then he comes of age, I give to him one negro man named
Hall, I give to my son Lewis one negro wench named Bet, likewise each
to have one feather bed, one horse briddle and saddle, two cows and
calves, one sow and pig apiece. I give to my daughter Sophia one negro
girl named Fanny, one feather bed, and furniture, two cows and calves,
horse and saddle. I give to my daughter Teree one negro woman named
Dilsey and two cows and calves, horse and saddle. I give to my daughters
Lotte, Sophia and Teree my tract of land in Franklin lying on old Tom
Creek to be divided as they come of age. I appoint my wife Sarah
Executrix with William Thompson Easter, my nephew Richard Easter, my
friend William Thompson, Senr. and Robert Thompson Senr. and Benjamin
Toliaforro executors. Dated 1791. Wit: Phillip Wray, Wells Thompson,
Stephen Ellington. Signed James X Easter. Recorded in Ord. Office.
Records Book 1791-1803, Page 13-17.

EATON

James Eaton. Land Warrant of James Eaton. Pack 114. Clerk of Court.
Pickens, S. C. By W. L. Keith Clerk. To any lawful surveyor you are
hereby authorized to lay out and admeasure unto James Eaton a tract
of land, etc. dated 1 Apr. 1850. Certified the 20 May 1850.

Lewis Eaton. Estate of Lewis Eaton. Box 49 #544. Probate Judge Office
Pickens, S.C. Est. admr. 9 Nov. 1858 by Lewis Reese, Asel Reeves, J. E.
Hagood who are bound unto W. J. Parson, Ord. in the sum of $1600.00.
Was late of Howard County, Indiana.

Joseph Eaton. Estate of Joseph Eaton. Box 92 #982. Probate Judge
Office. Pickens, S.C. Died 7 April 1877. Owned 32 acres in Anderson
Co., S.C. joining land of David Watkins, Maria Watson, R. G. Eaton
and others. Also 2 acres at five forks in Anderson Co. joining lands of

Casey, John Harper. Also land in village of Central, Pickens Co. Ch
& grand Chn. viz: L. Ross Eaton, Ephraim B. Eaton, John J. Eaton,
Amanda C. wife of Wm. Wilson, Margaret wife of John Harris, Lucinda
wife of J. P. Richey, Roswell Gaillard Eaton, John Davis, Eulalie
Davis, Leonidas Davis, Jane Maria Davis. The Davis Chn. are minors
under 14 years by a predeased dtr. All of S.C. except Lucinda P. Richey
of Ga. On 12 Aug. 1841 Wm. Eaton, Jr. and John Eaton of Lumpkin Co.,
Ga. Appointed Jas. Bruce of Cherokee Co., Ga. their attorney to
receive their part of the est. of Jas. Bruce Sr. of Pickens Co., S.C.
Lewis Eaton and wife Mary were heirs of William Abbott decd. and his
widow Julia Abbott of Pickens Dist. Dated 5 July 1858. Ref. Book A.
Page 228. Probate Judge Office. Pickens Co., S.C.

EDENS

Samuel Edens - Mary M. Edens. Deed from Samuel Edens to Mary M. Edens.
Pack 382 #4. Clerk of Court. Pickens, S.C. I Samuel Edens for
natural love and affection I have and bear to my wife Mary M. Edens
and one dollar, have granted, bargained, sold, etc.etc. unto Mary Edens
during her natural life and at her death to all my children share and
share alike. The tract of land lying on both sides of Oolenoy River adj
land of Margaret Edens, Samuel E. Sutherland, decd. containing 117
acres, conveyed to me by J. W. Southerland and Mary A. Cantrell on the
4 Jan. 1883. Dated 10 March 1885. Wit: J. C. Thompson, J. B. Clyde,
J. J. Lewis. Signed Samuel Edens. Filed 29 Apr. 1885.

William Edens. Estate of William Edens. Box 101 #1059. Probate Judge
Office. Pickens, S.C. He died 17 Jan. 1871. W. D. Edens, Saml S.
Edens made suit for letter of Admr. left the widow and 10 chn. Owned
the home place of 125 acres adj. land of Jas. Keith, Peggy Edens, and
others, #2 tract known as the Chastain tract of 75 acres adj. land of
Tyre L. Roper. Also on half interest in tract #3 known as the jet
survey of 200 acres adj. land of Ambrose Reid. All lying on waters of
Oolenoy River. Heirs: Widow Mary Edens, chn. John M. C. Edens of
Texas, Alexr. Edens, Sarah A. Edens, Warren D. Edens, Samuel S. Edens,
Rebecca Lynch wife of Nathaniel Lynch, Adaline wife of Vanb. Jones,
Eveline B. wife of barring (one place spelled Gassaway). Also the
heirs of the wife of Wilson Jones viz, Mary J. and Jas. P. Jones heirs
of Wm. J. Edens names unknown. The Judge called the wife of Wilson
Jones, Lydia A. Jones but A. Blythe in his recollection remembered it
as Deniza. 30 Mar. 1872 John M. C. Edens husband of S. B. Edens decd.
of Collins County, Texas appointed V. S. Jones of Pickens Co., S.C.
their attorney to receive money due them from the estate of Wm. Edens
decd. of Pickens, S.C.

Absolem Edens. Estate of Absolem Edens. Box 95 #104. Probate Judge
Office, Pickens, S.C. Est. Admr. 6 Sept. 1873 by Margaret Edens,
Saml. Edens, N. J. Williams who are bound to J. H. Philpot Ord. in the
sum of $1200.00.

S. M. - Mary L. Edens. Estates of S. M. and Mary L. Edens. Box 126
#5. Probate Judge Office, Pickens, S.C. Est. Admr. 5 Dec. 1895. By
T. J. Ligon, O. P. Field, M. D. Cantrell who are bound unto J. B.
Newberry, Ord. in the sum of $300.00 S. M. Edens died June 4, 1895.
Mary L. Edens died 3 Nov. 1895. T. J. Ligon the father and father-in-
law.

Edens Minors. Box 133 #5. Probate Judge Office. Pickens Co., S.C.
On 5 Dec. 1899 Allen K. Edens, H. A. Richey, T. R. Price are bound unto
J. B. Newberry Ord. in the sum of $400.00. Allen K. Edens gdn. for
Nora Rebecca Edens about 13 yrs. Margaret Queendora Edens about 11
years. Lula Victory Edens about 9 years. Kate Vilanta Edens about
7 years. Children of Warren D. Edens and wife Masours Edens decd.
Margaret Edens the grandmother.

Edens Minors. Box 10 #183. Probate Judge Office. Pickens Co., S.C.
On 7 June 1878 Margaret Edens, Saml. Edens, Allenk. Edens, J. M. Edens,

P. N. B. Edens are bound to W. G. Field Ord. in the sum of $1,000.00.
Margaret Edens gdn. for Elijah C. Edens, Warren D. Edens minors were
21 years in 1885.

Samuel Edens. Estate of Samuel Edens. Box 21 #251. Probate Judge
Office. Pickens, Co., S.C. Est. Admr. 7 Jan. 1848 by Alexander,
William Edens and W. Keith who are bound unto Wm. D. Steel, Ord. in the
sum of $8,000.00. Left 200 acres of land on Woolenoy Creek adj. lands
of Jacob Chastain, Jas. Keith and others. Heirs William, Alexander
Edens, Paschal Southerland and wife Esther, Jesse Adams and wife Polly,
Tyre L. Roper and wife Malinda. Paid Rebecca Chastain for dower $90.00.
Paid Wm. Edens expenses to Gilmore Co., Ga. $10.00.

Alexander Edens. Estate of Alexander Edens. Box 82 #866. Probate
Judge Office. Pickens Co., S.C. Est. Admr. 5 July 1869 by James M.
Edens, Margaret Edens, Saml. Edens who are bound unto I. H. Philpot,
Ord. in the sum of $2500.00 Admr. again 16 Jan. 1865 by Margaret Edens,
Jas. Burdine, Jas. Hagood, Andrew J. Anderson who are bound unto
W. E. Holcombe, Ord. in the sum of $20,000.00.

William & Alex Edens. Deed to William and Alex Edens. Box 105 #1099.
Pickens Co., S.C. Deed dated 9 Jan. 1843. Whereas Maxwell and Edward
Chastain did sell unto William and Alexander Edens and heirs of Abner
Chastain decd. For the sum of $200.00 did sell a tract of land
first granted to Henry Adams of one hundred acres on a branch of Oolenoy
Waters. Wit: Jesse Adams, John M. C. Edens. Signed Maxwell Chastain
and Edward X Chastain.

Alexander Edens. Deed to Alexander Edens. No Ref. Pickens Co., S.C.
Deed dated 9 May 1851. William Edens to Alex. Edens in the sum of two
thousand dollars for all that tract of land lying on the Oolenoy
Creek containing 350 acres. Wit: Vann S. Jones, John Lynch. Signed
William Edens.

Alexander Edens. Deed to Alexander Edens. No Ref. Pickens Co., S.C.
Deed dated 15 Feb. 1844 from Samuel Edens to Alexander Edens. In the
sum of $666.66 for all that tract of land lying on Oolenoy Creek con-
tianing 156 1/2 acres. Wit: F. N. Garvin, Paschal Sutherland.
Signed: Samuel Edens.

Alexander Edens. Alexander Edens died in Dec. 1864. Margaret Edens
the widow and 11 chn. viz; under 21 years. Mary Jane wife of Ira
Thomas Roper, William E. Edens, Crafton Alex. Edens, Elijah C. Edens,
Warren D. Edens, the last three under 14 years. Rebecca wife of
Nathaniel J. Williams, Samuel Edens, Ellen K. Edens, James M. Edens,
Pinkney N. B. Edens, Absolom B. Edens he died 8 Sept. 1872 who left no
widow or chn.

Samuel Edens. Pack 229 #9. Clerk of Court Office. Pickens Co., S.C.
On 18 June 1872 Samuel Edens by his malice aforethought did make an
assault upon of Dadison F. Mitchell with a certain gun in both hands
held to and against the said Mitchell did shoot off and discharge into
his belly at Pickens Court House from which mortal wound he died. That
James M. Edens also of said county was aiding and assisting the said
Samuel Edens. James A. McKee and William J. Hunnicut were with
Mitchell when he got killed.

EDGE

James Edge. Pack 610 #1. Clerk of Court Office. Pickens Co., S.C.
On 16 Oct. 1854 James Edge of Pickens Dist. was attached unto Joseph
Bennett who it is said is now absent from the state.

Littleton Edge. Book A, Page 226. Probate Judge Office. Pickens, S.C.
on 15 Mar. 1858 Littleton Edge and his wife Manerva living out of the
state were the heirs of Joseph Cox decd. and his widow Nancy Cox of
Pickens, Dist.

EDMONDSON

Edmondson. Deed Edmondson to Archer. Ref. Mesne Conveyance, Pendleton Dist. Book O Page 513 or 373?, Anderson, S. C. We Drucilla, Thomas and John Edmondson for $250.00 to us paid by John Archer do sell, release a tract of land lying on Middle fork of Brushy Creek of Saluda River. Being part of a tract granted to Samuel Means, by him to John Edmondson decd. containing 120 acres. Adj. lands of Pinckneys and John Archers. Dated 25 Feb. 1819. Wit: Rob. H. Briggs, Alexr. Sloan, Thomas Nichols, Christopher Nichols. Signed Drucilla X Edmondson, Thos. Edmondson, John Edmondson. Seals. Attested by Rob. H. Briggs before H. Terrell, J.Q. on the 12 May 1819.

Edmondson. Bond Edmondson to Vick. Pack 212 #1. Clerk of Court Office. Pickens, S.C. I M. S. Edmondson of Pickens Dist., S.C. am and firmly bound unto Howel Vick of Rabum County, Ga. in the sum of sixty dollars. Dated 10 Aug. 1832. Howel Vick sold unto Edmondson half of his interest in the rent land lottery in the state of Ga. and recd. thirty dollars for the same and confest judgment of the sd. Vick shall make good and lawful right to his half interest in sd. land by the first of Nov. next. Wit: Mathias Tally. Signed: M. S. Edmondson. seal.

EDWARDS

Thos. Edwards. Will of Thos. Edwards. Book B, Page 125-6. Probate Judge Office. Greenville, S.C. I Thos. Edwards of Greenville Dist. Knowing that it is appointed for all to die, etc.etc. I give to my son Thomas Edwards a tract of land, one negro boy named George, one horse and saddle and bridle, one bed and household furniture. One rifle gun etc. I give to my son Peter Edwards a tract of land, one negro girl named Vina. One horse, saddle and bridle, one bed and furniture, one rifle gun, etc. I give to my son Jesse Edwards a tract of land, one negro girl named Winna, one horse, saddle, and a bridle. One bed and furniture, one cow and calf, etc. I give to my son Lamech Edwards one negro girl named Hannah one mare saddle and bridle, one bed and furniture etc.etc. I give to my son John L. Edwards one negro girl named Lucy, one horse, saddle and bridle. On tract of land one bed and furniture, one cow and calf. Also one negro boy named Lewis, etc. I give to my son James M. C. Edwards one tract of land, one negro boy named Stephen, one horse, saddle and bridle, one bed and furniture, one cow and calf etc.etc. I give to my son Francis Edwards one negro boy named Sampson and one negro girl named Rachel, one bed and furniture, one horse, saddle, and bridle, one cow and cald etc.etc. I give to my son Edward Edwards one negro boy named Carlo and one negro girl named Mima, one horse, saddle, and bridle, one cow and calf, one bed and furniture etc. I give to my two youngest sons Francis and Edward the land where I now live. Their mother to live on it with her negroes during her life or widowhood, at her death land to be divided, let the branch divide with Francis is to have the upper part. The two youngest sons to have the land I bought from Sloan. I give to my wife Mary Ann Edwards my large family Bible and negroes Mary and Liza and Jerry & Adam and Tom and other items etc.etc. I appoint my sons Peter, Francis and Edward as Executors. Dated 8 July 1825. Wit: Robert Nelson, Lemuel Nelson, L. C. Reynolds, David Jackson. Signed Thos. Edwards, seal. Probated 20 Aug. 1832. Ref. also Apt. 3 File #150. Greenville, S.C.

ELDER

James Elder. Estate of James Elder. Box 31 Pack 675. Probate Judge Office. Abbeville, S.C. We Robert and Sarah Sterling and James McElwain and David Brown are bound unto John Thomas Junr. Ord. of 96 Dist. in the sum of five hundred pounds sterling. Bond dated 8 Oct. 1785. The appraisement of the estate was taken by Isaac Patton, William Eldre, Wm. Smith. No date given.

ELLENBURG

Martin Ellenburg. Estate of Martin Ellenburg. Box 68 #734. Probate Judge Office. Pickens, Dist. Est. Admr. 20 Feb. 1863 by Wm. Nimmons, John W. L. Cary who are bound unto W. E. Holcombe, Ord. in the sum of $1600.00. Left a widow and six chn. Heirs Widow Catharine, Elizabeth wife of Joe Chapman, Nancy Reaves, Adaline Mosely, John Ellenburg, Wm. Ellenburg, Jobery Ellenburg, Celey Ellenburg, Eli Ellenburg.

John Ellenburg. Estate of John Ellenburg. Box 86 #909. Probate Judge Office. Pickens, S.C. Est. Admr. 2 Mar. 1866 by Wm. R. Roberts, Jas. C. Roberts, H. A. H. Gibson who are bound unto W. E. Holcombe, Ord. in the sum of $200.00. Left a widow and three children.

Sarah Ellenburg. Sarah Ellenburg before her marriage to William Hunter of Pickens Co. she had by him 8 illegitimate chn. viz: William, John, Martha, Mary, Thomas, Washington, Henry and James Ellenburg. It was William Hunter desire in his will that they change their name to that of Hunter. Mary Ellenburg in 1903 ment. as the wife of a Gilstrap. Ref. Box 137 #13. Probate Judge Office. Pickens, S.C.

ELLINGTON

Ellington. Power of Attorney from Ellington and Coppenbarger. Apt. 4 File 245. Probate Judge Office. Greenville, S. C. "Know all men by these presents that we Johnathan Ellington and Downey Ellington originally Downey Downing and late Downey Hooper by intermarriage with Obadiah Hooper decd. but now Downey Ellington by intermarriage with the said Johnathan, Jacob Coppenbarger and his wife Polly Coppenbarger late Polly Hooper but now Polly Coppenbarger by intermarriage with the said Jacob. All of Sangamon Co., state of Illinois." Have authorized and appointed our friend William H. Salmon of the state of S.C. Greenville Dist. our attorney to use our name etc.etc. To call on John H. Goodlett Esq. the Admr. upon the estate of Thomas Hooper decd. all such money or sums of money due and coming to us as heirs at law of Obadiah Hooper who was one of the heirs of the late Thomas Hooper of the said state and dist. Dated 26 Apr. 1830. Wit: L. D. Matheny, Edward M. West. Signed: Johnathan X Ellington & Downey X Ellington. Jacob X Coppenbarge, Polly E. Coppenbarger.

ELLIOTT

James Elliott. Naturalization of James Elliott. No ref. Clerk of Court Office. Chester Co., S.C. To the Court of Common Pleas in Chester Dist., S.C. The petition of James Elliott sheweth that he is an alien and a native of Ireland and has resided within the limits of the United States between the 18 June 1798 and the 14 Apr. 1802 that he has continued to reside within the same ever since and he is desirous of becoming a citizen, etc. No other date given. Wit: J. Brevard. Signed: James Elliott. George Kenndy and James Harbson, J.P. made oath that Elliott is a man of good moral character, etc.etc.

Catharine Elliott. Power of Attorney of Catharine Elliott. Deed Book C-1, Page 61. Clerk of Court Office. Pickens, S.C. State of Georgia, City of Savannah. We Catharine Elliott of the State of S.C. the widow of late Capt. Barnard Elliott of said State and Sarah E. Habersham daughter of Elliott and wife of Richard W. Habersham of the city of Savannah, Ga. Catherine and Sarah sole heirs of Barnard Elliott decd. do hereby constitute and appoint Jesse P. Lewis Esq. of Pendleton Dist. in S.C. attorney at law and in our name and for our benefit etc.etc. To sell in fee simple to any person willing to pay sum set by said Jesse P. Lewis Esq. all that tract of land in said Dist. originally granted to Capt. Elliott for his military service. etc. Dated 17 Dec. 1832. Wit: B. E. Habersham. Signed Cathn. E. Elliott, Rich. W. Habersham, S. E. Habersham.

Elliott. Deed to Elliott to Gillison. Book C-1, Page 62. Clerk of Court Office. Pickens, S.C. State of S.C. Anderson Dist. We Catherine Elliott, Richard W. Habersham and wife of the State of Ga. in consideration of three hundred dollars paid by Elijah Gillison of Pickens Dist. do grant, sell and convey all that tract of land lying in Pickens Dist. on the waters of Coneross and Seneca being granted unto Capt. Barnard Elliott. Dated 22 Jan. 1835. Wit: J. S. Lorton, W. M. Ferrell. Signed Catherine Elliott, Richard W. Habersham and Sarah E. Habersham, seals. Attested by John S. Lorton before William L. Keith, C.C. 10 Mar. 1835.

William Elliott. Deed of William Elliott to James Hagood. Book B-1, Page 89. Clerk of Court Office. Pickens, Dist. I William Elliott of Pendleton Dist. and James Hagood Junr. of same Dist. Dated 28 Mar. 1821. For the sum of $700.00 paid by Hagood for 314 acres lying on both sides of Peters Creek waters of Saluda River, adj. land of Benjamin Clarks old line and across the mountain to the beginning. Wit: Henry Fendley, Young Potts. Signed William Elliott, seal. Attested by Henry Fendley before Samuel Scott, J.P. on the 3 Oct. 1831. Recorded by W. L. Keith, C.C.

William and John Elliott. Sheriff Deed of William and John Elliott land. Book B-1, Page 433. Clerk of Court Office. Pickens Co., S.C. I Samuel Reed former sheriff of Pickens Dist. by virtue of a Fieri Facias issued out of the Court of Common Pleas, held on the 8 Mar. 1830 at suit of Wallace and Davis to me directed that the goods and chattels lands and tenements of William and John Elliott be levyed in the sum of $40.25 for damage and cost. I have seized and taken land and tenements of said John Elliott lying on Peters Creek waters of Saluda River. Adj. land of Richard Goodlett, David Corbin, Elizabeth Brazel and Andrew Medlin, reference to an old deed from Samuel Mann to John Elliott. By virtue of the said writ of Fieri Facias have exposed to public sale and purchased by William L. Keith for the sum of $25.00 and ordered by his to make title to Barksdale Corbin. Dated 3 March 1834. Wit: W. M. Smith, James Knox. Signed William D. Sloan, S.P.D. Deed attested by James Knox by before William L. Keith, C.C. 12 Apr. 1834.

Elliott. Deed Elliott to Elliott. Book G, Page 257, Clerk of Court Office. Pickens, S.C. I William Elliott of Pickens Dist. for love and affection I have and do bear towards my son George R. Elliott of same Dist. Have granted, bargained and give unto said Elliott all that tract of land lying on waters of Little River, adj. lands of R. Maxwell the estate of Stribing and Major Seaborn containing ninety nine acres being part of an original grant to Crosby Miller. Dated 14 Jan. 1853. Wit: Thos. J. Keith, W. L. Keith. Signed William Elliott, seal. Deed attested by Thos. J. Keith before W. L. Keith, C.C. Dated 14 Jan. 1853.

Elliott. Deed Elliott to Elliott, Book G-1 Page 258. Clerk of Court Office, Pickens, S.C. I William Elliott of Pickens Dist. for and in consideration of ninety five dollars to James Elliott of the state and dist. aforesaid have granted, bargained, sold and released unto the said George W. Elliott a tract of land lying on branches of Seneca Creek, adj. lands of G. M. Stribling, R. Maxwell, G. R. Elliott containing ninety five acres. Dated 14 Jan. 1853. Wit: Geo. R. Elliott, Thos. J. Keith before W. L. Keith C.C. Dated 14 Jan. 1853.

Elliott. Deed Elliott to Maxwell. Book G-1, Page 304. Clerk of Court Office, Pickens, S.C. I William Elliott of Pickens Dist. for and in consideration of $150.00 paid me by Robt. Maxwell have granted, sold and released unto the said Robert Maxwell all that tract of land I purchased from the estate of Crosby Miller of Pickens Dist. on both sides of the road to Wm. Sloans Ferry on waters of Little River and Seneca Creek, containing 154 acres. Adj. lands of George Seabrook, George Elliott and others. Dated 1 Jan. 1853. Wit: George W. Elliott, Wm. Howard. Signed William Elliott, seal. I Thomas J. Keith, Dep. Clk. hereby certify all whom it may concern that Mrs. Martha Elliott the wife of William Elliott did this day appear before me and

and renounce, release and forever relinquish her claim to dower to
the said land. Dated 3 May 1853. Signed Martha Elliott. Recorded
same day.

Archibald Elliott. Estate of Archibald Elliott. Box 5 #187. Probate
Judge Office. Anderson, S.C. Est. Admr. 23 May 1804 by Mary Elliott,
William Gaston, Hugh Gaston who are bound unto John Harris, Ord. in
the sum of $2,000.00. One item of interest. Received 1 July 1806 of
Mr. William Gaston Admr. of Arch. Elliott decd. eight dollars in full
for six months schooling of two scholars Viz: John and Jinny Elliott
ending the 1 July 1806. Recd. by Robert Brackenridge.

W. E. T. Elliott. Box 34 #388. Probate Judge Office. Pickens, S.C.
Est. Admr. 25 May 1855 by David T. Holland who applied for the letter
of Admr.

Clarissa C. Elliott. Estate of Clarissa C. Elliott. Box 34 #389.
Probate Judge Office. Pickens, S.C. Est. Admr. 15 June 1855 by David
T. Holland, William Doyle who are bound unto W. J. Parson, Ord. in the
sum of $1400.00. Walhalla, S. C. 5 Nov. 1855 we the heirs of Clarissa
Elliott give our consent to sell the real estate of decd. viz: D. T.
Holland and Elizabeth Holland, Elizabeth Brewer, Susannah Doyle, W. T.
Holland. Owned 110 acres lying on waters of Choestoe waters of Tugaloo
River, adj. land of L. Towers, Capt. James Johns and others. On 15
Dec. 1859 Wm. Doyle states that he recd. a share of the real estate in
the life time of his wife now decd. To W. E. Holcombe, Ord. Sir: You
will make the titles to a certain piece of land purchased by my late
husband James Brewer decd. at Ord. sale as the real estate of
Clarissa Elliott decd. to Thaddeus S. Miller. Signed Elizabeth
Martin, Extrx.

William Elliott. Estate of William Elliott. Box 37 #423. Probate
Judge Office. Pickens, S.C. 16 Jan. 1855 D. T. Holland made suit for
letter of Admr. no other inf.

ELLIS

John E. Ellis. Estate of John E. Ellis. Pack 331. Clerk of Court
Office. Abbeville, S. C. To the Honorable the Chancellors. Your
Honors your oratrix Elizabeth Ellis complaining as follows, that John
E. Ellis the husband of your oratrix died the 16 May 1859 intestate
leaving a widow and fifteen living children and one dead son. viz;
Matilda wife of Turner G. Davis, Polly wife of Zachariah Hadden, Louanna
wife of James Strawhorn, Elizabeth Ellis, Christopher Ellis, John E.
Ellis, Joseph N. Ellis, Robert M. Ellis, Ebenezer P. Ellis, Benjamin
F. Ellis, William T. Ellis, Memminger M. Ellis, Amaziah R. Ellis, Luther
T. Ellis and Permelia S. Ellis the last four named are minors. Also
four minor children of Augustus E. Ellis decd. viz; John Calvin, James
Lucien, Mahala Elizabeth and Savannah Paratine Ellis. At the time of
his death John E. Ellis had considerable real and personal property
and that his sons Christopher and Ebenezer P. Ellis as administered
upon the estate and have enough to pay all debts. John E. Ellis had at
the time of death two plantations or tracts of land. One the home
place of eight hundred acres or more lying on Chickasaw Creek, waters
of Little River, bounded by land of Robert Ellis, Joseph Ellis, William
Ellis, Robert Pratt and others. The other tract called the Groggy
Springs Place, containing about seven hundred acres, lying on Jobs
Creek, waters of Long Cane, bounded by land of William Stevenson, Peter
Henry, John Cowan and others. Dated 25 May 1859. On another paper
children ages was given: Elizabeth of age, John Calvin age 10 years,
James Lucien age 8 years, Mahala Elizabeth age 6 years, Savannah
Paratine age 4 years, Memminger M. age 18 years, Amaziah R. age 17 years,
Luther T. age 16 years, Permelia S. age 14 years, Joseph N. Ellis
address was Acquilla P. O. Ga.

Ellis. Deed Ellis to Allgood. Book G-1 Page 46. Clerk of Court
Office. Pickens, S. C. Gideon Ellis, Senr. to Barnett H. Allgood both

of Pickens Dist. Dated 6 Jan. 1851. For the sum of one thousand
dollars for all that tract of land lying on both sides of Rices Creek
waters of Twelve Mile River. Containing 330 acres. Wit: John Gilstrap, Richard Underwood. Signed Gideon Ellis, seal. On 29 Nov. 1851
Lusey Ellis the wife of Gideon Ellis did release and forever relinquish
all her rights of dower... before John Bowen, N.P. seal.

Ellis. Deed Ellis to Mayfield. Book A-1 Page 336. Clerk of Court
Office. Pickens, S.C. Gideon Ellis to William Mayfield both of Pickens
Dist. Dated 1 Oct. 1830. For the sum of $500.00 for the tract of land
in the dist. and state aforesaid containing 270 acres. Originally
granted to John Boyd. Wit: Jac. Gearin, Pearson Mayfield. Signed
Gideon Ellis, seal. Attested before James Langston, J.P. by Pearson
Mayfield on 1 Oct. 1830.

Edmon Ellis. Will of Edmon Ellis. Book A Page 124. Probate Judge
Office, Union Co., S. C. I Edmon Ellis being very sick and weak in body
but in proper mind and memory etc.etc. Dated 14 Oct. 1800. I give to
my son William Ellis one third of my land joining his own land. I give
to my sons Jonathan and Edmon Ellis the other two thirds to be divided
between them, I also give to Jonathan one sorrel mare saddle and bridle
with one cow. I give to my beloved wife Mary Ellis the benefit of my
plantation and orchards during her life time. (No executor named).
Wit: Joshua Elliot, Peter Ellis, Jonathan Ellis, Hugh Cook, Ellender
Harvey. Signed Edmon Ellis. Recorded 12 Feb. 1801.

Robert Ellis. Will of Robert Ellis. Book D. Page 142, York County,
S.C. I Robert Ellis of York Dist. being sick and weak in body but of
perfect mind and memory, etc.etc. I will unto my beloved wife Mary
Ellis all that property particularized in our marriage contract which is
recorded in Yorkville to be hers in exect conformity as therein agreed
upon. I will to my daughter Sally Summer Ellis one negro named Stephen
and a boy named Austin, one feather bed and furniture, one spinning
wheel. I will to my son Benjamin negroes Luke and one child named
Esther to be dlivered to him at twenty one years old. I give to my
daughter Rebekah Ellis negroes Amy and Milly to be hers at age eighteen.
The land I hold by an Indian lease and land conveyed by marriage
contract to be Salley Summer Ellis to be hers at age eighteen or
marriage. The land on the Stony fork of Fishing Creek of 199 1/2 acres
to be my son Benjamin Ellis at the age of twenty one, land to be rented
out and applied to his support. If my negro George out lives my wife
he is to be given to Sally Summer Ellis. In case one of my children
dies its share to be divided between the other. In case all should
die then my estate to be divided between the male children of my
brother Thomas Ellis of Northampton County, N.C. I appoint John Workman
and David Hutchison my executors and guardian of all my children. Dated
3 Oct. 1814. Wit: Tho. Robertson, William Reeves, Robert Workman.
Signed Robt. Ellis, seal. Probated 26 Dec. 1816.

ELLISON

Robert Ellison. Will of Robert Ellison. Vol. 14 Page 215 Probate
Judge Office. Charleston, S. C. I Robert Ellison of Williamsburgh,
Craven Co. being sick and weak of body but of perfect mind and memory,
etc.etc. I give to my dear beloved wife one third part of my personal
property except one negro girl named Venice eldest child of Phebe and
one cow and calf. I will to my granddaughter Elizabeth Erwin eldest
daughter of John Erwin the named negro, I will to Mary McWhennay her
bed and board as long as my Executors think it convenient with one cow
and calf. Another fourth part to the children of John Erwin except
Elizabeth. Another part to the children of Mary Ellison wife of Hugh
Erwin. Another part to the children of Robert Ellison to be equally
divided between the two of them. I appoint and authorize John Erwin
and Hugh Erwin to sell two tracts of land, one on Jefferys Creek containing three hundred acres and the other on Kings Tree Swamp containing
three hundred acres. I will to grandson Robert Ellison the son of
Mathew Ellison one hundred acres I appoint my two sons in law John and

Hugh Erwin as my Executors. Wit: John McConnell, John Erwin Junr.,
Mary McWhoney. Signed Robert Ellison. Proved May 1772, same time
qualified John Erwin, Senr. as Executor.

Margaret Ellison. Will of Margaret Ellison. Box 42 Pack 1029. Probate
Judge Office. Columbia, S.C. I Margaret Ellison of town of Columbia,
Richmond Co. being of sound mind and memory, etc.etc. Pay my just
debts and be intered by my dear husband and a plain slab like on his be
put over my grave. I give to the Theological Seminary of the Synod of
S. C. $2,500.00 to be invested with the permanent fund to endow a
scholarship to be called the Joseph Ellison Scholarship to support one
indigent young man. I will to the Female Orphan House Society of
Columbia $1,000.00 to be invested in a permanent fund for the benefit
and support one girl at a time. I will $500.00 the interest for the
support of a missionary from the Presbyterian Church also $1,000.00 the
interest to support a Presbyterian Missionary laboring amongst the
colored people, both sums to be invested in permanent stock. I give
all my slaves to my beloved nephew Joseph Ellison Edger of Fairfield
Dist. on conditions the wish to live with him, if not they are to be
sold, having the liberty to choose their owner, with Joseph Ellison to
get the proceeds. I give to Joseph Ellison Adger of Fairfield Dist.
$4,000.00 in stock in Commerical Bank of Columbia with all plates and
chinia one bed and cloathes and my secretary and book case and books.
I give to my nephew William Cook Scott son of John S. Scott, the sum of
$2,000.00 in stock of the Bank of Charleston, to be continued invested
untill he comes of age. I give to my niece Elizabeth Margaret Wilson
$2,000.00 and at her death to go to her son John Player Wilson also my
mahogney ward robe. I give to my niece Margaret Cook the daughter of
John Ellison in Georgia $1,000.00. I give to my brother John Ellison
Senr. of Georgia $1,000.00. I give to Robert E. Ellison son of
William Ellison $1,000.00. I give to my brother James Ellison of
Georgia $1,000.00. I give the remainder of my furniture and beds and
cloathing and wearing apparel to be divided between my sisters viz;
Agnes Law, Jean Scott, Mary Quigley. I give the remainder of my
estate to my brother and sisters named John Adger, Agnes Law, Jean
Scott, Mary Quigley. I give to my niece Susan Jean Player $1,000.00 and
to my niece Mary Adger daughter of James Adger Jr. decd. I appoint
my friend William Law of Columbia and John Adger of Fairfield and John
S. Scott of Columbia to be Executors. Dated __ July 1845. Wit:
James Martin, Richard Oneal, W. E. Drennan. Signed Margaret Ellison.
        Codicil #1. If my niece Mary T. Adger should die before the age
of twenty one or leave lawful issue at the time of death the legacy
given her in caluse #15 shall go to my sister Mary Quigley. It is my
will and desire that my sister Agnes Law should retain, possess and
enjoy the house and lot I now live in. It is my will that the legacy
I gave to brother John Ellison Senr. to go to John Ellison Junr. It
is my will that my executors appropriate from my estate $1,000.00
toward building of a new Presbyterian Church in the town of Columbia.
Dated 12 April 1848. Wit: Andr. Crawford, Daniel Crawford, W. E.
Drennan. Signed: Margaret Ellison. The second Codicil. The legacy
given to Susan Jane Player in clause 15 having lapsed by her death, I
give the same sum to Mary Esther Thompson. Having subscribed the sum
of one thousand dollars toward the building of a new Pres. Church. I
hereby revoke the legacy given that purpose. Dated 23 June 1851. Wit:
Samuel Fair, James McMahon, William Donaldson. Signed: Margaret
Ellison. The first dodicil was attested to by And. Crawford on 15
May 1854 before James S. Guignard Ord. The will was attested by
Richard ONeale on the 17 May 1854 before James S. Guignard, Ord. The
second codicil attested by James McMahon on 17 May 1854. Before James
S. Guignard, Ord.

Mathew Ellison. Pack 641 #1. Clerk of Court Office. Pickens, S.C.
On 19 Sept. 1881 Mathew H. Ellison made oath that he is the father of
eight children whose mother has recently died. He lived in Pickens
Dist.

ELMS

John Elms. File 24 York Dist. No other inf. In 1848 John Elms and wife Malinda were heirs of Benjamin Withers decd. of York Dist.

ELMORE

Elizabeth Elmore. In equity. Pack 262. Clerk of Court Office. Abbeville, S.C. Your oratrix Elizabeth Elmore sheweth unto your Honors that Stephen Elmore her late husband was in his life time seized in fee simple a tract of land lying on Rockey Creek, containing 98 acres bounded by land of Willard Smith, William B. Dorn which he had purchased from Daniel New. Being informed and believes her husband gave a mortgage to Col. John Hearst now decd. That said Hearst estate has possession of said land. That her husband departed this life on the __ day __ 1850 leaving your oratrix his widow now about sixty three years of age and infirm and by the death of her husband she is entitled to her dower in the said land. The land is now in possession of William B. Dorn. There is a deed from Stephen B. Elmore to John Hearst for 89 acres with no date. Land on Westcoat Creek waters of Savannah River first granted to Elizabeth Hudnel. Adj. land of James Brown, Daniel Chambers, William Rowen, lands of Bennett, Harkness and John Smilly. No witness or signature on this deed.

ELROD

Quincy Elrod. Estate of Quincy Elrod. Book B Page 66. Probate Judge Office. Pickens, S. C. On 20 March 1861 Quincy Elrod decd. owned 50 acres of land in Pickens Dist. lying on Snow Creek. adj. land of J. A. Elrod, Moses Cain and others. Heirs Mary N. Elrod the widow and 6 chn. viz: John C. A. Elrod, Frances E. Elrod, George C. Elrod, Franklin W. Elrod, Elijah J. Elrod, Anna Q. D. Elrod, J. B. Sanders appointed gdn. of the chn.

EMBERSON

Emberson Minors. No ref. Abbeville, S. C. Martha E. Emberson now of the state of Miss. is entitled to a small sum of money from the estate of her grandfather John Osborne decd. in right of her mother or daughter of said Osborne. Whereas James Fair is gdn. of the sd. Martha E. and she sent Joel J. Cunningham a power of attorney on 21 Feb. 1859. Settlement of the estate of Frances A. Emberson a minor who is now of age and has intermarried with A. E. McClelland and recd. $115.68 from James A. Fair her gdn. In the settlement of the estate of John Osborne decd. It is decreed in favor of Eveline wife of John H. Emberson her share to be $215.26 one third of this to be deducted for Jno. H. Emberson the father of these wards. John Osborne and his daughter Eveline Osborne Emberson were both dead by 7 Jan. 1842. Eveline chn. were John William, Frances A. and Martha E. Emberson all under 14 years.

EMERSON

Moses S. Emerson. Pack 181 #23. Clerk of Court Office. Pickens, S.C. To the Honors Board of Commissioners: The undersigned most respectfully petition your board for a license to retail spiritous liquors by the drink at Cedar Rock for three months from the 18 day of Aug. 1869. Signed M. S. Emerson. We the undersigned recommend Moses Emerson as a suitable person to retail spiritous liquors at Cedar Rock. A. S. Smith, J. V. Duncan.

ENGLISH

English. Deed English to Foster. Pack 358. Clerk of Court Office. Abbeville, S.C. John English to John Foster both of Abbeville Dist. Dated 28 Sept. 1815. For the sum of $275.00 have sold, release all that tract of land containing 95 acres on the waters of Norris Creek being part of a tract granted to Samuel Foster Senr. Wit: Jno. Wardlaw, William McGraw. Signed: John English, seal. Attested by Jno. Wardlaw before Jno. Devlin, J.P. on the 19 March 1816. Recorded 20 July 1816.

Daniel English. Will of Daniel English. No Ref. Abbeville Dist., S.C. I Daniel English of Abbeville Dist. being in sound and disposing mind and memory etc.etc. I will and desire all my just debts be paid and my beloved wife Elizabeth to have all real and personal property during her natural life or widowhood. In case she marries my will is that my estate be divided between my eight children. I appoint my wife Executrix, my son in law John Sentell and Thomas Eaton and Jackson English my Executors. Dated 4 May 1853. Wit: Jacob Miller, Joseph X Philpot, Jas. M. Harrison. Signed Daniel English, seal. The heirs of Daniel English are viz: Hetha Dooly wife of George W. Dooly residing in Abbeville Dist., S.C. Rocelia Eaton wife of Thomas W. Eaton of Edgefield Dist., S.C. Lucinda wife of Hiram Jay resides in Georgia, Sarah wife of Wm. Hardin of Alabama. Jackson English resides in Union Town P. O. Morengo Co., Alabama. Frances wife of John Sentell of Abbeville Dist., S.C. Elizabeth wife of Reuben Morris of Louisiana. Amanda wife of B. F. Spikes of Georgia. There is a letter to the Executors of Daniel English estate. That she was a married lady, my husband is now living. I have four children viz: Anneliza about 14 years., Frances Elizabeth 8 years, Franklin Independence 2 years and John Giddy one year old. That she desires her share of her father's estate to come to her or her children and not be subject to any debts contract or liabilities of my husband or any future husband she may have. Dated 14 March 1860. Wit: John Sentell. Signed: Caroline Amanda Spikes. Stilesborough P.O. or Cartersville Cass County, Ga.

ERNEST

Betey Ernest. Pack 633. Clerk of Court Office. Equity records of Richard Burnine. Pickens, S.C. March 23, 1861 Betey Ernest wife of Jacob Ernest were living in Indiana. She was a daughter of Richard Burdine decd. of Pickens Dist. who died in 1860 and his widow Patcy Burdine. Same Ref. 26 June 1867. James R. Ernest of Terrehaut, Vigo County, Indiana, Mordecia H. Dicks and Candace Dicks his wife, Bethuel J. Dicks and wife Evalyn Dicks of Douglass County, Illinois were heirs of Jacob Ernest decd. of Indiana.

ERWIN

Jennie Erwin. Book B Page 83. Probate Judge Office. Pickens, S.C. On 10 Nov. 1865 Jennie Erwin wife of John Erwin a sister to John H. Black. decd. of Pickens, S.C.

Thomas Erwin. Land Warrant of Thomas Erwin. Clerk of Court Office. Pack 630 #35. Pickens, S.C. By James E. Hagood Clerk of Court. To any lawful surveyor you are authorized to lay out unto Thomas Erwin a tract of land etc. and return to my office within two months. Dated 7 Aug. 1858. Executed on the 12 Aug. 1858. For 26 acres. Signed T. B. Mauldin, D.S.

John Erwin. Estate of John Erwin. Box 95 #1005. Probate Judge Office. Pickens, S.C. John Erwin died 4 Nov. 1864. On 10 Feb. 1869 the estate owned 300 acres on Town Creek, waters of 12 mile River joining land of Judge G. Ferguson, Absolem Roper, H. J. Anthony and others. Heirs:

Nancy Erwin the widow, chn., Wm. Erwin of Tenn., Thos. Rewin of N.C.
John B. Erwin and Rachel Hendricks of Pickens Co. and heirs of Geo.
Erwin a predeased son who are all minors in N.C. 6 minors of Isaac
Erwin a decd. son of N.C. 16 Oct. 1872 Harriet E. Erwin of Transylvania
Co., N.C. was gdn. of Susan L., M. A., Mitchel, Sarah E., John and M. E.
Erwin. 24 Feb. 1783 M. L. Orr was gdn. for Esther, Sarah J., Rebecca
G., Mary H., John C. and Sophia H. Erwin minors orphans of Geo. Erwin
decd. all of Transylvania Co., N.C.

Erwin. Deed from Wm. and Thos Erwin to John B. Erwin. No Ref. Clerk
of Court Office. Pickens, S.C. We Wm. Erwin and Thomas A. Erwin to
John B. Erwin all of Pickens Dist. for the sum of $200.00 have granted,
sold and released unto John B. Erwin all our undivided rights, titles,
claim and interest in the real estate of John Erwin decd. lying on
both sides of Town Creek waters of 12 mile River. Dated 5 Feb. 1866.
Wit: Jesse Ashworth, T. W. Clark. Signed: William Erwin and Thomas A.
Erwin. Recorded 31 May 1869.

ESKRIDGE

Burditt Eskridge. Will of Burditt Eskridge. Box 32 Pack 701. Probate
Judge Office. Abbeville, S.C. I Burditt Eskridge of Collington County
Ninety Six Dist. Being well in health and of perfect mind and memory
etc.etc. I leave my loving wife the third of all the land I possess
during her life time. I leave my eldest son Samuel that land lying
on Red Bank. I leave my second son Grigesbey so called the land that
was surveyed for Jacob Smith joining Enoch Grigsbey. At my wife
deceased her third of the land I leave to my son Richard. My negroes
to be equally divided between Samuel and the child my wife is now with,
and if the child is a boy each of my other sons shall give to him one
hundred pounds a piece. I appoint my wife Enoch Grigsbe and Jacob
Smith to be Executors. Dated 23 March 1779. Wit: Jno. Davis, Jacob
Smith, Sarah Smith. Signed Burditt Eskridge. An inventory was made
5 Sept. 1782. by Wm. Lisson, David Nicholson, John Davis. Durditt
Eskridge was of Richland Creek in 96 Dist.

EUBANKS

Thomas Eubanks - William Eubanks. Deed Thomas Eubanks to William Eubanks
Book H Page 84. Pendleton Dist. Anderson, S.C. Thomas Eubanks to
William Eubanks for the sum of $200.00 paid by William Eubanks hath
grant, bargain, sell and release a tract of land containing one hundred
and three acres. Originally granted to John Brady 19 Feb. 1791. This
deed made 8 Feb. 1804. Wit: Peter Edwards, John X Eubanks. Attested
by Peter Edwards before John Wilson J.Q. The John X Eubanks that
witnessed the deed was the Senr. Dated 9 Oct. 1804.

Eubanks. Deed from Eubanks to Perry. Book E Page 123. Clerk of Court
Office. Greenville, S.C. I William Eubanks to Philip Perry both of
Greenville Dist. Dated 11 Jan. 1798. In the sum of thirty pds.
sterling have granted, sold, released all that tract of land containing
150 acres on the still house branch of Reedy River and on the South
side of Brush Branch. Joining land of Perry, the Turpin line, Sedgings
line and Hugh Roarks line. Wit: Daniel Ayers, Obediah Bolding.
Signed William X Eubanks. Attested by Daniel Ayers before Jesse
Carter. 3 Dec. 1798.

Elisha Eubanks. Estate of Elisha Eubanks. Box 26 #17. Probate Judge
Office. Union, S.C. The appraisement made 30 Jan. 1841 of the
personal estate. The appraisers are Jno. Jennings, John Gagory, Isaac
Gregory.

Thomas Eubanks. Deed to Thomas Eubanks from James E. Hix. Book W
Page 547. Clerk of Court Office. Union, S.C. James E. Hix to Thomas
Eubanks both of Union Co. Dated 3 Jan. 1855. In the sum of $300.00

Hix hath granted, sold and released all that tract of land lying on the
South side of Union Village containing about one acre beginning on the
main road, South by land of C. Gage, other sides by Dr. J. E. Hix.
Wit: R. V. Gist, J. G. McKissick. Signed: J. E. Hix, seal.

John Eubanks. Deed to John Eubanks from William Porter. Book O Page
160. Clerk of Court Office. Union, S.C. I William Porter to John
Eubanks both of Union Co. for the sum of $123.00 have sold, granted
and release all that tract of land containing 80 acres on the waters
of Turkey Creek branch of Tygar River joining land of Jesse B. Kennedies
line. Dated 13 March 1818. Wit: Joseph Howard, Absalom Davis.
Signed William X Porter. Proved on oath of Absalom Davis before
Pressley Williams, J.P. Dated 20 Apr. 1818.

Elisha Eubanks. Deed to Elisha Eubanks from Samuel Beaty. Book W
Page 132. Clerk of Court Office. Union, S.C. I Samuel Beaty for the
consideration of a due record for Devine worship and the accommodation
of Baptist Denomination of Christians, I have granted and conveyed unto
Elisha Eubanks, Mordecai Chandler and George Fant in trust all that
tract of land being on the East side of the main road leading to Cooks
Bridge and supposed to contain seven and one half acres adj. land of
Wm. Sheltons. It is understood that I Samuel Beaty shall have use of
the spring and reserves the school house and the privilege of one when
ever necessary. Wit: John D. Wood, B. Johnson. Signed S. Beaty,
seal. Dated 2 Oct. 1833.

Thomas Eubanks. Estate of Thomas Eubanks. Box 19 #7. Probate Judge
Office. Union, S.C. We John F. Smith, Enoch Smith are bound unto
John J. Pratt, Ord. in the sum of $200.00 to make a true and perfect
inventory of the goods and chattels of the estate of Thomas Eubanks
decd. Dated 8 Dec. 1831. A letter in pack "J. J. Pratt, Ord. Union
Dist. Sir, it is my request that you appoint my brother John F. Smith
administrator of my deceased husband Thomas Eubanks estate. Yours
Respectfully. Anna Eubanks" Sale of the personal property held
13 Jan. 1832. Anna Eubanks bought all items but smith tools, one bull,
one piggon. The appraisers were: John C. Valentine, Asbury Rochester,
Willson Tollison.

Aaron Eubanks. Pack 14 In Equity, Pickens Dist., S.C. In Nov. 1856
Aaron Eubanks was mentioned as the husband of Harriet Johns daughter
Henry Johns decd. and his wife Martha Johns of Pickens Dist.

Eubanks Minors. Box 31 Pack 25. Probate Judge Office. Union, S.C.
We Elisha Eubanks, Mordicai Chandler, John Eubanks are bound unto
J. J. Pratt, Ord. U.D. in the sum of one thousand dollars. This
obligation is such that the above bounden Elisha Eubanks guardian for
Henry, Nancy, Jonathan, Isaac and Letty Eubanks minors and shall
carefully bring up the said minors with necessary meat, drink, washing,
lodging, apparel and learning according to their degree, etc.etc.
Dated 16 Nov. 1834. The parents of these children not given.

Letty Eubanks. Estate of Letty Eubanks. No Ref. Probate Judge Office.
Union Dist. To Hon. J. J. Pratt, Ord. The petition of Henry Eubanks
praying for a letter of Admr. on the estate of Letty Eubanks decd.
She departed this life about the last of Sept. 1844, intestate, being
entitled to a distributive share in her grandmother estate Mrs. Lucy
Ann Townsend estate, and other interest which remain unsettled. Dated
17 Jan. 1845. Signed Henry Eubanks.

John Eubanks. Deed from John Eubanks to William Edward. Book M Page
113. Clerk of Court Office. Anderson, S.C. Pendleton Dist. I John
Eubanks to William Edwards both of said Dist. for the sum of $150.00 do
grant, sell, release a certain tract of land containing 95 acres
joining Bradley's line on Gooldon's Creek. Dated 8 Feb. 1804. Wit:
Peter Edwards, Henry X Edwards. No signature.

John Eubanks Senr. Deed from John Eubanks Senr. to James Parson. Book
H Page 5. Probate Judge Office. Anderson, S.C. Pendleton Dist. I
John Eubanks Senr. to James Parson both of said Dist. for the sum of

$150.00 do grant, sell, release 40 1/2 acres of land beginning at a
dogwood North to a branch not named, etc. Dated 9 Nov. 1803. Wit:
Edmond Parson, William Parson. Signed John X Parson.

EWART

John Ewart. Will of John Ewart. Box 1 Pack 11. Probate Judge Office
Union, S. C. I John Ewart of Union Co. being very sick and weak in
body but of perfect mind and memory etc.etc. Pay all debts be justly
and lawfully. I give to my brother Robert Ewart living in Scotland
all that tract of land containing 524 acres lying on the waters of
Broad River. I give to my brother Mathew Ewart living in Scotland the
tract of land of 150 acres joining to Union Court House formerly
bought of Joseph Jones. I give to my brother William Ewart living in
Scotland all that tract of land containing 923 acres lying on Brown's
Creek a branch of Broad River. I give to my aforesaid brother Mathew
Ewart all the tract of land containing 300 acres on Fennings Creek with
a mill standing thereon. I give to my two trusty and well beloved
friends Thomas Blasingame Esq. and Andrew Terrance that negro wench
called Dianh now living at Thomas Vances. The negro fellow called
Charles now in possession of Thorowgood Chambers be sold and the money
be disposed of at the discretion of my Executors. I appoint my two
trusty friends Thomas Blasingame Esq. and Andrew Terrance, Executors.
Dated 31 Aug. 1788. Wit: William Morgan, Isaac Bogan, Moses Collyer.
Signed John Ewart, seal. An inventory made 31 Jan. 1789.

Andrew Ewart. Estate of Andrew Ewart Box 31 Pack 684. Probate Judge
Office. Abbeville, S.C. This I purpose to be my last will and testament as I find myself to be sound in every faculty and member of my
body altho weak. Put my body by my father and mother. I allow my
brother-in-law Adam Stewart to settle my affairs. "First the four
pound ten note that James Gilmore owes I leave it to pay the expenses
of my coffin, nails and some liquor to give the people at my wake and
a dram just before the start with my corpes," The four pounds, note
I allow it for to pay Pat. White, Wm. Richard, James Calhoun, and
Daniel Garvin what remains of these two notes I will to my brother-in-
law for his trouble. Next my nephew James who I will make my heir on
account that he is the name of my father in the first place I will to
my nephew Jas. Stewart my land, my watch, my Bible, my gun, slate,
pen knife, ink stand, reding comb for ever. Next I will to my cousin
Andrew Milligan my clothes all but what I wear to the earth forever.
The two thousand wt. of tobacco that Thos. White owes I divide this
way, first my uncle Jas. Milligan I will one hoggeshead to him for my
boarding for ever to be his and the other thousand wt. I will to my
friends this way Jain and Thomas White each one hundred wt. Caty and
Andrew White each one hundred wt. to my old aunt Mary McBride and cousin
Andrew McBride one hundred wt. each to my cousins Hugh Rachel and Mary
Milligan each one hundred wt. or the price ot it I will to these my
friends for ever the last 100 wt. I will to my nephew Ann Stewart with
my box that my cloath is in and my hat forever to her her's. I will to
my nephew Mary Stewart my bed and all my bed clothes for ever. I will
to my sister Mary Stewart my fine cloath the box that my papers is in
for ever to be her's. I will to my nephew Adam Stewart my dictionary
with all my other books except my arithatic which I allow to James.
I will to my brother-in-law my case and razors to be his while he
lives and then I allow James to get them. My saddle and bridle I will
to my cousin Andrew Milligan to be his for ever. What pay is coming
for teaching school I will to my three smallest nephews to pay for
schooling to them what Robt. Lawson owes I will to them too all but one
pair of shoes to my uncle James Milligan. (This will is ended with a
prayer.) Dated 2 Apr. 1795. No witnesses. Signed Andrew Ewart.
Recorded 13 Sept. 1799.

Elizabeth Fant. Book A. Page 232. Probate Judge Office. Pickens,
S.C. On 8 Oct. 1858 Elizabeth Fant was a legal heir of Daniel J.
Chapman, decd. of Pickens Dist. (Probably a widow P.Y.) other heirs
were James Chapman, Miles Chapman, Caroline Chapman.

FARR

James Farr. Deed to James Farr from William Keith, C.E.P.D. D. Book
D-1 Page 155. Clerk of Court Office. Pickens, S.C. This indenture
made 7 Oct. 1839 between William L. Keith Esq. Commissioner of the
Court of Equity and James Farr of Greenville Dist. Whereas Keziah
Hunt, Julia Ann Hendrick and John Hendrick on the 20 June exhibit their
bill of complaint in the Court of Equity, against Esli Hunt, Alpha
Hunt, Rose Hunt, Pilot Hunt, John Hunt, McDuffie Hunt and Keziah Hunt
heirs and representatives of Lucy Hunt decd. The cause was heard at
June Term and did order adjudge and decree that the tract of land be
sold at public out cry by the Comm. Sale held 7 Oct. 1839 accordingly
to custom of auction. Did sell to James Farr for the sum of two
thousand and five dollars he being the highest bidder. For 368 acres
lying on Saluda River. With another tract of 39 acres that widow
Keziah Hunt purchased from Anderson Smith since the death of her
husband. Wit: P. Alexander, E. M. Keith. Signed William L. Keith
C.E.P.D. seal. Recorded 25 Nov. 1839.

Delilah Farr. Deed from Delilah Farr, at al. to George W. Farr. Book
K-1 Page 199. Probate Judge Office. Pickens, S.C. We Delilah Farr,
Frances M. Groce, James M. Farr, Thomas F. Farr, Baylus Farr, Elizabeth
Hunt, and Martin Hunt Junr. heirs of James Farr decd. of Greenville
Dist. For the sum of five thousand and fifty five dollars and seventy
five cents paid us by George W. Farr of Pickens Dist. All that tract
of land in Pickens Dist. on Saluda River contianing 561 3/4 acres.
Dated 20 June 1863. Wit: W. D. Therlheld, Frances A. Farr. Signed:
Delilah X Farr, Frances Groce, James M. Farr, Thomas J. Farr. Elizabeth
Hunt and Martin Hunt. On 3 Dec. 1863. Mrs. Elizabeth Hunt wife of
Martin Hunt Junr. appeared before Willis D. Therlheld, N.P. and Mag.
and did renounce, release her dower to the said land. Signed Elizabeth
Hunt. On 12 Sept. 1863 Mrs. Frances M. Farr wife of James M. Farr
and Mrs. Elizabeth P. Farr wife of Thomas J. Farr did appear before
W. D. Therlkeld, N.P. and Mag. did renounce, release and relinquish
her dower to the said land. Signed F. M. Farr and Elizabeth P. Farr.

James M. Farr. Estate of James M. Farr. Box 90 #945. Probate Judge
Office. Pickens, S.C. Est. Admr. 9 March 1881 by Frances M. Farr,
widow, John T. Gossett, G. W. Farr, Henry W. Farr who are bound unto
Olin L. Durant, Ord. in the sum of $1,000.00.

Maggie J. Farr. Estate of Maggie J. Farr. Box 10 #184. Probate Judge
Office. Pickens, S.C. On 12 May 1885 Frances M. Farr, Hannah E. Cox,
Jas. E. Cox are bound unto J. H. Newton, Ord. in the sum of $200.00
Frances M. Farr gdn. for Maggie J. Farr minor dtr. of Frances and J. M.
Farr.

Eloise May Farr. Estate of Eloise May Farr. Box 123 #11. Probate
Judge Office. Pickens, S. C. On 28 Nov. 1893 Henry W. Farr, Frances
Moore, Mrs. F. M. Farr are bound unto J. B. Newberry Ord. in the sum
of $90.00. Born 23 May 1886 dtr. of Marther E. Farr, H. W. Farr.

G. W. Farr. Estate of G. W. Farr. Box 127 #12. Probate Judge
Office. Pickens Co., S.C. I G. W. Farr being desirous before I die
of making and equitable disposition of such property as I may have, etc.
Pay all debts with money on hand or in bank or use any property for
this purpose. I give to my son John P. Farr that tract of land containing 146 acres on waters of Saluda River, adj. land of Ware, on
West by Pickens, Freeman and Davis. I give to my daughter Frances E.

Farr all that tract of land containing 198 acres on Saluda River.
Bounded on North by Ware, on West by Marion Bazils land. I give to
my daughter Delia Farr all those two tracts of land adj. each other on
Saluda River and branch waters containing 202 acres bounded by Marion
Brazil, Norris, Pink Gossett, S. M. Cox, John R. Gossett and Saluda
River. To sell all personal property and divide equally between my
chn. I appoint my son John P. Farr and Nephew E. M. Hunt my Executors.
Dated 13 Nov. 1896. Wit: Bertha McNabb, J. E. Farr, George McAdams.
Signed G. W. Farr. He died 10 Feb. 1897. Filed 24 Feb. 1897.

FAULKNER

Faulkner. Faulkner Inf. Pack 9. Equity Rec. of John and Wm. Spence.
Abbeville, S.C. John Faulkner married Mary Spence of Abbeville Dist.
who was a daughter of James Spence decd. Her father was the son of
James Spence Senr. decd. and his widow, Ann Spence who died 9 March
1854. Filed 28 Apr. 1856.

FENNELL

William M. Fennell. Estate of William M. Fennell. Book B Page 94.
Probate Judge Office. Pickens, S.C. On 27 Nov. 1865 William M.
Fennell decd. owned 70 acres of land on Hamby Branch of Three and Twenty
Creek, adj. land of H. J. Fennell, L. J. Hamilton and others. Left a
widow Mary A. E. Fennell who has intermarried with Harvey Jones. His
father Hardy J. Fennell and the following brothers and sisters viz:
Evaline Hollingsworth, F. G. Fennell, Thomas Hinton and wife Elizabeth,
Mary King and Martha Fennell all living in this dist. and Warren J.
Fennell. 27 Nov. 1865 W. J. Fennell and wife Martha Fennell heirs of
Sarah Chapman, decd.

FERGUSON

Thomas Ferguson. Will of Thomas Ferguson, Apt. 8 File 540. Probate
Judge Office. Greenville, S.C. I Thomas Ferguson of Greenville
Dist. being very sick in body but of sound mind and memory, etc.etc.
I give to my wife Rachael Ferguson one mare, saddle and bridle all my
stock of cattle and hogs. I give to my son Thos. Ferguson one iron
kettle, one mattock. All my clothing to be divided between my sons
Thos. and Burrel Ferguson. My writing desk I leave to Jesse Elrod.
There shall be no appraisement or inventory made of my estate. Make
wife Rachael Executrix and son Thos. Ferguson and son-in-law Jesse
Elrod executors. Dated 14 Jan. 1822. Wit: Jeremiah Cleveland,
Alfred M. Cleveland. Signed: Thos. Ferguson. Will proved 13 day
March 1822.

James Ferguson, Sr. Estate of James Ferguson, Sr. Box 17 #213.
Probate Judge Office. Pickens, Dist. Est. Admr. 17 Jan. 1848 by
Nancy, Judge G. Ferguson, W. L. Keith are bound unto Wm. D. Steel, Ord.
in the sum of $12,000.00. Settlement made 1 April 1850. Paid Nancy
Ferguson her share $2157.66. Paid Prior Alexander gdn. for Elizabeth
Jane Alexander $894.63. Paid John Ferguson $61.30 1/2. Paid James T.
Ferguson $259.91. Paid atty. for Nancy Barrett $678.43. Paid atty.
for Jas. and Mary Stephens $914.01 1/2. Paid Benton Freeman $785.96½.
Jane Freeman recd. property also. Prior Alexander married Elizabeth
Jane dtr. of James Ferguson. Mary Stephen a dtr. was of Union Co.,
Ga. and left 7 heirs.

Nancy Ferguson. Will of Nancy Ferguson. Box 21 #253. Probate Judge
Office. Pickens, S. C. I Nancy Ferguson being in a low state of
health yet of sound mind and memory. I will to my oldest daughter
Mary Stephens one hundred dollars. I will to my second daughter Jane
Freeman one hundred dollars. I give to my third daughter Nancy Barrett

one hundred dollars. I will to my oldest son John Ferguson one hundred
dollars. I will to my next son James T. Ferguson one hundred dollars.
I will to my granddaughter Elizabeth Alexander one hundred dollars as
the representative of my youngest daughter Elizabeth Alexander decd. All
other items and monies to go to J. G. Ferguson. I appoint J. G. Ferguson
my executor. Dated 4 Apr. 1850. Wit: Reese Bowen, Martin Barrett,
James Major. Signed Nancy X Ferguson. Proven 20 May 1850. (In proving
the will it states that she was about 80 yrs. old and died about three
weeks after will made.

James T. Ferguson. Estate of James T. Ferguson. Box 51 #561. Probate
Judge Office. Pickens, Dist. Est. Admr. 13 June 1859 by J. D. Ferguson,
E. A. Ferguson, Samuel Reid, Miles M. Norton who are bound unto W. J.
Parson, Ord. in the sum of $40,000.00. On 28 Jan. 1861 heirs were Anna
Ferguson widow, Benjamin Holder and wife E. M., James Ferguson, Joseph
Ferguson, McElroy Jameson and wife C. M., Elisha A. Ferguson, Afterty
Ferguson, William Ferguson. 27 Feb. 1861. Paid McElroy Jameson
guardian for F. A. E. Kirksey $2,338.75. 12 Sept. 1860. Paid Delilah
Ferguson $10.00.

John Ferguson. Estate of John Ferguson. Box 39 #443. Probate Judge
Office. Pickens, S.C. Est. Admr. 1 Sept. 1856 by James T. Ferguson,
Lemuel Thomas, Daniel Alexander who are bound unto W. J. Parson, Ord.
in the sum of $8,000.00 Est. Admr. again 13 June 1859 by Delila
Ferguson, Miles M. Norton, J. E. Hogood, R. E. Holcombe who are bound
unto W. J. Parson, Ord. in the sum of $8,000.00.

Elisha Ferguson. Will of Elisha Ferguson, Box 59 #635. Probate Judge
Office. Pickens, S.C. I Elisha A. Ferguson of the Hains Place in
Pickens Dist. being of sound mind and memory, etc.etc. I will to my
beloved wife the land known as the Hanis Place lying on Town Creek, adj.
land of E. H. Griffin, James Ferguson together with what is due me from
my father's place, during her natural life. Should she have an heir the
property to be its when my wife dies. If she have no heirs I wish my
effects to be disposed as follow. I wish all property to be sold and
divided as, E. M. Holder, brother Joseph five dollars, James five dollars,
sister Margaret C. Jameson five hundred dollars, brother Asterby five
dollars, William five dollars, Frances N. Kirksey five dollars, the
remainder to be divided my brothers and sisters and wife. I appoint
Noah Richardson to be Executor. Dated 8 May 1861. Jno. L. Templeton,
Samuel F. Templeton, Thos. H. Boggs. Signed E. A. Ferguson, seal.
Filed 2 Sept. 1861.

James Ferguson. Estate of James Ferguson, Pack 1-A In Equity. Clerk of
Court Office. S. C. Your orator Judge G. Ferguson sheweth to your Hon.
that James Ferguson departed this life 29 Dec. 1847. With considerable
real estate Tract #1 On Flat Creek and Toxaway River of 139 acres. #2
Known as Little horse pasture on Toxaway River of 113 acres. #3 known
as the Covington Place adj. land of James Crow of 868 acres. #4 In
Laurens Dist. known as the Babb place. All subject to distribution
amongst, Nancy Ferguson the widow. Mary Stevens wife of James Stevens
of Georgia. Jane Freeman wife of Benton Freeman, Nancy Barett widow
of Caswell Barett decd. on the 11 Dec. 1830, John Ferguson, the legal
heir of Elizabeth Alexander decd. she was the wife of Prior Alexander.
She died 20 June 1836. Leaving one child Elizabeth Alexander a minor
under 12 years and not represented by gdn. Filed 4 Feb. 1848. The
child was a niece of your orator Judge G. Ferguson. On 21 Nov. 1850
Prior Alexander recd. $80.10 for his ward Elizabeth Jane Alexander. On
4 Nov. John Ferguson recd. his share. No date giave on paper.

Andrew Ferguson. Will of Andrew Ferguson, Box 15 #194. Proabe Judge
Office. Pickens, Dist. I Andrew Ferguson Senr. Being weak in body
but of sound mind and memory, etc.etc. I will to my wife Mary the
plantation, goods, chattles during her natural life and after her death
to be sold and money equally divided between my children and legtees
of sd. estate. I will Sarah Ann Morehead one cow and calf, one bed
and furniture as her portion when she is eighteen years old. I also
give to her five dollars in store for dressing her as Exec. may think
fit. Sell off 150 acres between Jarrett and James Ferguson to pay

debts and expenses. Dated 28 Apr. 1843. I appoint Thomas Farmer of
Franklin Co., Ga. and James Ferguson as Executors. Wit: Jefferson
Dalton, Levi Tannery, Samuel Addis. Signed Andrew Ferguson, Senr.
Codicil. I will to my two grandchildren Andrew Rolan and Thadias
Warren Ferguson these two is to have an equal share, provided they
stay with their grandmother till 21. Proven 16 Nov. 1843.

John Ferguson. Warrant for John Ferguson. Pack 402 #2. Clerk of
Court Office. Pickens, S.C. On 17 Sept. 1883 George Hagood states
that on or about 3rd of Aug. 1883 just after a kind of family row at
my house with my step son John Ferguson did have him arrested for
carrying a concealed weapon.

Ferguson Minors. Box 2 #35. In Equity, Clerk of Court Office. Pickens
S. C. On 2 Sept. 1861 Delilah Ferguson, James E. Hagood, John Bowen
are bound unto Robt. A. Thompson C. in Equity in the sum of $6,000.00.
Delilah Ferguson gdn. for Nancy B. and Judge Harrison Ferguson children
of John Ferguson decd. Over 14 years of age. gdn. for John Earl
Ferguson, James Irvin Ferguson minors under 14 years, dated 17 Nov. 1859

Anna Ferguson. Estate of Anna Ferguson. Box 121 #2. Probate Judge
Office. Pickens, S.C. Est. Admr. 17 Jan. 1893 by John T. Ferguson,
J. E. Garrick, Juliuse Boggs who are bound to J. B. Newberry, Ord. in
the sum of $40.00.

Afterby Ferguson. Estate of Afterby Ferguson. Box 103 #1083. Probate
Judge Office. Pickens, S.C. Est. Admr. 6 Nov. 1872 by Sara Jane
Ferguson, James McAdams, Wm. M. Ferguson who are bound unto I. H.
Philpot, Ord. in the sum of $1,000.00. Afterby died in Sept. 1872.

Joseph D. Ferguson. Assault. Pack 604 #9. Clerk of Court Office.
Pickens, S.C. Mrs. Louisa E. Ferguson of Pickens Dist. made oath that
Joseph D. Ferguson did on 14 June 1866 attempt to shoot her with his
gun and also at the same time and place did assault her on the head
several times by striking her with his fist and also other injuries.
She further says that on Sat. the 11 Aug. he did attempt to shoot her
with a postol at the baptizing near Secona Church and did disturb a
religious assembly.

FIELDS

John Field Sr. Pack 124. Clerk of Court Office. Pickens, S.C. John
Fields, Sr. to Josiah Trotter both of Pickens Dist. Dated 18 May
1842. For the sum of $75.00 a tract of land of fifty acres on branches
of Georges Creek, waters of Saluda River. Wit: Benjamin J. Williams,
Eli Watson. Signed John Fields, Sr., seal. Attested by B. J. Williams
before J. M. Barton, M.P.D. 26 Aug. 1842.

John Fields, Sr. Will of John Fields, Sr. Box 11 #142. Probate Judge
Office. Pickens, S.C. I John Fields Sr. being weak in body but of
sound mind and memory etc. I give to my wife Rahab Fields the free
privilage of six hundred acres where I now live, to remain her right
and property during her natural life, then divided between my children.
I also give to Rahab negroes Isaac, Joanna and her two chn. Dick and Ben
to dispose as she pleases. Wife to have choice of stock, cattle, hogs,
horse, saddle, household furniture etc. All ready money and notes. The
rest and remainder to be sold and divided between my children (not
named here). I appoint Josiah Trotter executor. Wit: Levi, J. B.
Williams, Joel M. Walker, Eli Watson. Signed John Fields Sr., seal.

John Fields, Jr. vs. Exec. of John Fields, Sr. (No ref. given; this
is in Equity, no date). Clerk of Court. Pickens Dist. Pickens, S.C.
John Fields Jr. vs Josiah Trotter Exc. That his father was in advanced
age and could not recognize his own hand writing etc. That Trotter
exercised an influence over him etc. Eli Watson testifies that he
lived with Fields for about two months and he could go about the house
and was of sound mind. He died in Aug. 1842 leaving five heirs, viz:

John, Abner J. Fields, Susan wife of Michl Kenemore, Elizabeth Gibson, widow, Jane wife of Bailey Barton. On 19 Dec. 1843 John Fields Jr. states that Elizabeth Gibson was divorced who resided in Fayett Co., Ga.

John Fields, Sr. Estate of John Fields, Sr. Box 47 #521. Probate Judge Office. Pickens, S. C. Est. Admr. 22 April 1845 by Rahab Fields, W. L. Keith, James Laurance, John Ferguson who are bound unto Wm. D. Steele, Ord. in the sum of $8,000.00. Paid A. G. Fields share $124.12. Paid Susan Kennmore share $172.29. Paid Elizabeth Gibson share $52.87. On 2 Dec. 1846 Elizabeth Gibson was of DeKalb Co., Ga. Rahab Fields the widow cit. was pub. at Poplar Springs Church.

Joseph A. Fields. Estate of Joseph A. Fields. Box 11 #141. Probate Judge Office. Pickens, S. C. Est. Admr. 21 Mar. 1842 by Major John Arial, John Bowen, Wm. S. Birge, who are bound unto Jas. H. Dendy, Ord. in the sum of $1200.00. On 11 Jan. 1843 paid Mrs. Elizabeth Fields on an acct. owing by est. $15.65. This estate was Admr. again on 6 Mar. 1848 by Elizabeth Fields, widow, Reese, Thos. H. Bowen, Judge G. Ferguson who are bound unto W. D. Steele, Ord. in the sum of $18,000.00. No heirs given.

Jeremiah Fields. Estate of Jeremiah Fields. Box 47 #521. Probate Judge Office. Pickens, S. C. Jeremiah Fields was from Cherokee Co., Ga. He had seven tracts of land in S. C. totaling over 5,000 acres viz 1,000 acres on Big Laurel, 664 acres on Nine Times Creek, 794 acres on Big Eastatoe, 502 acres on Nixes Branch, 602 acres Big Eastatoe, 648 acres on Jocasse River, 265 acres on Devils Fork. Also 100 acres in Buncombe Co., N. C. On 25 May 1857 Elias E. and Elijah N. Fields as Admr. of the estate appointed Reese Bowen of Pickens Dist., S. C. as an attorney to sell the land. Heirs are John D. Fields, B. M. Fields, James N. Fields, Malinda wife of Joseph Donaldson, heirs of Joseph A. Fields, Mary wife of Amos L. Southerland, W. T. Fields and J. M. Fields of Pickens, S. C.

John D. Fields. Estate of John D. Fields. Box 56 #613. Probate Judge Office, Pickens, S. C. Est. Admr. 17 Oct. 1860 by Reese Bowen, James E. Hagood, W. N. Craig who are bound unto W. E. Holcombe, Ord. in the sum of $115.00. He was of Lumpkin County Georgia.

Fields Minor. Box 2 #37. In Equity. Clerk of Court Office. Pickens, S. C. On 10 Nov. 1848 John M. Fields a minor over 14 years son of Joseph and Elizabeth Fields. Reece Bowen his uncle gdn. Also gdn. of Wm. T. Fields. 17 Mar. 1857 Recd. of Admr. of Jeremiah Fields decd. $500.00

Rahab Fields. Estate of Rahab Fields. Box 98 #1027. Probate Judge Office. Pickens, S. C. I Rahab Fields being of sound mind and memory etc. I give unto Jane Elizabeth Thacker the tract of land I now live on lying on waters of Georges Creek adj. land of G. W. Higgins, A. McDuffie Hamilton and others containing 67 acres. To her and her heirs G. J. Thacker and Frances E. Thacker. I give to the said Jane Elizabeth all personal property of every kind whatsoever, bonds, notes, monies, etc. To pay all debts and receive all debts due me. I appoint Alfred M. Folger my sole executor. Dated 25 July 1868. Wit: Alfred M. Folger, Alonso M. Folger, Laura M. Folger. Signed Rahab X Fields. Will proven 14 Apr. 1870.

Abner G. Fields. Estate of Abner G. Fields. Box 104 #1085. Probate Judge Office. Pickens, S. C. I give to my beloved wife Jane Fields all my real estate also one bed and furniture for her use during her natural life. At her death to be divided between my two sons William G. Fields and O. Perry Fields. The land division as, start at the top of the ridge between A. G. Fields and Taylor Odell, running to 12 mile River etc. The land adj. Mary Alexander and John P. Perritt I give to son O. Perry, with William taking the other. They are come into full possession at the death of their mother. The personal property to be sold and divided between my daughters viz; Mary Fields, Milly Boyd, Martha Ariel, and my grand son James A. Lewis to share with my daughters. William to take care of his mother and be guardian of

James A. Lewis. I appoint William G. Fields my executor. Dated 23
May 1871. Wit: W. T. Odell, F. A. Miles, R. C. Clayton. Signed
Abner G. Fields. Will proven 15 July 1871.

Joseph Fields. Cruelty to animals. Pack 251 #5. Clerk of Court Office
Pickens, S. C. M. F. Hester sworn, I saw Joseph Fields whipping the
horse, there were whelps on him, wet with seat, this was in town, the
horse was trotting. L. C. Thornley sworn, that he was of the firm of
Hagood and Thornley & Co. He hired Joseph Fields the horse and buggy
to go to Cold Springs, he took the horse from the stable, I was at
Bruce store when he came by Capt. Griffin in a sweeping trot. He
passed through town and was gone about two hours. The horse had three
whelps and so stiff he could hardly come out the stalbe, this was
caused by over driving. Joseph Fields sworn, He went to Cold Springs
Church, and after preaching he went to his brother-in-laws. On 16
May 1894 he was found not guilty.

William G. Fields. Deed from William G. Fields to Bailey Barton.
Pack 228 #4. Clerk of Court Office. Pickens, S. C. Dated 22 Jan.
1835. William G. Field of Herd Co. in Georgia and Bailey Barton of
Pickens, S. C. In the sum of $100.00 do sell a tract of 125 acres
lying on South Fork of 12 Mile River waters of Keowee River. One part
being first granted to John Young 4 Sept. 1786, and another part
granted unto James Jett. Wit: Abner G. Fields and A. Akins. Signed
Wm. G. Field. Proved by Archibald Akins on 15 Mar. 1836.

John Fields, Sr. Deed to John Fields, Sr. from Wm. H. Terrell. Pack
228 #1. Clerk of Court. Pickens, S. C. Pendleton Dist. William H.
Terrell of Chattooga River to John Fields, Sr. of Pickens, S. C.
Dated 1 Apr. 1814. In consideration of $800.00, sell a tract of land
of 500 acres being part of two tracts from Charles Lay to G. W. Terrell
and William H. Terrell lying on 12 Mile River. Adj. Salmons and
Cammorn lands. Wit: Bailey Barton, William R. Cochran. Signed:
Wm. H. Terrell, seal. On 15 Jan. 1814 Cynthia Terrell relinquished
her rights of dower on the land before Joseph Davis, J.I.C.

John Field, Sr. Deed to John Field, Sr. from Aramanos Anderson. Pack
211 #13. Clerk of Court Office. Pendleton Dist. Dated 1 Feb. 1812
in consideration of fifty dollars for fifty acres lying on South fork
of 12 Mile River. Wit: Isaac X Anderson, John Garner. Signed
Aramanos Anderson, seal. Deed proven by John Garner before G. W.
Terrell, J.P. 10 Feb. 1812.

John Fields, Sr. Deed from John Fields, Sr. to Bailey Barton. Pack 226
#8. Clerk of Court Office. Pickens, S. C. Dated 29 Aug. 1822. John
Fields, Sr. to Bailey Barton and wife Jinny. For love and affections
which I bear toward my son in law and his wife, I do give, release a
tract of land containing five hundred acres, first granted to Charles
Lay from Lay to Terrell, from Terrell to Fields, lying on 12 Mile
River, adj. lands of Solmons and Earles & Cammorns. Wit: John D.
Fields, John Fields, Jr. Signed John Fields, Sr. Proved by John D.
Fields before John Clayton. 14 Dec. 1822.

William T. Fields. Dr. William T. Fields, affacavit, Pack 359 #4.
Clerk of Court Office. Pickens, S. C. "Personally appeared before me
W. T. Fields and made oath that he is a regularly licensed physician
living in Pickens Co. State aforesaid and that he is practicing medicine by authority of a diploma granted to him by the Medical College
of Charleston in the State of aforesaid." Sworn to before me this 31
May 1882. J. J. Lewis, C.C.P. Signed W. T. Fields.

                              FINCH

Isabella Finch. Will of Isabella Finch. Vol. 9 page 162. Probate
Judge Office, Charleston, S. C. I Isabella Finch of Charleston, S. C.
a widow, being infirm of body and of advanced age but of sound mind,
etc. I will my just debts be paid, and I will my negroes be sold with

all and singular my messuages lands and tenements whatsoever. I give
to Elizabeth Mackay, Lydian Mackay and Meek, Sarah Nelson and Thomas
Brickles the sum of twenty pds. to each and every of them. I give unto
Ann Remington the sum of one hundred pds. I give to her brother Robert
Remington one hundred pds. I give to Margret Glen fifty pds. I give
to Margaret Hamilton Forty pds. I will that one hundred pds. be put
on interest for the use of the Minister of the Scotch Meeting in
Charleston for ever. I give to Margaret Cofton twenty pds. I give to
Isabella Robinson twenty pds. I give to each of my executors one ring.
I give to my cousin Jennet Ackles in Ervine Scotland the best of my
wearing apparel. All the rest and residue I give to my cousin Robert
Ackles and John Ackles. I appoint Robert Ackles, John Remington,
William Glen and George Marshall executors. Dated 14 July 1757. Wit:
Wm. Pincknet, John Remington, Junr., I. Joyley. Signed Isabella X
Finch. seal. Proved in Court of Ord. 28 Aug. 1761.

FINDLEY

Hezekiah Findley. Estate of Hezekiah Findley. Book A, page 168.
Probate Judge Office. Pickens, S. C. to W. J. Parson, Ord. The
widow of said Findley petition for an order to sell the real estate of
the decd. on the waters of Shoal Creek of Saluda River. Adj. lands of
Roswell Hill, Pachel Norton and others. Containing 92 acres. His
heirs are Elizabeth X Crain, Martha J. Findley, Joseph Findley, John M.
Findley. Dated 20 Feb. 1857. Sale to be held on first Monday next on
credit of one year. Signed: W. J. Parson, Ord. The bond for this
estate in Box 39 #440. Est. Admr. 23 Nov. 1855 by David Freeman,
J. W. L. Carey who are bound unto W. J. Parson, Ord. in the sum of
$600.00. On 1 Jan. 1860 paid the widow her share $76.67. Paid David
Freeman gdn. for Martha, Joseph and John Finley their share $174.78.

Thomas W. Finley. Estate of Thomas W. Finley. Box 64 #689. Probate
Judge Office. Pickens, S. C. Est. Adrm. 6 Oct. 1862 by Levi N.
Robins, Joseph Burnett, Daniel Hughes who are bound unto W. E. Hol-
combe, Ord. in the sum of $500.00. He left a widow and 2 children.
No names given.

John Fendley. Estate of John Fendley. Box 83 #877. Probate Judge
Office. Pickens, S. C. I JOHN FENDLEY being of sound mind and perfectly at myself and in my right sences, etc.etc. I will to my two
daughters Lucinda Fendley, Mary Fendley my house, household furniture,,
one hundred acres of land, also one cow and calf. Also they may have
from my property to support them comfortably during their life. Dated
15 Apr. 1874. Wit: T. P. Looper, Joseph Looper. Signed John X
Fendley. Proven 7 Octo. 1880. On 15 Mar. 1881 paid the heirs of
Hezekiah Fendley decd. $390.20. Paid heirs of William R. Fendley
balance due them after deduction $302.50 value of land given by John
Findley decd. $87.70 paid the heirs of J. W. Findley balance due them
after deducting $315.50 value of land given by John Findley decd.
$74.70. Paid the heirs of Frankey Findley Decd. $390.20. Paid
Margaret Hollingsworth $390.20. John Findley died in Sept. 1880.
Owned 100 acres lying in Dacusville Township adj. lands of Joseph
Looper, Levi Wimpy and others.

Elizabeth Finley. Box 97 #1021. Probate Judge Office. Pickens, S. C.
On 30 Sept. 1869 Elizabeth Knox widow of John Knox decd. Now wife of
C. W. Finley states that John C. Knox died in 1864 leaving a widow
with children, all minor... not named.

Thomas M. Finley. Estate of Thomas M. Finley. Pack 325. Clerk of
Court Office, Abbeville, S. C. Abbeville Dist. To the Honr. the
Chancellors, Your orator William Henry Parker Esq. states. That on
7 Feb. 1849 Henry A. Jones Esq. of this Court acting under its order
made a case of Thomas M. Finley, Admr. and others against Alexander
Hunter Executor did sell a tract of land which Thomas M. Finley purchased for seven hundred dollars. Paying one half and giving a mortgage
for the other, payable one year from date. Land lying near Mount

Carmel, adj. land of Andrew Weed and others. The said Finley lived in
Overton Co., Tenn. departed this life in Sept. 1849. Leaving wife
Lititia Finley and chn. Nancy Jane, Oscar, Amanda all of age. Nevill,
Stephen, Sarah, Lucy and Granville all minors. Wife has been made Admr.
of the estate. A letter of Admr. for this state will be applied for
shortly. Filed 27 Feb. 1860.

Morning Jane Findley. Box 94 #992. Probate Judge Office. Pickens,
S. C. Morning Jane Findley on 20 Feb. 1886 ment. as an heir of Abel
Hendrick of Pickens Dist. Probably a daughter. Hendrick est Admr. 18
Sept. 1884.

FISHER

Nicholas Fisher. Will of Nicholas Fisher. Apt. 8 File 587. Probate
Judge Office. Greenville, S. C. I Nicholas Fisher, Sr. being in per-
fect mind and memory, etc.etc. I give to my beloved wife Elizabeth
Fisher one third of my lands, goods, and chattels during her life time
and after her decd. the land to be divided between my sons Thomas
Fisher and Nicholas Fisher. After my lawful debts are paid, I give to
my youngest son Nicholas a horse colt and my saddle the rest of my
stock to be divided between Thomas Fisher, Peggy Fisher, Anice Fisher,
Nicholas Fisher. I appoint John and Thomas Fisher my sole executors.
I give to my son John Fisher five shillings sterling. I give to my
son James Fisher five shillings sterling. I give to my daug. Mary Tubb
one shilling sterling. I give to my daughter Salley Cooksey one
shilling sterling. I give to my daughter Elizabeth McVey one shilling
sterling. Dated 2 Apr. 1794. Wit: Elijah Hutchinson, Elizabeth X
Hutchinson. Signed Nicholas Fisher, seal. N.B.... I appoint and make
James Tubb, Elizabeth Fisher, John and Thomas Fisher my Executrix and
Executors. No probate date given.

Mrs. Fisher. Heir of Mrs. Fisher. Box 94 #987. Probate Judge Office.
Pickens, S. C. L. C. Hester decd. whose est. was Admr. 10 Sept. 1866
in Pickens Dist. ment. as heirs, the heirs of a Mrs. Fisher. No other
names given.

FITZGERALD

Ambrose Fitzgerald. Will of Ambrose Fitzgerald Box 4 #47. Probate
judge Office. Pickens, S. C. I Ambrose Fitzgeraldbeing of sound and
disposing mind and memory. etc.etc. I desire that my just debts be
paid from the ready money that Mr. Aaron Terrel has for me, and a
receipt for the amount in the hand of Jesse Jenkins, after debts are
paid I give the remainder to my son Eli Fitzgerald. The land on Tugee-
loo River to be sold and the monies divided between sons Ambrose and
Dudley Fitzgerald, if the money is more than $200.00 the overplus to be
paid to granddaughter Julity Rowel, with one feather bed and furniture.
To my son Garret Fitzgerald one dollar in addition to what he has. To
my daughter Elizabeth Anderson one dollar in addition to what she has.
To daughter Anna Rowel one dollar in addition to what she has. The
rest of property to be sold and money divided between sons Thomas,
Ambrose, Dudley, Eli. I appoint Capt. David Sloan and son Eli Fitz-
gerald executors. Wit: Thomas Lamar, James Adair, Elizabeth Lamar.
Signed: Ambrose X Fitzgerald. Proven 5 May 1834 (Made 8 Apr. 1834)

FITZPATRICK

Michael Fitzpatrick. #12. Clerk of Court Office. Pickens, S. C. An
inquest was taken at Patsey Creek in Pickens Dist. The jury brought it
out that he came to his death by the visitation of God. James J.
Hunter says; I was passing Michael house, stopped to ask if his apples
was ripe, was door open, stepped to the door and saw him lying on the

floor, the same way the jurors saw him. I went straight home and told my father about it, this was the evening of June 30. Fredrick O. Herrin says that he stopped to ask for apples, and found Michael on the floor. He went to Mr. Cooks and told him, this was just before sunset June 30. John R. Cook says, that F. O. Herrin by his house and told that Michael was dead and that with his father and David Hunter they to Michael house and found it was so. That he never heard any threats against him. Enoc Cook says he was the decd. last Monday evening and he complained of being unwell. John Morton says; That William Welch told him that he and Fitzpatrick had a few hard words about a month ago. A. West says; About a month ago he told Welch that he and Fitzpatrick should live together and not argue. Welch said it he knew Fitzpatrick was the blame he would use him rudely, but nothing like taking him life.

Michael Fitzpatrick. Estate of Michael Fitzpatrick. Box 58 #632. Probate Judge Office. Pickens, S. C. Est. Admr. 30 July 1861 by John B. Morton, Ephraim M. Perry, H. R. Capehart who ard bound unto W. E. Holcombe, Ord. in the sum of $200.00.

FLEMING

John L. Fleming. Will of John L. Fleming, Box 61 #661. Probate Judge Office. Pickens, S. C. I John L. Fleming, do make this my last will and testament etc. I desire all just debts be paid. I will to my beloved wife Martha all my real and personal property during her natural life time, if she marry then my property be sold and divided between she and my children, share and share alike. Dated 15 Jan. 1862. Wit: J. Hagood, William X Finley, Z. C. Pulliam. Signed: John L. Fleming. Proven 26 May 1862.

FLOYD

James Floyd, Sr. Estate of James Floyd, Sr. Apt. 3 File 174. Probate Judge Office. Greenville, S. C. Dated 28 April 1797. Heirs were; William Floyd, Elizabeth Creemer, Sarah Dowdle, Nancy Elliott, James Floyd, Jr., John Floyd, Richard Jasper Floyd, Mary Lee, Lee Floyd, Milly Haise (or Hays). No other inf.

John Floyd. Estate of John Floyd. Box 72 #770. Probate Judge Office. Pickens Dist. Est. Admr. 2 Jan. 1864 by Madison F. Mitchell, Jas. E. Hagood, Allen Thrift who are bound unto W. E. Holcombe, Ord. in the sum of $4,000.00.

FOLGER

Dr. Alfred M. Folger. Box 113 #1084. Probate Judge Office. Pickens, S. C. Est. Admr. 6 Dec. 1880 by Orlando C. Folger, Elias Day, W. A. Lesley who are bound unto O. L. Durant, Ord. in the sum of $1,500.00.

Frank Folger. Estate of J. Frank Folger. Box 115 #18. Probate Judge Office. Pickens, S. C. Est. Admr. 7 June 1888 by J. McD. Bruce, A. W. Folger, W. W. Hagood, J. E. Boggs who are bound unto Jas. B. Newberry, Ord. in the sum of $7,000.00. He died 7 May 1888. A. W. Folger, a brother. J. McD. Bruce a nephew.

Earnest Folger. Estate of Earnest Folger. Box 116 #2. Probate Judge Office. Pickens, S. C. Est. Admr. 2 July 1888 by A. W. Folger, W. M. Hagood, J. E. Robinson, who are bound unto J. B. Newberry, Ord. in the sum of $218.662/3. A. W. Folger gdn. for Earnest Folger minor under 21 yrs. Son of J. Frank Folger.

Folger Minors. Box 116 #3. Probate Judge Office. Pickens, S. C. On 3 July 1888 J. McD. Bruce, J. E. Boggs, W. M. Hagood are bound unto

J. B. Newberry, Ord. in the sum of $537.32. J. McD. Bruce gdn. for
Lucie and Marie Folger minors under 21 yrs. Chn. of J. Frank Folger
decd. A. R. Newton Folger, Laura Folger O'Dell, Mary Folger of Easley,
S. C. were relatives.

Lena F. Folger. Box 142 #7. Probate Judge Office. Pickens, S. C. On
19 April 1904 Lena F. Folger recd. a share from the est. of Samuel G.
Higgins who died in Easley, 22 Dec. 1902.

R. C. Folger, M.D. Affidavit of R. C. Folger, M.ᴛ. Pack 359 #17.
Clerk of Court Office. Pickens, S. C. "Personally came before me
R. C. Folger who being sworn says that he graduated from the Atlanta
Medical College, Feb. 28, 1884, that he was born in Greenville, S. C.
and that he is now thirty (33) three years of age." Sworn before me
this 1 Apr. 1884. Signed R. C. Folger... by T. W. Folger, J.P.

FOOSHEE

Charles Fooshee. Estate of Charles Fooshee. Box 33 Pack 724. Proabe
Judge Office, Abbeville, S. C. I Charles Fooshee, Senr. being in perfect health and of sound mind and memory etc.etc. I have 258½ acres
in Laurens Dist. whereon Stokes Allin now lives. I give to my two
daughters by my first wife viz; Elizabeth Jay and Susannah Allin and
Susannah Allin to have one cow and calf, as I have helped them already.
I give to my son John Fooshee that tract of land I bought at sheriff
sale belonging to David Gaines, also two more tracts on the East side
of Cornaco and Wilson's Creeks, I bought of Marshel and the heirs of
Sion Green, also three negroes, called Simon, Edum, and Peter. One
cow and calf, feather bed and furniture. I give to my son Charles B.
Fooshee the tract of land whereon he now lives, on the West of Dudly
Richardson and James Ward, including the tract I bought from Jacob
Pollard South of Wilsons Creek, also three negroes called Stumpy, Jacob,
Judy, one feather bed and furniture, one cow and calf. I give to my
son William Fooshee the land I now live on with the house, 369 acres,
except my daughter Sarah Payn to have a comfortable room in my house
as long as she lives, except if Lewis Payn should come back and take up
with her or she should marry then she is to continue no longer. Sarah
Payn is to have 50 acres to work and if her two children stay with her
and help the land is be as theirs till they come of age. William to get
three negroes called Reubin, Rhody and Milley, with cow and calf, one
feather bed and furniture. I give to my daughter Sarah Payn three
negroes called Kitte, Samboy and Jurdon, one cow and calf, one feather
bed and furniture, the said property of Sarah Payn to be hers during her
natural life only, at death to be divided between her two children
Thomson Payn and Eliza Payn. I give to my daughter Patsey Cheatham
negroes called Peter, Amos and Samson, and fifty acres of land on the
South of the tract I bought from John Hatter, one cow and calf, one
feather bed and furniture. I give to my daughter Hennerita Richardson
negroes called Harry, Bill and Rachel and all the land between Dudly
Richardson and James Wards on Coronaco Creek of the Marshal tract. I
give to my daughter Fanney Boyd, the land I bought from John Hatter
except the 50 acres I gave to Patsey Cheatham, with three negroes called
Betsey, Benjamin, Jean. with one cow and calf, one feather bed and
furniture. I appoint my sons Charles B. and William Fooshee with my
son in law Dudly Richardson my executors. Dated 31 Mar. 1820. Wit:
Zachry Pulliam, William Calhoun, Nathan Calhoun. Signed Charles Fooshee.
Will proved 12 Mar. 1823 by Nathan Calhoun. The inventory was made
14 March 1823 by William Calhoun, Zachy Pulliam, Elihu Criswell, Nathan
Calhoun, Robert A. Cunningham. There is 10 pages to the sale, which
was held 27 Mar. 1823. With a total amount of $3,393.82½. In this
pack is another inventory for another Charles Fooshe dated 21 Dec.
1814. Total amount of $250.42½. Signed A. Houston, Joseph Calhoun,
J. Houston.

Charles B. Fooshee. Estate of Charles B. Fooshee. Pack 343. Clerk
of Court Office. Abbeville, S. C. In Equity. Your oratrix Joel
Fooshee and your oratrix Mary his wife and Sarah Fooshee widow. On the

13th instant Charles B. Fooshee, departed this life intestate leaving Sarah his widow and fiv living chn. viz; Mary your oratrix and wife of Joel Fooshee, James Fooshee, Washington Fooshee, Casen Fooshee, Rebecca Ann Fooshee. Martha another daug. who died before her father leaving a son John Fooshe who is still living. Land owned by Fooshee was, one tract of 460 acres on Wilsons Creek waters of Saluda River, adj. land of N. McCants, Esq. Griffin Golding, Winston Davis. another tract, called "Mill place" of 200 acres on Cornacre Creek and Saluda River, adj. Thomas B. Boyd, Nathan Calhoun. Another tract called "old place" of 200 acres, adj. Thomas B. Boyd, Francis Arnold. Admr. of Fooshee Est. has been granted to James W. Richardson and your orators believes that the personal estate will more than pay all debts. Filed 26 Jan. 1850. On another paper Capers (Casen) was 16 years old, Rebecca Ann 2 yrs. old, grandson John Fooshe about 7 years old.

FORD

Jesse Ford. Deed from Jesse Ford to Phillip Miller. Book O, Page 58. Clerk of Court Office, Greenville, S. C. Jesse Ford to Phillip Miller both of Greenville Dist. Dated 26 Oct. 1805. In the sum of 250 dollars sell and release a tract of land of 200 acres on the South side of Reedy Fork of Reedy River. First granted to Steven Ford, Drury Smith. Adj. lands of Elhana Burnes and Thomas Rice. Wit: John McElory, Junr. Daniel Ford, On 28 Oct. 1805 Phebey Ford wife of Jesse Ford appeared before Hudson Berry, J.Q. and renounce and released all rights to dower on the land. Signed Pheby X Ford. Deed recorded 17 Nov. 1824.

Daniel Ford. Will of Daniel Ford. Box 3 File 164. Probate Judge Office. Greenville, S. C. I Daniel Ford being of sound mind and memory etc.etc. I give to my beloved wife Mary Ford the whole of my estate both real and personal during her natural life or widowhood but in case she marry I give to my daughter Elizabeth McElroy a negro man named Jack and two boys named Dick and Jatts and one half of the stock and goods and chattels. I appoint my wife Executrix and James McElroy Executor. Dated 13 Dec. 1810. Wit: John McElroy, Micajah Berry, Hudson Berry. Signed Daniel Ford, seal. Probated 1 Aug. 1837.

Stephen Ford. Will of Stephen Ford. Box 3 #168. Probate Judge Office. Greenville, S. C. I Stephen Ford being of sound and disposing mind and memory, etc.etc. After paying just debts, I give to my granddaughter Polly Sullivan one bed and furniture. I then wish my executors to sell the whole of my estate both real and personal, when money is collected divide between my lawful heirs that is Milley and Thomas Owens, John Ford, Rebecca and Ananias Wallis, Patsey Owens, the heirs of Vicey and Charles Sullivan, Polly and Batey Chandler, James Ford, Stephen Ford, Daniel Ford, William Ford, Sintha and Benjamin Brewer, Keziah and William Thompson. I appoint my friend Micajah Berry and my brother Daniel Ford Executors. Dated 10 Dec. 1829. Wit: John McElroy, Hudson Berry Jr. Signed Staphen X Ford, seal. Probated 18 Jan. 1830.

Dolly Ford. Will of Dolly Ford. Box 30 Pack 30. Probate Judge Office. Spartanburg, S. C. I Dolly Ford widow of Capt. Manly Ford, decd. being of sound and disposing mind and memory, etc.etc. I give to Mount Pleasant Church five dollars of which I am a member to be paid unto the hand of Bowin Griffin. Pay all just debts. I give to my brother William Chumner one half of the estate. I give to my niece Nancy Inlow and heirs of her body the other one half. I give to Dolly Young daughter of my sister Sally Young the residue of my estate remaining of whatsoever kind. Dated 25 June 1849. Wit: John Poole, W. I. Brem, Y. J. Wingo. Signed Dolly X Ford, seal. Recorded 8 March 1854.

FORESTER

James M. Forester. Estate of James M. Forester. Box 63 #683. Probate Judge Office. Pickens, S. C. Est. Admr. 19 Sept. 1862 by Washington

Sheriff, Wm. Jones, L. V. Jones who are bound unto W. E. Holcombe, Ord. in the sum of $600.00. Left a widow and one child, no names given. 8 March 1864, Elizabeth Forester recd. share $119.68. 1 Apr. 1872 Elizabeth Watkins and David Watkins recd. part share from Alfred Sheriff exor. of Washington Sheriff decd. from estate of J. M. Forester decd.

FORKNERS

Timothy Forkners schedule. Pack 187 #31. Clerk of Court Office, Pickens, S. C. A schedule of all real and personal estate of Timothy Forkner who is now confined in the common jail of Pickens Dist. on a Writ Corpus adsatisfaciedum at the suit of the state for fine and cost. Two tracts of land of ten acres each, two beds and furniture, 2 spinning wheels, one oven and lid, one peecher, two rine tables, one loom, 1 puter dish, one execution for $19 on Aaron Nally, some knives, forks and spoons, some farm and carpenters tools, some old barrels and water vessels. He signed an affidavit that the list was a true account of his possession and that he had not leased sold any of the articles. That he will collect all deeds, vouchers, accounts relating to or concerning whatsoever, and as soon as possible after my discharge, and that I have not spent more than six shilling and three pence per annum out of my estate for my subsistance since I have been a prisoner, so help my God. Dated 29 May 1837. Signed Timothy Forkner.

FOSTER

John Foster. Will of John Foster. Apt. 3 File 159. Probate Judge Office. Greenville, S. C. I John Foster of Greenville Co. Dist. of 96 a carpenter, being weak in body yet of a sound mind and perfect memory, etc.etc. I will and positively order my debts be paid. I give to my dear wife three negroes named Sam, Cole and Lill together with the stock and household goods and at her decease to be equally divided between my children. I give to my daughter Mary Hendley one negro girl named Silvia. I give to my son John Crow Foster one negro named Cain. I give to George Singleton Foster one negro named Sheriff, sons John and George are to divide the two tracts of land I bought from John Hambleton and Robert Ramsey containing 246 acres. I give to my son Josiah Foster one negro named Carolina. I give to my son James Hacket Foster one negro named Limbrick. I give to my daughter Nancy one negro named Sall. I give to my son Robert Singleton Foster two negroes named Kitt and Sawyer. I give to my daughter Frances fifty acres of land at the lower end of the place I now live. I give to my sons James Hacket and Robert Singleton & Josiah Foster the place I now live on consisting of 300 acres. I appoint my sons John Crow Foster and George Singleton Foster Executors and Wife Executrix. Dated 9 Oct. 1787. Wit: Rich. Thompson, Dave Hidden, John X Rabun. Signed John Foster.

Robert Foster. Estate of Robert Foster. Box 35 Pack 761. Abbeville, S. C. Admr. bond dated 29 Sept. 1802 to Hannah Foster, Robert Griffin, John Shannon, Robert Gibson and Samuel Foster are bound unto Andrew Hamilton, Ord. in the sum of $10,000.00. Sale, held on 15-16-17 Nov. 1802 Fosters who bought Elijah Foster, Hannah Foster, Samuel Foster. On 1 March 1805 (the chn. that had gdn. were) Benjamin, Joseph, William, Margaret, John, James and Samuel.

Josiah Foster. Will of Josiah Foster. Pack 81. Clerk of Court Office. Pickens, S. C. I Josiah Foster of Pendleton Dist., S. C. being of sound mind and memory. First sell my stock or loose property to pay my just debts. I give to my wife Polly Foster life time or widowhood the use in any way or to sell any part for her use up to one half thereof. Except W. S. Harrison and his wife Polly to have a negro each. The other half I desire every nephew that is named for me and actually called for me, to have a negro or two hundred dollars each. The law books I have I give to Brown Foster, the remainder to be divided between James H. and Robert S. C. Foster and the chn. of the other brothers and sisters to share qual with James and Robert Foster. I appoint Wm. Simpson, Richard Harrison, Col. J. C. Kilpatrick Amr. (Execr) and wife Admrx. (Extrx) or any two of them. Dated 2 Nov. 1816. Wit: Aaron Shannon, R. H. Grant, Elijah Gillison, Eli X Latta. Signed Josiah Foster. On 27 Aug. 1821 Aaron Shannon appeared in open Court in Green Co., Ala. and after duly sworn acknowledged he saw Foster sign sd. will and he witnessed same. On the same day Reuben H. Grant acknownedged the will.

Alexander Foster. Deed of Alexander Foster to Basdail Darby. Pack 358. Clerk of Court. Abbeville, S. C. Dated 19 March 1822. In consideration of $285.00 paid to Alexander Foster by Basdail Darby both of said Dist. do sell release a tract of land of 61 acres on a branch of Norrises Creek. Originally granted to Samuel Foster, Sr. decd. Joining land of Basdail Darby, Samuel Foster, Nathaniel Cammorns, S. S. and John Fosters. Wit: James Foster, Saml. Foster. Signed Alexr. Foster, seal. No recording date given.

Samuel Foster, Sr. Estate of Samuel Foster, Sr. Box 34 Pack 733. Probate Judge Office. Abbeville, S. C. I Samuel Foster, Senior. Being old and inform of body of of sound disposing mind and memory. Pay all just debts. My will that my estate real and personal remain with my wife Sarah Foster during her natural life and after her death divided as: I will unto my grandsons Samuel and Robert Foster sons of Robert Foster decd. one negro man named Harrey. I will to my grandson John Slone 100 acres where he now lives, one negro named Lewis, also one cow and calf, one mare, etc. I will to my great grandson Samuel Foster Slone son of John Slone 30 acres. The land and negro to be kept by John Slone as long as he lives. I will unto grandson Alexander Senclar Foster son of Samuel C. Foster 100 acres and one half of the value of negro Nelly (she having the priviledge of choosing her master). The other half of Nelly value to be equally divided between Joseph, Elijah, Sarah, Margret and Frances Foster sons and daughter of my son Robert Foster decd. If Alexander S. Foster die without heirs, his share of Nelly value to go to his brother Thomas Jordan Foster. Thomas J. Foster to get negro named Mike, one horse, cow and calf, bed and furniture. I give to son in law Thomas Slone five dollars, with the other property I have given him. I give to son in law Samuel C. Foster five dollars with the other property I have already given him. I will to my daug. in law Jenny Foster the wife of son Robert Foster decd. five dollars, with the other property I have already given her. I appoint my friend Edmon Cobb and Ephraim Davis Executors. Dated 19 May 1825. Wit: John Slone, Samuel McElwain, Margaret M. Paul. Signed Samuel X Foster, Senr. Will proved by Samuel McElwain and Margaret M. Paul on the 12 Dec. 1825. Ephraim Davis, qualified as Exect. same date. The estate was settled on 1 Nov. 1847. Sarah Foster in Abbeville, S. C. Joseph Foster supposed to be dead. Elijah Foster in Pickens Dist. Margaret Foster married a Williams, absent. Frances Foster dead, Saml and Robert Foster both absent. The four chn. of John Slone decd. Alexr. S. Foster, absent. Thos. Jordan Foster absent. Another place. David Lesly recd. his share of his grandfather's estate, and Marcus Williams and wife Margret sell their share of Nelly value. The last dated 3 Dec. 1832. Wit: by Charles Calhoun, Elijah Teague. Signed Marcus Williams.

Samuel Foster Senr. Deed of Samuel Foster Senr. Pack 381. Clerk of Court Office. Abbeville, S. C. Whereas Samuel Foster, Senr. Esq. decd. intestate and the heirs have agreed and entered into bond authorizing John Foster and John English to sell or dispose of the real estate. We John Foster and John English both of Abbeville, Dist. in the sum of $91.50 to us paid by James Stuart do sell and release a tract of land of 61 acres, part of a grant of 350 acres granted to Saml. Foster lying on Norris' Creek, adj. land of Toliver Livingston and Jane Foster. Dated 5 Sept. 1814. Wit: And. Crawford, John Foster. Signed John Foster and John English. seal. Attested before Jno. Foster, J.P., by John Foster on the 5 Sept. 1814.

Mary Foster. Will of Mary Foster. Pack 81. Clerk of Court Office. Pickens, S. C. State of Alabama, Greene Co. I Mary Foster being in

sound mind and disposing memory, also in good health, etc.etc. First
collect all debts due me and pay all debts owed by me. I give and
bequeath unto my daughter Catherine (otherwise called Kitty) Harrison
and her eight children, viz; Elizabeth, James, Kitty or Catherine,
Harriett, Laura, Clarissa, Josiah and the youngest named Florence. The
whole of my estate both real and personal to be equally divided between
the nine above persons and no more. I appoint Kitty Harrison and grandson Slone Harrison Executrix and Executor. Dated 22 Feb. 1831. Wit:
Wm. J. VanDeGraaff, James A. Beal, J. C. Phares. Signed Mary X Foster.
State of Ala. Greene Co. Special term of Court. Dated 29 Dec. 1834.
Appeared Wm. S. Harrison one of the Exect. and recorded the will of Mary
Foster, decd.

George E. W. Foster, S.P.D. Deed from George E. W. Foster, S.P.D.
Book A-1 Page 5. Clerk of Court Office. Pickens, S. C. I George
Foster, Sheriff of Pendleton Dist. Whereas a writ of partition issued
by the Court of Common Pleas, at the instance of Burt Moore and wife
and others. Against Duke W. Glenn and others for the partition of the
real estate of William Glenn decd, etc. In the March term in the year
1826 the said writ was issued. One tract of 640 acres originally
granted unto John Vanderhorst dated 16 July 1784. Also another tract
of 90 acres being part of a tract granted unto Samuel Hand on the 5
Jan. 1798. At the sale Moses Hendrix paid $2,007.35¢ for the first
tract, and $2,002.00 for the last tract, being the highest and last
bidder. The land was on Oolenoy Creek of Saluda River. Wit: Joseph
Reid, D.R. Towers. Signed George E. W. Foster, Sheriff of Pend. Dist.
Recorded 27 Oct. 1828.

Foster Heirs. In Equity. Pack 81. Clerk of Court Office. Pickens,
S. C. Dated 18 March 1840. Recd. of N. J. F. Perry all our rights
of the estate of Josiah Foster decd. Being entitled to one seventh part
of one half by the sd. will of Josiah Foster decd. as chn of Frances
Grant a sister of the decd. Signed H. Grant, Nancy Grant, Richard
Harris, Elizabeth M. Harris. G. W. Grant. Also agent for R. H. Grant
and Mary H. Robinson. Josiah Foster was a brother to Robert S. C.
Foster and James H. Foster and a uncle of Davis Hunt and wife Harriet J.
Hunt, B. F. Perry, Josiah F. Perry, John Grant, R. H. Grant, Elizabeth
Harris and her husband Richard Harris. Nancy Grant, Polly Robinson,
J. B. F. Foster, W. E. Foster, Washington Foster, Columbus T. Foster,
Mary T. Foster on March 15, 1844 recd. a share from Josiah Foster estate
to which she was entitled as a granddaughter of Mary Hendley who was a
sister to said decd. Sarah P. Tolbert recd. a share also as one of the
grandchildren of Mary Hendley who was a sister to said decd. George
E. W. Foster, J. R. W. Foster, J. C. Foster 3 of the heirs of John
Foster decd. recd. a share from the estate. Recd. of Miles M. Norton
$15.00 being my part of the estate of Josiah Foster decd. inright of my
wife. Signed Sarah Cannan and H. L. Kennan. Dated 14 Mar. 1844.

FOUNTAIN

Simpson L. Fountain. In Equity, Pack 91. Clerk of Court Office.
Pickens, S. C. Simpson L. Fountain states that in 1858 he was much
in debt and was pressed by creditors etc. He applied to Alexander
Cryce Senr. and J. Gambrell Bryce. They loaned him $550.00 with
security of two slaves to wit, Leah and her child named Eade. The
Bryce men with Edwin M. Cobb of Anderson Dist. a dealer in slaves, and
that Cobb knew the slaves was on mortgage and not the property of
Alexander and Gambrell Bryce and they removed said negroes from the
state. Filed 4 Oct. 1859.

Simpson L. Fountain. Estate of Simpson L. Fountain. Book A Page
228. Probate Judge Office. Pickens, S. C. On 5 July 1858 the heirs
at law of Simpson L. Fountain were: Mary M., James, Wildey Fountain
minors, were heirs of William Abbott decd. and his widow Julia Abbott.

Joshua Fowler. Estate of Joshua Fowler. Box 4 #38. Probate Judge
Office. Pickens, S. C. Est. Admr. 4 Feb. 1833 by Wm. Jameson, Abraham
Burdine, Mark Freeman, Charles Durham who are bound unto Jas. H. Dendy,
Ord. in the sum of $2,000.00. On 19 Jan. 1833 Elizabeth Fowler widow
relinquished her Admr. to Wm. Jameson and Abraham Burdine. Cit. pub-
lished at Cross Road Meeting House. (The two admr. are not listed as
heirs) The heirs are: Elizabeth wife of Mark Freeman, Joshua Fowler,
Jr., decd., Thos. Fowler decd., heirs of John Leonard, Ruth wife of
Moses Cantrell, William Fowler, John Fowler who lived in Wayne Co., Tenn.
John's wife was Beddy Freeman, Josiah Fowler, Milly wife of Robert
Boyd decd. and Elizabeth the widow, Joshua Fowler owned 662½ acres on
George Creek, adj. land of Edmond Singeton, Samuel Hall and others.

Archibald Fowler. Will of Archibald Fowler. Apt. 3 File 161. Probate
Judge Office. Greenville, S. C. I Archibald Fowler being weak in body
but of perfect mind and memory, etc.etc. I will to my wife Edy Fowler
a child's part of my estate. My will that the six children of my
daughter Jessefy Pike decd. have no more than five dollars each. My
will that the balance of my estate, after paying my debts be divided
between my chn. Except my son West I. Fowler to have no more than
$200.00. The other heirs are; Mary Evans, Leah Mahaffey, Rachel Pike,
Louisa Miller, Luna Miller, Lavina Pool, John W. Fowler, Lovey Waldrop
and Alexander W. Fowler. I appoint my son John W. Fowler as Executor.
Dated 22 Feb. 1839. Wit: Lyn Walker, Thos. I. Dean, Isaac Walker.
Signed Archd. Fowler. Probated 1 June 1840.

Coleman Carlile Fowler. Land Warrant for Coleman Carlile Fowler. Pack
630 #5. Clerk of Court Office. Pickens, S. C. By J. E. Hagood, Clerk
of Court. To any lawful surveyor you are authorized to lay out unto
Coleman Carlile Fowler a tract of land. Dated 8 July 1859. Filed 10
Aug. 1859. The amount of land not shown.

FRANKLIN

Franklin Minors. Box 2 #37 In Equity. Clerk of Court Office. Pickens,
S. C. On 18 July 1838 Benjamin F. Sloan, W. H. D. Gaillard are bound
unto W. H. Harrison in the sum of $3600.00 as guardian for Elisa
Franklin a minor over 12 years. She dtr. of Wm. Franklin.

FRASIER

William H. & Mary Frasier. The Deposition of William H. and Mary
Frasier. Pack 655 #1. Clerk of Court Office. Pickens, S. C. In
Equity. Case of Samuel S. McJunkin vs Larkin Holbrooks and William
Bradberry. Dated 1852. Questions to William H. and Mary Frasier of
Walker or Blount County, State of Alabama. Do you know Larkin Hol-
brooks, yes, as a boy. Did you sign the sd. deed. Yes, with Randolph
Howard. Date of this deed 20 Dec. 1832. Deed #2. When and where was
this deed made. 4 Jan. 1843 at my house in Pickens Co., S. C. Where
did Roger Murphey then reside and when did he die. He resided in DeCalb
Co., Ga. I did not know he was dead. Where is Pinque H. Frasier now
and how old is he, and where did your son die and when. I don't
know where. He was born in Granville Co., N. C. about 1806-07. Wm.
H. my son died 13 July 1840 in Noxube Co., Miss.

Samuel & Bethshaba Frasier. Power of Attorney. Samuel & Bethshaba
Frasier. Box 27 #325. Probate Judge Office. Pickens, S. C. On 4 Jan.
1851 Samuel and Bethshaba of Hall Co., Ga. appointed Garner Evans of
Pickens Dist., S. C. as their lawful attorney to receive and recover
their share of the estate of Margret Prater decd. of Pickens Dist.
Who was late of the State of Alabama.

John Fraser. Estate of John Fraser. Box 33 #725. Probate Judge Office, Abbeville, S. C. I John Fraser being of a sound mind and memory etc. Sell all land first and pay just debts. I give to my sister Mary Jones twenty dollars, I give to my sister Easter Woods for the benefit of her son William Young the sum of two hundred and fifty dollars. The balance I give to my brother William. Dated 11 March 1807. Wit: Jas. Killough, Samuel Mitchel, Nath. Norwood. Signed John Fraser. Recorded 1 June 1807. Admr. to this will are: Brother William Fraser and friend Samuel Mitchel. On 26 Aug. 1809 before Andrew Hamilton, J.P. appeared Francis Young Senr. stated that Samuel Mitchel died in 1808 in the month of Dec. and that he was the Executor of the estate of John Fraser at the request of Wm. Fraser.

Donald Fraser. Estate of Donald Fraser. Box 33 #714. Probate Judge Office. Abbeville, S. C. I Donald Fraser do declare this to be my last will and test. I desire that all debts be paid first. I will to my son John all the tract of land whereon I now live and my negroes be divided between my wife Amy Fraser and my two chn. John and Margaret. In the division my dau. to have a double share of the negroes account of no land to her. If either child die without heir, the other to get all and if neither have an heir then my estate goes to my brothers and sister, John, William, and sister Isabella. If my wife be with child now and it be a boy, he is to share with brothers, if a girl to share with her sister. I appoint my wife Mary Allen Fraser executrix and brother John Fraser of Charleston, and George Bowie and James Wardlaw of this Dist. to be executors. Dated 12 Aug. 1807. Wit: John X Stuart, John Wilson, A. Ralston. Signed Donl. Fraser. Will proved by John Stuart before Tal. Livingston, Ord. on the 20 Apr. 1812. An inventory was made as: 29 negroes (not named), 8 horses, 30 head cattle, 20 sheep, 40 geese, 1 waggon and gear, household and kitchen furniture an old riding chair, and some old books, a set of store books and some notes of hand. The above property was seized by John Caldwell Sheriff soon after sd. Fraser death by an execution then in force against him by McBeth Henry and Co. sold sd. estate and did not pay off debts.

William Fraser. Estate of William Fraser. Box 34 Pack 743. Probate Judge Office, Abbeville, S. C. I William Fraser being weak in body but of sound mind and memory. First let my just debts be paid. I leave to William Young my bed and furniture, the rest of my property be sold and the money I now have be given to my two sisters Marey Jones and Ester Woods. I appoint Ezekiel Calhoun, Senr. and Ester Woods Executors. Dated 4 Jan. 1809. Wit: Thos. Ansely, E. Calhoun, Senr., Esther Woods. Signed Wm. Fraser, seal. Recorded 13 Jan. 1809. The appraisers were: Walter Ward, Nathl. Noewood, Francis Young, Archd. McKinley and Francis Carlile. Sale held 14 Feb. 1809.

John G. Fraser. Estate of John G. Fraser. Box 35 #771. Probate Judge Office. Abbeville, S. C. I John G. Fraser being of sound mind but infirm health, etc.etc. Sell my stock, crops, tools to pay my just debts. To my daughter Georgiana I leave $500.00 to be paid when she is married. Sell boy Jack and money paid to Thos. A. Sanders during life time, and at his death money paid to J. F. Livingston son of Dr. J. F. Livingston. I leave to J. F. Livingston a girl named Lavina. To Clara J. Fraser dtr. of John Fraser I leave the land on which I now live. To my mother I leave negroes Frank, Mourning, Flora, William, Patterson, Alexander, Maria and all further increase. To my wife negroes Leroy, Sandy, Lee, Harris, Jenny, Squire, Micklings and children Pompey and Taby and all increase, Winny and child Lucinda with all plate, furniture, books, monies. Dated 13 June 1838. Wit: J. C. Fowler, Jas. W. McAlister, John G. Gallaugher. Signed: John G. Fraser. N.B. I appoint J. F. Livingston, Executor. Proved by John Gallaugher before Moses Taggart, Ord. on the 5 Sept. 1840. Estate appraised on 25-26 Nov. 1840 by John Speer, Starling Bowen, Jas. H. Baskin and Wm. Campbell. Settlement of estate of Jno. G. Fraser decd. made 19 May 1842. Jno. G. Fraser died in August 1840.

James Frazier. Estate of James Frazier. Pack 35 #766. Probate Judge
Office. Abbeville, S. C. I James Frazier of Cedar Springs do make
this my last will and testament. I will my just debts be paid from the
crop of cotton made this year and the slaves that was sold to my by my
son James W. Frazier to wit: Beverly, Patty, Josephine, Elbert, Mary,
Lucretia, Jerry, Emily, Russell and Maria or as many as necessary to
pay my debts and no more. I give to my wife Charity Frazier in lieu
and bar of her dower, negroes Anne, Isabel, Peter, Charles, Charlotte,
Clara and her son Augustus and Violet and her dtr. Eliza. Note,
Charlotte is the child of Rachel. I also give to my wife one third
part of my plantation, stock, farm tools, household and kitchen furniture, she may stay in my dwelling house or have one built in such part
as she wish. I further give to my wife during her natural life to be
disposed of by will the following negroes Hiram, Caroline, Julia, Ellen
children of Violet, Henry and Washington children of Clara, also fellow
Anthony to be devised to my grandchildren. I give to my grandchildren
Henry, James A., Sarah A., Joseph, and Allen S. Walker children of my
decd. dtr. Jane Walker, one negro girl named Priscilla with her increase
and to each ten dollars. I give to my dtr. Lucretia S. Devlin and son-
in-law Robert Devlin the following negroes: Frank, Sally and her
children Lewis, John, Nancy, Emily, Sam and Oliver, also Harriet and her
chn. Martha and Josephine. I give to my son in law Robert Devlin and
nephew John F. Livingston the plantation on which I now live containing
782 acres, subject to the life estate of my wife, also the following
slaves: Dick, Willis, Lindsy, Tinsley, Flora, Sam also Patrick. I
give to Robert Devlin and John F. Livingston in trust all stock, tools,
furniture of every kind subject to provision to my wife. I charge my
whole estate real and personal to support my son Benjamin. I commit
the care of Benjamin to wife Charity. I give to my granddtr. Martha B.
Frazier one negro girl named Meriam. I also give to her four sisters
viz; Mary, Rebecca, Charity and Amanda the sum of ten dollars. I give
to Robt. Devlin and J. F. Livingston one negro girl named Sarah in
trust for the use of Edwin H. Frazier. Shoul dhtere be anything left
I give it to my granddtr. Tallulah H. Frazier. I appoint Thomas
Thomson the Executor. Dated 20 Aug. 1842. Wit: Lewis Smith, Lucretia
Fulton, Martha A. McClelland. Signed: James Frazier, seal. A cadicil
added: The land given to Robert Devlin and John F. Livingston was in
trust for James W. Frazier, James W. to get the rent and profit only.
Dated 22 Aug. 1840. Wit: A. H. Spence, John C. Red, Sam W. Cochram.
Signed James Frazier. Will proved 11 Oct. 1842, by Lewis Smith.
The inventory was held at Cedar Springs 24 Jan. 1843. by Bartholomew
Jordon, James L. Devlin, Lewis Smith, sworn appraisers.

James Fraser. Land Warrant for James Fraser. No ref. Abbeville, S. C.
From John B. Black, C.A.D. At the request of Cravin Fraser, I have
laid out for his son James Fraser, one hundred acres on Piney Creek in
Abbeville Dist. Dated 6 May 1841.

FREDERICK

Jacob Frederick. Land Warrant of Jacob Frederick. #168. Pack 114.
Clerk of Court Office, Pickens, S. C. By W. L. Keith, Clerk of Court.
To any lawful surveyor you are authorized to lay out and admeasire
unto Jacob Frederick a tract of land. Dated 21 June 1853. Executed
the within for 13 acres 24 June 1853. M. S. McCay, D.S. Recorded
29 June 1853.

George Frederick. Estate of George Frederick. Box 93 #979. Probate
Judge Office. Abbeville, S. C. Est. Admr. 30 Aug. 1867 by Cynthia
Frederick widow, Thos. L. Lewis, G. R. Cherry, W. A. Lay who are bound
unto W. E. Holcombe, Ord. in the sum of $1,500.00. Heirs; Sarah,
Martha J. Elijah E., Mary H., Susan E., Baylis E., Patrick, John
Frederick, W. D. Rochester and wife Rebecca C. owned 550 acres on
Martin Creek waters of Seneca River, joining land of Stephen Baldwin
and others. 21 Jan. 1868 Susan E. was ment. as wife of Joseph B.
Caradine who was out of the state.

FRICKS

Matthias Fricks. Land Warrant for Matthias Fricks. #149 Pack 114.
Clerk of Court Office. Pickens, S. C. By W. L. Keith, Clerk of Court
To any lawful surveyor you are authorized to lay out unto Matthias Frick
a tract of land. Dated 22 March 1852. Executed for 824 acres 26 March
1852. Tyre B. Mauldin D.S.

FREEMAN

David Freeman. Will of David Freeman. Box 74 #786. Probate Judge
Office. Pickens Dist., S. C. I David Freeman being weak in body but
of sound and disposing mind and memory. My wish that my exectuors sell
enough property to pay debts and no more. I want my beloved wife
Frances to have all that is left during her natural life, as a child
comes of age if there is any property to spare give them something. I
wish my executors to have power to appoint another to serve in place
of one dying. I appoint Abel Hendricks, William F. Fendley, Moses
Hendricks. Dated 23 Feb. 1859. Wit: A. R. Simmons, Railey Simmons,
G. M. Simmons. Signed David Freeman. Another note, Frances Freeman
died before David leaving 3 children one boy John T., Mary Susan who
married Columbus Jones and Martha Alice who married John Hood. David
married Elvira Findley 4 June 1861 by Thos. Looper Min. Elvira had
three chn. one dead and two living, they are David Marion and Thos.
Meredith Freeman they were twins. Elvira Findley had a sister Lucinda
Findley. On 29 Dec. 1835 Wiley Freeman and John Dean Jr. in right of
his wife Sally Freeman of Habersham Co., Ga. appointed Jas. Coward of
same Co. their attorney to collect their part of est. of John Freeman,
Sr. of Pickens Co., S.C.

Elizabeth Freeman. Pack 56. In Equity. Clerk of Court Office.
Pickens, S. C. Elizabeth Freeman was a dtr. of David Hendricks who
died in Sept. 1850 and his was Mourning Hendricks. She died some years
previous to her father. Her children were: Mary who married Henson
Looper, Martha who married Thomas Tompkins, David Freeman.

Benton Freeman. Will of Benton Freeman. Box 31 #363. Probate Judge
Office. Pickens, S. C. I Benton Freeman being in a low state of
health, but in my right mind and memory, etc.etc. I will to my wife
the home place during her natural life then to my youngest son the same
for ever. I also give to her a negro named Balass during her life
then to my two sons Barney L. and Benton S. Freeman. I give to my
wife Jane household and kitchen furniture of every kind, also provisions
for one year. Sell the other property to pay debts and funeral expenses
I appoint my friend and brother in law Judge G. F. Ferguson my Executor.
Dated 3 Nov. 1853. Wit: Jeptha Freeman, Moses X Clark, David Freeman,
J. G. Ferguson. Signed Benton Freeman. Codicil. I, Benton Freeman
wish to alter a small portion of my will. I devise one negro named
Chana to my wife Jane, also the boy named George to be kept for ten
years then to be sold. Dated 8 Nov. 1853. Wit: Reddin Freeman,
Jane Ferguson, J. G. Ferguson. Signed Benton Freeman. Proven 16 Dec.
1853.

Francis Freeman. Estate of Francis Freeman. Box 40 #453. Probate
Judge Office. Pickens, S. C. Est. Admr. 9 June 1856 by Levi N. Robins,
Nathan Gunnin, who are unto W. J. Parson, Ord. in the sum of $100.00.

Z. T. Freeman. Estate of Z. T. Freeman. Box 79 #845. Probate Judge
Office. Pickens, S. C. Est. Admr. 14 Nov. 1864 by Abel Hendricks,
Andrew J. Anderson, John W. L. Cary who are bound unto W. E. Holcombe,
Ord. in the sum of $400.00.

Mark Freeman, Sr. Will of Mark Freeman, Sr. Box 85 #901. Probate
Judge Office. Pickens, S. C. I, Mark Freeman, Sr., being of sound
mind and disposing memory. First pay my just debts. I will to my wife
Jane Freeman during her natural life all my personal property and real

130

estate, also I give to her forty acres of land where the home place is,
to dispose of in any way she sees fit. My son Drooury H. Freeman to
have fifty acres from the lower end of the home place. Daughter Haner
McClannahan, Huldy Wimpys, Milly Looper, Benjamin Williams and wife
Martha Williams, to have twenty dollars more than those heretofore
named, Dtr. Mahaly A. D. Freeman to have twenty dollars and the bed
she has made her self, in case Druah H. Freeman should die before he
receives his share then it goes to his daughter Laura or Louisa Jane
Freeman. I appoint A. J. Anderson, ___ Freeman, ___ Freeman, Executors.
Dated 1 Aug. 1863. Wit: J. Tra, S. E. Sutherland, Mary Anderson.
Signed: Mark X Freeman. Proven 13 Oct. 1865.

John Freeman. Estate of John Freeman. Book 1 page 3. Probate Judge
Office. Pickens, S. C. On 19 April 1830 he owned 175 acres. John
S. Edwards asignee of John and Francis Freeman legal heirs of John
Freeman at the time of his death viz; Fanny Freeman widow, Westly
Freeman, William Freeman, Alexander Freeman, John Findley in right of
wife, Jane Freeman, Sally Freeman, Wiley Freeman, John Fowler in right
of wife Bidy, Marshall Holley and wife Parthenia, Mary Freeman.

Freeman Minors. Box 132 #2. Probate Judge Office. Pickens, S. C. On
29 March 1898 Viola Freeman states that she is the wife of B. E. Freeman decd. and mother of his three children viz; Ollie D., age 9 yrs.,
Walton M. age 7 yrs., Zelie F. age years. B. E. Freeman son Jas. G.
Freeman, Empes Freeman a brother.

Barney L. Freeman. Estate of Barney L. Freeman. Box 93 #984. Probate
Judge Office. Pickens, S. C. On 8 Dec. 1877 Freeman owned land on .
Saluda River and on both sides of Ooleyroy Creek whereon he died and
Augustus Williams now lives. He had 500 acres adj. land of Wm. May-
field, Est. Philip Martin decd. Jas. Jones. Heirs; Mary J. Freeman
widow. Chn. Eliza J. Freeman, Geo. T. Freeman, John F. Freeman,
Lindsay B. Freeman minors under 14 years. Mary J. Freeman Jr., Wm. B.
Freeman, Jas. B. R. Freeman children over 14 years chn. by his first
wife. Benton S. Freeman brother to dec.

Reddin Freeman. Will of Reddin Freeman. Box 101 #1064. Probate Judge
Office. Pickens, S. C. I Reddin Freeman being in a low state of
health yet strong and disposing mind, etc.etc. After all just debts
and funeral expenses are paid. I will to my wife Nancy Freeman all
my real estate during her natural life. At her death to be divided as
follows (this is given). I will to my son William Freeman and my
son in law Warren Boyd the North half and I will to my son in law Philip
A. Porter and my grand son James T. Looper the South half, to be
divided between themselves. All personal property to wife Nancy during
her life and if any remains, I will all to the heirs of John and
Needom Freeman my two deceased sons each to have an equal share. I
will and direct my Executors to give heirs of John $200 dollars as I
have already given his same amount. I will and direct my Executors to
give heirs of Needom $300 as I have given him one hundred dollars,
This will make each an equal amount with them getting land. The saw
mill to be kept in operation in case some one will use it. I appoint
my son and sons in law William Freeman, Warren Boyd, Philip A. Porter.
Dated 9 Jan. 1869. Wit: E. H. Griffin, Junr., Benton S. Freeman,
Daniel Durham. Signed Reddin Freeman. Codicil #1. I forgot or neglected to mention my son William Freeman as having a share in my saw mill.
Therefore I acknowledge and declare he the said William my son did own
half of my sawmill and is entitled to half of all the benefits arising
there from. Dated 23 Jan. 1369. Wit: E. H. Griffin, Benton S.
Freeman, Daniel Durham. Signed: Reddin Freeman. Codicil #2. In the
will of 23 Jan. 1869, I gave to heirs of John Freeman $200 as taxes are
high, I now give to them $150 dollars. And to the heirs of Needom
Freeman, I now give them $250 dollars. Dated 20 Aug. 1870. Wit:
E. H. Griffin, Benton S. Freeman, Daniel Durham. Signed: Reddin
Freeman. Filed 28 Aug. 1371. In 1890 John Freeman and his sister
Georgia A. Aarons heirs were of Settendown, Forsyth Co., Ga.

Barney L. Freeman. Estate of Barney L. Freeman. Box 109 #1036.
Probate Judge Office. Pickens, S. C. Est. Admr. by Mary J. and Benton
S. Freeman were Admr. Left a widow and seven children. Est. Admr.
11 Mar. 1876.

Freeman Minors. Box 8 #128. Probate Judge Office. Pickens, S. C. On
16 Feb. 1870 Barney L. Freeman, Henry J. Anthony are bound unto I. H.
Philpot, Ord. in the sum of $200.00. Barney L. Freeman Gdn. for Mary
J., Wm. B., Jas. Freeman minors. Martha E. Freeman decd. the mother.
Wm. B. Freeman 21 years in 1881. Abraham Burdine decd. their grand-
father.

Freeman Minors. Box 4 #118. Probate Judge Office. Pickens, S. C. On
6 Jan. 1891 J. T. Looper, F. M. Morris, E. F. Looper who are bound unto
J. B. Newberry, Ord. in the sum of $120.00. J. T. Looper gdn. for
Barnette and Blythe Freeman minors. Barnett age 7 years. Blythe
Freeman age 5 years, children of Wm. Freeman decd. John Langston a
brother in law to minors.

Freeman Minors. Box 10 #164. Probate Judge Office. Pickens, S. C.
On 8 Oct. 1877 M. J. Freeman, J. R. Freeman minors over 14 years,
wanted John T. Anthony to be their gdn. Had interest in est. of B. E.
Freeman decd. In 1879 M. J. Roper and John Roper recd. share.

Freeman Minors. Box 11 #182. Probate Judge Office. Pickens, S. C.
On 24 Apr. 1883 Mary J. Freeman, D. E. Hendricks, J. R. Harris are
bound unto J. H. Newton, Ord. in the sum of $1715.84. Mary J. Freeman
gdn. for Eliza J. Freeman, Geo. T. Freeman, John F. Freeman, Lindsay B.
Freeman minor under 21 years.

J. B. R. Freeman. Box 137 #3. Probate Judge Office. Pickens, S. C.
Est. Admr. 3 Jan. 1901. by Amanda E. Freeman, W. B. Freeman, W. T.
Griffin who are bound unto J. B. Newberry, Ord. in the sum of $2,000.00.
Died 12 Dec. 1900. Lucinda C. Griffin recd. a share.

William Freeman. Estate of William Freeman. Box 118 #9. Probate
Judge Office. Pickens, S. C. Est. Admr. 30 Oct. 1890 by John T.
Langston, W. T. Meares, F. M. Morris, who are bound unto J. B. Newberry,
Ord. in the sum of $400.00. Died 29 Sept. 1890. John T. Langston a son
in law. 23 Feb. 1891. Paid J. T. Looper gdn. for Barnett and Blythe
Freeman minors $60.00. Paid Mary Freeman $30.00. Paid T. E. Langston
and Alice Jenings each $30.00. Paid 24 Jan. 1893 Elizabeth Langston,
Mary Gillespie share each $8.66.

Bennett Freeman. Estate of Bennett Freeman. Box 117 #14. Probate
Judge Office. Pickens, S. C. Est. Admr. 29 Apr. 1890 by E. M. Freeman,
W. B. Freeman, J. J. White who are bound unto J. B. Newberry, Ord. in
the sum of $2,000.00. 6 Feb. 1893 paid Mrs. Elizabeth White, Mrs. Lou
Watson, Ellen Freeman each a share of $158.39. Paid E. M. Freeman
gdn. for Wm. & John W. Freeman minors each $158.39.

Bernard Freeman. Estate of Bernard Freeman. Box 132 #1. Probate Judge
Office. Pickens, S. C. Est. Admr. 22 Sept. 1898 by E. Freeman, J. A.
Freeman, W. T. Field who are bound unto J. B. Newberry, Ord. in the sum
of $598.00. E. Freeman gdn. for Bernard M. Freeman, Endel D. Freeman
minors. Chn. of Corena Freeman widow of Robt. P. Freeman the son of
Jas. G. Freeman. Bernard M. Freeman 7 years. Endel D. Freeman 5 years.
Wilbur Freeman 3 years. Blanche R. Freeman 1 year old.

R. P. Freeman. Estate of R. P. Freeman. Box 128 #6. Probate Judge
Office. Pickens, S. C. Est. Admr. 6 Aug. 1897 by W. B. Freeman, Emps
Freeman, J. S. Freeman who are bound unto J. B. Newberry, Ord. in the
sum of $500.00. Died 10 May 1897. W. B. Freeman a brother.

J. G. Freeman. Estate of J. G. Freeman. Box 128 #5. Probate Judge
Office. Pickens, S. C. Est. Admr. 6 Aug. 1897 by W. B. Freeman, Emps
Freeman, J. S. Freeman who are bound unto J. B. Newberry, Ord. in the
sum of $1,000.00. Died 17 July 1897. W. B. Freeman a son...left 8
heirs: Emps Freeman, B. E. Freeman, Elvira Freeman, Margaret Hill,

W. B. Freeman, J. S. Freeman, Jane McAdams each bought land.

Joseph R. Freeman. Will of Joseph R. Freeman. Box 109 #1037. Probate
Judge Office. Pickens, S. C. I Joseph R. Freeman being of sound mind
and memory, etc. First I desire that two heads of horses with the money
on hand pay debts and funeral expenses. I give to my wife Caroline
Freeman all my estate both real and personal during her natural life
or widowhood. At her death or marriage I desire all my property be sold
and money divided between my children for ever. If she does marry she
to get one third of all money. I appoint my wife Caroline Executrix
and brother in law Benjamin J. Williams executor. Dated 16 May 1862.
Wit: J. W. Singleton, W. F. Looper, Joseph X. Looper. Signed Joseph R.
Freeman. Proven 4 Apr. 1876. On 8 Mar. 1877 paid W. W. Freeman, acct.
$7.25. Paid Jeptha Freeman on account $2.75.

Notes on Freeman. Book B, page 83. Probate Judge Office, Pickens, S.C.
On 10 Nov. 1865 Sarah Freeman wife of James Freeman was a sister of
John Black decd. of Pickens, S. C. Martha E. Freeman wife of B. L.
Freeman died on or about 5 Apr. 1862 in Pickens, S. C. Left a husband
and three minor chn. Mary J. Freeman, William B. Freeman, James R.
Freeman. She was a dtr. of Abraham Burdine who died before her father
Richard Burdine in Pickens Dist. Ref. Pack 633. Clerk of Court Office,
Pickens, S. C.

Drury and Nancy Freeman. Divorce of Drury and Nancy Freeman. #21 in
Equity. Clerk of Court Office. Pickens, S. C. Nancy vs Drury. She
was Nancy E. Burgess the dtr. of George R. Burgess. She and Drury
Freeman were married 5 Jan. 1860. They had one dtr. born 15 May 1861
named Lavinia Jane. She files her complaint on the 14 Dec. 1866. He
replied on 17 Apr. 1867. Verdict not given.

                              FULLER

Notes on Fuller. Box 132 #3. Probate Judge Office. Pickens, S. C.
Mrs. Annie H. Fuller recd. a share from the estate of Col. Columbus L.
Hollingsworth decd. whose est. was admr. 26 Jan. 1899 in Pickens, S. C.

                             GAINES

Richard Gaines. Will of Richard Gaines. Box 4 #36. Probate Judge
Office. Pickens, S. C. I Richard Gaines being afflicted in body but
of sound mind and memory, etc. I give to my dtr. Susanna Arnold one
negro named Lucrecy, one horse with saddle and bridle, one feather bed
and furniture, one cow and calf. I gave to my dtr. Patsy Murff, decd.
cow and calf and the feather bed, with a horse and saddle and bridle. I
now give to her heirs viz: Caty G. Murff, Wiley Murff, and Malinda
Murff each forty dollars at the death of my wife Mary. I give to my
son Henry P. Gaines one negro named Mary Ann, one horse and saddle and
bridle, feather bed and furniture, one cow and calf. I give to my son
Reuben Gaines, one negro named Amy, one horse, saddle and bridle, one
feather bed and furniture, one cow and calf. I give to my son Richard
Gaines, one negro named Milly, one horse, saddle and bridle, one feather
bed, one cow and calif. I give to my son Robert Gaines, one negro named
Orid, one horse and saddle and bridle, one cow and calf. I give to my
son James Gaines, one horse, saddle, feather bed and furniture, one cow
and calf and in lieu of a negro $250 dollars worth of land, to be laid
out on the lower end of the tract whereon I now live. I give to my
son Benjamin Gaines, one negro named Zedikiah, one horse, saddle and
bridle, bed and furniture, one cow and calf. I give to my dtr. Mary P.
Gaines, one negro named Lydia, one horse, saddle and bridle, bed and
furniture, one cow and calf. I give to my son Enoch G. Gaines one
negro named Clark Wiley, one horse, saddle and bridle, bed and furniture,
one cow and calf. The balance of my property I lend to my wife during
her life time, provided she raise and educate my two sons Enoch G. and
Elisha, and at her death be divided between my living children. I

appoint my wife Mary Gaines as Executrix and sons Reuben, James Junr., Henry Gaines as Executors. Dated 22 Nov. 1829. Wit: James Gaines, Benjamin X Morgan, Francis X Morgan. Proven 5 Mar. 1832.

Henry Gaines, Sr. Will of Henry Gaines, Sr. Box 16 $205. Probate Judge Office. Pickens, S. C. Being in decline of life and infirm of body but of sound and disposing mind and memory, etc. Revoking all other except two deeds made to my grand chn. to wit: Mariah and Henry P. Gaines, chn. of my son Robert Gaines. I give to my dtr. Caty Waggoner $200.00 to her and her heirs forever. I give to my dtr. Elizabeth Johnson $125.00 to her and her heirs forever. I give to my dtr. Nancy Dogan $200.00 with a deduction of $93.00 which she received. To my son Reuben Gaines being legacy of mother estate. I give to my dtr. Lucy Sims $19.91 to her and her heirs forever. The rest of my estate be sold and equally divided between following living chn. Nancy Dogan, Lucy Sims, Jonadab Gaines, Mariah Clardy to have her father part for her affection to her father in his affliction also Henry P. Gaines son of Robert Gaines and Mary P. Gaines dtr. of Richard Gaines. I appoint Robert Gaines and James Gaines, Esq. as Executors. Dated 5 Feb. 1828. Wit: James Gaines, Nancy X Gaines, Marindy J. Gaines. Signed: Henry Gaines. Codicil: For the concerning the maintainance of a negro woman named Lane profit of a certain tract of land whereon I now live. Beginning at a post oak corner of William Arnolds by the Meeting House a straight line to Robert Gaines line. After the death of Laner I give sd. land to grandson Henry Gaines son of Robert. Dated 19 May 1830. Wit: Mehala Thompson, Andrew Beller, James Gaines. Signed: Henry Gaines. Proven 2 Aug. 1830.

James Gaines. Will of James Gaines. Box 25 #298. Probate Judge Office. Pickens, S. C. I, James Gaines being of a sound mind and memory, etc. I give to my dtr. Marinda J. Gaines one feather bed, one cow and calf. I give to my dtr. Catharine J. Gaines, one feather bed and furniture, one cow and calf. I give to my dtr. Elizabeth A. Gaines one feather bed and furniture, one cow and calif. I give to my dtr. Frances P. Cann five dollars to make her equal with what I have given her. I desire my son Thomas H. Gaines to have a good English education to be paid from the estate, and a horse, saddle and bridle worth one hundred dollars. I give to my wife Nancy Gaines during her natural life all real, personal property, consisting of two hundred acres, negroes, household, kitchen furniture, stoch, horses, cattle, hoggs, waggon, tools, etc. At wife death son Thomas to have the plantation, with rest of property divided between my nine dtr. to wit: Sarah Campbell, Margaret B. Evatt, Philadelphia D. Mullinix, Mary K. Campbell, Marinda J. Gaines, Matilda Boggs, Catharine J. Gaines, Elizabeth A. Gaines and Frances P. Cann. I appoint Rev. Wm. G. Mullinnix and Aaron Boggs as executors. Dated 15 Nov. 1840. Wit: Thos. J. Zachary, J. A. Evatt, John G. Mullinnix. Signed James Gaines. Prove 6 Sept. 1841.

Henry Gaines, Esq. Estate of Henry Gaines, Esq. Box 35 #398. Probate Judge Office. Pickens, S. C. Est. Admr. 12 Jan. 1855 by Barnet S. Gains, Mariah Gains, Reuben Gains, James D. Gassaway who are bound unto W. J. Parson, Ord. in the sum of $4,000.00. On 4 Nov. 1856 paid note to E. G. Gains estate $17.45. Paid R. Gains acct. $40.70. Left widow and five chn. no names given. sale 12 Jan. 1855. Buyers: Mariah Gaines, B. S. Gaines, Robert Gaines, E. C. Gaines, Jas. Neal, R. J. Smith, Benj. Douthit, J. D. Elrod.

Enoch G. Gaines. Estate of Enoch G. Gaines. Box 37 $416. Probate Judge Office. Pickens, S. C. On 3 Sept. 1855 a letter of admr. was granted to Cornelius M. Sharp, Samuel Reid are bound unto W. J. Parson, Ord. in the sum of $1,000.00. Sale made 1 Nov. 1855. Buyers: Vashti Gaines, B. S. Gaines, Rev. Wm. McWhertor, etc.

Vashti Gaines. Widow. #13. In Equity. Clerk of Court Office. Pickens, S. C. On 26 March 1856. Vashti Gaines the widow of Dr. Enoch G. Gaines, decd. states that he died in 1850 with considerable real estate, one tract on East side of Keowee River containing 445 acres, adj. land of W. L. Keith, J. P. Benson and others, also a tract on both sides of Six Mile Creek containing 433 acres, adj. land of F. N. Garvin,

Elishe Lawrence and others. That Dr. Gaines left as his next of kin and distributee his brother Elisha Gaines who resides in Texas, and your oratrix his widow. She is desirous of possessing her share, etc.etc. On 14 Apr. 1858, Elisha Gaines of the State of Texas sell to Marcus M. Arnold his share of the estate of Dr. E. G. Gaines, decd. for $1,154.45¢. On 1 Jan. 1860 Milford Burriss and Vasthi Burriss recd. her share of Dr. Gaines decd. est.

Simeon Gaines. Estate of Simeon Gaines. Box 4 #43. Probate Judge Office. Pickens, S. C. Est. Admr. 20 Aug. 1833 by James O. Lewis, Benj. D. Duthrie, who are bound unto Jas. H. Dendy, Ord. in the sum of $200.00. Cit. pub. at Rock Spring Meeting House. Sale 21 Sept. 1833. Byrs. Nancy Gaines, Robert Gaines, Richard Harris, John Wooten, J. O. Lewis, Capt. John Abbet, John Abbet, Jr., Eli Cleveland, Anderson Blalock, Abner Armstrong, Joseph Beaty, John McWhorter, Nancy Gaines was a dtr. of Benjamin Armstrong decd. Her father will proven 13 Dec. 1832. She is survived by her brothers, Abner Crosby and Charles Armstrong and three sisters viz: Rebecca McWhotter, probably the wife of Ezekiel McWhorter who was Exor. of her father's will, Gillah Wooten and her husband John Wooten, Syntha Armstrong. The husband of Nancy Gaines was not mentioned in the will. Benjamin Cornelius Wooten was the son of Gillah and John Wooten. On 7 Jan. 1875 Benjamin Cornelius Wooten's widow, Charlotte Wooten was living at Tunnel Hill, Ga. She wrote a letter to the Ord. of Pickens Dist. stating that her husband B. C. Wooten had died in the war. Copy of letter in Armstrong file no. 11.

Robert Gaines. Estate of Robert Gaines. Box 77 #816. Probate Judge Office. Pickens, S. C. I Robert Gaines being of sound mind and memory etc. First pay all expenses be paid. I will to my granddaughter Mary Lieuezer Power all my personal property, one negro named Gibb, one bed, five chairs, table and some tools. I appoint B. S. Gaines, J. D. Gassaway and Reubin Gaines to be executors. Dated: 23 May 1863. Wit: J. D. Gassaway, Mahala Thompson, Susan F. Gaines, J. N. Arnold, Mary X Arnold. Signed: Robert Gaines. Proven 29 Feb. 1864.

Mary E. Gaines. Estate of Mary E. Gaines. Box 126 #9. Probate Judge Office. Pickens, S. C. Est. Admr. 7 May 1896 by R. G. Gaines, J. T. Gassaway, A. Ramsier who are bound unto J. B. Newberry, Ord. in the sum of $1,000. Died Jan. 1896. R. G. Gaines a brother in law.

George Galphin. Will of George Galphin. Box 40 #898. Abbeville, S. C. I George Galphin do make this my last will and testament, etc. It is my will that all every the legatees herein named or mentioned after my death be and remain from all manner of slavery and bondage. I will my muletto girl named Barbara be free, also I give to my muletto girls Rachel and Betsey (dtr. of a muletto woman named Sapho). I also give my half breed Indian girl Rose (dtr. of Nitehucky) her freedom. I also give her five cows and calves, two mares and colts. I give to Thomas Galphin son of Rachel Dupee all my household furniture and plates, ten mares and colts with half of all stock of cattle at Ogeehee. Also the use occupation and enjoyment of my grist mill and saw mill being on the North side of Town Creek, together with all land on the same side of the sd. creek of about one thousand acres. Also the use of my new ____ with four hundred acres belonging to it. Also the use of all land from Wm. Shaw's lower line upon Savannah River at the Spanish cutoff down the river to Mr. McGillvery's lower line of about 1300 acres. Also one tract of land on the side of the swamp in Georgia, which I bought from James McHenry. Also one thousand acres of ceded land. Also 350 acres of land upon Ogeehee which I bought from Patrick Dennison. Also a tract of land on the back swamp of 400 acres. Also the use and labor of the following slaves viz: Petersison and his wife Nanny and their chdn. Cato and wife Bess their chn. Michal and his wife Sarah their chn. Coffe and his wife Betty their chn. Derham and his wife Celia their chn. Goodfellow (a negro man) Sarah I had of James DeNeaux and her chn. Little Frank (a mustee boy), Davey (a negro man). Pompey and his wife and issue. Rachel (Friday's wife) and her chn. (Limitations are viz: The mill house land and slaves to sd. Thomas can only be will to his issue and to theirs issue. etc.) I give to Martha Galphin

(dtr. of Rachel Dupee) two tracts of land of five hundred acres each
lying and being above McRaes above Augusta, Ga. also two lots of land
in Augusta, also fifty acres in Augusta which I bought from John
Joachin where Gray lived. Also a tract outside of the swamp I bought of
Wade joining McHenry's land in Georgia. Also two thousand acres ceded
land. Also ten horses, seven mares with half the stock of cattle at
Ogeehee. Also the work and labor of the following slaves, viz: Dick
and wife Cleranda their chn. Billey and wife Dina their chn. Dutch,
Jenny, Rockey and their chn. Jemima and her chn. Deborah and her chn.
____ and his wife Juda and child. Trump and his wife Tina their chn.
Peter and his wife Silvia their chn. and Little Jacob. (Same limitations and restrictions for Martha slaves as on her brother Thomas's).
I give to George the son of Metawney (an Indian woman) ten horses, even
mares, also one third of all stock of cattle with his own, his sister
Judith's and brother John's mark or brand. Also the use of the old
brick house with one hundred acres of land. Also three hundred acres
joining below the old brick house. Also five hundred acres above the
Spanish cutoff on Savannah River in Ga. Also the mill on the South side
of Town Creek with one hundred acres. Another tract of one thousand
acres above the saw mill, to be held by them jointly. Also two thousand
acres ceded land. I also give to George the use and labor of the
following slaves viz: Coboy and his wife Sarah their chn. August a
muletto man and his chn. (except Rose whose freedom I have herein given.)
Moll and her chn. Kingston and his wife Darkey their chn. Grays Mark
and his wife Claranda and any issue she may have by him, Sue and her
chn. Joe and his wife Hannah their chn. Long John and his wife Sarah
their chn. Leander, Frank and Harry (Same limitations and restrictions
as the others). I give to John (son of Metawney) ten horses, seven
mares one third of all his own, his sisters Judith's and brother
George's mark or brand as they may find. Also I give to John a tract
of land upon Ogechee in Georgia called Old Town containing about 1500
acres. Also a tract below it that was John Sallers'. Also a tract
in the swamp called Dunifins place. Also two hundred acres joining it,
and the Joel Walker behind it. Also I give to John and his brother
George the saw mill on the South side of Town Creek with the land whereon it stands of about one hundred acres, with the land I run on the
South side above the mill of about one thousand acres, to be held by
them jointly. Also I give to John one thousand acres ceded land. Also
I give the labor of the following slaves, viz: Stepney and his wife
Margaret their chn. Phina and her chn. Mingo and his wife Maria their
chn. Ockera and his wife Cate their chn. Limerick, King, Nero, Golo
Peter a negro man, Olifer and his wife Cresha their chn. New negro
Dick, Peter (I bought of Joseph Butler) and his wife their chn, Sapho
(a muletto woman) her chn. (except her dtr. Rachel and Betsey whom ____
made free. New negro Jack, Bulley and Chevers negro man, also Delia
a half breed Indian woman, she to serve him for seven years, then be
free. On the day of her freedom John is to give her five cows and
calves. (Land and slaves to John has same limitations and restrictions
as the others.) I give to Judith (dtr. of Metawney) the use of the
upper half of three tracts of land, which was run from Mr. Newman line
down to the point containing in the whole about 1300 or 1400 acres with
the swelling house where she now lives called Silver Bluff. Also I
give to Judith two thousand acres ceded land. Also ten horses, seven
mares, also one third of the stock of her or her brothers George or John
where they may be found. Also the use and labor of the following
slaves viz: Marick and his wife Marcha their chn., Billey, Peter,
Cela (Mustees) her chn., Sally an Indian and her chn. Kelly, Abraham
and his wife Elcey their chn. Cyrus and his wife Sue their chn. Joe
and his wife Emma and their chn. Gabriel and his wife Minerva their
chn. Jacob and his wife Cloe their chn. Charlotte and her issue.
(Land and slaves to Judith same limitations and restrictions as the
others.) I give to Barbara (the dtr. of Rose decd.) the use of the
lower half of three tracts, which runs from Mr. Newman's line down to
the point containing about 1300 or 1400 acres. I also give to Barbara
two thousand acres of ceded land, also ten horses, seven mares, likewise
all cattle with her own brand or mark. Also the labor of the following
slaves, viz: Little March, Kate--that was his wife and their chn.
Ponpon, Jemmy and Betsy his wife and their chn. Ned and his sister
Dido (son and dtr. of Dido decd.) and her chn., Bidgo and Lib his wife.

Young Lib and her chn. Mina and Ellsey and their chn. Catch (a boy)
Santee Jemmy, Tom I had of Mr. McGillvery and his wife Hannah and their
chn. Indian Peter and his wife Caputhey and their chn. and Georgia
Bublin. (With same limitations and restrictions as the other legatees.)
I also give to Thomas negro named Abraham which I had of Mr. Barnard,
also Indian Prince. I also give unto Thomas my great guns, with my
silver mounted gun and pistols. The rest of guns I give to George and
John between them. The six named devisees and legatees viz: George,
Thomas, John, Judith, Martha and Barbara should die without issue the
share shall be divided between my Executors and the survivors of the
said legatees. It is my will that during their respective minorities
be maintained, clothed, schooled and educated out of the profit of the
estate. I give to David Holms ₤500 sterling also two tracts of land
on the long reaches where Galpin lived, and one tract on the long reaches on the Georgia side I bought of Benjamin Stedham and two thousand
acres ceded land. I leave to my sister Judith Galphin ₤150 sterling.
I leave to Catherine Galphin living in Ireland ₤150 sterling. I give to
my sister Margaret Holms ₤50 sterling, to each of her children living
in Ireland ₤50 sterling, and to her son Robert living here ₤50 sterling
and 100 acres ceded land. I give to Mrs. Taylor ₤50 sterling also 500
acres ceded land, and to each of her children five cows and calves. I
give to ___ Crossby ₤50 sterling, __ horse and side saddle, and to each
of her chn. ₤50 sterling and 500 acres ceded land, and a horse and mare
to each. I leave to my cousin George Rankin in Ireland ₤70 sterling.
I leave to George Noland ₤50 sterling and a horse. I leave to my Aunt
Lennard's daughter in Ireland ₤50 sterling. I leave to Cousin John
Trotter ₤50 sterling. I leave to Rachel (dtr. of Sapho) two negro men
and two negro women to be bought from the first ship that come in with
negroes. Also ten cows and calves, three mares and colts, one horse
and twenty pds. sterling. Also the tract of land where John Roton lived
called Claud's place between Macbean and Brier Creek. I leave to
Betsey one new negro man and woman to be bought for her. Ten cows and
calves, two mares and colts, one horse and a tract of land below the
cowpen. Thomas (son of Rachel Dupee) children are to be maintained and
schooled on the plantation till they marry or come of age. I leave to
Betsey Callwell (dtr. of Mary Callwell) one new negro wench, ten cows
and calves, two mares and colts, one riding horse and saddle, the tract
of land at the Three Runs at the old Stomp above Tims Branch and fifty
pds. Carolina Currency to be laid out in clothing for her. I leave
to all the poor widows and fatherless children within thirty miles of
where I live in the province of South Carolina and Georgia fifty pds.
sterling. I leave fifty pds. sterling to be shared among the poor of
Armagh in Ireland. I leave to Timothy Barnard ₤200 sterling. I leave
to all the orphans I beought up ₤10 sterling each and Billey Brown to
be bound out to a trade. I leave John McQueen and Alexander his
brother each a good riding horse and to each and their wives a ring. I
leave to Mr. Netherclift and his wife a ring. I leave to all my
executors a suit of mourning and a ring each. I leave Mr. & Mrs. Wylly
each a ring. I leave to their dtr. Suckey Wylly ₤50 sterling and a
suit of mourning. I leave to each of my sisters, their husband and
children a ring. I leave to Mrs. Campbell a ring. I leave to Mr.
Carlan Campbell a ring. I leave to Mrs. Fraser a ring and ₤10 sterling.
I give to Mr. Newman a ring and twenty pds. sterling. I give to widow
Atkins twenty pds. sterling and a ring. I give to her son William a
good riding horse, and to her dtr. a good pacing horse. I give to
Mr. & Mrs. Grierson each a ring. I give to Parson Seymour and his wife
each a ring. I give to George Parsons a likely boy to be bought from
the first ship that come in, and one of my best riding horses. I leave
to Quintin Pooler 500 acres of ceded land, and all the rest of my
cousin Poolers men and woman each a ring. I leave to Rachel Dupee the
use of one negro man called Foot, one negro wench called Charlotte and
her chn. and Martha Boy called Jacob. Rachel to get household and
kitchen furniture. I leave to my Sister Young in Ireland ₤50 sterling,
to each of her children ₤50 sterling, and to each 500 acres ceded
land, and five cows and calves, a horse and mare. I hereby appoint
James Parsons, John Graham, Lauchlin McGillvery Esqrs. John Parkinson
and sd. George Thomas, and John Galphin as Executors. Dated 6 April
1776. Wit: David ___, J.P., Michael Meyer, John Sturzenegger.

Signed: George Galphin. There is two codicils to the will, the first dated 14 Feb. 1778. He makes changes in land and slaves in both. Last one dated 16 March 1780. This will is torn into small pieces and full of holes. Any blank spaces in this abstract is due to a torn place.

GAMBRELL

Madden J. Gambrell. Estate of Madden J. Gambrell. Box 109 #1043. Probate Judge Office. Pickens, S. C. Est. Admr. 3 June 1876 by Maria E. Gambrell widow, Reid Gambrell, B. C. Johnson who are bound unto I. H. Philpot, Ord. in the sum of $2,000.00.

Madden J. Gambrell. Estate of Madden J. Gambrell. Box 94 #1002. Probate Judge Office. Pickens, S. C. Est. Admr. 5 Jan. 1885 by Burrell C. Johnson, J. J. Johnson, J. P. Payne who are bound unto J. H. Newton, Ord. in the sum of $800.00. 19 Nov. 1884 Burrell C. Johnson states that the widow Maria E. Gambrell died about six weeks ago.

Gambrell Minors. Probate Judge Office. Box 7 #70. Pickens, S. C. On 1 Sept. 1885 Burrell C. Johnson, J. P. Payne, Simeon Eskew are bound unto J. H. Newton, Ord. in the sum of $350.00. B. C. Johnson gdn. for Lela A., Mary R., Norah, Thomas J. and William Gambrell minors under 21 years. Chn. of Madden Gambrell, who owned real estate in Pickens and Anderson Counties. He died in Pickens Co. But their mother Maria E. Gambrell died in Anderson Co., S. C.

GANTT

Cador Gantt. Estate of Cador Gantt. Pack 345. Clerk of Court Office. Abbeville, S. C. Will of--I Cador Gantt being advanced in age and growing weak in body though of a sound mind etc.etc. I give to my beloved wife Sarah Gantt all real estate and other property of every description. Sell what may be necessary to pay my debts and just debts during my wife life, after the death of Sarah sell all property except negro Phillis, on such terms and conditions as best for all and apply as directed. I give to Joseph Pratt, Wm. Pratt, Josiah Burton, Tyra Gantt, James Pratt, David Pratt, Jacob Lollar, Yate Perkins, Richard Alexander and Sampson Gantt, to each two dollars. I give to Cador Gantt Milford (son of Mary Milford) the sum of $100.00. I also give to Gantt Wright (son of John L. Wright) the sum of $100.00. I wish my negro woman Phillis to be left free as the law of the country will admit, and the sum of fifty dollars, and I appoint my executors for her government. After paying all debts, I give the balance of the proceeds for the use of the Bible Society. I appoint my friend A. G. Latimer as executor. Dated 3 Aug. 1846. Wit: William S. Hampton, George W. Nelson, John Milford. Signed Cador Gantt. seal. In another paper in pack states that Cador Gantt died Nov. 1848 and his wife Sarah died 1858, They left no chn. just brothers and sisters. Filed 8 March 1860 by Thomas Crawford Admr. with the will annexed of Cador Gantt decd. Gantt by his will named B. Latimer as Executor who has also died leaving part of said will not executed. The Bible Society named in the will is for the Court to decide, Gantt was a member of the Abbeville, Edgefield Union Bible Society, this is the one which claims the fund in question. Gantt was a member of the Little River Baptist Church. His brothers and sisters are: Giles Gantt died in S.C. chn. unknown. John Gantt died in N.C. chn. unknown. Frederick Gantt died in S. C. chn. Cynthia Wakefield wife of Hezekiah Wakefield decd. and John Gantt of Anderson Dist. Tira Gantt lived in Indiana, left chn.: Calvin, Newton, James, Crowther, William, Martha and Sarah maybe others. Britton Gantt lived in Indiana, chn. unknown. Abagail wife of Lenard Saylors, Saylors, Sarah wife of a Perkins lived in Ala., Elizabeth wife of Jacob Tolar (maybe Lolar) lived in Ala. left chn: Hugh, William, Elizabeth, Martha, Sarah and Mary. Amey wife of a Saylors lived in

Tenn. chn. unknown. Nancy wife of a Alexander lived in Tenn. chn.
unknown. Viney wife of John Townley lived out of state, chn. unknown.
Brothers and sisters of Mrs. Cador Gannt are: Mary wife of Josiah
Burton living in this Dist. chn. John Burton, Peter Burton, Mary
wife of Joshua Ashley living out of State. Joseph Pratt, decd. with 5
chn.; Amy wife of Samuel Young resides in Ga., Sarah wife of William
Young of this Dist. William Pratt and Elizabeth wife of John
McConnell both of this Dist. William Pratt lived in Kentucky left
nine chn. one was Susannah who married Tira Gantt brother of intestate.

Nicey Gantt. Estate. Book B Page 30. Probate Judge Office. Pickens,
S. C. On 7 Aug. 1858 the heirs of Nicey Gantt were Caroline Gantt,
John Gantt, William Gantt, Alexander Gantt. were heirs of a John A.
Childress decd.

Martin Gantt. Land Warrant to Martin Gantt. Pack 630 #16. Clerk of
Court Office. Pickens, S. C. From J. E. Hagood, Clerk, to any lawful
surveyor or to Thomas D. Garvin, Dep. Sur. You are authorized to lay
out for Martin Gantt a tract of land, etc. Dated 23 Feb. 1863.

GARNER

John Garner. Deed from John Garner to John Field, Sr. Pack 211 #17.
Clerk of Court Office. Pickens, S. C. John Garner to John Field, Sr.
both of Pendleton, Dist. Dated 10 Apr. 1820. In the sum of $450.00
paid in hand by Field Sr. for 100 acres lying on Brandy Creek waters of
Twelve Mile River on the West side of sd. creek, adj. land of Sammons
line, Salmon line, March Banks land. Wit: Bailey Barton, Richerson
Frazer, Elizabeth X Gibson. Signed John Garner, seal. Deed attested
by Richerson Frazer before Bailey Barton, J.P. 10 Apr. 1820. On 11
Jan. 1821 Jenny Garner wife of John Garner appeared before Barton and
renounce, released and relinquished her dower forever. Signed Jenny X
Garner. Bailey Barton, J.P.

Henry Garner. Estate of Henry Garner. Pack 128. Clerk of Court Office.
In Equity. Pickens, S. C. James Garner states that Henry Garner died
in Pickens Dist. in 1848. Owned 100 acres on 18 mile Creek bought from
Robert Anderson, Jr. Also 96 acres bought from Robert Baker on north
branches of 18 mile Creek. Also 130 acres bought from Thomas Garvin on
West side of Little 15 Mile Creek. He left a widow Nancy and six chn.
viz; Polly widow of Thomas Boggs decd. Mahala wife of Hardy Fennel,
Ruhama widow of Barnett Neighbors decd. Matilda wife of John Garner,
James Garner, heirs of Sylvania Boggs decd. the wife of Aaron Boggs
to wit. Josiah N. Boggs, James A. Boggs, William Garner and wife
Matilda, Henry G. Boggs, Munro Boggs, John Mullenax and wife Elizabeth,
Madison Boggs, Martha Boggs. Filed 21 June 1849. On 7 Feb. 1849 Aaron
Boggs states that Martha Boggs is over 12 years and Madison Boggs is
over 14 years. A Power of Attorney from William A. Mullinax and Sylvania
Mullinax of Monroe County, Miss. appoints Aaron Boggs as their attorney
to collect, receive or drawn any money or monies from the estate of
Henry Garner decd. Dated 17 Dec. 1850. Signed Wm. A. Mullinax and
Sylvania Mullinax. Signed at Aberdeen, Miss. before D. W. Sadler, J.P.

Nancy Garner. Will of Nancy Garner. Box 24 #288. Probate Judge
Office. Pickens, S. C. I Nancy Garner being in the full possession
of my mental faculties but infirm from age and feeble in health, etc.
I hereby give to my two dtr. my real and personal property and cash I
may have or be entitled to. Rhuama wife of Barnet Neighbors now decd.
and Matilda wife of John Garner. To be divided between them. I appoint
John T. Sloan of Pendleton Village my executor. Dated 25 June 1849.
Wit: Ezekiel Madden, A. M. Boggs. Signed Nancy X Garner. Proven 24
Feb. 1851.

Starling Garner. Estate of Starling Garner. Box 17 #216. Probate
Judge Office. Pickens, S. C. Est. admr. 24 July 1848 by Wyatt Garner,
Daniel Fullerton, Wm. C. Lee who are bound unto Wm. D. Steel, Ord. in
the sum of $600.00. He owned 155 acres on Coneross Creek adj. land of

John C. Gordon, B. W. Burns, Henry McDaniels and others. Heirs: Sarah the widow, Wyatt, Henry M., T. R., Mary, John, Starling, C. C., Harriet, James M., Sarah J., and William R. Garner.

GARRETT

Matthew Garrett. Power of Attorney of Matthew Garrett. (No ref. given Sarah Dill died in Greenville Dist.) We Matthew and Sarah Garrett of Jackson Co., N. C. this day appoint Elijah Dill of Greenville Dist., S. C. our agent and attorney in fact to collect, receive and receipt from the estate of Sarah Dill decd. Dated 17 June 1856. Wit: William Garrett. Signed Matthew Garrett and Sarah Garrett. Same day came James Fisher before John Wilson, J.P. and on oath that he was acquainted with Sarah Garrett and knew her to be a lawful heir of Sarah Dill. Signed: John Wilson, J.P.

Garrett. Deed from Garrett to Reeder. Box 94 #995. Probate Judge Office. Pickens, S. C. I Joel W. Garrett of Bankes Co., Ga. to James H. Reeder of Pickens, Co., S. C. in the sum of $150 paid by Reeder all my half of a certain tract of land lying on the West side of Crooked Creek. Adj. land of Stephen Garrett. The other half owned by John R. M. Cannon, Munro Cannon, James Hunnicutt containing 25 acres. Dated 17 Feb. 1864. Wit: A. Bryce, Sr. W. M. Woodin. Signed J. W. Garrett. Per C. H. Speares, Atty.

Garrett. Deed from Cannon to Garrett and Neal. Same ref. as above. Pickens, S. C. I John R. M. Cannon in the sum of ___ paid Charles Neal and Stephen Garrett, all that tract of land whereon Warren R. Cannon now lives, lying on the West side of Crooked Creek. Dated 17 July 1861. Wit: J. C. Fringe, G. A. Taylor. Signed John R. M. Cannon, seal. In another paper, the heirs of Stephen Garrett are: Martha Garrett widow, Vilanta wife Frasier McCartee, Milton, Harrison, Elizabeth, Warren, Franklin, Bluford Garrett. McCartee and Milton Garrett lived out of State.

David Garrett. Estate of David Garrett. Box 73 #778. Probate Judge Office. Pickens, S. C. Est. admr. 8 Feb. 1864 by Elizabeth Garrett widow, Samuel Chapman, Wm. N. Craig who are bound unto W.E. Holcombe, Ord. in the sum of $1200.00. On 19 Feb. 1858 David Garrett and his wife Elizabeth Chapman were heirs of Joshua Chapman decd. and his wife Elizabeth Chapman of Pickens Dist.

Garrett. Asaault Garrett vs Blake. Pack 220 #28. Clerk of Court Office. Pickens, S. C. On 30 July 1880 William Garrett made oath that Joseph Blake did assault upon his wife Garrick, by coming into his house in a rude manner. I told him not to come into my house. He went off and soon came back with three clubs. He keep my awake all night, his wife was at my house. The next morning about one half hour by sun he seized my wife and tried to drag her out of the house, saying at the time God dam you I am going to take you out of here. I ordered him three times to let go of her, he would not do it and I struck him over the head with an axe and knocked him down.

GARVIN

Thomas Garvin. Estate of Thomas Garvin. Book 2 page 32. Probate Judge Office. Pickens, S. C. To J. E. Hagood, Ord. We the legal heirs of Thomas Garvin decd. Petition your Court to sell the real estate consisting of two tracts. #1. on Laurel Fork of Keowee River, adj. land of Henry Morton and others containing 1030 acres. #2. tract on Mile Creek, adj. land of B. Hagood, F. N. Garvin, and others containing 350 acres to be sold for a division among the heirs. Dated 18 Nov. 1859. Signed F. N. Garvin. Heirs were: F. N. Garvin, Betsy wife Samuel Smith, Ann wife of E. W. Merritt, Thos. D. Garvin, Matilda wife of Samuel Parson, Ferdela wife of Robert Johnston, Green S. Garvin,

Marilda wife of James H. Evatt.

Thomas Garvin. Land Warrant to Thomas Garvin. Pack 630 #183. Clerk of Court Office. Pickens, S. C. By W. L. Keith, Commissioner of Locations for Pickens Dist. To any lawful surveyor you are authorized to lay out unto Thomas Garvin a tract of land not exceeding ten thousand acres, etc. Warrant Certified 8 Aug. 1853. Executed for 2473 acres.

L. Armes Garvin. Will of L. Armes Garvin. Box 81 #861. Probate Judge Office. Pickens, S. C. I L. A. Garvin being of sound mind and memory, etc. I give to my wife Sarah Jane Garvin all my real and personal property, and all monies due me for her use and benefit during widowhood and at death to go to my son Lue Armp Garvin after just debts are paid, by selling personal property first. I appoint Joseph J. Norton and Neuriden A. Garvin as executors. Dated 23 Apr. 1864. Wit: W. B. White, W. H. Thomas, N. B. Lusk. Signed: L. Armp Garvin, seal. Proven 20 July 1864.

Frederick N. Garvin. Will of Frederick N. Garvin. Box 107 #1117. Probate Judge Office. Pickens, S. C. I Frederick N. Garvin being weak in body but of sound mind and memory, etc. First pay my just debts and funeral expenses. To my dtr. Lucy Hannah Brock all that tract of land on Camp Creek of 381 acres ref. to land on plat made by Thomas D. Garvin 13 July 1853. Also horse John. To Mandanna wife of Benajah Williams a tract of land #16 and 18 of estate of Saml. Maverick decd. on Camp Creek and 12 Mile River being 462 acres. To Sarah Jane wife of Franklin Orr two tracts of land #1 tract on a branch of Praters Creek waters of 12 mile River and a part of Six Mile mountain containing 400 acres ref. by a plat made by J. J. Garvin in Dec. 1874. #2 tract on head waters of Camp Creek, adj. land of Bloomer Merck, and land willed to Lucy Hannah Brock, containing 362 acres. I give to Mary E. wife of W. B. Boggs two tracts of land. #1 tract, on a branch of Shoal Creek near Six Mile Mountain of 426 acres. #2 tract, on waters of Todds and Six Mile Creeks adj. land of R. F. Morgan, J. King, F. L. Garvin, known as the cross road tract, containing 327 acres. To my son F. L. Garvin a tract of 662 acres, also one tenth of the income from the saw mill to be set up by Joseph Simmons and W. J. N. Benton. All other property both real and personal or mixed to son F. L. Garvin, who is to pay all debts and funeral expenses, and pay dtr. Sarah Orr $150 and to dtr. Mary E. Boggs $75. I appoint my son F. L. Garvin as executor, the one tenth part of saw mill income to pay him for managing my will. Wit: W. E. Holcombe, J. C. C. Boggs, J. N. Arnold. Signed F. N. Garvin, seal. Proven 19 Feb. 1875. Lucy Hannah Brock was admr. of W. O. Brock decd. est. 20 Mar. 1878. Paid Mary E. Hunnicut and Malinda Russell $10.00 each.

F. L. Garvin. Estate of F. L. Garvin. Box 131 #5. Probate Judge Office. Pickens, S. C. Est. admr. 25 Apr. 1898 by Marietta Garvin, C. L. Dean, W. B. Cook who are bound unto J. B. Newberry, Ord. in the sum of $200.00. He died 26 Jan. 1898. Marietta Garvin the widow.

Jesse Garvin. Estate of Jesse Garvin. Box 115 #7. Probate Judge Office. Pickens, S. C. Est. admr. 9 Nov. 1887 by Aaron Garvin, B. J. Johnson, Isaac Hallums who are bound unto J. B. Newberry, Ord. in the sum of $40.00. He died 24 July 1887. Aaron Garvin a son.

F. N. Garvin. Deed of Assignment F. N. Garvin to George W. Rankin. Pack 38. Clerk of Court Office. Pickens, S. C. for the better securing of certain debts due and owing by me, do grant, bargained, sold and released unto G. W. Rankin all my real estate (17 tracts of about 10,000 acres) together with six negroes named, Sally, Harry, Sampson, Phillis, Henry and Lucy with all stock of all kinds and household furniture. Dated 1 Oct. 1860. Wit: W. E. Holcombe, W. N. Craig. Signed: F. B. Garvin, seal.

Fredrick N. Garvin. Pack 122. In Equity. Clerk of Court Office. Pickens, S. C. George W. Garvin assignee of the estate of Fredrick N. Garvin. That the sd. Garvin in fee simple a tract of land on waters of Chauga, adj. land of George Seaborn, John West containing 138 acres.

Whereas F. N. Garvin and William Welsh entered into a sale of said land on 1 June 1857 for $400. Garvin to make deed when full amount was paid Having bought cattle, hogs, sheep also from Garvin, with a balance of only $188 for the total. Garvin on 1 Oct. 1860 did deed unto G. W. Rankin the said land. Filed 14 May 1861.

Addella Hyden. Estate of Addella Hyden. Box 50 #549. Probate Judge Office. Pickens, S. C. Est. admr. 25 Sept. 1859 in Pickens Dist. was formerly Addella Garvin of Georgia.

GARY

Thomas R. Gary. Estate of Thomas R. Gary. Box 109 #1040. Probate Judge Office. Pickens, S. C. I Thomas R. Gary being of sound mind and memory etc. I will that my just debts be paid. I will to my wife Elizabeth Gary all my real and personal property as long as she remains a widow, and use the property for her comfort and raising and education my legal heirs. If she marry both real and personal property to be sold and she take a child part. I will to my two youngest dtr. (not named) when they grow up or marry to have an equal share with my other heirs who are already married and gone. They are to receive a good cow and calf, beds, furniture and fifty dollars in money. Dated 11 Dec 1869. Wit: N. R. Reeve, D. A. Green. Signed: Thomas R. Gary. Filed 15 May 1876.

Mary A. Gary. Estate of Mary A. Gary. Pack 310. Clerk of Court Office. Abbeville, S. C. To the Honr. the Chancellors: The petition of Mary A. Gary sheweth that she is the mother of William Gary son of the late Thomas R. Gary decd. a minor under the age of choice about thirteen years old. That he is entitled to a share of his father estate, and is unable to manage. Your petition pray she may be made gdn. of said child. Filed 13 June 1854.

Samuel A. Gary. Will of Samuel A. Gary. Box 120 #13. Probate Judge Office. Pickens, S. C. I Samuel Gary being of sound mind and disposing memory, etc. First pay all just debts and erect a good monument over my grave, similar to the one over my son Thomas, and at the death of my wife Lucinda erect one similar over her grave. After the debts are paid I will to my wife all my personal property of every kind including money on hand, notes due me, accounts owning me. I will to my wife all my property in the town of Liberty, consisting of two half acre lots opposite the Presbyterian Church in fee simple forever. I will to my wife the rest and residue of my real estate during her natura life, then to be sold, and the funds arising from the sale. I bequeath unto the Baptist Orphanage one hundred dollars. To Miss Amanda Jane Mayfield the sum of $250. To the heirs of E. S. Griffin and Sallie now decd. the sum of $200 to be divided between them. To Jane Singleton wife M. P. Singleton the sum of $100. To Elizabeth Craig wife of J. A. Craig the sum of $100. To the heirs of Thomas R. Gary the sum of $100. To Samuel Gary Higgins son of John A. Higgins the sum of $50. To Samuel Gary Boggs son of B. F. Boggs the sum of $50. To the heirs of Alexander and Sallie Robinson the sum of $100. I desire my executors t retain $100 to keep in repair the family graveyard, a good fence around it. I appoint my wife Lucinda B. Gary Executrix and J. M. Stewart, E. S. Griffin as Executors. Dated 8 Dec. 1891. Wit: J. H. Newton, G. W. McClannahan, J. A. Boggs. Signed: Samuel A. Gary. He died 11 Jan. 1893. Will filed 28 Jan. 1893.

GASSAWAY

Thomas Gassaway, Jr. Estate of Thomas Gassaway, Jr. Box 3 #22. Probate Judge Office. Pickens, S. C. Est. Admr. 7 Nov. 1831 by Robert, Christopher and Wm. Kirksey are bound unto Jas. H. Dendy, Ord. in the sum of $400.00. Cit. Published at Liberty Meeting House. States that

Mrs. Gassaway objected to Stephen Perry being admr. and recommended
Robert Kirksey be in his place. Sale 19 Nov. 1831. Byrs: Hannah
Gasaway, Chas. Thompson, Daniel Gasaway, Wm. Garner, Thos. Evatt, John
Russell, Frederick Garvin, Daniel Grant, Jas. Martin, Waymon Holland,
David Cherry, Henely Evatt, Saml. Smith, Robt. Kirksey, Coleman Gasaway.

Henry Gassaway. Estate of Henry Gassaway. Box 48 #535. Probate Judge
Office. Pickens, S. C. On 26 Jan. 1858 the heirs petition the Court
to sell the real estate of the decd. He had 213 acres on Long Creek
waters of Chattoga River, adj. land of Jonas Phillip, John Maxwell and
others. Heirs John Gassaway, James Gassaway, Rachel Gassaway, William
Gassaway, Jeremiah Sutton and wife Sarah, Heirs of Elizabeth Butt,
Wesley Gassaway, Ira Gassaway, Bryant Bandy and wife Phebe, Henry
Lowery and wife Sara, Jonas Phillips Sr. and wife Manervia, James C.
Lee and wife Harriett, Nathan Phillips and wife Mahala, Edward Williams
and wife Mary, David Rochild or Rothild and wife Susan, Silas Conn or
corn and wife Sarah. Jacob Butt Jr. Henry Gassaway bought tract #8
on Long Creek, paying one fourth part agreeable to the act, on those
directing the sale of land ceded by the Cherokee Indians to S. C. given
under my hand at the house of Ephraim Massey. 10 March 1818.

Thomas H. Gassaway. Estate of Thomas H. Gassaway. Box 36 #409. Probate Judge Office. Pickens, S. C. Est. admr. 5 Jan. 1855 by James D.
Gassaway, John Easley, who are bound unto W. J. Parson, Esq. Ord. in
the sum of $3,000.00. On 18 Dec. 1854 James D. Gassaway and Clara
Glassaway applied for letter of admr. Left a widow and three children
(no names given).

John W. Gassaway. Estate of John W. Gassaway. Box 27 #324. Probate
Judge Office. Pickens, S. C. Est. admr. by Tyre B. Mauldin, Wm. Robin-
son who are bound unto Wm. D. Steele, Ord. in the sum of $400. Mrs.
Candace Gassaway bought at sale.

Candace Gassaway. Estate of Candace Gassaway. Box 50 #550. Probate
Judge Office. Pickens, S. C. Est. admr. 30 Sept. 1859 by S. H. Johns,
James E. Hagood, R. A. Thompson who are bound unto W. J. Parson, Ord.
in the sum of $300.00. James S. Gassaway, Mrs. Harriet Ward, Nathaniel
Ward bought at sale.

Joseph S. Gassaway. Guardianship for Joseph S. Gassaway. Box 1 #30.
Probate Judge Office. Pickens, S. C. On 29 July 1852 Candis Gassaway
wanted Leonard Towers to be gdn. of her son Joseph Simpson Gassaway
a minor. On 26 Jan. 1853 recd. of Joseph Grisham admr. of est. of
Wm. Simpson decd. $104.57.

Matilda Ann Gassaway. Guardianship of Matilda Ann Gassaway. Box 2
#44. Probate Judge Office. Pickens, S. C. On 24 Feb. 1854 Jas. D.
Gassaway, H. L. Gains are bound unto W. J. Parson, Ord. in the sum of
$500.00. James D. Gassaway gdn. for Matilda Ann a minor over 14 years.
Matilda Ann and Jas. D. Gassaway had a interest in est. of Wm. McDow
decd. also Gr.chn. of Thos. Gassaway decd. On 18 Dec. 1861 Matilda Ann
ment. as wife of F. H. Thurber.

Joseph S. Gassaway. Will of Joseph S. Gassaway. Box 127 #11. Probate
Judge Office. Pickens, S. C. I Joseph S. Gassaway being of sound mind
and memory, etc. I desire my debts be paid, each of my heirs to bear
an equal portion thereof. I give to my dtr. Mary Eliza Gassaway, my
sons Charles Lee, Thomas Traywick, and Paul Deway Gassaway the mill and
mill seat of about five acres. I give to Mary about 25 acres on the
public road leading to Centeral, Bed and furniture, cow known as Mollie
calf. I give Charley Lee one half of the Campbell tract of about
40 acres. I give to Thomas the other half of the Campbell tract. I
give to Paul about 25 acres lying on 12 Mile River. I give to my wife
Julia C. to have free and full access to and control of the real and
personal property. My sons do not sell the property until after the
death of my wife. Dated 22 July 1887. Wit: J. R. Williams, W. E.
Bellotte, T. W. Folger. Signed: Joseph S. Gassaway. He died 14 Mar.
1897. Filed 27 Mar. 1897.

Thomas H. Gassaway. Estate of Thomas H. Gassaway. Box 1 #30. Probate
Judge Office. Pickens, S. C. On 28 Aug. 1875, he owned 200 acres on
12 Mile River, adj. land of T. J. Robinson, C. N. Reed. Heirs: C.
Gassaway widow, Mary J. R. wife of Benjamin Madden, John E. and Thomas
H. Gassaway minors.

Warren W. Gassaway. Guardianship of Warren W. Gassaway. Box 2 #40.
Probate Judge Office. Pickens, S. C. On 24 Feb. 1854 Reubin Arnold,
H. L. Gains are bound unto W. J. Parson, Ord. in the sum of $300.
Reubin Arnold gdn. for Warren Washington Gassaway a minor under 21 years.
Had interest in est. of Wm. McDow decd. 5 Mar. 1855 recd. of G. W.
McDow admr. of Capt. W. McDow decd. $80.80.

Thomas Gassaway. Will of Thomas Gassaway. Box 31 #359. Probate Judge
Office, Pickens, S. C. I Thomas Gassaway being of a sound mind and
memory, etc. First pay just debts. I will to my beloved wife Darcas
during her life or widowhood, a negro named Juliet, also use of
dwelling house with as much land as she may think necessary for the
comfortable support of herself and negroes, also as much kitchen and
household furniture as she may select for her use. I will to my son
Samuel F. a negro boy named William. I will to my son James D. a bed
and furniture, and a bureau, and the tract of land on which he now
lives, of about 150 acres. I will to my dtr. Lucinda wife of Allen C.
Harbin a negro girl named Amy, after her death to her heirs if any, if
not, then the sd. Amy to revert to the heirs of son John W. Gassaway.
I will to my son Thomas H. a negro boy named Elijah and a bookcase. I
will to my son Joseph Smith, all land lying East of road from Pendleton
to Mauldins Ford on 12 Mile River, being part of the Campbell place and
a part of the homestead whereon are the mills, also another tract of
about 200 acres on 12 mile River known as the Todd land. Also negro
named John, with a bed and walnut bureau and a sorrel horse. I will
to my dtr. Darcas Ann a negro girl named Mariah, a cow and calf, two
feather beds and furniture, all the land lying on West side of road from
Pendleton to Mauldin Ford on 12 Mile River. I will to my son Enoch B.
a negro boy named Henry. I will unto my son James D. in trust for use
and benefit of my dtr. Elizabeth the wife of Jesse C. Crenshaw, the
tract of land of about 80 acres, on which she now lives for which I
have this day paid J. T. Sloan the sum of $250. I will also intrust
for sd. Elizabeth the sum of $250 with interest from this date. James
D. to keep the money on interest and pay that amount annually unto
Elizabeth. I will to my granddaughter Matilda Gassaway (dtr. of decd.
son Wesley) a negro girl named Rebecca. I will that at my wife's
death her negro Juliet may choose which of my children she desires to
go to and who she may choose becomes the owner. If my brother Daniel
present a claim or demand against my estate, my executors to prosecute my claim to the real estate of my father James Gassaway died seized
with. I appoint my son James D. Gassaway and my friend Henry L. Gains
Executors. Dated 8 Nov. 1853. Wit: John T. Sloan, Dennis Sullivan,
M. R. Boggs. Signed Thomas Gassaway. Will proved by D. Sullivan before W. J. Parson Ord. 13 Dec. 1853. Recorded also in will book #1,
page 170-171. Pickens Dist., S. C.

Enoch Benj. Gassaway. Deed from Enoch Benj. Gassaway and wife to W. L.
Kieth. Pack 228 #2. Clerk of Court Office, Pickens, S. C. Elisha
Laurence on 25 Nov. 1842 delivered to W. L. Kieth and G. W. Liddell
a deed of trust for certain property to be held by same as trustees
for the only use, benefit of his wife Martha Laurence during her
natural life. After her death to the use and benefit of her heirs.
The trustees have power to sell any part to pay debts of sd. Elisha
Laurence. We Benjamin Gassaway and Artimissa his wife who is one of
the heirs of Martha Laurence of Cobb Co., Ga. have consented that the
remainded of the property that has not been sold to pay the debts of
Elisha Laurence or given to the heirs of sd. Martha heirs by this Court
of Equity who have removed from this State to the State of Texas. Do
hereby release and for ever discharge the sd. W. L. Kieth and G. W.
Liddell, etc. Dated 16 Oct. 1852. Wit: J. P. Smith, John E. Smith.
Signed Artimissa Gassaway and Enoch B. Gassaway, seals.

John W. Gassaway. Land warrant for John W. Gassaway. #22. Clerk of Court Office. Pickens, S. C. By W. L. Kieth, Clerk. To any lawful surveyor you are authorized to lay out unto John W. Gassaway at tract of land not exceeding ten thousand acres. Dated 22 Jan. 1842. Executed 25 Jan. 1842. Recorded 22 March 1842.

John W. Gassaway. Estate of John W. Gassaway. Box 27 #3254. Probate Judge Office. Pickens, S. C. Est. admr. 5 May 1845 by Tyre B. Mauldin, William Robinson who are bound unto W. D. Steele, Ord. in the sum of $400.00. 20 Aug. 1852 Amt. recd. of Joseph Grisham Exor. of est. of William Simpson $500.00. Mrs. Candace Gassaway, Thomas Gassaway etc. bought at sale.

Dorcas Gassaway. Estate of Dorcas Gassaway. Box 49 #543. Probate Judge Office. Pickens, S. C. Est. admr. 19 Oct. 1858 by James D. Gassaway, Sidney McDow, Zachariah Powers who are bound unto W. J. Parson, Ord. in the sum of $600.00.

James D. Gassaway. Box 2 #38. In Equity, Clerk of Court Office. Pickens, S. C. In 1860 James D. Gassaway states that Elizabeth dtr. of Thomas Gassaway decd. and wife of Jesse Crenshaw is desirous of removing to Ga. B. P. Vandirier of Franklin Co., Ga. trustee for sd. Elizabeth.

Gassaway Notes. Pack 31 #4 and Pack 13. Clerk of Court Office. Pickens, S. C. On Oct. 5, 1829 William W. Gassaway was ment. as the husband of Cosby Curtis dtr. of Naaman Curtis decd. and his wife Milly Curtis. Henry Gassaway on 28 March 1808 deeded to John Simpson 770 acres on Six Mile Creek.

GATEWOOD

Richard Gatewood. Will of Richard Gatewood. Book not given. Page 56. Elberton, Georgia. I intent with God leave to go to Georgia it may please God I never return if not my desire that after my debts are paid all the rest of my estate I lend to my wife during her widowhood all but as much to those children not married to have equal to those that is married and at her death to be equal divided if any child die their share to be equal divided with brothers and sisters. Dated 10 Dec. 1789. Wit: Peter Cashwell, Joseph Higginbotham, John Ham. Signed: Richd. Gatewood, seal. Recorded 4 Nov. 1794. and granted letter of admr. to Betty Gatewood and John Gatewood.

GEORGE

John George. Will of John George. Book 1 Page 28. Probate Judge Office. Union Co., S. C. I John George of Union County, being in good and perfect memory and in my right mind, etc. I give to my son John George the plantation where he now lives, one horse colt ten months old. I give to my dtr. Mary 200 acres where she now lives, one sorrel colt, six head of cattle and my loom. I give to my son Thomas the plantation where I now live, with one bay horse six years old. I give to my loving wife my gray horse, four cows and calves during her life or widowhood, then to be divided between the chn. To my wife and Thomas all the rest of my goods and chattles, the funeral charges to be paid by Thomas. Dated 16 March 1791. Wit: John Jasper, John McWhirter, Charles X. Homes. Signed: John George.

GIBSON

Luke Gibson. Estate of Luke Gibson. Box 30 #347. Probate Judge Office. Pickens, S. C. Est. admr. 6 June 1853 by John Bowen, James W. Hughes who are bound unto W. J. Parson, Ord. in the sum of $200.00.

Jane A. Gibson. Warrant for Assault Jane A. Gibson. Pack 268 #1.
Clerk of Court Office. Pickens, S. C. On 2 Dec. 1857. Jane A. Gibson
wife of Robert Gibson made oath that Thomas Gibson, Samuel Nichols,
Jr., and David Gibson came to her house on 28 Nov. last and demanded
possession of the house in a violent manner and told me to leave and
that they would kill me if I didn't give it up. I shut the door and
they tore some boards from it in an attempt to get in, they threw a
bucket of water against the door and cursed me.

Absalom Gibson.   Estate of Absalom Gibson.   Box 40 #446. Probate Judge
Office. Pickens, S. C. Est. admr. 20 June 1856 by Zachariah Gibson,
H. A. H. Gibson, E. E. Alexander who are bound unto W. J. Parson, Ord.
in the sum of $1600.00. On 12 Jan. 1857 the heirs wanted the real
estate sold for a division which was 460 acres lying on both sides of
Little River waters of Keowee River adj. land of Col. Jeptha Norton,
John Cape Hart and others. Land originally granted to Jacob Capehart.
Heirs: Mary wife of Abner Lewis, Sabina Groan, Hiram Gibson, Vilanty
Cobb, heirs of Lela Boon decd. Boon heirs are out of state. On 24
Dec. 1858 paid Mrs. Valanty Lewis $483.46.

Duke Gibson.   Inventory of Duke Gibson.   Box 45 #501. Probate Judge
Office. Pickens, S. C. An inventory made 23 June 1853 by J. B. Sutherland, Umphrey Rogers, L. C. Young. (No other papers.)

Zachariah Gibson. Will of Zachariah Gibson. Box 62 #501. Probate
Judge Office.   Pickens, S. C. I Zachariah W. Gibson being of sound
mind and disposing memory, etc.etc. I desire as soon as possible pay
my funeral expenses and just debts. I give to my loving Father and
Mother (Hiram and Catherine Gibson) all my property both real and
personal. I do appoint my uncle Zachariah Gibson executor. Dated 18
July 1861. Wit: Z. W. Green, D. L. Craig, J. E. Hagood. Signed
Z. W. Gibson. Proven 28 July 1862.

Nancy Gibson. Nancy Gibson Heir. Book A Page 222. Probate Judge
Office. Pickens, S. C. On 21 June 1858 George Gibson and wife Nancy,
Elijah Gibson and wife Polly were heirs of Thomas Alexander decd. of
Pickens Dist.

Andrew J. Gibson. Assault. Pack 220 #8. Clerk of Court Office.
Pickens, S. C. On 8 June 1859 Vaney Whitfield took out a peace warrant
for Andrew J. Gibson stating he had struck her on the face with his
fist.

GILBERT

Dr. John J. Gilbert. Estate of Dr. John J. Gilbert. Box 40 Pack 893.
Abbeville Dist., S. C. Admr. bond dated 12 June 1818 in the sum of
15 thousand dollars. We James L. and S. Pettigrew, George Bowie and
Alexander Bowie are bound unto Teliaferro Livingston, Ord. Est. appraised 15 June 1818 by Dale Palmer, Stephen Gilbert, Joshua Hill.

Sarah B. Gibert.   Box 40 Pack 894. Probate Judge Office. Abbeville,
S. C. Admr. bond dated 5 Oct. 1836. We James F. Gibert, Dyonitus M.
Rogers, and James Taggart who are bound unto Moses Taggart, Ord. in the
sum of 30 thousand dollars. Cit. pub. at Willington Church. Statement
of the settlement of the estate of Stephen Gibert and Sarah B. Gilbert
immerged in one. After the death of Stephen Gibert, Sarah B. Gibert
administered. During her admr. the property was not sold nor divided.
After her death James F. Gibert Administered on her Administration. The
property was not sold in his hands but finally divided in the following
manner: By mutual consent the legetees of the said estate were: James
F., Elizabeth H., Stephen F., Peter L., and John A. Gibert we entered
into the following resolution, to agree and oblige ourselves to abide
by the division and appraisement of Robert Brady, James Taggart, D.
Rogers, Robert McCraven, S. Reid who at our request have agreed to
appraised and divide the property of the above estates. Dated 1 Dec.

1841. Wit: John S. Reid. Each heir signed the above. (Some places
the name was spelled Gilbert.)

Samuel Gilbert. The following is a letter from a lady in Lawrenceburg,
Ky., no date, searching for a Samuel Gilbert in 96 Dist., Spart. Co. in
1790. He was born in Md. or Va. 1752 and died Madison Co., Ky. 1820.
Son of Jarvis Gilbert and Elizabeth Preston M. 1735. Jarvis was son of
Gervais Gilbert and his first wife Margret ___? Samuel had a treasury
warrant for land in Madison Co., Ky. was Lincoln when granted. In
1795 from Pendleton Dist., S. C. he appointed Wm. Irvine of Madison
Co., Ky. his attorney to transact business of his grant, on which he
settled on a short time later. His first wife named was Rhoda ___?
In "Wallace Gen. and Data on Peter Wallace and wife Elizabeth Woods."
by Geo. Seldon Wallace, is ment. that one married a Samuel Gilbert. He
married second time to Susannah Elam in 1813 and they had two boys
possibly twins. In his will chn. named William, Samuel Jr., Amelia
Clements, Stephens, Mary Quick, Patsy Kavanaugh, Sally Oldham, Betsy
1st married John Gilbert, her cousin, second marriage Timothy Burgess.
Chn. by second wife, Jarvis Elam and Jephtha Rice Gilbert. Betsy in
1850 census gives her birth as Georgia in 1783. Samuel bro. and sis.
are, Margaret b. 1736, Martha b. 1737, Garvace b. 1738, Sarah b. 1741,
Preston b. 1743, M. Jemimah Cock in Bedford Co., Va. 1769. Hannah b.
1755, m. Alexander Gibbs in Bedford Co., Va.

GILLBEAU

Andrew Gillbeau. Will of Andrew Gillbeau. Box 40 Pack 884. Probate
Judge Office. Abbeville, S. C. I Andrew Gillbeau being weak in body
but of perfect mind and memory etc. I will and demise that all my
debts be paid. If I die before my wife she is to keep all my estate
both real and personal during her life time. I will to my dtr.
Susannah Boushalon $40.00. I will unto Eliser supposed to be the
dtr. of James Gillbeau, begotten by Liddy Billot $70.00. I will to my
son James Gillbeau one dollar. I will to my son Peter Gillbeau all
the balance of my estate. I appoint my son Peter Gillbeau as executor.
Dated 18 Feb. 1806. Wit: Chas. Hathorn, Elevserour X Covin, Peter
Covin. Signed Andrew Guilbeau. Recorded 21 Feb. 1815. (No more inf.)

GILES

John Giles. Will of John Giles. Will Book ___ Page 50. Elberton, Ga.
I John Giles of the county of Elbert in Georgia. Being in perfect mind
and memory. First I will that my debts be paid. I give to my loving
wife one horse and mare, the horse called Jack, two cows and calves,
the house I now live in and the plantation on which it stands, during
her natural life. The rest of my property of all kinds be divided
between my children, My grandchild Jonathan Gray to share equal with
my chn. I give my negro man Daniel I give to my wife. After the death
of my wife the property she may have to be equally divided between my
children and the grandchild above ment. Except withhold fifteen pds.
from dtr. Wells, I have given her and her husband Jerimiah Wells that
amount before. I appoint my wife executorix and William Hobby as
executor. Dated 12 Apr. 1794. Wit: Andrew Elliet, John X McNeel,
Benj. Ragland, Saml. M. Thomson. Signed: John Giles. Recorded the
will of John Giles, 28 July 1794.

GILKEYSON

Wm. Gilkeyson. Will of Wm. Gilkeyson. Box 36 Pack 791. Abbeville,
S. C. I William Gilkeyson being in sound mind but weak in body, etc.
etc. I will to my beloved wife Rebekah one negro woman Jinney, one
negro girl Syntha one negro boy Webster. Nine head of cattle, one
horse, one filley, all my household and kitchen furniture, all my

147

plantation tools for the use of supporting my children (not named),
sell negro Jack, one gray mare, one black cow and calf to pay off my
debts, if not enough wife to choose other items to sell. I appoint my
wife Rebeckah Gilkeyson Executrix and Wm. Pyles as executor. Dated 19
Feb. 1828. Wit: George Mattison, Geo. W. Reeve, Wm. P. Martin.
Signed: William X Gilkeyson. Wm. Pyles qualified as Exec. 10 March
1828. Estate appraised 15 Mar. 1828 by Wm. Reeve, Thomas Norwood,
John Mattison.

GILLILAND

John Gilliland. Will of John Gilliland. Pack 217 #1. Probate Judge
Office. Pickens, S. C. I John Gilliland being of good health and
sound mind and disposing memory. First pay my just debts and funeral
expenses. I give to my beloved wife Elizabeth Gilliland all my real
and personal property during her natural life or widowhood. Should my
wife die or marry all my property both real and personal be divided
between John Roper the son of Absolom and Malinda Roper and Robert
Banks the son of Warren T. Banks my two nephews. He states that his
wife was Elizabeth Banks. Dated 1 Jan. 1862. Wit: George Hendricks,
Riley Simmons, F. E. Hendrick. Signed: John X Gilliland, seal. Will
proved by George Hendrick on 2 Mar. 1863, before W. E. Holcombe, Ord.

GILLISON

Israel Gillison. Article of Agreement, Israel Gillison. Pack 382 #1.
Clerk of Court Office. Pickens, S. C. Agreement dated 10 March 1828,
between Israel Gillison and David Sloan both of Pickens Dist. Sloan
leases to Gillison three tracts of land to tend and cultivate as he may
think proper until the first day of January next. Gillison is to clear
up all the swamp land on the South side of the creek, and the old
field to be drained. Wit: Wm. D. Sloan. Singed: D. Sloan and Israel
Gillison.

GILLISPIE

James Gillispie. Estate of James Gillispie. Box 40 Pack 882. Probate
Judge Office. Abbeville, S. C. Est. admr. 10 Nov. 1795 by Elizabeth
Gillispie, widow, Lowry Gillispie, Andrew Pickens, John Harris of Flat-
woods are bound unto Judge at Abbeville Court in the sum of one thousand
pds. sterling. Est. appraised 5 Dec. 1795 by James Caldwell, Joseph
Lemaster, Andrew Pickens. Byrs. John Robison, Abraham Pickens, Gabriel
Pickens, Lowry Gillispie, Jonathan Pickens, Margret and Elizabeth
Gillispie, Joseph Vernon, Stuard Baskin, Capt. Linton, David Gillispie,
John Allison, Phanny Gillispie, John More, John McNeil, Thomas Wilson,
John Campbell, Harris Jones, Cary Evans, Lewis Howlin, Nehemiah Vernon,
Mason Izard, Patrick Cain, Wm. Walker, Robert Smith, Wm. Love, Francis
Cummins, Wm. Dunlap, Samuel Green, Francis Drinkard, Robert Dennomn,
Francis Sutherland, Hugh Baskin, Wm. Harris, Wm. Gillispie. Cit.
published at Rockey River Church.

GILREATH

William A. Gilreath. Estate of William A. Gilreath. Box 10 #165.
Probate Judge Office. Pickens, S. C. Est. admr. 31 Jan. 1883 by Emma
Gilreath, J. H. Ambler, J. L. Ambler who are bound unto J. H. Newton,
Ord. in the sum of $200.00. Emma Gilreath gdn. for Wm. A. Gilreath
minor under 14 years. Son of Emma, and Benjamin J. Gilreath decd. of
Greenville Co. his father.

GILSTRAP

William Gilstrap. Deed of William Gilstrap. Pack 383 #2. Clerk of
Court Office. Pickens, S. C. William Gilstrap to Jasper N. Hawthorne
of Abbeville Dist. In consideration of fifteen hundred dollars have
granted, sold and released all that tract of land on which William
Gilstrap now lives containing 274 acres lying on Rices Creek waters of
twelve mile River, adj. land of Elihu Griffin, Joseph Young, Bright
Gilstrap, Jeremiah Durham, Danl. Durham and Isaac Millers. Dated 4
Sept. 1851. Wit: R. Norris, A. S. Smith. Signed Wm. Gilstrap, seal.
Dilley Gilstrap the wife of William Gilstrap relinquish her dower before
John Bowen, N.P. on 26 Feb. 1852.

Mary Gilstrap. Heir. Box 137 #13. Probate Judge Office. Pickens,
S. C. On 25 March 1903 Mary Gilstrap recd. $164.47 as her share from
estate of William Hunter decd. She was Mary Ellenburg his illegitmate
dtr. before her marriage and of his wife Sarah Ellenburg.

Gilstraps. Statements of Gilstraps. Box 137 #8. Clerk of Court
Office. Pickens, S. C. Benson Gilstrap states that he was 31 years
old the 28th last March and the son of Hardy Gilstrap. His present
wife is my step mother, married in 1866 she was Esther Reed. Her
guardian was Mattison Reed. David F. Gilstrap states that I am 27 years
old on 27 March next. I married Reuben Ellis dtr. Ann, Peter Gilstrap
was a brother to Hardy Gilstrap. William Smith married a niece of Hardy
Gilstrap. John Gilstrap was a brother to Hardy Gilstrap. John W.
Gilstrap states he is a son of Peter Gilstrap and a nephew of Hardy
Gilstrap. Hardy Gilstrap states the last time he married the widow
Luvinia Hawthorne. Wiley Gilstrap a son of Hardy died about 10 years
ago and was not married. Dated 28 Oct. 1879.

Hardy Gilstrap, Sr. Estate of Hardy Gilstrap, Sr. Box 113 #1092.
Probate Judge Office. Pickens, S. C. Est. admr. 11 Mar. 1882 by
W. A. Lesley, J. C. Griffin, J. B. Newberry who are bound unto O. L.
Durant, Ord. in the sum of $2,000.00. B. B. Gilstrap, E. O., and G. W.
Gilstrap bought at sale.

Hardy Gilstrap, Jr. Estate of Hardy Gilstrap, Jr. Box 11 #175. Probate
Judge Office. Pickens, S. C. Est. admr. 11 March 1882 by W. A. Lesley,
J. C. Griffin, J. B. Newberry who are bound unto O. L. Durant, Ord. in
the sum of $2,200.00. Whereas on 28 Feb. ___ W. A. Lesley gdn. for
Hardy Gilstrap, Jr. a minor under 21 years son of Hardy Gilstrap.

Leuvina Gilstrap. In Equity, Box 2 #39. Clerk of Court Office.
Pickens, S. C. Camplaint for dower, Leuvina Gilstrap states that
she was married to Hardy Gilstrap decd. In April 1863. Previous to
said marriage she was the widow of Jasper N. Hawthorne decd. About
the age of 21 years. Wm. Hamilton was her father. John M. Hendrick a
brother in law.

Hardy Gilstrap. Land Warrant of Hardy Gilstrap. Plat Book C Page 2.
Clerk of Court Office. Pickens, S. C. By request of Hardy Gilstrap
and by consent of David Gilstrap, I have surveyed a tract of land on a
branch of Rices Creek waters of 12 mile river. Containing 62 acres
Dated 20 Nov. 1872. J. B. Clayton, Surveyor.

GIVENS

Daniel Givens. Will of Daniel Givens. Will Book D Page 38. Probate
Judge Office. York, S. C. I Daniel Givens, Sr. of York Dist. being
of sound mind and memory, etc. I give to my dtr. Eleanor one cow and
calf and her increase that is called hers, that was bestowed to her by
James Tiner, one sow, one spinning wheel, one feather bed, and furniture.
I give to my wife Lucy Givens during her natural life all my land and
personal property, after paying the above legacy to my dtr. Eleanor, and
payment of my just debts. At my wife decease her property is to be

taken over by my son Edward Givens all together. I appoint my wife
Lucy Givens sole executrix. Dated 18 March 1809. Wit: J. A. Whyte,
Mary G. Whyte, E. Bayless. Signed Daniel X Givens, seal. Probated
2 Jan. 1815.

William Given. Will of William Given. (No ref. given) York Co., S.C.
I William Given, I will to the four minor chn. of Samuel E. Given decd.
in equal shares negroes Jim and wife Caroline and their chn. Thomas,
Harriet, Milly and Jean. The negroes to be hired until the youngest
comes of age. I will to William Poag (son of Joseph Poag) my gold
watch. I will to my neice Mary Harriet Poag $100 to be paid 12 mos.
after the sale of my estate. The balance of my estate be sold to pay
debts and (furnishing a slab lettered with gold leaf to my grave) be
equal divided between my sisters Polly Ash, Esther Poag, Isabella Walker,
Margaret Sadler. I appoint Zenas A. Walker executor. Dated 25 Nov.
1844. Wit: I. L. Howe, J. M. Moore, John Burris, Signed: William
Given, seal. Probated 3 Dec. 1844.

GLASGOW

James N. Glasgow. Guardianship. In Equity, Pack 77. Clerk of Court
Office, Abbeville, S. C. He is a minor of twenty years old the son of
James Glasgow, decd. has about seven hundred dollars, and a small sum
from the estate of John Hunter, his former guardian lately decd. He
wish that William H. Belcher be appointed his guardian. This was done
25 Jan. 1855.

GLENN

Duke W. Glenn. Assault. Pack 270 #6. Clerk of Court Office. Pickens,
S. C. On 1 Sept. 1839 Pickens Turner made oath that D. William Glenn
did on 1 Aug. last assault him on the forehead with a rifle gun and
inflicted on him a severe wound.

Duke W. Glenn. Estate of Duke W. Glenn. Box 17 #215. Probate Judge
Office. Pickens, S. C. Est. admr. 7 Feb. 1842 by Noble Glenn, Alfred
Hester, Henry Williams who are bound unto Jas. H. Dendy, Ord. in the sum
of $2500.00. Cit. publ. at Peters Creek Church. Paid 1844 James Glenn
his share $146.67. Paid 1845 Annah Glenn the wid. $700.34. Paid 1848
Warren W. Glenn his share $112.75. There was two more chn. William and
Robert A. Glenn (In Book A, page 79 the last two chn. are listed as
minors, with Noble Glenn as gdn.)

D. W. Glenn. As Heir. Apt. 2 File 82. Probate Judge Office. Pickens,
S. C. On 8 Aug. 1826 D. W. Glenn recd. a legacy from estate of Philemon
Bradford decd. of Greenville Dist.

W. D. Glenn. Estate of W. D. Glenn. Box 122. #13. Probate Judge
Office. Pickens, S. C. Est. admr. 20 April 1898 by J. P. Glenn, T. S.
Glenn, W. M. Smith, John C. Watkins who are bound to J. B. Newberry, Ord.
in the sum of $500.00. J. P. Glenn a brother. Est. admr. again 15
June 1893 by John M. Glenn, Thos. S. Glenn, J. P. Glenn who are bound
unto J. B. Newberry, Ord. in the sum of $5,000.00. John M. Glenn a
brother. Died 6 May 1893, was of Liberty, S. C. J. P. Glenn was of
Equality, S. C. S. Carrie Smith recd. share.

GOLDEN

N. G. Golden. Bond. Pack 249 #31. Clerk of Court Office. Pickens,
S. C. We N. G. Golden and P. Alexander of Pickens Dist. are bound unto
Elias Lotts in the sum of sixty eight dollars, the said bond or bill of
attachment dated 5 Sept. 1842. Whereas the sd. bound N. G. Golden
hath this day sued out a writ of attachment against the said Elias

Lotts before W. L. Keith, CC for the Dist. aforesaid. Now the condition
of the obligation is such that is sd. N. G. Golden shall satisfy and pay
Elias Lotts and discontinue his sd. suit also all damages which shall
be recovered of illegally sueing. Signed N. G. Golden, seal.
P. Alexander, seal.

GOLDING

Richard Golding. Estate of Richard Golding. Box 41 Pack 928. Probate
Judge Office. Abbeville, S. C. Admr. Bond we Reuben G. Golding,
Charles B. Foosbee and Harris Y. Gillam are bound unto David Lesly, Ord.
in the sum of four thousand dollars. Dated 2 Nov. 1842. Whereas R. A.
G. Golding of Abbeville Dist. being a minor leaving considerable
personal estate and some negroes and some money the estate being
liable to waste and abuse, your petitioner prays for a letter of
admr. as a brother of the decd. and at the request of other parties,
Dated 15 Oct. 1842. R. G. Golden. Est. appraised 31 Dec. 1842 by William Eddins, C. B. Foosbee, Larkin Carter. Parties interested in estate
of R. A. G. Golding, R. G. Golding Gdn. John M. Golding, N. C.
Golding, W. D. Mounts (mounce) and wife Louvenia. Dated 12 Apr. 1844.
Mrs. Willey D. Mounce the mother of the decd. received $285.80.
Nimrod (R. C.) C. Golding lived in Lousiana.

GOLDSMITH

William Goldsmith, Senr. Estate of William Goldsmith, Senr. Apt. 3
File 198. Probate Judge Office. Greenville, S. C. Elizabeth Goldsmith made as inventory of Wm. estate 22 March 1834 for $420.00. The
sd. Wm. Goldsmith had made an inventory for his father property he had
received on 18 Jan. 1834. In the amount of #133.00. Turner Goldsmith
made an inventory of property of Wm. Goldsmith. total amount of $184.00.
Sally Goldsmith (now Willingham) made an inventory of Wm. property in
the amount of $22.00. Thomas Goldsmith made an inv. of Wm. property in
the sum of $190.50. William and Lucy made an inv. of Wm. property in
the sum of $122.50. Heirs of Wm. Goldsmith are: Elizabeth the widow.
Thomas Goldsmith, heirs at law of Polly Howard, William Daugherty and
Lucy his wife, Wm. B. Willingham and Sally his wife, Wm. Goldsmith,
Josiah Greee and Milley his wife, Turner Goldsmith, Thomas McCresry
and Elizabeth his wife, the heirs at law of John Goldsmith decd. You
are appear at Greenville Dist C. H. to show cause why the real estate
of Wm. Goldsmith on the waters of Durbins Creek and Enoree River containing 400 acres adj. land of John Greer, John S. Westmoreland and
others, should not be sold and divided. Date 7 Dec. 1835. Chn. of
John Goldsmith are: Elizabeth, Milley, Massey, Turner, Mariah Goldsmith,
Thomas Goldsmith will serve as gdn. for these chn. Polly Howard chn.
Lemuel, James, Lewis, Nancy, Polly, Elijah, Fatima Benjamin F. Howard.

GOODE

Richard Goode. Deed of Richard Goode. Deed Book A Page 116-117.
Mesne Conveyance, Greenville, S. C. This indenture made 27 Nov. 1786.
Between Richard and Rebekah Goode of North Carolina and William Nelson
of Greenville County, S. C. In consideration of forty five pds. sterling doth grant, bargain sell and release a tract of land lying and
being in 96 Dist. on Golden Grove Creek waters of Saluda River, being
100 acres, part of a grant dated 21 Jan. 1785 unto Richard Goode.
Wit: Isaac X Wilson, James Moor. Signed: Richd. Goode and Rebekah
Goode, seals.

GOODLETT

Hiram Goodlett. Will of Hiram Goodlett. Putnam Co., Ga. (At the top
of page 3-184 this may be book and page.) I Hiram Goodlett being low
in health, but in perfect mind and memory, etc. etc. I will my just
debts be paid from the money due me and the balance to be divided
between my two sisters Mahalah and Betsey Goodlett. I will unto my
brother Jesse Goodlett four of my largest hogs. I will to my brother
Zion Goodlett my young mare also all my stock, hogs, except the four
above named, also my trunk and wearing apparel. I appoint my brother
Spartan and Zion Goodlett executors. Dated 15 June 1814. Wit: John
Harper, Jeremiah Watts. Signed: Hiram Goodlett, seal.

GOODWYN

John Goodwyn. Deed of John Goodwyn, Pack 656 #2. Clerk of Court
Office. Pickens, S. C. This indenture made 24 July 1789 between
Captain John Goodwyn of Greenville Co. and Benjamin Cleveland Esq. of
Pendleton Co. In consideration of sum of five shillings current money,
the receipt whereof is acknowledged hath sold, bargain and released a
tract of land of 300 acres in Pickens Co. on Tugulo River, adj. land of
Robert Looney and Tugalo River, others sides vacant. Granted unto John
Goodwyn Esq. 15 Oct. 1784. This is a lease and release. Wit:
Alexander Ramsey, Joseph Jenkins, John Boles. Signed Jno. Goodwyn,
seal.

Nathaniel Gordon. Will of Nathaniel Gordon. Box 12 #158. Probate
Judge Office. Union Co., S. C. I Nathaniel Gordon calling to mind the
uncertainty of life do make this my last will and testament. I will
to my granddaughter Sarah Canter or Cantes one beaureau looking glass
table and two chairs. I will to my granddaughter Louisa Gordon one
table and bed and bed clothing, two chairs. After my death I will my
negro named Betty be sold and the money divided as follows fifty
dollars to each of my grandsons, Marian, William and Jefferson Gordon
sons of A. W. Gordon, if any thing left over, give to my dtr. in law
Treasey Gordon, she is to get kitchen ware, such as pots and earthen-
ware. The same to be in care of Treasey for her two dtr. called
Sarah and Louisa when they need the same. If it be lawful for me to
give any thing to my girl Betty my will and desire that fifty dollars
keep for her use in the hands of Reuben Coleman, Sr. I appoint Reuben
Coleman, Executor. Dated 23 Apr. 1842. Wit: Samuel Hodge, S. A.
Haman, Moses Hodge, Signed: Nathaniel X Gordon. Proven in Pickens Dist.
31 Jan. 1844.

John L. Gordon. Constable. Pack 634. #198. Clerk of Court Office.
Pickens, S. C. On 9 May 1846 John L. Gordon of Pickens Dist. was
appointed a constable by Wm. C. Lee a M.P.D.

GOSSETT

John T. Gossett. Will of John T. Gossett. Box 119 #2. Probate Judge
Office. Pickens, S. C. While I have strength and ability to do so
with sound mind and memory. I will my just debts and funeral expenses
be paid as soon as conviently. I will to my grand children Frances
Medora Folger, Carrie Keith, Robert Keith the chn. of my decd. dtr.
Edna Caroline Keith, together with the heirs of my grandson John Keith,
collectively the following tract of land of 200 acres, adj. land of
George Davis field, Elizabeth Gossett's line, Gus Keith spring, to be
divided five ways viz: granddaughter Frances Medora Folger two fifths,
grand dtr. Carrie Keith one fifty, to grand son Robert Keith one fifty,
and the heirs of my grand son one fifth. I will unto my grand son
E. K. Gossett one half interest in my house and lot in Easley whereon
my son J. R. Gossett now lives. I give to my wife Elizabeth Gossett
one cow, one horse and buggy and such property as she may need. I give

to my grand son Augustus Keith the sum of five dollars. After paying
just debts and funeral expenses both real and personal estate be sold
and divided between chn. and gr. chn. Another gr. child is ment. as
Mary Rudcliff. I appoint my son John R. Gossett and John Gossett my
nephew. Dated 19 Dec. 1888. W. T. Wyenton, D. W. Belt, Carroll
Wilson. Signed John T. Gossett. Filed 30 Jan. 1892. R. A. Keith,
Nellie E. Keith in Nov. 1893 of Richmond, Va. recd. a share. 1 Jan.
1893 Mary Dunn recd. a share from her grandfather estate.

GRADY

John W. Grady. Attachment Bond. Pack 417 #4. Clerk of Court Office.
Pickens, S. C. I John W. Walker, agent for John W. Grady of the state
of Georgia, are held and bound unto William Warwick late of Georgia and
Lumpkin Co. in the sum of 150 dollars to be paid to the said William
Warwick. Dated 11 Dec. 1848. This day John W. Walker applied to the
Clerk of Court in Pickens Co., S. C. for an attachment against William
Warwick. Signed Jno. W. Walker, seal, agt. for Jno. W. Grady.

GRANT

J. W. Grant. Estate of J. W. Grant. Box 78 #830. Probate Judge Office.
Pickens, S. C. Est. admr. 29 Aug. 1864 by Rebecca M. Grant, Samuel J.
Adams, James Neal who are bound unto W. E. Holcombe, ord. in the sum of
$2,000.00. left a widow and four children (not named).

A. B. Grant. Deed of A. B. Grant. Pack 13. Clerk of Court Office.
Pickens, S. C. A. B. Grant of Pickens Dist. on 7 July 1841 deeded to
Elisha Gaines 217 acres on six mile Creek. Letticia Grant his wife.

William Grant. Estate of William Grant. Book B Page 50. Probate Judge
Office. Pickens, S. C. On 11 Oct. 1860 William Grant decd. of Pickens
Dist. owned 134 acres on Little Beaverdam Creek, adj. land of Robert
Tribble, William Hunt and others. Nancy Grant widow, heirs: William
Grant, Mary wife of Tully Simmons, George Grant, Martha C. wife of Jordan
Simmons, Bird C. Grant, Noah W. Grant, Pressly A. Grant, Nancy E. Grant.
Bird C., Noah W., Pressly A., Nancy E. Grant minors under 21 years.
Robert O. Tribble, guardian.

James Grant. Will of James Grant. Box 30 #353. Probate Judge Office.
Pickens, S. C. I James Grant being of a sound mind and desirous to
prevent all jarring that might otherwise take place amongst my children
make this my last will and testament. I will my just debts and funeral
expenses be paid first. I will to my two sons James W. and Willis each
a cow and calf, a sow, and bed and furniture. I will to my two dtr.
Sidey and Sarah each a cow and calf, a sow, a bed and furniture. The
land not to be sold for twelve years so to four above chn. that are
minors can become of age or marry. Twenty five dollars to go to grand
son Augustus Rodolfus Grant, the balance to be divided between all my
children. I appoint my two sons A. B. and Jas. W. Grant my executors.
Dated 19 June 1850. Wit: F. N. Garvin, Daniel J. Chapman, Andrew X
Neal. Signed: James X Grant. Proven 7 Feb. 1853.

GRAY

James Gray. Estate of James Gray. Box 40 #877. Probate Judge
Office. Abbeville, S. C. I James Gray of Abbeville County and 96
Dist. being in perfect health of body also sound mind and memory, etc.
I leave to my only daughter Marget Gray otherwise Marget Ellis my large
Bible and household furniture. I leave to my two grand sons James Gray
Ellis and John Lindsey Ellis a tract of land on Long Cane containing
200 acres to be divided between them, with other property that is a
negro Bob and one wagon and one horse, to be kept by their father if

best. James Gray Ellis get the small Bible, and chest. John Lindsey
Ellis my large pot. I appoint Robert Ellis, and Robert Lindsey as
executors. Dated 23 Feb. 1796. Wit: John Murphy, John Lindsey, James
Ellis. Signed: James X Gray. Recorded 28 March 1797.

John Gray. Estate of John Gray. Box 159 #4314. Probate Judge Office.
Abbeville, S. C. I John Gray being in sound mind and memory etc. It
is my will the tract of land I now live on be divided into four parts.
He describe the lines for division, dtr. Mary to get the part with the
pond. Son James to get the old house place, Claudius to get the part
with the dwelling house on which I now live. Son Joseph to get the
part next to James Grays. I give to my dtr. Anna the remainder of the
South west quarter of sec. #5, in the State of Alabama Green County.
After taking off the ten acres I have already give to son Allen. The
South East quarter to be sold and money divided between James, Joseph,
Mary and Claudius. As personal property, the cash, notes due me and
negro woman Celia to remain together for benefit and support of Anna
if she remaines single and my minor chn. My library to be equal divided
between my chn. Celia is to stay on the place until James becomes of
age, then she Celia to be hired out until the year 1834 to support my
son Lewis in his collegiate course, not to exceed $800. My dtr. Patsey
to receive from time to time as she needs help, if her husband dies,
and she stays near, she to get $800 or more. I appoint Alexr. Houston,
Esq., John Presley, Allen and James Gray executors. Dated 1 Sept. 1826.
Wit: James Gray, Andrew McClane, Anna C. Gray. Signed John Gray.
Sale made 17 Dec. 1829.

Frederick Gray. Estate of Frederick Gray. Box 36 Pack 793. Probate
Judge Office. Abbeville, S. C. I Frederick Gray being of sound mind
and memory, etc.etc. I give to my wife Mary one hundred acres at a
place I called Equipt whare, I last built and marked to be laid out for
her during her natural life. The remainder of real and personal propert
to be sold and divided into equal parts. My wife to have one part. The
chn. of my decd. dtr. Jane Thomas one part. The chn. of decd. son Henry
Gray one part. My granddaughter Elizas Klugh one part, surviving chn.
are: George Gray, William Gray, John F. Gray, Mary An Marshall, Cloutte
Boyd, F. Jefferson Gray, Washington R. Gray. I appoint my sons William
and J. F. Gray executors. Dated 24 Nov. 1836. Wit: Williamson Norwood, David F. Cleskey, Alex Hughes. Signed Frederick X Gray. Est.
Appraised 16 Dec. 1837.

James A. Gray. Estate of James A. Gray. Box 36 Pack 792. Probate
Judge Office. Abbeville, S. C. Admr. bond dated 19 Dec. 1834. We
James Wiley, Samuel Huston, William H. Harris are bound unto Moses
Taggart, Ord. in the sum of $12,000. Cit. pub. at Bulah Church. Est.
appraised 7 Jan. 1835 by Thomas Douglass, Michel Wilson, William Paul,
Elizabeth Gray widow, others red. Hamelton Hill gdn. of George Pauls
minor chn. Egnis D. and Margaret M. Gray minors, Mary d. wife of
John R. Martin, Nancy A. and Andrew Gray. John W. and Zechariah Gray.

John Gray. Revolutionary Pension Claim. Probate Judge Office. Pickens
S. C. A declaration in order to be placed on the pension list, under
the act of the 18 March 1818. Pickens Dist., S. C. On the 7 March
1829 appeared in open Court, John Gray aged sixty nine years, being duly
sworn according to law doth make the following declaration, in order
to obtain a pension under the act of 18 Mar. 1818 and 1 May 1820. John
Gray enlisted in the city of Augusta, Ga. in the month of June 1781, in
the U. S. service in what was called State Troops in the State of
Georgia, served out this enlistment and was discharged on the 10 June
1782 near Savannah, Ga. Previous to that enlistment he had been in the
service as a Minute Man eighteen months. That he was in the Florida
expeditions during that time. When he enlisted in 1781 he joined Capt.
Stallions Company of Cavalry, attached to Col. James Jackson Reg. but
commanded most of the time by General Wayne. He was constantly employed
during the time of this enlistment on the Continental Establishment.
That until late years he could make a support for himself and family,
he thought he could do without applying to the government for help, as
gaining Independence he was amply compensated for all his toils. I

have not disposed in any manner by gift or sale with intent thereby so
to deminish it as to bring myself within the provisions of the act of
Congress, passed 18 Mar. 1818. His assets are one cow and yearling, one
bed and a few articles of household and kitchen furniture, a few hogs
say ten or eleven, and a few farm tools the whole amount would not
exceed fifty dollars at a fair price. Since the act of 1818 he bought a
horse on credit and had to sell him to make the payment. He has in his
family wife Aairy, and dtr. Patsey and her child. Patsey age is about
thirty five years old. Sworn before and in open Court. John X Gray.
By Daniel E. Houser, Judge Presiding. John Gray appeared in open Court
and declares he was acquainted with William Entrekin (now of Anderson
Dist.) during the war and served in the same company under the same
officers, except he thinks Entrekin has mistaken in his declaration the
grade of the Subatten? officers as this deponent thinks Henry? was a
Lieutenant and Ezekiel Stallions Ensigs, he thinks him correct in all
other respects. Signed John X Gray. I Richard Gannt Presiding Judge
of the Court of Sessions and Common Pleas. That he believes John
Gray to be a man of good character and entitled to credit from the
representations, but not personal acquaintance with him myself. Signed:
Richard Gantt, Judge. Samuel Ramsey of Abbeville Dist. sworn that he
and John Gray served in the same outfit, and that John Gray enlisted a
few days before he, and served until 10 June 1782 and was discharged
about twelve miles from Savannah, Ga. Signed: Samuel Ramsey. We the
undersigned of the Dist. of Pendleton hereby certify that we are well
acquainted with John Gray and have been for many years. That we believe
him to be a man of veracity. We believe him from his own statement
to have been engaged in the service of his country during the war of
the Revolution and know him to be in extremely indigent circumstances
and entitled to a pension from the service. Dated 24 Oct. 1827.
Signed: Thomas Lamar, J.P., Nathan Boon, J.P., seal., Francis Jenkins,
David Russell, James Cannon, John McWhorter, Esq., Zachariah Hall, John
Crge(?), Wm. Dodd, Wm. Hall, Andrew Kelly, Jacob R. Cox.

GREEN

Peter Green. Estate of Peter Green. Box 40 Pack 879. Probate Judge
Office. Abbeville, S. C. I Peter Green being low in state of health
but of sound mind and memory, etc. First pay just debts and funeral
expenses. I give to my dtr. Sarah Bell (Beal) one shilling in addition
to what I have already given to her. I give my dtr. Martha Moore one
shilling with what I have given her. I give to my two sons Philemon
and Sion Green the whole of the following personal property to be divided
between them. Four negroes Sukey, Lucy, Abram, Rose, one wagon and gear,
three horses, sixty head hogs, and all the debts due me at my decease.
I give to son one good feather bed and twenty barrels of corn. I give
to my dtr. Rebecca Eddins a negro named Milley, two feather beds already
in her possession. In order to care for my wife Thamer and two chn. now
living with me Polly Beal and Sarah Beal, my son Philemon should have
the care of them, I give him in addition to what already (line torn
from page) raise the two girls Polly and Sarah Beal (line torn again)
hundred and fifty acres with the whole remaining part of household
furniture. I appoint my sons Philemon and Sion Green executors. Dated
16 Dec. 1794. Wit: Julius Nichols, Thomas X Anderson, John Bell, Junr.
Signed: Peter X Green. Recorded 27 March 1797. Est. Appraised by
James Chiled, Nimrod Chiles, Robert Sample. Dated 8 Sept. 1797. Valued
$1300.00.

Thomas Green. Estate of Thomas Green. Box 39 #861. Probate Judge
Office. Abbeville, S. C. Admr. bond dated 1 Oct. 1784. We Elisha
Green, Joseph West and William Plumer are bound unto John Thomas Junr.,
Ord. of 96 Dist. in the sum of two thousand pds. sterling. Whereas
admr. of the goods and chattels of the late Thomas Green decd. was
lately committed by the sd. John Thomas Junr. unto sd. Elisha Green and
shall well and faithfully admr. the goods and chattels of sd. decd.
Sale held 1 Nov. 1784. Those who bought at sale viz: Tabitha Green,
Elisha Green, John Pool, Jonathan Barson.

Sarah Green. Estate of Sarah Green. Box 39 Pack 853. Probate Judge Office. Abbeville, S. C. I Sarah Green being weak in body but of perfect mind and memory. etc. I will my just and lawful debts be paid. My will that my Black woman Cate and her five chn., Hanah, Charlotte, Lydia, Rhoda, Cicley together with all my household furniture be sold and money divided between my chn. viz: James Green, George, Thomas, Frances Cullins, Elizabeth Sims, and Nancy Shirley. The chn. are to share and share alike. I appoint my sons James and George Green executors. Dated 11 Jan. 1809. Wit: Not. and J. Rosamond, Dudley Mabrey, Bartholomew X Mabrey. Signed: Sarah X Green. Recorded 13 Feb. 1809. Est. appraised by Wm. X Robartson, Robert X Robartson, Eaton Mabry. on 18 Feb. 1809. Sale held same day.

Henry Green. Deed of Henry Green to Benj. Clardy. Book F Page 62. Clerk of Court Office. Henry Green to Benjamin Clardy both of Washington Dist., Pendleton Co., S. C. This indenture made 11 Jan. 1796. Henry Green and Carolina his wife in consideration of one pd. five shillings good and lawful money of S. C. for a tract of land containing 230 acres on Haricane Creek a branch of Saluda River. Being part of a tract granted unto Henry Green on the 17 Nov. 1791. Wit: Smith Clarridy, Ambrose Hudgens. Signed: Henry X Green and Carolina X Green. Deed attested by Smith Clarridy before William Countz, Esq. on 6 July 1796.

Henry Green. Deed of Henry Green to Isaac Devenport. Book F Page 138. Clerk of Court Office. Washington Dist., Pendleton Co., S. C. Whereas Henry Green of Washington Dist., Pendleton Co. and Isaac Devenport of 96 Dist. Newberry Co. This indenture made 17 Apr. 1793. In consideration of one shilling and six pence current money of the State. Henry Green and Carolina his wife sell all that tract of land containing 676 acres lying on the waters of Hurricane Creek waters of Saluda River. First granted unto Henry Green on 4 Nov. 1791, adj. land of Andrew Brown, Joseph Smith and Johnston land. Wit: William Fariss, John Kirby. Signed: Henry X Green and Carolina X Green. Attested by John Kirby before ___. On 23 Sept. 1797.

John Green. Deed of John Green to Elizabeth Smith. Book F Page 392. Clerk of Court Office. Pendleton Co., S. C. John Green to Elizabeth Smith both of Pendleton Co. Dated 5 Juen 1801. In consideration of thirty pds. sterling paid by Elizabeth Smith for five acres lying on branches of Rockey Creek of Savannah River. Adj. land of George Anderson John Green and Thomas Green, George Nelson. Wit: Daniel X Pitman, Andrew Barkley. Signed John Green. Deed attested by Daniel Pitman before Robert M. Cann, J.P. on 19 Nov. 1801.

Joseph Green to Isham Green Deed of Joseph Green to Isham Green. Book E Page 68. Clerk of Court Office, Pendleton Co., S. C. Joseph Green to Isham Green both of Pendleton Co. Dated 1 May 1798. In consideration of three hundred dollars paid by Isham Green for a tract of land on six and twenty mile Creek waters of Savannah River. Originally granted to John Mills (no date). Wit: Benjamin Harris, Hugh Mills. signed: Joseph Green, seal. Recorded 25 Sept. 1799.

Sion Green. Estate of Sion Green. Box 39 Pack 855. Probate Judge Office. Abbeville, S. C. By Andrew Hamilton, Ord. Whereas Elizabeth Green and Nimrcd Overby applied for a letter of admr. of the goods and chattels of Sion Green decd. as the next of kin. The letter and bond dated 27 Jan. 1802. Sale held on 17 Feb. 1802.

Burwell Green. Estate of Burwell Green. Real Estate Book, Page 26. Probate Judge Office. Pickens, S. C. The heirs of Burwell Green decd. on 9 June 1836 thought it best to sell the real estate lying in Pickens Co., S. C. As many of the heirs are out of State. Heirs are: Asa A. Green, John O. Green, Phoebe Green widow, Margaret wife of Archibald Walker, Lucy the wife of Garland Hardwick, Elizabeth the wife of Jeremiah Gibson, Jane Caldwell, William Green, Burwell Green, Lewis T. Green. Green owned 200 acres on Ccneross waters, adj. land of John Adair, 257 acres on Chauga, adj. land of Almond Powell, 93 acres, adj. land of Abner Honea and Samuel Hunt on waters of Choestoe, 82½

acres on waters of Beaverdam, adj. land of Earle and William Ward,
290 acres adj. land of estate of Earl and others. 200 acres on the
waters of Choestoe adj. land of Widow May and Samuel Moseley Esq.
Being satisfied it to the benefit of all to sell the above property.
Notice will be given for eight weeks. Dated 13 June 1836.

GRISHAM

Elizabeth Grisham. Will of Elizabeth Grisham. Box 15 #199. Probate
Judge Office. Pickens, S. C. I Elizabeth Grisham being old and infirm
in body but in my proper senses and perfect mind and memory, etc. I
will all my ready money and notes to be divided into nine equal parts
among my bodily heirs viz; Mary wife of Ancel Roe, Nancy wife of David
Jarret, Kizziah wife of Thomas Alexander, Sally wife of Richard Crogan,
Elizabeth wife of Gabriel Barns, Hannah wife of William Alexander,
Emelia wife of Fountain Alexander, Sarah Hix my grand dtr. wife of
Elisha Alexander, Diana wife of Abraham Stewart. I appoint Daniel
Alexander my executor. Dated 29 Nov. 1844. Wit: Wm. J. Parson,
___bert Stewart, ___tson Stewart, ___ Durham. Proven May __, 1845.

Grisham Family. Notes on Grisham Family. Pack 606 #1. Clerk of Court
Office. Pickens, S. C. On 21 June 1841 the heirs of John Grisham decd.
in right of their mother Martha Grisham decd. were heir of William
Halbert, Sr. decd. of Anderson Dist.
On 8 Aug. 1826 the heirs of William Grisham recd. a legacy from est. of
Philemon Bradford decd. of Greenville Dist. Apt. 2 File 82. Probate
Judge Office. Greenville, S. C.

HACKETT

Elijah Hackett. Estate of Elijah Hackett. Equity papers. Pack 12.
Abbeville, S. C. Elijah Hackett died 1 Dec. 1853. Left a widow America
E. Hackett and two chn. Anna Hackett who has since died, and Ella C.
Hackett who was born after the death of her father. At the time of
death he owned a tract of land on Cuffee Town Creek in Abbeville Dist.
containing 200 acres. He also left the following brothers and sisters,
William Freeman Hackett age 38 years old, Elizabeth wife of Lemuel Bell,
Augusta G. Hackett age 28 lives in Edgefield Co., S. C. His father and
mother are both dead. Ann Moore wishes her land surveyed, she lives in
Edgefield Co., S. C. about 6½ miles from New Market on the road. Mrs.
Hackett resides at Phoenix P. O. Edgefield, S. C.

Ella C. Hackett. Estate of Ella C. Hackett. Pack 371. Clerk of Court
Office. Abbeville, S. C. The petition of Augustus G. Hackett shews
that Mrs. America E. Hackett was appointed guardian of the person and
estate of her infant dtr. Ella C. Hackett at the June Court of Equity
for the year 1853. But sd. America E. Hackett is now desirous that your
petitioner Augustus G. Hackett should be appointed gdn. of the estate of
sd. minor Ella C. Hackett. That the sd. minor has an estate of four or
five thousand dollars, and she is not quite three years old. Filed
8 June 1857.

HADDEN

Robert Hadden, Sr. and Jr. Estate of Robert Hadden, Sr. and Jr. both
in Box 47 Pack 1080. Probate Judge Office. Abbeville, S. C. Est. of
Robt. Hadden, Sr. We Jane Hadden widow, John Lindsey and William Ross
are bound unto the Judge of Abbeville Co. Court in the sum of 500 lbs.
Dated 12 Sept. 1791. Inv. made 26 Sept. 1791 by James Stevenson, Wm.
Ross, John Cowan.

Robert Hadden, Jr. Estate of Robert Hadden, Jr. Box 47 Pack 1080.
Probate Judge Office. Abbeville, S. C. An inv. made 1 Nov. 1788 by

James Stevenson, Wm. Ross, Ezekiel Evans, Sale held 7 Feb. 1791 byr.
Wm. Mayn, Wm. Hadden, Alexr. McCleskey, James McCoullough, James Bracken-
ridge, James Wardlaw. Settlement made 10 June 1799. Paid Esther
Hadden a legatee, Wm. Hadden a legatee, Jean and Mary two legatees,
Paid Jean Hadden alias Mayn and her third of est. William Mayn was admr.
of Robt. Hadden, Jr. est.

Hadden Family. Hadden Family in Lindsay Cemetery 2 miles south of Due
West, S. C. Abbeville Co., S. C.
  Abram Haddon, born 8 Feb. 821, died 21 Oct. 1864 (spelled with O)
  Hannah Haddon born 18 Nov. 1821, died 1 May 1869.
  Permelia P. Haddon, born 12 Nov. 1848, died 5 June 1863.
  Winube? Haddon, born 28 July 1845, died 2 Aug. 1865.
  Thomas Luther Haddon, born 10 Apr. 1847, died 3 Nov. 1905.
  Elizabeth A. Key, wife, born 27 Nov. 1845, died 9 June 1927.

                              HAGOOD

William Hagood. Deed of Gift from William Hagood. Pack 224. Clerk of
Court Office. Abbeville, S. C. This indenture made 1 June 1808 between
Wm. Hagood of Edgefield Dist. and John Marshall Moore Trustee appointed
by Wm. Hagood for the intent and purposes hereafter mentioned. For and
in consideration of love and affection which he the Wm. Hagood hath for
his dtr. Susan Ambler the wife of James Ambler. To provide more amply
for the support of sd. Susan and the children of her body by her present
or any future husband she may have. For further consideration of five
dollars now paid by John Marshall Moore the receipt whereof is acknowledged and for other good causes and consideration, Wm. Hagood hath
given unto John Marshall Moore the following negroes, Nidelicit, Jenny
and her child Clarissa. The negroes are to be kept by Moore and his
heirs in trust and not be subject to his debts or use. She to enjoy
the work and service or the same to hire out and thus wages to receive
and same to aplly to her only use. At her death to be divided between
her chn. of her body only. Wit: Wm. M. Johnson, Gideon Hagood.
Signed: Wm. Hagood, seal. Personal appeared Wm. M. Johnson before
Julius Nichols, J.P. Sworn saith he saw Wm. Hagood sign the above will.
Dated 24 Oct. 1808.

Hagood Notes. Pack 654-1. In Equity. Allen Robertson. Clerk of
Court Office. Pickens, S.C. On 7 Apr. 1855 Lydia Hagood widow of
Osborne Hagood and residing in Gilmer County, Georgia. Dtr. of Allen
Robertson decd. who died in 1854 and of his widow Catherine Robertson
of Pickens Dist.

Benjamin Hagood. Estate of Benjamin Hagood. Box ___ # ___. Probate
Judge Office. Pickens, S. C. I Benjamin Hagood being of sound mind
and memory, etc. I will to my beloved wife Adaline Hagood during her
natural life one half of the plantation whereon I now live, and the
following negroes, Harry, Molly, Gilbert, Clarissa, Peter, Harriett,
Gilbert, Jr., Berry Carolina nd two chn. and any increase she may have
and Jerry. Also my grist mill tract of land, lines given adj. land of
Thomas and Porters. My children to get their milling done without toll
Wife to have any stock, farm tools, household and kitchen furniture she
may think needed to keep up the farm, with one thousand dollars in cash.
I give to my son James E. Hagood the plantation where he now lives,
being the same I bought from John Burdine, and the following negroes.
Dilce, Torrence, Tom and Jane and two negro boys Jack and Bill the
negroes now in his possession. To my oldest dtr. Elvira C. Robinson.
I will the following negroes Miles, Mary and Martha. To my second dtr.
Elmina E. Hagood I will the tract of land called Ceasers Head containing 480 acres, with the house on Turn Pike Road. To my third dtr.
Eliza I will one negro girl named Mariah. To my son John H. Hagood one
half of the plantation whereon I now live, and at the death of his
mother he is to get her half. All debts to be paid from money collected
and due me. As each child becomes of age or marry they are to receive
its share. I will to Benjamin Holder the balance of the land whereon
he now lives known as the Amber Tract with three negroes Yancy, Jack Jr.,

Lydia. (No exectr.) Dated 23 July 1852. Wit: L. C. Craig, E. H. Griffin, W. D. Steel. Filed 18 Feb. 1865. Est. admr. 27 Feb. 1865 by James E. Hagood, Robt. A. Thompson, W. L. Grisham who are bound unto W. E. Holcombe, Ord. in the sum of $100,000.00. Died 2 Feb. 1865.

J. R. Hagood. Estate of J. R. Hagood. Box 94 #1000. Probate Judge Office. Pickens, S. C. Est. admr. 3 Mar. 1885 by W. M. Hagood, P. McD. Alexander, J. Frank Folger who are bound unto J. H. Newton, Ord. in the sum of $1,000.00.

Jerry Hagood. Estate of Jerry Hagood, Box 113 #1086. Probate Judge Office. Pickens, S. C. On 9 July 1881 Hester Lawrence wanted J. J. Lewis to be admr. of her father Estate.

Buck Hagood. Estate of Buck Hagood. Box 144 #5. Probate Judge Office. Pickens, S. C. He died 26 April 1901. A. J. Boggs the admr.

James E. Hagood. Estate of James E. Hagood. Box 144 #10. Probate Judge Office. Pickens, S. C. I James Earle Hagood being of sound mind and disposing memory, etc. I desire my body be buried at my family grave yard on my 12 mile plantation near my wife and chn. and my ancestors, and that my family have placed over my remains a good marble tomb as near as can like the one over my wife's grave, and my family are hereby requested and directed to always keep a good neat fence enclosing same well painted. I desire my executors to collect all monies due me and pay debts which I may owe. I give to my three dtr. Mary Elizabeth Alexander, Lucie Virginia Bruce, Fannie Miles Hagood, my 12 mile plantation known as my home place or Burdine tract, containing 700 acres, also that portion of my father's place which is now attached to my home place, which I bought from brother John H. Hagood, containing 220 acres, together with all horses, mules, stock, farming tools, and crops at time of my death. Place to be kept in good order and in the family as long as possible. I give to my dtr. Fannie Miles Hagood my house and lots in Pickens where I now live, and all land on the North of the road going to Benjamin Holder and one half of the household and kitchen furniture, the other half to dtr. Virginia Bruce. I give to all my children the mill tract, they are to use and retain it jointly. I give to my son Benjamin Adger Hagood all that portion of land which I bought at Haynes' sale, known as Kelly Hill; all of my office furniture, safes, law books, both in my office and in Charleston, it my will and desire that the office furniture and books shall not be charged against him in the final settlement of my estate. To my dtr. Lucie Bruce, the Folger house and lots in Pickens, also three other lots containing about two acres each. I give to my dtr. Elizabeth Alexander one half of lot #24 containing two acres North of her lot. I desire that each of my children share equal, I have given some items of value, that I have entered in the "Family Book" I charge them to enter into said book and at the price therein stated. I appoint my two sons William Milliken Hagood and Benjamin Adger Hagood as executors. Dated 11 Sept. 1897. Wit: J. J. Lewis, John L. Thornley, Thomas K. Price. Signed: J. E. Hagood, seal. Filed 4 June 1904. Died 29 Apr. 1904.

Eliza Ann Hagood. Will of Eliza Ann Hagood. Box 48 #1108. Probate Judge Office. Abbeville, S. C. (only part of will found) I Eliza Hagood make this my last will and testament. I bequeath unto my aunt Eliza McGowen my horse, barouche and harness for her sole use and benefit. I give to my uncle Richard Hagood my tract of land containing two or three hundred acres in Abbeville Dist. on the waters of Cuffer Town Creek, adj. land of Maximillian Hutchenson, Mr. Barbor, Mr. William Stalworth. I give to my cousins, Henry Chiles, Mary G. Chiles, Robert Chiles and Caroline Eliza McGowen all remaining property, after paying my debts to be divided between my cousins as my executor sees fit. (The year 1839 is written on top of will.)

Randolph Hagood. Estate of Randolph Hagood. Box 45 #1001. Probate Judge Office. Abbeville, S. C. We Rebecca Hagood, Garland Chiles, Thomas Marsh, Thomas Livingston and Benjamin Chiles are bound unto Moses Taggart, Ord. in the sum of $4,000.00 dollars. Dated 18 Nov.

1820. Citation published at Cambridge, S. C. Inv. made 14 Dec. 1820
by Joab Wilson, Wm. Harison, Wm. Hackett. Sale held 15 Dec. 1820.
byers: Wm. Stallsworth, Elbert Henderson, Wm. Campbell, Dr. Wm. Chipley
Robt. Kay, David Griffin, Thos. Stallsworth, Mukins Hollaway, Wm. Dover,
Wm. Mitchell, Thos. Henderson, David Tedders, Saml. Henderson, Jno.
Lee, Edmund Stallsworth, Jeremiah Wilson, Peter Lee, Richard Hagood,
Eli Henderson, Vincent Griffin, Col. John Moore, Saml. Turner, Rebeca
Hagood, Wm. Sales, Mary Crow, John Foster, Danl. English, James Amber,
Garland Chiles, Stephen Witt, George Hagood, Robt. Burns, Hugh Oliver.
Expend. 1824 cash sent to Hamburg for clothing for Eliza Ann Hagood.

HAIRSON

William Hairson. Will of William Hairson, No Ref. Probate Judge
Office. Abbeville, S. C. (First part of will not found.) I give to
my beloved wife one negro woman named Oney, one horse called Dick a
saddle and bridle, two cows and calves, one sow and pigs, two beds and
furniture, farm tools she may need, with enough feed to do twelve
months. The rest of my estate sold by my executors to pay just debts.
At the death of my wife the whole of my estate be sold and divided
between my chn. except my son Peter Hairson, I will one dollar, and
Jane Brown my dtr. I will the same and nothing more. An equal division
to be made between James Hairson, Agness Martin, John Hairson, William
Hairson and Thomas Hairson. I appoint my trusty friend James Lomax and
John Brannan Executors. Dated 18 March 1808. Wit: James Lomax, Junr.,
Steth Howlet, Elijah Thomas. Signed William Hairson, Senr. Recorded
9 Apr. 1808. Inv. made 13 Apr. 1808 by John Hairson, Archibald Douglass
Wm. Bell.

James R. Hairson. Estate of James R. Hairson, Box 48, Pack 1107.
Probate Judge Office, Abbeville, S. C. I James R. Hairson being weak
in body but of sound mind and memory etc. I allow my executors to sell
as much of my estate to pay debts. I allow the remainder to go to my
wife Jane Hairson to do as and dispose in any manner as she may think
best. I appoint my wife as executrix and John Keller executor. Dated
5 July 1827. Wit: G. Lomax, B. Johnson, S. Williams. Signed James R.
Hairson. Jane Hairson, qualified as exrix. 22 Jan. 1835. Inv. made
24 Jan. 1835 by W. B. Arnold, Jesse C. Beasly, B. Johnson.

Jane Hairson. Estate of Jane Hairson. Box 131 Pack 3799. Probate
Judge Office. Abbeville, S. C. I Jane Hairson being frail in body but
of sound and disposing mind. I give to my nephew James Wesley Johnston,
son of Telever Johnston all my slaves viz: Rebecca, Jane T., George
W., John B., Mary Ann, Rhody S. and Edney Frances with all their
increase and none of them to be sold or parted from each other. It is
my desire that all my real and personal property, except the slaves be
sold by my executors, pay all just debts and my grave well furnished,
the remains to be divided between viz: Toliver Johnston, Thos. Johnston
Rachel Martin, William Gray son of John Gray decd. William Gray son of
James Gray, decd. Mary Ann Thompson and Sarah Jane Lomax daughter of
John and Elizabeth Lomax. I appoint my friend David Keller, Esq.
Dated 4 June 1853. Wit: John W. Lomax. Garlington Owens, Elizabeth
B. Lomax. Signed Jane X Hairson. A power of attorney from Thomas
Johnson of Panola County, State of Miss. appointing John Adams of
Abbeville Dist. as his attorney to collect and all sums of money from
David Keller the executor of Jane Hairson estate. Dated 24 July 1855.
A power of attorney from James H. and Rachael Martin his wife of Tippah
County, State of Miss. to collect all money from David Keller as
Executor of Jane Hairson estate. Dated 2 Aug. 1856. Signed J. H.
Martin and Rachel Martin.

HALBERT

William Halbert, Sr. Estate of William Halbert, Sr. Pack 606 #1.
Clerk of Court Office. Pickens, S. C. On 21 June 1841 Charles Garrison

William Halbert, Jr. admr. of the estate of William Halbert, Sr. of
Anderson Dist. made their first returns, left 13 chn. John Sherrill
in right of his wife, Susannah Ackers widow of Peter Acker decd., Joel
Halbert, John Halbert, James Halbert, Joshua Halbert, William Berry in
right of his wife, David Berry in right of his wife. Heirs of Enos
Halbert decd.. heirs of Arthur Halbert decd. Heirs of John Grisham
decd. in right of their mother Martha Grisham decd. Heirs of Charles
Garrison in right of his wife.

HALL

Nathaniel Hall. Will of Nathaniel Hall. Book C Page 104. Probate
Judge Office. Anderson, S. C. I Nathaniel Hall of Pendleton Co.
being very sick and weak in body but of perfect mind and memory. First
pay my just and lawful debts. All that estate that was deeded to me
by John Falkner as may be seen on records in Laurence (Laurens) County
office, if ever it is obtained shall be equally divided among all my
chn. I give one negro named Suly and her dtr. Jenny   I give unto my
wife Elizabeth during her natural life, and after her death to be
divided among all my chn. Like wise all my lands, household, kitchen,
stock of all kinds shall be for my wife Elizabeth use, except one
sorrel colt named cross, I give to my son Nathaniel. The other boys are
to stay with their mother till they are twenty years of age. Then to
get a saddle and bridle with a young creature as the stock will afford.
At the death of my wife the whole estate to be divided between all my
chn. I appoint my brother Fenton Hall and John Hall as executors.
Dated 19 Oct. 1793. Wit: Robert Norris, Jos. Erwin, Benjamin Hall.
Signed: Nathl. Hall, seal. Proven in open Court on oath of Benjamin
Hall 24 Jan. 1797.

John Hall. Estate of John Hall. Box 45 Pack 1012. Probate Judge
Office. Abbeville, S. C. We Sarah Hall, widow, Thomas Hodge, Francis
Hodge and Wm. Dunlap are bound unto the judge of Abbeville Court in the
sum of five thousand dollars. Dated 6 Nov. 1797. John Hall was a
merchant. Inv. made 29 Dec. 1797 by Dunken Campbell, Thomas Pringle,
Francis Hodge. Buyers at sale: Sarah Hall, Robert George, Michael
Cain, Francis Hodge, Wm. Hudgen, Gordon Lippard, Wm. Holmes, Hugh Dawson,
Saml. McClellon.

Fleming Hall. Estate of Fleming Hall. Box 43 Pack 960. Probate Judge
Office. Abbeville, S. C. We David Hall, Fenton Hall, John Davis are
bound unto Moses Taggart, Ord. in the sum of one thousand dollars.
Dated 18 Feb. 1832. Appraisement made 6 Mar. 1832 by Bartley Tucker,
John Davis, William Pitts. (letter).. "Storeville, S. C. Nov. 2,
1842. This is to certify that David Hall deposited in the post office
a letter enclosing the right end of $50 bill of the bank of Hamburg.
I mailed for him to John Ward Ripley in Miss. A. Thomson, P.M.
Storeville.."

(Guardianship) State of Mississippi Co. of Tippah. At a Probate Court
in the town of Ripley on the first Monday in March 1843 Hon. R. R.
Thomas the presiding Judge. The following preceedings were had wit.
Fenton B. Hall and Laurel V. Hall minors heirs of Fleming Hall decd.,
formerly of Abbeville, Dist. S. C. and late of Carroll County, state
of Tenn. Exhibited their petition in this Court praying the Court to
appoint Margaret Hall a citizen of said County as their Guardian. It
appearing to the Court that she is a suitable and proper person etc.
Bond was set for $200 with Nathaniel Hobson and William Shetley as
security, as filed in the Clerk office. Signed Haywood Bowers, Clerk
of Tippah Co., Miss. (Another letter) Dated 7 June 1844 from Ripley,
Miss. Margaret Hall to her brother Mr. David Hall of Anderson Court
House. She enquires of her sister Elizabeth Hall. Fleming Hall estate
was settled 19 May 1842, left a widow and 7 distributees. One of the
distributees was a Jesse Hall.

Jesse Hall. Estate of Jesse Hall. Box 6 #66. Probate Judge Office.
Pickens Co., S. C. I Jesse Hall being weak in body and afflicted with

disease but being in perfect mind and memory, etc. I give to my wife
all my personal estate of during her natural life or widowhood on
express conditions that it be keep on the plantation whereon I now live
for the common use and support of herself and the four chn. Viz:
Mary, Nancy, Ruth, Henry. On conditions that anyone or more than one
should marry or leave the family they shall have an equal share of
what remains of the property at that time. I give to my son Thomas
Hall the tract of land whereon I now live on conditions he care for my
wife and children which remains single and support his mother during
her natural life, and to take charge of his brother George and support
him during his natural life. I have other children who are not named
in this will, who are dear to me, but have been provided an equal share
with the others. I appoint Thomas Hall and Zacheriah Hall Executors.
Dated 2 Apr. 1833. Wit: D. Sloan, Richard Harris, William X Hall.
Signed Jesse X Hall. Proven 4 Nov. 1833. (In the same pack) Admr.
este. of Ann Hall 5 June 1843 by Francis Burt, J. A. Doyle who are
bound unto Jas. H. Dendy, Ord. in the sum of $1,400.00.

Catherine Hall. Estate of Catherine Hall. Box 53 #582. Probate Judge
Office. Pickens, S. C. Est. admr. 7 May 1860 by James Hall, George
W. Vanzant who are bound unto W. E. Holcombe, Ord. in the sum of $100.00.
Was late of Cobb Co., Ga.

Hugh Hall. Will of Hugh Hall. Bxo 54 #189. Probate Judge Office.
Pickens, S. C. I Hugh Hall being in a low state of health with death
before my eyes tho of sound disposing mind and memory, etc. I give to
my beloved wife Mary Hall household and kitchen furniture, items named.
To my grand dtr. Mary Collins three bed quilts, one sheet, one counter-
pin, one stand of curtains and ten dollars in cash. The remaining part
to be sold and pay just debts and equal divided between my wife and two
dtr. Salena Spensor and Sarah Thompson. I appoint my friend R. A.
Gilme executor. Dated 23 Feb. 1860. Wit: E. Collins, Daniel Butler,
William X Norris. Signed Hugh X Hall. Proven 30 Apr. 1860. On 20
Feb. 1868 paid Mary Norris, Sarah Thompson, Salena Spensor each in full
$6.27.

Francis M. Hall. Estate of Francis M. Hall. Box 65 #703. Probate
Judge Office. Pickens, S. C. Est. admr. 3 Nov. 1862 by Zachariah Hall,
Wm. S. Grisham, D. Biemann who are bound unto W. E. Holcombe, Ord. in
the sum of $300.00.

John E. M. Hall. Note on John E. M. Hall, who was living in Central,
S. C. in 1885 and the son of Mrs. M. A. Hall. Ref. Pack 277 #3. Clerk
of Court Office. Pickens, S. C.

Frances E. Hall. Bill of Alimony, Frances E. Hall vs. Samuel James H.
Stark. Pack 4. Clerk of Court Office. Abbeville, S. C. Your oratrix
Frances E. Stark of Anderson Dist. the wife of Samuel James H. Stark
of Abbeville Dist. by Ezekiel Hall of Anderson Dist. her father. On
the 15 Feb. in this present year (1852) your oratrix intermarried with
Samuel Stark in the house of Ezekiel Hall by the Rev. Mr. Rice. Stark
lived in her father house for about a month and started collecting his
clothes and other articles, and said he was leaving for Texas or
California. He is said to be worth about ten thousand dollars and she
wish alimony. Filed 9 March 1852. Settled by arrangement of the
parties the 17 May 1852.

Zach, Ruth, William, Sarah Hall. On 28 Nov. 1859 Zach Hall and wife
Ruth, William Hall and wife Sarah Hall were heirs of Francis Jenkins
decd. of Pickens Dist. Also Daniel Hall and wife Caroline were also
heirs. Ref. Est. of Francis Jenkins. Book B, page 42 On 1 June 1818
Drury Morris decd. of Greenville Dist. in his life time deeded property
to Sarah Hall Ref. Apt 6 File 346. Probate Judge Office. Greenville,
S. C.

James E. Hagood. Warrant for Land. Pack 603 #38. Clerk of Court
Office. Pickens, S. C. By James E. Hagood, Clerk of the Court, to any
lawful surveyor, you are hereby authorized to lay out unto Fenton H.
Hall a tract of land not exceeding one thousand acres. Dated 12 Nov.

1860. Executed 15 Nov. 1860 for 52 acres. Warrant for land. Pack
603 #89. This warrant executed 20 Feb. 1860 for 225 acres. Filed 16
Apr. 1860.

Fenton Hall, Sr. Estate of Fenton Hall, Sr. Box 116 Pack 3437.
Probate Judge Office. Abbeville, S. C. Est. admr. 2 Nov. 1848 by
Jesse W. Norris, Robert B. Norris, John Clinkscales, Ezekiel Hall who
are bound unto David Lesly, Ord. in the sum of $3,000.00. Died 23 Oct.
1848. (A letter) from Crawfordville, Miss. dated August 25/72. Dear
Mother and sisters and brothers, a few lines to let you know me and
Rebecca is well hoping these lines come to hand it may find you well
received your letter of the 10 of Aug. was glad to hear from you
Mother wanted me to let you know about my claim on the land you can sell
or rent which is best you think How is G. W. Hall and his family
How is William Hall is he still living at the same old place where is
W. N. Hall and the rest of the family where is Sarah and what is she
doing How is the Preachers at First Creek and Rocky River I am going
to send for my letter I think I will settle myself here Give my best
respect to Uncle Billy Tucker and Aunt I remain your son and brother
until death... Signed J. D. Hall. Letter written to Miss Mary D.
Hall, Centerville, Abbeville County, S. C.

HALLUMS

William Hallums. Estate of William Hallums. Box 9 #111. Probate
Judge Office. Pickens Dist. Est. admr. 14 Dec. 1829 by Thomas Hallum,
Jr., James C. Griffin, Wm. Bowen, Madison C. Livingston.

Bazzel Hallum. Land grant to Bazzel Hallum. Plat Book C page 4.
Clerk of Court Office. Pickens, S. C. grant for 100 acres on 18 mile
creek, dated 1 Aug. 1785.

Richard Hallum. Will of Richard Hallum made 29 Jan. 1848. Proven 8
Jan. 1849. He lived in Pickens Dist. Wife Elizabeth Hallum, chn.
John Hallum, A. C. Hallum, Eliza A. Prater, Elizabeth McCain, Thomas J.
Hallum. Wit: John Maxwell, John T. Sloan, Green Stephens. J. B.
Prather and Robert McCain recd. a legacy of $100.00.

Nero Hallum. Estate of Nero Hallum. Box 140 #6. Probate Judge Office.
Pickens, S. C. Est. admr. 29 Nov. 1902 by Isaac Hallum, B. H. Callahan,
T. H. Hunter who are bound unto J. B. Newberry, Ord. in the sum of
$1400.00. Died 1 Nov. 1902

Thomas Hallum. Will of Thomas Hallum. Box 53 #579. Probate Judge
Office. Pickens, S. C. I Thomas Hallum being of sound body and mind
and of perfect understanding. I will and desire that my executors put
up a marble stone at the head and foot of my grave, also at the head
and foot of my wife Margaret grave. I will just debts and funeral
expenses be paid. I will to my dtr. Mary Ann my negro boy Ellick, one
horse, saddle and bridle and one burow that I have now. I will to my
dtr. Julia A. Smith one negro boy named Henry also sixty-five acres of
land, a part of the tract I now live on, adj. land of Warren Smith and
on the Hobord line and the Chapman line. I will to my dtr. Sary Emily
Hunter in trust to her and her heirs one negro woman named of Charity
and a tract of land of seventy acres, adj. land of Mavrick land,
Warren Smith to be in trust for the special use and benefit of her and
the natural heirs of her body. I will to my dtr. Martha Adeline Kalaham
a negro boy named John. I will to my dtr. Margaret Malinda a negro girl
named Caty and one horse and saddle and bridle. I will to my dtr.
Melinda Naomia a negro girl named Harriet, one horse, saddle and
bridle. I will to my dtr. Jane a negro woman named Ann and child
named Ann Mariah, one horse, saddle and bridle. I will and desire my
negro Sam to work on the place for the single girls, if they marry he
can choose his home among my chn. My negro boy Jess shall work for the
single girls, if they marry he is to be sold. I will my personal
property any other real estate be sold and money divided between my
four single dtr. I appoint my son in law Warren Smith and John W.

Kallaham as executors. Dated 29 Nov. 1859. Wit: John H. Bowen, W. P.
Hunt, John Bowen. Signed Thomas Hallum. Proven 17 Feb. 1860. Settle-
ment made 24 Dec. 1863 paid Aeneas Hunter and wife Emilia C. $263.06.
Paid John Williamson and wife $263.06.

Thomas Hallum. Land Warrant of Thomas Hallum. Pack 114. Clerk of
Court Office. Pickens, S. C. By W. L. Keith, Clerk of any lawful
surveyor you are authorized to lay out unto Thomas Hallum a tract of
land not exceeding ten thousand acres. Dated 3 Sept. 1849. He
received 950 acres, certified 30 Oct. 1849.

HAMBY

James Hamby. In Equity for Rape. Pack 650 #8. Clerk of Court Office.
Pickens, S. C. On 5 Jan. 1829 James Hamby was charged as having reped
his dtr. Elizabeth Hamby a child about 12 or 13 years old. Sarah Hamby
was also a witness in said case.

HAMILTON

Leonard S. Hamilton. Deed, Leonard S. Hamilton. Book C-1 Page 1.
Clerk of Court Office. Pickens, S. C. Deed from Leonard S. Hamilton
to William Odell both of Pickens Dist. Dated 14 Apr. 1834. In the sum
of $595. Hamilton sell, bargain, release 170½ acres lying on Goldens
Creek of 12 Mile River, being part of two tracts, one granted unto
Samuel Martin in 1787, the other granted unto John Brady in 1789 who
sold to Aaron Boggs Sr. then to Aaron Boggs, Jr. then to Leonard
Hamilton. The other Samuel Martin to Absolem Martin to Wm. Mayfield to
Isiah Prator to Leonard Hamilton. Wit: Thos. D. Garvin, Lot X James.
Signed Leonard S. Hamilton seal. Attested by Thos. D. Garvin before
F. N. Garvin, J.P. on 30 Aug. 1834. Recorded 1 Sept. 1834.

David Hamilton, Sr. Estate of David Hamilton, Sr. Box 7 #89. Probate
Judge Office. Pickens, S. C. I David Hamilton being far advanced in
my time of life and frail but of sound mind and memory, etc. I give
to my wife Jane two beds and their furniture, the plantation and house
on which I live, and one half of the amount of the sale of my property.
I give to my son Andrew Hamilton one hundred and eight acres on which
he now lives for his support but not subject to his disposal or debts,
but to be the property of my grandson Alexander Hamilton his son in
fee simple. I give to my two granddaughters Margaret and Jane Hamilton
a tract of land on Goldens Creek of 38 acres. It is my will that my
personal property be sold on twelve months credit, except my man Cegar
not to be sold, but to live with my children not as a slave, also my
woman Malinda to stay with my wife during her life time, she also may
choose the one of my chn. she wish to live with not as a slave. At
the death of my wife the plantation to be sold and divided as, one third
to my dtr. Margret Peatee and one third to Mary Kirkpatrick, the
remaining third to my granddaughters Margaret and Jane Hamilton. After
my debts are paid the balance as thirty dollars to each of our chn.
Elizabeth Perrons, Andrew Hamilton, David L. Hamilton, Mary Kirkpatrick,
Margaret Prater and Bershaba Fraser. I appoint Maj. Andrew Hamilton,
Col. David K. Hamilton, Thomas G. Boggs my stepson as Executors.
Dated 20 Feb. 1830. Wit: J. L. McCann, Fielding Fennell, Rt. McCann
D. Chamblin. Signed David Hamilton, seal. N.B... The forgoing last
will and testament of David Hamilton was not proven by a subscribing
witness as is usual, they being absent from the State. Proven on oath
of Col. David K. Hamilton one of the executors. James H. Dendy, Ord.
Proven 7 Nov. 1837. Legatees paid on 19 Jan. 1839. Jarrett Parson and
wife Margaret, Andrew W. Kirkpatrick, Samuel Fraser, Shelby Bates,
Jane P. Hamilton, David A. Hamilton. (In will Perrons was written
but expend papers it is Parson) Elizabeth, Margaret, Jarret Parson,
Jane Hamilton was mother of T. G. Boggs, Margaret Bates and John E.
O'Dell.

Jane Hamilton. Will of Jane Hamilton. Box 11 #145. Probate Judge
Office. Pickens, S. C. I Jane Hamilton being of sound and disposing
mind and memory. I desire that the negro woman Maria and her two
youngest chn. Susan & Isaac, and the negro woman Julia and her youngest
child Celia be sold to pay my debrs and funeral expenses. The remainder
of the money be divided between my chn. Elizabeth Odell, John R. Boggs,
Thomas G. Boggs, George W. Boggs. I desire that the others negroes be
divided into four equal lots, a lot for each child. Negroes are:
Harriet, Thomas, Antony, Simpson, Billy, Berry, Eliza, John Westly,
Green, Emily and Anderson. I give to my son Thomas G. Boggs one black
cow. I give to my dtr Elizabeth Odell one feather bed. I give to my
daughter in law Jane Boggs one feather bed. I give all my bed clothing
and wearing apparel be equally divided between my dtr. Elizabeth Odell
and my dtr. in law Jane and Elenor Boggs. Dated 6 Jan. 1843. Wit:
Aaron Boggs, A. E. McDonnell, Allen Fuller. Signed Jane X Hamilton.
A Codicil added the next day. The codicil states that she had made a
deed of gift for the negroes that was to be divided by lots, her dtr.
Elizabeth Odell is to get twenty five dollars in cash to make her lot
of negroes equal with the others. Dated 7 Jan. 1843. Wit: Allen
Fuller, A. E. McDonnell, Wm. S. Williams. Signed Jane X Hamilton.
Will proven 23 Jan. 1843.

William Hamilton's Minors. Estate of William Hamilton's Minors. Box
47 Pack 1091. Probate Judge Office. Abbeville, S. C. We Luke Hamilton,
James D. Houston, James H. Taylor are bound unto T. A. Taggart, Ord. in
the sum of $2,000.00. Dated 9 May 1836. Whereas Luke Hamilton of
Anderson Dist. was made gdn. of Wm. Hamilton a minor under 14 yrs. Same
date, We James D. Houston, George W. Liddell, Hudson Prince are bound
unto T. G. Taggart, Ord. in the sum of $2,000.00. James D. Houston was
made gdn. of James Hamilton, Luke Hamilton, Elizabeth and Sarah Hamilton.

Thomas Hamilton. Will of Thomas Hamilton. Box 47 Pack 1070. Probate
Judge Office. Abbeville, S. C. I Thomas Hamilton of 96 Dist. being
weak of body but sound mind and memory. I leave to my son John Hamilton
the plantation once belonging to Ballinger and now in his possession
and the tract of land joining to Mr. Beard which he once sold to Mr.
Montgomery and a negro boy named Joe. I leave to my dtr. Margaret
Hamilton the tract of land which I now live on, also negro named Jude,
all household and kitchen furniture, stock, cattle, etc. The rest of
my personal property to be sold and pay debts and funeral expenses if
any left over divided between my chn. John Hamilton, Thomas Hamilton,
Saray Turner and Margaret Ray, that my dtr. Margaret Hamilton may
dispose of the tract of land when and how... (This is all of this will
that I could find. The year 1789 was written on top of paper. J.E.W.)

Capt. John Hamilton. Estate of Capt. John Hamilton. Box 45 Pack 1015.
Probate Judge Office. Abbeville, S. C. I John Hamilton of Abbeville
Dist. being weak in body but of sound mind and memory, etc. I leave to
my beloved wife Mary Anne Hamilton the plantation whereon I now live,
containing 335 acres with all household and kitchen furniture, the
sorrel mare and young bay horse of what crops, stock, cattle as she may
need for her and the family support. Also the negro Hannah during
her widowhood, the rest of my negroes to be keep or hired out as my
executors may think best. To each of my dtr. Mary, Isabella, Elizabeth
Anne, and Sarah Waddel when they come of the age of eighteen I give one
horse and saddle valued at one hundred dollars, and a bed and furniture.
To my son Thomas Twining when he comes of the age of twenty one yrs.
the plantation affd. unless his mother should remain a widow then she
shall hold one third of sd. land. If she think best to keep negroes
and farm tool, stock to support the family and schooling of my chn. to
be taught by a good English scholar as to reading, writing and arith-
metic. I appoint my wife and John Caldwell Esq. as Executors. Dated
26 Nov. 1805. Wit: Fras. Carlile, Wm. Davis. Signed John Hamilton.
Recorded 26 Dec. 1805. Est. appraised by Joseph Bickley, Fras. Carlile,
John Harris, Those who bought at sale: Robt. Allen, Senr., Thos.
Ward, John Scudday, John Dickey, Arch. McKinley, Jno. Caldwell, Wm.
Richeson, Burel Morris. Benj. Terry, Robt. David, Pleasant Wade, Aaron
Jones, Francis Moore, Colo. Carlile, Thos. B. Craigh, James Bickley,
John Linch. Lewis Howland.

Waddy Hamilton. Estate of Waddy Hamilton. Box 100 #1048. Probate Judge Office. Pickens, S. C. Est. admr. 20 Apr. 1870 by G. H. Symmes, Whitner Symmes, F. V. Clayton are bound unto I. H. Philpot, Ord. in the sum of $100.00. Died 25 Dec. 1869.

Lemuel Hamilton. Will of Lemuel Hamilton. Box 116 #17. Probate Judge Office. Pickens, S. C. I Lemuel G. Hamilton do make this my last will and testament, etc. I will and desire the tract of land I may die with be held by my wife Clemenia during her natural life (having conveyed to my chn. certain tracts of land). At the death of my wife my executors to sell the land. From this money give my dtr. Chloe Jane Cureton two hundred dollars as she has not been advanced by me as much as the other chn. The rest and residue be divided between my chn. Mary Lucretia Hunt, Chloe Jane Cureton, Hester Ann Cureton, Effie C. Brown, Whitten A. Hamilton and Andrew Hamilton. The household and kitchen furniture of every description, I will to my two dtr. Mary Lucretia Hunt and Effie C. Brown to be divided by themselves and without the intervention of my executors. I appoint my two sons Whitten A. Hamilton and Andrew R. Hamilton my executors. Dated 24 Apr. 1886. Wit: J. J. Lewis, F. V. Clayton, J. B. Hinton. Signed L. G. Hamilton seal. Filed 31 May 1889. Paid 14 Jan. 1897 Mrs. Jane C. Cureton, $200. Mrs. Jessie J. Carpenter dtr. of Mrs. M. L. Hunt decdl $70.78.

A. M. Hamilton. Estate of A. M. Hamilton. Box 119 #4. Probate Judge Office. Pickens, S. C. Est. admr. 4 Feb. 1892 by C. E. Hamilton, A. M. Boggs, W. E. Griffin who are bound unto J. B. Newberry, Ord. in the sum of $1,000.00. Died 29 Dec. 1891 C. E. Hamilton a son.

Warren Hamilton. Will of Warren Hamilton. Box 129 #13. Probate Judge Office. Pickens, S. C. I Warren Hamilton being of sound mind and disposing memory, etc. I will to my beloved wife Caroline Hamilton during her natural life all my property both real and personal, and at the death of my wife, I will all of sd. property to my two sons Milton and William Hamilton to share and share alike. I will my just debts be paid with my own and my wife funeral expenses be paid from the estate. I appoint my son Milton Hamilton as executor. Dated 20 April 1896. Wit: W. H. Merck, J. H. Hudson, J. P. Carey. Signed: Warren Hamilton, seal. He died 19 Sept. 1897. Filed 4 Oct. 1897.

Notes on Hamiltons. Notes on the Hamilton from "Loose Papers" Pickens Co., S. C. Jean Boggs, widow of Joseph Boggs. On 24 Jan. 1807 after her marriage to David Hamilton of Pendleton Dist. entered into a covenant. Jean Hamilton formerly Jean Boggs widow, woman in York Dist. of the other part. David Hamilton died in 1830. Both parties had chn. by a former marriage. On 8 Dec. 1841 David A. Hamilton of Jackson County, Ga. appointed Leonard S. Hamilton of Anderson Dist. and from all persons the debts that are owing to me. 19 Dec. 1846 Mr. Steele please pay Cyrus E. Hamilton $27.00 for service done for me and others. Signed: Andrew W. and Mary Kirkpatrick.

David Hamilton. In Equity. Box 3 #88. Clerk of Court Office. Pickens Co., S. C. To their Honor the Chancellor: The petition of Garner Evans sheweth that a certain tract of land in the sd. State supposed to be the property of the late David Hamilton, being the tract whereon one Celia Hamilton resided at the time of his death. Was lately sold by order of the Court of Ordinary for the purpose of partitions amongst the heirs of David Hamilton decd. application being A. W. Kirkpatrick and wife and Edmund Parson and wife. The land was sold and your petitioner bought sd. land for $400 and same paid unto James H. Dendy, Ord. Celia Hamilton set up a claim in her own right in the same Court the verdict was that David Hamilton was not at the time of his death siezed of the premises. Therefore your petitioner asked for a refund of his money from the sd. James H. Dendy, Ord. who refused alledging that a portion had been paid over to the distributees. Your petitioner is advised that the said Dendy, Ord. has applied these funds to his own individual use. That he has only disbursed the sum of $211. to A. W. Kirkpatrick, Samuel Frazer, Leonard S. Hamilton, J. W. Hamilton, C. E. Hamilton, Shelby Bates, Jane Hamilton, Thomas R. Hamilton. Also a Power of Attorney from Samuel Frazer of Hall Co., Ga.

appointed David H. Frazer his attorney to collect and receive any
money from the estate of David Hamilton decd. Dated 19 Dec. 1840.

William Hamilton. Estate of William Hamilton. Box 95 #1001. Probate
Judge Office. Pickens, S. C. Est. admr. 4 Sept. 1868 by Robert E.
Holcombe, R. A. Christopher, W. T. Davis, who are bound unto W. E.
Holcombe, Ord. in the sum of $2,000.00. Widow Sarah Jane. He owned
land on Georges Creek adj. land of Tilmon Miller, Thomas Grangers,
Addington and others. Heirs, Nancy Benson, Terrel Hamilton, Griffin
Hamilton of Texas. Warren Hamilton.. Leuvina Gilstrap wife of Hardy
Gilstrap.. Cynthia Jane wife of John Hendricks.. Harrison Hamilton,
McDuffie Hamilton, Mary Malinda Hamilton appointed J. P. Reid Esq. as
her attorney. Nancy G. wife of Hugh Dickerson (she may be the Nancy
Benson) Malissa Long, Margaret Ann wife of James M. Field of Gordon Co.,
Ga. James Hamilton son of Terrel Hamilton. On 13 June 1872 Rachel C.
Hamilton of Floyd Co., Ga. and gdn. also of Nora J. Hamilton a minor
of same Co. appointed W. Fields their attorney. On 11 Nov. 1870 Malissa
McCoy, Mahala Hamilton, Caroline Hamilton, Wm. S. Smith, Franklin
Smith, Mrs. Wm. Smith, Elizabeth Chandler, Judy McWhorter, Mrs. Geo.
Manning, John R. Gossett, Mrs. Brachins, were ordered to appear in court.
Same pack, on 1 Oct. 1870 James M. McCoy shows that Wm. A. McCoy,
Malinda A. McCoy, Lawrence E. McCoy, Annice C. McCoy are minors under
14 years and entitled to a share of their grandfather's est. Wm.
Hamilton decd.

Major Andrew Hamilton. Estate of Major Andrew Hamilton. Box 21 #255.
Probate Judge Office. Pickens, S. C. Est. admr. 29 Oct. 1849 by
A. M. and Lemuel Hamilton, Benj. Hagood, John Ariail, Elihu Griffin,
Wm. Hunter who are bound unto Wm. D. Steele, Ord. in the sum of
$40,000.00. A. M. Hamilton a son, Melinda Archer, Wm. Hunter, B. F.
Mauldin, L. A. Osborn, James J. Shumate recd. property during his life
time. (Shumate, Mauldin was from Anderson Dist.) 21 Nov. 1849 paid
Ellen, Emily and Mary A. Hamilton their share $126.75. Paid John
Thompson $120.00.

Jane P. Hamilton. Pack 58 #6. Clerk of Court Office. Pickens, S. C.
On the 23 Sept. 1835 Jane P. Hamilton a single woman appeared before
James Osborn a Justice of Peace and on oath saith that on the 13 Apr.
now last pass at the home of Shelvy Bates in the Dist. of Pickens was
delivered of a male child and that Robert Johnston of said Dist. a
trader did get her with child.

J. P. Hamilton. Power of Attorney from J. P. Hamilton and wife. Pack
218 #6. Clerk of Court Office. Pickens, S. C. We J. P. Hamilton and
his wife Harriet A. Hamilton and Wm. M. Gawley and wife L. E. Gawley
of Carrel Co., Miss. Have appointed Zachary C. Pulliam of Pickens
Dist., S. C. our true and lawful attorney to demand, ask, sue recover
receive, etc. all sum or sums of money from the estate of Russel
Cannon decd. late of Pickens Dist. as the legal representatives of
William Cannon decd. late of Kemper Co., Miss. in the hands, power or
possession of the admr. of Russel Cannon decd. Dated 26 Apr. 1858.
Signed J. P. and H. A. Hamilton, Wm. M. and L. E. Gawley.

Christiana Hamilton. Estate of Christiana Hamilton. Pack 341. Clerk
of Court Office. Abbeville, S. C. Your orators E. Lewis Davis of the
State of Georgia and Joseph A. David of the State of Alabama. That
their mother departed this life on 26 Dec. 1849. She was at that time
the wife of Joseph A. Hamilton, by whom she had two chn. Alice Orean
Hamilton about seven years old and Anna E. Hamilton about five years
old. Christiana having been married before to Joseph Davis by whom
she had three chn. Your orator Eli Lewis Davis, Joseph A. David and
Benjamin F. Davis, now a minor of the age of fifteen years old. After
the death of her first husband she received one third of his estate or
about $10,000 she purchased a lot and house in Abbeville village,
bounded on the North by David Lesly, now owned by Henry A. Jones, Esq.
On the South by James Alston on West by Main Street leading to
Augusta. On said lot Joseph A. Hamilton and his wife lived until
about two years before her death when the lot and house was sold by
the sheriff and was bought by Nathaniel J. Davis. N. J. Davis made a

deed to your orators E. Lewis and Joseph A. Davis so their mother could enjoy and use and benefit from her property. At the time of her death she was free from debts and no admr. has been taken out upon her estate. Your orators desire a partition be made of the house and lot, between the chn. of Christiana Hamilton decd. Filed 8 Apr. 1851.

L. G. Hamilton. L. G. Hamilton vs C. M. Taylor. In Equity #3. Clerk of Court Office. Pickens, S. C. Whereas C. M. Taylor made a note to Ransom Duke for the sum of four hundred dollars, dated 24 Oct. 1857, payable on the 25 Dec. 1858. With Lemuel G. Hamilton as surety, giving a mortgage on his share of the real estate from his father James Taylor decd. estate. His mother was Charlotte Taylor and he had a brother F. Cicero Taylor. The mortgage was on one third of 402 acres on 23 Mile Creek, adj. land of L. G. Hamilton, Widow Williams and others. C. M. Taylor had left the State, and not paid his note. Filed 11 March 1859.

Alexander C. Hamilton Minors. Estate of Alexander C. Hamilton Minors. Box 47 Pack 1089. Probate Judge Office. Abbeville, S. C. Guardianship bond. We James E. Wilson, Joseph Eakins, Thomas Graves are bound unto Moses Taggart, Ord. in the sum of twelve thousand dollars. Dated 28 Oct. 1835... whereas James S. Wilson made guardian of Joseph A. Alexander, Samuel S. and Harriet E. D. Hamilton also for Ann A. Hamilton, Expend. of Samuel S. Hamilton 12 Feb. 1839 for a draft to Randolph Macon College $150.00. Paid for Alexr. Hamilton 8 Jan. 1838 to James Shackelford treasurer of Cokesburg School $48.00. Paid for Joseph A. Hamilton 6 Jan. 1836. J. V. Shanklin treasurer Board of Director of Manuel Labor School in Pendleton $27.50. Recd. 5 July 1838 share of brother Richard A. Hamilton decd. estate $177.86. Paid for Saml. Hamilton 2 July 1838 John Logan treasurer of Greenwood Academy $18.00. Paid Randolph Macon College $178.62½. Paid stage passage from Abbeville to Milton, N. C. $12.00. Recd. 16 Jan. 1841 from James S. Wilson gdn. for Anna A. Hamilton who is now my wife and in right of whom I now give receipt for $1827.15 in full of her father Alexander C. Hamilton and her brother Richard A. Hamilton estates. Signed James H. Giles. Recd. 3 Sept. 1837 from James S. Wilson admr. of A. C. Hamilton decd. estate $16.06 my dist. share. Signed John Bowie. John Bowie share was thru a marital right.

Notes on Hamiltons. Catharine A. Hamilton wife of Col. Paul Hamilton was the niece of a Collin Campbell of Beaufort Dist. in 1850. See Campbell will #14. Jeremiah Hamilton died in Union Dist. 1814 sons, William, Joseph and Hampton Hamilton, dtr. R. Legg wife no name given. Will 21... William Hamilton was the father of Nancy G. Benson widow of William P. Benson of Pickens Dist. who later married Hugh Dickson. Ira Griffin Hamilton was a brother to Nancy G. Benson.

Jeremiah Hamilton. Will of Jeremiah Hamilton. Box 7 Pack 46. Probate Judge Office. Union Co., S. C. I Jeremiah Hamilton of Union Dist. being of sound mind and memory, etc. I give to my three sons, William, Joseph and Hampton all my real estate, consisting of three surveys joining into one tract to be divided between them, executors are to value the land so they may divide my estate between my sons and dtr. I give to my wife one negro girl named Henrietta and one negro boy named Tom, one feather bed and covering, three cows and calves to be chosen by herself. I give to my dtr. the residue of my negroes until by fair valuation to be equal with my land, after which they shall be divided between all my chn. with my wife taking an equal part. I give to my wife my best work horse. I give to my son Hampton my young filly, with a feather bed and furniture. I give to my dtr. R. Legg one feather bed and furniture, with one cow and calf. I will Capt. Bernard Glenn and Geo. Phillips as executors and my wife executrix. Dated 19 Oct. 1810. Wit: Park Dugan, Saml. O. Johnson. Signed Jeremiah Hamilton. Proven by Doctr. George Phillips and recorded 28 Feb. 1814. Wm. Rice, Ord.

HAMPTON

Richard Hampton. Estate of Richard Hampton. Pack 3001. Clerk of
Court Office. Abbeville, S. C. To the Honr. Hugh Rutledge, William
James, Waddy Thompson Judges of the Court of Equity. Your oratrixes
Joanna Ogilie, William Hampton and wife Charlotte. Show to your Honr.
that Richard Hampton of Edgefield Dist. decd. the father of your oratrixes did on the 14 July 1789 make a deed of gift for the natural
affection he bore to his chn. to wit: Gale Hampton, Charlotte Hampton,
Joanna Ogilie late Hampton (your oratrixes), Lucy Hampton, Mary
Hampton, Edward Hampton, Richard Hampton. He did give, grant and
deliver unto his chn. and their heirs the following articles to wit:
Negroes Dick, Hannah, Judy, Nancy, Simon, Cresey and other personal
property that the chn. are to share equal. Their father departed this
life 25 Dec. 1801. He have been supported by his five oldest dtr. in a
decent and respectable manner, with the two youngest sons in like
manner, they are now of full age. That Mary has intermarried with
Ludwell Bacon of Horse Creek, and that Lucy resides with Ludwell Bacon,
and that the youngest brother Richard resides at Meliner C. Leavens-
worth also in Horse Creek, that Gale Hampton now resides near Columbia
in Richland Dist. And that Edward resides at the High Hills of Santee
in Sumpter Dist. Your oratrixes complaining that all children are of
full age that not any division of the said property contained in the
deed of gift as yet taken place so as to give equal share of the
property to the (No more of this in notes).

HANES

John Hanes. Will of John Hanes. Box 8 #98. Probate Judge Office.
Pickens, S. C. I John Hanes being weak in body but of sound mind and
memory, etc. I give to my wife Susannah Hanes all my estate both real
and personal to sell, trade or dispose of all or any part during her
natural life. At her death the estate to be divided between my two
children Lidia Ann and Wm. John Flaven. I appoint my wife executor.
Dated 11 Apr. 1838. Wit: John Bowen, John Farr, Richard Burdine.
Signed John X Hanes. Proven 18 June 1838.

HANKS

Frances Hanks. Pack 646 #6 & &. Clerk of Court Office. Pickens, S.C.
Frances Hanks age about 95 years died in Poor House in Pickens Dist.
in 1860. Elizabeth Hanks age about 50 years was living in Poor House
in Pickens Dist. on 18 Oct. 1861. Elizabeth died in 1862. (This name
was written Hawks in one place.)

HANNA

Robert Hanna. Power of Attorney from Robert Hanna. Pack 381. Clerk
of Court Office. Abbeville, S. C. I Robart Hanna of Rowan Co., N.C.
being son James Hanna decd. late of S. C. am seised in fee of and all
that tract of land lying in 96 Dist. and in the Long Cain Settlement
which was left me by my father. I do appoint Vincent Tabb of the
County of Rowan in N.C. my true and lawful attorney, to lease, sell or
demise or whatever we thinks proper. Dated 13 Apr. 1811. Wit: J. H.
Fruling. Signed Robert Hanna. Recorded 8 June 1812.

HANNAH

Robert Hannah. Estate of Robert Hannah. Box 47 Pack 1078. Probate
Judge Office. Abbeville, S. C. I Robert Hannah of Newberry Dist.

being very sick and weak in body but of sound mind and memory. I give
to my dtr. Nancy Chapman one cow and calf named swaney and one acre of
land next to themselves. I give to my wife Jenney Hannah the milk of
a cow and her food body ready, one heiffer calf to be reared on the
place till it is a cow. I leave one dollar toward clearing the land
for the Meeting House and grave yard. I give to Charlie Burton my son
in law all my land and wordly goods, he paying all my just debts, I
likewise leave the money that I payed Sam Chapman for the land if he
does not make a right according to his bargain. I appoint Charles
Burton my Executor. Dated 8 Jan. 1787. Wit: Robert Moore, Chas.
Thompson. Signed Robert Hannah. Proven 25 Jan. 1787. Inv. made 30
Jan. 1787 by Abraham Thompson, Charles Thompson, John Barlow.

Jane Hannah. Estate of Jane Hannah. Box 45 Pack 1016. Probate Judge
Office. Abbeville, S. C. I Jean Hannah of Abbeville Dist. being sick
and weak of body but of a perfect mind and memory etc. I give to my
sister Agnes McRay twelve dollars. I give my niece Mary McRay. I give
nephew John McRay my hat. I leave to my niece Jenet McRay six yards
stuff?, I give to Elender McRay the rest of my effects. I appoint my
niece Elender McRay my executrix. Dated 13 Dec. 1801. Wit: Nathl.
Bailey, Robert Evans. Signed Jean X Hannah. Recorded 17 Feb. 1802.

HANNON

Richard L. Hannon. Estate of Richard L. Hannon. Box 8 #107. Probate
Judge Office. Pickens, S. C. Est. admr. 29 July 1839 by Wm. Holcombe,
Elijah Watson. Citation published at Poplar Springs Church. (A
letter dated 22 July 1839 signed Wm. Holcombe) Dear Sir: Richard
Hannon a young man died a few weeks back living at Pendleton leaving a
very small property, had several brothers and sisters and living in
different states, with one sister here in Pickens Dist. who married
A. C. Campbell, he had some things at the Campbells' that has been sent
to me already. I will fill out the papers if Esq. Dendy will send them.
The estate is less than $400 and will do it as an accomedation of
friends and creditors. I can not come to court house until after the
muster. Signed Wm. Holcombe.

HARBIN

Thomas W. Harbin. Will of Thomas W. Harbin. Box 31 #362. Probate
Judge Office. Pickens, S. C. I Thos. W. Harbin do make this my last
will and testament. I will that the tract of land known as the Cross
Road tract be sold and money applied to my debts. I will that a tract
of land from where I now live be sold and $900 be sat aside as a legacy
for my sister Polly Harbin to be applied to her support and maintenance
and at her death be equal divided between my chn. Henry F. and Morgan
Harbin. I will the remainder of the aforesaid tract on which I now
live, with negro man named Ned and a negro woman named Milly, with the
stock of horses, hogs, cattle, farming tools, household and kitchen
furniture be set apart from the raising and maintaining of my minor
chn. when my youngest becomes of age to be equal divided between them.
I will to my son Wiley R. Harbin a negro named Isaac and the horse
and saddle and bridle he now has. I give to my dtr. Sarah C. Harbin a
negro girl named Martha and a bed and furniture. I will to my son
Samuel V. Harbin a negro named Clark, a horse saddle and bridle, a bed
and furniture. I will to my dtr. Mary E. Harbin a negro girl named
Mariah and a bed and furniture. I will to my son John M. Harbin a
negro named Eliza, a horse saddle and bridle and a bed and furniture.
I give to my son Andrew P. Harbin a negro boy named Andrew a horse
saddle and bridle, a bed and furniture. I will to my son Elias N.
Harbin a negro named Arch, a horse saddle and bridle, a bed and furni-
ture. I will to my dtr. Harriet R. Harbin a negro girl Carry and a
bed and furniture. I appoint Wiley R. Harbin, Morgan Harbin and Henry
F. Chandler as Executors. Dated 19 Aug. 1853. Wit: Elijah Land,
F. M. Cleveland, Fanny Chandler X Her Mark. Signed T. W. Harbin.

Thomas W. Harbin. Minor chn. were: Sarah Harbin about 20 years old.
Samuel V. Harbin a minor about 19 years old. Mary E. Harbin a minor
about 17 years old, John M., Andrew P., Elias N. Harbin minors each
under 14 years. Harriet Harbin a minor under 12 years old. Thomas W.
Harbin bought a tract of land on 11 Aug. 1849 described in his will
as the home tract which was sold by the heirs of the decd. Morgan and
Wiley Harbin charged that the deed was defective and insufficient as
A. P. Reeder who married Harriet Swift dtr. of Nancy Swift, who died
before the deed was made, nor has his wife relinquished her rights.
Samuel Knox who married Mary Swift. Laban E. Leard (Laird) married
Harried C. Harbin, Henry Chandler married Frances Harbin dtr. of
Thomas W. Harbin decd. Each signed the deed without theirs wifes
joining therein or relinquishing their rights. Polly Harbin was an
idiot. On 29 Aug. 1848 Moses W. Simmons and his wife Harriet were
residing in Talledega Co., Ala. On 21 Jan. 1848 Laban E. Laird and
Harriet his wife were living in Tippah Co., Miss. (This Harriet ment in
her power of attorney as being a grand dtr. of Thomas W. Harbin.) The
heirs of Nathaniel Harbin decd. viz: Morgan P. Harbin who resides in
Miss., Henry F. Chandler and wife resides in Georgia, Mary Swift who
married Samuel Knox resides in Franklin Co., Ga. Ref. Pack 5 Clerk of
Court Office. Pickens Co., S. C.

HARDIN

Carol Hardin. Will of Carol Hardin. Box 46 #509. Probate Judge
Office. Pickens Co., S. C. Robert Carol Hardin made his will 5 July
1857. Proven 19 Oct. 1857. Wife Rebbeca Hardin brother John Hardin,
chn. ment. no names. Wit: B. F. Reeder, Samuel Reeder, J. R. Cleveland.

HARMON

Thomas Harmon. Estate of Thomas Harmon. Pack 365. Clerk of Court
Office. Abbeville, S. C. To the Chancellors of the said State. Your
oratrix and orators, Stephen W. Willis and Susan his wife, Charles M.
Freeman and his wife, Alexander A. Laramore and his wife Esther,
Anthony Harmon. Shewth that Thomas Harmon departed this life intestate
many years ago with land of about seven hundred acres lying on Savannah
and Little River joining land of William Harmon, Frederick Edmonds,
James Banks, Charles M. Freeman, Ellington Searles and others. leaving
the widow Mary Harmon... chn. Susan Willis, Cynthia Freeman, Esther
Laramore, Anthony Harmon, Frances the wife of Dr. Socrates N. G. Ferguson, Dicy the wife of James Banks... John Harmon, William Harmon,
Appleton G. Harmon, and Luke Harmon. The admr. was committed to John
and Appleton Harmon for the personal estate, this has been done. The
real estate to remain till the death of the widow. Her death was in
the month Nov. 1862. Her estate was admr. by Appleton Harmon and your
Orators and oratrixs. Heirs are Susan wife of Stephen Willis, Cynthia
wife of Charles M. Freeman, Frances Furguson wife of Socrates N. G.
Ferguson, Dicey wife of James Banks, John Harmon, William Harmon,
Esther wife of Alexander A. Laramore, Anthony Harmon, Appleton G.
Harmon, Mary Harmon a minor the only child of Emanuel Harmon decd. and
William Harmon, Pickens Harmon and Cornelia Crawford chn. of Luke
Harmon decd. Filed 21 July 1863. In 1863 Dr. Ferguson and wife
Frances and Wm. Harmon, Pickens and Mary Harmon were living out of
State.

HARPER

William Harper. William Harper to William Hester. Pack 4-A Clerk of
Court Office. Pickens, S. C. Whereas Abraham Crenshaw decd. will to
his wife Nancy the use of the land on which Crenshaw then lived during
her natural life. I William Harper have since married Nancy, now for
and in consideration of sixty five dollars paid to me by William Hester

and Abraham Crenshaw exclusive of the part of said plantation now in possession of Alexander Copeland to be inherited and cultivated by Hester and Crenshaw during my life. Hester and Crenshaw shall not unnecessarily destroy the timber or damage the land in any way. Dated 14 Marhc 1813. Wit: Isaac McAdams, Alexander Copeland. Signed William Harper, seal. Joseph G. Evetts purchased the land from Abraham X Crenshaw and William Hester on 3 Oct. 1823. Wit: B. J. Earle, Wm. Choice.

HARRALSON

Moses Harralson. Deed from Moses Harralson to chn. Book A, page 2-3. Clerk of Court Office. Marion, S. C. This indenture made between Moses Harralson and his chn. dated 17 Aug. 1789. The chn. are Rebeckah, Isom, Jesse, Sealah, Paul. For natural love and affection and five shillings sterling money doth grant. sell and confirm the following negroes: Rebeckah one negro named Phillis, To Isom one negro named Peg, to Jesse one negro named Will to Sealah one negro girl named Mary, to Paul the first child born of Gillen, Moses Harralson is to hold said negroes during his life time. Wit: Abigal and Lewis Harralson. Signed Moses Harralson. Recorded 25 Apr. 1800.

HARRIS

Rev. John Harris. Estate of Rev. John Harris. Box 107 Pack 2895. Probate Judge Office. Abbeville, S. C. I John Harris of Abbeville Dist. mindful of my approaching mortality and being in my rational powers do make this my last will and testament. I give to my son Handy Harris that tract of land I took up lying on the Savannah River between lands of Peter Collins and John Calhoun Esq. I give to my second son John Harris that tract of land on which he now lives. I give to my second dtr. Elizabeth Erving the wife of Joseph Erving the tract of land where I now live, on conditions that Joseph Erving make me and my heirs a title for a negro boy or man between the ages of sixteen and thirty within the term months from the date hereof, also permit me to use the peach trees now standing in the surfery, also the apple trees now fit to be transplanted. I give to my oldest dtr. Anne Handy McCurdy a tract of land lying on the flag-reed?, I also give to my grand dtr a negro girl named Sal. The two tracts of land lying on the Keowee River be sold by my executors and make the dtr. equal. I give to my youngest son Thos. Harris (part of page torn off) that tract of land I bought from Charles Collins except one third part reserved to the use of my wife during her natural life or widowhood. I also give to my beloved wife Mary Harris another tract of land joining the above tract of 70 acres, also all personal property during her natural life or widowhood. I appoint my wife Executrix, and son Handy Harris executor. Wit: Robert Hall, John Bowie, Joseph Weson. Will proven 5 Apr. 1790. Will not dated. (No other papers in file.)

James A. Harris. Estate of James A. Harris. Box 43 Pack 967. Probate Judge Office. Abbeville, S. C. We Thomas P. Martin, Thomas Heron, William Robertson are bound unto Taliaferro Livingston, Ord. in the sum of ten thousand pds. sterling. dated 27 Jan. 1816. Citation published at Rockey River Church. Inv. made 23 Feb. 1816 by Richard Covington, William Harris, William Covington. Byr. at sale, held 4 Mar. 1816. George Patterson, Hiram Tilman, Meredith McGee, Wm. Harris, Solomon Blackwell, Alexr. Oliver, Saml. Scott, John C. Oliver, Wm. Whipple, Joseph Simpson, Robert Aken, Jourdon Ramey, Richard Covington, Thomas Caldwell, Ester Harris, J. C. Bole, Wm. Covington.

William Harris. Estate of William Harris. Box 47 Pack 1069. Probate Judge Office. Abbeville, S. C. I William Harris of Abbeville Dist. being considerable advanced in age and at present under a lingering disorder which threatens my life, but of sound mind and memory. I order my body buried in my own grave yard. I order my just debts

called in and enough stock sold to pay. I give to my wife Margret the
plantation on which I now live, also my negroes Maseck, Cloey, Dick
during her natural life likewise my stock, tools, household furniture,
and at her death they are all to be my youngest son Alexander. I give
to my three oldest sons John Mayney Lesley and Robert Long five dollars
each. To my son S. William Harris I gave my negroes Tye and Philas also
ten pds. sterling. To F. Robert I gave Bulltown plantation exclusive
of what is South of the river, paying General Anderson and Andrew
Hamelton as agreed heretofor, also one bed and furniture. To my son
Samuel I give one bed and furniture also my wearing apparal. To my
dtr. Margret I leave my negroes Dina and Tobea, also one bed and furniture, and my young mare, two cows, six sheep. I order my grand child
Margaret Lesley be schooled and to have a bed and furniture, saddle
and creature valued at ten pds. sterling. I hereby appoint Margret
Harris my wife executrix and John Caldwell my executor. Dated 12 March
1796. Wit: Henry Long, John Harris. Signed William Harris. Recorded
26 March 1798. Inv. made 26 Apr. 1798 by James Caldwell Senr.,
Joseph McClesky, Samuel Mitchell. Sale held on 26 Apr. 1798... byr,
Royal Lipford, Dudley Jones, James Armstrong, Robert Davis, Samuel
Harris, Christopher Brooks, John Harris, Wm. Caldwell Senr., Henry Long,
John Drinkard, John Drinkwater, Robert Green, Charley Holland, James
Holland, James Harris, Joseph Black, Mary Lesley, Wm. Beard, Josiah
Stricklin, Thomas Tinsley, Frances Cummins, Wm. Russell, David Madden,
Peggy Harris, Joseph Brown, Jacob Clark, Donald Frazer.

Handy Harris. Will of Handy Harris. No ref. Probate Judge Office.
Anderson, S. C. I Handy Harris of Pendleton Dist. being weak in body
but of sound mind and memory, etc. I give to my sister Anna McCurdy
the tract on which she now lives. The principal part was granted unto
McCurdy in his life time, the rest was granted unto me the whole I
give unto her, except which I sold unto Mr. Montgomery upon his paying
unto me or my executors $405.93 with interest from 1 Jan. 1805 until
the sum is paid, allowing ten years to pay. I give to my wife Ann all
my personal estate my goods, chattles, bonds, notes and book accounts
to be at her disposal after paying all my just debts. I give unto my
son Nathaniel Harris all my land in Pendleton Dist. lying on Little
Beaver Dam, allowing my wife the use of land during her life time.
I give to my two dtr. a tract of land in Abbeville Dist. which I bought
from William Callahan to be theirs after the death of my wife. It is
my will that my executors have the tuition and direction of my son
Nathaniel until he is of the age of twenty one years old. I will
my executors purchase for my two dtr. when they come of age, each a
large well bound Bible, a hymn book, that is approved by the General
assembly of the Presbyterian Church, also Pike and Howard case of
village sermons, one half dozen silver table spoons and one half dozen
tee-spoons. I appoint my wife brother John and Brother Thomas Harris
with brother Joseph Irwen my executors. Dated 27 May 1805. Wit:
William Davis, Mary Harris, Martha Harris. Signed Handy Harris. Proved
on oath of Martha Harris that she was Doctr. Handy Harris sign the within will, same day qualified Ann Harris and Thomas Harris as executors.
Dated 17 July 1805. John Harris, Ord.

James S. Harris. File 324. Probate Judge Office. Anderson, S. C.
James S. Harris made his will 13 June 1836 was living in Anderson Dist.
will probated 5 Sept. 1836. Wife was Sarah Harris. He had a former
wife that was decd. name not given. Children were Mary E. Harris,
William L. Harris, James C. Harris, Jane Amanda Harris, Thomas Alonzo
Harris, Terrissa A. E. Harris. His son James C. was willed the Watt
tract of land. M. B. Clark of Abbeville Dist. was the exor of will.

Nathaniel Harris. Will of Nathaniel Harris. Will Book Page 41. Probate Judge Office. Anderson, S. C. I Nathaniel Harris of Anderson
Dist. being of sound mind and memory but weak in body etc. I desire
all my debts be paid out of the notes and accounts, after paying debts
and funeral expenses, I give to my wife Susan the house and lot on which
I now live in Pendleton Village and a tract of land adjoining the lot
containing thirty acres. With it one carage, two horses, stock of
hogs and cattle, household and kitchen furniture, and farm tools except
one four horse waggon. Likewise I give to her negroes Adam and a

woman named Hannah and her third child named Henry, during her natural life, I give to my wife a legacy of one thousand dollars. I give to my son Edwin Handy Harris fifteen hundred dollars, to be paid when he arrives at the age of twenty one years old. I give to my son George Reese Harris fifteen hundred dollars to be paid when he arrives at the age of twenty one years old. I wish that a portion of the income of the estate be used to defray the necessary expenses incurred by him in getting his profession. I give to my dtr. Mary L. Harris a negro girl named Lucy and a boy named Mat, and five hundred dollars when she is twenty one years of age. I give to my dtr. Lucsa Ann Harris three negroes named George, Alick, Jamima. Also five hundred dollars given her when she marry or at age of twenty one. All the rest of my property not already mentioned and disposed of I desire to be sold and money divided between my heirs. I appoint my wife Executrix, and my friend David Cherry and Thomas Cherry as executors. Dated ___ May 1837. Wit: Wm. Hubbard, John B. Sitton, A. H. Ruse. Probated 31 July 1837.

William Harris. In Equity #38. Clerk of Court Office. Abbeville, S. C. To the Chancellors of the sd. State. Your Oratrix Elizabeth Harris on the second day of Feb. 1860. William Harris being the son of your Oratrix being involved in debts and desiring to make some provision for himself and family. Executed a certain deed in trust to your Oratrix. Supposing that the debts of the sd. William Harris would not exceed three thousand dollars, when the debts were called upon they amounted to six thousand dollars, and having the deed in trust, she failed to have inserted in the sd. deed an express power to sell part of the trust estate for this purpose. Your Oratrix prays that all the creditors of William Harris whose debts may be called in and proven to this Court, and a decree of this Court to sell as much of the property as will be sufficient to pay outstanding demands. Filed 25 May 1860. A letter in the file to Wm. Hill Esq. of White Plains near Springs Grove P.O. S.D. 1 Feb. 1861. That he had a note on William Harris in the amount of $346.73. He may learn more particulars from a man named Mr. James Creswell whom I sent. Signed John D. Williams.

Joseph H. Harris. Estate of Joseph H. Harris. Book B Page 68. Probate Judge Office. Pickens, S. C. On 16 Feb. 1863 Joseph H. Harris decd. owned 169 acres in Pickens, Dist. on branches of Beaverdam Creek adj. land of S. C. Reeder, Elias Earle and others. Heirs Mary M. Harris the widow and 3 minor chn. James E. Harris, John E. Harris, Lucy A. Harris.

Benjamin B. Harris. Land Warrant #31. Pack 630. Clerk of Court Office. Pickens, S. C. By James E. Hagood, Clerk to any lawful surveyor you are authorized to lay out unto Benjamin B. Harris a tract of land not exceeding one thousand acres. Dated 9 Apr. 1860. Executed for 147 acres 12 Apr. 1860... filed the 16 Apr. 1860.

HARRISON

John Harrison, Sr. Estate of John Harrison, Sr. Box 6 #80. Probate Judge Office. Pickens, S. C. Est. admr. 2 Feb. 1836 by Thos. and John Harrison, William Jolly, Thos. W. Harbin who are bound unto Jas. H. Dendy, Ord. in the sum of $6,000.00. James R. Smith a preacher of the Gospel states that the citation was published at the Block Meeting House 31 Jan. 1836. He owned two tracts of land in Pickens Dist. One of 300 acres where he lived at time of death and where the widow now lives this tract on Tugaloo River being a Soldiers Bounty originally granted to Edward Lowry. Another tract of 300 acres on waters of Choestoe Creek adj. land of John Messer, J. F. Perry and John Jolly. He left a widow Naomi and 11 chn. Hugh and Robert Harrison, Nancy the wife of Solomon O'Kelly, Mary (Polly) the wife of W. W. Short, Celia the wife of John Robertson, Stacy the mother of James H. Robertson (Husband not given) the only her only heir, she died before her father, Matilda Harrison, Elizabeth the wife of Squire Hughes, Thomas Harrison, Sinah (Lenah) Maddox heirs, she departed this life before her father,

her heirs are: Thomas, John, Martha all minors, John T. Harrison, Mary Brookshire. Note that there is also a Mary Short. On the 24 Jan. 1837 John T. Harrison being sworn that, Hugh and Robert Harrison, Short and wife Polly, John and Celia Robertson, John Maddox all resides out of the state.

Thomas Harrison. Estate of Thomas Harrison. Box 9 #122. Probate Judge Office. Pickens, S. C. Est. admr. 24 Nov. 1841 by Martin Harrison, N. J. F. Perry, Aaron Terrill who are bound unto James H. Dendy, Ord. in the sum of $16,000.00. Citation published at Bethel Church. Nancy Harrison the widow. Chn. are, Clara the wife of Aaron Terrell, L. D. Harrison, Lydia the wife of S. D. Dortch, Shadrack Harrison, Martin Harrison, Mary the wife of Josiah Stovall, Hepsey (Hessy) the wife of Elam Farmer, Catherine the widow of ___ Blair, Elizabeth heirs, the late wife of John Legrand, the late Thomas Harrison owned two tracts of land. One tract of 450 acres where he lived at death and the widow now lives lying on Tugaloo River, adj. land of Joseph Shealor, George Cleveland and others. The other tract of 450 acres on Choestoe Creek waters of Tugaloo River adj. land of Bingham Leathers, Cleveland Marett and others. He also owned land in Ga. Paid 1 Jan. 1842 taxes for Georgia land for two years $1.50.

Land Warrant of Martin Harrison. Pack 630 #40. Clerk of Court Office. Pickens, S. C. By J. E. Hagood Clerk. To any lawful surveyor you are authorized to lay out unto Martin Harrison a tract of land not exceeding one thousand acres. Dated 2 March 1866. Executed for 145 acres on a branch of Cane Creek waters of Tugaloo River. Filed 30 Apr. 1866.

William S. Harrison. Power of Attorney of William S. Harrison. Pack 81. Clerk of Court Office. Pickens, S. C. The State of Alabama; Greene County. I William S. Harrison, Executor of the last will of Mary Foster late of Greene Co. Ala. Have appointed Samuel G. McClanahan of Greenville Dist., S. C. to be my true and lawful attorney, to ask demand, sue for, receive and recover from the estate of the late Josiah Foster of the State of S. C. From the sale of the real estate of Josiah Foster by virtue either of his will or of Mary Foster his widow and devisee. Dated 28 Sept. 1840. Wit: William Walton, David R. Chiles. Signed W. S. Harrison. In 1831 Catherine Harrison was the dtr. of Mary Foster of Greene Co., Ala. had 8 chn. Elizabeth, James, Kitty or Catherine, Harriet, Laura, Clariss A., Josiah and Florence Harrison. Wm. S. Harrison was the execr. of her mother's will.

E. W. Harrison. Pack 74-A. Letter. Clerk of Court Office. Pickens, S. C. Fayette County, Tenn. 22 Feb. 1842. This will inform you we are enjoying good health. Harriet is at my house at this time and expect to continue till fall, then go out to brother John she is inclined to go to school as there is one convenient. I have been in the section were Uncle David Wrights family formerly lived. They have all moved away except his oldest dtr. who is living in Miss. the balance in Stewart Co. of this State (Tenn.) Uncle Chattron Wright lives in Macon County, Ala. near Tuskegg. I will write cousin Claton about his brother. Your brother E. W. Harrison. On March 27, 1843 $10.10 in full of the distributive share of the within named E. W. Harrison to the estate of James Wright decd. Benjamin Holland.

Maj. James W. Harrison. Land Warrant for Land to Maj. James W. Harrison and James Atkins #46. Page 114. By W. L. Keith, Clerk to any lawful surveyor you are authorized to lay out unto Maj. James W. Harrison and James Atkins a tract of land not exceeding ten thousand acres. Dated 18 Jan. 1843. Executed 24 Jan. 1843 for 607 acres.. certified 10 Feb. 1843.

HARVICK

William Harvick. Will of William Harvick. Box 107 #2874. Probate Judge Office. Abbeville, S. C. I William Marvick of Abbeville Dist. do make and ordain this my last will and testament. I desire my

executors pay and discharge all my just debts. I give to my brother
Nicholas Harvick all my land in the Arkansas Territory also all my
money and all money due me. My saddle I give to my nephew William
Harvick and my trunk and all cloths. I give to my brother Jacob Harvick
the sum of five dollars. I give to my sister Polly the wife of Andrew
Warnick the sum of five dollars. I appoint Nicholas Harvick executor.
Dated 21 May 1824. Wit: Orville Tatom, Maj. B. Clark, Williamson
Norwood. Signed Wm. Harvick. Will proved on oath of Williamson Norwood
before Moses Taggart, J.Q. on ___ Aug. 1824.

HATTER

Benjamin Hatter. Will of Benjamin Hatter. Box 45 Pack 1002. Probate
Judge Office. Abbeville, S. C. I Benjamin Hatter being weak in body
but of perfect mind and memory. He owed a debt to Boyce and Johnson
and Oneel of Charleston and how to pay the debt by the ones due him
from others in Abbeville. No wife is named. Only one son Richard is
given, he is a minor in 1820 when the will was made (only part of will
in notes).

HAWTHORNE

Anna Hawthorne. Power of Attorney of Anna Hawthorne. Pack 79. Clerk
of Court Office. Pickens, S. C. I Anna Hawthorne of Pickens Dist.
have appointed Joseph J. Norton, Esq. to collect, recover, receive,
etc. any money from Lemuel Reid executor of the estate of John R.
Wilson decd. of Abbeville Dist. Dated ___ May 1866. Signed Anna
Hawthorne.

Betsey Hawthorne. Estate of Betsey Hawthorne. Box 47 #1092. Probate
Judge Office. Abbeville, S. C. Guardianship Bond. We Alexander
Foster, Enos Crawford, John Pressly are bound unto Moses Taggart, Ord.
in the sum of one thousand dollars. Dated 1 Feb. 1828. Whereas
Alexander Foster was made guardian of Betsey Hawthorn a minor under 14
years of age.

Hawthorne. Notes on the Hawthorne. Tombstone inscription, taken from
Lindsey Cemetery, 2 miles South of Due West, Abbeville County, S. C.
Sarah Jane Hawthorne dtr. of Joseph J. and Ann Hawthorne. Born 15
Apr. 1826. Died 28 Nov. 1848. Hardy Gilstrap of Pickens Dist.
Married the second time the widow Luvina Hawthorne. From a paper dated
28 Oct. 1879. Ref. Pack 641 #8. Clerk of Court Office. Pickens, S.C.

Jasper Hawthorne. Estate of Jasper Hawthorne. Box 64 #693. Probate
Judge Office. Pickens, S. C. Est. admr. 20 Oct. 1862 by Wm. Hunter,
Andrew Hunter, Henry J. Anthony who are bound unto W. E. Holcombe, Ord.
in the sum of $5,000.00. Expend. 4 May 1867 paid W. B. Hutchins gdn.
in full for Tinsey Anna Ellis $385.78. 10 Feb. 1871 paid Anna
Hawthorne $730.00. 6 Jan. 1874 paid H. Gilstrap for wife $950.00.

Anna Hawthorne. Estate of Anna Hawthorne. Box 105 #1104. Probate
Judge Office. Pickens, S. C. I Anna Hawthorne being of sound mind
and memory etc. I desire enough of my property be sold to pay my
debts and funeral expenses. I will all the tract of land in this County
known as the Jeremiah Durham tract to my dtr. Constantia C. Hutchins
and her heirs forever. After my death I desire my executors sell my
home tract of land together with all personal property and divide the
proceeds with all my chn. and their lawful heirs, except my two dtr.
Mary D. Pruett and Susannah M. Martin who has had their shares heretofore out of my estate. Dated 19 Aug. 1870. Wit: W. R. Brown, Bright
Gilstrap, W. E. Welborn. Proved 20 Jan. 1874. On 3 Apr. 1877 paid on
funeral expenses of Mrs. Elizabeth Matthews decd. who died without
heirs and was a legatee $73.35. L. A. Durham recd. share. Chn. viz.
Jane Johnson of Panola Co., Miss. Mrs. Amarylie E. Crawford of Abbeville Co., S. C. Jasper Hawthorne decd. whose chn. are Sarah A. Durham,

Deborah D. Bown, Belle R. Smith, Jasper L. Hawthorn last three under 21 years. Deborah A. McLlwain decd. who left 1 son A. Thomas McLlwain. C. C. Hutchins of Pickens Co. Elizabeth A. Mathews who died in Abbeville Co., S. C. 22 Feb. 1875 without heirs or husband. Mary D. Pruett decd. of Texas. Susan M. Martin decd. of Miss. who had one dtr. living, Jane Johnson of Sardis, Miss.

Sarah E. Hawthorne. Estate of Sarah E. Hawthorne Box 123 #10. Probate Judge Office. Pickens, S. C. Died Sept. 1892. J. L. Hawthorne her husband and admr. (no other info.)

Hawthorne Minors. Box 10 #154. Probate Judge Office. Pickens, S. C. On 10 May 1876 Luvina Gilstrap, Hardy Gilstrap, R. E. Holcombe are bound unto R. E. Holcombe, Ord. in the sum of $1,000.00. Louvina Gilstrap gdn. of D. D. Hawthorne, R. R. Smith, L. N. Hawthorne minors under 21 years. Paid on 7 Feb. 1879 for land for Bell Smith formerly Hawthorne $75.00.

Robert Hawthorne. Estate of Robert Hawthorne. Pack 78 In Equity. Clerk of Court Office. Pickens Co., S. C. Whereas Moses Cain, William Hardin, John Baylis Myers and H. A. Cole assignee of William Hardon as follows. Robert Hawthorne on the 14 Feb. 1859 sold to the above a tract of land in Pickens Co. which formerly belonged to the estate of Josiah F. Perry decd. The tract of land lies on the branches of Snow Creek, waters of Conneross Creek, waters of Seneca River. Robert A. Hawthorne and Thomas D. Long made and executed their bond at the same date for two thousand dollars to the above named. To Moses Cain 91 acres. To John B. Myers 96 acres. To William Hardin 92 acres. Wm. Hardin sold and transfered his land to H. A. Cole of Pickens Dist. Robert A. Hawthorne soon after the execution of the bond entered the Army of Confederate of America and was killed in the battle around Richmond whilst gallantly charging at the head of the Company of infantry which he commanded. After his death E. P. Verner Esq. took out letter of admr. upon his est. Capt. R. A. Hawthorne died leaving a widow Mrs. Emma Hawthorne and one infant child Ida Hawthorne. Filed 5 May 1864.

Joseph J. and Anna Hawthorne. Estate of Joseph J. and Anna Hawthorne. Pack 178 Clerk of Court Office. Abbeville Dist., S. C. This deed of trust made 4 Sept. 1845. Between Joseph J. and Anny Hawthorne of one part and John R. Wilson and Robert Ellis trustee of the second part and Andrew Prewit and Polly his wife and Alexander A. Miller and Elizabeth his wife, and William Martin and Susan his wife, and Toliver Johnson and Jane his wife, Orpha Hawthorne, Jasper Hawthorne, Deborah Hawthorne, and Constantia Hawthorne of the third part. Anna Hawthorne had a life estate of her and her chn. from her father the late Isaac Cowan will. "I give and bequeath unto my daughter Anny Hawthorne, Franky and three chn. viz. Susan, Thomas and Bethany and to remain hers for life and at her death to be equally divided between her heirs." The slaves has been sold in the amount of $3,695.00. and has been secured in the hands of one Alexander A. Miller. Wit: James Cowan, D. O. Hawthorne. This deed signed by Joseph J. and Anna Hawthorne, John R. Wilson, Robert Ellis, Andrew and Mary J. Prewit, A. H. and Elizabeth Miller, William Martin, Toliver and Jane S. Johnson, James F. and Amryles E. Crawford. Seals.

Anna Hawthorne. Estate of Anna Hawthorne. Plat Book C, page 2. Clerk of Court Office. Pickens, S. C. By request of Hardy Gilstrap and by consent of David Gilstrap, I have surveyed a tract of land in Pickens Co. on Rices Creek waters of 12 mile River. Containing 62 acres. Dated 20 Nov. 1873. J. B. Clayton, Surveyor. The above tract of land belongs to the estate of Anna Hawthorne never having been executed by order of C. L. Hollingworth. Dated 1 Dec. 1874.

HAYNES

John Haynes. Estate of John Haynes. Box 28 #333. Probate Judge
Office. Pickens, S. C. Est. admr. 3 Apr. 1848 by Jesse Haynes, Miles
M. Norton who are bound unto Wm. D. Steele, Ord. in the sum of $300.00.
Paid Mary Haynes, Harrison Haynes, Nathaniel Haynes, Nancy A. Haynes,
Harper Haynes, Rebecca Haynes, Andrew Haynes, Sarah P. Haynes, Mary
Haynes, Dorcas A. Haynes their share of said estate. (Mary is given
twice, one may be the widow.)

Sheriff Haynes. Estate of Sheriff Haynes. Box 17 #212. Probate Judge
Office. Pickens, S. C. On 25 Sept. 1848 Mary Haynes the widow applied
for a letter of admr. He lived in Pickens Dist. on Wolf Creek had 363
acres in the home tract, adj. land of Christopher Kirksey, Griffin
Breazeale. Another tract on Town Creek adj. land of James Ferguson,
Griffin Breazeale of 67 acres. On 15 Oct. 1855 Andrew P. Haynes a
minor recd. $164.78 by his guardian J. H. Amber. Same date J. G.
Ferguson recd. $493.34 as gdn. for minors Dorcas A., Mary A., Sarah P.
Haynes from their father estate. On 3 Oct. 1853 Nancy Haynes recd.
$69.70. from her father est. On 1 Nov. 1852 Jesse Haynes recd. $209.11
from Sheriff Haynes Est. On 2 Oct. 1855 Rebecca and T. W. Alexander
recd. $69.70 in full from Sheriff Haynes est. On 3 Jan. 1853 Nathaniel
Haynes recd. in full $209.11 from Sheriff Haynes est. On 3 Oct. 1853
W. D. Steele recd. his full share $209.11 from Sheriff Haynes est.
On 1 Feb. 1856 P. M. and N. A. Alexander recd. $69.70 their full share
of the est.

Haynes Family. Notes on Haynes Family. Tombstone inscriptions, taken
from Eakin Cemetery, Central Community, Abbeville, S. C. Nancy Jane,
Dtr. of G. W. and S. P. Haynes, born 2 July 1879, died 25 Sept. 1879.
An infant son of G. W. and S. P. Haynes, born and died 25 Oct. 1892.

Susannah Haynes. Estate of Susannah Haynes. Box 25 #295. Probate
Judge Office. Pickens, S. C. Est. admr. 7 June 1852 by John Bowen,
J. A. Doyle, John Gossett who are bound unto Wm. D. Steele, Ord. in the
sum of $2,000.00. Paid 8 April 1854 Pickney Gossett his share $312.00.
Paid M. J. F. Haynes his share $312.00.

Haynes Minors. In Equity, Box 2 #41. Clerk of Court Office. Pickens,
S. C. On 3 Sept. 1855 J. G. Ferguson, G. R. Burgess, J. H. Ambler are
bound unto Robert A. Thompson Clerk of Equity, in the sum of $600.00.
J. G. Ferguson Gdn. of Dorcas A. Haynes under 12 years and Sarah P. and
Amry Adaline Haynes both over 21 years.

Haynes Minors. Box 10 #166. Probate Judge Office. No County given.
On 28 Jan. 1883 Rev. W. B. Singleton gdn. of Robert Hanes son of
Richard Hanes of Anderson Co., S. C. Richard died about 1865 left two
sons Alexander C. Hanes and Robert Hanes the latter a minor of 19 years.

Haynes Minors. Box 8 #131. Probate Judge Office. Pickens, S. C.
On 18 Feb. 1898 Harper Haynes Sr. and Annie M. Haynes, J. T. Brown are
bound unto J. B. Newberry, Ord. in the sum of $437.20. Harper Haynes
gdn. of Taylor Haynes, George H. Haynes minors under 21 years. Chn. of
sd. Harper and Annie Haynes.

HAYS

David Hays. Notes on David Hays. Real Estate Book A, page 29. Probate
Judge Office. Pickens, S. C. David Hays of Pickens Dist. married
Barbara Hendricks the dtr. of Moses Hendricks Sr. and his wife Susan.
Her father estate was admr. on 30 Jan. 1837 they were married at this
time. In a schedule of property dated 14 July 1838 David Hays recd.
from Moses Hendricks est. one cow and qalf for $13.00. One bed and
furniture for $10.00. There is a note in Moses Hendricks estate file
of David Hays. "Mr. J. H. Dendy, Sir please to let Moses Hendricks
have my part of the money which are coming to me for the land of Moses

Hendricks decd. this 8 March 1838 David Hays" This note written in
his own handwriting.

Abram Hays.(bootlegging) Pack 213 #3. Clerk of Court Office. Pickens
S. C. On 19 May 1856 Willis Haley a lawful Constable made oath that he
is and ifnormed that Abram Hays did on the first day of Jan. last at
the sale of Mrs. Martha Wright expose to sale or cause to be sold by
a boy in his employment, spiritous liquors in quantities without a
license.

Thomas Hays. Real Estate. Pack 654.#2. Clerk of Court Office.
Pickens, S. C. On 10 Sept. 1841 Margaret Hays the widow of Thomas Hays
decd. states that her husband owned 1,000 acres on Conneross Creek.

Elizabeth Hays. Pack 289 #6. Clerk of Court Office. Pickens, S. C.
on 3 Sept. 1858 Elizabeth Ann Hays residing with her mother Jans Carson
at the Falls on Little River in Pickens Dist. A single woman made oath
that on the 28 Aug. last past at her mother home she was delivered of
a male child with dark eyes and black hair and that William John Hunnicutt a carpenter is the father of said child.

James Hays. Estate of James Hays. Box 33 #376. Probate Judge Office.
Pickens, S. C. Est. admr. 29 Dec. 1854 by O. H. P. Fant, William S.
Woolbright who are bound unto W. J. Parson, Esq. in the sum of $400.00.
Slae 13 Jan. 1855. Buyers Wm. S. Woolbright, W. Haley, Abram Hays,
Malissa Hays. Paid Eliza Hays $3.60. Paid James H. Hays $3.60.

Robert Hays. Estate of Robert Hays. Box 33 #381. Probate Judge
Office. Pickens, S. C. Est. admr. 29 Dec. 1854 by Elizabeth Hays, Wm.
S. Woolbright, O. H. P. Fant who are bound unto W. J. Parson, Ord. in
the sum of $1200.00. Abram Hays, Wm. Hays, Elizabeth Hays bought at
sale.

Charles H. Hays. Estate of Charles H. Hays. Box 34 #395. Probate
Judge Office. Pickens, S. C. Est. admr. 26 Jan. 1855 by Wm. S. Woolbright, James George who are bound unto W. J. Parson, Ord. in the sum
of $400.00. Paid account of Elizabeth Hays $2.50. Paid John N. Hays
decd. account $2.43. Buyers at sale Anderson Hays, Wm. S. Woolbright,
Wm. Hunt, George Grant.

Solomon Hays, Sr. Will of Solomon Hays, Sr. Box 39 #445. Probate
Judge Office. Pickens, S. C. I Solomon Hays Senr. do make this my
last will and testament, etc. I wish my body be buried and my debts be
paid. I will to my dtr. Charlotte Hays one feather bed and kitchen
furniture, also one cow and calf with twelve head of hogs. I will to
my dtr. Mary Massingill one hundred acres of land of the lower end of
my tract where I now live to be hers during her life time then to her
son Benjamin Hays, Also to Mary five dollars in cash. To my son
Solomon Hays one hundred acres of land whereon he now lives, also one
feather bed and small wagon. I will to Mary Elizabeth Hays dtr. of
Benjamin Hays one heiffer yearling. I appoint my sons Solomon and
Benjamin Hays my executors. No date. Wit: W. W. Robinson, James
Gilliland, Benjamin Hagood. Signed Solomon X Hays. Proven 15 Oct. 1855.

Elijah Hays. Estate of Elijah Hays. Box 69 #738. Probate Judge
Office. Pickens, S. C. Est. admr. 16 March 1863 by George Hendricks,
Henry J. Anthony, James E. Hagood who are bound unto W. E. Holcombe,
Ord. in the sum of $3600.00. Solomon Hays, Elizabeth Hays, Elizabeth
Crain and the widow, no name given, bought at sale.

Benjamin Hays. Estate of Benjamin Hays. Box 89 #944. Probate Judge
Office. Pickens, S. C. Est. admr. 8 Feb. 1867 by Elizabeth Hays,
Roswell Hill, James R. Harris who are bound unto W. E. Holcombe, Ord.
in the sum of $300.00.

Elizabeth Hays. Estate of Elizabeth Hays. Box 98 #1026. Probate
Judge Office. Pickens, S. C. Est. admr. 20 Sept. 1870 by George
Hendrick who is bound unto I. H. Philpot, Ord. in the sum of $200.00.

Sarah Hays. Will of Sarah Hays. Box 121 #4. Probate Judge Office.
Pickens, S. C. We Malindy Hays, Sarah Hays and Suse Ann Evet being old
and infirm and desiring that our real and personal property be disposed
of in a way satisfactory to our selves. We make this our last will and
testament and first it is our will that our goods and effect real and
personal, be used for our benefit as long as we or either of us lives
and no part to be sold or disposed of as long as we or either of us
lives and when all of us dies save one it is our will that she may
dispose of all that we own in any way that she may desire. Dated 4
Dec. 1888. Wit: J. A. Robinson, E. A. Lawson, T. S. Massingill.
Signed Malindy X Hayes, Sarah X Hayes, Suse Ann X Evet. Filed 14 April
1893. (The above will not abstracted.)

William Fields Hays. Estate of William Fields Hays. Box 9 #139.
Probate Judge Office. Pickens, S. C. Est. admr. 10 Jan. 1872 by
George Hendrick, Barney L. Freeman, D. E. Hendrix who are bound unto
I. H. Philpot, Ord. in the sum of $1400.00. George Hendrick gdn. of
Wm. F. Hays a minor under 14 years son of Elijah Hays who died in 1863
and his widow died in Aug. 1870.

                              LADD

John Ladd. Estate of John Ladd. Box 73 #777. Probate Judge Office.
Pickens, S. C. Est. admr. 18 Jan. 1864 by Salathiel Ladd, James
Cantrell, T. R. Price, Alexander Edens who are bound unto W. E. Holcombe, Ord. in the sum of $2500.00... left seven heirs. Recd. 24 March
1864 Pleasant Ladd old note $121.00. Paid Rilla Howard $500.00.

Thial Ladd. Estate of Thial Ladd. Box 110 #1054. Probate Judge
Office. Pickens, S. C. Est. admr. 28 Aug. 1876 by John L. Gravely,
John T. Jones who are bound unto H. I. Philpot, Ord. in the sum of
$200.00. On 11 Jan. 1879 Milly Ladd, Thia M. Ladd, recd. shares.
T. A. Hudson the wife of John F. Hudson recd. a share. Left eight
heirs; Jane Ladd, Elizabeth Stansell, Adaline Redmond and the heirs of
Amos Ladd decd., Sarah Gravely recd. a share.. P. E. Ladd recd. a
share. On 1 March 1877 J. M. Akins of Transylvania Co., N. C. states
that Thial Ladd is indebted to him and that he is not a resident of this
State. A letter in the file to Mr. John L. Gravely, Prices, P. O.
Pickens Co., S. C. from his cousin P. E. Ladd of Banks Co., Ga. He
request that Gravely send his money to him at the same P. O. letter
dated 31 July 1879. Another letter to Mr. John L. Gravley, he called
him a friend and is from J. M. Odell of Hall Co., Ga. and states that
Mr. P. E. Ladd was at my house now. no date.

Charity Ladd. Charity Ladd to Jackson Arter. Pack 309 #1. Clerk of
Court Office. Pickens, S. C. In the County Commissioners Court...
That Jackson Arter your complainant and petitioner. That Milton Arter
is a son of Charity Ladd born without wedlock and is now about ten
years old, whose mother now has two more chn. of illegal birth, all of
whom has no home of their own, and depend upon their mother for
support. That your petitioner is the grandfather of Milton, and has
cared for him from his mother breast, when his mother gave him to me,
and is still willing that he remain until he is of full age. That if
the Court approves the Bond of Indenture herein applied for, he will try
to raise and educate him and that he will be a comfort to him in his
old age and the sd. Milton will inherit a reasonable part of his estate
both real and personal at the age of twenty one. Signed: Jackson X
Arter. Wit: E. E. Kennemore. Dated 16 Oct. 1875.

                              LAMB

David Lamb. Will of David Lamb. Vol. 35, Page 708. Probate Judge
Office. Charleston, S. C. I David Lamb of Charleston city, merchant,
being of sound and disposing mind and memory, etc. I will my just
debts and funeral expenses be paid. I give to Mrs. Joan Christie, the

wife of Alexander Christie and unto her son David Lamb Christie the sum
of five hundred dollars, this legacy is to be for her sole use and shall
dispose of the same as she pleases. I give to my two nephews James and
Peter Robertson the sum of five hundred pds. sterling. I give to my
three nieces Janet Cunningham, Margret Miller, and Katharine Sampson,
dtr. of my sister Katherine Miller, three hundred pds. sterling a
piece. I give to my three sisters Katherine Miller, Christian Lamb and
Margret Robertson during their natural life, an annuity or clear
yearly sum of fifty pds. to be paid to them severally in half yearly
payments of twenty five pds each at the turns of Whitsunday and
Martainmas in every year during their natural life. The said sisters
resides in or near Aberdour Fife Shire Scotland. I give to my friend
William McGavin and Isabella his wife, or their heirs three hundred
pds. sterling. I give to the Presbyterial Church in the city of
Charleston of which I have long been an elder the sum of one thousand
dollars. I give to my dear dtr. in law Mary Lamb the sum of five
hundred dollars. And unto dear grandchildren Mary and Janet Lamb the
sum of four thousand dollars a piece. I give the rest and residue
and remainder of my estate to my two sons David and James Lamb to be
divided equally between them. I appoint my sons David and James Lamb
my executors. Dated 7 July 1820. Wit: M. King, Samuel G. Barker,
Henry Campbell. Signed David Lamb. Proved 17 June 1822.

Thomas Lamb. Will of Thomas Lamb. Vol. 34 Page 230. Probate Judge
Office, Charleston, S. C. I Thomas Lamb of Charleston, S. C. school
master, being weak in body but of sound mind and memory, etc. I will
all my messuage and tenament situated in the town of Columbia, S. C.
unto Michael Odonovan, his heirs and assigns forever. He the said
Michael Odonovan paying my just debts and funeral expenses. Dated 1
Dec. 1819. Wit: Samuel Segle, W. Veitch, John Neman. Signed Thomas X
Lamb. Proved 14 Dec. 1819.

                                 LANEY

Richard Laney. Pack 645 #4. Clerk of Court Office. Pickens, S. C.
Richard Laney died in the poor house in Pickens Co., S. C. in 1862.
Age 41 years.

                                 LANGLY

Carter Langly. Estate of Carter Langly. Apt. 9 File 639. Probate
Judge Office. Greenville, S. C. I Carter Langly being in low state
of health but of sound mind and memory. I give to my dtr. Anne Langly
a negro boy named Jacob, one mare called Judy, two feather beds and
furniture, two cows and calves, thirteen head of hogs, four head of
sheep and the balance of the household and kitchen furniture, I give
to my son Thomas Langly one negro boy named Tolbert, one feather bed
and furniture... I give to my dtr. Easter Leaster one negro boy named
Edmon, one feather bed and furniture. I give to my two dtr. Ann and
Easter all the tract of land whereon I now live agreeable to the heirs
called for by the deeds. I appoint my son Thomas Langley and Street
Thurston Executors. Dated 8 Dec. 1820. Wit: Carey W. Jackson, Peter
Gerard. Signed Carter X Langly. Will proven by Peter Gerard before
Spartan Goodlett, Ord. on 4 Feb. 1823. There is two others negroes in
the inventory, not named in will. Pomp, Cinda. Notes on hand on
Street Thurston, Lamuel Laflin and Allen Marshal due, Aaron Kemp due,
Marino and Harden Roberts due 25 Dec. 1823, Samuel Magnue due, George
Stewart due, Cornelius Stewart, Alford Gilbreath, Thomas Edward Junr.,
Enoch Sparks, Joel Bruce, Noah Nelson, William Stewart due, Jesse
Waddle due, Bird Street, William Ducan, Joshue Stewart, Thomas Brown
due, Thomas Barnett, Miles Southern, John Snanden, Creasia Robertson,
George Gilbreath, Gipson Southern, William Thurston Sr., Anvil Runnels,
Leroy Burns, Elijah Dill.

Solomon Langston. Deed from Solomon Langston. Book F page 48. Clerk
of Court Office. Laurnes, S. C. Dated 23 Oct. 1795. From Solomon
Langston to Henry Langston both of Laurens Co., S. C. in consideration
of thirty pds. sterling, hath given, granted and sold a certain tract
of land lying and being on the North side of a branch of Enoree, called
Coxes Creek, being part of a grant granted unto Christian McCuller.
Dated 18 July 1795. Wit: Gabl. Bumsass, Jesse Holder. Signed Solomon
Langston seal. Laurnes Co. 96 Dist. This day came Jesse Holder and
made oath he saw the above deed signed. Dated 20 July 1795. Wit:
Rogers Brown (Justice). (The date at top of deed may be date recorded.)

Henry Langston. Deed from Henry Langston. Book H Page 230. Clerk of
Court Office. Laurnes Co., S. C. From Henry Langston to Solomon Langston both of Laurnes Co in consideration one hundred dollars, have
granted, bargained and sold all that tract of land containing 54 acres
lying in Laurnes Co. Originally granted unto John Blackstock. Dated
13 April 1806. Wit: Thomas Lynch, Joseph Addir. Signed Henry Langston,
seal. Proved on oath of Joseph Addir before J. A. Elmore, J.Q.
Dated 2 June 1807.

Solomon Langston. Deed from Solomon Langston Book F Page 60. Clerk
of Court Office. Laurnes, S.C. Solomon Langston to Samuel Stiles both
of Laurnes Co., S. C. for and in consideration of fifty pds. sterling
hath granted, bargained and sold that tract of land containing 250
acres on a branch on the South side of Enoree, called Cox's Creek. adj.
land of Jesse Holder, James Miller and Angus Campbell. Dated 27 Oct.
1795. Wit: Solomon Langston, Jesse Holder, Solomon Holder. Signed
Solomon Langston. Proven 27 Oct. 1795. Recorded 16 Nov. 1795.

Solomon Langston. Deed. Book F Page 149. Clerk of Court Office.
Laurnes, S. C. Solomon Langston to Bennet Langston both of Laurens
Co., S.C. In consideration of twenty pds. sterling hath granted,
bargained and sold all that tract of land containing 125 acres lying
and being the dividing ridge between Enoree and Duncans Creeks. Adj.
land of William Cooper, Anthony Millers. Dated 29 Oct. 1796. Wit:
Mathew Brown, Ephraim Christopher. Signed Solomon Langston. Proved
29 Oct. 1796. Before Roger Brown, J.P.

Asa Langston. Deed from Asa Langston. Book H Page 183. Clerk of
Court Office. Laurnes, S. C. Asa Langston to Leonard Beasley both of
Laurnes Co., S.C. In consideration of $130.00. . hath granted, bar-
gained and sold all that tract of land containing 30 acres being part
of two tracts adjoining each other. Originally granted to Robert Hannd
and Abraham Holland. Dated 8 Aug. 1806. Wit: Turner Richardson,
John Miller. Signed Asa Langston. Sarah Langston relinquished all her
interest and estate. Before me J. A. Elmore, J. Q. Dated 25 Aug.
1806. Signed Sarah X Langston.

James Langston, Jr. Deed to James Langston, Jr. Book A-1 Page 167.
Clerk of Court Office. Pickens, S. C. This indenture made between
John Reid and James Langston Jr. both of Pendleton Dist. S. C. Dated
29 Dec. 1797. In consideration of thirty pds. current money of this
state, doth grant, bargained, sell a tract of land containing 200
acres lying on the South side of Little River. Originally granted
3 Dec. 1792 to ___. Wit: James Smith, Joshua X Holden. Signed
John Reid. Proved by James Smith before Henry Burch J.P. 19 Mar. 1800.
Recorded 17 Aug. 1829 and examined by William L. Keith, C.C. & R.M.C.

James Langston. Deed to James Langston. Book A-1 Page 191. Clerk of
Court Office. Pickens, S. C. I John Moore of the State of Ga. Elbert
C. to James Langston of Pendleton Dist., S. C. In consideration of
$250.00 have granted, bargained and sold 106 1/4 being part of an
original grant given to Ferdinand Hopkins lying on Rices Creek. Adj.
land of Joel Morton. (No more of this deed found in the notes.)

LATHAM

John Latham. Estate of John Latham. Box 6 #72. Probate Judge Office. Pickens, S. C. Est. admr. 12 Sept. 1836 by James Latham, John Brown, Abraham Burdine who are bound unto James H. Dendy, Ord. in the sum of $18,000.00. Citation published at Peters Creek Church mentioned James Latham as a son... one paper mentions eight legatees, no names given. Estate sale 15 Nov. 1836. Buyers James Latham, George Latham, John Farr, John Latham, Sinkler Latham, Anthony Latham.

Polly Latham. Estate of Polly Latham. In Equity Pack 633. Clerk of Court Office. Pickens, S. C. On 23 Mar. 1861 Polly Latham decd. wife of John Latham died before her father. Her father Richard Burndine died in Sept. 1860. Her heirs were: Patcy Smithwick and her husband T. H. Smithwick... John W. Latham, Richard M. Latham, Abraham P. Latham, Anthony G. Latham, Samuel W. Latham, Jane E. Pettit and her husband James E. Pettit all who resides in Georgia.

LATIMER

Latimers Minors. Box 56 Pack 1346. Probate Judge Office. Abbeville, S. C. Guardianship bonds. We Lemuel Trible, Ezekiel Trible, Hugh N. Huston are bound unto Moses Taggart, Ord. in the sum of $2,000. Dated 25 Feb. 1840. Whereas Lemuel Trible was made gdn. of Richard T., Catherine C., and James N. Latimer minors under 21 years. They are chn. of Benjamin Latimer decd. We James Latimer, Lemuel Trible and Lydwell Williams are bound unto Moses Taggart, Ord. in the sum of $1,000. Dated 6 Sept. 1830. Whereas James Latimer was made gdn. of Thaddeus, Caroline and James Latimer minors under 14 yrs. On the back of both bonds it mentioned they were chn. of Benj. Latimer decd.

Latimer Minors. In Equity, #44. Clerk of Court Office. Abbeville, S. C. M. B. Latimer was made gdn. of Mary K. Latimer, C.C.A. Latimer, Charles A. Latimer in 1852. He was gdn. of James S. Latimer in 1862.

Albert Latimer. Estate of Albert Latimer. Box 128 Pack 3472. Probate Judge Office. Abbeville, S. C. Est. admr. 21 May 1849 by Micajah B. Latimer, C. T. Latimer, B. N. Latimer who are bound unto David Lesley, Ord. in the sum of $6,000.00. Petition to admr. the estate of Albert G. Latimer who departed this life intestate leaving a widow and five minors (not named). On 12 May 1849 S. A. Latimer widow said she was willing for M. B. Latimer to admr. her late husband est. The appraisement was had 23 May 1849 by Stephen Latimer, James B. Kay, William S. Hampton, Bennet McAdams, Magt. A. D. He had four negroes viz: Bob, Charles, Nimrod, Emeline.

LAWSON

Jonas Lawson. Estate of Jonas Lawson. In Equity, Pack 3203. Clerk of Court Office. Abbeville, S. C. To the Honr. Hugh Rutledge, William James, Waddy Thompson, Henry W. Desaussure and Theodore Gaillard Esqs. Judges of the Court of Equity. Your orator Benix Howland and your Oratrix Peggy Howland, that your oratrix father Jonas Lawson lately decd. made his will on the 11 Apr. 1806. Ordered that the whole of his estate after paying his debts be divided equally between his children, viz: Margaret or Peggy Nash, James, Jesse, Robert, Jonas, Arthur and Elizabeth Lawson and appointed James, Jesse and Robert as executors. That the sale of the estate amounts to $2487.65. That the executors are not collecting and paying over to the heirs as they ought. And that your oratrix father was the admr. of the estate of Henry Lawson of the State of Georgia, that your oratrix is entitled to eighty dollars of said est., which was never paid (Henry was a son of Jonas Lawson, Sr.) and each time she applied to the executors, they refused, pretending that a large debt against the estate that would absorb the whole of the estate. Filed 19 Sept. 1809.

LAY

<u>Charly Lay</u>. Deed of Charly Lay. Deed Book I Page 177. Pendleton
Dist. Anderson, S. C. I Charly Lay for in consideration of $220 paid
in hand by George Washington and William H. Terrell. Both of Pendleton Dist. Dated 2 Aug. 1803. Doth sell, bargain, release all that
plantation or tract of land lying on the South side of 12 mile river.
Containing 200 acres. Wit: Jamey Jett, Demony Pew, John Simmons.
Signed Charly X Lay. On the third day of Aug. 1803 Ann X Lay released
and relinquished her dower to the above land. Recorded 19 March 1808.

<u>Charles Lay</u>. Estate of Charles Lay. Box 2 #11. Probate Judge Office.
Pickens, S. C. I Charles Lay being of sound and memory do make and
ordain this my last will and testament. I give to my wife Nancy Lay
one negro woman named Renday and one negro man named Lace, also two
feather beds and bed clothing with the other household and kitchen
furniture and my sorrell mare and colt, and her saddle and bridle. I
give to my sons David, John, James, Charles F. and William Lay each to
keep the property I have given them. I appoint my son William Lay as
executor. Dated 20 Feb. 1829. Wit: Elihu Creswell, Robert H. Creswell
John Knox. Signed Charles X Lay. The will was proved on 20 April 1829
and was contested by Nathaniel Lynch and others. In the May term of
Court Lynch withdrew his caveat and the case was dismissed. On the back
of will Anderson Keith received or bought $203 worth of items, under
this William McKinney received or bought $137 worth of items. Then
under this "William McKenney to be equal with Keith $66" (These two
with Lynch may be son in laws?)

<u>Nero Lay</u>. Deed of Nero Lay. Pack 350 #6 Clerk of Court Office.
Pickens, S. C. I Nero Lay for and in consideration of $200 in hand
paid Elizabeth Lay, do sell and convey my entire crop of corn, fodder
and cotton growing on my place and the land I rented from Elizabeth Lay
during the present year. That I will pay to Elizabeth Lay two bales of
lent cotton weighing 500 pds. each and fifty bushels of corn by the
15 day of Oct. Inst. This deed or contract made ___ Feb. 1879. Wit:
C. P. Barrett, G. W. Singleton. Signed Nero Lay.

<u>James Lay</u>. Will of James Lay. Box 54 #194. Probate Judge Office.
Pickens, S. C. I James Lay being of sound mind but feeble in body, etc.
I desire my wife Elizabeth to have and hold during her natural life or
widowhood and no longer. The tract of land whereon I now live, and the
mill tract, the Ned Norton tract and the Lemuel Nicholson tract. Also
the following negroes Ben, Nice, Bob, Cale, George and Lucinda. Also
provision for one year, for her negroes and stock. Her choice of
twelve hogs, fifteen head of sheep, four milk cows, one mare called
"gray," two mules, beck and sal. All the beehives, ten best hogheads,
the whole amount of gears and farm tools, blacksmith tools, and household and kitchen furniture. My executors is to buy a suitable wagon
for her use. They are also to put two thousand dollars on loan giving
her the interest for her support. At her death the items given to her
to be divided between my heirs. If she should marry then immediately
the whole of my estate be sold and she to get a child part. I instruct
my executors to execute deeds to my son Jesse Lay for the land he now
resider on, known as the William Deadman tract, the Moss and Gilly
tract in conformity with the terms of sale being three thousand and
five hundred dollars. I give to my heirs at law the rest of my real
and personal property, to be divided equal between them (not named).
I appoint Samuel Livengood as guardian of my granddaughter Josephine
Livengood to receive her share of my estate. I appoint my son Charles
Middleton Lay executor. Dated 8 Feb. 1860. Bennett Moody, A. B. Grant
E. M. Perry. Proven 21 June 1860.

<u>Charles Middleton Lay</u>. Will of Charles Middleton Lay. Box 75 #799.
Probate Judge Office. Pickens, S. C. I Charles Middleton Lay being of
sound mind and memory, etc. First all my lawful debts and funeral

expenses be paid. To my beloved wife 200 acres of land, commencing
on the 18 mile creek at a place known as the Maverick old bridge, up
the creek to Matilda Walkers land, then westly and South to make a
tract for her (Square or nearly so) this to include my home place and
building, also five hundred dollars. The balance of my estate to be
keep in charge of my executor until my youngest child becomes of age,
then to be sold and divided between my living children. I desire that
all my personal property be keep on the place to support the family
except the notes, stock and accounts. It is my earnest request that
my executors pay attention to the education of my children and see
each to get a good English education for this purpose I appropriate
any funds in their hands. All bills and burial expenses of either
myself or any member of my family white or black, doctors bills, and
providing comfort and welfare of my family. I appoint my friend J. B.
Sitton, of Anderson Dist. and J. E. Hagood, and my son William Lay to
be executors. Dated 5 Dec.1863. Wit: E. Madden, W. W. Hollingsworth,
W. W. Knight. Signed C. M. Lay. Filed 1 Jan. 1864. Heirs Widow
Elizabeth Lay, chn. Mattie A. Hester, Mary A. Martin, Myra R. Lay,
James F. Lay, Caroline A. Lay, Susan E. Lay, Charles W. Lay, Letty E.
Newton.

Nero Lay. Box 124 #1. Probate Judge Office. Pickens, S. C. I Nero
Lay being of sound mind and memory, etc. I give all my estate after
my debts are paid to my sons Joseph Lay, Samuel Lay, James Gantt and
Belle Willerby. I appoint the five named legatee as executors. Dated
10 Apr. 1893. Wit: Wm. Watson, John Craine, Edward X Crook. Signed
Nerro Lay per Wm. Watkins. Filed 26 May 1893. Others heirs Savilla
Lay the widow, H. J. Martin brother in law. Settlement in 1900 Savilla
Lay, Mary Lay, Birdie Lay, Sallie Lay, James Lay.

                               LEE

James Lee. Power of Attorney from James Lee. Pack 417 #6. Clerk of
Court Office. Pickens, S. C. The State of Alabama, St. Clair Co. I
James Lee of said State and county legal guardian of Joseph, Sargent J.,
and Avarilla Griffin minors heirs of the estate of Bailey Griffin decd.
who was the son of Sargent Griffin late of Pickens Dist., S. C. who
departed this life before sd. Sargent Griffin decd. Have made, constitute and appoint James E. Hagood of Pickens Dist., S. C. my true and
lawful attorney for me in my name as guardian of said minors and heirs
of Sargent Griffin decd. Dated 13 March 1860. Wit: Samuel Dillard,
John W. Juzer. Signed James Lee, seal.

James Lee, Jr. In Equity, Pack 439 #2. Clerk of Court Office. Pickens,
S. C. On the 13 Oct. 1859 personally appeared James Lee, Jr., Henry
Lee, James Lee, Sr. before me L. Rogers Mag. Each indebted to the State
of S. C. in the sum of $300 each to be levied on their goods and chattels
if the said James Lee, Jr. shall fail in performing the condition under
written; the condition of this recognizance is such that if James Lee,
Jr. pay the sum of twenty five dollars annually for the support of a
bastard child begotten of Malinda Calhoon until such child shall be of
age of twenty one years, then this recognizance to be null and void or
else to remain in full force. The child was born 1 day of August 1859.

Drucilla Lee. Will of Drucilla Lee. Vol. 1 Page 48. Probate Judge
Office. Union, S. C. I Drucilla Lee widow of Union Dist. being weak
in body but of sound mind and memory, etc. I desire my just debts be
paid out of personal estate. I give to my helpless child ___ my feather
bed and furniture and all my real estate consisting of a tract of land
bought of Gillumm Williams consisting of 100 acres on a branch of
Frenchman Creek waters of Enoree River whereon Jones lives and to be
disposed by my executors for the support of said helpless child. I
give to my son Thomas Lee and Catherine, Robert, Mick, Jobe and
William Lee five shillings each of my personal estate. I give to my
son Joseph and two dtr. Delilah and Drucella Lee the remainder of my
personal estate consisting of household and kitchen furniture and stock
at the disposal of my executors. I appoint my trusty friend Mark

Murphy, ___ Murphy, and my son Michael and Robert. Dated 3 May 1814.
Wit: Sampson Gilliam, Elizabeth X Duncan, Larry X Green, Damaus Jackson.
Signed Drucilla Lee, seal. Proven 5 Sept. 1814.

LENDERMAN

Peter Lenderman. Estate of Peter Lenderman. Apt 8 File 595. Probate
Judge Office. Greenville, S. C. On 7 Jan. 1841 John Lenderman was
mentioned as the admr. of the estate of Peter Lenderman decd. of Greenville, S. C. Heirs; Barbary Lenderman, widow, Henry Lenderman in Alabama, Hiram Hyde and wife Nancy out of State, Thomas Hyde and Polly his
wife in George. ___ David and Caroline his wife in Tenn., John Kelly
and his wife in Texas, John Stagner, your petr., Catherine Lenderman,
William Smith and Priscilla his wife in Alabama.

LESLEY

Lesley Minors. #25. Clerk of Court Office. Abbeville, S. C. In 1842
James L. Lesley was the guardian of Eliza Lula Lesley, a minor. On
5 Jan. 1857 she was mentioned as wife of James M. White. James L.
Lesley the father of said minor.

William Lesley. Real Estate Book A, Page 29. Probate Judge Office.
Pickens. William Lesley married Rosana Hendricks a daughter of Moses
Hendricks Sr. decd. of Pickens Dist. They were already married when
her father estate was admr. on 30 Jan. 1837. They received one cow and
calf, one bed and furniture, two sheep, one hog. In Hendricks File is
a note of William Lesley "Three days after date I promise to pay
Moses Hendricks Senr. the just sum of forty dollars for value received
of him as witness my hand and seal 24 July 1830." Wit: Alexander
Clark. Signed William X Lesley.

LIGON

Ligon Minors. Pack 26. Clerk of Court Office. Abbeville, S. C.
In 1868 Eliza M. Ligon was the guardian of Louisa M. Ligon, Langdon
Cheves Ligon, Elizabeth E. Ligon, Joseph Allen Ligon, Richard C. Ligon
all minors. Were children of Joseph Ligon decd. On 19 Feb. 1876
E. E. King recd. her full share of said estate.

LINDSAY

John Lindsay. Estate. No Ref. Probate Judge Office. Abbeville, S. C.
(This is the last part of a letter to James Lindsay, Esq. of Abbeville,
S. C. from Alamon Nash, his resident not shown.)... said estate of
John Lindsay decd. and to make full and final settlement with you as
acting executor, which shall and will be satisfactory to us. Therefor
dear brother we expect you to fully compensate yourself for your trouble
and make up any demands or accounts which you may have against our son
Abner A. Nash, and any in the neighborhood. Also reserve to yourself
what you may require and think the mare worth which John brought to this
country, she cannot be rode or use her hoof is coming off she may or
may not be of service when that comes off after the foregoing deduc-
tions if any please pay over the remainder to John T. Nash, his
receipt will and shall be valid. Your ever loving and affectionate
brother and sister. Dated 9 Dec. 1842. Signed Alamon Nash and Jane
Nash--- Legatees of est. of John Lindsay decd. Recd 11 Jan. 1843 from
James Lindsay exor of John Lindsay decd. $141.40 in full of the legacy
in right of my wife Ally Lindsay. Signed Daniel Pruit.

Lindsay Minor. Pack 20 Clerk of Court Office. Abbeville, S. C. In 1856 P. A. Lindsay was the guardian of A. B. C. Lindsay a minor. On 9 Jan. 1856 recd. from J. Bonner admr. of estate of James Lindsay decd. $1836.29. On 9 Nov. 1860 paid expenses of ward in Philadelphia $300.00. A. B. C. Lindsay was of age in 1861.

Samuel Lindsay. Samuel Lindsay vs Jesse W. Norris. Pack 11. Clerk of Court Office. Abbeville, S. C. Abbeville Dist. In Equity, Your orator Samuel Lindsay formerly of Lowndesville in the Dist. and State aforesaid now of Elberton, Ga. That on or about 11 Dec. 1854 your orator made with Jesse W. Norris a contract for the sale of a house and lot in Lowndesville, on main street, bounded on South by lot owned by James M. Latimer Esq. formerly owned by Dr. A. B. Arnold, and by a cross street known as Walnut or Bell street for the sum of $600. Your orator received a note on W. A. Giles in the sum of $232.86. This is all that has been paid. Dated 28 Apr. 1856.

LIPSCOMB

Lipcomb Minors. Pack 42. Clerk of Court Office. Abbeville, S. C. On 14 Mar. 1836 John Lipcomb was guardian of Thomas Lipcomb and James W. Lipscomb, sons of N. Lipscomb decd. of Abbeville Dist., S. C. Recd. July 1836 of John D. Williams Exor of Col. James Williams legacy from said estate $391.36. 11 Jan. 1837 recd. from Stanmore Brooks guardian on settlement, this account due from estate of Thomas Lipscomb Exor $48.67.

LITTLETON

Solomon Littleton. Deed to Solomon Littleton. Deed Book B Page 24-25. Mesne Conveyance Office, Greenville, S. C. This indenture made 17 Feb. 1789 between Thomas Lewis and Solomon Littleton both of Greenville Dist. In consideration of fifty pds. sterling, hath bargained, sold and confirm a tract of land containing fifty acres on the Saluda River. Being part of a tract of two hundred acres granted to James Gore on the 4 July 1785, and conveyed from Gore to Lewis the 10 July 1788. Wit: John Lewis. Signed T. Lewis, seal.

LOCKHART

James Lockhart. Estate of James Lockhart. Box 57 Pack 1357. Probate Judge Office. Abbeville, S. C. I James Lockhart being weak in body but of perfect mind and memory. etc. First if desire my just debts and funeral expenses be paid. I will to my son Joel Lockhart four negroes named, Negro girl Lucy, negroes boys Hardy, George and Lewis, I will and bequeath that my son Joel pay to John Green Clay as trustee for his mother Polly Clay four hundred dollars to be paid in four installments of fifty dollars each. I will to my son Joel Lockhart as trustee for my dtr. Nancy Ashworth one tract of land lying in Elbert County, Ga. the same whereon she now resides, to remain in the hands of the trustee, Executor or admr. until her death, then to be divided between the heirs of her body. I will to my son in law Simeon Clay five dollars. I will to my son in law Noah Ashworth five dollars. I appoint my son Joel Lockhart and William Pressly my executors. Dated 2 May 1843. Wit: Van A. Lawhon, Martin A. Bowie, William A. Pressly. Signed James X Lockhart, seal. Proved on oath of William Pressly on 8 July 1843 before David Lesly, O.A.D. Estate was appraised on the 15 Aug. 1843 by Van A. Lawhon, William A. Pressly, Jno. W. Conner, Tilman Lomax.

Logan Minors. Pack 24. Clerk of Court Office. Abbeville, S. C. In
1862 Dr. John Logan was guardian of Mary Susan Alice Logan and William
E. Logan minors. Paid funeral expenses 7 Jan. 1863. Paid 3 March 1858
for articles in Newberry Village $5.00. Paid for articles bought in
Columbia $2.25. For board at Glenn Springs two weeks and traveling
expenses in summer of 1857 $10.50. Cash recd. from est. of Louisa
Logan $9.82. In Feb. 1855 Recd. from admr. of est. of W. W. Logan
$56.00. W. R. Logan was of age in 1870. Paid his tuition at school
at Greenwood $17.00.

Logan Minor. Estate of Logan Minor. Pack 302. Clerk of Court Office.
Abbeville, S. C. Received of Dr. John Logan former guardian of my
wife Jane, the title to a tract of land belonging to my wife, known
as the home tract, where on Mrs. Barbara Logan resided at the time of
her death. Containing four hundred and seventy five or eighty acres.
Dated 2 Oct. 1839. Signed Wm. C. Black. On Jan. 1, 1837 amt. for
tuition of Jane Logan at Greenwood Academy $20.00. Expenses in
getting to Yorkville School $17.87 1/2.

Sarah and Isaac Logan. In Equity, Pack 385. Clerk of Court Office.
Abbeville, S. C. To the Honr. Chancellors: Your oratrix Sarah Logan
the wife of Isaac Logan by her next friend James W. Fooshe. That your
oratrix and Isaac Logan were married on the 9 March 1843. That within
three years after marriage without any provication or course inflicted
violence upon her person, and frequently afterward until the month of
June 1860 when a merciless beating drove her from his house for several
weeks to houses of relatives. His pretended penitence, and fair
promises, she returned to his house and resumed her duties as his wife.
Then on 28 Sept. 1861 he threatened her life that she sought safety and
refuge in the house of her brother John B. Sample, when he pursued her
with his gun. To avoid the legal siding with your oratrix, he executed
a deed conveying a tract of land of 150 acres and two slaves. Appointed
her brother as trustee to execute the deed. Your oratrix leased out
the slaves to one Robert Mathis for $25.00 per year. Within a few
weeks Isaac Logan forcibly took possession, and think he will remove
them from this State. A Mrs. Calhoun is the mother of Mrs. Logan.
Filed 20 June 1862.

Andrew J. Logan. Estate of Andrew J. Logan. In Equity, Pack 465.
Clerk of Court Office, Abbeville, S. C. To the Honr. Chancellors:
Your oratrix Louisa Logan a feme sole and Huldah Riley a feme sole (an
unmarried woman) infant dtr. of Louisa Logan under the age of twenty
one. That Andrew J. Logan departed this life 20 April 1850 leaving in
full force his will and test. Frederick B. Logan was executor and has
management of the estate. The will sheweth that A. J. Logan the husband
of your oratrix and father of Hulda Riley directed that after his death
his executor was to sell all the surplus land and stock, keeping a
small farm to support his family, until the youngest child becomes of
age. The executor has sold the property held by A. J. Logan and has
purchased another place containing 217 acres, and nine negroes is all
that is left in the possession of your oratrix. The said property
lies on Curtail, and is adj. by land of William Smith, Silas Ray and
known as the Hughey Place, the land purchased is worn out and impossible
to make a support upon it, and that the estate is more indebted now
than when A. J. Logan died. The negroes are viz: Ephraim about fifty
years, Jess about forty years, Waller about twenty five, Will about
twenty two, Dick eighteen, Rose a woman thirty eight years, Sallie
about twenty with two chn., John and Charles... Your Oratrix and
Huldah Riley your complaint and Lucy Logan, William Logan, Tyler Logan
are the legatees under the will of A. J. Logan. Tyler the youngest in
his eleventh year, Huldah the eldest is in the eighteenth year. Filed
10 May 1860.

Thomas Long, Sr. Will of Thomas Long, Sr. Apt. 8 File 555. Probate
Judge Office. Greenville, S. C. I Thomas Long being sound in mind
but weak in body, etc. I will and desire that my beloved wife Rachel
Long shall have and enjoy all my land now held by me lying on the South
side of Rock Creek or Stoney Creek, together with my son Young living
on same with his mother during her life time or widowhood, at her
death to be his in fee simple. She (the wife) is to have use and
enjoyment of my stock the brown mare she rides as her own at her death
all to be divided between my heirs. Dated 4 June 1824. Wit: Henry
S. Walker, Michel Robins, Rebecca X Croft. Signed Thomas Long. Proven
by Michael Robins and Rebecca Croft before S. Goodlett, O.G.D. on the
4 Oct. 1824.

John Read Long. Will of John Read Long. Box 53 Pack 1254. Probate
Judge Office. Abbeville, S. C. I John Read Long being of sound and
disposing mind and memory, etc. First pay my just debts from the
estate. I lend unto my beloved wife Sally Long during her natural life
all that tract of land whereon I now live, also four negroes: Peter,
Nan, Betty and Lyley also as much of my stock, cattle, hogs, sheep as
she think sufficient, and the use of household and kitchen furniture.
I have in times past given unto my son Harrison Long $500 in cash, this
to be counted in his share. I have given unto my dtr. Elizabeth
Shirley a negro by name Nelson with his service, I value at $1200 to be
counted in her share. I have given unto my dtr. Lucy Swanzy decd. one
negro named Hatten with his service I value as $1200 to be counted in
her share. The following four negroes I value as: Toney value $900,
Armstead value $900, Isaac value $900, Tom value $800. These shall be
drawn for by Nancey Greenlee, Harrison Long, Ruben Long, Nicholas Long,
Alcey Sample, the ones that draws one of the above negro shall be counted
as I have valued. The one that not get a negro in said drawing shall
have two negroes: Nacee value at $600 and Annica value at $400 for a
total of one thousand dollars. The remainder of my estate to be sold
on twelve month credit and divided between my six chn. viz: Nancey
Greenlee, Betsey Shirly, Harrison Long, Reuben Long, Nicholas Long,
Alcey Sample and the chn. of Lucey Swanzy decd. I appoint my beloved
wife Sarah Long executrix and son Reuben Long and Joel Lipscomb Esq.
Executors... Dated 12 Jan. 1819. Wit: Alexr. Sample, John Pulliam,
Robert Young. Signed John Read X Long. Proved on oath of Alexr. Sample
before Moses Taggert, O.A.D. on 15 March 1819.

James Long. Estate of James Long. Box 55 Pack 1302. Probate Judge
Office. Abbeville, S. C. I James Long being in a low state of health,
but of sound mind, etc. First pay my just debts out of my estate. I
give to my grand daughter Lucy Hodges one negro girl named Charity and
a negro boy named Ishmael, one horse, saddle and bridle, a cow and calf,
bed and furniture. It is my desire that she should live with her
grand mother during her life, should she marry before the death of her
grand mother the property left to her to be subject to her call
(several words worn from page too dim to make out) The remainder of
my property I lend unto my beloved wife Margret Long both real and
personal during her life, then sold and money divided equal between my
three dtr. Betsey Long, Frankey Hodges and Lucy Anderson. I appoint
my wife executrix and friends John Weatherall, Hugh Dickson as Executors. Dated 20 Aug. 1807. Wit: John Hodges, George Weatherall,
Marshal Weatherall. Signed James Long. Receipt, 13 Jan. 1813. For
my wife Frances Hodges the sum of $1864.67 her legacy left her by her
father James Long decd. Wit: George Weatherall. Signed William X
Hodges. Receipt 19 Mar. 1811 the sum of $50.00 being the balance of
a legacy left my wife Lucey Wardlaw (then Lucey Hodges) by her grandfather James Long. Wit: Polley Weathall. Signed Robert Wardlaw for
Lucey Hodges. Receipt. 20 Jan. 1813 in the sum of $1864.67 the share
of Betsey Long legacy from her father James Long decd. Wit: Gabl. Long
Signed: Wm. Long. Receipt. 20 Jan. 1813 in the sum of $1864.67.
Lucey Anderson legacy from her father James Long decd. Wit: Gabl.
Long. Signed Richard L. Anderson. The estate was appraised 28 Oct.
1807. Negroes named viz: Tom, Anbrem, Moses, Aaron, Girl Matilda,

Charity, Boy Solomon, Boy Gilbert, Boy Ishmal, woman named Moll and inft. son George. Appraisers, Robert Wardlaw, John Hodges, John Richey, Samuel Anderson, Gabriel Long. Those who bought at sale... William Long, Richard Anderson, William Hodges, John Weatherall, Hugh Dickson, Pleasant Wright, John Adams, John Conner, William Fuller, John Hodges, Robert Wardlaw, Nathaniel Rosamond, Joseph Hackney, Gabriel Long, James Henderson, James Graham, Samuel Anderson, William Henderson, John Long, Nathaniel Rowlen, Bartholomew Mabry. Sale held 22-23 Nov. 1809.

William Long, Sr. Estate of William Long, Sr. Box 125 Pack 1684. Probate Judge Office. Abbeville, S. C. I William Long, Sr. being of sound and disposing mind and memory, but weak in body, etc. I give to my dtr. Elizabeth Long one hundred acres of land to be laid out North of the tract embracing the dwelling house, also all my household and kitchen furniture, my stock of cattle, hogs, sheep, and horses, one carriage, farm tools, one year provision, one negro named Edmund, during her natural life, and at her death, I give to my dtr. Elizabeth fifty acres of her mother land that embracing the house and one side board. And to dtr. Margret the other fifty acres during her natural life, and at her death to be divided between my lawful heirs, except my son Reuben and his heirs who is to have no part nor share of it. I will the balance of my land to be sold and all just debts paid and equal divided between my heirs, except my son Reuben and his heirs to whom I will ten dollars which is all I intend him to have of my estate. I appoint my son William Long and friend W. P. Martin executors. Dated 16 Nov. 1847. Wit: Geo. Mattison, Jesse Gent, Wm. P. Martin. Signed Wm. Long, Sr. Abbeville Dist. To F. W. Selleck, Esq. The petition of Wm. P. Martin sheweth that William Long, Sr. departed this life on the 18 instant, your petition is mentioned as a executor, not wishing to act in the capacity etc. Dated 23 Jan. 1852. W. P. Martin. Appraisement and inventory had on 9 Feb. 1852. The appraisers were Stephen Latimer, Donnald, Wm. W. Mosley, N. R. Reeve, W. J. Mattison. Sale held, 10 Feb. 1852. Longs who bought at sale; William Long, Sarah M. Long, James Long, Margret E. Long, Elizabeth Long.

Frances Long. Estate of Frances Long. Box 128 Pack 3475. Probate Judge Office. Abbeville, S. C. The estate of Frances Long was admr. 20 Nov. 1846 by J. W. H. Johnson, D. Calhoun and Thomas Stewart who are bound unto David Lesly, Ord. in the sum of eight thousand dollars. Frances Long died intestate Oct. 1846, had a dtr. who died many years before her mother who left an only daughter, which granddaughter named Hazel Smith having two great grand children and died after Mrs. F. Long and the great grand chn. are now living (two words not plain) or either of them get any thing of Mrs. F. Long estate. Frances Long chn. are living. The grand dtr. Mrs. H. Smith died after the sale of the personal property, but before the sale of the land. A citation to settlement. In the Ordinary Office the 4 Sept. 1848. To Hezel Smith and T. R. Puckett to make distribution of the est. of Frances Long decd. Signed David Lesly, Ord. A power of attorney from Thomas Polly and Mitchell B. Hopper of the County of Perry state of Alabama, do make and appoint Thomas Abercrombie of said county and state, who is about to go to the state of South Carolina. To be our lawful attorney, to use name and rights and interest from the estate of Frances Long (formerly Frances Pucket) while widow of Richard Puckett late of Abbeville Dist. in right of our respective wives, to wit: Permelia F. Polly formerly Permelia F. Abercrombie now wife of said Thomas Polly and Martha A. Hopper formerly Martha A. Abercrombie now wife of said Mitchell B. Hopper both daughters of Mary Abercrombie formerly Mary Puckett who was the wife of said Thomas Abercrombie and the dtr. of said Frances Puckett but who is now decd. to sue, demand, recover and receive our legacies or share etc. Dated 7 Aug. 1848. Signed Thomas Polly and Mitchell B. Hopper, seals. John Cunningham was Clerk of Court and John P. Graham Judge of Probate. In the final settlement of the estate of Frances Long decd. held in the Ord. office 12 Sept. 1848 at Abbeville, S. C. "Present J. W. J. Johnson, Admr. and distributee in right of his wife, Thomas R. Puckett, Wyatt W. Puckett, Thomas Abercrombie representing under power of attorney, Permelia Frances wife of Thomas Polly and Martha Agness wife of Mitchell B. Hopper two of his children by Mary a daughter of Mrs. Long and as guardian under an appointment

in Alabama of James Redding and Thomas Jabez, Hazel Smith who married
Mary Frances, daughter of Mrs. Long. Perelia died before Mrs. Long
leaving one child the said Mary Frances who survived the grand mother
and died leaving a husband. The said Hazel Smith and two children
Eliza Frances and Marshall R., J. W. H. Johnson representing under
power to attorney Elizabeth Ramsey. Absent: Robertson residing in
Georgia. Negroes listed in the appraisement viz: man Sam, woman Nancy,
man Enuck, Martha and her two chn. boys Henry and Sam, man Milford,
woman Emily, girl Many, boy Charley. Signed D. Calhoun, Thomas Stuart,
Franklin Miller, Benj. X Busbee. Dated 8 Dec. 1846.

Robert Long. Revolutionary Claim. Book E Vol. 11 Page 73. No other
ref. Robert Long was living in Laurens Co., S. C. in July 1833, has no
record of his age, only told by his mother that he was born in County
of Antrim, Ireland about year 1763, when four or five months old father
came to Pennsylvania, thence two years later moved to the place where
he now lives. His father died when he was about four years old. Had
one brother who died in 1776. Fathers people came from Scotland originally, and were Presbyterians (Called covenanters) his family in
Charles the second time fled to Ireland to escape his persecution.
Lived in a neighborhood of Whigs during Rev. war. He was on the East
Florida Expedition. Served under Capt. Joseph Greer. Capt. James
Dillard. Col. Levi Carey, Col. Haynes Regt. Brig. Gen. Andrew Williamson. Was in the battle of Cowpens. The siege of Charleston. "Not
expecting any advantage but liberty." Paid $40 per month.

LOVE

John Love. Estate of John Love. Box 55 Pack 1306. Probate Judge
Office. Abbeville, S. C. Patrick Calhoun administer the oath of an
administratrix of John Love estate to Elizabeth Love his widow. No
date or other information.

LOONEY

John Looney. Estate of John Looney. Box 19 #235. Probate Judge
Office. Pickens, S. C. Est. admr. 17 Apr. 1848 by Wm. S. Grisham,
Miles M Norton who are bound unto Wm. D. Steele, Ord. in the sum of
$400.00. Jane Looney a daughter of decd. wants Wm. S. Grisham to admr.
on the est. She was from West Union, S. C. Sett. made 2 Jan. 1849.
Paid Jane Looney $14.12 3/4. Paid Osborn and Elizabeth Manning
$14.12 3/4. Paid James Palmer and wife Dorcas $14.12 2/3. Paid John
Miller and wife Sarah $13.12 3/4. Paid Rachel Dennington $12.13 3/4.

LOMAX

Augustus Lomax. Estate of Augustus Lomax. Pack 338. Clerk of Court
Office. Abbeville, S. C. To the Honr. Chancellors: The petition of
W. James Lomax a committee that by order of this Court was on 29 July
1858 to govern the person and affairs of Augustus Lomax who has been
found to be of unsound mind and incapable of goerning himself and his
estate. After one year your petitioner has paid out over five thousand
dollars in debts with about the same amount left to be paid. The
estate has a house and lot in Abbeville and the plantation of about
three hundred acres of very poor land, and thirty negroes, ten of
whom are hands. The overseer of the plantation is Thomas Mobley.
Dated 2 Nov. 1859.

William Anderson Looper. Estate of William Anderson Looper. Box 99
#1039. Probate Judge Office, Pickens, S. C. Martha Malisa Looper
states that her husband Wm. Anderson Looper died 3 Mar. 1871... left a
widow and three minor chn. viz: Wm. Laurence Orr Looper age 4 years,
James Franklin Looper age 3 years, Mazie Anderson Looper age 3 months.
Dated 5 Sept. 1871. Robt. McWhorters the admr.

Augustus Looper. Estate of Augustus Looper. Box 99 #1044. Probate
Judge Office. Pickens, S. C. Est. admr. 30 May 1871 by A. Melissa
Looper, Jas. Lewis who are bound unto I. H. Philpot, Ord. in the sum
of $800.00. Widow Melissa Looper. Paid 11 Dec. 1871 Malissa Singleton
formerly Looper. Sale held 24 Oct. 1871 buyers. Thomas Looper,
Malissa Looper, William Hunt.

Jeremiah Looper. Estate of Jeremiah Looper. Box 114 #1105. Probate
Judge Office. Pickens, S. C. Est. admr. 14 Nov. 1885 by Mary M.
Looper, widow T. P. Looper, H. M. Looper who are bound unto J. H.
Newton, Ord. in the sum of $1200.00. He died 12 Aug. 1885. Paid 7
Aug. 1908. Mrs. S. M. Turner, T. J. Looper, M. A. Looper each share
$97.74.

Joseph Looper, Sr. Will of Joseph Looper, Sr. Box 130 #9. Probate
Judge Office. Pickens, S. C. I Joseph Looper, Sr. being in good
health and of sound and disposing mind and memory, etc. First pay my
just and honest debts. I direct my beloved wife Sarah Looper have one
hundred acres of land, including the house and buildings where I now
live, all the household and kitchen furniture she may want during her
natural life or widowhood. I direct my admr. to appoint five freeholders to divide my land into seven equal lots, also my personal
property lotted by the same freeholders. With each heir making their
choice and paying into the estate if the lot is above their equal share.
Pay unto Elvira Freeman, Sarah A. Singleton, Mary Hendrix, Martha Edens
and Matilda Chastain one hundred dollars before the division to make
them equal with the ones who has had rent free land. Then I direct
that the remainder be equally divided between each and every of my
heirs as named below. To Elvira Freeman her share, my son Wm. F. Looper
decd. to his heirs Emer Looper, Burdine Looper, Perry Looper. To my
son T. P. Looper his share, to my dtr. Sarah A. Singleton her share, to
my son Samuel Looper his share, to my son H. M. Looper his share, to my
son Joseph Looper his share, to my son Jeremiah Looper his share, to
my dtr. Mary Hendrex her share, to my dtr. Elisabeth Griffin decd. her
heirs, Tempy Griffin, Sarah Griffin her share, to my son G. B. Looper
his share, to my dtr. Martha Edens her share, to my dtr. Matilda
Chastain her share, to my son John Looper his share. I appoint my sons
T. P. Looper and H. M. Looper, Executors. Dated 25 Dec. 1878. Wit:
David Hendricks, George W. Cox, D. C. Freeman. Signed Joseph X
Looper, seal filed 23 May 1898. Others who received from the est. viz:
Malissa Barr, J. E. Looper, Lillie A. Edens, Mary Bridges, S. E. Child-
ress, Joe Edens, Eva Edens, Eula Edens, Lena Edens, Delar Hendricks,
Bird Looper, Sarah J. Childress, J. W. Singleton, Emma Childress.

Samuel Looper, Jr. Estate of Samuel Looper, Jr. Box 89 #943. Probate
Judge Office. Pickens, S. C. Est. admr. 12 Nov. 1866 by Mary J.
Looper, widow, Redin Rackley, Andrew J. Anderson who are bound unto
W. E. Holcomb, Ord. in the sum of $400.00. He was from Dacusville, S.C.

Sloan Looper. Estate of Sloan Looper. Box 8 #130. Probate Judge
Office. Pickens, S. C. On 22 Oct. 1870 James F. Caulley, Wm. M.
Jones, Geo. W. Owens are bound unto I. H. Philpot, Ord. in the sum of
$100.00. James F. Caulley gdn. of Sloan Looper minor under 21 years.
On 21 Oct. 1870 Mary J. Caulley formerly Mary J. Looper and mother of
Sloan Looper infant son of Samuel Looper, Jr. decd. is entitled to an
interest in est. of Daniel Looper decd.

W. A. Looper. Estate of W. A. Looper. Box 99 #1039. Probate Judge
Office. Pickens, S. C. Est. admr. 29 Mar. 1871 by J. Perry Looper,

Robert McWhorter, John W. Major who are bound unto W. H. Philpot, Ord. in the sum of $800.00. Jeramiah Looper, J. Perry Looper, Malissa Looper bought at sale.

Solomon Looper. Estate of Solomon Looper. Box 101 #1061. Probate Judge Office. Pickens, S. C. I Solomon Looper being of sound mind and memory do publish this my last will and testament, etc. I give my beloved wife Judath W. all that she got from or may get from her own people, as her own property to do as she think best. I give to my dtr. Margaret my large bureau, one cow and calf, one sow and pigs. I give to my grand dtr. Evaline (Margaret daughter) my small bureau and what is on it viz three images. I also want my land divided into five equal lots of eighty acres each. My personal property, household and kitchen furniture, farm tools, to be divided between my children and my wife to take a child part. I appoint John A. Robinson and Joseph Looper as executors. Dated 6 Jan. 1866. Wit: J. F. Smith, W. C. Jones, J. W. Brown. Signed Solomon X Looper, seal. Proven 6 Nov. 1871. Paid 22 Jan. 1873 Elisha and Nancy Robinson as per receipt $344.86. Paid Sarah and Margaret Hood as per receipt $344.86. On 20 Dec. 1871 paid Elizabeth Crane, D. M. Keith, Martha Robinson, Judia Ann Keith, Harriet A. Freeman, Lurania Smith, Judeth W. Looper, Margaret Looper, Mary Braswell and husband Wm. Braswell as per receipt $344.86 each.

Hassie Looper. Estate of Hassie Looper. Box 10 #158. Probate Judge Office. Pickens, S. C. On 14 Nov. 1876 James T. Singleton, Malissa Singleton James Lewis are bound unto I. H. Philpot, Ord. in the sum of $330.00. James T. Singleton gdn. of Hassie Looper a minor under 14 years. Dtr. of Augusta Looper decd. and Malissa Singleton. Feb. 1890 paid Hassie Winchester, nee Looper $155.50. One paper Harriet Looper.

William F. Looper. Estate of William F. Looper. Box 95 #1001. Probate Judge Office. Pickens, S. C. Est. admr. 1 March 1869 by Thomas P. Looper, D. C. Freeman, J. W. Singleton who are bound unto Irvin H. Philpot, Ord. in the sum of $600.00. 16 March 1869 paid note on Sarah Satterfield $100.50.

Daniel Looper, Sr. Estate of Daniel Looper, Sr. Box 33 #385. Probate Judge Office. Pickens, S. C. Est. admr. 2 April 1860 by Jeramiah Trainham, Robert F. Morgan, J. W. L. Cary who are bound unto W. E. Holcombe, Ord. in the sum of $210.00. Joice Looper the widow. Property was given during his lifetime to Rachel Prichett, Mary Dunkin, Carolina Phillips his dtrs. Had notes on John Pritchett, Daniel Looper, Jr., Joseph Looper, Solomon Looper. On 9 Nov. 1855 Joice Looper wanted R. F. Morgan to be the gdn. of her six minors chn. viz; Elender P. Looper, Elizabeth Looper, Rachel Looper, Samuel Looper, Arminda A. Looper, Mary Looper. Owned 198 acres of land on waters of Carpenters Creek waters of Saluda River, adj. land of Larkin Hendricks Esq. Solomon Looper and others. Arminda was the wife of Charles Holcombe in July 1860. Heirs were: John Pritchett and wife Rachel, Henry Duncan and wife Mary, John L. Rackley and wife Ellender, Charles Holcombe and wife Arminda A., John M. Pinson and wife Joicey Elizabeth, Samuel Looper, Peter Phillips and wife Carolina. A letter... State of Georgia. Whitfield Co. 12 Sept. 1871. Mr. Solomon Looper (First part about the weather and crops) -- Sol you said that they was some money in the office there belonging to the estate of Caroline Phillips, they was no admr. on Caroline things she was not in debt. She married a man named Danl. or David Buff and he keep all she had, no heirs but fathers heirs, so I close your brother till death. (Signed) John and Rachel Pritchett. The Pritchett lived at Varnels Station, Ga.

James Perry Looper. James Perry Looper and Benson Gilstrap applied for license to keep a tavern and retail spiritous liquors at the house whereon we now live at the fork of the Greenville and Pickensville road just outside of the corporate limits of the village of Pickens for 12 months from this day. Dated 3 May 1869.

Martha Lyon Minor. #22. Clerk of Court Office. Abbeville, N. C. In 1864 Margaret C. Lyon was guardian of Martha Lyon, on 9 Dec. 1860 Margaret C. Lyon in account with James Lyon. 9 Dec. 1860 to amount recd. from J. H. Wideman $874.14. Was gdn. of Thomas J. Lyon. We the undersigned called on by Margaret C. Lyon guardian, and Martha F. Lyon and James W. Lyon to examine and appraise the tract of land now owned by the said Margaret C. Lyon, appraised the land containing three hundred and forty two acres at $7.50 per acre, or $2565.00. We recommend that the parties Martha F. and James W. to whom the land has been assigned receive the tract jointly. Dated 16 Sept. 1875. Signed George L. Patterson, Henry Mosley. Wit: J. H. Wideman.

Elijah Lyon. Estate of Elijah Lyon. Box 56 Pack 1347. Probate Judge Office. Abbeville, S. C. I Elijah Lyon being of sound mind and understanding. I give to my wife Phebe Lyon all of my real and personal property after paying my debts. After the death of my wife I give to my grand daughter Mary Ann Lyon a negro girl named Eliza, and to my grand son Nathaniel N. Lyon one negro girl named Martha, also to my grand son James F. Lyon a negro named Rachel To my wife grand son Franklin W. Norwood a negro boy named Ellis. I give to my son Elisha Lyon five dollars. After the death of my wife all the remaining of my property to be equally divided between my son William Lyon and my dtr. Mary Norwood. I appoint my step son John Norwood executor. Dated 15 Nov. 1842. Wit: Nathan Gunnin, William J. Hammond, Lewis Rich. Signed: Elijah X Lyon. Proven 7 Jan. 1843. John Norwood died after the proving of this will and the 27 May 1845 when it states that he was decd. Nathaniel Norwood and L. Smith was executors of John Norwood est.

John Lyon. Estate of John Lyon. #220. Clerk of Court Office. Abbeville, S. C. To the Honr. Chancellors: Your oratrix Lucy E. Lyon the widow of John Lyon decd. departed this life in the month of Oct. 1853, leaving the widow and one child Jane G. Lyon now the wife of Benjamin C. Reynolds. John F. C. Settle (or Little) was named admr. of the estate. Her husband was much embarrassed with debts, a sale of the personal property has been held leaving considerable amount of debts still unpaid. The real estate lying on Rockey Creek waters of Savannah River, containing three hundred acres. Your oratrix is informed that there will be a small amount over after the debts are paid, but will not exceed the one third value of the land... (no more on this item).

MABRY

Andrew J. Mabry. Bottlegging, Pack 214 #4. Clerk of Court Office. Pickens, S. C. On 29 Jan. 1857 Andrew J. Mabry was found guilty of retailing whiskey without a license.

MACKIE

Thomas Mackie. Will of Thomas Mackie (No ref. given) Elbert County, Georgia. I Thomas Mackie of the State of Georgia, Elbert Co. being weak in body, but in perfect mind and memory, etc. I give to my wife Rosannah a third of the plantation that I now live on during her life time. The other two thirds to my sons John and William Mackie. At the death of my wife, her third to fall to my son John Mackie. I give to my wife Roseannah one black mare, three cows and these are to be maintained from the plantation, and one negro named Hager. At the death of my wife, Hager is to go to my dtr. Marthew Pleaman during her life time, then to go to her dtr. Janiet and Rosannah Fleman. I give to my sons Samuel and William one negro called Cat, one negro boy named Isach, one negro woman named Joan and child named Sam. I give to my son William Mackie one bay horse and my still, and five dollars.

To my dtr. Rachel Strictland five dollars, to my dtr. Mary Hemphill
five dollars, to my dtr. Rosannah Templeton five dollars, to my dtr.
Marthew Flemings five dollars, and my clothes to Thomas Breesy. I
appoint my sons John and Samuel Mackie as my executors. Dated 23 July
1796. Wit: Samuel Hopkins, Elijah Hopkins. Signed Thomas Mackie.
Recorded 2 Apr. 1797. By W. Higginbottom Reg.

MADDEN

E. M. Madden. Estate of E. M. Madden. Box 78 #828. Probate Judge
Office. Pickens, S. C. Est. admr. 25 Aug. 1864 by Opheia A. Madden,
James N. Arnold, Ezekiel Madden who are bound unto W. E. Holcombe, Ord.
in the sum of $2,000.00.

B. F. Madden. Estate of B. F. Madden. Box 86 #911. Probate Judge
Office. Pickens, S. C. Est. admr. 23 March 1866 by Robert A. Thompson,
C.E.P.D.? are bound unto W. E. Holcombe, Ord. in the sum of $200.00.

Ezekiel Madden. Estate of Ezekiel Madden. Box 88 #931. Probate Judge
Office. Pickens, S. C. Est. admr. 1 Oct. 1866 by Nathaniel M. Madden,
Thomas D. Garvin, John B. Clayton who are bound unto W. E. Holcombe,
Ord. in the sum of $600.00.

Temperance W. Madden. Estate of Temperance W. Madden. Box 107 #1024.
Probate Judge Office. Pickens, S. C. On 2 June 1875 owned tract #1
the old homestead on waters of 12 mile River, adj. tract #2 lands of
J. B. Clayton, Samuel Parson and others containing 350 acres. Heirs
R. A. Madden, E. J. Madden, Martha T. wife of A. M. Boggs, Sarah wife
of Zoch Smith, Naomi wife of James Moseley, Mary A. wife of J. J. Garvin,
Louisa M. Arnold, Harriet wife of John Wilson reside out of State.
Malissa wife of John Hallum, Thomas E. Madden, D. B. Madden. Heirs
at law of E. M. Madden decd. viz: John, Ferdelia and Walker Madden who
are minors under 21 years. Nathaniel M. Madden petitioner against
Thomas E. Madden. On 15 Dec. 1876 N. S. Moseley recd. share. A Deed
of Gift Elisha Merritt Deed of Gift to Temperance W. Madden. State
of Georgia, Hall County. I Elisha Merritt of state and county aforesaid
for and inconsideration of the love and good will and one dollar paid
by my nephew Nathaniel M. Madden do give in trust for my sister
Temperance W. Madden wife of Ezekiel Madden all the rights I have in
and to a negro named Washington now in my possession. I purchased said
negro from Ezekiel Madden and to terminate at the death of Ezekiel
Madden he having a life estate in the said negro by virtue of a deed
of gift made by Nathaniel Merritt unto the said Temperance W. Madden
and her bodily heirs. Dated 22 Sept. 1847. E. Merritt. Wit: H. C.
Langford, D. Garvin.

John Madden. Estate. 51-8. In County Court. Laurnes Court House.
Laurnes, S. C. The last and testament of John Madden decd. presented
in open court proven by Richard Pugh and Ann Madden and ordered to be
recorded. Dated 17 Feb. 1796.

MAJOR

Epps Major. Estate of Epps Major. Pack 132. Clerk of Court Office.
Pickens and Plat Book 4 Page 133. Clerk office. Anderson, S. C. Epps
Major of Pendleton Dist. now Pickens Dist. was born 3 Jan. 1772 and
died between 12 Apr. 1827 and 1 May 1827. His wife was Susannah Teague
they married 28 Oct. 1802. Had 8 chn. in all. Made his will 12 Apr.
1827 will proven 28 May 1827. Before he made his will he had given to
his oldest dtr. Dorothy Major the wife of John McWhorter her part of
his estate or $150.00 in property. He gave to his wife Susannah all his
real and personal property during her life or widowhood for her support
and the children until they became of age. Then the tract of land
whereon he lived he devised to his two sons George H. Major and Elijah
Major. Susannah Major took possession of the plantation and raised

her family with the rent and profits, she died 12 Jan. 1852. George
Major one of the sons died soon after his father, in April 1828, having
never married. The land was on Rices Creek, waters of 12 mile river,
adj. land of Carwell Hester, Elihu Griffin and others, containing 267
acres. Heirs: Dorothy G. wife of John McWhorter, Nancy S. wife of
Mabry Mauldin, Elijah T. Major, Rebecca wife of William Ellis, Sarah
wife of Alvey or Alvah Jones, Elizabeth wife of James Jones, Mary Ann
wife of Jonathan Lee who died in the year 1850, heirs of Mary Ann Lee;
Nancy Rebecca Lee, George Nelson Lee, Mary J. Lee, Martha E. Lee, James
Olin Lee. On 17 Sept. 1856 Alvah Jones and family, James W. Jones and
family, William Ellis and family, and Jonathan Lee and James Olin Lee
with their family had moved to Blount Co., Alabama. The tract of land
was sold to Hardy Gilstrap for $1500.00. David Hendrix who witnessed
Epps Major will was a brother in law having married his sister Sarah
Major. On file in Anderson, S. C. is an old plat for Susannah Major by
John Bowen D.S. for the lcoation of her land, plat dated 3 March 1828,
containing 267 3/4 acres, adj. land of David Hendricks, James Langston
and Millers land.

Major chn. Major chn. as minors. Pack 46. Clerk of Court Office.
Abbeville, S. C. On 12 Feb. 1861 Matilda L. Major was guardian of
Martha Ella Major, Anna Rebecca and Samuel Gamewell Major. They
received on 12 Feb. 1861 $1040.79 from the est. of Samuel B. Major
decd. On 12 Jan. 1877 Anna Rebecca Watson released her mother from the
guardianship. Samuel G. Major was of age in June 1870.

Major Chn. Minors. Pack 48. Clerk of Court Office. Abbeville, S. C.
On 12 Feb. 1861 Robert W. Major was gdn. of Isabella M., Emma J.,
Joseph M., Mary L. Major. He received $990.16 from Matilda Major Admr.
of est. of Samuel B. Major. Robert W. Major was also gdn. of Samuel H.
Benjamin and Bella Benjamin. And M. L. Greene and J. W. Greene. The
Greene minors recd. from Mary L. Major.

James Major. Will of James Major. Box 77 $821. Probate Judge Office.
Pickens, S. C. I James Major being in a low state of health, but of
sound mind and memory. After my just debts and funeral expenses are
paid I give to my beloved wife Elizabeth Major all my property both
real and personal during her life or widowhood. Should she marry I
direct my property be sold and she to have an equal share with my chn.
I direct my executors to give to my dtr. Lucia Ann and son James enough
to make them equal with the others that I gave them as found in the gift
book. Stephen A. Major (one of the executors. Part of the will is
torn off.) Dated 13 March 1863. Wit: J. G. Ferguson, Anner Latham,
W. E. Welborn. Proven 17 May 1864.

MANSELL

Samuel & Robert Mansell. Power of Attorney of Samuel and Robert Mansell
Pack 106. Clerk of Court Office. Pickens, S. C. State of Georgia,
Cherokee Co. We Samuel and Robert Mansell for divers good causes and
consideration, have ordained and constituted and appointed Lemuel
Mansell of said State and County our true and lawful attorney in fact
for his and our own proper use and benefit. To receive from the Ord.
or any other person having money or effects due us from the est. of
James Mansell late of Pickens Dist., S. C. Dated 15 Apr. 1848. Wit:
Uriah Stephens, Wm. P. Hammond, J.P. Signed Samuel & Robert Mansell.

MANTZ

Christopher W. Mantz. Estate of Christopher W. Mantz. Pack 349.
Clerk of Court Office. Abbeville, S. C. To the Honr. Chancellors:
Your orator David Glover of Edgefield Dist. That Christopher W. Mantz
of Abbeville Dist. being possessed of a considerable real and personal
estate, did make and publish his last W-T... That the testator departed
this life near the end of Dec. in 1851. Will was probated 5 Jan. 1852

by John W. Hearst as executor. Mary P. Mantz the widow having been
appointed executrix, dpclined to qualify. The said Mary P. Mantz took
possession of the estate of her decd. husband, and continued in possession of the property until her death, which occurred on or about ___ day
of ___ 1856... Mary P. Mantz leaving her will nameing your orator as
executor and qualified as such on the 8 Sept. 1856. Immediately upon
her death of the said testatrix the said John W. Hearst proceeded to
take possession of the property mentioned by the said C. W. Mantz in
his will. In the will of he bequeat many articles to her grand niece
Harriet Glover and grand nephew Vandall M. Glover chn. of your
orator, and to sell others, that under the will of her husband should
be given to said chn. and not sold. The orator prays for an order of
understanding as to which will is valid, and who is to stand for debts
or profits. Filed 27 March 1857. Statement of John Cothran Esq.
Sworn says, that C. W. Mantz settled the place on which he died in 1821
or 1822. Thinks the Mantz were married in 1823, always understood Mrs.
Mantz carried property, does not know how much. In 1829 lived at Mrs.
Aproul.

MARCHBANKS

Margaret Marchbanks. Power of Attorney. Margaret Marchbanks. Pack 218
#6. Clerk of Court Office. Pickens, S. C. State of Texas, Tarrant
County. I Margaret Marchbanks, widow, and formerly Margaret Cannon.
This day constituted and appointed A. G. Fowler of the same place, my
lawful attorney in fact to apply for, receive and receipt for all
monies, land, or other property and effects, that I may be entitled to
as heir of Russel Cannon decd. and of Ransom Cannon decd. and of Jane
Cannon decd. widow of Russel Cannon, all of whom died in Pickens Co.,
S. C. Giving and granting to my said attorney and his substitute, full
power to do and perform all acts necessary as if I might or could do
myself were I present, etc. Dated 27 Feb. 1857. No witness. Signed
Margaret Marchbanks, seal. Margaret Marchbanks appeared before G.
Nance, C.C.C.T.C. per M. Mathews, Deputy. The above Power of Attorney
was certifyed by Seaborn Gilmore, Chief Justice, Tarrant Co., Texas.
On 6 Mar. 1857. On the 6 March 1857 A. G. Fowler of State of Texas,
Tarrant Co. By virtue of the authority to me given by the foregoing
power of attorney do substitute B. W. Ball of the State of S. C. and
Laurens Dist. as attorney in my stead to do perform, execute all and
every act or thing that I might, etc. Signed A. G. Fowler, seal.
Attested same date, before Thos. M. Mathews, Dep. Clk. and S. Gilmore,
Chief Justice .T.C.....

MARET

John Maret. Will of John Maret. Box 60 #654. Probate Judge Office.
Pickens, S. C. I John Maret do make this my last will and testament. I
will to my wife Frances Maret all the property I may possess at my
death during her life or widowhood. At her death or marriage everything is to be sold and divided between my nine chn. seven sons and two
dtr. I will to my son Robert W. Maret a bed and furniture and a desk,
my little shot gun, and four dollars and fifty cents. I will to my two
dtr. Rutha A. and Matilda A. Maret to have fifteen dollars when called
for. I appoint my sons George W., William M. and Robert W. Maret as
executors. Dated 5 Nov. 1861. Wit: J. E. Maret, D. S. Maret, Fell
Cleveland. Signed John Maret. No probate date.

Stephen Maret. Estate of Stephen Maret. Box 28 #329. Probate Judge
Office. Pickens, S. C. I Stephen Maret being of sound mind and
memory, etc. It is my will that my jsut debts be paid. It is my will
that my wife Lucy Maret have all my property both real and personal,
household and kitchen furniture, with all stock and the present crop
that is now growing during her natural life. It is my will and desire
that my dtr. Harret M. and Martha F. Maret to have sixty dollars each
from the estate after the death of my wife. It is my will that my sons

Middleton A. and Wiley H. Maret each to have ten dollars from my estate
after the death of my wife, this is to make the four equal with the
older chn. After the death of my wife all my property put at public sale
and money divided between all my chn. I appoint my sons Cleveland and
Andrew J. Maret as executor. Dated 8 July 1852. Wit: A. P. Reeder,
David S. Stribling, James Hodges. Signed: Stephen Maret. Proven 1 Nov.
1852.

MARION

Nathaniel Marion. Estate of Nathaniel Marion. Box 67 Pack 1623. Probate Judge Office. Abbeville, S. C. I Nathaniel Marion being of sound
and disposing mind and memory. I give unto my wife Mrs. Jane Marion
the lot and ten acres of land at Cokesbury whereon I now live, the
household furniture, and stock of cattle. My carriage and one pair of
horses and the following negroes, Snow, Sary, Peter a carpenter, Mary
his wife, Kitty, Frances, David, Susy, Esther, Sam and old Mariah to her
during her natural life, the divided between my heirs. I give unto
E. M. Tarrant in addition to land, the following negro. Sarah and her
increase. I give to my son John S. Marion in addition to the negroes
given him by deed the following, Auber a woman, and her child Mary,
a man called John Jingo, a woman called Catey. I give to my son
Nathaniel P. Marion the following negroes, July a carpenter, Mary Ann his
wife, Sue, Molly, Chance and Beck their chn. Nanny, Hannah, Louisa,
Nancy, Thomas a child, Betsy a child and James the son of Peter the
carpenter and Mary his wife. I give to my dtr. Jane Elizabeth Marion the
following negroes, Patricia, Lizett, Jacob, Silvey, Andrew, Melia,
Lancaster, Abbegale, Cittrus, Charles, William and old Sucky. I give
to my son Nathaniel P. and my dtr. Jane Elizabeth Marion each the sum
of five hundred dollars in bank stock forever. I desire my negroes
Blacksmille, Peter and Princess be sold and the money divided between
E. M. Tarrant, John S. Marion, Nathaniel P. Marion and Jane Elizabeth
Marion. I appoint my friend James Shackelford, and my son in law
John R. Torrant executors. Dated 2 May 1836. Wit: F. Connor, O. A.
Williams, W. C. Anderson. Signed Nathl. Marion. Proved 27 July 1839.
Inventory was made 10 Sept. 1839 by A. P. Pool, Stephen Ross, George
Holloway. There is part of a marriage settlement (no date) that she
Mrs. Jane Marion nee McCants, the widow of Nathaniel McCants, Esq. Her
chn. by the first marriage are Nathaniel, Robert James, Mary Louisa
McCants, who was the wife of George H. Round, Ann Elizabeth Holland the
wife of Nathaniel Holland by his father Dr. John Holland... Allen G.
McCants, Victoria Jane the wife of D. Sanders, Amanda D. Winter wife of
Charles W. Winter, Lois R. wife of Dr. Asa W. Greggs, John S. McCants,
Robert G. McCants the last five by their brother Allen G. McCants as
agent. The children Nathaniel Marion had by a former wife are: Louisa
Charlotte Marion, she died intestate while a minor. John Samule Marion,
Elizabeth the wife of M. W. Tarrant.

MORRIS

Samuel Morris. Will of Samuel Morris. Box 68 Pack 1675. Probate
Judge Office. Abbeville, S. C. I Samule Morris being weak in body,
but of sound and disposing mind and memory. I will that my just debts
and funeral expenses be paid punctually I will to my beloved wife
Margret Morris all my land including the plantation on which I now live
with the Davidson place, also one bay mare during her natural life. I
will to my four chn. viz: Louisa M. Morris, James H. Morris, Elizabeth
Morris, Sarah Jane Morris, each to get seven hundred dollars. I do
empower my executors to bring the balance of my property to sale, and
giving my wife one third, and divided the balance equally between all
my chn. Two not named before Mariah M. Morris, Samuel T. Morris I
appoint my faithful friends executors, Archibald Kennedy, Dr. Geo. W.
Presly. Dated 30 July 1841. Wit: John Ruff, Henry Fosbrook, John
Riley. Signed: Samuel Morris. No proven date given.

Alexander Martin. Estate of Alexander Martin. Box 58 Pack 1387.
Probate Judge Office. Abbeville, S. C. I Alexander Martin of Newberry
Dist. being called into the service of the United States of America,
being of sound and disposing mind and memory. Collect all debts to pay
my just and due debts if not sufficient sell enough of the property to
do so. The balance of my estate both real and personal I lend to my
wife Agnus Martin during her life or widowhood. At her death or marriage all my property to be equally divided between my children (not
named). I appoint John Martin and James Caldwell as executors. Dated
30 Jan. 1814. Wit: John M. Morris, W. M. Rutherford, Thomas Gordon.
Signed: Alexander Martin. Inventory made 4-5, 10 Jan. 1832. By
Samuel Watt, Wm. Lesley, Samuel A. Jack. Citation published at Upper
Long Cane Church. Exped. Recd. from Gordon Martin $11.00. James P.
Martin, Richard Martin.

Absalom Martin. Estate of Absalom Martin. Book A Page 54. Probate
Judge Office. Pickens, S. C. Personal appeared before me William
Odell, Thomas D. Garvin being duly sworn that the real estate of Absalom
Martin is not worth one thousand dollars, and is best for the parties
to sell and divide the money. To the heirs of Absalom Martin viz:
Edy Martin the widow, Rutha the wife of John M. Hendrix, Elizabeth the
wife of Dudley Wooton, Margret the wife of Claborn Wilkerson, Rachel
Martin, Juda Martin, Lydia Martin, Mary Martin, the last three being
minors, with Thomas D. Garvin Guardian. The sale of the real estate of
Absalom Martin decd. consisting of 95 acres lying on Goldens Creek in
Pickens Co. Adj. land of Wm. Bogg, Henry Sergeant and Mary Holland.
Sale to be held on the first Monday in July 1844.

Benjamin Martin. Deed from Benjamin Martin and others to Thomas Harbin.
Book A-1 Page 417. Clerk of Court Office. Pickens Co. We Benjamin
Martin, Gideon Smith, James R. Wyley Attorney of John H. Cleaveland,
Hudson Greenwood, Micajah Bryan and Moses Shannon. In rights for our-
selves in consideration of $4,056. to us paid by Thomas Harbin, do sell
a tract of land of five hundred acres. On the North East side of Tugalo
River and on Chaugo Creek, being part of a tract whereon Col. Benjamin
Cleaveland last resided. Adj. land of James R. Wyley and Sandford,
Henry Shell Aline, and Absalom Cleaveland. Dated 4 Jan. 1827. Wit:
Benja. C. Wyley, Thos. F. Gordon, Ellis Sparks. Signed: B. F. Martin,
Gideon W. Smith, James R. Wyley, agent for John H. Cleaveland, Hudson
Greenwood, Micajah Bryan, Moses Shannon.

John Martin. Estate of John Martin. Box 68 Pack 1673. Probate Judge
Office. Abbeville, S. C. Admr. bond, we Robert Martin, James Cowan
and William Dunn are bound unto David Lesley, Ord. in the sum of $1,000.
Dated 2 Jan. 1843. The petition of Robert Martin sheweth that his father
died in the year 1817 leaving a widow Sarah and the following chn.
William, James, Elizabeth, Samuel, Nancy, Robert and Sally the wife of
Andrew Webb, she being decd. leaving two chn. and a brother named John
Martin decd. leaving no widow or chn. Your petitioner prays for a
citation from this Court to admrs. Dated 19 Dec. 1842. The estate
settled in 1844 with the widow taking one half.

Gideon Martin. Estate of Gideon Martin. Box 10 #129. Probate Judge
Office. Pickens, S. C. Est. admr. 22 Nov. 1841 by Elijah Martin,
Pleasant Alexander, Robert Craig, who are bound unto James H. Dendy,
Ord. in the sum of $3,000. Cit. read at Carmel and Providence Churchs.
Est. admr. again 21 Dec. 1840 by Margaret Martin, Garner Evans, James
Mauldin of Georgia. Edy Martin bound unto Jas. H. Dendy, Ord. in the
sum of $6,000. Margaret Martin was the mother of decd.

Phillip B. Martin. Will of Phillip B. Martin. Box 103 #1084. Probate
Judge Office. Pickens, S. C. I Phillip B. Martin being of sound and
disposing mind and memory. First pay my just debts and funeral expenses.
I give to my beloved wife Elmira E. Martin all my estate both real and
personal during her natural life or widowhood. In case she marry she
is to have one half of my estate and the chn. the other half. If she

survive my chn. she is to have their share, or the whole of the estate.
I appoint my friend and brother in law James E. Hagood executor.
Dated __ Aug. 1866. Wit: R. K. Pace, C. W. Pace, J. W. Pace. Signed
Phillip B. Martin, seal. Filed 6 Jan. 1872.

James G. Martin, Minor. Box 11 #165. Probate Judge Office. Pickens,
S. C. In 15 July 1882 George W. McClanahan is bound to James H. Newton,
Ord. in the sum of $500. He the guardian of James G. Martin a minor
age 16 years.

William Waddell Martin. Box 127 #2. Probate Judge Office. Pickens,
S. C. I William Martin, famer of Pickens Co. First I direct my just
debts and funeral expenses be paid. I give, and devise all my real and
personal property or may possess at the time of my death of my dear wife
Sarah Elizabeth Martin. During her life or widowhood, for her support
and comfort. Having already given to my six oldest chn. a considerable
portion of my estate, I now give them one dollar each, one year after
the death of their mother, they are: Sarah Milly Susannah Stewart,
William Alfred Martin, Lucy Hannah Spearman, Mary Renick Garvin
Spearman, Martha Elizabeth Adams, Willie Ann Matilda Martin. I will
and devise to my four youngest chn. to wit. Warren Columbus Martin,
Deborah Ette Martin, Laura Maoma Martin, Silas Abraham Clayton Martin
the entire residue and remainder of my estate at my death and the death
or marriage of my wife, to share and share alike. I appoint Dr. Silas
W. Clayton, Executor. Dated 20 Feb. 1882. Wit: Joab Mauldin, J. K.
Kirksey, James P. Cary, C. L. Hollingsworth. Signed: Wm. W. X. Martin,
seal. Died 18 Aug. 1896. Filed 14 Sept. 1896.

William Martin. Will of William Martin. Box 109 Pack 3041. Probate
Judge Office. Abbeville, S. C. I William Martin of Abbeville Dist.
being weak in body but of sound and disposing mind and memory, etc.
I will my just and lawful debts be paid. I will to my nephew William
Marshall Moore one bed and clothes also one gun. I will to my nephew
William Bird Martin (son of Nancy and George W. Martin) "all the
residue of my estate as the only pledge of that brotherly love I can
possibly so well for their kind and endearing treatment to me from
the earlist dawn of my residence with them to the present moment."
I appoint my brother George Washington Martin my executor. Dated 4
Dec. 1817. Wit: Thomas McMillan, Andrew X Smith. Signed Wm. Martin.
Proved by Thomas McCillan before Thom. Livingston, Sr., Ord. the 15
Jan. 1818.

Robert Martin. Estate of Robert Martin. Box 65 Pack 1581. Probate
Judge Office. Abbeville, S. C. I Robert Martin of Abbeville Dist.
being weak in body, but of sound mind and memory, etc. I will to my
beloved wife Jannet Martin one third part of my land, one bald faced
mare, saddle and bridle, one bed and beding. I will to my son James
Martin 92 acres of land, one horse, saddle and bridle, one bed and
beding. I will to my dtr. Jean 92 acres of land, one horse, saddle
and bridle, one bed and beding. I will to my dtr. Mary 92 acres of
land, one horse, saddle and bridle, bed and bedin. I will that my
beloved wife have all under her care till my chn. becomes of age or
marry, she to be careful in having the children educated in a decent
manner. I appoint my wife as Executrix. Dated 9 May 1810. Wit: David
Pressly, Tho. Gillespie, Anny Gillespie. Signed: Robert Martin, seal.
An appraisaic of the estate of Robert Martin was held on the 12 Oct.
1810 by David Pressly, Nathl. X Strickland, Tho. Gillespie.

Janett Martin. The will of Janett Martin. Box 65 Pack 1564. Probate
Judge Office. Abbeville, S. C. The last will of Janett Martin late of
Rockey River in the Dist. of Abbeville. Declared by her by word of
mouth the 28 Nov. 1811. "It is my will and desire that David Pressly
be my sole executor of my whole estate that he take immediate charge
thereof and that he take care of my children and do the best he can for
them." These words were spoken by Janett Martin decd. spoken before
us. Signed Joseph Scott, Ann X Pressly, Easter X Pressly. This done
in my presence. Talo. Livingston, Ord. A.D.... The above citation
was read before the congregation at Dimond Hill Church. 9 Dec. 1811.

James Martin. Estate of James Martin. Box 13 #439   Probate Judge
Office. Anderson, S. C. Est. admr. 26 March 1802 by John Mauldin,
Burgess Reeves, Maulding Reeves who are bound unto John Harris, Ord. in
the sum of $4,000. Citation published at Rockey River Meeting House.
Appraisers are Robert Dowdle, George Reid, James Nash. Sale held 14
May 1802. Buyers: James Taylor, James Garner, Taply Oldham, William
neonard, John Crain, James South, William Hillhouse, Caleb Hall, William
Taylor, Ephraim Herrin, Patrick Norris, William Waddle, Martin Hall,
Adam Huffman, Charles Hayney, John Mauldin, Ambrose Nicholls, Stephen
Hayney, Daniel Williams, Abner Keaton, James Hartnes, James Campbell,
Thomas Garner, George Reed, Ansell Jarrett, Samuel McAdams.

Thomas Martin. Estate of Thomas Martin. Box 13 #452. Probate Judge
Office. Anderson, S. C. Est. admr. 5 Sept. 1831 by Jacob Martin,
William Martin, Ezekiel Murphrey who are bound unto John Harris, Ord.
in the sum of $10,000. Citation pub. at Big Creek Meeting House. He
left a widow and nine chn. names not given. Notes due the est. by
Abraham Martin, Edmand Martin, John Harris, John Towns, Ezekiel Murphey,
Anderson Crains. Sale of the est. held 18 Nov. 1831. Buyers: Wilburn
Duckworth, William Martin, James Martin, Widow Martin, Ezekiel Murphy,
Robert White, Bayles Wadkins, J. B. Earl, William Bryant, James Tugnell,
Humphrey Rodgers, Robert Richardson, Simon Bryant, William Rodgers, Jr.,
Larkin Rodgers, Benjamin Duckworth, Jeremiah Rodgers, William Erskine,
Abram Martin Senr., Abram Martin, Jr., John Golden, Alfred Moore, Moses
Welburne.

David Martin. Estate of David Martin. #2936. Probate Judge Office.
Anderson, S. C. I David Martin of Anderson Dist. do make this my last
will and testament. I will to my wife Pheby Martin during her life time
or widowhood, all my estate for her support and to raise the chn. At
her death or marriage to be divided between my chn. It is my desire
that each son to have sixty dollars when he come of age. I give to my
dtr. Sally Gables two cows and calves, one side saddle, two tables, one
new spinning wheel, one bed and clothing. I appoint my son James O.
Martin and John Spearman my executors. Dated 4 Jan. 1842. Wit: David
Whitman, David Martin, John A. Martin. Signed: David Martin. Will
proved before John Martin, Ord. A. D. 7 Feb. 1842. The estate of
David Martin was admr. 8 April 1850 by John A., Edmund S., David Martin
and Levi Gable who are bound unto Herbert Hammond, Ord. in the sum of
$1,000. To the Honr. W. W. Humphreys Judge of Probate. Your petitioner
John A. Martin sheweth that his father David Martin departed this life
in the year 1842, leaving a will by the provision of which his wife is
to have the land to support herself and his chn. nameing his son James
O. Martin and John Spearman as executors. Qualified as such on the 7
Feb. 1842. In the year 1849 the executor James O. Martin departed this
life, and in 1850 the surviving executor departed this life. In the
year 1857 his mother, the widow of David Martin departed this life.
Under the letter of admr. dated 8 Apr. 1850 to your petitioner will pray
for a sale of the real estate, consisting of one tract containing 114
acres, adj. land of Dr. James Spearman, John James, Howard, F. S. Hall,
lying on Conoe Creek waters of Little Generostee waters of Savannah
River. Heirs: Sarah the wife of Levi Gable, Robert G. Martin, heirs
at law of James O. Martin to wit, R. Harrison Martin, Louiza J. Martin
who are of age and J. J. Martin a minor, all who resides in this state.
David and E. S. Martin resides beyond the limits of this state, Edmond
S. Martin resides out of state. Filed 19 Aug. 1869. John A. Martin.

Abraham Martin. Estate of Abraham Martin. Box 12 #421. Probate Judge
Office. Anderson, S.C. Est. admr. 13 Jan. 1809 by Thomas Martin and
Joshua Kees both of Anderson Dist. who are bound unto John Harris, Ord.
in the sum of $2,000. Citation pub. at Mount Pizgah Church, 8 Jan. 1809.
The sale was held 20 Apr. 1816 buyers: Joseph Duckworth bought a gun,
Thomas Martin bought a plow, Mrs. Anne Martin bought the rest. She
may have been the widow.

John C. Martin. Estate of John C. Martin. Pack 8 Page 17. Equity
Records. Clerk of Court Office. Abbeville, S. C. John C. Martin died
in June 1854. Admr. was granted to Benjamin Y. Martin Esq. of Abbeville Dist. on 14 Oct. 1854. He owned a tract of land on Pennys Creek

and Little River waters of Savannah River contianing 2,850 acres adj.
land of George B. Clinkscales, John A. Donald, Nicholas H. Miller,
Alexander McCoy, James T. Liddell and others. He was living on this
land when died. Left a widow Mary A. Martin and the following chn.
Luther L. Martin a minor about 19 years, Mary E. Martin a minor about
16 years, John M. Martin a minor about 14 years, Thomas P. Martin a
minor about 13 years, Sarah A. Martin a minor about 12 years, Samuel
Starke Martin a minor about 10 years, William B. Martin an infant a
few months old. Filed 20 Apr. 1855.

MASON

Ambrose Mason. Estate of Ambrose Mason. Box 12 #420. Probate Judge
Office. Anderson, S. C. He made a will dated 4 Apr. 1837. Proven 5
June 1837. Witt: James Young, Sr., Jesse Bradberry, Abraham Meridith.
Ment. estate of Jenny Payne. Expend. 25 July 1849 paid Lucinda Mason
$19.19 1/2... 24 Oct. 1849 paid Ester Mason $14.40, 25 July 1849 paid
Mary Mason $19.19 1/2, same date paid Kitty Mason $19.19 1/2, 1 Feb.
1845 Elijah Kees of Pickens Dist. saith that Elizabeth Cox was his
half sister and had a female illegimate child and when about three years
old she married James Mason and the child took the name of Nancy Mason
and when the child came to maturity she had a illegimate female child
Milinday and she married John Vills, Jr. and the said child Malinday
is about to try to become one of the heirs of Ambrose Mason decd. James
Bradberry of Habersham County, Ga. married a sister of Ambrose Mason.
Dated 17 Jan. 1842. William King of Anderson applied for letter of
admr.

Joel Mason. Estate of Joel Mason, Apt. 13 #148. Probate Judge
Office. Oconee Co., S. C. On 26 Sept. 1861 Frances Mason recd. $26.18
her share of her husband Joel Mason decd. estate. Heirs were: Milly
the wife of B. C. Whiseant, Mary W. the wife of Samuel Lyles, Martha Ann
the wife of D. L. Lyles, Charles W. Mason, all residents of Pickens
Dist. and of age except Charles Mason. Dated 19 Oct. 1859. Land Warrant
to Joel Mason. #96 Pack 114. Pickens Co., S. C. By Wm. L. Keith,
Clerk to any lawful surveyor you are authorize to lay out and admeasure
unto Joel Mason a tract of land not exceeding ten thousand acres.
Dated 24 July 1847. Executed 26 July 1847. Certified 5 Aug. 1847.

John W. Mason. Estate of John W. Mason. Apt. 84 #897. Probate Judge
Office. Oconee Co., S. C. Est. admr. 6 Dec. 1897 by Wallace W. Cornog,
W. C. Mason, J. R. Earl who are bound unto E. L. Herndon, Ord. Oconee
Co. in the sum of $518.00. John W. Mason died 9 Apr. 1897 in Franklin
Co., Ga. His widow was Julia Mason, chn. are John W. and Carry C.
Mason minors under 14 years. Had half interest in 128 acres known as
the Cleveland Place in Center Township. Oconee Co. Adj. land of
William Cleveland, B. J. Maret, Robert Isbell and E. C. Maret.

MASTERS

Thomas Masters, Jr. Estate of Thomas Masters, Jr. Box 3 #25. Probate
Judge Office. Pickens, S. C. Est. admr. 3 Jan. 1831 by Aaron Roper,
D. W. Glenn, Sargeant Griffin who are bound unto James H. Dendy, Ord.
in the sum of $1500. Sale held 26 Jan. 1831. Buyers D. W. Glenn, Wm.
Masters, Nathl. Collins, Noble Glenn, Tilmon, Aaron Roper, Wm. Chastain,
Simeon Burgess, Reuben Roper, Wm. Eliot, Davis Dowthit, Yearby Corbin,
Wm. Southerland, Hezekiah Anderson, Robert Dowthit, Catherine Masters
the widow, Wm. Stafford, Richard Masters, John Allen. He had 250 acres
of land on Saluda River that was sold in 1833. He left a widow and
three minors. Catherine Masters widow, Rosey Catherine, Austin Edward,
Amanda M. Masters minors under 14 years.

Masters Minors. Box 1 #18. Probate Judge Office. Pickens, S. C. On
1 April 1844 Matthew Keith, Allen Keith, Sr. are bound to James H.
Dendy, Ord. in the sum of $324.00. Mathew Keith gdn. of Rosey Masters,

Amanda Masters, Austin E. Masters minors over 14 years. Chn. of Thomas
Masters decd. (Loose papers) on 18 Mar. 1837 Wm. Masters and wife recd.
share from est. of William Allen decd.

MATHIS

Thomas E. Mathis. Thomas E. Mathis, Petition. Pack 239. Clerk of
Court Office. Abbeville, S. C. To the Honr. the Chancellors: The
petition of Thomas E. Mathis sheweth that he is a minor about 18 years
old. That his father Luke Mathis died many years ago and he being
entitled to a share of the estate. His mother Isabella Mathis was
appointed his gdn. and received his share of the est. His mother and
gdn. lately died intestate, and he is entitled to a share of her est.
He pray that his brother in law Charles B. Griffin be appointed his
gdn. Filed 13 June 1855.

MATTHEWS

John Matthews. Bill of account. Pack 230. Clerk of Court Office.
Abbeville, S. C. To the Honr. the Chancellors: Your oratrixes Elizabeth A. Matthews and Amarellir Crawford of the dist. aforesaid. On
30 Aug. 1859 John Matthews then the husband of your orator, did give,
transferred, paid and delivered to David O. Hawthorn five thousand
dollars in trust. "to have and to hold the same and to pay out the
interest annually to Elizabeth Matthews his wife during the term of her
natural life" and in further trust should the said Elizabeth survive
the said John Matthews, then at the death of Elizabeth to be paid out
to the brothers and sisters of Elizabeth at the time of her death, also
the chn. of Susan Martin a per decd. sister is to share equal. David
O. Hawthorn accepted the money, with S. W. Agnew and C. M. Sharp as
sureties, on the 25 Dec. 1859 executed the bond to secure the payment
of $350 annually and to secure the corpus of the trust. John Matthews
the donor was killed at the battle of Chickamingo, Ga. in Sept. 1863.
(Part of the bond torn) from another paper the legatees are: David
O. Hawthorn, Mary D. Pruitt, S. White Agnew, Toliver Johnson and wife
Jane, Wm. Hutchins and Constantine C. his wife, Thomas McIlwain,
Sallie A. Hawthorn, Drucilla Hawthorn, Arabella Hawthorn, Joseph L.
Hawthorn. Filed 25 April 1868.

John Matthews. Box 65 Pack 1586. Probate Judge Office. Abbeville,
S. C. I John Matthews being very sick in body, but of perfect mind.
I do leave to widow (two lines torn. In 1950 Miss Young copied this
record as widow Agness Calhoun) the use of my crockery ware, my china
set, cups and saucer, the use of milk cow until called for by my son
Isaac. I leave the remainder of my estate to my son Isaac. I appoint
my brother Isaac Matthew, Alexr. Noble as executors. Dated 21 Oct. 1793.
Wit: Wm. Colhoun Senr., Nancy Colhoun Senior. Signed John Matthews.
Recorded 25 March 1794. Majr. Alexr. Noble, James Noble, James
Milligan, William Clahoun, William Deal, this is to you or any three of
you to repair to all such places as directed by Isaac Matthews Executor
of John Matthews estate, to make a true and perfect inventory and
appraisement of the same etc. Dated 25 March 1794. Signed: James
Wardlaw, D.C.C. These were certified by Flm. Bates J.P. the 18 Apr.
1794.

Victor Matthews. Estate of Victor Matthews. Box 64 Pack 1550. Probate
Judge Office. Abbeville, S. C. I Victor Matthews being sick and weak
in body, but of perfect mind and memory, etc. I give to my beloved
wife Isable her third of the moveable estate and her living on the
land while a widow. Also I give to my three sons, John, James, Isaac
my land, with the remainder divided amongst my children that is
unmarried, the boys and girls to get alike, as to my married dtr.
Esther Ann, Elizabeth Rebekah, I leave five shillings each. I appoint
Isable and Joseph Matthews as executors. Dated 31 Dec. 1795. Wit:
William Weagworth, Samuel McNeily, Moses Edmiston. Signed: Victor

Matthews. Recorded 25 March 1796. To William Wedgworth, John Lumbis, John Irwin, John Conner, Thomas Pool, you or any three of you to repair unto all places as directed by Isable Matthews executrix. Dated 5 March 1796. Signed: James Wardlaw, D.C.C. The above appraisers were certified before. Charles Devenport, J.P. The inventory and appraisement was held 26 April 1796. With the sale on 24 April 1798. Buyers are: Isbel Matthews, David Black, John Fleming, Thomas Davis, James Fleming, James Campbell, Moses Edminston, Thomas Bartee, John Sims, William Brown, James Wedgworth, William Buchanan, Alexander Sample, Joseph McNeeley, John Wilson, Carr McGeehee, Robert Johnson Gulley, Thomas Cobb, Robert Buchanan, James Parker, Stephen Watson, John Blackburn, John Irwin, Isaac Logan.

Jane Matthews. Estate of Jane Matthews. Box 61 Pack 1432. Probate Judge Office. Abbeville, S. C. Whereas Josiah Crammer and Margret Chevas have applied to this Court for a letter of admr. of the est. of Jane Matthews as the next of kin. Dated 30 Oct. 1798. Signed James Wardlaw, D.C.C. Citation read at Rockey Spring Meeting House 28 Nov. 1798. To John Pettigrew, Andrew Weed, William Gray, Reuben Weed and Peter Tulton, you or any three of you are to repair to all places directed to by Josiah Crammer and Margret Chevas admr. of Jane Matthews decd. Dated 5 March 1799. Signed James Wardlaw, D.C.C. The inventory was held on the 13 April 1799, by Andrew Weed, John Pettigrew, William Gray...

Richard Matthews. Estate of Richard Matthews. Box 62 Pack 1475. Probate Judge Office. Abbeville, S. C. Admr. bond made to Lytteton Myrick as admr. with Samuel L. Watt, John Bowie, Jr. are bound unto Moses Taggart, Sr. Esq. Ord. in the sum of $1,000. Dated 17 Nov. 1823. The inventory and apprisement was made the 18 Nov. 1823 by Garland Chiles, William Collier, John W. Williams, Richard M. Todd. The sale was held 1 Jan. 1824 buyers are: Robert Chatham, John Sale, Jr., William Collier, James L. Mayson, Dudly Richardson, Charles S. Patterson, Elihu Creswell, James Wardlaw, Ira Griffin, Larkin Chiles, Seth Wilbourn, A. Steward, A. Sample, M. Holloway, William Eddins, C. C. Mayson, Jos. Griffin, James Coleman, John D. Williams, Albert Waller.

Joseph Matthews. Estate of Joseph Matthews. Box 109 Pack 3020. Probate Judge Office. Abbeville, S. C. I Joseph Matthews being sensible but sick in body, etc. I give to my beloved wife Rachel, two beds and furniture, also two cows and calves, also her living from my plantation during her natural life. With all tools for the farm and kitchen furniture, also one horse as she may want to cultivate some land afterward the horse to go to son David. I give son John one half of my tract of land, on which he now lives, the other half I give to son David. I give to my dtrs. Rachel, Elizabeth and Ann, five shillings each. I appoint my sons John and David as executors. Dated 15 Nov. 1832. Wit: J. E. Glenn, Jesse Calvert, Robert Buchanan. Signed: Joseph X Matthews. Will proved before Moses Taggart, Ord. by Jesse Calvert, on the 6 Dec. 1826.

John Matthews. Estate of John Matthews. Box 118 Pack 3489. Probate Judge Office. Abbeville, S. C. We David Matthews, William Truwit, J. C. Willard are bound unto David Lesly, Ord. in the sum of $500. Dated 10 Nov. 1848. That David Matthews admr. of the estate of John Matthews decd. to make a true and perfect inventory of said est. The petition of David Matthews sheweth that his son John Matthews died intestate, in Miss. without wife or children, having as his heirs at law your Pet. his father and two sisters, leaving in your petitioner hand a note of $251.11 as all his estate. Dated 27 Oct. 1848. One sister was Sarah Matthews and the other sister had married Wade Sutlesworth or Holligworth (written both ways).

John Matthews. Estate of John Matthews. Box 145 Pack 4115. Probate Judge Office. Abbeville, S. C. I John Matthews enjoying good health and of sound mind and memory. I do hereby give to my wife Nancy Matthews all my land and negroes and all other property I may have at my death, for her during her natural life, at her death to my dtr. Mary A. Dabbs, and the chn. of John Matthews Dabbs my grandson. Dated

10 Jan. 1858. Wit: Andrew Cobb, Joseph Milford, Martin Delany. Signed
John Matthews. Filed 20 Jan. 1858. [This name is written Mathis in
some places.] The inventory and appraisement was made 28 Jan. 1858.
Slaves named: Man Denis, Elbert a carpenter, boy Stephen, boy Addem,
woman Fanny, Lathy & two chn. Jimmy & Macknel, Hesteran & one child
Harvy, girl Ellen, girl America, girl Caroline.

MATTISON

Martha Mattison. Estate of Martha Mattison. Box 144 #11. Probate
Judge Office. Pickens, S.C. I, Martha S. Mattison being of sound
mind and memory... I desire and direct all my just debts be paid without delay. . . I give to my husband R. J. Mattison five dollars to be
paid by my executors, I give to my four children Floid O. Mattison,
Anny Mattison, Mary Caroline Mattison and Tecora Mattison all my
property both real and personal to be equal divided between them. My
real property consisting of one tract lying and being on twenty three
mile Creek in Pickens Co. containing 158 acres, deeded me by my husband
R. J. Matthews. I appoint my son Floid O. Matthews as executor. Dated
4 Aug. 1899. Wit: A. C. Sutherland, Kate Sutherland, W. L. Sutherland.
Signed: Martha S. Mattisson. Proven 20 June 1904. In Dec. 1905
Annie M. Cox recd. and Tekos M. Mattison recd. a share.

Daniel Mattison. Petition. Pack 353 #2. Clerk of Court Office.
Pickens, S.C. To the Honr. Chancellor. Your petitioner Daniel
Mattison sheweth that he is the guardian of William Southerland a
minor age thirteen years, John N. Southerland a minor age seven, and
Sarah Jane Southerland a minor age nine, whose parents are both dead.
Your petitioner sheweth that he is resident of Anderson Dist. his permanent place of abode, to make his annual return to this court causes him
much travel and expense and loss to time. He respectfully asks leave
of this Court to be transfered to the Anderson Dist. Court, and to make
his annual return to the Court of Equity of that Dist. Signed Daniel
Mattison. Filed 1 April 1861.

MAULDIN

Jane Mauldin. Estate of Jane Mauldin. Box 14 #177. Probate Judge
Office. Pickens, S.C. I Jane Mauldin being in common health and of
sound mind and memory, etc. I give to my son Samuel Mauldin one
feather bed and furniture, with the addition of one Marsails quilt to
it. I give to my son Benjamin Franklin Mauldin one feather bed and
furniture with the addition of Marsails quilt to it. I give to my son
James Lawrence Mauldin one feather bed and furniture with the addition
of two figured counterpains to it. I give to my son Joab Mauldin one
feather bed and furniture with the addition of two figured counterpains.
I have given the balance of my children (not named) at various times
as much as I intend them to have. I appoint my two sons Samuel &
Benjamin Mauldin as executors. Dated 31 Aug. 1835. Wit: Sarah
M. Roberts, Jane E. Liddell, Jno. Watson. Signed: Jain X Mauldin.
Proved by John Watson before Jas. H. Dendy, Ord. on the 27 Nov. 1843.
The est. was settled and legatees paid 7 Jan. 1845.

Milton Mauldin. In Equity. #35 Clerk of Court Office. Pickens, S.C.
To the Honr. Chancellors: Your orator Joab Mauldin sheweth that Milton
Mauldin the father of your orator departed this life the 4 July 1860
intestate. He having five tracts of land to wit, #1 The Norton tract
containing 354 acres, adj. land of Lot Kennemore, Joel Bradley James
McCollum... #2 Known as the Dover tract of 81 acres, adj. land of Lot
& Elias Kennemore, A. R. Taylor... #3 Known as the Gillstrap tract of
50 acres, adj. land of John Ryal, A. R. Taylor and the Norton tract.
Known as the Kennemore tract of 40 acres, #5 known as the Moses
Kennemore tract of 134 acres. The land is subject to distribution
among the heirs. viz. Sarah Mauldin the widow, Martha O. the wife of

Jeremiah Looper, Loretta the wife of James B. Hester, Joab (your orator) Elbert, Wm. A., Samuel, Elias E., Perrin, Sarah E. Mauldin. The last six are minors under the age of 21 years. That the personal property will be greatly more than to meet all just debts and demand. He prays for a partition of the land, and that guardian ad litem may be appointed for the minors. Filed 16 Aug. 1860.

William P. Mauldin. Land Warrant for William P. Mauldin. Pack 630 #8. Clerk of Court Office. Pickens, S. C. By J. E. Hagood, clerk, to any lawful surveyor you are authorize to lay out unto William Mauldin & Fenton H. Hall a tract of land not to exceed one thousand acres. Dated 22 Sept. 1859. Executed 24 Sept. 1859 for 764 acres. Filed 29 Oct. 1859.

Joab Mauldin. Deed of Joab Mauldin. Box 130 #4. Probate Judge Office. Pickens, S. C. This deed from Joab Mauldin to Thomas Henderson both of Pendleton Dist. Dated 29 May 1817. In the sum of $475 do sell, grant, bargain, release all that tract of land lying on the South side of Little Georges Creek containing eighty acres. Conveyed to me by heirs of James Duff decd. known as the Mize place, adj. land of Archibald Mahans, Thomas Henderson or his son John. Wit: Samuel A. Easley, Jane L. Briggs. Signed: J. Mauldin.

Tyre B. Mauldin. Land Warrant for Tyre B. Mauldin. #147. Clerk of Court Office. Pickens, S. C. By W. L. Keith, Clerk, to any lawful surveyor, you are authorize to lay out unto Tyre B. Mauldin & Joseph Fricks a tract of land not exceeding one thousand acres. Dated 22 March 1852. Executed for 88 acres, 26 March 1852. Certified 29 March 1852.

Milton Mauldin. Estate of Milton Mauldin. Box 55 #596. Probate Judge Office. Pickens, S. C. Est. admr. 6 Aug. 1860 by Joab Mauldin, Perrin Odell, Robert A. Thompson who are bound unto W. E. Holcombe, Ord. in the sum of $12,000. Mrs. Sarah Mauldin the widow. Heirs: Martha O. the wife of Jeremiah Looper, Lucetta, the wife of James B. Hester, William A. Mauldin, Elias E. Mauldin, Perrin Mauldin, Sarah Mauldin were ordered to appear at the Court house for a final settlement on 15 Dec. 1863.

Mauldin Minors. In Equity, Box 3 #62. Clerk of Court Office. Pickens, S.C. On 15 Dec. 1863 Joab Mauldin, Jeremiah Looper, W. N. Craig are bound to Robt. A. Thompson, C. in E. in the sum of $4,200. Joab Mauldin Guardian of Perrin Mauldin, Sarah E. Mauldin minors under 21 years. Joab Mauldin their brother. On 19 Apr. 1873 Wm. J. Smith, Thos. H. Smith, Joab Mauldin are bound unto I. H. Philpot, Ord. in the sum of $1170.00. William J. Smith her husband, and gdn. of Sarah E. Smith a minor under 21 years. nee Mauldin.

Mauldin Minors. In Equity, Box 3 #64. Clerk of Court Office. Pickens, S. C. On 15 Dec. 1863 Jeremiah Looper, Joab Mauldin, James E. Hagood, are bound to Robert A. Thompson, C. in E. in the sum of $4200.00. Jeremiah Looper gdn. of William A. Mauldin, Elias E. Mauldin minors under 21 years. Jemeriah Looper their brother in law and lived in Wolf Creek, S.C. The minors were over 12 years.

Tyre B. Mauldin. Land Warrants of Tyre B. Mauldin. #113 & 126. Clerk of Court Office. Pickens, S. C. By W. L. Keith, Clerk, to any lawful surveyor you are authorized to lay out a tract of land unto Tyre B. Mauldin & James Cox #113 not exceeding one thousand acres. Dated 5 Oct. 1849. Executed for 503 acres, and certified the 17 Nov. 1849. #126 to Mauldin only, dated 10 March 1850. Executed for 289 acres. 14 March 1850. Date certified not given.

Joseph G. Mauldin. Estate of Joseph G. Mauldin. Box 72 #767. Probate Judge Office. Pickens, S. C. Est. admr. 30 Oct. 1863 by Sarah Ann Mauldin widow, W. N. Craig, James E. Hagood who are bound unto W. E. Holcombe, ord. in the sum of $500.00.

Mauldins. Notes on Mauldins. Box 52. #568. Probate Judge Office.

Pickens, S. C.   Advancements were made to Deborah R. Hollingsworth now
Mauldin by James J. Hollingsworth whose est. was admr. the 7 Nov. 1859
in Pickens Co., S.C.   Real estate book B, page 94.   Probate Judge Office.
Pickens, S. C.   On 27 Nov. 1865 Josephine A. Mauldin the wife of Andrew
Mauldin was the dtr. of Sarah Chapman decd. of Pickens Co., S. C.

Elbert Mauldin.   Estate of Elbert Mauldin.   Box 72 #766.   Probate Judge
Office.   Pickens, S. C.   Est. admr. 7 Dec. 1863 by Joab Mauldin,
Jeremiah Looper, James B. Hester who are bound unto W. E. Holcombe,
Ord. in the sum of $4,000.   Paid 15 Dec. 1863 J. Looper expenses bring-
ing remains home from Virginia $144.25.   left 8 heirs... names not given.

Godfrey Mauldin.   Estate of Godfrey Mauldin.   Box 74 #787.   Probate
Judge Office.   Pickens, S. C.   Est. admr. 18 Dec. 1863 by Mathew Mansell,
R. E. Holcombe, B. F. Morgan who are bound unto W. E. Holcombe, Ord.
in the sum of $4,000.   On 7 Oct. 1867 Mathew Mansell & wife recd.
$40.03.   On 29 Feb. 1864 Sarah Hughes recd. $160.30.   Was grandfather
of Alfred Mauldin, Mariah J. Leath.

Godfrey Mauldin.   Box 94 #988.   Probate Judge Office.   Pickens, S. C.
On 31 Oct. 1866 owned 164 acres situated on the line of Pickens &
Anderson Dists.   Adj. land of Joel Ellison & others.   Heirs James
Mauldin, John McClanahan & wife Fannie Mauldin a sister of said decd.
had the following chn. Reuben Garvin, Elias Kimsey, John Godfrey,
Auora Elizabeth, William Harrison McClanahan whom all determined to
seek homes in the West or South West, left their father in 1870 in Coffee
Co., Tenn. and first settled in Arkansas then afterward to Duncan,
Missouri thence to Clarksville, Arkansas thence to Guess Honi, Texas,
and their mother being unwilling to be separated from her children left
her husband and went West with them.   John McClanahan being unwilling
to sacrifice his property remained at his home in Tenn. and altho for
several years he heard from them regularly, yet for the past 10 years
notwithstanding his frequent letters to them and also to others in their
neighborhood he has been wholly unable to hear from or learn anything
of them in consequence of which he has been induced to believe, that they
have died or gone to parts unknown and when last heard from in the fall
of 1875 they were residing at or near Robbinsville Post Office, Guess,
Prarie, Texas.   19 Feb. 1887 Mary S. White, Gilla Mauldin, J. W. Mauldin,
A. N. Stone of Douglass County, Ga. were heirs of Godfrey Mauldin,
Mary S. White a niece, Gilla Mauldin being the widow of John W. Mauldin
who was a nephew, A. N. Stone being the husband of S. E. Mauldin decd.
who was a niece of Godfrey Mauldin.   Jane Wood decd. a sister and her
heir Isaac N. Wood, Godfrey Wood, Jane Wood, Fanny Wood, Sarah Hughes.
Heirs of Taliaferro Mauldin and heir of Francis Mauldin, not incorporated
in petition making 8 heirs in all.   John McClanahan states that he was
72 years old the 28 Sept. 1885, by occupation a farmer, native of S. C.
and lived there until he went to Tenn. in the fall of 1851.   I was
married to Fannie Mauldin on Thursday before Xmas 1839.   Her parents were
both dead when I became acquainted with her, they said her father's
name was John Mauldin.   We had fiven chn. Reuben Gardin both the fall
of 1840, Elias Kimsey born the fall of 1842, as well as I recollect.
John Godfrey born 1845, Ann Elizabeth I think she was born in 1849.
William Harrison born in Tenn. in 1852.   All the others were born in
S. C.   Mary Jane born in 1855.   Franklin born in 1847.   I relate the
age from memory, at home I have a dim record, which I neglected to bring
with me, not knowning their age were wanting.   None of my family are
with me, they left me in the fall of 1870, they went to Blufton, Ark.
where they remained in 1871-72 thence to Missouri in 1873 Duncan being
their P. O. they moved back to Ark. near Clarksville in 1874 thence that
fall to Texas and lived that year in Texas 1875 and after that lost
sight of them and have not heard of them since.   The boys the older
ones were of age and the country being poor barren where we lived they
were desirous of going West and improving their condition.   These were
the only reason for leaving me.   I last heard from them at Robinsville,
Texas in 1875 and they were all there as far as I know, they had not
separated.   At that time John wrote that he was going to tend about 50
acres in corn and cotton.   Mary Jane and Franklin died in the fall of
1861 in about 10 days of each other.   In the fall of 1875 John wrote
that they were not satisfied & was going to leave but had not decided

where they would go to. I was to sick to answer, latter in the fall I
wrote a reply but have never heard from them. I wrote to the P. M.
at Robinsville various times but never recd. any reply and have not got
any letter from them or any news. I never treated my wife crudelly
or bad, she left because she wanted to be with her chn. There has never
been any application by me for divorce from the bonds of matrimony or
from bed and board, nor has she ever applied either so far as I know.
James C. Davis being 40 years of age, farmer and who have lived in
Coffee Co., Tenn. states that he have known John McClanahan 27 years and
for 25 years had lived in a quarter of a mile of him, the other two
years lived further apart. Isaiah Fleming age 56 years who lived in
Manchester, Coffee Co., Tenn. a machanic had lived there about 45 years
and states that he knew John McClanahan about 30 years. For 28 years
lived within one mile and a half of him. Have lived in Manchester about
7 or 8 miles of him. (The above deposition was copied as Miss Young
has written, by, when, where she does not show, may be in the Godfrey
Mauldin material in Pickens Co. C. H.)

Joab Mauldin. Estate of Joab Mauldin. Box 130 #4. Probate Judge
Office. Pickens, S. C. Est. admr. 30 Dec. 1897 by J. M. Mauldin,
J. MD. Bruce, J. J. Lewis who are bound unto J. B. Newberry, Ord. in the
sum of $2,000. Died 30 Nov. 1897. J. M. Mauldin a son.

Mauldin Minors. Box 126 #2. Probate Judge Office. Pickens, S. C. On
13 Nov. 1895 E. E. Mauldin, A. M. Mauldin, A. M. Norris, W. S. Lewis
who are bound unto J. B. Newberry, Ord. in the sum of $75.00. E. E.
Mauldin guardin of Nannie Mauldin et al. Nannie Mauldin 18 years,
Sallie Mauldin 17 years, Earl Mauldin 16 years, Eliza Mauldin 14 years,
Willie Mauldin 12 years, children of E. E. Mauldin. Their mother nee
Ellen Anderson is dead. Entitled to share of est. from their ancestor
Freeman Lay the executor of whom resides in Canton, Ga. where est. is
situated. (In one paper Willie is written William.)

William J. Mauldin. Deed of William J. Mauldin. Pack 225 #3. Clerk of
Court Office. Pickens, S. C. This deed between William J. Mauldin of
the County of Jackson West Florida and Thornton Benson of Pickens Dist.,
S.C. Dated 21 Feb. 1831. In consideration of sixteen hundred dollars,
do sell, bargain, release all that tract of land lying on the South
fork of George Creek it being part of the tract of land owned by
Joab Mauldin which fell to William J. in a division of estate of Joab
Mauldin containing 553 1/2 acres. Adj. land of Henderson Maverick,
Huff Easley and others. Wit: Francis M. Mauldin, Robert Bowen.
Attested by Robert Bowen before James Osborn J. Q. on the 27 July 1831.
On the 14 Dec. 1833 Martha L. Mauldin the wife of William J. Mauldin,
released, renounce, and forever relinquish all her rights, and interest
or claim of dower on the land... before James Osborn, J.Q.

                            MAXWELL

John Maxwell. Estate of John Maxwell. Box 65 Pack 1568. Probate Judge
Office. Abbeville, S. C. I John Maxwell of Abbeville Dist. being
frail in body, yet being in my perfect senses, judgment, mind and
memory, etc. I will and ordain all my just debts be punctual paid. I
will and give to my wife Jane Maxwell, all the plantation I now live
on, and all I possess on said land. During her widowhood or life time.
If she remarries she to have as the law provides. I also will and
ordain that a tract of land lying at or near the Golden Grove in
Greenville Co., S. C. be sold and the price used to purchase slaves
to work on the plantation I now live on, for the support of my dear wife
Jane. I will that none of my moveable property be disposed of or give
away during her life or widowhood. After the death of my wife I give
to my eldest son Robert Maxwell, oldest son John Maxwell the value of
ten pds. in property. I give to my son George Maxwell the plantation
whereon I now live to him and his heirs forever, also the expenses of
one year schooling in the (torn). . . I will and give to my son
Charles Maxwell the tract of land containing 200 acres, lying in the

County of Laurens, where John Williamson did live to him and his heirs
forever. I will and give to my son William Maxwell five shillings, I
also leave it to my executors to give him more if his behaviour deserves.
I give to my dtr. Sarah one horse and one saddle at her marriage. I
give to my dtr. Nancy one horse. I will and give all my estate of stock
and household and kitchen furniture to my sons John, Hugh and George,
and my dtr. Nancy and Sally if of good behaviour at their Mother's
decease. I appoint my trusty friend Robert Maxwell, Jane Maxwell, and
Robert Sloane as executrix and executors. Dated 25 Aug. 1792. Wit:
John Stephens, Robert Sloane, Thomas Shirley Marfret X Stephens.
Signed: John Maxwell. Will was proven by Robert Sloane on the 16
Dec. 1806 before Andrew Hamilton O.A.D. Again by Thomas Shirley on
5 Jan. 1808 before Andrew Hamilton, O.A.D. Est. appraisers were John
Finley, Dr. Thomas Taylor, Edm. Ware, and made the 13 Jan. 1807.

John Maxwell. Land Warrant of John Maxwell. #114. Clerk of Court
Office. Pickens, S. C. From W. L. Keith, Clerk, to any lawful surveyor
you are authorized to lay out a tract of land unto John Maxwell a tract
of land not exceeding ten thousand acres Dated 27 Feb. 1843. Executed
for one thousand acres 22 Apr. 1843. Certified 23 Apr. 1843.

MAY

John May. Will of John May. Vol. 10, page 730. Probate Judge Office.
Charleston, S. C. I, John May, of Edisto Island, being very sick in
body but of perfect and sound mind and memory, etc. First I will my
just debts and funeral expenses be paid. I will that my negro wench
Pegg be kept to attend my son William May during his minority. I will
all the rest except my wearing apparel be sold at public sale, and the
money put out on interest to be given to my son William when he arrive
at the age of twenty one years, and not before. If he dies before
arriving at the age of 21, my whole estate to be equal divided between
my beloved Mother Martha May and my sister Martha Seabrook. I appoint
my brother in law Benjamin Seabrook, executor. Dated 23 Sept. 1765.
Wit: Andrew Townsend, Sam. Roberson, Kanaway Norton. Signed: John
May. Proved 25 Oct. 1765.

Martha May. Will of Martha May. Vol. 15, page 362. Probate Judge
Office. Charleston, S. C. I Martha May of Edisto Island in Colleton
Co., S. C. widow, being sick and weak in body but of perfect and sound
mind and memory. I give to my sister Charity Russell the sum of
sixty pds. current money of the province. I give unto Christopher
Koon one negro boy named Sambo when he come to the age of twenty one.
I give unto Elizabeth Koon one negro girl named Subina and all my
wearing apparel, one feather bed, one bolster, two pillows, one pr.
sheets and one blanket when she arrives at the age of eighteen or marry.
All the rest of my estate be sold at public vendue, and pay my just
debts and funeral expenses. The remainder to be divided into halves
one half to be put on interest for Christopher and Elizabeth Koon, this
half to be divided between them. The other half I give to all my grand
children to be divided between them. I appoint my friend Benjamin
Seabrook and Kannaway Norton executors. Dated 11 Nov. 1772. Wit:
Andrew Townsend, Abraham Bush. Signed: Martha May. Proved 8 Jan.
1773. Kannaway Norton execr.

James May. Will of James May. Vol. 11, page 68. Probate Judge Office.
Charleston, S. C. I James May being sick and weak but of perfect sense
and memory, etc. I give to my two sons John May and James May a tract
of land containing 350 acres to be equal divided between them by my
executors, which land I now live on. I give to my son John one bed and
furniture, likewise to my son James. I give to my three chn. John, Lucy
and James all my stock of cattle, hogs and horses to be equally divided
between them. I give to my dtr. Lucy one bed and furniture. I give
to my wife the plantation which I live on during her widowhood and
after all my just debts are paid. I appoint my wife Elizabeth May as
executrix and John Thomas Junr. my executor. Dated 15 Apr. 1767.
Wit: Thomas Taylor, Nathan X Mils, Martha X Taylor. Signed: James May.
Proven 11 May 1767.

John May. Will of John May. Vol. 27, page 867. Probate Judge Office. Charleston, S. C. I John May of Chyhaw, planter, St. Bartholomew's Parish, do make this my last will and testament. To my nephew James Graves I give my riding horse and double barrel gun. To Mrs. Elizabeth Anson, I leave the use of the house free of rent during her life time. I do emancipate and make free my two negroes Nancy and her dtr. Mary. I give to my son Henry William May (alias) Henry William McGuire my whole estate both real and personal forever. In case he should die before he attains seventeen years, at which time I make him of age, and take possession of my whole estate, if he should die before he attains seventeen years. I give to Mary McGuire the following negroes. Negro man and his wife Betty with their chn. Limus, Sally, Harry. Also Hannable and his wife Cumbo and their chn. Affey, Daniel, Fortune. Also Mingo and wench Rachel. Also my gray horse, my chesnut horse called Jim, with a mare called Nancy with one half of my stock of cattle, sheep, hogs with the household and kitchen furniture. I do emancipate and make free my negro carpenter fellow Will. If Henry William McGuire should die, my nephew James Graves shall have the whole estate after taking out the above legacies. I appoint my friend Mary McGuire, executrix to my est. during her widowhood and I further appoint my nephew James Graves and friend Philip Smith executors. Dated 14 Dec. 1798. Wit: John Minott, Barnet Cohen, Robert Scott. Signed: John May. Proved 1 Aug. 1799.

James May, Senr. Will of James May, Senr. Vol. 27, page 733. Probate Judge Office. Charleston, S. C. I James May Senr. of Edisto River, Charleston Dist... being of sound mind and memory, etc. I give to my beloved wife Patty May my plantation whereon I now live, also the tract I bought from Joell Spell both containing 400 acres, also all negroes, stock of every kind, household and kitchen furniture I may possess at the time of my decease, reserving enough for the education and maintain-ance of my children during their minority. After the death or marriage of my wife and my youngest son becomes of age, the same shall be divided in the following manner. I give to my son John May the land that as my wife, to him and his heirs forever. If John dies without issue the land is to go to my son Robert May. I give to my son Redden May my negro man named Stephen. I give to my son Jacob May twenty five pds. sterling at the division of my est. I give to my son James May my negro named Jacob. I give to my son Robert May my negro named Will. I give to my son John May my negro named Abner. I give to my dtr. Mary Ratliff my negro wench named Nancy, and her child called Rose. I give to my dtr. Patty May my negro wench named Roda, and her child named Rachell. As to the other negroes I may have at time of my decease to be equal divided between all my chn. except my son Jacob May. I give to my son Reddin May a tract of land containing 200 acres lying and being on the North side of Boxes Branch being part of a tract of 400 acres whereon said Reddin May now lives. I give to my son Robert May the other half of said tract, to him and his heirs forever. If any of my children die before my wife, their share to be equal divided except unto Jacob May. I here by enjoin and require my wife and executors hereafter named to give my youngest children sufficient and necessary education. I appoint my wife Executrix and my son James May and my friend Joseph Rogers and Daniel H. Milhouse executors. Dated 28 Dec. 1796. Wit: John Moore, Charles DeWitt, William X Crafford. Signed James X May, Senr. Proved 13 Aug. 1798.

John May. Will of John May. Vol. 46, page 339. Probate Judge Office. Charleston, S. C. I John May being now of sound mind and memory, but sick in body, etc. First I will all my lawful debts and funeral expen-ses be paid. I will unto my dear wife Mrs. Margaret May one third of my estate both real and personal and to my two dear chn. John and Eliza May the balance of my estate, that is the other two thirds. It is my last will that it is properly and honestly executed. I appoint the Rev. P. O'Neill my lawful executor. Dated 21 Dec. 1853. Wit: James Hewley, Peter Lee, Patrick X May. Signed: John May. Proved before George Buist, Esq. O.C.D. 7 Dec. 1853.

John May. Will of John May. Vol. 48, page 502. Probate Judge Office. Charleston, S. C. I John May do hereby make this my last will and testament, etc. I give to my son James W. May, my house and lot at #3 Liberty Street. One hundred and five shares in the fireman ins. Co., one bond from Theo. S. Gourdin for one thousand five hundred dollars secured by mortgage on lot in Meeting Street and one thousand dollars in cash. I give to my mother and sister during their natural life the interest on thirty shares on the Bank of Charleston, old issue, at their death to go to son James W. May. I give to my wife, one lot #62 on Queen Street, one lot and house and house # 64 Queen Street, One lot on Sullivans Island and seven servants viz; Quash and his wife Mary, Eliza Bachus, Isaac, Charley and Morris. I give to my wife 480 shares in the Farmer and Exchange Bank during her natural life, then to my son James W. May. I appoint my wife executrix and son James W. May and J. Seigling, Jr. executors. Dated 11 July 1856. Wit: H. L. Pickney, W. J. Laval, John B. Gray. Signed: John May. Proved 8 Aug. 1859.

Margaret May. Will of Margaret May. Vol. 49, page 565. Probate Judge Office. Charleston, S. C. This is the last will and testament of Margaret May widow, I give to my friend Catherine R. Mood wife of John R. Mood my house and lot on Norman St. with my feather bed, pillows, and bolster. The house and lot between Comming and Saint Philip St. to be sold and all my just debts and funeral expenses paid. I give to Sprint Street Church twenty five dollars, twenty five dollars to the Sabath school, twenty five dollars to conference, and twenty five to the missionary. The balance of the money be divided between my friends Josephine Hyder, Elizabeth C. Arnold, Susan A. Ayers, and Elizabeth Jones the wife of John H. Jones and Ann H. Bradley. I give to Ann H. Bradley a half dozen silver spoons. I appoint my friends John H. Jones and John R. Mood, executors. Dated 16 Aug. 1859. Wit: H. F. Borneman, R. W. Dunning, Peter F. Dunning. Signed: Margaret May. Proved 22 Nov. 1859.

Laura J. May. Will of Laura J. May. Box 92 #4588. Probate Judge Office. York Co., S. C. I, Laura J. May of York Co. do declare this my last will and testament. I will all my property to my four children Annie B., Blanche, Charlie, and Mary Ann May to share and share alike, subject to the trust and power given to my executor. He to sell, use dispose of any of my estate to benefit my children. I appoint my beloved brother William M. Frew to have guardianship custody, and tuition of each of my chn. and the management and possession of their estate during their minority, and that he shall exercise the utmost deligence and care in and about the moral and education of each. I appoint my brother William M. Frew as my executor. Dated 20 Aug. 1885. Wit: W. B. Wilson, Fred H. London, Hattie May. Signed: Laura J. X May. Proved 26 Oct. 1885.

William S. May. Estate of William S. May. Box 27 #1152. Probate Judge Office. York Co., S. C. Est. admr. 27 Oct. 1854 by Alexander F. Fewell, Alexander Powell and Archibald J. Barron who are bound unto John M. Ross, Ord. in the sum of $20,000. Martha Ann the wife of A. F. Fewell his dtr. On 27 Aug. 1863 paid Mrs. A. May in part her share of est. $135. . . On 15 Jan. 1857 paid Arabella May her share of $4441.44 who was also the guardian of Mary J. May, R. T. May, H. L. May and W. S. May each who received $1480.48 as their share.

May Minors. Box 107 #4895. Probate Judge Office. York Co., S. C. On 11 Mar. 1890 Charles W. Frew, S. S. Frew, S. T. Frew who are bound unto the Ord. in the sum of $11,500. Charles Frew the guardian of Blanche May, Charles May and Mary May who are minors over the age of 14 years.

Samuel Mays. Will of Samuel Mays. Box 106 #8. Probate Judge Office. Orangeburg Co., S. C. Will probated in 1899. Wife: Patsy Mays. Wit: Thos. H. Tatum, W. P. Brunson, J. W. Bowman.

James M. Mays. et al. Box 36 #13. In Equity. Clerk of Court Office. Spartanburg, S. C. Whereas James M. Mays, Robert L. Mays, Elizabeth P.

Mays and Lelia Mays the widow of Thomas G. Mays decd. Complainants
filed their bill in the Court of Equity in Sptg. Dist. against Emily C.
Mays infant dtr. of Thomas G. Mays for a partition of the real estate
of Matthew Mays decd. consisting of 260 acres in one tract joining lands
of George Storey, Edward Carroll. Dated 25 Nov. 1854. Matthew Mays
died 21 Apr. 1841. His chn. were: Robert L. Mays, James M. Mays,
Elizabeth P. Mays, Emily C. Mays infant dtr. of Thomas G. Mays decd.
Matthew Mays during his life time deeded to James M. Mays and Thomas G.
Mays a tract of land of 80 acres each.

Caleb Mays. Real Estate. Book A, page 38. Probate Judge Office.
Pickens. I, Martha M. Mays, wife of Caleb Mays decd. having no bodily
heirs, being the main heir, do petition this Court for a sale of the
land belonging to Caleb Mays decd. Dated 4 June 1839. In Equity.
Martha M. Mays, applicant vizt. Horace Naremore & Caleb Babbitt,
defendants (relation not given). Land to be sold, 600 acres on the
Walton ford road leading from Pickens C. H. to Clarksville, Ga. known
as Double Cabins. 281 acres lying on Battle Creek granted to Caleb
Mays. 100 acres granted to James Doran and sold to Caleb. 81 acres
on Brass town Creek. Dated 9 Sept. 1839. Jas. H. Dendy, Ord.

Meedy Mays, Jr. Estate of Meedy Mays, Jr. Pack 347. Clerk of Court
Office. Abbeville, S. C. To the Honr. Chancellors; Your oratrix Mary
Elizabeth Mays sheweth that Meedy Mays, Jr. lately her husband, departed
this life on the 11 Jan. 1849 leaving as heirs, your oratrix the widow
and two chn. John Mathew Mays about four years old and Lucretia Ann
Mays about two years old. At the time of his death he was possessed
with a tract of land containing four hundred acres on Saluda River, adj.
land of Capt. J. W. Warem, George Higgins, Robert Smith. Admr. of the
decd. est has been granted to Larkin Mays and Henry Mays. Filed 21 May
1850.

Meedy Mays. Deed to Meedy Mays. (No ref.) Abbeville Dist., S. C.
Deed from John Williams to Meedy Mays. Dated 17 Nov. 1843. In consideration of $220 do sell, bargain, grant, release all that tract of land
containing 40 acres, lying on Little Mulberry Creek waters of Saluda
River, adj. land of William Pope, Greyham and Hoskinson. Wit: John C.
Waters, John C. Fowler, Signed: John Williams, Rebecca X Williams
relinquish all dower as the wife.

Meedy Mays. Deed to Meedy Mays. (No ref.) Abbeville Dist., S. C.
Deed from Larkin Mays. Dated 12 July 1845. In consideration of $100
do sell, bargain, grant and release to Meedy Mays all my part of that
tract of land lying and being on Little & Big Mulberry Creek waters of
Saluda River containing forty or forty five acres. Adj. land of
William Pope and John Williams, on the North side of the road that leads
to Smith bridge. Wit: Thos. Rosamond and John Rosamond. Signed:
Larkin Mays.

Meedy Mays. Deed to Meedy Mays. (No ref.) Abbeville Dist., S. C.
Deed from William Pope to Meedy Mays. Dated 17 Nov. 1844. In consideration of $214 do sell, grant, bargain and release all that tract
of land containing fifty acres lying on Little Mulberry Creek, waters
of Saluda River. Adj. land of Meedy and Larkin Mays, George Higans,
Robert Smith, John Williams. Wit: John Williams, John C. Waters.
Signed: William Pope. Margret X Pope signed as the wife and relinquish
her dower to the land the 27 Nov. 1844.

Meedy Mays. Deed to Meedy Mays. (No ref.) Abbeville Dist., S. C.
Deed from James Graham son of Will. Dated 13 Nov. 1844. In con-
sideration of $750 do sell, bargain, grant and release to Meedy Mays
all that tract of land lying on Little and big Mulberry Creek waters of
Saluda River. Containing 225 acres. Adj. land of George Higens,
James Graham son of James John Huskerson and John Williams. Wit:
Thos. Rosamond, Elihu Campbell. Signed: James Graham, Senr.
Thursey X Grayham the wife of James Graham relinquish her rights of
dower on the 12 Dec. 1844.

Meedy & Larkin Mays. Deed to Meedy & Larkin Mays. (No. ref.)
Abbeville Dist., S. C. Deed from George Pope. Dated 4 Nov. 1843.
In consideration of $200 do sell, grant, bargain and release to Meedy
& Larkin Mays all that tract of land lying on Little and Big Mulberry
Creek waters of Saluda River, containing forty or forty five acres.
Adj. land of Beachams, William Pope. Wit: Thos. Rosamond, Samuel
Graham. Signed: George Pope--Mary X Pope the wife of George Pope who
relinquish her dower to the land the 17 Nov. 1843. In another deed
James Graham is said to be the son of William Graham Senr. and the deed
was witnessed by Wm. Graham, Jr. Dated 9 Nov. 1839.

Thomas Mayes. Will of Thomas Mayes. Box 3 Pack 26. Probate Judge
Office. Union, S. C. I Thomas Mayes of Union Co., S. C. Being weak
in body but of perfect mind and memory, etc. First I will my just
debts and funeral expenses be paid. I will to my son Thomas Mayes
the whole of my blacksmith shop and tools. I will that my son John
Mayes shall be paid twenty pds. sterling by my son Edward Mayes who is
to have the plantation whereon I now live, with the crops that is upon
the ground, on condition of him paying the twenty pds. to Thomas. The
remainder of my estate to be equal divided between the whole of my chn.
Margaret, Thomas, John, Edward, Jane and Elizabeth Mayes. I appoint
James Meane, Senr. and my sons Thomas and Edward the executors. Dated
26 Aug. 1797. Wit: Samuel Clowney, Henry White, James Mayes. Signed:
Thomas Mayes. The above will was proved by oath of Samuel Clowney the
11 Dec. 1801, before Jas. W. Woodson, Clerk. Thos. Brandon.

Edward Mayes. Will of Edward Mayes. Box 24 #24. Probate Judge Office.
Union, S. C. I Edward Mayes, of Union Dist. being of sound mind and
memory, etc. I desire a portion of my estate, as the family think best,
be sold and pay my just debts and funeral expenses. I give to my dtr.
Dorcas one sorrel colt, one bed and furniture and a burrow. I give to
my dtr. Sarah one burrow and one bed and furniture. I give to my son
Samuel one bay colt. My two bound children Munrow and Sarahann I want
my wife to have the care of and the benefit of them. The rest of my
estate both real and personal I leave to my dear wife Rachel during
her life. At her death the whole to be divided between John, Dorcas,
Sarah, and Samuel. I appoint my son John executor and Dorcas as executrix. Dated 24 Sept. 1838. Wit: William Long, John H. Roundtree,
Alexander Campbell. Signed: Edward Mayes. Will proved on oath of
Wm. Long, Esq. before J. J. Pratt, Ord. on the 5 Nov. 1838.

Robert P. Mayes. Will of Robert P. Mayes. Bundle 175 #15. Probate
Judge Office. Sumter, S. C. I Robert Peterson Mayes being daily
reminded by failing health of body, I do whilst yet of sound mind and
memory, etc. I appoint my wife Caroline J. Mayes, my son James E.
Mayes and son in law Edward B. Muldrow to be my ___. First I desire my
executors sell enough to pay in full my debts. I will and bequeath
all my estate both real and personal and to be sole heir during her life
time, with full power to distribute the estate among the children (not
named) during her life time or after her death. Dated 17 Oct. 1881.
Wit: M. P. Mayes, Sr., R. A. Chandler, Jr., F. J. Mayes. Signed:
Robert P. Mayes. Filed 28 Feb. 1882.

Matthew P. Mayes. Will of Matthew P. Mayes. Bundle 173 #5. Probate
Judge Office. Sumter, S. C. I Matthew Peterson Mayes of Sumter Co.
In view of my advanced age and the certainty of death and whilst my
mental powers are yet sound and my reason unimpaired, etc. I do hereby
enjoin it upon my executors hereinafter named to settle my worldly
affairs according to the terms and specifications herein set forth.
I give to my four dtrs. Mrs. Mary H. Cooper, Mrs. Margaret E. Bethune,
Mrs. Sarah J. Grant, Mrs. Frances A. Burgess the sum of four hundred
dollars each. I give to my three sons, James A. Mayes, Robert P. Mayes,
and Thomas A. Mayes the sum of two hundred dollars each. I give to my
wife Martha M. Mayes my Piano Forte and one hundred dollars, to be paid
from the funds on hand. The balance of my estate both real and personal,
and of every kind, I give to my son Matthew Peterson Mayes and to my
wife Martha M. Mayes, to be theirs jointly during her life time, then
to my son Matthew P. Mayes for his sole use and benefit. I appoint Dr.

Thomas L. Burgess and Matthew P. Mayes my lawful executors. Dated 28
May 1872. Wit: J. W. Hudson, J. E. Atkins, H. M. Reames. Signed:
Matw. P. Mayes. Recorded 19 Dec. 1878. Matthew Mayes died about 1
Nov. 1878.

Caroline J. Mayes. Will of Caroline J. Mayes. Bundle 180 #16. Probate
Judge Office. Sumter, S. C. The last W & T of me Caroline J. Mayes
of Sumter Co., S. C. Being daily reminded of the uncertainty of life,
which are experienced as age increases. I desire to leave my executor
some plain instructions. First I have already given and conveyed to
my children, James E. Mayes, Mrs. Elizabeth Muldrow, R. Charlton
Mayes and William M. Mayes each a portion of my property as are equal
to a full share for each of them as distributees of my estate, I can
now give them my Love, Affection and my prayers. I will and instruct
my executors to see that my lawful debts are paid in full before my
estate passes out of their hands. I will the remaining property after
the debts are paid to my two sons George G. Mayes and Robert P. Mayes
to be equal divided between them, as soon as the younger becomes of
legal age, the property is to be keep together for their joint use and
benefit until that time arrives for the division. I appoint my son
James E. Mayes and my son in law Edward B. Muldrow to be my executors.
Wit: W. D. Rhodes, J. M. Bradley, F. J. Mayes. Signed: Caroline J.
Mayes. Filed 17 Nov. 1887.

Samuel J. Mayes. Will of Samuel J. Mayes. Box 82 Package 5. Probate
Judge Office. Union, S. C. I Samuel J. Mayes of Union Dist. being of
sound mind and memory, etc. I give to my beloved wife Elizabeth B.
Mayes all my property during her natural life, and at her death as I
hereinafter direct. I give to my two grand sons, Joseph Adolphus and
William James Frances Mayes one full share of my est. to be equal
divided between them, when they become of age, or the death of my wife.
I give to my granddaughter Ann Hyatt, daughter of Amanda Hyatt decd.
one half share to remain in care of my executor until she is of age.
I give to Susan Hyatt and her children one full share. I give to Mary
McDowell Mayes one full share. I appoint my son Daniel Wallace Mayes,
executor, and also one full share. Dated 6 Jan. 1868. Wit: J. H.
Williams, C. S. Greenleaf, Gordon Williams. Signed: Samuel J. Mayes.
Proven in common form by the oath of Gordon Williams, this 9 May 1892
before James M. Gee, J. of P.

Dorcas Mayes. Will of Dorcas Mayes. Box 82 Pack 21. Probate Judge
Office. Union, S. C. I Dorcas Mayes of Union Co., S. C. Being of
sound mind and memory, do make this my last W & T so help me God. I
give to my nephew John Wesley Scott all my estate both real and personal
credits or monies forever. My real estate consist of one half of the
place upon which I now live. I appoint my nephew John Wesley Scott my
sole executor. Dated 23 Jan. 1892. Wit: W. H. S. Harris, Isabella
Storey, C. M. Rodgers. Signed: Dorcas Mayes. Will proved before
Judge of Probate, James M. Gee. By W. H. S. Harris the 20 July 1893.

Thomas G. Mayes. Will of Thomas G. Mayes. No Ref. Spartanburg Dist.
I Thomas G. Mayes, being weak in body but of perfect mind and memory
and understanding. First I will my just debts be paid. I give to my
dear wife Celia one half of the remaining property of which she is to
school Emily Caroline so as to make her a tolerable good English
scholar. With all household and kitchen furniture and a cow if she
need one. I give to my dtr. all remaining property to be managed by
my executor until she becomes capable of managing her own business.
I leave the tract of land in the hands of my executors, if they think
best to let stand or rent it out to support the family do so. I
appoint Daniel G. Storey executor. Dated 12 Aug. 1843. Wit: George
Sparks, Thomas P. Storey, James M. Mayes. Signed: Thomas G. Mayes.
No proven date.

MAYFIELD

Pierson Mayfield. Deed from Pierson Mayfield. D 1, page 263. Clerk of
Court. Pickens, S. C. Deed dated 29 July 1840. Pierson Mayfield to
Lyman Thayer both of Pickens Dist. in consideration of $360, have sold,
bargained, granted and released all that tract of land whereon I now
live containing 50 acres lying on Brushey Creek waters of Saluda River.
Being part of the tract of land whereon George Edmundson formerly
lived. Wit: Robert Emerson, Benjamin Mauldin. Signed: Pierson
Mayfield. Attested by Robert Emerson before James Henderson, J.P. the
10 Aug. 1840. Recorded 31 Aug. 1840.

Reuben Mayfield. Deed from Reuben Mayfield. Book D, page 322. Clerk
of Court Office. Pickens, S. C. Deed dated 13 Feb. 1841. Reuben
Mayfield to Isreal Mayfield both of Pickens Dist. in consideration
$250, have granted, sold, bargained and released all that tract of land
lying on Wolf Creek waters of 12 Miles River. Adj. land of James
Mansell and widow Cannon and others. Wit: Robert F. Morgan, James W.
Lewis. Signed: Reuben Mayfield. Attested by James W. Lewis on the
13 Feb. 1841 before W. L. Keith, Clerk of Court. Recorded 16 Feb.
1841.

Isreal Mayfield. Deed from Isreal Mayfield. Book DL, page 407. Clerk
of Court Office. Pickens, S. C. Deed dated 14 Nov. 1840. Isreal
Mayfield to Reuben Mayfield. In consideration of $500 have granted,
sold, bargained and released all that tract of land containing 177
acres lying on the branches of Goldens Creek waters of 12 Mile River.
Originally granted to Henry Norton on the 3 Dec. 1792. Wit: John E.
Odell, William Odell. Signed: Isreal Mayfield. Attested by John E.
Odell on the 2 Oct. 1841 before William Smith J.Q. Recorded 12 Oct.
1841.

George Mayfield. Deed from George Mayfield. Book S, page 395. Clerk
Office. Greenville, S. C. Deed dated 4 Oct. 1837. George Mayfield to
Abner Mayfield. In consideration of $425 have bargained, sold, granted
and released all that tract of land where I now live containing 70
acres lying on the South side of Frowhock Creek waters of South Tiger
River. Adj. land of James Wilson, William Bright. Wit: Walker Mayfield, W. Wood. Signed: George Mayfield. Attested by Walker Morgan
(written this way) on the 26 May 1838, before William Cunningham, J.P.
Signed: Walker Morgan.

John Mayfield. Estate of John Mayfield. Apt. 41, file 54. Probate
Judge Office. Greenville, S. C. I John Mayfield of Greenville Dist.
do make this my last will and testament. I will my just debts be paid.
I give to my wife Elizabeth Mayfield during her life my plantation of
320 acres, her choice of three slaves, one half of my stock, one half
of all tools and furniture to enable her to make a crop. I will and
direct that the shares belonging to my dtrs. Bidsey Pollard and Elizabeth Long be put out on interest and the interest paid to them annual.
I will and direct that the balance of my estate and at the death of
my wife the whole be sold and proceeds divided between my children
except the two above named (others not named). I appoint Josiah
Kilgore executor. Dated 15 Jan. 1847. Wit: Geo. W. Sheppard, John
Tarver, James Henderson. Signed: John X Mayfield. Will proved by
John Tarver on 8 March 1852 before L. M. McBee, O.G.D. Recorded the
8 March 1852.

William D. Mayfield. Estate of William D. Mayfield. Box 4, File 19.
Probate Judge Office. Greenville, S. C. I William D. Mayfield of
Greenville Dist. being of sound mind and memory, etc. First I will
and direct that all my just debts be settled. It is my will that all
my estate be sold by my executor, I give him power of selling my land
together with all other goods and chattels as soon as possible after
my decease and after my debts are paid. That my wife Nancy C. Mayfield
receive one third of my entire estate personal and real. It is my will
that my son James Henry Mayfield shall receive the remaining two thirds

of my estate. I will that Manly Bright be and is hereby appointed my
executor and guardian of my son James Henry Mayfield having full power
to act for him till he is of age. Dated 12 March 1860. William
Dickson, B. F. Mayson, L. W. Mayfield. Signed: W. D. Mayfield. Will
proved by L. W. Mayfield before Robert M. Kay Esq. Ord. on the 25 March
1860, same day qualified Manly Bright as executor. Est. appraised the
16 April 1860. A. Davis, L. W. Mayfield, James Wilson.

Isaac Mayfield. Deed from Isaac Mayfield. Book D, page 190. Clerk
Office. Greenville, S. C. This indenture made between Isaac Mayfield
and Armon Gibson both of Greenville County, 96 Dist. In the sum of
100 pds. sterling hath granted, sold, bargained and release a tract of
land lying on both sides of the North fork of Saluda River, containing
200 acres as granted unto John Henderson on the 20 Jan. 1785. Wit:
John Motlow, Thomas X Speiggs. Signed: Isaac Mayfield. Deed attested
by John Motlow before George Salmon Esq. was presented and recorded this
26 Jan. 1796.

Daniel Mayfield. Deed to Daniel Mayfield. Book L, page 143. Clerk
Office, Greenville, S. C. This indenture made between William Brown
to Daniel Mayfield both of Greenville Dist. Dated 7 Nov. 1816. In
consideration of fifty dollars hath sold, bargain, granted and release
all that tract of land containing fifty acres on cane brake branch of
Enoree River. Wit: David Vaughan, Polly Vaughan. Signed: William X
Brown. Deed attested by David Vaughan before Andrew McCrary J.Q. on
the 13 July 1820.

George Mayfield. Deed to George Mayfield. Book S, page 167. Greenville, S. C. This indenture made between William Bright to George
Mayfield both of Greenville Dist. Dated 30 Dec. 1835. In consideration of $250 have sold, granted, bargained, and release all that tract
of land whereon I formerally lived containing seventy acres, lying on
the South side of Frowholk Creek waters of South Tyger River. Adj.
lands of James Akins, James C. Green, John McHickur, William Robbs, Jr.
and William Blasingame, Sheriff. Wit: Phillip C. Lester, Reuben Owens.
Signed: William Bright. Deed attested by Phillip C. Laster before
Josiah Kilgore, J.Q. On the 13 July 1836. On 3 Aug. 1836 Sarah Bright
the wife of William Bright did relinquish her dower on the above land.

MEEKS

Athe Meeks. Deed from Athe Meeks. Book F, page 77-78. Clerk Office.
Greenvillle, S. C. This indenture made between Athe Meeks and John
Barnett both of Greenville Dist. Dated 30 Sept. 1797. In consideration
of eighty pds. sterling, have granted, sold, bargained and released
unto John Barnett a tract of land on which I now live, whereas in and
by two granted, one dated 1 May 1786, for 440 acres in 96 dist. on
branches of Horse Creek waters of Reedy River. The other grant dated
7 Aug. 1786 for 470 in 96 dist. on branches of Mountain Creek waters
of Saluda River. Now the said Athe Meeks convey to John Barnett 335
acres. Wit: James Thompson, Abraham Ellis. Signed: Athe Meeks. No
recording date.

John Meeks. Will of John Meeks. Box 49 Pack 5. Probate Judge Office.
Laurens, S. C. I John Meeks being at this time sick of body but of
perfect mind and memory. I leave to my loving wife Ellinor Meeks
all my estate both real and personal for her use and support during her
life time or widowhood, after my lawful debts and funeral expenses are
paid. It is my desire my chn. shall share equal in my est. I direct
and order that as my children marry my executor shall give them one
cow and calf, one feather bed and furniture and $30 in cash and other
property if it can be spared without injuring my widow. At the death
of my widow the land be divided among my chn. William, Betsey, Nancy,
Jenny, Samuel, John, James Meeks. Negroes to be divided by my executors except my son William, I wish my executors to pay his share of the
___ (torn) in other property or in cash if it seems best. I appoint my

beloved wife Ellinor Meeks, Charles O'Neall and William Rowe my sole executors. Dated 13 Dec. 1802. Wit: John Cook, Durey Sims, Benjamin Cason. Signed: John Meeks. Will proven by John Cook and Duery Sims before David Anderson, Ord. on the 6 April 1803.

MELEAR

<u>Robert H. Melear</u>. Will of Robert H. Melear. Box 35 #410. Probate Judge Office. Pickens, S. C. As life is uncertain and death is sure, I Robert H. Melrear being in sound mind but feeble in health do make this my last W & T. I give to my loving wife Sarah all my household and kitchen furniture, one cow and calf and some hogs as my executor think she may need for a year support. I wish all my tools and books, with my cattle and hogs and my tract of land lying in Pickens Co. be sold by my executor on such credit as he think best. I wish my executor pay my debts or as many as he can from the proceeds. I wish James E. Hagood obtain from the pension office a land warrant, that he pay all expenses on said warrant, and the remainder of said warrant to be placed at a credit on an execution which he has against me in the Sheriff's Office at Pickens C. H. It is my will that James E. Hagood shall act as my executor. I wish my executor if he has any money in hand after paying my debts to retain it and give it out to my wife only as she may actually need it for her support. I wish my executor to have any money or property after the death of my wife Sarah. I wish my executor to collect all my debts or as many as he can. Dated 10 May 1854. Wit: L. A. Edge, Andrew J. X James, Mary A. Perry. Signed: Robert H. Melear. No probate date.

MERCK

<u>Daniel Merck</u>. Estate of Daniel Merck. Box 26 #315. Probate Judge Office. Pickens, S. C. Est. admr. 11 Oct. 1852 by Emilia Merck, W. L. Keith, who are bound unto W. J. Parson, Ord. in the sum of $2,000 Owned land on Reedy Fork waters of 12 Mile River. Adj. land of Joshua Chapman, Carter Clayton and others. Heirs: Emilia Merck the widow. Bloomer Merck, Daniel Merck. Rachel the wife of Jacob Chapman, Martha Jane the wife of Vincent James, and the heirs of Mary Banks, Rachel J. Banks entitled to a share from her grandfather. James George, Silas Kirksey were the commissioners named to divide the land.

MERIAM

<u>Henry & James Meriam</u>. Deed from Henry & James Meriam. Pack 401 #4. Clerk of Court Office. Pickens, S. C. We Henry M. Meriam of Jacksonville, Ala. and James A. Meriam of Cass County, Ga. for and in consideration of our note given back to us for the sum of $500 by Anderson Smith of Pickens Dist. Having granted, sold, bargain, and released unto Anderson Smith all that tract of land lying on 12 Mile River, being part of three grants, the same land deeded to us by said Anderson Smith on the 13 Aug. 1834 as recorded in Book C, page 5, Pickens Co., S. C. Dated 25 Nov. 1840. Wit: John E. Clark, T. B. R. Hillin and Thos. Coskey, J.P. Signed: Henry M. Meriam and James A. Meriam, seals.

MERIWEATHER

<u>Robert Meriweather</u>. Estate of Robert Meriweather. Box 67 #1624. Probate Judge Office. Abbeville, S. C. We John Meriweather, Joseph Meriweather, Dabney McGehee are bound unto John Hamilton, Ord. in the sum of five thousand dollars. Dated 2 July 1810. An appraisement was made 31 Aug. 1810. Slaves named: George, Anthony, Ann, Pegg, boy

Jack, girl Annaca, boy Isham. Notes due the estate on, Benjamin Childs,
Francis Meriweather, Joseph Meriweather, Armstrong Heard, Richard
Heard, Peter McMahan, William Spearman, Thomas Heard, Isaac Logan,
William Heard, Junr., James Galagly, Nicholas Moor. Sale held on 21
Sept. 1810. Buyers: John Meriweather, Thomas Brightman, Alexander
Sample, John McGehee, John Logan, Thomas Weir, James Cobb, Nicholas
Meriweather, Nathan Lipscomb Junr., Dabney Puckett, John Long, Lewis
Conner, Dr. Zachary Meriweather, William Hackett, Francis Meriweather,
Archd. Frith, Robert Shotwell, Alexander Stewart, Larkin Whitton,
Joseph Foster, Abraham Pool, John Waters, Samuel Hughson, Michael Ward,
Mary Gaines, David Thomas, Zeri Rice, Edmon Stephens, Benjamin Johnson,
Benjamin Hatters, Capt. James Pitts, Thomas Osborn, Humphrey Klugh,
Nancy Payne, James Pettus, Chars Devenport, Jonathan Swift. The only
person who may be an heir was Caroline Meriweather who in 1814 clothing
was paid for by admr. and in 1818 paid Dr. Zach. Meriweather for
Caroline Meriweather.

Francis Meriweather.   Estate of Francis Meriweather.   Box 62 Pack 1476.
Probate Judge Office.   Abbeville Dist.   I Francis Meriweather being in a
low state of health but perfectly in my mind and senses, etc.   I give
to my wife Mary Meriweather during her natural life the tract of land
whereon I now live with all appurtainances thereon and after her death,
I give said land to my son John and his heirs forever.   This tract has
over 100 acres of land, I give to my wife during her life twelve negroes
of her choice and stock with household and kitchen furniture and one
half of a mill I purchased of Colo. Nicholas Eveleigh's estate and a
third of my land adj. the mill, and a third of a tract lying on Rockey
Creek I bought from the same est.   I give my son Zachary Meriweather
half of 417 acres I bought from Eveleigh's estate on Rockey Creek.   I
give to my son Nicholas Meriweather my half of a tract of land containing 350 acres with a mill thereon we bought in copartnership of the
est. of Colo. Eveleigh's.   I give to my dtr. Ann M. McGehee in the state
of Virginia a negro named Fillis and her offsprings, Judy, Nanny,
Peter, London and Susan.   Whereas my dtr. Mary Conner is departed this
life my desire is that her chn. shall have her part under the pro-
tection of John Conner the father, until they marry or come of age.
I appoint my sons John Meriweather, Zachary Meriweather and Nicholas
Meriweather my executors.   Dated 7 June 1793.   Wit: John Logen, Junr.,
William X Gains.   Signed: Fran. Meriweather.   A Dedimus Potestatum
(to act in the place of a Judge) was issued to Julius Nichols Esq. to
administer the oath of Executors to Capt. John Meriweather, Dr.
Zachary Meriweather, Nicholas Meriweather of the estate of Francis
Meriweather decd.   Dated 12 Sept. 1793.   Signed: James Wardlaw, D.C.C.,
On the same day John Chiles, Leonard Waller, Thomas Levingston and Capt.
Richard Pollard were duly qualified as appraisers.   Signed: Julius
Nichols, J.P.   Negroes listed as: Will, London, Burges, Ceasae,
Fanny, Lucy, Milly, Boy Ned, Moses, girl Jenny, Charles, Davy, Amey,
Meriah, Winna, Queen, Minna, Rachel, Tom, Patrick, Fillis, Anne, Tom,
Hannable, Esther, Aleck, Hager, Christian Snella, Alse, Winston,
Fielding, Daniel, Woman Anne, girl Anne, Sam, Isaac.   Notes due the
estate, George Tyler of Virginia, George Brightman, John Logan Senr.,
Mary Mitchel, James Calhoun, James Gains, Benjamin Eddins Junr., Capt.
John Calhoun, Jean McGill, Elijah Moore, James Heard, William Gains, Joh
Talbert, Robert Mitchel, W. C. Carlile, Wm. Nicholas, E. Ramsey,
Micajah Stevens, David Gains, Peter Green, Jonathan Beesly, William
Wardlaw, Stephen Heard, Mayson Mitchel.

Nicholas Meriweather..   Estate of Nicholas Meriweather.   Box 60 Pack
1427.   Probate Judge Office.   Abbeville, S. C.   I Nicholas Meriweather,
being strong in body and sound of memory, do make this my last W & T.
Feelings as I do the warmest paternal affection for all my chn. both
Mary Ragland Meriweather and Sally Meriweather, Dtr. of Sarah Meriweather my first wife, and William Bickley Meriweather, John Lewis
Meriweather, Eveline Meriweather, Nicholas Meriweather, and Charles
Waller Meriweather by Mary Meriweather my second wife.   Had not Mary and
Sally already inherited by the will of their grand father (not named)
estate equal if not superior to what I shall be able to give to the
rest of my chn., another consideration of equal weight, Mary and Sally

218

have arrived at years of maturity while the rest of my chn. are yet infants, etc. First I do will that all my just and existing debts be paid. That the balance of my estate both real and personal shall be and remain in the power and at the disposal of Mary Meriweather my wife, for the joint use and benefit of her and my chn. (named the chn. of the second wife.) Should my widow marry she shall have the choice of any seven negroes, and the use of my land, at her death the negroes to desend to the above named chn. in fee simple, likewise the land to my sons, in equal share in fee simple. I appoint my wife executrix and John Bickley, Junr. and John Scudday. Dated 30 Nov. 1809. Wit: Joseph Meriweather, Lewis Conner, Andrew Logan. Signed: Nicholas Meriweather. We the undersigned appraisers appointed by Moses Taggart, Ord. to appraise the estate of Nicholas Meriweather decd. Dated 15 April 1831. Signed: John Logan, Samuel Crawford, Joseph Foster, Robert Buchanan, Charles Neely. Downs Calhoun applied for a letter of admr. on the estate of Nicholas Meriweather decd. dated 28 March 1831. Letter published at Providence Church on the 3 April 1831. Negroes named in the inventory, Paul, Thornton, Milley, Winston, Mary and child, Anne and two chn. John and Isaac, Winney, Jackson, Wesly, Albert. Sale held 25-26 April 1831. Buyers, William Meriweather, John Anglin, William Buckhanan Senr., Nicholas Meriweather, William Calhoun, Nathan Calhoun, Charles Neely, John Logan, John Irvin, Robert Buchannon, Samuel Crawford, Stanley Crews, Walter Anderson, William Leek, John Turner, Brackston Smith, James Franklin, James Patterson, Thos. B. Byrd, Richard Griffin, William Taggart, Thomas Smith, Francis Logan, Thomas Morgan, William Crawford, John W. Parker, John B. Davis, Jimison Millford, George Freeman, Robert Crawford, John Roman, William Oneal, David Stuart, M. T. Stuart, Wiley Watson, John Foster, Smith Roman, Joseph Foster, James Hearston, Thomas West. In the paid out receipts, one Paid for pailing in graveyard of Nicholas and Mary Meriweather (second wife died before him).

Thomas Meriweather. Deed to Thomas Meriweather. Book 33 page 381. Clerk of Probate. Edgefield, S. C. We Archey Mayson and Elihu Creswell trustees for Elizabeth Swift late Elizabeth Ball decd. and Jonathan and William Swift to Thomas Meriweather Esq. both of Edgefield Dist. Dated 22 Nov. 1816. Dated 22 Nov. 1816. In consideration of $143.50 have granted, sold, bargain and released one tract of land containing 137 acres lying on waters of Stephens Creek on the East side of the road leading from Long Cane to Augusta. Wit: Austin Pollard, James Mayson. Signed Arc. Mayson and Elihu Creswell trustees, Jonathan Swift and William Swift. On 25 Nov. 1816 Mary Swift the wife of Jonathan Swift and Mary Ann Swift the wife of William Swift renounce, release, and forever relinquish their dower to the said land. Before Thomas Anderson J.O. Deed attested by James L. Mayson on the 25 Nov. 1816 before Thomas Anderson J.Q.

Thomas Meriweather. Deed from Thomas Meriweather. Book 40, page 111. Clerk of Probate, Edgefield, S. C. Deed from Thomas Meriweather to Dr. George Graves both of Edgefield Dist. Dated 8 April 1820. In consideration of $165 hath sold, bargained, granted and released all that tract of land containing 91 acres, lying on both sides of the road leading to Taries ferry being part of a tract of 118 1/2 acres granted to William Swift on 5 Feb. 1787. Adj. lands of John Middleton and George Graves. Wit: James Thomas, Jefsy X Sharpton, William Thomas. Signed: Thomas Meriweather. On the 3 May 1820 Margaret Meriweather the wife of Thomas Meriweather renounce, release and relinquish her dower to the sd. land before Charles Hammond, J.Q. Deed proved the same date by James Thomas before Charles Hammond, J.Q.

Thomas Meriweather. Deed to Thomas Meriweather. Book 30, page 419. Clerk of Probate. Edgefield, S. C. Deed from Susannah Barksdale, widow to Thomas Meriweather both of Edgefield Dist. Dated 13 July 1811. In consideration of $3,804.00 hath granted, sold, bargained and released all that tract of land containing 929 acres lying on Stephen Creek, adj. land of Henry Wares, est. of James Thomas, Jeff Sharpton. Originally granted 50 acres to Joseph Chatwin on 3 Sept. 1754. 100 acres to John Scott on the 5 April 1765, 500 acres to James Simpson

Esq. on 12 July 1771, 147 acres to Alexander Oden on the 1 Feb. 1790.
Also 100 acres to Daniel Barksdale the 7 March 1791. Wit: Charles
Bufsey, Henry Ware, Robert Ware, Jr. Signed: Susannah Barksdale.
Proven on oath of Charles Bufsey before Robert Ware J.Q. on the 13 July
1811.

Waller B. Meriweather. Minor. Pack 49. Clerk of Court Office.
Abbeville, S. C. On 6 Feb. 1833 E. R. Calhoun was gdn. of Waller B.
Meriweather a minor. Recd. 6 Feb. 1833 of Downs Calhoun Admr. of
Nicholas Meriweather decd. my father part of my legacy. 27 June 1831
Stanley Crews was gdn. of Belinda Meriweather a minor.

                                NALLY

Nally Minors. Box 144 #3. Probate Judge Office. Pickens, S. C. On
16 Dec. 1903 W. T. Nally, J. M. Laboon, G. S. Barr are bound unto J. B.
Newberr, Ord. in the sum of $410.48. W. T. Nalley gdn. of James A. and
Vernessia Nally minors. Chn. of Matilda C. Nally decd. James A. age
about 16 years. Vernessia Nally under 10 years.

John W. Nally. Admr. Bond of John W. Nally. Box 118 #6. Probate
Judge Office. Pickens, S. C. John W. Nally died 3 April 1890. George
W. Hendricks a son in law. J. M. Stewart the admr.

                              NEDARMAN

John Nedarman. Will. Book A, page 169. Probate Judge Office. Union,
S. C. I John Nedarman being very sick and weak in body, but of perfect
mind and memory, etc. First it is my will that all my debts and funeral
expenses be paid. I give to my dearly beloved wife Sarah, all my land
and tenements with all my household goods. I ordain William McClure and
John Briggs to be my only executors. Dated 7 Oct. 1793. Wit: Thomas
Harris, Martha Harris, Elias Bezley. Signed: John Neadarman. Will
was proven on the 10 Sept. 1803 on oath of Edward Dodd states that he
had acquaintance with the hand writing of John Nedarman and the within
will is his own writing. He believe that the witnesses are deceased.

                                 NEAL

John Neal, Jr. Will of John Neal, Jr. Box 35 #402. Probate Judge
Office. Pickens, S. C. I John Neal, being sick in body but of sound
and disposing mind and memory. etc. I desire my executor to pay all
my just debts and funeral expenses. I give to my beloved wife Sarah
Neal all the tract of land whereon I now live, lying on 12 Mile River.
Adj. land of Samuel Smith, A. Wemms, J. F. Maw and others, containing
243 acres to hold the same during her life time or widowhood. I give
to my wife Sarah all my ready money notes and accounts, together with
all stock of horses, cattle, hogs, sheep, tools with household and
kitchen furniture during her life time or widowhood. Should my wife
marry I direct my executor to sell all my land and property and divide
the same between all my children (not named) share and share alike.
After the death of my wife, executor to sell all property left after
raising my chn. and equally divide between all my chn. I appoint my
wife Sarah Nela executrix, and my friend Silas Kirksey executor. Dated
27 Jan. 1853. Wit: James Lawrence, W. L. Keith, Thomas R. Brackenridge. Signed: John X Neal. Proven 11 Oct. 1854. Expend. 13 Jan.
1857 by amount of property valued to dtr. Eliza as per appraisement &
receipt $44.50.

John Neel. Will of John Neel. Box 5 #64. Probate Judge Office.
Pickens, S. C. (only the first page found in notes). I John Neel of
Pickens Dist., S. C. being in sound and disposing mind and memory, etc.

I desire that my executors after my death sell such of my property as they think best and out of the money pay all my just debts and funeral expenses. I give to my dtr. Sarah Copeland the sum of one dollars. I give to my dtrs. Margaret Hillian, Mary Hillian, Martha Weems, to my sons, James, John and Andrew all and singular the real and personal property of whatever kind to be divided between the last six mentioned children. I appoint my son James Neel and my son in law Andrew Weems as executors and to sell or divide the property after giving my dtr. Sarah one dollar.

Martha Neel. Will of Martha Neel. Box 142 Pack 4004. Probate Judge Office. Abbeville, S. C. I Martha Neel, now feeble in body, but of sound and disposing mind and memory. I will all my just debts and funeral expenses be paid. My object is to secure my dtr. Mary Adalaide now the wife of Augustus Lomax. I give all my property both real and personal for her sole use and not subject to any control, or indebtedness of her present or future husband, to better effect this, I will and bequeath to my friend Attorney H. A. Jones Esq. the following slaves viz: Lotty, and her chn. Eliza, Lem, Belton, Cilla, Pressly and Alice, also Dina and her child Edy and Edy's chn. Tom, Hariet and her child Jim, Phebe, Dilce, Bill and Sally, also Harriett and children Ellen, Easter and Ike and also Nat to my friend and his heirs forever in trust. With the right and power of my dtr. to disposing thereof by her last will and testament. I further will all my interest in and to the estate of my late husband John P. Neel of Newberry Dist. yet unsettled. I appoint my friend H. A. Jones Esq. executor. Dated 29 Oct. 1855. Wit: B. P. Hughes, Wm. H. Parker, J. A. Allen. Signed: M. C. Neel. Proven 29 Nov. 1855.

NEELY

William Neely. Estate of William Neely. Box 70 Pack 1716. Probate Judge Office. Abbeville, S. C. I William Neely, being in a low state, but in perfect mind and memory. My will and desire is that my just debts be paid. It is my will and desire that my four youngest sons viz; Jubelous, Sanders, Beauford and Oswell each to have a saddle worth thirteen dollars, when my executors think most proper I consider to make them equal with their elder brothers. My will and desire that Sally Samuels shall have a bed and furniture, when she marry, and the sum of twenty dollars. My will and desire that my dtr. Judah shall have a bed and furniture to make her equal. The balance of my estate to my beloved wife Polly Neely to do and act as she and the rest of my executors may think proper for the support of my minor children during her life. At the death of my wife, my estate to be sold, and my children each and every one equal. I appoint my wife Polly Neely Executrix and my sons Charles Neely, and William L. Neely executors. Dated 6 Sept. 1821. Wit: James Franklin, Alex. Sample, Robert Bartrim. Signed: William Neely. Proved by Alex. Sample on the 4 Feb. 1822. The est. was appraised 23 Feb. 1822 by John B. Sample, James Franklin, Alex. Sample, Robert Bartrim.

William Neely. Will of William Neely. Vol 14, page 255. Probate Judge Office. Charleston, S. C. I William Neely of Craven County and St. Mark Parish, being sick in body but sound in mind and judgment, etc. I give to my well beloved dtr. Christian Neely a tract of land containing 250 acres adj. the land I now live on, originally granted to me in my name. Also a negro named Peg and a negro child named Major, one horse and a woman saddle, five cows delivered to her at the day she marry. I give to my well beloved wife Sarah Neely all the plantation where I now live, likewise one negro Man called Tom and one woman named Mary, during her natural life or widowhood, I further give to my wife all her wearing apparel, one bay horse and her saddle, I further give to my wife all my household furniture, farming and other tools, all stock of cattle, hogs during her natural life or widowhood. I give to John Phillips one hundred acres of land where he now lives. I give to my brother Christopher Neely one hundred acres of land, situated on

Burbons Creek. I order my executors to sell one negro woman named
Cerah, one hundred and fifty acres of land I purchased from Joseph
Hutchinson, my waggon still and three horses for the payment of my
debts and to my brother Robert Neely. I give to my brother John
Neely five shilling sterling. I appoint my brother George Neely and
my friend John Caldwell of little River executors. Dated 26 Oct. 1771.
Wit: Wm. Anderson, Jas. Coch Murphy, Ailes McGin. Signed: William
Neely. Proved 1 May 1772.

Jean Neely. Will of Jean Neely. Book G, page 3. Probate Judge
Office. York Co., S. C. I Jean Neely, being in a low and declining
state of health but of sound and disposing mind and memory, etc. The
two thirds of the land I was entitled to, that has been sold to James
McMeans be conveyed to him. The other third I give to my dtr. Elizabeth
McNair and at her death the same to my grand children Jean and Rachel
McNair and to no other person. I give to Jean McNair my mare and my
cow to Rachel for their kindness to me. I appoint James McMeans my
executor. Dated 12 May 1819. Wit: Jackson N. Henry, William Henry.
Signed: Jean X Neely. Recorded 30 Dec. 1820.

Elizabeth Neely. Will of Elizabeth Neely. Book G, page 337. Probate
Judge Office. York Co., S. C. Last will and testament of Elizabeth
Neely made this 19 Jan. 1831. I give all and singular, the property I
hold and possess to my son Tillotson S. Neely. Without any other
reserve whatever. Allowing him to have me decently intered. I appoint
my son Tillotson S. Neely my sole executor. Wit: Joseph W. McCorkle,
William Neely, Elizabeth X Steel. Signed: Elizabeth X Neely.
Probated 28 March 1831.

William Neely. Will of William Neely. Book 3, page 34. Probate Judge
Office. York Co., S. C. I William Neely being at this time of sound
and disposing mind and memory. I will that my just debts and funeral
expenses be paid from money on hand. I leave unto my nephew Tillotson
S. Neely, son of my sister Elizabeth Neely the land whereon I now live,
on the following conditions, that he hold and use it, or sell it for
his own advantage, if he does not sell it, or dies without issue then
the land is to return to the lawfull heirs of the Neely family. I also
leave to my nephew Tillotson S. Neely the whole of my personal property,
stock, household and kitchen furniture, together with all money on hand.
I appoint Tillotson S. Neely as executor. Dated 27 Oct. 1841. Wit:
Joseph W. McCorkle, Samuel Steele, John Workman. Signed: William
Neely. Probated 14 Feb. 1842.

William Neely. Estate of William Neely. Box 57A Pack 1552. Probate
Judge Office. Chester, S. C. Est. admr. 5 March 1852 by James F.
Wherry, John N. Neely, and David C. Crawford who are bound unto the
ordinary of Chester Co. in the sum of $6,000.00. Expend: 15 Dec.
1855 paid Samuel Neely $110.00. 20 Dec. 1855. Paid Ellias Neely
$25.00. Return 6 Jan. 1862. Paid John L. Neely $257.25. Paid John N.
Neely $280.14. Paid Robert Davinson $280.14. Paid James H. Neely
$280.14. Paid P. P. Neely $257.25. Paid S. E. Neely $257.25. Paid
Irene T. Neely $280.14. Paid Margaret A. Neely $25.50. Paid Matthew
Lynn $259.27. Return of 1855 mentioned, G. H. Neely, Mary N. Neely,
Sarah E. Neely, P. P. Neely. 10 March 1853 paid Rachel Neely $15.93.

Jonathan Neely. Will of Jonathan Neely. Book G, page 75. Probate
Judge Office. York, S. C. I Jonathan Neely being weak in body but of
sound and perfect mind and memory, etc. First I give to my wife Mary
Neely her maintenance from the plantation whereon I now live, as long
as she remains my widow, also one negro girl named Dine, all the household furniture, one horse and saddle, two milk cows, one loom. The
rest of my property after paying my debts to be equal divided between
my children viz: Peggy Eliza., Thomas M., Jonathan M., Nancy Amaline,
James C. Neely. It appears that my wife is pregnant and if the child
lives to share with the others. I appoint James Carrothers my executor.
Dated 26 Dec. 1821. Wit: Chas. Robertson, Leven Benton. Signed:
Jonathan Neely. Probated 31 May 1822.

William Neely. Will of William Neely. Box 52 #1822. Probate Judge
Office. Camden, S. C. I William Neely of Camden Dist. being weak in
body, but of sound and perfect mind and memory, etc. First I will and
desire that my just debts and funeral expenses be paid. My will and
desire that my beloved wife Mary Neely have her living and support off
the plantation I now live on during her widowhood or natural life.
With full power and free priviledge of my dwelling house, and to let or
rent the said plantation if occassion shall require it to be for the
supportion and raising of my young family, with the benefit and service
of two negroes named Tom and Simon. Also I give to my dear wife one
third of my personal estate and one forth of my household furniture
forever. I give to my son Samuel Neely one forth part of the personal
est. and at the decease of my wife I give to the said son the negro
Simon forever. I give to my son William Neely the tract of land whereon
I now live containing 200 acres, being half of the tract first patent'd
line not yet run. I give to sd. son one fifth part of my personal est.
and at the death of my wife to him negro named Tom. I give to my three
dtr. viz; Elizabeth, Mary and Catherine each one fourth part of my
household furniture and one fifth part of my personal est. to each of
them forever. I desire that each receive their share at the appraisement without any sale. The part set aside for my aged parents be
continued to them during their natural life. I will that James Miller
of 96 Dist. shall see that the line of division be run on the land. And
that my brother in law John Anderson of Camden Dist. have a deed for
the land he now lives on containing 200 acres. I appoint James Miller
and my wife Mary Neely executors. Dated 10 Oct. 1778. Wit: William
Smith, John Steel, Samuel Neely. Signed: William Neely. Recorded
25 Dec. 1783.

Elizabeth Neely. Will. Will 23. Probate Judge Office. York, S. C.
Elizabeth Neely of York Dist. died in 1841. Chn. Elizabeth McElwee,
Nancy Warren, Benjamin Neely, Bequeath to Jane Thomasson, Drusilla
Simpson, Joseph Miller, grand dtrs. Rachel, Lilla and Eliza Miller.

Henderson Neely. Estate of Henderson Neely. Box 34 #1437. Probate
Judge Office. York, S. C. Est. admr. 6 Nov. 1833 by John A. Brown,
John Brown Sr., Samuel C. Brown who are bound unto Benjamin Chambers,
Ord. in the sum of $1,000.00. Wit: published at Bethesheda Church.
Hance Neely bought at sale.

Neely Minors. Box 48, #2091. Probate Judge Office. York, S. C. On
19 Feb. 1823, Wm. Carothers, James Carothers are bound to the Ord. in
the sum of $3,000.00. Wm. Carothers guardian of Mary Ann, James W.,
Thomas C., Elias H., George N., Betsey C., Nancy C., John M., and Peggy
C. Neely minors of Thomas Neely decd. Margaret Neely of Maury Co., Tenn.
the widow of Thomas Neely decd.

Violet Neely. Estate of Violet Neely. Box 40 #1710. Probate Judge
Office. York, S. C. Est. admr. 28 Mar. 1859 by Robert L. Neely, G. E.
M. Steele, A. C. Hutchinson, D. B. Miller are bound to John M. Ross,
Ord. in the sum of $8,000.00. On 28 June 1875 W. T. Neely and D. F. E.
Neely of Warren, Bradley Co. Arkansas recd. share of said estate.

David Neely. Estate of David Neely. Box 34 #1438. Probate Judge
Office. York, S. C. Est. admr. 30 Dec. 1835 by Benjamin Dunlap, James
P. Dunlap, H. G. Massey who are bound unto Benjamin Chambers, Ord. in
the sum of $500.00.

Samuel W. Neely. Estate of Samuel W. Neely. Box 34 #1439. Probate
Judge Office. York, S. C. Est. admr. 16 Nov. 1835 by Thomas M. Neely,
James Carothers, William Carothers who are bound unto Benjamin Chambers,
Ord. in the sum of $2,000.00. Cit. published at Ebenezer Church ment.
that Samuel W. Neely decd. was a minor of Jona Neely decd. Nancy A.
Neely recd. her distr. share. Johnanthan N. Neely, James C. Neely
recd. shares. James M. Cline was a minor heir.

Robert Neely. Estate of Robert Neely. Box 61 #2803. Probate Judge
Office. York, S. C. Est. admr. 24 March 1804 by Sarah Neely, Robert
Neely, John Neely, Wm. Chambers who are bound unto Alexr. Moore, Esq.
Ord. in the sum of $5,000.00.

Robert Neely. Estate of Robert Neely. Box 33 #1405. Probate Judge
Office. York, S. C. On 7 July 1858 Robert S. Neely of Chattooga Co.,
Georgia appointed John Alexander of the same state his attorney to
receive his share from est. of Robert Neely of York Dist., S. C. On
3 Aug. 1857 Myles Neely son of Robert Neely transfered all his rights
and titles to est. over to John Dulin. On 1 April 1856 Miles Neely,
Robert S. Neely, Madison Neely, Hance Neely, Robert Turner and wife
Minerva, James Turner and Wife Angelina, Hiram Gilbreath and wife Mary
Ann, David Stradley and wife Mary, Peter S., Suaan, and Henry C.
Bodenhamer legal heirs of Robert Neely. Owned 216 acres on Fishing
Creek. Henderson Neely since dead leaving his child Mary who married
David Stradley and his widow who married Peter S. Bodenhamer the widow
afterwards died leaving as her heirs, her husband Peter Bodenhamer and
chn. Harriet, William, Suana and Henry C. Bodenhamer and David Stradley
and wife Mary all whom resides out of State except Robert Turner and
wife, Hance Neely, Madison Neely. On 2 Sept. Hiram H. Gilbreath and
his wife Mary Ann were of Chattooga Co., Georgia.

Thomas Neely. Estate of Thomas Neely. Box 33 #1386. Probate Judge
Office. York, S. C. Est. admr. 9 March 1819 by John S. Forbes,
Hartwell Adkins, Zaccheus Adkins who are bound unto Benjamin Chambers,
Ord. in the sum of $3,000.00. Left a widow Jean Neely and 5 chn.
Jackson Neely, Matthew Neely, Robert Neely, Elizabeth McNair were
children.

Annie G. Neely. Minor. Box 70 #3495. Probate Judge Office. York,
S. C. On 3 April 1871 J. F. Workman, R. H. Workman, R. W. Workman are
bound unto S. B. Hall, Ord. in the sum of $800.00. J. F. Workman guar-
dian of Annie G. Neely minor child of W. W. Neely decd. of Chester Dist.
Grandaugther of J. Frank Workman.

Mathew Neely. Minor. Case #50, file 2166. (No county given, State of
S. C.) On 25 Feb. 1828 John S. Moore, Samuel Moore and Thomas Moore
are bound unto John Taylor Governor of S. C. in the sum of $1,200. John
S. Moore guardian of Mathew Neely, Jr. minor... also Stenson Neely,
Samuel M. Neely, minors of Mathew Neely decd.

Robert Neely. Minor. Box 50 #2184. Probate Judge Office. York, S. C.
On 4 Feb. 1823 Lemuel Thomason, Wm. Thomason, Isaac R. Harris are bound
unto John L. Wilson Ord. in the sum of $1,000.00. Was of N. C. Lemuel
Thomason gdn. of Robert Neely minor orphan within the age of 21 years.
Son of Martha Neely decd.

John Neely. Estate of John Neely. Box 4 #168. Probate Judge Office.
York, S. C. Est. admr. 12 Dec. 1845 by Mary C. Neely, Wm. D. McFadden,
Oliver P. McCullough, Samuel Reid who are bound unto J. M. Ross, Ord.
in the sum of $2,500.00.

Mary Neely. Estate of Mary Neely. Box 4 #169. Probate Judge Office.
York, S. C. Est. admr. 9 April 1846 by Thomas M. Neely, James C. Neely,
Jonathan M. Neely who are bound unto John M. Ross, Ord. in the sum of
$1,000.00. Est divided into four shares.

Sam Neely. Marriage of Sam Neely. Box 66 #3120. Probate Judge Office.
York, S. C. "I hereby acknowledge myself bound to Alex Moore Esq. in
the penal sum of one hundred dollars to keep the sd. Alex Moore harm-
less upon account of his granting a license to join in marriage Sam
Neely and Jean Black. Witness my hand this 6 day of May 1801. Samuel
Williamson."

William Neely. Estate of William Neely. Box 52 #1823. Probate Judge
Office, Camden, S. C. Est. admr. 15 May 1783 by Jane Walker, Philip
Walker, John Walker who are bound unto Henry Thompson, Ord. in the sum

of 3,000 pds. sterling. Jane Walker was next of kin.

Thomas Neely. Estate of Thomas Neely. Box 33 #1387. Probate Judge
Office. York, S. C. Est. admr. 2 April 1819 by Jonathan Neely, Samuel
Carothers and James Carothers who are bound unto Benjamin Chambers, Ord.
in the sum of $3,000.00

Thomas Neely. Estate of Thomas Neely. Box 33 #1384. Probate Judge
Office. York, S. C. Est. admr. of Thomas Neely by William McGuown,
Daniel Laney and John Steel Forbes who are bound unto Benjamin Chambers,
Ord. in the sum of $1,000.00. In the same package the following, 9
Sept. 1815 Samuel Neely, John A. Gebie and John Adams all of York
Dist. are bound to Benjamin Chambers in the sum of $500.00. Samuel
Neely bound guardian of the personal estate of Luske Davis a minor
within the age of 21 years. (1 May 1818).

Harriet S. Neely. Estate of Harriet S. Neely. Box 31 #1308. Probate
Judge Office. York, S. C. Est. admr. 13 Dec. 1855 by Eliza A. Neely,
John S. Moore, G. R. Ratchford, John H. Adams who are bound unto John
M. Ross, Ord. in the sum of $30,000.00.

Samuel Neely. Estate of Samuel Neely. Box 61 #2802. Probate Judge
Office. York, S. C. Est. admr. 14 Oct. 1788 by Jane Neely, Thomas
Neely, Henry Creswell, Robert Smith who are bound unto the Ord. in the
sum of 500 pds.

Rev. Thomas Neely. Estate of Rev. Thomas Neely. Box 61 #2801. Probate
Judge Office. York, S. C. Est. admr. 2 Jan. 1812 by Martha Neely,
John Minter, William Givin, Samuel Givin, James Feemster who are bound
unto Alexr. Moore, Esq. Ord. in the sum of $3,000.00.

David F. Neely. Estate of David F. Neely. Box 14 #588. Probate
Judge Office. York, S. C. Est. admr. 22 Oct. 1850 by Violet Neely,
Jesse Brumfield, Joseph J. Daniel who are bound unto John M. Ross, Ord.
in the sum of $4,000.00. D. S. Neely bought at sale. . .

Daniel S. Neely. Box 16 #686. Probate Judge Office. York, S. C.
Est. admr. 23 Oct. 1851 by Cynthia Neely, A. Whyte, J. P. Creighton
who are bound unto J. M. Ross, Ord. in the sum of $3,000.00.

Benjamin Neely. Estate of Benjamin Neely. Box 23 #978. Probate Judge
Office. York, S. C. Est. admr. 10 April 1854 by Eliza A. Neely, G. W.
Williams, D. H. Thompson, J. H. Adams, G. R. Ratchford, J. M. Anderson
and John S. Moore who are bound unto J. M. Ross, Ord. in the sum of
$80,000.00. Est. divided between three chn. and widow.

D. Frances Elizabeth Neely. Minor. Box 28 #1190. Probate Judge Office.
York, S. C. On 15 Sept. 1854 Violet Neely, J. Monroe Anderson, W. J.
Bowen are bound unto J. M. Ross, Ord. in the sum of $740.00. Biolet
Neely guardian of her dtr. a minor. The dtr. entitled to a legacy from
estate of John Brumfield decd.

Robert Neely. Estate of Robert Neely. Box 34 #1436. Probate Judge
Office. York, S. C. Est. admr. 5 Nov. 1832 by Andrew McWhorter,
John S. Moore, Robert M. Williams who are bound unto Benjamin Chambers,
Ord. in the sum of $2,000.00. Cit. published at Independence Church.
2 June 1832 Violet and Henderson Neely applied for letter of admr.

T. Madison Neely. Box 25 #1072. Probate Judge Office. York, S. C.
Est. admr. 17 Jan. 1880 by J. F. Wallace, J. A. L. M. Stewart, Wm. J.
Neely who are bound unto J. A. McLean, Ord. in the sum of $1,000.00.
Est. divided between the widow and three chn.

Thomas Neely. Estate of Thomas Neely. Box 34 #1425. Probate Judge
Office. York, S. C. Est. admr. 21 June 1822 by James Carothers, Samuel
Carothers, Wm. Carothers who are bound unto Benjamin Chambers, Ord. in
the sum of $3,000.00. Margret Neely recd. a share. 8 Nov. 1828 Mary
Ann Neely of Maury Co., Tenn. was an heir. Margret Neely was gdn. of

James W. Neely, Mary Ann Edwards nee Neely, Hazel W. Edwards all of Maury Co., Tenn. chn. of Thomas Neely decd.

Alexander P. Neely. Estate of Alexander P. Neely. Box 34 #962. Probate Judge Office. York, S. C. On 13 Feb. 1854 Wm. E. Kelsey, John Dickey, John McFadden, Samuel Reid, Wm. D. McFadden who are bound unto J. M. Ross, Ord. in the sum of $3,000.00. Wm. E. Kelsey gdn. of Alexr. P. Neely a minor, Hyder A. D. Neely Minor.

Matthew Neely. Estate of Matthew Neely. Box 33, 1383. Probate Judge Office. York, S. C. Est. admr. 5 Feb. 1816 by Obadiah Alexander, Margaret Neely, Thomas Neely, Lemuel Thomasson, Hermon Alexander are bound unto Benjamin Chambers, Ord. in the sum of $4,000.00. Citation published at the burial of David Neely on the 28 Jan. 1816. Left a widow and seven chn. In 1821 John Neely was in Tenn. Margaret Neely the widow. Samuel Stevenson and wife Hannah heirs of the decd.

John McCreee Neely. Estate of John McCree Neely. Box 34 #1434. Probat Judge Office. York, S. C. Est. admr. 4 Jan. 1830 by Wm. Carothers, Wm. Allen, Wm. Thorn who are bound unto Benjamin Chambers, Ord. in the sum of $1,000.00... was of Tenn. Paid Margret Neely of Tenn. proven account $26.50. Was an heir of Thomas Neely decd. On 17 May 1830 paid Abner Houston atty. of Mary or Marg? Neely and gdn. of James W. Neely and Atty. of Mary Ann Edwards each $14.59. On 14 Dec. 1829 John L. Cheeks of Maurey Co., Tenn. states that he was acquainted with John M. Neely and that he died in Oct. about the 20th last.

AMZI NEELY. Minor. Box 50 #2154. Probate Judge Office. York, S. C. on 20 Feb. 1818 John Minter, James Feemster, J. Wm. Jamison are bound unto Benjamin Chambers, Ord. in the sum of $10,000.00. John Minter gdn. of Amzi Neely a minor within the age of 21 years an orphan.

Martha Neely. Will of Martha Neely. Box 33 #1385. Probate Judge Office. York, S. C. I Martha Neely of York Dist. widow being sick and weak in body but of a sound and disposing mind and memory, etc. I give to my dtr. Clarinda my new callico bed quilt. To my dtr. Clarissa I give my wrought counterpane. To my son Amzi Neely I give my gold watch, leaving said watch in care of my brother James Feemster till my son arrives at the age of twenty one years. I desire the remainder of my property be equally divided between my three chn. and that the said property be keep and not sold except such articles as may be unprofit-able to be kept, James Feemster and John Minter be the judges. I appoint John Minter as executor. Dated 19 Feb. 1814. Wit: Margaret Fair, Nancy X Egger. Signed: Martha Neely. Probated 28 Feb. 1814.

William Neeley. Estate of William Neeley. Bundle 77 Pack 9. Probate Judge Office. Barnwell, S. C. Est. admr. 6 Dec. 1840 by George J. Reed, Jesse Rice, Samuel Overstreet and Hugh Reed who are bound unto O. D. Allen Esq. Ord. in the sum of $5,000.00. Left four small chn. no names given.

Mrs. Eleanor Neeley. Estate of Mrs. Eleanor Neeley. Bundle 81 Pack 5. Probate Judge Office. Barnwell, S. C. Est. admr. 17 Jan. 1842 by George J. Reed, Jesse Rice, William Butto, Jr. who was bound unto O. D. Allen Esq. Ord. in the sum of $1,500.00. George Reed was admr. of estate. Left four children, no names given.

NEIGHBORS

Franklin Neighbors. On 20 Oct. 1863 Franklin Neighbors age 72 years and Darcus Neighbors age 48 years. were living in the poor house in Pickens Co. Ref. Pack 645 #3. Clerk of Court Office. Pickens, S. C.

Mary E. Nelson. Estate of Mary E. Nelson. Box 52 Pack 1832. Probate Judge Office. Camden, S. C. Est. admr. 14 Aug. 1849 by Richard Nelson, William Nelson, John Thompson, John Warren who are bound unto the Ordinary in the sum of $1600. Mary E. Nelson wife of Richard Nelson died 28 March 1849, and was entitled to a share under the will of her grandfather William Cook, and the other chn. of James Cook decd. Left three minor chn. Elizabeth L. Nelson age 5 years, John Alexander Nelson age three years and six months, Mary Ann Nelson age 10 months. Mary E. was a dtr. of James Cook decd.

Richard Nelson. Estate of Richard Nelson. Box 52 #1833. Probate Judge Office. Camden, S. C. On 17 Nov. 1865 William Taylor states that Richard Nelson and Margaret his wife died intestate and he applied for letter of administration.

Ruth Nelson. Abstract of Ruth Nelson will. Box 52 Pack 1835. Probate Judge Office. Camden, S. C. Will dated 22 June 1850. Proven 20 July 1857. Daughter Jane Love. Executor John B. Mickle. Wit: James Love, Sr., Rutledge Love, Robert Love.

Walter Jasper Nelson. Minor. Box 52 #1836. Probate Judge Office. Camden, S. C. On 12 Oct. 1871 John H. Hartz was appointed guardian of Walter J. Nelson a minor age 15 years. He was also an heir of Jasper Christiansen of Charleston, S. C. He was born 11 Oct. 1855 in the city of Philadelphia.

Samuel E. Nelson. Will of Samuel E. Nelson. Box 135 Pack 11. Probate Judge Office. Sumter, S. C. I Samuel E. Nelson of Sumter Dist. being of sound mind and memory, etc. I give to my beloeved wife Amarintha C. Nelson the use of my Acton plantation near Atatesbourgh during her natural life or while she is a widow with all my household and kitchen furniture, carriage, horses, hogs, cattle and sheep. She is to have use of all negroes at the Acton place, at the time of my death, also fifteen hundred dollars to be paid her on the first day of Jan. each year. My son James M. Nelson having been provided for, is not to have any part of my estate. I give to my sons Patrick Henry Nelson and Samuel Warren Nelson all my real estate on Santee in Claredon County to be divided as, Patrick Henry to get the plantation called indigo hill, on the West side of the dividing line made by Stephen H. Boykin surveyor on the 22 Dec. 1843. With Samuel Warren to have the eastern side of said line called the Goshen plantation, with all tools, cattle, horses, mules, to be divided between them. I give to my grand son Samuel Nelson Burgess the sum of five thousand dollars to be paid him at the age of twenty one years. I give to my sons James M. Nelson, Patrick Henry Nelson, Samuel Warren Nelson in trust fifty negroes and two tracts of land, one tract bought from McKnight decd. est. also a small tract adj. purchased from the Sumters, also for the use of my dtr. Camiller Agnes Nelson. I appoint my son James M. Nelson guardian of my sons Patrick Henry and Samuel Warren Nelson and my wife guardian of my dtr. Camilla A. Nelson. I appoint my sons executors James M. Nelson, Patrick Henry Nelson and Samuel Warren Nelson in this order. Dated 25 March 1845. Wit: John Watson, W. E. Richardson, John B. Miller. Recorded 3 Nov. 1852.

John J. Nelson. Minors of John J. Nelson. Box 52 Pack 1829. Probate Judge Office. Camden, S. C. On 22 June 1874 Frank P. Beard was appointed guardian of James Nelson, English Nelson, Joseph Nelson, Mary Nelson, John Nelson, Mattie Nelson, Maggie Nelson, and William Nelson. Sarah Nelson wife of John J. Nelson. Paid 10 Dec. 1873. J. S. Nelson $96.00.

Levi Nelson. Estate of Levi Nelson. Box 52 Pack 1830. Probate Judge Office. Camden, S. C. Est. admr. 25 May 1857 by Asa Evans, William Kelly, James Team who are bound unto the Ordinary in the sum of $2,000.00. He died in April 1857. Owned 100 acres lying near Oakey

Ford on head waters of Swift Creek bounded by land of John Workman,
Tabitha Bradley. Heirs, Samuel Nelson, Elizabeth wife of William
Kelly, James Nelson, Rachel wife of John Kniper. The heirs of Granwell
Nelson (not given). The last three are out of State.

Martha Jane Nelson. Estate of Martha Jane Nelson. Box 52 #1831.
Probate Judge Office. Camden, S. C. Est. admr. 24 April 1869 by
Frank Nelson, Charles Bowen, John A. Chesnut, John A. Boswell who are
bound unto the Ordinary in the sum of $1,500.00. Frances Nelson states
that his mother died the 10 Jan. 1859.

Mary Nelson. Will of Mary Nelson. Box 74 Pack 12. Probate Judge
Office. Sumter, S. C. I Mary Nelson of Claredon County, being in perfect health, mind and memory. I give to my brother Sam. Edgar Nelson
the following negroes: Pegga, Letty, Mitty, Young Peggy, Febby,
Dranford, Betsey, Maria, Renoldo, Davy, George, Frasher, Jack with all
my household furniture, one feather bed and one half of my stock of
cattle to him and his heirs forever. I give to my nephew Miles
Hampton Plowden negroes Stepney, Molira, one feather bed and furniture,
and the remaining part of my stock of cattle to him and his heirs
forever. I give $100 from my estate to my niece Mary Nelson Plowden.
I give $100 from my estate to my niece Mary Potts. I give $100 from
my estate to my niece Mary Conyers. I give to my nephew Samuel James
Nelson $100 from my estate. I give to my nephew Samuel John Murray
$100 to be paid from my estate. I give to Mary Nelson Taylor $100 to
be paid from my estate. But the whole of my property is to remain in
the possession of my mother during her natural life and no longer. I
appoint my brother Samuel Edgar Nelson Executor. Dated 21 July 1809.
Wit: Samuel E. Plowden, Samuel and Thomas Potts. Signed: Mary
Nelson. Recorded 7 Jan. 1819. On another paper the heirs is given as
James Nelson, Samuel James Nelson, Isaac Montgomery and his wife Mary,
Samuel E. Plowden, Mary C. Conyers, William Plowden, Gabriel Plowden,
Miles H. Plowden, Frances E. Plowden, Hannah Plowden, Mary Nelson
Taylor, William Potts Sr. and Matilda his wife, Elizabeth Murray, the
heirs of Ann Plowden decd., Samuel J. Murray, Mary E. Potts.

E. C. Nelson. Estate of E. C. Nelson. Box 73 Pack 9. Probate Judge
Office. Sumter, S. C. Est. admr. 17 June 1833 by Capt. John Wither-
spoon, A. R. Ruffin, Josiah B. Mores who are bound unto the Ordinary
in the sum of $3,000.00. Citation published 16 June 1833 at Midway
Church.

John Nelson. Estate of John Nelson. Box 73 Pack 8. Probate Judge
Office. Sumter, S. C. Est. admr. 25 May 1805 by Samuel P. Nelson, who
is bound unto William Taylor, Ord. in the sum of $500.00. Estate
appraised by James Nelson, Samuel E. Nelson, Samuel E. Plowden.

General Patrick Henry Nelson. Estate of General Patrick Henry Nelson.
Box 155 #6. Probate Judge Office. Sumter, S. C. Est. admr. 15 Nov.
1864 by Emma S. Nelson, S. Warren Nelson, John Cantey who is bound unto
the Ordinary in the sum of $160,000.00. Patrick Henry Nelson died
22 June 1864. Left a widow Emma S. Nelson and two infant chn. Patrick
Henry Nelson and Camilla A. Nelson.

James M. Nelson. Estate of James M. Nelson. Box 155 #5. Probate
Judge Office. Sumter, S. C. Est. admr. 15 Nov. 1864 by Sarah R.
Nelson, his widow, W. B. Murray, S. Warren Nelson, who are bound
unto the Ordinary in the sum of 60 thousand dollars. He died on the
17 Dec. 1855. Expeditures for Dec. 13, 1858. Paid, Miss Emma J.
Nelson $16.30, paid Lizzie Nelson $12.42, paid J. Murray Nelson $3.67,
paid S. E. Nelson $2.04, paid J. M. C. Nelson $2.04.

William Nelson. Estate of William Nelson. Box 52 Pack 1837.. Probate
Judge Office. Camden, S. C. Est. admr. 4 Dec. 1856 by Jean Nelson his
widow, James Teams, William L. Picket who are bound unto the Ordinary
in the sum of $5,000. William Nelson died 10 Oct. 1856. Partition
made 27 Dec. 1858, mentioned Richard Nelson, Elizabeth Owens the wife
of Issac Owens, Francis Nelson, Amanda Nelson, George Nelson, Emma

Nelson, Ranson Nelson, Sarah Nelson the last two are minors. Owned 225 acres on 25 miles Creek North side being part of a grant formerly belonging to John Bowen bounded by land of Emanuel Parker, Mrs. McGraw, George R. Hunter and others.

W. R. Nelson. Estate of W. R. Nelson. Box 52 Pack 1838. Probate Judge Office. Camden, S. C. Estate admr. 29 Nov. 1879 by Jane C. Nelson, J. L. Mickle, J. McClair, Alice P. McClair who are bound unto the Ordinary in the sum of $2,000.00. He died 12 Sept. 1879.

NEVELL

James A. Nevell. Land Warrant of James A. Nevell. #71 Pack 114. Clerk of Court Office. Pickens, S. C. By W. L. Keith, Clerk, to any lawful surveyor you are authorized to lay out unto James A. Nevell a tract of land not exceeding ten thousand acres. Dated 7 Oct. 1844. Executred 9 Oct. 1844 for 1,150 acres. John O. Grisham. Certified 22 Oct. 1844.

Joseph E. Nevill. Bond for Title for land. Pack 108. Clerk of Court Office. Pickens, S. C. I Joseph E. Nevill of Clayton, Ga. am held and bound unto John W. Terry of Laurens Dist., S. C. in the sum of four thousand dollars. Dated 24 Feb. 1857. Condition are that Joseph E. Nevill shall make a certain deed unto John W. Terry for a tract of land of 202 acres lying on Cane Creek in Pickens Dist. adj. land of J. E. Nevill, Dr. L. B. Johnson, Capt. Andrew Dickson, and Issac Bradwell... Terry is to pay $500 per year. Wit: John O. Watson, Robert A. Steele, Jr. Signed: Joseph E. Nevill. Nevill filed a bill for relief on 1 April 1859. The defendant paid part of the notes on the land, but failed to pay the rest. Bond executed 1 Aug. 1859.

Jesse Nevill. Will of Jesse Nevill. Box 11 #138. Probate Judge Office. Pickens, S. C. Jesse Nevill of Pickens Dist. made his will 13 Sept. 1838. Was proven 25 July 1842. No wife mention. Chn: Alexander Nevill, William Nevill, James Nevill, Rebecca Price, Wenneford Beck. Bequeathed to Edward Coffee and his wife Elizabeth a negro girl. May have been a dtr.? Wit: John Adair, Enos A. Shields, Wm. H. England.

NICHOLAS

Julius Nichols. Estate of Julius Nichols. (No ref. given). Probate Judge Office. Abbeville, S. C. (First part of will not in notes.) ..."of our marriage contract and that in lieu of all dower in my lands and so forth." At her marriage or death the negroes, stock of cattle, horses, household furniture, hogs, still etc. be sold to the highest bidder, and the money divided between my grand chn. that is to say chn. of Sukey Moore, Betsey Cooper, Molley Jones, Lucy Marshall, Julius Nichols, Bobby Hunt and to William Nichols (and to Thomas Nichols an equal part with the rest), Thomas Nichols to have sixty dollars paid from my estate it being in full for one year labour while he lived with me. I appoint my wife Patty Nichols executrix and my son Julius Nichols Executor. "With the discretionary power to inclose my family buring ground in any manner they may think proper." Dated 23 Jan. 1803. Wit: Zachy. Pulliam, James Johnson, Gillam Sale. Signed: Julius Nichols. Recorded 8 Mar. 1804. Inventory made 31 May 1804 by James Pulliam, Zachy. Pulliam, James Johnson.

John Nichols. Estate of John Nichols. Box 70 Pack 1724. Probate Judge Office. Abbeville, S. C. Admr. Bond, 96 Dist., S. C. We Joshua Petty and Zachariah Bullock are bound unto John Thomas, Jr., Ord. in the sum of two thousand Pds. sterling dated 3 April 1784. An inventory made 17 April 1784 by Nathaniel Jeffries, Adam Potter, John Garrard.

William Nichols. Estate of William Nichols. Box 70 Pack 1734. Probate
Judge Office. Abbeville, S. C. Admr. Bond, Abbe. Dist., S. C. We
Benjamin Y. Martin, Jacob Martin and John C. Martin who are bound unto
Moses Taggart, Ord. in the sum of $10,000. Dated 2 Dec. 1839. Inven-
tory made 30 March 1840 by Andrew Giles, Thomas Cunningham and Alexander
Hunter. Expends; 10 Nov. 1839 by cash paid expenses in removing negroes
from Athens, Ga. to Abbeville Dist., S. C. $8.00. Paid 1 March
Mathew Young treasurer of Mineral Spring $28.17.

NICHOLSON

Ira R. Nicholson. In Equity, Pack 103. Clerk of Court Office. Pickens
S. C. Issac Holden and Jane his wife, nee Nicholson, sheweth that Ira
R. Nicholson died owning considerable real estate viz: Tract #1 the
Chattooga old town tract containing 600 acres, lyong on Chattooga
River in Pickens, Dist. on the Georgia line. Tract #2 containing 300
acres adj. tract #1. Now subject to division amongst the heirs, viz;
his widow Jane Nicholson and twelve chn. to wit, Evan Nicholson, Mary
the wife of Josiah Barker, Sarah the wife of James Loveless, Martha the
wife of William Holden, Harriet the wife of James Jackson Pell, William
Nicholson, Malinda the wife of Mordecai Cox, Mira the wife of Jesse
Lay, Silas Nicholson, Bailey Nicholson, Bailus Nicholson, Jane the wife
of Isaac Holden, filed 15 March 1851. Evan Nicholson was appointed gdn.
of Bailey Nicholson a minor over the age of 14 years, Evans
Nicholson, James Loveless and wife, William Holden and wife, William
Nicholson, Mordicai Cox and wife Bailus Nicholson were all living in
Georgia.

Hannah Nicholson. Will. Box 12 #154. Probate Judge Office. Pickens,
S. C. In the Court of Ordinary, 13 Feb. 1843. Three witnesses intro-
duced for the proving of a noncupative will of Hannah Nicholson decd.,
Nathan Lusk on his oath saith that on the 30 Dec. 1842 he was at the
residence of Hannah Nicholson a short time before her death, with him
was his wife Rosananh Lusk, and Deborah Massingale. She said that all
her effects to go to her son Ben, including some debts owing her, and
she wished Ben to be mericiful in making collections. Some one mentioned her clothing, she observed the women might divide them themselves.

Hannah Nicholson. Real Estate. Book A, page 46. Probate Judge Office.
Pickens, S. C. To the Court of Ordinary: Benjamin Nicholson sheweth
that he is entitled to a share of the land of Hannah Nicholson decd.
and he prays for an order for the sale etc. Dated 13 March 1843. She
had 100 acres lying on waters of Little River adj. land of John Holden
and others. Heirs: Benjamin Nicholson, Issac Nicholson of Missouri,
Jacob Nicholson of Arkansas, William Nicholson, Elizabeth the wife of
Joel Holden of Georgia, Mary the wife of William Queen of North Carolina
Lucinda the wife of Martin Moody, Hannah the wife of Bennett Moody,
Deborah the wife of Dread Massingale.

Bailus Nicholson. Land Warrant. #36, pack 630. Clerk of Court
Office. Pickens, S. C. J. E. Hagood, Clerk to any lawful surveyor you
are authorized to lay out a tract of land unto Bailus Nicholson not
exceeding ten thousand acres. Dated 17 May 1858. Executed for 519
or 579 acres. Filed 15 June 1858.

Lillie Nicholson. Estate of Lillie Nicholson. Box 114 #1108. Probate
Judge Office. Pickens, S. C. Lillie T. Nicholson on 1 June 1901
recd. a share from the estate of Mary Holden decd. of Pickens Dist.

NIEBUHR

John P. Niebuhr. Will of John P. Niebuhr. Box 34 #386. Probate Judge
Office. Pickens, S. C. I J. P. Niebuhr of Walhalla, being of sound
mind and understanding, but weak in body, etc. I do hereby will and

order that my executrix hereinafter named have have full and complete
power and authority, to hold and keep all of my estate, both real and
personal or mixed, until a more favourable time for the sale thereof.
I desire first my just debts to be paid. I give and bequeath to my
dear wife Rebecca Niebuhr to her support and use and for the support
and use of my children untill they shall be of lawful age. I hereby
appoint my wife Rebecca Niebuhr my executrix. Dated 13 Sept. 1854.
Wit: H. W. Kuhtmann, D. Biemann, Herman Knee. Signed: John P. Niebuhr.
Proven 29 Sept. 1854.

Rebecca Niebuhr. Will. Box 66 #720. Probate Judge Office. Pickens,
S. C. I Rebecca Niebuhr of Walhalla, being of sound mind and memory,
etc. After my just debts are paid the residue of my estate, both real
and personal, I give to my three chn. Henry, Peter and Carolina to be
divided between them equal, share and share alike. I hereby give to the
executors of this my last will to be the guardian of my children, with
full power to sell any or all of my property and to reinvest the proceeds or part thereof to the best of their judgement. I appoint Herman
Knee and H. W. Kuhtmann to be executors of my will and gdn. of my chn.
Dated 31 Oct. 1862. Wit: D. Biemann, H. Fagen, A. E. Norman. Signed:
Rebecca X. Niebuhr.

NIMMONS

William Nimmons. On 6 Feb. 1843 William Nimmons was appointed a
constable of Pickens Dist. Pack 634 #153. Clerk of Court Office.
Pickens, S. C.

Winny Nimmons. Real Estate. Book A, page 171. Probate Judge Office.
Pickens, S. C. Isabella Nimmons petitions the Court to sell the real
estate of Winny Nimmons as one of the heirs at law. Winny Nimmons had
26 1/2 acres on the waters of Conney Ross, adj. land of Abner Shuttles,
John Hardin and others. The others heirs are: Margaret the wife of
Abner Shuttles, Eleanor Nimmons, Martha the wife of Ebenezer Thomas,
Sarah the wife of Elijak Emery. Dated 7 March 1856.

James M. Nimmons. Deed from James M. Nimmons. Book E-2, page 117.
Clerk of Court Office. Pickens, S. C. James M. Nimmons to James M.
Winchester both of Pickens Dist. Dated 12 Nov. 1880. For the sum of
$200 do bargain, sell and release a tract of land lying on Nine Times
Creek, waters of Little Eastatoe, adj. land of J. M. Winchester,
Daniel Winchester and others. Containing 350 acres, known as the Darb
Nix place, sold on first Monday in Dec. 1877 as the homestead of Sarah
Nix. Wit: S. R. Fisher, M. C. Winchester. Signed: J. M. Nimmons.
Deed was attested by M. C. Winchester before James M. Stewart, Trial
Justice P. D. on the 12 Nov. 1880. Same date Phralba Nimmons the wife
of James M. Nimmons and voluntarily renounce, release and relinquish
her right of dower in the said land. Before James M. Stewart, Trial
Justice, P. C.

NOBLE

William Noble.. Estate of William Noble. Pack 4020. Clerk of Court
Office. Abbeville, S. C. To the Honr. the Chancellors: your orator
William P. Noble sheweth that on ___ day of Oct. 1823 William Noble
late of this dist. died intestate, seized with considerable real and
personal property. Leaving as his heirs, his widow Rebecca Noble, and
the following chn. your orator William P. Noble, who is twenty one years,
Andrew A. Noble, Samuel Noble, Ezekiel Noble, Joseph Noble, the four
last named being minors, the first two over fourteen years, the last two
under fourteen year, Rebecca Noble has a letter of admr. Your orator
is desirous that the negroes belonging to the estate be divided, with
the widow taking one third and your orator one fifth of the other two
thirds. Dated 22 June 1829.

Rebecca Noble. Estate of Rebecca Noble. Box 69 Pack 1697. Probate
Judge Office. Abbeville, S. C. We William P. Noble and Patrick Noble
are bound unto Moses Taggart, Ord. in the sum of $7,000.00. Dated 16
March 1831. The inventory was made the 19 March 1831 by M. Waddel,
Wm. Calhoun, Nathl. Harris, Paul Rogers. Negroes, man Charles, Jack,
Sesor. Girl Rose, Hannah, Luesia and old woman Nelly, girl Lidda and
boy Hazard. Sale held 21 March 1831. Buyers. A. Noble, W. P. Noble,
Charles Vaughn, Dr. E. Gibert, Dr. N. Harris, George Patterson, Col. P.
Noble, John G. Arnold, Pall Rogers, J. P. Covan, William P. Noble, Mary
H. Noble, L. Gillibo, H. Sturt, Thomas Morrow, M. Breazell, Joseph
Bushelong.

James Noble. Estate of James Noble. Box 70 Pack 1707. Probate Judge
Office. Abbeville, S. C. I James Noble of Abbeville Dist. being of
sound mind and memory, but weak in body. I give to my dear wife Mary
Ann one negro named Sarah in fee simple, with one third part of the
land including my dwelling house and clear lands, and one third of my
moveable estate during her widowhood or natural life. I will my two
sons James and John to have the whole of my land at the death of my
dear wife. The whole of my moveable property to be divided between my
four chn. James, John, Mary and Sarah when they come of age. My will
is that my outstanding debts and ready money be applyed to the education and maintainance of my children and wife. I appoint my brother
Alexander Noble and friend Joseph Calhoun executors. Dated 5 Nov. 1796.
Wit: Flm. Bates, William Noble, Nancy McFarland. Signed: James Noble.
Recorded 8 Nov. 1796. The appraisement was made 19 May 1797, by
Benjamin Howard, J. McCarter, William Gray. Negroes, Man Ben, woman
Dinah, Dot, Nance, Sall, Sarah, boy Isaac, Simon, Bill, girl Hannah.

John L. Noble. Estate of John L. Noble. Box 69 Pack 1704. Probate
Judge Office. Abbeville, S. C. I John L. Noble being of sound mind
and disposing memory. I give unto my two sisters Mary Baskin and Sarah
Baskin and their heirs 100 acres of land adj. land of Ezekiel Calhoun,
Esq. I give to my nephew James Noble and his heirs all the rest and
residue of my land, provided he has heirs of his body, if not land to
be equal divided between my two sisters Mary and Sarah. I give to my
sister a negro man named Bill, for her use only, and not subject to any
debts or contracts of her husband Thomas S. Baskin. I give to my
sister Sarah a negro man named Jim and a negro woman named Lizzy, upon
payment of $200 to my sister Mary. I give to my nephew James Noble a
negro boy named Tooman, the rest and residue of my personal property
of what ever kind except my household and kitchen furniture, with such
a part of my cattle, hogs, sheep as may be necessary for the support
of my sister in law Betsey Noble. I appoint my friends John Baskins
and Patrick Calhoun the executors. Dated 26 May 1816. Wit: J. Calhoun
Jos. Hutton, Patrick Calhoun. Signed: John L. Noble. Will proved 23
Sept. 1816. In the inventory and appraisement he is called Dr. John
L. Noble, with a medicine furniture and case and bottles. Appraiser
were J. Calhoun, Jos. Hutton, Wm. Moseley, J. Houston, J. W. Simonds.
Expenditures of the est. from 4 Jan. 1817 to 21 Ma. 1821. Paid:
John McCelwee, John E. Norris, Benjamin Finney, Vincent McCelhaney,
Andrew Norris, Thomas S. Baskin, Mathew Brewer, Alexander Houston,
Robert McComb, William H. Caldwell. Paid negro Bill for work on Dr.
Noble house. John Gray, Majr. Chiles (sheriff), Robert Bates, Dr. Casey
Joseph Calhoun Jr., Joseph Hutton, Dr. Waddle, William Moseley, Robert
Brown, Andrew Milligan, Fanney Calhoun, Samuel McLouch, William Scot,
Jr., Mrs. McCormick, Alexander Noble, Archibald Stokes, Capt. Rogers,
John Saxon, Nathaniel Norwood, Capt. William Robertson for surveying
and platting. William H. Caldwell for taxes for year 1819. Peter B.
Rogers for taxes for 1820. Returned 24 Sept. 1821.

Patrick Noble. Estate of Patrick Noble. Box 119 Pack 3518. Probate
Judge Office. Abbeville, S. C. I Patrick Noble First Lieutenant of
dragoons in the U. S. Army, do make this my last will and testament, etc
I give to my sister Elizabeth Bonneau Noble my entire estate real and
personal forever, excepting and reserving the following legacies herein
named. I will and direct my executors to purchase four (4) gold watches
worth about $150 each--one to be given to my brother Ezekiel Pickens

Noble. One to be given to my brother Edward Noble. On to be given to
my brother Alexander Noble. One to be given to my brother Samuel
Bonneau Noble. Also I direct my executor to purchase for my sister
Floride C. Cunningham a tea set of silver, viz a silver sugar dish,
silver cream pot, silver tea pot, set to cost about $150. I direct my
executors to purchase for Mary M. Noble my brother Edward wife a
silver urn, to cost fifty dollars. I direct my executors to pay over to
Ezekiel P. Noble sixty dollars to purchase for his son Patrick Noble
when he arrives at the age of sixteen (item not in notes). I further
will to Lieutenant John Love 1st. Dragoons U. S. A. my Mexician mustong
in charge of Lt. Chapman, Ft. Gibson Arkansas. I give to my brothers
Edward, Alexander, and Samuel B. Noble my trunks, boxes and clothing,
also my accountments as officer of the U. S. Army. I appoint Edward
Noble Executor. Dated 25 Dec. 1848. Wit: L. T. Bratton, B. P. Hughes,
T. B. Dendy. Signed: P. Noble, Lt. Drags. Will proven on oath of
B. P. Hughes before David Lesly, Ord. A. D. on the 20 Jan. 1849. State
of S. C., Abbeville Co. To Jones F. Miller, Esq. Probate Judge in and
for said Co. The petition of J. L. Perrin shows: That he is the duly
elected clerk of the Court of Common Pleas etc. That Patrick Noble Jr.
late of the County and State. Departed this life (no date) leaving his
last will and testament, which was duly proved, and admitted to probate and same is now on file. That Edward Noble the executor was
qualified, and after having partially administered the est. he died,
and the est. has not been fully administered. It has come my knowledge
as Clerk of the Court of Common Pleas. The fact that no application
for letter of admr. De Bonis Non Cum (of goods not yet administered on)
and there is now no legally appointed representative of the said
Patrick Noble Jr. by reason of which fact, your petitioner, as Clerk
of the Court, hereby makes application forletter of admr. Your
petitioner alleges that an amount is due the estate, by the U. S.
Government account of continuous service as a soldier, that your
petitioner is not informed as to the exact amount due the est. Therefore your petitioner prays for a letter of admr. issued to him etc.
Dated 10 June 1910. Signed: J. L. Perrin, Clerk of the Court of
Common Pleas, Petitioner.

NORRIS

Jasper J. Norris. Estate of Jasper J. Norris. Pack 323. Clerk of
Court Office. Abbeville, S. C. The state of Alabama, Dallas County:
To the Honr. Thomas G. Rainer Judge of Probate of said County and State.
Your petitioner Jasper J. Norris of said Co. and State, show that he
has a dtr. under the age of fourteen years, named Fanny Lula Norris
who is entitled to the sum of $1,000 from her mother estate in the
State of S. C. which is in the hands of Thomas Chatham admr. of the
mother estate, or money may be filed in some Court in said County. A
bond of two thousand dollars is executed, and he prays for gdn. of said
minor. Dated 5 Sept. 1857. J. J. Norris.

Robert Norris. Will of Robert Norris. Book 1 page 228. Probate Judge
Office. Pickens, S. C. I Robert Norris being in a reasonable state of
health, mind and memory. I give whatever land I may have at my death
to my wife Elizabeth Norris to be for her use and support of the family
during her life time, at her death the property to be for our little
son Jesse P. Norris. All money, notes, and accounts that I may have,
I give to my wife Elizabeth which she will pay my debts if any. All
other property as household, stock, etc, with a negro girl which my
wife had when we married, which she has a deed for. Nor do I make any
claim to other personal property we may have or the money we laid out
for land, as she is entitled to a home of her own. Dated 25 June 1856.
Wit: John Ariail, Micajah Miller. Signed: Robert Norris.
Proven 20 Jan. 1857.

Edward Norris. Inquest of Edward Norris. Pack 115. Clerk of Court
Office. Pickens, S. C. An inquest held at Farrs still house in
Pickens Dist. on 7 July 1861 before John R. Gossett Magistrate, acting
as coroner, upon the view of the body of Edward Norris of Pickens. The

jury; R. E. Bowen, Wm. Atkins, Pinkney Gossett, John T. Gossett,
Tillman Miller, Abel Bishop, Henry Wade, Charles Roper, Henry Lark,
M. Cothran, Washington Farr, Wm. Haynes who being charged and sworn do
say that the decd. came to his death by a wound inflicted by a knife in
the hand of George Trannum, on the 6 July 1861. Those who testify on
oath were Wilson N. Turner, H. C. Hunt, Dr. W. R. Jones, Jerry M. Clements.

NORTON

Edward Norton. Estate of Edward Norton, In Equity. #46. Clerk of
Court Office. Pickens, S. C. To the Honr. the Chancellors; Your orator
James Mulliken and wife Malinda. Sheweth that Edward Norton departed
this life intestate, seized and possessed of a valuable real estate.
A tract of land containing 356 acres in Pickens, Dist. That the land
is subject to division among Martha Norton the widow and eight chn. to
wit: The heirs of Zepporah Forbes decd. who intermarried with William
Forbes leaving chn. viz: Elmina, Adolphus and Nelson Forbes, residing
in the State of Miss. The heirs of Malissa Forbes decd. who intermarried with Samuel Forbes, leaving four chn. viz: Jepthah, Eliza and
George and the name of the fourth unknown to your orator, who is residing in the State of Georgia. Sarah the wife of Robert Wilson, Malinda
your oratrix, Jeptha Norton, Elizabeth the wife of William Wilkinson,
Lucinda the wife of Joseph Taylor, Mathurza the wife of Robert Emmerson.
Filed 20 Feb. 1851. Edward Norton land was about three miles from
Pickensville, S. C.

(Loose Paper) Macon County, N. C. (no other ref.) (Not abstracted)
Mr. Dendy, Sir I understand that you wish to pay over some money to
the legal representatives of Gidon Nortons children that you have in
your hands of William Norton decd. money that arose from the sale of
said land of said decd. land I have wrote to Cal. Norton to collect
what is due to the seven younger children of said Gideon Norton and by
paying to him this order shall be a receipt to you. For the amount paid.
Dated 21 Dec. 1832. Signed J. Howard. Personally appeared Martin
Norton who sworn saith that John Howard was appointed gdn. for the 7
of the minor chn. of Gideon Norton decd. which he had by his last wife.
Dated 1 April 1833, Pickens Dist., S. C.

William Norton. Family record of William Norton. No ref. William
Norton, Born 22 May 1822 in S. C. Died 28 Feb. 1879 at Guntown, Miss.
(Lee Co.) Buried at Cambelltown Cemetery, Guntown, Miss. Married
Jane Hawthorne, born 9 March 1826 in S. C., died 12 Aug. 1905 at
Guntown, Miss (Lee Co.), buried at Guntown, Miss. Children: William
Palaski, Edward, Corinne, Ella, Liza, Olin Perry, Eugene Clifton
Norton. Jane Hawthorne was the dtr. of Andrew Cowan Hawthorne and Polly
Barmore of Due West, S. C. Wm. Hawthorne and wife came to Miss. in 1857.

Richard Norton. Bastardy. Pack 271 #3. Clerk of Court Office.
Pickens, S. C. In Oct. 1832 Letty Perkins a single woman made oath
that in Pickens Dist. on the 10 Aug. 1828 at Pickens Court House she
was delivered of a female bastard child and that Richard Norton is the
father of said child.

Elias Norton. Legacy. Box 29 #337. Probate Judge Office. Pickens,
S. C. Elias Norton recd. property from the est. of John Holden Esq.
decd. whose est. was admr. 7 June 1852 in Pickens Dist.

Henry Norton. Grant. Pack 35. Clerk of Court Office. Pickens, S. C.
On 29 Nov. 1838 Rial Kennemore of Pickens Dist. sold 177 acres to
Isreal Mayfield lying on branches of Golden Creek waters of 12 Mile
River, granted to Henry Norton on 3 Dec. 1792.

Miles M. Norton. Deed from Miles M. Norton. Pack 75. Clerk of Court
Office. Pickens, S. C. This indenture made the 29 May 1848 between
Miles M. Norton Commissioner of the Court of Equity, and Madison F.

and Sarah Mitchell all of Pickens Dist. Whereas James M. Reid on 15
Sept. 1847 exhibit his bill of complaint against Sarah Reid and other
heirs of Stephen C. Reid decd. for partition of the real estate. Sarah
now the wife of Madison F. Mitchell. Whereas Miles M. Norton Comm.
do sell, bargain and release unto Sarah and Madison M. Mitchell a tract
of land known as the Pickensville tract, containing 265 acres that
Stephen C. Reid bought from Elijah Watson. Being the place Stephen C.
Reid died and where Madison F. Mitchell now lives. Wit: George Head,
W. D. Steele. Signed: Miles M. Norton, C.E.P.D.

Henry Norton to Edward Norton. Deed from Henry Norton to Edward Norton.
Pack 225 #4. Clerk of Court Office. Pickens Dist., S. C. Henry
Norton to Edward Norton both of Pendleton Dist. in consideration of
$40.00 do sell, grant, bargain and release a tract of land containing
200 acres on braches of Golden Creek on the South side. Adj. land of
Dover and Gadsons. Dated 7 Sept. 1808. Wit: George X Cannemore,
Thomas Lorton. Signed Henry Norton. On 21 Feb. 1809 Martha Norton did
voluntarily renounce and relinquish her dower to the land to Edward
Norton before John Willson J.Q. Recorded 1 March 1809.

William Norton. Real Estate. Book A, page 1. Probate Judge Office.
Pickens, S. C. William Norton decd. real estate 650 acres valued at
$1,000 dated 2 Nov. 1829. Heirs; Edward Norton, Jephtha Norton,
Barak Norton, Susannah the wife of Albert Robbins, Katharine the wife
of William Bevert, Lydia Norton, Heirs of Henry Norton, Lathe Norton in
right of her husband Gideon Norton, heirs of Sampson Norton decd.

NORWOOD

Williamson Norwood. Estate of Williamson Norwood. Pack 336. In
Equity. Clerk of Court Office. Abbeville, S. C. Will: I Williamson
Norwood being of sound mind and memory. I give to my grand children,
Joseph, Caroline Mary Clark, the chn. of my dtr. Caroline Clark decd.
the following negroes, Starlin Sally and his wife Martha, and her child
Lucius, Nat, Middleton, Carren, John (Field) and Amanda his wife,
Wade, Elijah, Little Dick and Miona his wife, Sarah, William, Angeline
bought in Hamburg, Cloe and her chn. Tom and Moses, Lewis Graves and
Nelly his wife and her chn. Reubin, Eliza and Jackson, George, Melinda
and her children Reubin, Ahepherd, Mahala and Alexander, one man Abram,
one man Harry and his wife Dolly, and son Alexander. I give the named
negroes in trust to M. B. Clark for his use till the chn. attain legal
age. I give to my son James A. Norwood that portion of my land enclosed
in his fence, with the right to the Young place, that I bought from
Frances Young and the tract I bought from George McDuffie. With the
following negroes to wit, Eliza and her chn. Sarah, John, Henry, Frances,
Eliza, Mary, Eveline also Juliana and her chn. Paul and Eveline also
Salley and her child Polley, also one yellow boy Charles son of Rachel.
I am desirous of setting free my negro woman Rachel and her chn.
Asbury, Catherine also Delia and her child Melanethon but the law does
not permit so I give them to my son James in trust, he to see carefully
to their interest and benefit and if opportunity should offer to the
chn. an education as he think best or removing them to a free state.
I give to my grand chn. the children of my dtr. Mary E. Belcher decd.
all that tract of land certified by John Speers, Esq. the 25 Feb.
1847. Containing 789 acres. I give said land in trust unto my son
James A. Norwood and John A. Calhoun for the use and benefit of the chn.
I give to my dtr. Sarah M. Calhoun all that tract of land containing
1795 acres as in platt of John Speers Esq. Wit: Nathaniel Norwood,
Thomas L. McBryde, A. B. Arnold, A. Hunter. Signed: Williamson
Norwood. Dated 17 Apr. 1857 (must be 1847). On 2 June 1854 Warren P.
Belcher a student of the South Carolina College. That his grandfather
died about the last of July 1848. Leaving two chn. living Sarah A.
Calhoun and James A. Norwood with two dtr. decd. Caroline Clark and
Mary A. Belcher, that he is the eldest of Mary Belcher chn. there are
six other who are minors, William W., Williamson H., John H., Henry C.,
James N., Mary A. Belcher. Warren P. prayes for a accounting of the
estate.

John Norwood. No ref. Abbeville Dist. (Last page only one found.)
Fourth: I give to my son John 100 acres lying on the head waters of
Mill pond, and the use of the saw mill and grist mill for two years.
Then my son Andrew to attend both mills, when Theophilus come of age
he will keep the mills, and if Daniel recieves any more education than
is common I allow the executors to consider it in dividing the est.
I leave my son Samuel four sheep. To my dtr. Jean Gutherie a cow and
calf. Executors: John Miller, Hugh Reid, William Cunningham. (No
date on this page of will.) Recorded 26 March 1796. Sale made 13 July
1798. Buyers, John Norwood, William Crawford, Samuel Norwood, James
Watts, John Tucker, James Stuart Baskin, Blakley Norwood, William
Grady, Matthew Robertson, William Emberson, Robert Lindsey, Alexander
McCoy, James Stark, Samuel Black, John Miller.

PACE

John & Richard Pace. Deed from John & Richard Pace. Book G, page 1.
Mesne Conveyance Office. Spartanburg, S. C. We John and Richard Pace
to John D. Young all of Spartanburg Dist. dated 20 Dec. 1799. In the
sum of $239.44 have sold, bargained, granted and released, all that
tract of land on the South side of North Tyger River, being one half of
the tract granted to John McElhany and Frances Dodds containing 100
acres. Adj. land of Shields Bookers, John D. Young and the est. of
Wm. Benson decd. and Richard Pace's land. Wit: Gab. Benson, Jno.
Jamison. Signed: John & Richard Pace. Deed attested before James
Jordon, J.P. by John Jamison on the 22 May 1800. Wit: Martha Well.

Richard Pace. Deed to Richard Pace. Book D, page 456. Mesne. Conveyance Office. Spartanburg, S. C. This indenture made between Nicholas
Waters of Union Co. and Richard Pace of Spartanburg Co. Dated 13 Nov.
1795. In the sum of fifty pds. sterling, hath granted, sold, bargained
and release 100 acres on the South side of North fork of Tyger River.
Adj. land of Thomas Collins, John Leech, and John McLehany. Land
originally granted to John McElhany on 4 May 1796. Wit: Joshua Downs,
John X Pace, William Kelley. Signed: Nicholas Waters. Deed attested
before Isham Foster, J.P. by Joshua Downs on the 19 July 1795.

John Pace. Deed to John Pace, Book B, page 177. Mesne Conveyance
Office. Spartanburg, S. C. Deed from John Fincher of Union Co. and
John Pace of Spartanburg, Co. Dated 24 Jan. 1788. In the sum of fifty
pds. sterling for a tract of land whereon John Pace now lives, containing
100 acres, it being part of a tract for which Mr. Francis Dod got a
grant dated 24 Oct. 1767. Mr. Dod conveyed unto Fincher all that lies
West of the Tyger River. Wit: Jeremiah Lucas, John Oslin, John X
Fowler. Signed: John X Fincher.

Stephen Pace. Deed to Stephen Pace. Book H, page 202. Mesne Conveyance
Spartanburg Co., S. C. This indenture made between William Poole and
Stephen Pace both of Spartanburg Co. Dated 26 Oct. 1801. (William
Poole an ironmaster.) In consideration of $100.00 have granted, sold
and release 100 acres on the South side of Tyger River. Originally
granted to John Rosin the 5 June 1786, sold by him to William Poole.
Wit: John X Wood, Aries Brown. Signed: William Poole. Attested before
Isham Foster, J.P. by John Wood on the 24 Aug. 1802.

Jeremiah Pace. Deed to Jeremiah Pace. Book O, page 65. Mesne Conveyance. Spartanburg, S. C. This indenture made between James Kilgore
and Jeremiah Pace both of Greenville Dist. Dated 8 Aug. 1809. In the
sum of $200.00 do grant, sell, bargain and release a tract of land
containing 200 acres, being part of a grant of one thousand acres
granted to Pennel Wood on the North side of Maple swamp Creek waters of
Tyger River. The land where Ellis Reynolds now lives. Wit: John
Grier, Richard Locke. Signed: James Kilgore. On the 9 March 1811.
Kezekiah Kilgore the wife of James Kilgore appeared before Reubin
Barrett, J.Q. and renounce, release and relinquish her dower to the
above land.

Jonathan Pace. Deed to Jonathan Pace. Book 19, page 240. Reg. of Deeds Office. Asheville, N. C. This indenture made between Moses Martin of Clay Co. State of Kentucky and Jonathan Pace of Buncombe Co., N. C. Dated Nov. 13, Anno Domini. In consideration of $200.00 hath bargained, sold and released a tract of land containing 200 acres, being a tract granted unto Joseph Williams in 1793 lying on North Pacolate. Adj. land of Maberns Line, including the old mill and the place whereon Jonathan Pace now lives. Wit: Daniel Pace, Burrell Pace, Samuel Evans. Signed: Moses Martin. Proven in open Court by Daniel Pace the 25 Aug. 1834. Test John Miller, Clk. By N. W. Woodfin, D. C.

Burrel Pace. Deed from Burrel Pace. Book I, page 412. Mesne Conveyance. Spartanburg, S. C. Deed between Burrel Pace and John Shands both of Spartanburg Dist. Dated 24 Jan. 1804. In consideration of $150.00 have bargained, sold and release a tract of land containing 100 acres, granted to Pace 1 Jan. 1787, adj. his own land, and other sides vacant. Wit: Wm. L. Allen, Thos. Woodruff. Signed: Burrell Pace. Attested by William Lindsey Allen before W. Lancaster, J.Q. on the 13 Aug. 1804.

Jeremiah Pace. Deed from Jeremiah Pace. Book S, page 262. Mesne Conveyance Office. Spartanburg, S. C. I Jeremiah Pace of Buncombe Co., N. C. to William Miller of Spartanburg Dist., S. C. Dated 1 Jan. 1816. In consideration of $300 have granted, sold, bargain and released a tract of land containing 200 acres, it being part of a tract of 1000 originally granted to Pennel Wood on the North side of Maple Swamp Creek, waters of So. Tyger River. Including the tract where Miller now lives. Wit: Benjamin Wood, John Wood. Signed: Jeremiah Pace. Deed proved by Benjamin Wood before Thomas Wood, J.Q. on the 20 Aug. 1821.

Richard Pace. Deed from Richard Pace. Book G, page 137. Mesne Conveyance. Spartanburg, S. C. This indenture made between Richard Pace and William Traylor both of Spartanburg Dist. Dated 20 March 1800. In consideration of $250.00 doth grant, sell, acknowledge by this deed a tract of land containing 60 acres being part of a tract granted to John McElhenny on the North Fork of Tyger River. Wit: Isaac Snoddy, John Pace, John Traylor. Signed: Richard Pace. Proven by Isaac Snoddy before Isam Foster, J.P. on the 26 Apr. 1800.

Sarah Pace. Estate of Sarah Pace. In Equity. Pack 353. Clerk of Court Office. Abbeville, S. C. To the Honr. Chancellors. Your oratrix Lucinda Jane Cannon a minor. With Philip Cromer as gdn. the grandaughter of Sarah Pace decd. who died in 1855 leaving a last will and testament, which Thomas Easkin was appointed executor. But that will was lost or destroyed was not admitted to probate. On the ___ day in 1855 John Davis was duly appointed admr. of the est. An effort was made in the Court of Ordinary to establish the said will, but failed. An appearl was made and their verdict among other things gave three negroes, named Hester, Adaline, Frankie to your orator, but to remain in the hands of Mr. Breazeal until full age or marriage. Your orator is unable to account for said negroes or their rent, stock has been sold without account. etc. etc. Filed 22 Apr. 1859. On another paper dated Jan. 1850 Louisa Pace was appointed gdn. of Lucinda J. Cannon, Louisa Pace married Eakin Breazeal and Lucinda was living with her, but she now lives with her father, and James Irwin has been named her guraidna. (There seem to be more than one will of Sarah Pace, seem to be three.)

Jeremiah R. Pace. Deed from Jeremiah R. Pace. Book 11, page 63. Reg. of Deeds Office. Asheville, N. C. This indenture made between Jeremiah R. Pace of Buncombe Co., N. C. and Thomas Ballard (resident not given). Dated 1 Aug. 1816. In consideration of $200.00 hath granted, sold and bargained a tract of land lying on the West side of French Broad River, containing 290 acres. Adj. land of James Brittons, James Rutledges and McNitts corner. Wit: B. Brittin, Rheuber Ballard. Signed Jeremiah Pace. Proven in open Court July term. 1817. Jno. Miller, Clk.

Stephen Pace. Estate of Stephen Pace. Apt. 6 File 375. Probate Judge Office. Greenville, S. C. On the 21 Nov. 1809 John Pace and John Wood applied for a letter of admr. of the est. of Stephen Pace decd. An account dated 29 Dec. 1820 gives Jane Pace the widow as Jane Bruton as administratrix of said est. Total from sale and sundry persons $411.03 1/4. In her return of 19 March 1833 she paid John Pace acct. $14.00. Her share as widow $143.40 3/4... leaving a total of $286.82 1/4 This same amount she charge the estate for raising and schooling six small chn. since the year 1809. Signed: Joab Bruton, admr. and Jane Bruton Admrix. The heirs, Maiden the wife of Seth P. Pool, Anne the wife of Benjamin Lynch, Frances the wife of Clabourn P. Pool, James L. Pace, William Pace and John Pace.

Leander Pace. Estate of Leander Pace. Apt. 24 File 9. Probate Judge Office. Greenville, S. C. To Honr. S. J. Douthit, P.J.G.C. The petition of John F. Hightower shewth that he is admr. of Leander Pace decd. est. who died about the year 1862. Leaving his widow Lousana now Lousana Forrester, Henry T. Pace a son, Elizabeth C. Pace, now Reid a minor. The date set for a final settlement is 11 May 1880.

PADGETT

John Padgett. Estate of John Padgett. Pack 259. Clerk of Court Office. Abbeville, S. C. To the Honr. the Chancellors; Your orator John R. McCord and your oratrix Belinda McCord. That in the year 1839 John Padgett died intestate with considerable real and personal property Leaving two chn. Mary Ann and Louisa Padgett both minors and your oratrix Belinda Padgett the widow, who in the year 1841 married John R. McCord. Ezekiel Rasor and Abner H. Magee took out letter of admr. upon the est. They took possession and sold the personal property and were also appointed gdn. of the minor chn. All debts are paid from the said sale with considerable amount for the distributees, also a tract of land containing 270 acres on the waters of Turkey Creek, adj. land of Nicholas Ware, R. V. Posey, Richard Wardlaw, Letty Wilson, Filed 8 Feb. 1845.

Nancy Padgett. Pack 457 #16. Clerk of Court Office. Pickens, S. C. Nancy Padgett of Pickens Dist. made oath before Thos. H. Bowen, Mags. for sd. dist. this 8 Dec. 1849 sayeth that on 2 Aug. 1849 at her mother' house she was delivered of a female bastard child dark eyes and black hair and that Alvin Allgood did get her with child. Taken the day and year above written before me Thos. H. Bowen M.P.D. Signed: Nancy X Paget.

PALMER

Hellen Palmer. Estate of Hellen Palmer. Pack 388. Clerk of Court Office. Abbeville, S. C. To Honr. the Chancellors; Your orator John Marion Palmer sheweth that Robert M. Palmer his father of this state and Dist. on 10 April 1848 by deed duly executed conveyed to William A. Wardlaw of same State and Dist. twenty negroes with their increase, Basil and his family Hannah Caty, Sucky, Grace, Harriet, Marcus and Rena and Anthony and his wife Lines and her chn. Sam and Cyand Simeon and his family Molly, John, Mack, Billy, Dave, Harry and Jinney in trust. For the sole and separate use of his wife Hellen St. Julien Palmer during her life and at her death to her children to share and share alike. Your orator further sheweth that his mother died in June 1857 leaving the following chn. between whom the aforesaid...? (No more could be found in the notes.)

PARKER

Charles Parker. Estate of Charles Parker. Pack 256. Clerk of Court
Office. Abbeville, S. C. To the Honr. the Judge of the Court of
Equity; Your orator and oratrix, John Parker, Josiah Parker and Nancy
Parker. That on ___ 1823 Charles Parker departed this life intestate,
possessed with a tract of land containing 200 acres, bounded on South
by Robert Smith, West, by Dabney Wansley, North by John S. Allen, East
by Hugh McLin, leaving no issue, but a widow your oratrix Nancy and your
orators his brothers Thomas Parker, James Parker, also brothers and
Sarah Parker the widow and Thomas Parker, Sarah Parker, Margaret
Parker, Jane Parker, Catharine Parker, Stutly Parker, Matthew Parker,
Nancy Parker, Mary Parker, and Charles Parker the chn. of Mathew Parker
an other brother now deceased before the testate, Nancy Parker who is
the wife of Robert Blithe and Mary Parker who is the wife of James
Birmingham which said Nancy and Mary are sisters of the intestate.
Filed 23 May 1825. Abbeville Dist., S. C. Personally appears Alexander
Hunter who being sworn say he was personally acquainted with Mathew
Parker the brother of Charles Parker decd. that he once lived in this
Dist. afterwards removed to the State of Georgia, and that he heard
that he was killed in the late war with Creek Indians, and of this
fact he has no doubt, but surely believe that he was killed about that
time. Dated 8 June 1826. Signed: A. Hunter. Before Patrick Noble,
J.P.

Elmyra Parker. Pack 288 #1. Clerk of Court Office. Pickens, S. C.
(Peace Warrant). In 1845 Elmyra Parker was the wife of William Parker
of Pickens Dist.

PARKS

William Parks. Will of William Parks. Book 3 page 253. Probate Judge
Office. York, S.C. I William Parks of York Dist. being sick in body
but of sound mind and memory, etc. I give to my son in law John
Alderson and his wife Mary, one half of my tract of land including the
improvements and the spring of water, where said John now lives on the
West side of Steel Creek. I give the other half of my tract of land
to my son Joseph Parks, including the improvements and the spring of
water where I now live on the East side of Steel Creek. I give to
my son Henry Parks twenty dollars. Also to my grand son William
Clawson ten dollars, when he arrives at twenty one years. I appoint
my son Joseph Parks and John Alderson executors. Dated 26 Dec. 1851.
Wit: R. Stewart, A. J. Giles, S. H. Giles. Signed: W. Parks.
Probated 3 Nov. 1852.

James T. Parks. Estate of James T. Parks. Box 136 #5. Probate Judge
Office. Orangeburg, S. C. James T. Parks, Jr. was the son of Annie
E. Parks age 5 years and residing with his mother. His father James T.
Parks is now dead. Had an interest in an insurance policy. Dated 3
Aug. 1906.

George Park. Will of George Park. Book A, page 192-193. Probate
Judge Office. Union, S. C. I George Park of Union Co. being weak in
body yet in sound mind and memory. First I ordain that all my just
debts be paid. I leave to my loving wife Margret Park my house, her
bed and clothing and dresser furniture and such household utensils to
use them her life time in widowhood, if capable and if she should prove
frail and helpless that James Park shall take special care of her, and
then to possess all my worldly substance as my rightfull heir after
her death. I appoint James Park my sole executor to receive the profits
so as to sufficiently provide for his mother support either in health
or sickness or old age. Dated 23 June 1804. Wit: Ephraine McBride,
Samuel Davidson, Tabitha Davidson. Signed: George Park.

James Park. Will of James Park. Box 17 Pack 11. Probate Judge Office.

Union, S. C. I James Park of Union Dist. farmer, being in sound
mind and memory, etc. After my burial charges and all lawfull debts
are paid from the money due the estate. I order that my wife Jean enjoy
the dwelling house and such furniture as she shall think useful for her
and farming tools sufficient to tend as much land as may support her,
with horses, cows, hogs, sheep and negroes Ester, Polina, Jerry and
Abner to remain with her during her life. Sell Violet and her two
chn. Winny and ___. If the others negroes mind not my wife they are to
be hired out, and rent the land. Heirs, James, Joseph, George, Jean
married husband not named, Margret--married husband not named, Matthew,
Thomas, Ephraim. I appoint my trusty friends Joseph Quinn, Andrew
Leeper executors. Dated 18 Feb. 1828. Wit: John Wright, James S.
McWhirter, Mary G. Wright. Signed: James Park. Recorded 24 Aug.
1829.

PARSONS

James Parson. Estate of James Parson. Box 63, #684. Probate Judge
Office. Pickens, S. C. I James Parson, calling to mind the certainty
of death and the uncertainty of life, etc. I will that my just debts
be paid. I will to my beloved wife Marie L. Parson during her natural
lfie or widowhood the tract of land I now live on. Adj. the land of
Aeneas Hunter. D. Grice, J. C. Parsons, Stock, crops, household items,
also negroes Caroline and my negro boy. Also all the property she
brought here. At the death of my wife, property to be sold and divide
between my children. I appoint my sons Samuel and J. C. C. Parson as
executors. Dated 25 Oct. 1855. Wit: D. Grice, J. C. Boggs, J. C.
Grice, Z. Smith. Signed: James Parson. Proven 18 Aug. 1862. Heirs:
Samuel Parson, Thos. Parson, W. J. Parson, heirs of Sarah Adcock decd.
viz: L. B. Parson, James Adcock, Cynthia Neighbors, Carolina Dean,
Eliza A. Garner, Mary S. Mayfield, John B. Parson, F. C. Parson, Wm. G.
Parson, Malinda the wife of Watson Stewart.

James T. Parson. Estate of James T. Parson. Box 73 #784. Probate
Judge Office. Pickens, S. C. Est. admr. 17 Feb. 1864 by Mary A.
Parson, Samuel Parson, Charles Thompson who are bound unto W. E.
Holcombe, Ord. in the sum of $2,000.00. In 1869 Mary A. Parson was the
wife of James Dobson.

Manoh Parson. Estate of Manoh Parson. Box 100 #1061. Probate Judge
Office. Pickens, S. C. Est. admr. 11 Nov. 1886 by S. W. Clayton, H. A.
Richey, T. C. Robinson who are bound to J. H. Newton, Ord. in the sum
of $400.00. Mrs. Parson, James Parson, bought at sale.

J. J. Parson. Guardian of J. J. Parson. Box 11 #168. Probate Judge
Office. Pickens, S. C. On 24 Jan. 1881, D. G. Parson, D. R. Evans,
Samuel Parson are bound to O. L. Durant, Ord. in the sum of $300.00.
D. G. Parson gdn. of J. J. Parson minor under 21 years. Dtr. of Thomas
Thompkins decd. D. Garvin Parson her husband.

Samuel Parson. Will of Samuel Parson. Box 91 #969. Probate Judge
Office. Pickens, S. C. I Samuel Parson being of sound mind and disposing memory, etc. I desire all my debts and funeral expenses be
paid. I will to my beloved wife Sarah M. Parson during her natural life
or widowhood the tract of land whereon I now live containing 323 acres,
one wagon, two horses, two cows, one brood sow, and all growing crops,
etc. All notes, accounts and ready money. After the death of my wife,
I will and devise to my son David G. Parson the land, stock and tools
that she possessed. I will to my grand son Lowry G. Parson the son of
Benjamin, one bed and stead and furniture, in addition to his interest
in the est. in right of his father... I will to my grand daughter
Marietta dtr. of S. A. A. Parson, one bed stead and furniture, as a
special legacy, also to my daughter in law Hannah R. Parson the widow
of Benjamin Parson one cow as a special legacy. The remainder to be
divided between my chn. except David G. Parson, each to account for
what I have given them so they may be all equal out of the fund. I

appoint my son Samuel A. A. Parson and my son in law Samuel Chapman
executors. Dated 11 March 1875. Wit: Robert R. Todd, W. Eaton, W. E.
Holcombe. Signed: Samuel Parson. Probated 6 Oct. 1833. In Feb.
1887, Aubrey Brewer, Mary M. H. Chapman, Laura E. Rackley, Anna M.
Haynes, T. G. Parson, Susan M. Boroughs, Sarah Arnold each recd. from
the est.

PATTERSON

James Patterson. Estate of James Patterson. Box 74 Pack 1812. Probate
Judge Office. Abbeville, S. C. I James Patterson of Long Cane, planter,
being sick and weak in body, but of perfect mind and memory. I give to
my daughter Jenet Carswell forty shillings, to her dtr. Jean McCormice
three pds. and to each of her other chn. forty shillings. I leave to
my son Alexander Patterson all that tract of land on which he and I
now lives. I leave to my son Josiah Patterson that tract of land known
as the Crawfords place on the Bold Branch. I leave to my grand daughter
Anges Mills and Kethrine Graves 100 acres of land known as the Bradys
old place branch to be equal divided between them, also my bed and
beds to be equal divided between them, also my apparal to be divided
between my sons. I leave to my grand son James Patterson son of Josiah
my shot gun, and to my grand son James son of Alexander my rifle
gun. I leave to Mr. Dickson preacher of the gospel a good cow and calf.
I leave to my son Josiah my large Bible, the rest of my books divided
between my sons Josiah and Alexander and grand daughters Agnes Mills
and Kethrine Graves. I appoint my son Josiah Patterson and beloved
friends William McGaw and John Patterson executors. Dated 7 Aug.
1795. Wit: William Carson, John Betty, Robert X Howard.
Codicil added the 18 Aug. 1795. Having satisfied I have rather
lavish in my bequethmants to my son Alexander and for other causes,
I order the sum of twenty four pds. to be deducted from his legacy and
given to my dtr. Jennet Carswell. Wit: William Carson, Robert X
Howard. Signed: James Patterson. Recorded 10 Nov. 1795. Est.
appraised the 16 Nov. 1795. Sale held 2 Dec. 1795. Buyers, Thomas
Carswell, Andrew Taylor, Samuel McKiney, John Hearst, Robert Carson,
Josiah Patterson, John Davidson, Alexander Patterson, David Neilson,
Alexander White, Caleb Jennings, George Crawford, James McBride, John
McCreevan, John Beaty, William Robison, Charles Beaty, Alen Bailey,
John McGraw, James Ross, Thomas Stewart, Archibald Thomson, Robert
McDonald, John Mathison, John Conner, William Abel, Jacob Free, Robert
Lawson, Andrew Brown, Agnes Mills, Joseph Abel, Joseph Houston,
Timothy Russell, William Carson Jr., James Hill, William Deal, Jeremiah
Rogers, William Williamson, Mrs. Sarah Pettegrew, John Kennedy. Three
negroes boys, Fedd, Jack and Bob. One negro woman Bett in sale.

Thomas Patterson. Estate of Thomas Patterson. Box 3 #23. Probate
Judge Office. Pickens, S. C. Est. admr. 13 Dec. 1830 by Clary or
Clavy Patterson, John Davis, Alexander Ramsey who are bound unto James
H. Dendy, Ord. in the sum of $500.00. Inv. made 13 Dec.1830 by James
Morrison, Joshua Garrett, Stephen Baldwin. On 1 Aug. 1837 Dudly R.
Patterson, Syntha Patterson his wife of Franklin Co., Ga. of the one
part and Willia. Robinson of Pickens Dist. of the other part for the
sum of $125.00 do convey unto Wm. Robinson one sixth part of a tract
of land whereon Nicholas Hunt lived and died on the waters of Peters
Creek, adj. land of Martin Whitmire, Thomas Singleton, Joseph Robinson.
(Loose Papers). On 27 Feb. 1841 James Patterson recd. $15.00 in part
payment of the legacy due to his mother Elizabeth Patterson of Georgia
she being an heir of Wm. Baker decd.

Joel Patterson. Land Warrant of Joel Patterson. #159. Clerk of Court
Office. Pickens, S. C. By W. L. Keith, Clerk, to any lawful surveyor
your are authorize to lay out unto Joel Patterson a tract of land not
exceeding ten thousand acres. Dated 1 Aug. 1852. Executed for 13
acres on 19 Aug. 1852. Certified 29 Nov. 1852.

PEGG

Eliza Pegg. Ref. #61-Basement?. Pickens, S. C. On 20 March 1858
Eliza Brazeale was mentioned as the widow of Griffin Brazeale of Anderson, now the wife of James B. Pegg of Anderson, S. C. she was the
daughter of Bailey and Jean Barton. She had six children by her former
husband Griffin Breazeale decd. viz: Nancy J., Sarah A., Mary B.,
Eliza A., Jestine A., Camilla Brazeale all whom lived in Anderson Dist.
with her.

PELOT

Charles M. Pelot. Pack 344. Clerk of Court Office. Abbeville, S. C.
To the Honr. the Judge of Dist.Court. Your orator Lewis D. Merrimon
sheweth that Charles M. Pelot of the said Dist. departed this life
intestate in the year 1863 leaving the only heirs his chn. James M.
Pelot, Joseph Pelot, Susan Pelot, Sallie now the wife of ___ Epps, the
heirs of Thomas Pelot decd. heirs unknown, Cornelia wife of ___ Mulinax
and Eliza Pelot and Julia Pelot. The admr. on the est. was committed
to your orator who has not been able to find any personal effects.
Pelot was indebted unto the est. of James M. Perrin decd. and others.
The decd. Pelot was seized and possessed with a tract or lot containing
about 10 acres in the town of Greenwood, S. C. adj. land of W. P. Mc-
Kellar and W.C. Venning with the value of about $300. Your orator
prays for a sale of the real property to pay the debts. Your orator
is informed that the heirs are now residing beyond the limits of this
State. Filed 22 Aug. 1867.

PERKINS

Joshua Perkins. Estate of Joshua Perkins. Box 74 #794 A. Probate
Judge Office. Pickens, S. C. On 2 Nov. 1859. Josiah Perkins and
Hannah Perkins made oath that Joshua Perkins died intestate. Owned 319
acres lying in the fork of Tugaloo River and Chauga Creek, adj. land of
Jabez Jones, Robert Gilmer and others. Heirs, his widow Hannah Perkins
and eight chn. viz: Josiah, William, Augustus, Mary, Moses, Samuel,
Harriet Elizabeth, Martha Adaline Perkins. (Note on one paper Hannah
was written Johanna, this was in the letter of admr. dated 15 Dec. 1856.

William Perkins. Estate of William Perkins. Box 62 #672. Probate
Judge Office. Pickens, S. C. Est. admr. 18 Aug. 1862 by Daniel Butler,
W. W. Leathers, Samuel D. Armon who are bound unto W. E. Holcombe, Ord.
in the sum of $1,000.00. Left a widow and two chn. On 29 Feb. 1864
paid R. A. Thompson gdn. for the minors. John H. and Amanda M. Perkins
each $123.68. America D. Perkins bought at the sale.

Samuel Perkins. Estate of Samuel Perkins. A Minor. Box 74 #794.
Probate Judge Office. Pickens, S. C. Est. admr. 29 Feb. 1864 by Robert
A. Thompson who is bound unto W. E. Holcombe, Ord. in the sum of
$700.00.

Perkins Minors. Guardian of Perkins Minors. Box 6 #100. Probate
Judge Office. Pickens, S. C. On 29 Feb. 1864 Robt. A. Thompson, John
W. L. Cary are bound unto W. E. Holcombe, Ord. in the sum of $500.
R. A. Thompson gdn. of John H. and Amanda A. Perkins minors under
21 years. Chn. of Wm. and A. B. Perkins. On 5 Aug. 1861 Hannah
Perkins gdn. of Herriett E. and Martha A. Perkins Minors under 12 years.
On 23 Nov. 1863 John H. Perkins was five years old and Amanda was three
years old. Hannah was also gdn. of Samuel and Moses Perkins minors over
12 years.

Samuel Perrin. Estate of Samuel Perrin. Box 75 Pack 1833. Probate
Judge Office. Abbeville, S. C. I Samuel Perrin of Abbeville Dist.
being of sound and disposing mind and memory. It is my desire that
my executors sell whatever of my est. either real or personal, and that
the money arising be applied to my funeral expenses and my just debts.
Except not to sell land South of the Adamson Survey, which I wish
reserved as a house for my wife Eunice and my minor chn. The remainder
to keep together on the plantation to support my wife and children. If
my wife should marry or move away I give her two negro men and two
negro women, to be chosen by herself. I will to my daughter Elizabeth
Lee Perrin a special legacy, because she has stayed longer with the
family than any of the rest of my chn. The legacy is negroes David,
Lucinda, Achlin and Caroline and one sorrel mare called weine. I
will that my son Thomas C. Perrin shall have a negro boy. I appoint
my sons Henry William Perrin and Thomas Chiles Perrin guardian of my
minor chn. viz; Lewis, Mary Ann, Agnes, Samuel and James Perrin. I
appoint my sons Henry and Thomas Perrin executors. Dated 27 Aug. 1828.
Wit: John F. Pelot, John Chiles, Samuel Pressly. Signed: Samuel
Perrin. Will proved by John Chiles before Moses Taggart, Ord. the
3 Nov. 1828. Executors qualified same day.

James M. Perrin. Estate of James M. Perrin. No ref. Probate Judge
Office. Abbeville, S. C. I James Perrin being of sound mind do make
this my last will and testament. My executor to pay all debts. I
give to my wife all my silver plate. I give to my eldest son Joel
Perrin my library of literary works, also the portrait of his mother,
grand father and grandmother. I give to my beloved wife during her
natural life my house and lot in the village of Abbeville, where we now
live. After the death of my wife, I wish my house and lot be sold at
appraised value, the privilege to be given the oldest son first to buy,
if h- declines then the next son and so on. By the will of Edward
Tilman the father of my wife, the negroes I received on my marriage,
have been settled upon her and her children, and are not part of my
estate. I appoint my brother Thomas C. Perrin executor and ask as a
favor that he will act as the gdn. of my son Joel. Dated 7 Feb. 1863.
Wit: M. McDonald, Wm. H. Parker, B. Johnson. Signed: James M. Perrin.

Burrell Perritt. Will of Burrell Perritt. Box 49 #538. Probate Judge
Office. Pickens, S. C. I Burrell Perritt of Pickens Dist. being of
sound mind and memory, etc. First I will my lawful debts be paid. I
give to my wife the tract of land I now live on known as the Isaac
Murphree place also the land adj. I bought from the Wm. Murphree est.
also I give to my wife five slaves viz: Sanders, Agness, Berry, Andrew,
and Caroline with all my household and kitchen furniture, all stock of
horses, cattle, hogs, and tools. After the death of my wife, I give the
above property to my son John, if John should die before his mother the
property is to belong to the children of my son John. If the family
think best sell negro boy Andrew to pay debts. I give to my son in
law J. B. Wright one dollar in money. I request my son help his mother
superintend and manage her out door business. I appoint my neighbour and
friend Green Fields executor. Dated 24 April 1858. Wit: Wm. Hunter,
C. C. Porter, P. M. Porter. Signed: Burrell Perritt. Proven 24 Jan.
1859.

John P. Perritt. Will of John P. Perritt. Box 124 #16. Probate Judge
Office. Pickens, S. C. I John P. Perritt being of sound and disposing mind and memory. My executor to pay my just debts and funeral
expenses. I give to my son Andrew P. Perritt my home place on which I
now live, on conditions that he give me and my wife Dacus A. Perritt
a comfortable support, the same house and one acre of land on which it
now stands, and give us medical attention as we may need during our

natural life, and to give my other three children the sum of four
hundred dollars to be divided between them, viz; Daniel A., Elizabeth
A. Murphree, Levina J. Alexander, Giving Andrew twelve years to pay
said sum. Dated 3 April 1894. Wit: T. A. Williams, J. D. Cureton,
Jesse Crenshaw, J. M. Stewart. Signed: J. P. Perritt. Filed 22 Oct.
1895. (Died 6 Oct. 1895).

PARROTT

Jeremiah Parrott. Will of Jeremiah Parrott. Box 142 #1. Probate Judge
Office. Pickens, S. C. I Jeremiah Parrott being of sound mind and
disposing memory, etc. First pay all debts and funeral expenses. I giv
to my wife Milley Parrott all my real and personal property, with all
notes, accounts of every nature and kind. At the death of my wife my
executors sell my plantation in one or more tracts as they may think
best. The heirs of my son John A. Perritt settle the accounts and
notes I hold against him for advances made him during his life time,
then shall they be equal with the balance of my chn. I appoint my wife
Milly Perrett Executrix and my son in law Isaac Gravely and David A.
Parrett executor. Dated 9 Sept. 1895. Wit: M. F. Hester, Elisha
Gilstrap, J. H. G. McDaniel, J. M. Stewart. Signed: J. S. Parrott.
        Codicil. Dated 20 Nov. 1897. I Jeremiah S. Parrott desire to
change or add this to my foregoing will. That at the death of my wife
my executors may hold my plantation from sale until they in counsel
with each others think the time has come to divide the land into tracts
and sell the same hereinbefore. Wit: J. M. Stewart, J. S. Hendricks,
W. R. Lawrence. Signed: J. S. Parrett. Filed 25 July 1903.
(Note the different spelling in this name.)

PERRY

Lemuel A. Perry. Marriage Contract between Lemuel A. Perry and Lucinda
Harris. Box H-I, page 214. Clerk of Court Office. Pickens, S. C.
A marriage contract entered into between Lemuel A. Perry and Lucinda
Harris. Whereas it is the will of Lemuel A. Perry that his daughter
Nancy E. McMahan and his son Jesse R. Perry should be sole heirs at
his death of so much real estate herein mentioned. viz; all the tract
of land lying North of the road known as the Pickens road leading from
the Court House to Ligons bridge to be equal divided between the two
at his death. The heirs of Lucinda Harris relinquish all rights or
claim to the same. The land South of said road to remain the property
of Lemuel A. Perry to use or dispose of as he may see proper. Also it
is agreed that the said Lemuel A. Perry is to have nothing to do with
her children except Amanda and that he be not liable to take care of or
maintain them. Dated 15 Aug. 1848. Wit: Benjamin Mauldin, Rucker N.
Mauldin. Signed: Lemuel A. Perry. Lucinda X Harris. Deed proven on
oath of Benjamin Mauldin before Joshua Jameson M.P.D. on the 2 March
1857.

Nancy E. McMahan. Deed of Assignment, Nancy E. McMahan. Book K, page
664. Clerk of Court Office. Pickens, S. C. Whereas Lemuel A. Perry
did on the 15 Aug. 1848 sign a deed of gift bequeathing to Nancy McMaha
and Jesse R. Perry a certain tract of land to be equal divided between
them. Now be it known inconveyance of other arrangements, that Nancy
McMahan does freely relinquish all claims to her portion of said deed
and all claims to any portion of the personal and real estate of the
said Lemuel A. Perry for ever. Nothing herein contrained shall be
construed as impairing the claim of the heirs of the said Jesse R. Perr
to their portion of said deed. Dated 26 Dec. 1865. Wit: D. Grice,
John G. Brown. Signed: Nancy E. McMahan. Proved on oath of John G.
Brown before Jno. R. Gossett Mag. P. D. on the 17 March 1866. Recorded
2 April 1866.

L. A. Perry to Elvyn E. Perry. Deed from L. A. Perry to Elvyn E. Perry. Book 2, page 136. Clerk of Court Office. Pickens, S. C. I, L. A. Perry to Elvyn E. Perry both of Pickens Dist. Dated 9 May 1878. In the sum of sixty dollars have bargained, granted, sold and released a certain tract of land on the branches of George creek waters of Saluda River. Adj. land of McMahan, Elbert E. Perrys line to E. Ray Perry line. Wit: J. F. Barnes, E. R. Perry. Signed: L. A. X Perry. Proven on oath of J. F. Barnes before F. A. McMahan, N.P. on the 9 May 1878. Recorded 29 Aug. 1878.

L. A. Perry to E. Ray Perry. Deed from L. A. Perry to E. Ray Perry. Book D, page 138. Clerk of Court Office. Pickens, S. C. I, L. A. Perry to E. Ray Perry both of Pickens Dist. Dated 9 May 1878. In the sum of thirty dollars have granted, bargained, sold and released a certain tract of land, beginning at a rock on the road from Greenville to Easley, the description is set forth more fully in a plat prepared by T. A. McMahan D.S. containing five acres. Wit: J. F. Barnes, D. W. X Harris. Signed: L. A. Perry. Deed proven by J. F. Barnes before F. A. McMahan, Mag. P. D. on the 9 May 1878. Recorded 29 Aug. 1878.

L. A. Perry to Elbert E. Perry. Deed from L. A. Perry to Elbert E. Perry. Book D, page 137. Clerk of Court Office. Pickens, S. C. I, L. A. Perry to Elbert E. Perry both of Pickens Dist. Dated 9 May 1878. In the sum of sixty dollars, have granted, bargained, sold and released a certained tract of land, beginning at a rock in the road from Greenville to Easley, said rock on McMahan corner then to a stake on E. Ray Perry corner... containing five acres. Wit: J. F. Barnes, E. R. Perry. Signed: L. A. X Perry. Deed proven on oath of J. F. Barnes before F. A. McMahan, J.P. on the 9 May 1878. Recorded 29 Aug. 1878.

L. A. Perry to John Perry Martin. Deed from L. A. Perry to John Perry Martin. Book A, page 528. Clerk of Court Office. Pickens, S. C. I, Lemuel A. Perry for and in consideration of terms and stipulation herein after expressed have deeded, granted, bequeathed and conveyed unto John Perry Martin, infant child of Narcisa Francis Martin a certain tract of land, commencing at a rock on the road leading from Lemuel A. Perry house South, to R. E. Holcombe. Land is a forty rod square or ten acres, being entirely surrounded by land of Lemuel A. Perry who the reputed father of the said John Perry Martin in consideration that the said Marcissa Francis Martin does not prosecute the said Lemuel A. Perry for bastardy to the said John Perry Martin. Conditions that if Narcissa Francis Martin should vacate and leave the premises among the minority of John Perry Martin that she ceases to have any control of the said premises, but it is to be controlled by Lemuel A. Perry for the use and support of the said child, until he is lawful age when he will have control. Dated 20 Oct. 1868. Wit: John R. Gosett, John H. Nally. Signed: Lemuel A. Perry. Deed proven by the oath of John R. Gossett before R. E. Holcombe, J.P. on the 13 May 1871. Recorded the 6 Sept. 1871.

L. A. Perry. Deed of gift from L. A. Perry, et al. Book K, page 665. Clerk of Court Office. Pickens, S. C. This is an agreement between L. J. Perry, J. H. Becknell, J. D. Becknell and L. A. Perry, Lucinda Perry and Irbey L. Perry. L. A. Perry have this day made a deed of gift to the heirs of J. R. Perry decd. viz; Frances E., Lemuel A., Eubla C. and James W. Perry for seventy two and a forth acres of land, and this is to certify that this deed is to be a final settlement between all the parties concerned, that the said L. A. Perry or his heirs shall never have and claim on the land of the other parties, viz; L. J. Perry, J. H. Becknell and J. D. Becknell does agree that they will never have any claim of the L. A. Perry estate both real or personal for ever. Dated 31 Jan. 1866. Wit: John Brown, James N. McMahan. Signed: L. J. Perry, J. D. Becknell, L. A. Perry, Lucinda X Perry, I. L. X Perry. Proven on oath of James N. McMahan. Before Jno. R. Gosett, Mag. P. D. on the 17 March 1866.

John C. Perry to L. A. Perry. Deed from John C. Perry to L. A. Perry. Book E, page 258. Clerk of Court Office. Pickens, S. C. John C. Perry

to L. A. Perry both of Pickens Dist. Dated 15 Feb. 1845. In consideration of $78.00 have granted, bargained, sold and release a tract
of land containing twenty six acres lying on a branch of George Creek
waters of Saluda River. Adj. land of L. A. Perry, John C. Perry and
Samuel Nickols. Wit: John Brown, George W. McMahan. Signed: John C.
Perry. On the 20 March 1845 Rebeca Perry the wife of John C. Perry did
renounce, release and relinquish her dower on the land before John
Brown, N.R.P.

Lemuel A. Perry. Will of Lemuel A. Perry. Apt. 86, Pack 915. Probate
Judge Office. Pickens, S. C. I Lemuel A. Perry being of sound mind
and disposing memory, etc. First I direct my just debts and funeral
expenses be paid as soon as possible. I will and desire that my three
children viz; Emma Etny, Elvin Easley, and Ella Cornelia Perry shall
have my lot #1 whereon the dwelling house stands containing 32 1/2.
Bounded by McMahan, John Perry Martin, and the Greenville road. Except
my wood shop which is to be the property of my three sons viz; Elvin
Easley, Elbert Earle, and Ellie Ray Perry to work the shop where it
stands or move it if they desire, and Mrs. Lucinda Perry to have a home
during her natural life or widowhood. I will and desire that John
Perry Martin shall have lot #2 containing 4 1/2 acres. I will and desire
that Nancy Emily McMahan shall have lot #3 containing 30 1/4 acres. I
will and desire that Maryann Nally shall have lot #4 containing 17
acres, bounded by Holcombe land and land of Jesse Perry decd. heirs.
I will and desire that Elbert Earle Perry shall have lot #5 containing
10 acres, and that Ellie Ray Perry shall have lot #6 containing ten
acres. I will and desire that my son Irby Leland Perry shall have my
rifle gun and black horse mule (Jack). I will the remainder of my
personal property be divided as Ella Cornelia Perry to have my bay
horse (Bob). Elvin Easley to have my bay mare (Molly). Elbert E.,
Elvin E., Ellie R. Perry shall have my shop, carpenters tools, lathe,
saw, wagons, stock, crops, rent shall belong to the parties owning
the home place, except one hundred dollars worth of crop which Elbert E.
Perry shall take possession and pay to Adellee Perry Martin as follows
that is to say ten dollars on the first day of Jan. for ten years, in
case of her death the balance unpaid shall fall back to my heirs. I
appoint my son Elbert Earle Perry my executor. Dated 14 June 1878.
Wit: J. F. Barnes, E. T. Holcombe, R. E. Holcombe. Signed: Lemuel
A. X Perry. Proven 27 May 1879.

Benjamin Perry. Will of Benjamin Perry. Box 11 #143. Probate Judge
Office. Pickens, S. C. I Benjamin Perry being of sound mind and memory
but advanced in age. I give to my beloved wife Nancy Perry all my
lands, houses & tenements on the North and East of Choestoo Creek,
being the land which I now live on, to have and hold during her natural
life and no longer. I also give to my wife one negro boy named Solomon,
also negroes Sal, Ned, Charlotte, Jack and Tom and all my household
and kitchen furniture, all my stock of horses, cattle, all notes,
debts due and moneys at my death. I give to my son Nathaniel James
Foster Perry negroes which are already in his possession and was given
him at his marriage, viz; Jane, Rachel, Clary and Porpha and all their
increase I also give him all my land on the South and West side of
Choestoo Creek, being the land whereon he now lives. I give to my dtr.
Harriett J. Hunt the following negroes, viz; Tom, Chaney, Vina and Mary,
which are now in possession of her and her husband James Hunt. She is
also to get Solomon a boy given to Nancy till death. I give to my son
Benjamin Franklin Perry the following negroes, viz; Sheriff and Lucy.
I also give unto him whatever money or advances I have already given
him in obtaining his education. I give to my son Josiah F. Perry the
following negroes, Sawyer, Trulove, Mary and Tilly and their chn. I
also give unto Josiah F. and his heirs after the death of my wife Nancy
all my lands, houses on the North and East side of Choestoo Creek. I
appoint my wife Nancy Executrix and son Josiah F. executor. Dated 26
March 1837. Wit: V. M. Harrison, John H. Messer, William Jolly,
Signed: Benjamin Perry. Proven 5 June 1843.

John C. Perry. Estate of John C. Perry. Box 13 $166. Probate Judge
Office. Pickens, S. C. Est. admr. 13 June 1845 by A. G. Welborn,
J. M. Welborn who are bound unto Wm. D. Steele, Ord. in the sum of

$600.00. Left widow Rebece A. Perry and four chn. Elizabeth, Sarah A., Holbert, Julia Perry.

Jacob B. Perry. Estate of Jacob B. Perry. Box 19 #231. Probate Judge Office. Pickens, S. C. Est. admr. 3 Feb. 1845 by Mary Ann, Ephraim Perry, Samuel A. Porter who are bound unto Wm. D. Steele, Ord. in the sum of $500.00. Citation pub. at Six Mile Meeting house. Left widow Mary Ann, chn. mention names not given. Paid on 2 Feb. 1849 Mary Porter proven account $19.00. Mary Ann & Stephen Perry bought at est. sale.

Josiah F. Perry. Estate of Josiah F. Perry. Box 17 #217. Probate Judge Office. Pickens, S. C. Est. admr. 27 Nov. 1848 by Major B. F. Perry of Greenville, S. C. R. S. C. Foster, D. Hoke who are bound unto Wm. D. Steele, Ord. in the sum of $20,000.00. On 13 Nov. 1848 Maj. B. F. Perry states that his brother Josiah F. Perry died on Thurs. last, leaving no widow but three small chn. Expend. 1859 Susan Long, Emma Hawthorn and Anna Perry each $1014.59.

Perry Minors. Box 1 #29. Probate Judge Office. Pickens, S. C. On 6 Jan. 1851 A. G. Welborn and Wm. Austin Cason of Anderson Dist. are bound unto W. D. Steele, Ord. in the sum of $1100.00. A. G. Welborn gdn. of Sarah A. Perry, Elizabeth Perry (and Rebecca Kennemore) for Holbert Perry, Julia Perry minors under 21 years. On 10 Dec. 1849 Nancy Elizabeth Pery over 12 years. John C. Perry the father. 6 Jan. 1851 cash recd. due J. C. Perry from Tenn. $5.00

Perry Minors. Box 3 #79. In Equity, Clerk of Court Office. Pickens, S. C. On 6 Jan. 1851 Col. A. G. Welborn gdn. of Elizabeth, Sarah A., Holbert and Julia Perry minors. 21 Apr. 1852 paid Wm. A. Cason husband of Elizabeth $135.00. On 10 Dec. 1849 Rebecca Kennemore late Rebecca Perry the widow of John C. Perry decd. wanted Col. A. G. Welborn to be gdn. of her two chn. under age of choice fiz; Holbert and Julia Perry. 10 Dec. 1849 Sarah A. Perry under 12 years.

W. A. Perry. Estate of W. A. Perry. Box 124 #5. Probate Judge Office. Pickens, S. C. Est. admr. 13 Dec. 1894 by J. T. Darwin, J. D. Kennedy, J. F. Whisenant who are bound unto J. B. Newberry, Ord. in the sum of $1,000.00. He died 10 Sept. 1894. John T. Darwin a brother in law.

Jacob B. Perry. Estate of Jacob B. Perry. Box 55 #600. Probate Judge Office. Pickens, S. C. On 14 Dec. 1859 he owned 200 acres on Mile Creek waters of Keowee River, adj. land of John Dodson, W. J. Parson and others. Heirs Mary A. Perry the widow, and Elvira the wife of James A. McKee, Elmina M. the wife of William J. Hunnicutt.

E. M. Perry. Estate of E. M. Perry. Box 71 #765. Probate Judge Office. Pickens, S. C. I, E. M. Perry being of sound mind and disposing memory, do make this my last will and testament, etc. I desire my executrix to pay my just debts and funeral expenses with the first monies that come into her hands. I give to my loving wife Mary Ann and my dutiful son James Answell Perry at my death all my real and personal estate, money, and notes and everything which I have to them for their use, comfort and support. I appoint my wife Mary Ann Perry executrix and my son James Ansell Perry executor. Dated 23 April 1863. Wit: J. E. Hagood, Z. Gibson, L. N. Robin. Signed: E. M. Perry. Proven 24 Aug. 1863.

Ephraim Perry. Deed from Ephraim Perry. Pack 296. Clerk of Court Office. Pickens, S. C. Ephraim Perry to Ephraim M. Perry both of Pickens Dist. Dated 28 Jan. 1850. For and in consideration of the natural love, good will and affection, which I have for my son E. M. Perry, have granted, sold, release all that tract of land lying on North prong of Little River, according to a plat made by Benj. Lyord dated 3 March 1821. Adj. land of myself, W. L. Keith, C. B. Moses and others. Wit: W. M. Morton, E. M. Keith. Signed: Ephraim Perry. Deed attested by oath of W. M. Morton before E. M. Keith, N.P. on the 28 Jan. 1850. Recorded 4 Feb. 1850.

Ephraim Perry. Deed from Ephraim Perry. Pack 296. Clerk of Court Office. Pickens, S. C. I Ephraim Perry to A. R. Perry both of Pickens Dist. Dated 24 Dec. 1853. For and in consideration of the natural love and affection which I have for my son A. R. Perry, have granted, sold and released, one half of the plantation or tract of land on which I now live, lying on the North Prong of Little River, waters of Seneca River. One half of said tract previously deeded to my brother E. M. Perry, adj. land of E. M. Perry, James Lay, John Knox, Malin Morgan. Containing 113 acres. With the following promises that I Ephraim Perry and my wife Casanda Perry am to occupy possess and enjoy the same during our natural life and at the death of both A. R. Perry is to have full possession. Dated 24 Dec. 1853. Wit: John Knox, Joseph W. Kelly. Signed: Ephraim Perry. Deed attested by the oath of Joseph W, Kelly before John Knox M.P.D. on the 24 Dec. 1853. Recorded 5 March 1854.

W. W. Perry, J. Q. Perry. Power of Attorney from W. W. Perry, J. Q. Perry. Pack 218 #6. Clerk of Court Office. Pickens, S. C. We W. W. Perry and J. Q. Perry of Pickens Co., Alabama have constituted and appointed Zachary C. Pulliam of Pickens Dist., S. C. as our lawful attorney for us, to use our name, and may ask, demand, sue for recovery and receive all sums of money, debts, dues accounts etc. Form the estate of real and personal of Russel Cannon late of Pickens Dist., S. C. Dated 30 June 1858. Wit: W. T. White, R. D. Daniel. Signed: W. W. Perry, J. Q. Perry.

PORTER

Mary Porter. Will fo Mary Porter. Box 24 #290. Probate Judge Office. Pickens Dist., S. C. As life is uncertain and death is sure, I make this my last will and testament. I give to my dtr. Mary Ann Perry one bed stead and feather bed and furniture and one stand of curtains one large chest and one side saddle. I also give my son James Porter two dollars and fifty cents in money, I also give to my son Bassell S. Porter one white cow and one small pot. I give to my son Samuel A. Porter two feather beds and furniture, one clock, one cupboard and all cooking ware, etc. I appoint my son Samuel A. Porter and James E. Hagood executors. Dated 20 Jan. 1851. Wit: Martin Gant, Isam X Simmons. Signed Mary X Porter. Proven 2 April 1851.

Samuel G. Porter. Estate of Samuel G. Porter. Box 117 #12. Probate Judge Office. Pickens, S. C. Est. admr. 9 Jan.1890 by James M. Porter, Thomas R. Price, W. N. Bolding who are bound unto J. B. Newberry, Ord. in the sum of $75.00. Died in Aug. 1889.

Basiel S. Porter. Estate of Basiel S. Porter. Box 123 #9. Probate Judge Office. Pickens, S. C. I Basiel S. Porter being of sound mind and disposing memory, etc. I will and desire my executrix as soon after my death as possible to pay my just debts with funeral expenses. I give to my loving wife Vashti Porter during her life or widowhood, all my property both real and personal, for the support and education of my wife and children. I appoint my wife executrix. Dated 13 July 1863. Wit: J. E. Hagood, Willie Waldrop, Benjamin Hagood. Signed Basiel S. Porter. Filed 22 May 1894.

John T. Porter. Will of John T. Porter. Box 123 #8. Probate Judge Office. Pickens, S. C. I John T. Porter being of sound mind and disposing memory, etc. I desire my executrix as soon after my death as practicable to pay my just debts and funeral expenses with the money I may leave, if not enough, she is to sell such of my personal property as she think best. I give to my beloved wife Sarah J. Porter all my real and personal property. I desire after the death of my wife all my property be sold and the money equal divided between all my children. I appoint my wife exeuctrix. Dated 28 Dec. 1892. Wit: J. B. Clyde, W. G. Rollins, J. M. Stewart. Signed: John T. X Porter. Filed 8 Jan. 1894.

B. S. Porter. Estate of B. S. Porter. In Equity, Pack 243 #6.
Clerk of Court Office. Pickens, S. C. In the Court of Common Pleas;
Nancy E. Sanders, Hannah Sanders, Martha Waldrop, and Mary Roper,
Plaintiffs vs. W. R. Price, Defendant. Teh Plaintiffs shows that in
the year 1894 B. S. Porter died intestate seized of all that tract
of land on waters of 12 Mile Creek, adj. land of W. R. Prices, J. H.
Porter estate of John T. Porter and others containing 150 acres. That
the plaintiffs are heirs at law of said B. S. Porter decd. and are
entitled to a one twelfth interest in said land. There is 32 acres
that is subject to partition among the plaintiffs etc. And for such
others and further relief as may be just. Date filed not given.

PETTIGREW

George Pettigrew. Estate of George Pettigrew. In Equity, Pack 315.
Clerk of Court Office. Pickens, S. C. "Will" I, George Pettigrew of
Abbeville Dist. being weak in body but of perfect mind and memory, etc.
First I will and desire my debts and funeral expenses be paid. I give
to my dtr. Sarah Oliver $600 which she has already received and a negro
girl named Olly. I give to my dtr. Margaret Robison $300 which she has
already received, also a negro woman named Easther and child Della Ann,
Margaret Robison dtr. Mary Emily to get negro Dilly Ann. I give to my
son John Even Pettigrew $315 which he has already received, also one
negro named Isaac. I give to my son Robert H. Pettigrew the tract of
land whereon he now lives, also negro named Elijah. I give to my dtr.
Rosa Anna Brownlee $350, also negro girl named Milla, she has already
received the money, also two boys named Edman and Joe. To my grand
children Mary T. Paskel and Sarah J. Paskel, I give negro woman named
Sharlot and at the death of their grand mother my will they are to have
their mother part, to be left in the hands of John Brownlee till they
become of age or marry. I give to my son George P. Pettigrew two
negroes boys Dave and Alexander, also all my real estate where I now
live, at the death of my wife, my personal estate is to be sold and
divided between all my chn. except Perry he is to have no part. As I
think the land is a good portion. I appoint my son Robert Pettigrew
and son in law John Brownlee executros. Dated 1 March 1839.
Wit: Joel Lockhart, John Robinson, S. T. Baskin. Signed: George
Pettigrew.
    Codicil. Dated 27 June 1843. I will to my son Robin Pettigrew
on negro boy named Lewis in place of the one that died. I give to my
beloved son Perry one negro named Frank also 250 acres of land from
the upper end of this tract. My will is that negroes Jeff, Allen and
Siller be sold to settle debts, with the cotton crop. I will to my
wife negroes viz; Ben, Fanny, Cole, Sarah, Lillan, Harriet and Black
Harriet, Redler, Wiley, Augustus, and Pegga and Alfred. Wit: Joel
Lockhart, F. Y. Baskin, John N. Brown. Signed: George Pettigrew.
In the Equity case the widow is Mary Pettigrew and that Margaret Robinson was a widow, and that John Pettigrew lived in the State of Georgia,
Sarah the wife of Robert Oliver lived in the State of Miss. and the
grand chn. Mary and Sarah Jane Pashell the chn. of dtr. Jane, are minors
living in Miss. with their father.

PETTY

Ambrose Petty. Will of Ambrose Petty. Box 4 #45. Probate Judge Office.
Pickens, S. C. I Ambrose Petty being of sound mind and memory, but in
a bad state of health. I will that so much of my personal est. be
sold to satisfy all my just debts and funeral expenses. The residue and
remainder of my est. both real and personal shall remain together for
the use and benefit of my wife and chn. until the youngest one comes of
age, then sell to the highest bidder and each to have an equal share.
I appoint my wife Polly executrix and my trusty friend Bailey Barton
executor. Dated 14 March 1834. Wit: David Mosly, Hiram Haynes,
Elizabeth X Cantrell. Signed: Ambrose Petty. Recorded Mar. 1834.

George Petty. Deed from George Petty. Book E, page 222. Union Court House, S. C. George and Lydia Petty to Benjamin Stockton both of Union Co. Dated 30 Dec. 1797. In consideration of Forty Pds. sterling, have sold, bargain, alien and released all that plantation being on a ridge between Thickety and Gelkin Creek. Now in possession of George and his wife Lydia Petty, containing 72 acres. Wit: Lewis Ledbetter, Mary Harrington, Millenton Ledbetter. Signed: George Petty and Lydia X Petty. Deed attested by oath of Millenton Ledbetter before Charles Sims J.P. on the 3 April 1798. Recorded same date.

James Petty. James Petty from Peter Club. Deed Book 19, page 38. Union Courthouse, S. C. I, J. Peter Club of the State of Kentucky County of Christian to James Petty of Union County, S. C. In consideration of $500 have bargained, sold and delivered my right of title of a negro woman named Rachel, about twenty nine years of age, also a negro boy child called Jo about three years old, also one negro girl child called Hannah about six months old. Dated 22 Sept. 1809. Wit: Jacob Peeler, Samuel Jefferies. Signed: Jeter X Club. Deed attested by Jacob Peeler before John Jefferies, J.Q. On the 22 Sept. 1809. Recorded on 2 Oct. 1809.

Joshua Petty. Deed from Joshua Petty. Deed Book N, page 179. Union Courthouse, S. C. I Joshua Petty to John Littlejohn both of Union Co. Dated 1 Dec. 1814. In consideration of $120.00 have granted, bargained, sold and release a certain tract of land lying on both sides of Polcat a North branch of Thickety Creek. Adj. land of Jacob Guytons and Joshua Petty. Containing 40 acres being part of the tract conveyed to Petty by Charles Wood. Wit: Wm. Goudelock, John Littlejohn. Signed: Joshua Petty. Deed attested on oath of Wm. Goudelock before John Jefferies J.Q. on the 22 April 1815. Recorded on the 20 May 1816.

James Patty. Deed from James Patty. Deed Book R, page 91. Union Courthouse, S. C. James Petty to Davis Whelchell both of Union Co. Dated 22 Dec. 1820. For and in consideration of fifty dollars have granted, bargained, sold and released all that tract of land lying on Davis Whelchells line from a post oak to a dividing line made by Samuel Jeffries, this land originally granted to John Bird and bounded by its own line, but being a part of James Petty had taken off by an old survey. (Amount not given.) Wit: Henry Tate, Joshua Petty, John Whelchell. Signed: James Petty. Deed attested on aoth of Joshua Petty before ___. On the 8 April 1822. Recorded same date.

Joshua Petty. Deed from Joshua Petty. Deed Book T, page 163. Union Courthouse, S. C. I, Joshua Petty to John Jeffries Senr. both of Union Co. Dated 30 Jan. 1829. In consideration of $507.00 have granted, bargained, sold, released all that plantation where Joshua Petty now lives, lying and being on waters of Gilroys and Alston Creek, waters of Broad River. Containing 338 acres. Wit: James Jeffries, Samuel Jeffries. Signed: Joshua Petty. Deed attested on oath of James Jeffries before W. H. Collet. On the 7 Feb. 1829. On the 9 Feb. 1829 Rebeca Petty released and forever relinquished her dower to the above land. She being the wife of Joshua Petty. Before Nicholas Carey, J.Q. Recorded 20 March 1829.

Lydia Petty. Lydia Petty Dower. Book T, page 155. Union Courthouse, S. C. On 9 Feb. 1829 Lydia Petty renounce, released and relinquished her dower to land she and her husband Robert Petty sold unto Joshua Petty. Before Nicholas Carey. Recorded 2 March 1829. Signed: Lidy X Petty.

Lizzy Petty. Lizzy Petty dower. No Ref. May be same as above, date same. Union Courthouse, S. C. Elizabeth Petty the wife of James Petty, renounce, release and relinquish her dower on some land sold to Joshua Petty. Before Nicholas Carey. Dated 9 Feb. 1829. No recorded date. Signed: Lizzy X Petty.

PHILLIPS

<u>John Phillips.</u> Will. Will Book 1, page 3. Richmond Co., Georgia.
Augusta, Ga. I John Phillips being weak in body but of sound mind and
memory, etc. I will is all my just debts and funeral charges, and
charges of proving this my last will be paid. I give to my son George
one negro named Drummon. I give unto my dtr. Sophiah one negro named
Dick. I give to my son Hillery one negro named Sam. I give to my dtr.
Verlindo one negro named James. I give to my son Jeremiah one negro
woman named Fanney. I give to my dtr. Ruth one negro named Toady. I
give to my dtr. Mary one hundred pds. sterling to be raised out of my
est. My desire is that when my youngest child comes of age to act for
herself, that my land may be sold, and the money divided equally between
my chn. whose name are above written. I appoint my wife Ruth, my son
George and Jacob Beal executors. Dated 28 March 1777. Wit: John
Henderson, William Fenn, Tobitha X Harris. Signed: John Phillips. Will
proven on the 16 Aug. 1777 on oath of John Henderson and William Fenn
before William Jackson Esq. Reg. of Probate of Richmond Co., Ga. On
same date qualified executors.

<u>John W. Phillips.</u> John W. Phillips. Assault, Pack 213 #2. Clerk of
Court Office. Pickens, S. C. On 7 July 1857 R. W. Folger made oath
that John W. Phillips did on 4 July 1857 at Pickensville, S. C. commit
an assault on him by striking him repeated blows upon the head with a
large club and did attempt at the same time draw a Colt repeator which
was concealed upon his person and shooting at his breast at a distance
of not more than five paces, and that R. J. Gilliland was an accessory
to the offence by furnishing the said Phillips with a pistol.

<u>John W. Phillips.</u> Assault, Pack 213 #2. Clerk of Court Office.
Pickens, S. C. On 26 Oct. 1857 John W. Phillips was found guilty for
unlawfully whipping a slave.

<u>John Phillips.</u> Legacy, Will 41. Charleston, S. C. John Phillips
was bequeathed 100 acres of land from the will of William Neeley of
Charleston, S. C.

<u>Rachel Phillips.</u> Book B, page 86. Probate Judge Office. Pickens,
S. C. On 20 Nov. 1865 Rachel Phillips wife of Levi Phillips was a
dtr. of Christopher Whisenant decd. of Pickens Dist.

<u>Jonas Phillip.</u> Land Warrant. Pack 630 #13. Clerk of Court Office.
Pickens, S. C. By J. E. Hagood Clerk, to any lawful surveyor you are
authorized to lay out unto Jonas Phillips, Jr. a tract of land not
exceeding one thousand acres. Dated 16 Jan. 1860. Executed for 544
acres on the 21 Jan. 1860 by Tyre B. Mauldin, D.S. filed 27 Jan. 1860.

<u>Levi Phillips.</u> Land Warrant. Pack 630 #3. Clerk of Court Office.
Pickens, S. C. By James E. Hagood Clerk. To any lawful surveyor you
are authorized to lay out unto Levi Phillips a tract of land not
exceeding ten thousand acres. Dated 1 Oct. 1858. Execution of, or
recording not given.

PHILPOT

<u>John W. Philpot.</u> Estate of John W. Philpot. Box 69 #743. Probate
Judge Office. Pickens, S. C. Est. admr. 6 April 1863 by Joseph
Philpot, James E. Hagood who are bound unto W. E. Holcombe, Ord. in the
sum of $2500.00. Expend: 22 April 1863 paid for transporting corpse
from Richmond, Va. and fare for negro boy $197.50.

<u>James V. Philpot.</u> Estate of James V. Philpot. Box 103 #1075. Probate
Judge Office. Pickens, S. C. Est. admr. 23 March 1872 by Isabella
Philpot, W. B. Lawrence, James H. Lawrence who are bound unto I. H.
Philpot, Ord. in the sum of $1,000.00. Isabella Philpot the widow.
Left two chn. both minors.

Joseph Philpot. Estate of Joseph Philpot. Box 113 #1097. Probate
Judge Office. Pickens, S. C. Est. admr. 5 May 1883 by Elisha H.
Lawrence, Elias E. Mauldin, Chas. P. Barrett who are bound unto J. H.
Newton, Ord. in the sum of $400.00. Mrs. Lou Philpot bought at sale.

Pickens

Robert Pickens. Estate of Robert Pickens. Pack 534. Probate Judge
Office. Anderson, S. C. Anderson Dist. We the undersigned being chosen
by Andrew and Robert Pickens executors of the will of Robert Pickens
decd. to appraise certain negroes belonging to the est. for division
among the legatees, viz; Charles to estate of John Pickens, Cato to
John Smith, Jane to Margaret Pickens, Anderson to Elizabeth Pickens,
Allen to Mary Bowman, Milly to Dorcas Paris, Jackson to Ann Bolding.
Dated 13 Dec. 1830. Signed: J. Douthit, J. L. McCann, J. Smith.

Eliza Pickens. Will of Eliza Pickens. Box 53 #570. Probate Judge
Office. Pickens, S. C. I Eliza Pickens, while in sound mind and
memory, and desirous of making a disposition of my whole estate, etc.
I direct my executor to pay my just debts from sale of all property
not herein bequeathed. I give to my dtr. Mary B. Anderson for her sole
and separate use only. My waiting woman Nanny, Ellick and John chn. of
Sally decd. with their increase, also my bedroom furniture, my
carriage and horse, my table and bed linen, my silver cup and silver
ladle, my table and tea set, and my castors. Also all my right and
interest in the property setforth in the schedule made by Robert
Anderson on the 9 Sept. 1854, under the Prison Bounds Acts, to Thomas J.
Pickens and John Maxwell, at whose suit he was arrested, in consideration of which he was discharged. On the same day John Maxwell assigned
to my self and Thomas J. Pickens his interest therein, which will
appear by the records. At the death of my daughter I will the above
property and interest to her children then living. To my son Thomas J.
Pickens I give my two negroes William and Joe. To my son Andrew C.
Pickens I give two negroes Tom and Nelson for and during his life only,
at his death the two are to go to dtrs. Rebecca M. Pickens and Eliza B.
Pickens, if either dies without heirs, they are to go to the survivor,
and if both dies without heirs they are to go to Son Ezekiel Pickens.
The two above negroes are not in any way be security for any debts,
credits, or pledge for his debts of my son Andrew, if so they are
immediately to vest in and belong to my two dtr. I appoint my son
Thomas J. Pickens, executor. Wit: R. F. Simpson, W. Simpson, S. S.
Cherry. Signed: Eliza Pickens. Will proven on oath of R. F. Simpson
before W. E. Holcombe, Ord. on the 18 Jan. 1860.

Abram Pickens. Box 115 #16. Probate Judge Office. Pickens, S. C. He
died 1884. J. J. Lewis was admr. No other papers.

W. H. Pickens. Estate of W. H. Pickens. Box 141 #3. Probate Judge
Office. Pickens, S. C. Est. admr. 23 Feb. 1903 by R. F. Smith, W. L.
Pickens, J. E. Robinson who are bound unto J. B. Newberry, Ord. in
the sum of $6600.00. Late of Easley, S. C. Died 30 Jan. 1903. Heirs
Mrs. L. J. Pickens, the widow. Chn. W. L. Pickens, E. F. Pickens,
R. O. Pickens, J. A. Pickens, Rufus H. Pickens.

PILGRIM

Sidney Pilgrim. Box 60 #649. Probate Judge Office. Pickens, S. C.
Est. admr. 21 March 1862 by Jefferson Pilgrim, Samuel Chapman who are
bound unto W. E. Holcombe, Ord. in the sum of $70.00.

Mitchel Pilgrim. Box 114 #1101. Probate Judge Office. Pickens, S. C.
On 27 Dec. 1882 J. J. Lewis was admr. He died 14 Nov. 1882. J. E.
Pilgrim a son.

PITTS

William Pitts. Land Warrant. Pack 630 #21. Clerk of Court Office. Pickens, S. C. I, James E. Hagood, Clerk, to any lawful surveyor you are authorized to lay out a tract of land unto William Pitts not exceeding ten thousand acres. Dated 26 July 1860. Filed 20 Aug. 1860.

John B. Pitts. Estate of John B. Pitts. In Equity, Pack 104. Clerk of Court Office. Pickens, S. C. On 18 May 1863 Catherine the wife of Pleasant S. Mahaffey sheweth that her father John B. Pitts died the 27 Sept. 1862 leaving considerable real estate. Admr. was granted to Andrew Bolt who is proceeding to settle up the est. At his death Pitts possessed a tract of 160 acres on waters of Conneross Creek. Leaving a widow, Elizabeth Pitts, Chn. Catherine the wife of Pleasant S. Mahaffey, Martha Jane the wife of Andrew Bolt, Lucinda S. the wife of Nathan A. Gray, Drury Y. Pitts, William M. Pitts, Mary T. Pitts, Sarah A. Pitts, the last three are minors residing in Pickens Dist. Andrew Bolt resides in Laurens Dist.

POE

Richard Poe. Estate of Richard Poe. Box 29 #336. Probate Judge Office. Pickens, S. C. I Richard Poe, know that life is uncertain and death is sure, etc. I leave my daughter Lucinda Harris all my land so long as she lives then to her children, also my personal property after my debts are paid. I appoint Benton Freeman my executor. Dated 26 Oct. 1843. Wit: B. Hagood, Josia M. Dean, James E. Hagood. Signed: Richard X Poe. Under the will is "I, Mary Poe acknowledges the within full satisfaction." Dated 1 Nov. 1843. Wit: Jeptha Freeman. Signed: Mary X Poe. Will proven on oath of Josia (Jas.) M. Dean on 4 Nov. 1845. On 25 Dec. 1853 Benton Freeman states that Lucinda Harris is now dead. On 1 March 1852 Nathaniel Harris states that Richard Poe bequeath to his mother Lucinda Harris a tract of land and at her death to her chn. Had 245 acres lying on Town Creek adj. land of Daniel Hart, Solomon Mays, Riley Lawson. Children, John Harris, Dorcas Harris, James Harris, Sarah Harris, Carter B. Harris, and myself Nathaniel Harris.

POER

David Poer. Real Estate. Book A, page 13. Probate Judge Office. Pickens, S. C. The real estate of David Poer is to be sold and a division to be made. To the widow Frances Poer, heirs; James M. Poer, Martin Dickson, William Rother, James M. Poer, Assignee for Isaac Holden, Green B. Gilaspie. James M. Poer gdn. ad litm. for Emila Poer and Frances Poer minors of decd. Dated 15 Nov. 1834.

PONDER

James M. Ponder. Will of James M. Ponder. Box 81 #860. Probate Judge Office. Pickens, S. C. I James M. Ponder being of sound mind and memory. I will and desire that my whole estate both real and personal shall remain in the hands of my wife Elvira Ponder, subject to controll of my executor until my oldest son come of age, I will my estate be divided into fourt equal parts of same value. When my oldest son James M. Ponder become of age he to get his share. Then when my second son becomes of age he William Jefferson Ponder to get his share. The share for my dtr. Elizabeth Mildria Ponder to be keep by my wife and Martin Hunt Sr. till my dtr. marry or is of age. The other share for my wife this one to be the home place. If she marry the sons or a son shall buy or trade for the home place as they wish.

I appoint my wife Elvira Ponder executrix and my father in law Martin
Hunt Sr. executor. Wit: J. T. McDaniel, J. M. Watson, Robert McKay.
Signed: J. M. Ponder. Proven 3 Nov. 1863. (Will made 20 Dec. 1861.)

Nancy E. Ponder. Will of Nancy E. Ponder. Box 126 #11. Probate Judge
Office. Pickens, S. C. I Nancy E. Ponder do make, ordain and publish
my last will and testament. I will and devise all my property both real
and personal to my husband W. J. Ponder in trust however, to hold, use,
enjoy and control for his life time, for a home for himself and our
children. At the death of her husband the property is to be the chn.
share and share alike. I appoint my husband W. J. Ponder executor.
Dated 22 Jan. 1895. Wit: G. W. Bowen, B. J. Williams, Jr., A. Blythe.
Signed: Nancy E. Ponder. Died in 1895. Filed 18 July 1896.

Ponder Minors. Chn. Box 7 #133. Probate Judge Office. Pickens, S. C.
On 3 May 1899, W. J. Ponder, Henry Briggs are bound unto J. B. Newberry,
Ord. in the sum of $100.00. W. J. Ponder gdn. for Leota Talu and Thomas
Ponder both over 14 years old and James Ponder under 14 years.

Mrs. N. F. Ponder. Box 137 #6. Probate Judge Office. Pickens, S. C.
On 11 Oct. 1900 J. M. Stewart Admr. On 8 Oct. 1900 Adam C. Welborn
Atty. states that Wm. J. Ponder married the last time N. F. Hunt the
wid. of James Hunt who was a brother of E. Marion Hunt. That she has
been dead more than six months.

James M. Ponder. Box 10 #155. Probate Judge Office. Pickens, S. C.
On 30 Oct. 1878 W. J. Ponder, George McAdams, E. M. Hunt are bound
unto W. G. Field, Ord. in the sum of $2,000.00. W. J. Ponder a brother
of J. Martin Ponder. Wm. J. Ponder, Elvira Ponder, Elizabeth Thomas
the heirs all of age. Elvira Ponder his mother. He was a man without
a family.

POOL

William P. Pool. Estate of William P. Pool. Apt. 12 File 27. Probate
Judge Office. Greenville, S. C. I William P. Pool being of sound
and disposing mind and memory, but weak in body, etc. I give to my
wife Anny P. Pool all my land South of the old Buncombe Road, together
with all houses, stock, household and kitchen furniture, farm tools
during her natural life. I give to my son Seth P. Pool and his heirs,
after the death of my wife Anna all my land South of old Buncombe Road,
with all houses, stock, farm tools, household and kitchen furniture.
The said son Seth to have use of said land and utentials during the
life time of my wife. I give to my son John P. Pool one half of my
land lying North of old Buncombe Road. I give to my son William P.
Pool one half of the land lying North of old Buncombe Road. I give to
my son Erwin P. Pool one dollar by reason of these having had their
part. I give to my dtr. Rebecca Stephens one dollar by reason of these
having their part. I appoint my son Seth P. Pool executor. Dated 16
April 1838. Wit: John Moon, Nancy T. Moon, H. J. Gilreath. Signed:
Wm. P. Pool. Proven by Hardy J. Gilreath before Jno. Watson, O.G.D. on
the 6 Aug. 1849.

Micajah Poole. Estate of Micajah Poole. Box 73 Pack 1783. Probate
Judge Office. Abbeville, S. C. I Micajah Poole being of sound and
disposing mind and memory, but weak of body, etc. I desire my just
debts and funeral expenses be paid. I give to my son Robert Poole
shall have the tract of land whereon I now live, supposed to be 360
acres, by paying my son in law Robert Young $650.00. I give to son
Robert a negro woman called Lucinda also my desk and silver watch. I
have advanced my son in law about $750.00 in times past, with the
money from Robert, shall be considered as much as the land given to
son. I give to my dtr. Nancy Young a negro woman named Pat, my others
negroes are to be divided in value. I appoint Alexander W. Adams,
Francis White as executors. Dated 3 Sept. 1819. Wit: Joel Lipcomb,
Alexander Stuart, W. Wier. Signed: Micajah Poole. Proven on oath of

Alexander Stuart before Moses Taggart, Ord. on the 20 Dec. 1819. Sale
held the 13 Jan. 1820. Buyers: Humphry Clew, Jordan Williams, Robert
Pool, William Henderson, John N. Sample, Randle Bagget, James Leach,
David Steward, Pasen Davis, James Leach, Alexander Stewart, Jacob
Youngblood, Abselem Willsen, Benjamin Roberts, John Adams, John Hagood,
Joel Lipcomb, Clem Mitchell, James Anderson, William Loveless, Elizabeth
Buzbee, Lewis Conner, Henry Bishop, Drury Willson, Benj. Smith, Jabez
Johnson, Thomas Gaines, Thomas Brightman, Samuel Davis, Aron Pinson,
Zachary Smith, Jesse Colbert, Thomas Jones, Frances White, Mrs. Maberry,
J. R. Rayner, Daniel Perdue, John Crawford, James Leach, John Logan,
William Beasley, James Franklin, Robert Young, admr. settlement made
on 16 Dec. 1822.

PORTER

John Porter. Estate of John Porter. Box 71 Pack 1754. Probate Judge
Office. Abbeville, S. C. I John Porter, being of sound and disposing mind and memory. I will that all my just debts and funeral
expenses be paid. I order that my plantation in Winston County,
Orangeburg Dist. near the white pond lying on pond branch and Yarrow
Branch, containing 661 acres be sold. My desire is my family stay
together on the plantation which they now live as long as they can in
peace and quiteness. I will the moveable property to be sold to the
highest bidder. My wife Elizabeth to get her third part, with the
remainder divided between my three sons, Samuel Norwood Porter, Hugh
Porter, John Porter. I appoint my friend James Watts executor with my
wife Elizabeth Porter executrix. Dated 27 Dec. 1798. Wit: James
Jones, Benjamin X Simpson, Thomas X Winn. Signed: John Porter.
Recorded 20 Dec. 1803. Est. appraised on 25 Jan. 1804. By Thomas
Edwards, George Conner, James Pettus.

John Porter. Estate of John Porter. Box 71 Pack 1754. Probate Judge
Office. Abbeville, S. C. I John Porter, being of sound and
disposing mind and memory, but weak in body, etc. I desire my plantation be sold with my notes and accounts to pay my just debts and funeral
expenses and if this is insufficient, I desire my executor sell all my
personal property except my carriage and horse, if this insufficient
they are to sell my negro family of Temperance, Jeffrey, Luvinda and
William can be sold without separation. If the sale of my slaves
not needed they are to go to my wife Mary E. A. Porter. Wife to get
carriage and horse with the negroes she had when we married viz;
Peggy, Felord, Jemima and Bina. I desire my brother Hugh Porter shall
have the $110 due me on the 25th of Dec. also my watch. I appoint my
wife executrix and friend Capt. Daniel Norwood and my brother Hugh
Porter executor. Dated 19 Sept. 1824. Wit: C. B. Porter, Andrew S.
Porter, Hugh Porter. Signed: J. Porter. Proved on oath of Charles B.
Porter before Moses Taggart, Ord. on the 6 Dec. 1824. Sale held 22
Dec. 1824. Buyers: Flemine Wiley, Henry Kerr, Hugh Porter, Abram
Lights, Wm. Lomax Esq., John Adams, Captain Downey, Benjamin Adams,
Robert Conn, Hiram Moore, Wm. Sanders, Abram Lites, Robert C. Wilson,
John Gibson, John Norris, Matthew Foster, Johnana Porter, Lewis Lawson,
Luke Matthews, James W. Pettus, Wm. Crowmer, James Wilson, Wm. Marsh,
James Jorden, James Akins, Wm. Ray, Aron Lomax, Silas Cooper, Henry
Weems, John White, Francis Young, Randell Edwards. Hugh Porter, Executor.

Elizabeth Porter. Estate of Elizabeth Porter. Box 74 Pack 1804.
Probate Judge Office. Abbeville, S. C. I Elizabeth Porter being sick
and weak of body but of perfect mind and memory, etc. I give to my
son Rev. Alexander Porter one dollar and I will unto Elizabeth Lesly
my dtr. my plantation on which I now live, and the crop, except the
cotton. I will that money in Rev. Mr. Porter and John Cochrans hands to
pay the remainder of the price of the land, and Elizabeth to divide
my clothes with her sister Martha. I will that Andrew English get one
dollar and leave Hugh English one cow with her calf, and to Nancy
English I leave one cow named gentel with her calves. I will Sarah
Porter to have ghe black heffer of her choice, and one for Samuel

Lesly. I allow Sarah Porter to live with Elizabeth Lesly. I will my negro Dave to live with Elizabeth Lesly seven years and then have his freedom. Dated 18 June 1806. I appoint Reuben Weed and Hugh McBride executors. Wit: Nathaniel Weed, Robert McBride. Recorded 1 July 1806.

James Porter. Estate of James Porter. Box 74 Pack 1815. Probate Judge Office. Abbeville, S. C. We Sarah Porter (widow) John Gray, and Thomas Brightman are bound unto the Judges of Abbeville Dist. in the sum of $1,000.00. To make a true and perfect inventory of the good and chattels of James Porter decd. Dated 11 June 1798. Sale of est. was held 14 Aug. 1798. Buyers: Sarah Porter, Robert Smyth, John Gibson Robert Lumbus, William Bell, Abner Cotton, Elijah Lyon, Arthur Morrow, Robert Jones, Andrew Gray, George Conner, John Shotwell.

Samuel Porter. Estate of Samuel Porter. Box 74 Pack 1795. Probate Judge Office. Pickens, S. C. I Samuel Porter, being of sound and disposing mind and memory, but weak in body. I desire enough of my property be sold to pay my debts and funeral expenses. After my debts are paid I give to my wife Susanah Porter all the remainder of my personal property, as long as she lives, at her death I desire the property she left be sold and the money divided into six shares. One share to Jane L. Brownlee, and one share to Susanah M. Dobins, the remaining shares to Sinthy M. Dobins, P. Dobins and Eliza A. Dobins. I give all that tract of land where widow Nancy Porter now lives containing 170 acres to the heirs of Andrew R. Porter. I give my son Samuel Porter all that tract where on I now live, containing 250 acres. My sons Hugh Porter, John Porter, Richard Porter have received their share of my estate. I appoint Sugar Bonds and Samuel W. Beaty executors Dated 4 May 1833. Wit: James Cosper, F. Y. Baskin, Thos. X Crofford. Signed: Samuel X Porter. Will proven on oath of F. Y. Baskin before Moses Taggart, Ord. on the 11 Dec. 1836. A letter to D. Lesly, Ord. of Abbeville Dist. Dated 19 Jan. 1842 to Mr. Sugar Bonds of Jefferson Court House, Jackson Co., Ga. States that the widow was to have the personal property during her life time. She died in 1841 leaving nothing worth admr. on. Your petitioner is desirous to have an order for the sale of the est. of her son Samuel Porter decd. ordered by him to be sold at her death. Signed: Sugar Bond. One negro in sale named Tempy. Some expenses of the est. Jain Brownlee paid for keeping Susanah Porter the widow. Paid for moving the widow from S. C. to Jackson Co., Ga. On 15 Oct. 1841 the funeral expenses for Susanah Porter $8.00.

A. R. Porter. Minors. Box 76 Pack 1857. Probate Judge Office. Abbeville, S. C. We James S. Harris, James H. Baskin and James Wiley all of Abbeville Dist. each or all of us are bound unto Moses Taggart, Ord. in the sum of $1,000. Dated 5 Jan. 1835. Whereas a letter of guardianship to the personal ests. of John Harris Porter, Samuel S. Porter, Hugh L. Porter, R. M. Porter, Jane E. Porter minors of A. R. Porter decd.

Andrew R. Porter. Estate of Andrew R. Porter. Box 72 Pack 1765. Probate Judge Office. Abbeville, S. C. On 11 Dec. 1830 James Cosper received a letter of admr. on the est. of A. R. Porter decd. With him was Thomas Bigbie, R. E. Porter, Hugh M. Prince, as bondsman. The est. was appraised the 16 Dec. 1830 by Stephen, R. E. Porter, Hugh M. Prince. Sale held 17 Dec. 1830. Buyers: James Cosper, Stephen Jones, Wm. Arnot, Robert Peddigrew, Hugh Porter, widow Porter, Wm. Callwell, James Harris, Richard Porter, Stephen Shackleford, John Harris Michael Kenneda, Edward Beville, Mathew Young. Negroes named in sale Jane, Frank, Easter.

Hugh Porter. Minors. Box 76 Pack 1858. Probate Judge Office. Abbeville, S. C. John Brownlee, William Brownlee and Robert F. Black are bound unto Moses Taggart, Ord. in the sum of $20,000. Dated 18 March 1828. Whereas John Brownlee was made guardian of Susan, William B., Sarah Ann, John Owen and Samuel Porter minors of Hugh Porter under the age of fourteen years. A note settlement Est. of S. A. Porter a minor (now decd.) by John Brownlee his gdn. before the Ord. on 25 June 1843.

Present Jno. Porter the gdn. only he having notified M. J. D. and wife
Sarah A. the surviving distributees residing without the State.

James Porter. Estate of James Porter. Box 75 Pack 1834. Probate
Judge Office. Abbeville, S. C. We John Moragne, Isaac Moragne and
Edward Collier are bound unto Taliaferro Livingston Esq. Ord. in the
sum of $2,000. Dated 4 March 1818. Whereas John Moragne will make a
true and perfect inventory of the est. of James Porter decd. The
citation was publickly read at Liberty Meeting House on the 4th Sabbath
in Jan. 1818. Saml. Cartledge. Est. was appraised by Isaac Moragne,
Mackerness G. Williams, J. L. Gibert. Sale was held 23 Mar. 1818.
Buyers, David Porter, Wm. Cain, John Furgison, John Moragne. (In this
sale was four cotton gins with about fifty saws.)

David Porter. Estate of David Porter. Box 73 Pack 1774. Probate
Judge Office. Abbeville, S. C. We James O. DeVall, Peter B. Moragne
and Nathaniel Harris are bound unto Moses Taggart, Ord. in the sum of
$10,000. Dated 15 March 1836 whereas James O. DeVall admr. on the est.
of David Porter decd. shall make a true and perfect inventory of the
goods and chattels and credits, etc. The sale was held 5 March 1836.
Slaves sold, Major, Harriet and child, Boy Stephen, Lewis. Settlement
in part of David Porter est. 22 June 1846. Present at settl. the admr.
J. P. DeVall, James Carter who married Mary Ann, James W. Porter,
Maclin Porter, William Wilson who married Frances, William Wilson
petition this day to be gdn. of William C. Porter and Neri B. Porter
two minors under 14 years. Absent Martin and wife who is the widow
and David S. Porter minor. Recd. 13 July 1846 J. O. DeVall admr. of
David Porter $32.00 in full of all rent of land to date inright of my
wife thirds. Phares Martin.

Hugh Porter. Estate of Hugh Porter. Box 76 Pack 1862. Probate Judge
Office. Abbeville, S. C. I Hugh Porter being weak in body yet of
perfect mind and memory, etc. I demise and bequeath to the heirs of my
son James one dollar, I give to my son Philip one dollar, I will to the
heirs of my dtr. Vilet one dollar, I will to my dtr. Margery one dollar,
I will to my son William one dollar, I will to my dtr. Mary one dollar,
I will to my son Hugh one dollar, I will to my son John one dollar,
I will to my dtr. Martha her main bridle and saddle, also two feather
beds, also one half of my household and kitchen furniture, and half
of my cattle, I will to my son Samuel all that tract of land where I
now live, also his horse and the sorrel mare, half of my cattle and
household and kitchen furniture. I will to my grand dtr. Mary Chiles
Brightman one feather bed and furniture when she marry or becomes
eighteen years, Samuel is to pay my just debts. Dated 2 May 1808.
Wit: John Donald, Alex. Spence, Hugh Porter Jr. Signed: Hugh Porter.
Recorded 18 July 1808. (Note: No executor named in will.) We Hugh
Porter Jr., John Brannan are bound unto Andrew Hamilton, Ord. in the
sum of $5,000. Dated 18 July 1808. One inventory was taken the 1 Aug.
1808, amount of inv. $646.10 signed Robert Smyth, Andw. Gray, John
Donald. Another inventory was made the 25 Aug. 1813. total of this one
$7,331.10. Signed: William Chiles, John Harris, James Henderson.
Negroes at sale: Jenny and child, Ceaser, Mary Amy and child, Julia,
Elsey, Milly, Jack, Burrow, Talla, Moriah and Celwal, Jack, Sam, Tenor
and child Aenius, Silvey, Kelly. Sale held 16 Nov. 1813. Buyers:
Vincent Griffin, Mary E. Porter (the widow), John Conner Esq.,
Phillemon Ogletree, Samuel Porter, Joab Wilson, Pleasant Thurman,
Samuel Caldwell, James Wedgeworth, John Harris, John Hearst, Horatio
Mantz, David Rush, Robert Foster, Joseph Walker, Joseph Hearst, James
Walker, William Lummus, Garrett E. Groce, John Swansey, James Forrest,
William S. Alexander, Samuel Ramsey, James Bullock, Alexander Spence,
Richard Gaines, James Puckett, Talliferro Livingston, George Holloway,
Jared E. Groce, Robert Ethridge, Ira Griffin, Allen Glover, William
Chiles, William Hutchison, Stephen Witts, Ezekiel Glover, John Swillin.

Hugh Porter. Estate of Hugh Porter. Box 76 Pack 1863. Probate Judge
Office. Abbeville, S. C. I Hugh Porter being of sound mind and dis-
posing memory, but weak in body, etc. I desire that my negro named
Sharlott and three head of horses be sold to pay my just debts and

funeral expenses. The balance of the money from notes and accounts be put on interest to benefit my wife Sarah Porter and the chn. If my wife should marry then I desire my executors order a sale of all my real and personal property, giving my wife one third of the money from the sale, with an equal division of the rest. My negroes Mint, Henery, and Ned, Prince. H. B. Black is to attend to the suit I have entered against Hugh Maxwell. I appoint my wife Executrix and my friend John B. Black and Wm. Brownlee executors. Dated 15 Dec. 1824. Wit: Richard E. Porter, Moses Rutherford, Hugh Porter 2nd. Will proven on oath of Richard E. Porter before Moses Taggart, Ord. the 6 June 1825. One sale held on the 12 Aug. 1825. Buyers: Archd. Mauldin, David Robertson, Richard Porter, Jesse Goodwin, Coldwell Howie, Col. W. Coldwell, John Winfield, Lee Branton, James H. Baskin, Andrew Porter, William Brownlee, W. K. Patten. Sale held 6 Jan. 1830. Buyers: Thomas L. Harris, Thomas Linton, James Kelly, Robert Cown, John Brownlee, Kindred Kichens, Archey Moldon, John Martin, John White, Thomas Patterson, L. B. Shackleford, Kindred Kitchen, George Petigrew, M. Shackelford

RACKLEY

William Rackley. Estate of William Rackley. Box 10 #128. Probate Judge Office. Pickens, S. C. Est. admr. 7 Sept. 1841 by Reden Rackley, Larkin Hendricks, Henson Hunt who are bound unto James H. Dendy, Ord. in the sum of $1200.00. Left a widow and nine chn. Paid 20 Jan. 1845, Winney E. Rackley, $5.00, paid Eliza C. Rackley $17.75, paid Adaline Rackley $5.00, Cit. published at Cross Road Church. Sale held on 10 Nov. 1841, buyers, Warren, Lewis Rackley. Paid Mary Rackley the widow her share. Warren B. his share, Eliza and Adaline their share. Reden Rackley his share and he was gdn. of five minor chn. Winney E., William B., Mahala C., John L., and James L. Rackley.

Rackley Minors. Box 1 #12. Probate Judge Office. Pickens, S. C. On 27 Jan. 1846 Reden Rackley, Henson Hunt, Daniel Looper are bound unto Wm. D. Steele, Ord. in the sum of $660. Reden Rackley gdn. of Adaline, Winney E. William B., Mahala C., John L., James L. Rackley minors. By the 21 March 1860 James L. Rackley was decd. and that Warren Rackley was an heir. Also Taylor Richerds and wife, and Wm. Dacus.

W. Benson Rackley. Estate of W. Benson Rackley. Box 98 #1030. Probate Judge Office. Pickens, S. C. Est. admr. 22 Aug. 1870 by Reden Rackley, J. E. Hagood, W. O. Singleton who are bound unto I. H. Philpot, Ord. in the sum of $200.00. Owned 150 acres on Shoal Creek waters of Saluda River, adj. land of H. M. Looper, G. W. Julin. Heirs, Reden Rackley, Mahaley C. Rackley, Lucretia Dacus, Adaline Rackley, John Rackley, James Rackley, Mary Rackley, Thomas Rackley, R. T. Richards and wife Eliza, who resides in Georgia, Wm. Benson Rackley of Illinois, Malissa Rackley of Georgia, Thomas Martin and wife Manerva of Laurens Co., S.C. John L. was a brother. He died 12 May 1870.

Reden Rackley. Deed from Reden Rackley. Pack 416 #6. Clerk of Court Office. Pickens, S. C. Reden Rackley to William Hester and Z. H. Smith all of Pickens Co. For the sum of $600.00 have granted, sold, released a tract of land containing 100 acres. No water course given. Dated 18 Aug. 1881. Wit: I. H. Philpot, W. C. Dacus. Signed: Reden Rackley. Proven on oath of I. H. Philpot before R. Rackley, N.P. on the 18 Aug. 1881. Certified 26 Sept. 1882.

Reden Rackley. Estate of Reden Rackley. Box 97 #1027. Probate Judge Office. Pickens, S. C. Est. admr. 1 April 1886 by Wm. O. Singleton, H. C. Hunt, G. T. Hendricks, W. T. Field who are bound unto J. H. Newton, Ord. in the sum of $600.00. He died 16 Dec. 1885. Wm. O. Singleton a son in law.

RAMEY

Thomas Ramey. Thomas Ramey Land Warrant. Pack 630 #23. Clerk of
Court Office. Pickens, S. C. To any lawful surveyor you are authorized
to lay out a tract of land unto Thomas Ramey not exceeding one thousand
acres. Dated 20 Aug. 1860. Executoed 31 Aug. 1860 for 455 acres.
Filed 6 Sept. 1860.

David Ramey. Estate of David Ramey. Box 33 #379. Probate Judge
Office. Pickens, S. C. Est. admr. 10 Nov. 1854 by Abel Robin,
E. E. Alexander who are bound unto W. P. Parson, Ord. in the sum of
$400.00.

John Rampey. Estate of John Rampey. Box 118 #14. Probate Judge Office.
Pickens, S. C. Est. admr. 4 Sept. 1891 by J. M. Stewart, R. A. Hester
who are bound unto J. B. Newberry, Ord. in the sum of $400.00. Died
11 June 1891. Heirs, J. F. Rampey, J. M. Rampey, H. M. Rampey, M. C.
Gains.

Rampey Minors. Box 122 #5. Probate Judge Office. Pickens, S. C.
On 6 March 1893, Mrs. Frances C. Rampey, W. H. Perry, J. T. Youngblood
are bound unto J. B. Newberry, Ord. in the sum of $110.00. Mrs. F. C.
Rampey gdn. of S. Q. Terra Rampey, W. J. Mcd Rampey, Henry S. Rampey,
Joseph A. Rampey, Hattie L. Rampey, Anna C. Rampey minors under 21 years.
S. Q. Teera Rampey born 29 Dec. 1874, W. J. Mcd Rampey born 12 June
1876, Henry S. born 9 Dec. 1879, Joseph A. born March, Hatty L. born
23 Dec. 1883, Anna C. born Nov. Chn. of Levy McDuffi Rampey decd. and
Frances C. Rampey. On 6 May 1898 W. J. and Nannie Rampey recd. share
from est. of John Rampey decd. their grandfather. On 13 March Tecora
Williams recd. share from her grandpa Rampey est.

RANKIN

John Rankin. Estate of John Rankin. Box 81 #863. Probate Judge Office.
Pickens, S. C. Est. admr. 19 Dec. 1864 by Eliza M. Rankin, William
Todd, John Sharp who are bound unto W. E. Holcombe, Ord. in the sum of
$2,000.00. (Loose papers) On 7 Jan. 1840 Sarah Rankin wanted Mr.
Dendy to pay Andrew Kelly what was due her from her father est.

REAMS

Josiah Reams. Estate of Josiah Reams. In Equity, #45. Clerk of
Court Office. Pickens, S. C. To the Honr. the Chancellors: Your oratrix Mary Reams sheweth that Josiah Reams the husband of your oratrix
departed this life in 1858 being seized and possessed with a small
real and personal estate. The real est. consisting of 232 acres adj.
land of J. W. Crawford and John E. Calhoun and others. Heirs at law
are: Mary Reams the widow and seven chn. viz; William, Elizabeth,
Felix, Martha, Hasseltine, Monroe, Caroline Reams all minors under 21
years. The last two under the age of 21 years. A letter of admr. was
granted to Aaron Boggs. Your oratrix is desirous of enjoying her share
of the real estate by division or sale, and that a guardian ad litem
may be appointed to represent the interest of the minors. Filed 21
May 1860. On 27 July 1866 Mary Reams sold to Aaron Boggs all her
interest in the land of her late husband Josiah Reams. She received
$267.00 her her share. In 1854 Josiah Reams bought from Aaron Boggs
a tract of land for $1500 giving three notes of $500 each. Reams died
in 1858 having not paid off all the notes, this was done with the sale
of the real estate. 1 Dec. 1868, Elizabeth the wife of T. S. Crenshaw
and Martha the wife of James P. Martin recd. each $65.65.

Monroe and Caroline Reams. Minors. Box 123 #7. Probate Judge Office.
Pickens, S. C. On 24 Mar. 1869 James P. Martin, T. P. Campbell, W. S.
Wilson are bound unto I. H. Philpot, Ord. in the sum of $262.00. James

P. Martin gdn. of Monroe and Caroline Reams minors under 21 years. Chn. of Josiah Reams decd.

REDMAN

John Redman. Deed from John Redman. Deed Book D, page 150. Mesne Conveyance. Greenville, S. C. Deed from John Redman of Spartanburg Co. and James Cooper of Greenville Co. Dated 31 Jan. 1795. In consideration of one hundred pds. good and lawful money, doth grant, bargain, sell and release a tract of land of 640 acres, originally granted to sd. John Redman on the 21 Jan. 1785. Land lying in Greenville Co. on Derbuns Creek. Wit: Isham Harrison, Samuel Cobb, John X Howard. Signed: John Redman. Proven before Humphrey Cobb, Esq. on oath of Isham Harrison on the 12[?] Aug. 179__.

Reuben Redman. Deed from Reuben Redman. Deed Book S, page 577. Mesne Conveyance. Greenville, S. C. This indenture made between Reuben Redman and John West both of Greenville Co. For the sum of $350.00. hath sold, bargain, release a tract of land containing 200 acres lying on Brushy Creek, being part of the original grant of Paul Abner, dated 1 Jan. 1785, also part of a grant of Aaron Kemp, Bigby Branch also on land. Wit: Daniel Pike, Matthew Hudson. Signed: Reuben Redman. Dated 29 Dec. 1834. Proven by Matthew Hudson before Richard Thruston, J.Q. on the 7 Jan. 1839.

Alexander Redman. Deed from Alexander Redman. Deed Book R, page 124. Mesne Conveyance, Greenville, S. C. Deed from Alexander Redman to John Ross both of Greenville Dist. Dated 5 Oct. 1832. In consideration of $200.00. I hereby acknowledge a certain tract of land containing 104 3/4 acres lying on Brushy Creek waters of Enoree River. Wit: Caleb Green, Jesse Green. Signed: Alexander Redman. Proven on oath of Jesse Green before Caleb Green, J.P. on the ___ Oct. 1832. Recorded the 9 Oct. 1832.

William Redman. Deed from William Redman. Deed Book R, page 124. Mesne Conveyance. Greenville, S. C. Deed from William Redman to Alexander Redman both of Greenville, S. C. Dated 6 March 1829. In consideration of $100.00. I hereby acknowledge a certain tract of land containing 104 3/4 acres lying on Brushy Creek waters of Enoree River. Wit: Peter Shockley, Lyn Watson. Signed: W. Redman. Note: In the above deed it is expressly understood that the said William Redman reserves to himself and his wife Fanny Redman the entire privaledge and exclusive right of the present dwelling house, and as much land as he may think proper to cultivate during each of their natural lives, same being agreed unto by Alexander Redman. No date. Same wit. This deed proven on oath of Lyn Watson before J. McDaniel on the 8 Oct. 1832. I James McDaniel Clerk of Court and j . P. do hereby certify that Marian Redman the wife of William Redman? did this day appear before me and renounce, release and forever relinquish her dower. Dated 8 Oct. 1832. Recorded 9 Oct. 1832. (Note: Marian Redman may be another wife of William Redman, as William and Fanny Redman was to live on the land their natural life. As this is the same date as the deed made to John Ross. Marian maybe the wife of Alexander Redman.)

Francis Redman. Deed from Francis Redman. Deed Book S, page 37. Mesne Conveyance. Greenville, S. C. Deed from Frances Redman to Matthew Hudson both of Greenville Dist. Dated 19 Dec. 1833. In consideration of $150.00. Do grant, sell, bargain and release a tract of land containing 200 acres lying a branch of Brushy Creek waters of Enoree River. Near where James Ward lives, and Bigby branch on land. Being part of the grant of Lunsford Hudson and part of Aaron Kemp grant. Wit: Eliza X Perkins, Mourning X Redman. Signed: Francis X Redman. Proven on oath of Reuben Redman saith that he was present and saw Francis Redman sign the within deed. Before Caleb Green, J.P. on the 3 Feb. 1834. Recorded the 4 Jan. 1836.

Robert Redman. Deed from Robert Redman. Deed Book G, page 20. Mesne
Conveyance. Greenville, S. C. Deed from Robert Redman of Greenville
Dist. to Francis Sittle of the County of Fauqier in Virginia. Dated
12 Jan. 1803. In consideration of twenty five pds. four shillings
money of Virginia, have bargain, sold and released a tract of land
containing 150 acres lying on Brush Creek, being the same I bought brom
Joseph McAfee. This deed is to be in full effect if said Sittle or
his heirs do pay the full amount promise, if not then to be null and
void. Wit: George Wallis, Fielding X Wigginton, Benjamin Young. No
signature.

Robert Redman. Deed from Robert Redman. Deed Book I, page 208. Mesne
Conveyance. Greenville, S. C. Deed from Robert Redman to Feilden
Southern both of Spartanburg Dist. Dated 21 Oct. 1811. In considera-
tion of $350.00 have grant, sold, bargain and release a tract of land
containing 150 acres lying in Greenville Dist. on Brushy Creek being
part of a grant to Henry Hughes, dated 5 Feb. 1787. Adj. land of
Moses Kemp, Johnson Line, Aaron Kemp Land. Another part granted
to Paul Abner on Bigby Branch on Wm. Redman line. Wit: Reuben Redman,
William Redman. Signed: Robert Redman. Proven on oath of Reuben
Redman before P. Hudson, J.P. on the 1 Oct. 1811. Recorded the 20
July 1813.

William Redman. Estate of William Redman. Apt. 6 File 408. Probate
Judge Office. Greenville, S. C. I William Redman being very sick
and weak in body but of perfect mind and memory, etc. I give to my
beloved wife Frances the whole of my estate both real and personal
during her natural life, and at her death to dispose of as she may
think fit. I appoint my wife Frances Redman executrix and Mathew
Hudson executor. Wit: Reuben Suddeth, L.-F. Hudson, Reuben Redman.
Signed: William X Redman. Proven by Matthew Hudson before Jno. Watson,
Esq. Ord. on the 13 Apr. 1832. An appraisement was made on 13 April 1832
by Jesse Shockley, John X Ross, John Rains.

REEDER

Elizabeth Reeder. Estate of Elizabeth Reeder. Box 26 #305. Probate
Judge Office. Pickens, S. C. I Elizabeth Reeder being of sound mind
and memory, etc. I will and desire my just debts, if I have any, be
paid. It is my will and desire that after my death if my mother should
be alive that she shall have the use and benefit of my property, during
her natural life or widowhood, not to sell or dispose of in any way.
After the death or marriage of my mother, my property to be equal divided
between the following persons, viz; my brother Lewis W. or N. Reeder,
my brother Samuel C. Reeder, my brother A. P. Reeder, my brother James
H. Reeder, my brother B. F. Reeder, my sister Amanda F. Messer. Also
my desire that the negroes if possible be keep in the family. I give
to my name sake Clarisa Elizabeth Reeder and Rebecca Elizabeth Messer
one bed and furniture each. I give to my sisters Matilda Harbin and
Mary Cleveland one dollar each if demanded in thirty days. I appoint
my brothers S. C. and A. P. Reeder executors. Dated 13 March 1851.
Wit: C. H. Spears, William Jolly, A. Hester. Signed: Elizabeth Reeder.
Proven 3 Nov. 1851. On 28 Oct. 1852 Wiley W. Harbin, Samuel C. Harbin,
Mary E. Harbin, S. V. Harbin, John Harbin, A. P. Harbin, Harriet R.
Harbin were ordered to prove the will of said decd. Moses Masser was
the husband of Amanda Messer.

Lewis W. Reeder. Estate of Lewis W. Reeder. Pack 231 $4. Probate
Judge Office. Pickens, S. C. On 19 Feb. 1859 Margan Harbin recd.
$183.89 in full, of the share of Andrew P. Reeder in the real estate
of Lewis W. Reeder decd. On 4 Oct. 1858 B. F. Reeder recd. $179.19
his share from Lewis W. Reeder est. This was witnessed by Harriet
F. Reeder. On 4 Oct. 1858 M. S. Messer and A. F. Messer recd. $179.19
their share from the est. of Lewis W. Reeder decd. On 4 Oct. 1858
Samuel C. Reeder recd. his share $179.19. On 2 May 1859 W. R. Harbin
recd. his share $23.30. On 30 March 1859 S. V. Harbin recd. share

$23.18. On 26 Dec. 1859 Mary E. Harbin recd. share $24.37. On 29 Oct. 1859 Sarah C. Hunt and William Hunt recd. their share $24.09. On 4 Oct. 1858 Mary Cleveland recd. her share $179.19. I, James H. Reeder of Pickens Dist. for the sum of $167.46 to me paid by Mrs. Elizabeth Martin of the same Dist. (the receipt whereof is hereby acknowledge) have bargained, sold and assigned all my rights, title and interest in the real estate of my brother Lewis W. Reeder decd. be my full share, due from the Commissioner in Equity in Oct. 1858 with interest. Dated 13 Jan. 1858. Wit: J. G. Bryce, A. F. Reeder. Signed: James H. Reeder.

Thomas Milton Reeder. Will of Thomas Milton Reeder. Box 9 #117. Probate Judge Office. Pickens, S. C. Will dated 27 Feb. 1840 in Pickens Dist. Proven 11 April 1840. Executors Samuel C. Reeder. Wit: Morgan Harbin, Wm. McCart, Elias E. Harrison. Half Bro. Joel Reeder, half sister Sarah Ward. Desire that my brother Benjamin F. Reeder, Amanda F., Elizabeth Reeder have negro boy. After death of my mother my interest be divided between Lewis W. Reeder, Andrew P. Reeder, Ha. Reeder, sisters Matilda Harbin and Mary Cleveland.

Jonathan Reeder. Estate of Jonathan Reeder. Box 12 #163. Probate Judge Office. Pickens, S. C. Est. admr. 11 April 1845 by F. N. Garvin, Robert Johnston, Samuel Parson, Wm. Reeder, C. H. Brock who are bound unto Wm. D. Steele, Ord. in the sum of $30,000. Sally Ward wife of Wm. Ward was an heir. On March 28, 1845 Jefferson Allen as Atty. for Joel, Providence Reeder, Elizabeth Smith nee Elizabeth Reeder made suit for letter of admr.

Sarah Reeder. Estate of Sarah Reeder. Box 37 #417. Probate Judge Office. Pickens, S. C. Est. admr. 1 June 1855 by B. F. Reeder, J. W. L. Carey, Alexander Bryce, Sr. who are bound unto W. J. Parson, Ord. in the sum of $1200.00

Andrew P. Reeder. Will of Andrew P. Reeder. Box 38 #426. Probate Judge Office. Pickens, S. C. I, A. P. Reeder being of sound mind and memory, etc. I will all my just debts be paid. I give to my son Thomas Milton Reeder two negro boys twins brothers named William and Jack, he is to account for them at true value in the final settlement. I desire that he get my long shot gun and my white handle razor to be carefully reserved in safety for him and he is not to account for them in the final settlement. It is my desire that all my negroes be keep unsold with my wife for the support of herself and my chn. My desire that my chn. be schooled agreeable to the means I may leave on hand. If any of my dtr. should marry they are to get an equal share of my est. valuation. If any of my negroes become unmanageable in any way they are to be sold and the money put on interest for the benefit of my wife and chn. My desire is that all stock, farm tools, household and kitchen furniture to remain with my wife for her use and support my chn. If my wife think best, executors to sell all real est. and she may buy a small place near her family and friends, or she may sell some of my land and pay debts. It is my will that negro Harrison and Polly that is joint property of myself and my brother, be sold and if any debts remain against the firm of A. P. & S. C. Reeder for the debts be satisfied and the remaining divided between my brother and my est. Any debts due the firm, my share to be put on interest. All land may be sold except one half acre reserved for a family burial ground. I appoint my friends Samuel Knox and Morgan Harbin executors. Dated 11 Jan. 1856. Wit: Balus Hix, J. H. Maret, Jno. H. Maxwell. Signed: A. P. Reeder. Proven the 2 June 1856.

Lewis M. Reeder. Estate of Lewis M. Reeder. Box 40 #455. Probate Judge Office. Pickens, S. C. Est. admr. 14 March 1856 by B. F. Reeder, Samuel C. Reeder, E. M. Keith, J. W. L. Carey who are bound unto W. J. Parson, Ord. in the sum of $7,000.00. Left seven heirs no names given.

REEVE

Lewis Reeve. Will of Lewis Reeve. Vol. 16, page 175-176. Probate
Judge Office. Charleston, S. C. I Lewis Reeve of Granville County St.
Helenah Parish, do make this my last will and testament, etc. I desire
my estate be keep together till the following legacies be paid. I
give to my cousin Mary Barnwell seven hundred pds. currency and one town
lot known in the plat of the town of Beaufort by number 332. I give to
my cousin Phebe Barnwell seven hundred pds. currency and town lot in
the aforesaid town by number 128. I give to my cousin Ambrose Reeve
of Ashford, in Kent, son of Thomas Reeve one hundred and fifty pds.
sterling, and to my cousin ___ Reeve (son of aforesaid Thomas and
brother of above mentioned Ambrose Reeve) who in 1767 lived at Dover one
hundred and fifty pds. sterling. I give to my friend William Weight of
St. Helenah my horse buck and my two roan mares of English breed. I
desire that four hundred and twenty pds. be put on interest for the
above mentioned. I give my wench Nanny her freedom, with the use of
four acres of land, and the interest from the above amount be paid to
said Nanny yearly. The remainder of my est. to be divided between my
sister Sarah Gibbs and Ann Carson, if said Ann Carson should die, her
share will go to her son James Stuart. I appoint my friends Robert
Gibbs, James Carson, John Barnwell, son of my uncle Nathaniel Barnwell
executors. Dated 27 April 1771. Wit: John Joiner, Robert Porteous,
Alexander Cumine. Signed: L. Reeve.

Asel Reaves. Box 116 #14. Probate Judge Office. Pickens, S. C.
Letter of admr. granted to J. M. Stewart 4 Feb. 1888. Hiram Reaves
was first appointed admr. on 11 May 1883. Hiram died some time later.

Hyram Reaves. Estate of Hyram Reaves. Box 114 #12. Probate Judge
Office. Pickens, S. C. Est. admr. 3 Dec. 1888 by W. R. Price, H. B.
Hendricks, John W. Thomas who are bound unto J. B. Newberry, Ord. in
the sum of $50.00. Died 28 Oct. 1887.

Hiram Reeves. Box 117 #5. Probate Judge Office. Pickens, S. C.
Owned 190 acres on Cove Creek water of Big Eastatoe joining land of
Harrison Powell and vacant land. Wm. R. Price the admr. Heirs, his
widow Liddie Reeves, chn. Sarah A. Thomas, W. J. Reeves, D. H. Reeves,
L. S. Reeves, J. H. Reeves, A. C. Reeves, R. T. Reeves, H. R. Reeves,
the following of whom are minors viz; J. H. Reeves, A. C. Reeves, D. H.
Reeves, R. T. Reeves, L. S. Reeves, H. R. Reeves the first two are
over the age of 15, the last four under that age.

REID

George Reid. Estate of George Reid. Box 109 Pack 3119. Probate Judge
Office. Abbeville, S. C. I George Reid of the Dist. of 96 being of
sound mind and memory, etc. I give to my dtr. Rose Bowie the wife of
John Bowie Esq. my negro wench named Bet. I give to my dtr. Ann Baskins
wife of Capt. William Baskins Esq. my negro wench named Mille. I give
to my dtr. Margaret Reid wife of Hugh Reid my negro wench named Senna.
I give to my son Samuel Reid three head of horses, four cows and calves
which he formerly recd. also a negro fellow named Adam, likewise the
money to buy negro wench Kett. Also the plantation that he now lives
on which I purchased from Joseph Salvadore for him. I give to my son
Alexander Reid four negroes named Munmuth, Phillis his wife, a negro
boy Tom, a negro wench named Prue. I give to my son Joseph Reid four
negroes named Premiss, Boson, Isaac, and Hannah. It is also my will
that mill with all the land that belongs to it be euqally divided
between my two sons Alexander and Joseph, and that neither of them shall
have it in their power to mortgage, allien, sell or dispose of any
part without the other consent. Likewise the two horses they claim
will be their own property. Also all other personal property, cattle,
horses, cows, etc. household and kitchen furniture to be divided between
Alexander and Joseph. I will my wearing apparel to my son Samuel. I

also recommend Polly McGee to care for my two sons Alexander and Joseph and that they will help her, and give her some thing. I give to my sons Samuel the plantation lying on waters of Hen Coope containing 320 acres. I appoint Majr. John Bowie Esq., Capt. Hugh Wardlaw and Capt. William Baskins Esq. to be guardian or overseer of this will, and if dispute or controversy happen amongst my sons, that it will be their determination also that what is to be done. Dated 23 Nov. 1786. Wit: James Reid, John Bowman, John Wardlaw. Signed: George Reid. Proven 6 April 1790.

Joseph Reid. Will of Joseph Reid. Box 2 #15. Probate Judge Office. Pickens Dist. I, Joseph Reid of Pendleton Dist. being of sound mind and memory and understanding. I will that all my just debts are paid as soon as possible. To my son Thomas Baskin Reid I give all the land I own on the East side of Keowee River, opposite where I now live, containing 650 acres, in two tracts one granted to John Ewing Calhoun Esq. and the other to Jesse Speers, also two negroes boys named Ransom and Gaston, also one half of my farm tools. I give to my son Samuel Reid all the plantation whereon I now live, lying on the West side of Keowee River, containing 900 acres, in two tracts, one granted to Maj. Felix Warley and the other to myself. With one half of the farm tools and four negroes named Jack, George, Reuben, Saxton. I give to my beloved wife Issabella Reid, two negroes named Bose and Hannah, and all my household and kitchen furniture, and all my stock of every kind during her natural life. At the death of my wife all the furniture, stock that may remain with the negroes, may be sold and the proceeds shall be equally divided among my six dtr. viz; Margaret Baskin, Mary Gates, Elizabeth Reid, Issabella Lawrence, Rose Gates, and Sarah Hartgrove Reid. To the before mentioned negroes Bose and Hannah and her issue, it is my sincere desire that they may be retained among my family, and not go from among my children. And I do hereby request my executors to adopt some plan if possible not to let them be sold out of the family. To my son Joseph Reid I give on negro named Isaac and one negro woman named Prue and two boys named Edward and Milton and a horse worth one hundred dollars. I confirm to my dtrs. Margret Baskin, Mary Gates, Issabella Lawrence and Rose Gates all the property which I have given them. To my dtr. Elizabeth Reid I give two negroes named Jane and Louisa, and a horse of one hundred dollars value and two feather beds and furniture. I give to my dtr. Issabella Lawrence one horse of one hundred dollars value and what she has heretofore received. To my dtr. Rose Gates I give one horse of one hundred dollar value, with what ever she has received. To my dtr. Sarah Hartgrove Reid I give two negroes girls named Syntha and Mariah, one horse of one hundred dollars value, with two beds and furniture. The rest of my estate I direct to be sold and the proceeds with the money due me to pay any debts and funeral expenses. I appoint my wife Issabella Reid executrix and exeuctor. Dated 5 Aug. 1820. Wit: Nathan Boon, Patsey Boon, James Guthrie. Signed: Joseph Reid. Proven on oath of Patsey Curtis, one of the subscribing witnesses before James H. Dendy, O.P.D. dated 15 Dec. 1828. Recorded 15 Dec. 1828. (Note: Patsey Boon must have married a Curtis between 5 Aug. 1820 and the 15 Dec. 1828.)

Stephen C. Reid. Estate of Stephen C. Reid. Pack 250. In Equity, Clerk of Court Office. Box 12 #162. Probate Judge Office., Pickens, S. C. Est. admr. 25 March 1845 by Bailey Barton, W. L. Keith, P. Alexander, Wm. J. Gantt who are bound unto Wm. D. Steele, Ord. in the sum of $16,000.00. In equity, James M. Reid states that Stephen C. Reid died intestate and owning considerable real estate, one tract at Pickensville, known as the Pickensville tract containing 265 acres, one tract known as the Wiley Cantrell tract containing 145 acres, the home tract containing 200 acres, being part of a tract conveyed by William Hood to S. C. and J. B. Reid upon which S. C. Reid formerly lived, another tract known as the Wilson Tract containing 100 acres as appears by deed of Samuel Wilson, another tract known as the Peter Weaver tract containing 200 acres. Left a widow Sarah and seven chn. viz; Adaline the wife of B. F. Lawrence, George McDuffie Reid, Mary Reid, Esther Reid, Joseph B. Reid, Stephen C. Reid, all of whom are minors. Filed 15 Sept. 1847. James M. Reid may be a son?

Melinda C. Reid. Estate of Melinda C. Reid. Box 14 #188. Probate
Judge Office. Pickens, S. C. Est. admr. 10 Aug. 1846 by Nathaniel
Reid, W. L. Keith, who are bound unto Wm. D. Steele, Ord. in the sum of
$1,500.00.

F. M. Reid. Estate of F. M. Reid. Box 21 #256. Probate Judge Office.
Pickens, S. C. Est. admr. 28 Oct. 1850 by Wm. M. Jones, Clayton N.
Reid who are bound unto Wm. D. Steele, Ord. in the sum of $200.00.

Joseph Reid. Estate of Joseph Reid. Box 21 #256. Probate Judge Office.
Pickens, S. C. Est. admr. 9 June 1851 by Samuel Reid, Miles M. Norton,
W. L. Keith who are bound unto Wm. D. Steele, Ord. in the sum of $5,000.
Samuel Reid was a son of Joseph and Isabella Reid. Legatees; Thomas B.
Reid, Wm. C. Baskin, James Lawrence, Charles, Mary Gates, Alexander E.
Ramsey, Jehu Starrett.

Nathaniel Reid. Nathaniel Reid, Bastardy Bond. Pack 439 #20. Clerk of
Court Office. Pickens, S. C. On the 12 Oct. 1853 appeared beofre me
Joseph B. Reid, N.P. for Pickens Dist. Nathaniel Reid, Crafton Keith,
William H. Reid who acknowledge themselves to be indebted to the State
of S. C. in the sum of $600 each. Whereas at a late term of the Court
of General Sessions Pickens Dist. sd. Nathaniel Reid was convicted as
being the father of a (male) bastard child begotten on the body of Mary
Phillips, spinster, born 22 June 1852. Now the condition of this is
such that Nathaniel Reid shall annually pay twenty five dollars for the
maintainance of the said child until he attains the age of twelve
years. Signed: Nathl. Reid, Crafton Keith, William H. Reid.

Saml. Reid. Deed from Saml. Reid, Sheriff. Book A-1 page 309. Clerk
of Court Office. Pickens, S. C. I Samuel Reid, Sheriff. Whereas by
vertue of a fieri facias (an execution to be levied on the goods of a
debtor) issued out of the Court of Common Pleas held in Pickens Dist.
on the second Monday in March 1829. At a suit of William Whitten to
me directed commanding me that the goods and chattels of Allen Stephens
to levy the sum of eighty two dollars damage and cost, have seized and
taken of the land and tenements and all that undivided title and
interest he has in the tract of land of the late Samuel Stephens decd.
on the waters of 12 mile river. Sale was held and William Whitten
bought same for $25.00. Deed dated 9 March 1830. Wit: George E. W.
Foster, Jared Kirksey. Signed: Saml. Reid S.P.D. Deed attested on
oath of Jared Kirksey before William L. Keith Clerk of Court. Dated
2 Aug. 1830.

Isabella Reid. Estate of Isabella Reid. Box 24 #286. Probate Judge
Office. Pickens, S. C. Est. admr. 9 June 1851 by Samuel Reid, Miles
M. Norton, W. L. Keith who are bound unto Wm. D. Steele, Ord. in the
sum of $8,000.00. Heirs, Thomas B. Reid, Charles Gates, W. C. Baskin,
James Lawrence, Jehu Starrett, Alexr. E. Ramsey.

Rebecca Reid. In Equity. Box 3 #73. Clerk of Court Office. Pickens,
S. C. On 18 June 1846 Rebecca Reid wife of J. B. Reid late Rebecca
Keith shews that she is entitled to a share of a tract of land containing
about 200 acres lying on Oolenoy Creek, waters of Saluda River. Mrs.
Mary Keith decd. her mother. Cornelius Keith decd. her father.

Reid Minors. Box 3 #73. In Equity. Clerk of Court Office. Pickens,
S. C. On 5 March 1860 James M. Reid, Thomas J. Keith, James E. Hagood
are bound unto Robert A. Thompson, clerk of Equity in the sum of
$4,000.00. James M. Reid gdn. of Esther R. Reid, Stephen C. Reid minors
under 21 years. James M. Reid their brother. In 1869 Esther R. was
wife of B. B. Gilstrap. Geo. M. Reid decd. their former gdn.

Ambrose Reid. Box 96 #1010. Probate Judge Office. Pickens, S. C.
Est. admr. 12 July 1869 by Clayton N. Reid, A. M. Roper, Wm. M. Jones
who are bound unto I. H. Philpot, Ord. in the sum of $600.00. Oliver
C. Reid a son lived out of State. Do not know whether said O. C. Reid
alive or not. Sarah Reid widow of Ambrose Reid. Alfred M. Reid decd.
an heir. On 17 Oct. 1870 paid Rebecca Prince acct. $15.00. Left 7

chn. Clayton N. Reid, Abigail Roper, Telitha the wife of Wm. M. Jones,
resides out of State, Alfred Reid, Jane B. The wife of Barton Griffin,
Olive C. Reid, and Lawrence C. Reid the only child of ___ Reid decd.
Who resides out of state. Know that we Jane B. Griffin an heir of
Ambrose Reid decd. and Barton Griffin my husband both of Union, Miss.
Have appointed E. H. Griffin of Pickens Dist., S. C. our attorney to
receive our right from the said est. Dated March 1874. R. C. White,
A. H. Fox witness to the said power of attorney. Appeared a N.P. in
Lee Co., Miss. 24 Mar. 1874. Ambrose Reid owned 462 acres on Adams
Creek adj. land of James H. Ambler and Cornelius Keith and others.

Reid Minors. Box 3 #78. In Equity. Clerk of Court Office. Pickens,
S. C. On 7 May 1849 Madison F. Mitchell, P. Alexander, E. Alexander
are bound unto M. M. Norton in the sum of $1,400.00. M. F. Mitchell
gdn. of Geo. McDuffie Reid minor over 14 years. On 27 Jan.1848 Wm.
L. Keith, Saml. Reid, Jas. Lawrence are bound unto M. M. Norton in the
sum of $2,400.00. W. L. Keith gdn. of Joseph B. Reid, Geo. McDuffie
Reid minors under 21 years. On 4 July 1853 Jas. M. Reid states that
Stephen C. Reid a minor under 14 years and Esther Reid a minor under
12 years. Geo. M. Reid brother to Jas. M. Reid took over as gdn. as
Jas. M. Reid was about to remove from the State. On 17 Oct. 1855 Geo. M.
Reid, John Bowen, Jas. E. Hagood are bound unto Robert A. Thompson,
Ord. in the sum of $4,000.00. Geo. M. Reid gdn. of Mary E. and Esther
R. Reid minors under 21 years. Gdn. also for Stephen C. Reid a minor
under 21 years.

Nathaniel Reid. Estate of Nathaniel Reid. Box 102 #1073. Probate
Judge Office. Pickens, S. C. I Nathaniel Reid of Pickens Dist.
knowing that men must die, and being of strong mind as is usual of men,
etc. I desire that as soon after my death as will be convenient to
my executors, that they sell to the hgihest bidder all my personal
and real property, that is all property and all money I may have on
hand, that they distribute the same to my heirs as follows, after
paying my funeral expenses and just debts. I give to my son Harrison
C. Reid one sixth part, to my son William H. Reid one sixth, to my dtr.
Elizabeth Williams one sixth, to my son Roswell Reid one sixth, and to
my three grand children which is the heirs of my decd. son Warren D.
Reid to wit, dtrs. Neeley, Margret Missouri and Warren D. Reid one
sixth part, which will be divided into three equal parts. "To my dtr.
Mary Hawkins, I give her nothing herself." but desire her share be given
to her trhee chn. viz; Warren D. Keith, Allen Keith and Rebecca Jones.
I therefore give to sd. Rebecca Jones one half of the one sixth, and
the other half be divided between the other two grand chn. "It may be
asked why I gave my daughter Mary nothing my answer is she has not
treated me as a father, and just so is the reason why I gave nothing
to her daughter Margaret she does not treat me as I think she should
and I have therefore given the part she would of been entitled to, to
my three grand children as above." I appoint my son Wm. H. Reid and
my friend William M. Jones executors. Dated 2 Jan. 1872. Wit: J. B.
Reid, Isaac Williams, Signed: Nathl. Reid. On front of will was
written. "This paper purposting to be the last will and testament of
Nathaniel Reid, was this day presented for probate, and was declared
void for want of a third witness 25 March 1872. Signed: J. H. Philpot,
Judge of Probate. On the same day W. H. Reid petitioned the Court for
a letter of admr. upon the estate of Nathl. Reid decd. dated 25 March
1872. Same was issued by the Judge. On 22 June 1874 heirs; Martha H.
Reid now Whelchel of Missouri, W. H. Reid, Roswell Reid of Greenville,
S. C., Mary Hawkins and Betsey Williams and Warren D. Reid of Pickens,
Nelly Reid, Warren Joseph Reid of Greenville, S. C., Harrison Reid of
Arkansas. Elizabeth Williams recd. her share in presence of Isaac
Williams, James Jones share of the Edens estate $133.50.

Lawrence O. Reid. Minor. Box 9 #136. Probate Judge Office. Pickens,
S. C. On 16 Oct. 1871 Clayton N. Reid, Wm. M. Jones, Joab Mauldin are
bound unto I. H. Philpot, Ord. in the sum of $300.00. Clayton N. Reid
gdn. of Lawrence O. Reid minor aged 15 years and a citizen of Hart Co.,
Ga. Son of Shelton Reid son of Ambrose Reid decd. of Pickens, S. C.
Clayton N. Reid of Pickens Co., S. C. his uncle. On 7 Aug. 1871
Sarah Reid recd. $88.842 her share of Ambrose Reid est.

Hugh Reid. Estate of Hugh Reid. Box 82 Pack 2009. Probate Judge Office. Abbeville, S. C. I Hugh Reid of Abbeville, Dist. being at an advanced age but of good health, and sound mind and understanding. I will my just debts be paid as soon as possible. I give to my son George Reid my negro woman called Sun, and two hundred dollars. I give to my dtr. Margery Miller wife of Ebenezer Miller ten dollars, having given her a full portion already. I give to my dtr. Margerat Miller, widow of Joseph Miller decd. one hundred and fifty dollars. I give to my dtr. Elizabeth Wilson ten dollars, having given her a full portion already. I give to my dtr. Rebecca Barr the wife of Rev. W. H. Barr my negro girl Malinda on condition that she pay her brother James Reid $75.00, not being able to make an equitable distribution without this condition. I give to my son James Reid of the State of Indiana, Union Co. one quarter section of land, lying in said State and County, adj. the land whereon he now lives, containing 160 acres. Also I give him one negro called Isaac. I give to my son Samuel Reid all that tract of land whereon I now live, consisting of several adj. tracts containing about 900 acres. I also give him negroes Bob and Alfred and Jesse and Hannah. I heretofore give to my son Samuel the rest and residue of my estate, except my saddle which I give to my son James. I appoint my son Samuel Reid and my son in law Robert C. Wilson executors. Dated 15 May 1829. Wit: Mary G. Lesly, Hugh Kirkwood, Wm. Bowie. Signed: Hugh Reid. Will proven on oath of William Bowie and Hugh Kirkwood before Moses Taggart, Ord. on the 7 Aug. 1829. In 1831 Margret Miller is living in Mississippi.

Notes on Reid Family. George Campbell Read of the United States Navy recd. a legacy from the will of Hugh George Campbell of Charleston, S. C. in 1820. M. H. Reid and wife recd. a share from the est. of Moses Hendricks of Pickens Dist. His est. was admr. 12 Nov. 1855.

Joseph B. Reid. Deed from Joseph B. Reid. Book A-1, page 99. Clerk of Court Office. Pickens, S. C. This deed made between Joseph B. Reid and Chilion Packard both of Pickens Dist. Dated 19 Nov. 1828. In consideration of $300 have granted, sold, and released all that tract of land lying on Carpenter Creek, water of Saluda River. Containg 198 acres, adj. land of Stephen Reid, Joseph B. Reid and John Keith. Wit: Lemuel Keith, J. M. Keith. Signed: Joseph B. Reid. Rebecca Reid appeared before Baily Barton, J.Q. and renounced, released and relinquish her dower to the above land. Dated 29 Nov. 1828. Recorded same date.

Nancy Reid. Deed to Nancy Reid. Book A-1, page 292. Clerk of Court Office. Pickens, S. C. This deed made between Charles F. Lay and Nancy Reid both of Pickens Dist. Dated 22 Dec. 1829. In consideration of $500 have granted, released, sold all that tract of land containing 131 acres lying on Tomosse Creek waters of Little River. "To have and to hold all and singular the premises before mentioned unto the said Nancy Reid and her children, Susannah, Elizabeth, Sarah, Polly and Nancy for ever." Wit: W. M. H. White, John Knox. Signed Charles F. Lay. Proven on oath of John Knox before John McWhorter, J.P. on the 9 June 1830. Recorded 17 June 1830.

Nathan Reid. Deed to Nathan Reid. Book F-1 page 85. Clerk of Court Office. Pickens, S. C. This deed made between Peter Weaver of Georgia State suposed and Wallon & Nathan Reid of Pendleton Dist. Dated 23 April 1804. have bargain, sold, granted and released a tract of land in Pendleton Dist. on a branch of Oolenoye Creek, containing 100 acres it being part of a tract surveyed for Wm. Reid and himself in partnership with John Hawks and conveyed from Hawks to Weaver. Wit: Daniel Blyth, John Stevenson. Signed: Peter Weaver. Proven on oath of Daniel Blyth before Colen Campbell, J.P. dated 19 June 1804.

J. B. Reid. Release of land by J. B. Reid. No ref. Clerk of Court Office. Pickens, S. C. I, J. B. Reid, do by these present relinquish and deliver over to Stephen C. Reid all my right, title and interest in the tract of land within mention it being part of the legacy given to us from the est. of our father Nathaniel Reid decd. agreeable to a

division between the heirs. Dated 20 Oct. 1842. Signed: J. B. Reid.
Recorded 5 April 1848. (Both of these deeds may be on same page.)

Nathan Reid, Sr. Deed from Nathan Reid, Sr. Book B-1 page 153.
Probate Judge Office. Pickens, S. C. This deed made between Nathan
Reid, Sr. and Nathan Reid Jr. both of Pendleton Dist. Dated 10 Aug.
1816. In consideration of $200 have granted, sold, and released a tract
of land lying in Pendleton Dist. on waters of Oolenoie Creek, containing
100 acres, it being part of a tract granted unto Robert Wilson, dated
5 Nov. 1787. Wit: John Keith, John Mackey. Signed: Nathan Reid, Sr.
Proven on oath of John Keith before Nathan H. Camler, J.P. Dated 10
Aug. 1816. Recorded the 12 March 1832.

Joseph B. Reid. Power of Attorney to Joseph B. Reid. Book C-1 page
163. Clerk of Court Office, Pickens, S. C. I William Hood of Franklin
Co., in the State of Ga. Have appointed and authorized Joseph B. Reid
of Pickens Co., S. C. my attorney for me and in my name to use, inter
into, possess, or take possession of a messuage or tract of land commonly
known as the Sally Ford tract lying on the South West side of Sally Ford
branch. Originally granted unto James Jett dated 1 Sept. 1806, containing 534 acres, also in my name to convey, sell all or any part of
said messuage on any terms as he shall seem meet for me. Dated 12 Nov.
1830. Wit: James H. Hood, Attest. Ann Southerland. Signed: William
X Hood. Proven on oath of Ann Southerland before William L. Keith, Clk.
C. on the 5 Sept. 1835. Recorded 15 March 1836.

Joseph B. Reid. Deed from Joseph B. Reid. Book C-1 page 164. Clerk of
Court Office. Pickens, S. C. This deed made between Joseph B. Reid
and Mary Howard, widow, both of Pickens Dist. Dated 8 Aug. 1833. In
the sum of $25.00 have granted, sold and released a tract of land con-
taining 25 acres, lying on the West side of a branch known as Sally
Fords branch, which is a branch of Adams Creek. It being part of a
tract granted unto William Hood, adj. land of James Gillaland Smith,
Stephen C. Reid, C. Packard. Wit: Richard Goodlett, Joel Jones.
Signed: Joseph B. Reid. Proven on oath of Joel Jones before William
L. Keith, Clerk of Court. Dated 5 Sept. 1835. Recorded 15 March 1836.

RICE

John Rice. Will of John Rice. Vol. 1 Page 300. Probate Judge Office.
Marion Co., Marion, S. C. I John Rice, do make this my last will and
testament. First to pay my just debts. I give to my beloved wife
Elizabeth Rice during the term of her natural life the plantation whereo
I now live, also two negroes named Crisy and Descey, also all horses,
cattle, hogs, etc. After the death of my wife as follows, Negro
Descey to my grandaughter Mary Elizabeth Phillips daughter of Katharine
Phillips. To Jane Davis wife of George Davis the land I gave to my
wife containing 500 acres on the Out Back Swamp of Catfish, also negroes
Mary, Dolly, Prince, and Will. To my dtr. Katharine Phillips wife of
Zachariah L. Phillips a tract of land called the River Swamp lying in
Marion County containing 512 acres, also negroes Susan, Bob, Caleb,
and Sam. I give to Mary Davis wife of Abijah Davis, negroes Sally,
Irene, Ebby, Peter and Harry. There is a debt due by H. Davis of
Alabama when it is collected, I desire it to be equal divided between
my heirs. I appoint George Davis and my friend E. B. Wheeler executor.
Dated 20 Sept. 1836. Wit: H. G. Wall, James Wall, Washington Wall.
Signed: John Rice. Recorded the 14 July 1837.

Zenus Rice. Estate of Zenus Rice. Apt. 9 File 669. Probate Judge
Office. Greenville, S. C. To Honr. John Watson, Esqr. Your petitioner
sheweth that Zenus Rice their father late made a will but failed to
order a sale of the real estate. Your petitioner pray for a sale and
a division among the heirs, the deeds call for 210 acres adj. land of
Mrs. Chandler Robert Scott, and others lying on waters of horse creek.
Originally granted unto Charles Sullivan and Benjamin Arnold. The
heirs are ten. Elizabeth the wife of Clement Traynum, Charity Rice,

Thomas Rice, Clement Rice, Vencent Rice, Susannah the wife of Jolly
Atkins, Scily Eastes, Benjamin Thomason and his wife Temperance, Nancy
the wife of George Balwin, Delia the wife of John Richards. Eight of
the legatee when last heard from lived in Georgia. Charity Rice a
minor. Dated 27 Oct. 1845. John C. Sullivan was made gdn. ad litem
for Charity Rice.

Rice Family. Notes on the Rice Family. Book A Page 222. Probate Judge
Office. Pickens, S. C. On 21 June 1858 Jordon Rice and his wife
Emila were heirs of a Thomas Alexander decd. of Pickens Dist. Book B
Page 83. Probate Judge Office. Pickens, S. C. On 10 Nov. 1865 Anna
Rice wife of Isaac Rice a sister to John H. Black decd. of Pickens
Dist. Pack 647 #7. Clerk of Court Office. Pickens, S. C. Jordan
Rice and his wife Milly Rice of Pickens Co. were heirs of Thomas and
Mary Alexander decd. 1 Sept. 1891.

RICHARDS

Adam Richards. Estate of Adam Richards. Book A page 107. Probate
Judge Office. Pickens, S. C. To the Ordinary of Pickens Dist. Your
petitioner heirs of Adam Richards decd. sheweth that we wish you to
have the land belonging to the estate of Adam Richards sold and a
division of the proceeds to the heirs. viz; Watson Collings and Mary
Collings, T. P. Richards, F. M. Jones, S. T. Richards, E. A. Richards,
James T. Richards, J. B. Richards, Eliza Richards... Watson Collings
was made guardian ad litem for E. A. Richards a minor. Dated 1 Jan.
1849.

Adam Richards. Estate of Adam Richards. Box 8 #106. Probate Judge
Office. Pickens, S. C. Est. admr. 7 Nov. 1839 by Mary Richards,
Cleveland Maret, Wm. Janes, Frederick Moss who are bound unto James
H. Dendy, Ord. in the sum of $12,000.00. Cit. Pub at Beverdam Meeting
House. Expend: Jas. F. Richards to Mary Collins nee Mary Richards to
lent money sent to him in Kentuckey in the year 1845. $50.00. On 23
Nov. 1850 paid T. P. Richards $30.00. 4 June 1844 paid Mary P. Richards
$150.00. 8 June 1847 paid John B. Richards $219.00. 3 June 1844 paid
Susan T. Richards $150.00. 6 Nov. 1852 paid Elizabeth Richards $490.54.
1 Jan. 1849 E. A. Richards minor under 21 yrs. wanted Watson Collins
to be her gdn.

Thomas Richards. Estate of Thomas Richards. Box 10 #127. Probate
Judge Office. Pickens, S. C. Est. admr. 3 May 1841 by Wm. Todd, John
Rankins, James A. Doyle, P. Alexander who are bound unto James H.
Dendy, Ord. in the sum of $1,000.00. Cit. pub. at Bethel Church.
Heirs; Robert Brackenridge and wife, Hugh and Jane Erskine, Wm. Richards,
James Todd. On 28 May 1842 James Todd the brother-in-law of Jane
Erskine wife of Hugh Erskine recently of Pickens Dist. but now
residing in Tenn. is entitled to a share in the est. of her father Thos.
Richards decd. That she has a large family of chn. to support and is
desirous of returning to this State, alleging that her husband often
abandons her for months together. It is stated he is a man of inte-
merate habits, and that unless the little pittance to which she Jane
Erskins is entitled is sent to her only it will be squandered. On the
request of Mr. James Todd a tract of land was laid off for Hugh Erskins
containing 79 1/4 acres in Anderson Dist. on Broadway Creek waters of
Rockey River. Surveyed on the 31 Jan. 1844 by Asa Clinkscales Dep. Sur..

RICHARDSON

William Richardson. Will of William Richardson. Will Book C Page 124.
Probate Judge Office, Camden, S. C. I William Richardson of Bloom Hill,
being in perfect mind and memory, etc. First I desire my just debts
be paid from sum due me in bonds. The remainder I will to my wife in
lieu of her dower one thousand pds. sterling paid out of the bonds

and other specialitis I have on interest, the said sum to be paid whenever she pleases to demand and to be wholey subject to her disposition.
To each of my dtr. born before the date of this will I give the sum of
one thousand pds. sterling to be paid each on the day each attain the
age of twenty one years. Any children born after the date of this will,
shall be supported by the income of my estate for their maintenance and
bringing up. The estate it to stay together until two of my sons attain
the age of twenty one years at which time the whole of my personal
est. shall be divided between all my chn. If wife marry she to get only
the sum of 1000 pds. When the youngest son become of twenty two years I
give the whole of my real property be equal divided between them, if
only one son attain that age he is to get the whole..." and as it
always had an advection to the name of Richardson I desire and request
that my children would change it for Rich which is a short easy wrote
name and first aylable of my name and if they me or respect my memory
they will acknowledge no other name." I appoint my wife during her
widowhood Executrix and my friend Charles Cotesworth Pinckey, John
Pringle, John Chesnut, John Smyth and all my sons as they attain the
age of twenty one years executors. Dated 1 Dec. 1785. Wit: Eliy or
Eliz? Fly, Joseph Dukes, Recoke Waning. Signed: Wm. Richardson.

William Richardson. Deed from William Richardson. Book A Page 235.
Clerk of Court Office. Camden, S. C. An agreement made this 8 April
1795 between William Richardson and Burwell Boykin, whereas two thousand acres lying on the waters of Watree river known as the Richland
Plantation the property of the late William Richardson decd. was put
up for sale by the Sheriff of Camden Dist. The highest bidder was
William Richardson. Now it is agreed between the parties that Richardson will give up the tract unto Burwell Boykin permit him to take the
Sheriff title for the land on these terms. One thousand pds sterling to
be paid in the course of one fortnight, and the other thousand to be
paid the first day of April next, with all money due Richardson and Wm.
Magrant. The three are to have possession until next January, the to
be delivered to Boykin who is to make a title to a small part of the
high land of about 300 acres unto heirs or Executor of Samuel Boykin
decd. This being part of an agreement made between Wm. Richardson decd.
and Samuel Boykin decd. With Richardson agrees to procure him a full
and ample vencietion of dower from Ann Richardson to all and every
part of the tract of land. Wit: B. Bincham. Signed: Wm. G. Richardson and B. Boykin. Proven on oath of B. Bincham before Francis Boykin,
J.P. on the 1 June 1797.

John P. Richardson. Book M Page ___. Clerk of Court Office. Camden,
S. C. I James Drakeford of Kershaw Dist. to John P. Richardson of
Sumter, Dist. Dated 23 Dec. 1829. In consideration of $600.00 have
granted, bargained, sold and released all that tract of land containing
100 1/2 acres being part of a tract granted to James Berkley for 250
acres, lying on the East side of the great road leading from Camden to
Lancaster, and on the West side of Big Flat Creek, adj. land of
William McDowell and James Chesnut. Wit: Jon. M. De'Saussure, Jno.
J. Blair. Signed: James Drakeford. Proven on oath of John J. Blair
before Thomas R. Evans Clk. on the 23 Dec. 1829.

John P. Richardson. Mortgage to John P. Richardson. No ref. Clerk
of Court Office. Camden, S. C. James W. Cantey to J. P. Richardson,
J. B. Richardson, Jr. and R. J. Manning and Jno. Cantey. I James W.
Cantey, of Kershaw Dist. am indebted to John P. Richardson, James B.
Richardson, Jr., Richard J. Manning and John Cantey, by note of land in
the sum of $2,000.00...cash advanced...For better securing the payment
of the said sum, with lawful interest have bargain, sold and in plain
open market the following fifteen negroes viz; Hester, John, Cindar,
Juacco, Edy, Paul, Charity, Billy Amy (old) Preston, Clarisse, Sam,
Ned, Honoris Caraboo. Dated ___ April 1833. Wit: Jno. J. Manning,
Thos. Salmond. Signed J. W. Cantey. Proven on oath of John J. Manning
before John J. Baird, J.P. on the 12 April 1833.

William Richardson. Deed from William Richardson. Book F Page 25.
Clerk of Court Office. Camden, S. C. This deed made between William

Richardson of Camden Dist. and Ann his wife and Honr. John Rutledge
of Charleston. Dated 4 Jan. 1785. In consideration of eleven hundred
pds. sterling have granted, bargain, sold and released all that plantation or tract of land containing 300 acres, lying in Craven County on
the South side of Watree River, formally of James Michie all other sides
vacant when surveyed, also all that tract of 150 acres on the South side
of Wateree River bounding and butting to the above tract on the South-
east side. Wit: Eliza Fley, Isham Moore. Signed: Wm. and Ann
Richardson. Proven on oath of Elizabeth Moore who saith that she was
present and saw William and Ann Richardson sign the within deed, before
John Horan, J.Q. on the 2 Feb. 1809. To Mr. Isham Moore and Joseph
Duke, whereas William and Ann Richardson did on 4 Jan. 1785 made a
deed to Honr. John Rutledge, Esq. That Ann Richardson is unable to
make the trip to Charleston, it has been suggested to us that both or
one of you are hereby commanded and fully authorized and empowered to
go to the said Ann and take such release, renunciation and acknowledge-
ment as she shall make before you, and to be certified to associate
Justices. Witnessed before the Honr. J. F. Grimke, Esq. Associate
Justice. Signed: R. Rutledge, Atty.

William Richardson. Estate of William Richardson. Pack 354. Clerk of
Court Office. Abbeville, S. C. In Equity. 96 Dist. Feb. Term 1819.
Wm. Richardson et al vs. The Exors of Tol. Bostick. Whereas Stephen
Bostick intermarried with the widow of Wm. Richardson decd. and admr.
on his estate. With Toliver Bostick and Thomas Pool as securities to
the Ord. for the faithful admr. Pool became dissatisfied and made
application to the Ord. to be released from the suretyship. No more
genealogical information in paper.

Thomas Richardson. Will of Thomas Richardson. Box 59 #2070. Probate
Judge Office. Camden, S. C. I, William Richardson, of Craven Co.
being very sick of body but of perfect mind and memory, etc. I give to
my wife Margaret Richardson all my household goods and moveable estate,
with one negro such as she may choose, to be at her disposal at her
decease. I also appoint and ordain her one of my executrix, also her
third of my 200 acres of land that I now live on at Little River during
her life. I give to my son William Richardson two pds. current money of
this State, to be paid after my lawful debts are paid. I give to my
son Thomas Richardson, Jr. two pds. current money of the aforesaid
state, I also appoint him as my executor. I give to my dtr. Jennett
Kennedy two pds. after my debts are paid. I give to my dtr. Mary
Richardson fifty pds. to be paid her by my son Samuel Richardson two
years after my decd. But if she dies before she marries to fall to the
disposs of my wife ... (Only page found in notes.)

George Richardson. Estate of George Richardson. Box 59 #2068. Probate
Judge Office. Camden, S. C. To Honr. Isaac Alexander Ord. of Kershaw
Dist. The petition of Elizabeth Richardson executrix of the last will
of George Richardson decd. states that a number of articles appear to
her unnecessary for the purpose of raising the family, particularly
the saddle tools and many plantation tools, etc. prays for a sale at
public vendue on Saturday the 31 day of Aug. 1805... at the dwelling
house of the decd. Dated 16 Aug. 1805. Signed: Elizabeth X Richardson.
The estate was appraised on the 13 Aug. 1805 by Daniel Kirkland, Samuel
Kirkland, Benjamin Dawson.

Richard Richardson. Deed from Richard Richardson. Book C Page 115.
Clerk of Court Office. Kershaw, Dist. I Richard Richardson a black-
smith to Thomas Whitaker both of Kershaw Dist. dated 12 April 1800.
In consideration of $200.00 have bargain, sold, grant and released all
that tract of land containing 230 acres, originally granted unto John
Richardson for 200 acres on the 24 Oct. 1766. Adj. land of John
Rutledge Esq. and Ogivie's land, and on South side by Wateree River.
Wit: Burwell Boykin Jr., S. Brown. Signed: Richd. Richardson.
Proven on oath of John Bodkin Jr. before Samuel Mathis J.Q. on the
15 Oct. 1800.

William Richardson. Estate of William Richardson. Box 80 Pack 1975.
Probate Judge Office. Abbeville, S. C. By Taliaferro Livingston Ord.
Whereas Charles Johnson made suit to me for a letter of adme. on Wm.
Richardson decd. est. Dated 10 Jan. 1812. Citation published at
Rockey River Meeting House. 12 Jan. 1812 by me A. Hunter. Warrant of
appraisement. This is authorize and empower you or any three of you
to make a list of the goods and chattels of Wm. Richardson decd. as
directed by Charles Johnson admr. Dated 18 Jan. 1812. Signed: Nathl.
Beever, Christopher Brooks, Edward Tilman, David Carr, Isaac Bowles.
Those who bought at sale, Rebekah Richardson, Charles Johnson, John
Ellington, Jesse C. Bouchell, Lewis Howland, Thomas S. Baskin, Freeman
Wilis, Thomas Boyd, John Boyd, John Gent, Philemon Beauford, R. Richardson, Robert Akins, Wm. Bradshaw, Wm. Ward, Robert Jimmerson, Berryman
Loftis, Jacob Martin, Thomas Tinsley, John Richardson, Dudley Jones,
Joseph Wilson, D. Gillaspie, John Camron, Tolo. Leviston. A petition of
Green C. Richardson sheweth that he is a son of Wm. Richardson decd. and
that the admr. was granted unto Charles Johnson who died without an
account for his admr. Your petitioner prays that Alexander Hunter
executor for Johnson decd. be cited to appear on a fix day and render
an account of the admr. of Richardson decd. ated 21 Sept. 1840.
Benjamin Y. Martin representing the heirs of Wm. Richardson decd.

James W. Richardson. Estate of James W. Richardson. Pack 386. Clerk
of Court Office. Abbeville, S. C. To the Honr. the Chancellors. Your
orator John W. Fooshe a minor about 16 year of age by Winston W. Davis
his next friend... I nt year 1852 James W. Richardson then a citizen
of this Dist. was appointed guardian of your orator on the 22 June
1852, with John W. Fooshe and J. Thornton Carter as sureties. That
James W. Richardson as gdn. received money into his hands from the estat
of Charles B. Fooshe the grand father of your orator. The amount your
orator thinks is about two thousand dollars, and he has removed from the
State of S. C. without accounting for the same, and is living in the
State of Georgia. Your oator prays that his gdn. and his sureties be
held accountable for the money. Dated 19 April 1858.

Noah T. Richardson. Estate of Noah T. Richardson. Box 64 #691. Probat
Judge Office. Anderson, S. C. I Noah Richardson of Anderson Dist. bein
of sound and disposing mind and memory, etc. I direct that all my
funeral expenses and just debts be paid. I give to my son Charles P.
Richardson one negro named Harrison and eight hundred dollars in cash
to make him equal with others. I direct my executor to give each of my
sons sixteen hundred dollars upon their reaching the age of twenty one
years to make them equal with the others. I devise to my executor in
trust to each of my dtr. Charity Emaline and Frances Elizabeth two
negroes girls to be selected at their marriage or at age of twenty one
years. I direct my executors when my youngest child reaches twenty one
years. that my beloved wife Hester Richardson receive a negro man and
woman to be selected by her from the negroes belonging to the estate at
that time, one hundred acres of land, including the house where I now
live, also anything in the way of stock, furniture provision, etc. I
direct my executor to sell or divide the residue of the estate and equal
divide among all my children. I appoint my wife Hester Richardson
executrix and my son J. F. Richardson executor. Dated 18 Aug. 1862.
Wit: B. F. Mauldin, Aaron Welborn, Ezekiel Murphy. Signed: Noah
Richardson. Proven 17 Oct. 1862. Expend: On 26 June 1879 paid T. J.,
A. N., M. B., Clark, E. B. Richardson each $1,000.00. Owned three
tracts of land, 112 acres deeded by Hester and J. F. Richardson to
E. B. Richardson, on 12 Aug. 1877, 125 acres deeded by Hester Richard-
son to T. J. Richardson on 8 Nov. 1878, 13 acres deeded to E. B.
Richardson by Hester Richardson 8 Nov. 1878.

Charles P. Richardson. Estate of Charles P. Richardson. Box 113 #1094.
Probate Judge Office. Anderson, S. C. Est. admr. 22 Sept. 1882 by
Albert Newton Richardson, Enoch B. Richardson, J. C. Griffin who are
bound unto Olin L. Durant, Ord. in the sum of $1,000.00. A. N. Richard-
son a brother to decd.

Hester Richardson. Estate of Hester Richardson. Box 127 #10. Probate Judge Office. Pickens, S. C. I Hester Richardson being of sound and disposing mind and memory and understanding etc. I give to my son Enoch B. Richardson the twenty acres of my home place, which adj. his, this being his part of my home place. I devise all rest and residue of my home place to my six chn. viz; Matthias, Newton, Clark, Emmie McDaniel, Thomas J. and Frances E. Hyde and the four children of my decd. son John F. Richardson, to wit; Ada, Bula, Carrie and Noah Richardson. I give to my dtr. Mary C. Hendrick the sum of five dollars, which is all of my estate I intend her to have. The rest and residue of my estate of every nature I devise to my seven chn. (Mary not named) I appoint my son Newton Richardson executor. Dated 21 Dec. 1883. Wit: G. G. Wells, R. T. Jaynes, J. I. Earle. A codicil made the 6 Feb. 1896. "I desire to strike out section third and charge section second so as to read my seven children instead of my six, namely, Mary C. Hendricks, Mathias Richardson, Newton Richardson, Clarke Richardson, Emmie McDaniel, Thomas J. Richardson, Frances E. Hyde. Witness to the codicil J. J. Watkins, J. L. Williams, W. B. Brooks. Filed 22 Oct. 1899.

Noah T. Richardson. Land Warrant of Noah T. Richardson. Pack 630 #29. Clerk of Court Office. Pickens, S. C. I J. E. Hagood, Clerk, to any lawful surveyor you are authorized to lay out unto Noah T. Richardson a tract of land not exceeding ten thousand acres. Dated 13 April 1860. Filed 28 April 1860.

RIDDLE

Joseph Riddle. Estate of Joseph Riddle. Box 81 Pack 1993. Probate Judge Office. Abbeville, S. C. I Joseph Riddle being low in health but sound in mind do ordain this my last will and testament, etc. To my beloved wife Elizabeth Riddle I give one third of all my personal property consisting of notes, household and kitchen furniture, stock and the use of the plantation whereon I now live during her natural life, and at her death to be equal divided between my two dtr. Margaret and Elizabeth. The tract of land lying in the neighbourhood of Willington, containing 200 acres, I wish to be sold and the money divided betwixt my four daughters, viz; Mary McCombes, Margeret Riddle, Martha Chevis, Elizabeth Riddle. I appoint Patrick Calhoun my executor and my two dtr. Margeret and Elizabeth Riddle Executrix. Dated 30 Dec. 1811. Wit: James Calhoun Jr., James Noble, Wm. Jones, W. T. Shackelford. Signed: Joseph X Riddle. Proven on oath of James Noble before Talo. Livingston, Ord. on the 17 Jan. 1812. Estate appraised on the 6 Feb. 1812.

Riddle Notes. Box 95 #1002. Probate Judge Office. Pickens, S. C. On 1 Jan. 1888 Mary J. Riddle recd a share from the est. of William Hester, Jr. who died 20 Aug. 1864. Was a dtr. of decd.

RIGDON

Rigdon Minors. Box 5 #80. Probate Judge Office. Pickens, S. C. On 21 Aug. 1860 Gabriel Rigdon, James E. Hagood are bound unto W. E. Holcombe, Ord. in the sum of $9106. Gabriel Rigdon gdn. of Wm. Henry Harrison Rigdon a minor. On 22 May 1848 Gabriel Rigdon, Noble Glenn are bound unto W. D. Steele Ord. in the sum of $600.00. Gabriel Rigdon gdn. of his son Wm. H. H. Rigdon minor under 14 years. James Southerland decd. his grandfather.

Matilda Rigdon, fornicator. Pack 220 #27. Clerk of Court Office. Pickens, S. C. On 24 March 1842 Archibald Akens made oath that Sarah and Harvey Rigdon the chn. of Matilda Rigdon are likely to become chargeable to the State and ordered her to appear in Court to give an account of said bastard children.

RIGGINS

Powell Riggins. Estate of Powell Riggins. Box 13 #170. Probate Judge Office. Pickens, S. C. Est. admr. 7 July 1845 by Allen Riggins, Isaiah Wood, Daniel Alexander who are bound unto Wm. D. Steele, Ord. in the sum of $300.00. Expend; Paid Andrew Riggins $2.42, paid William, James Riggins each $2.42, paid the widow her share $10.88. Probably Sarah Riggins who bought at sale. On 14 May 1854 Edy Riggins recd. share.

Allen Riggins. Will of Allen Riggins. Box 101 #1068. Probate Judge Office. Pickens, S. C. I Allen Riggins being of sound mind and memory, etc. First pay my funeral expenses and my just debts. I give to my beloved wife Nancy M. Riggins all the tract of land whereon I now live, also the tract I purchased from Anthony Stewart, with all my personal effects, and that Nancy Riggins to have free use and control of all my property, during her natural life, at her decd. to be divided between my heirs (not named). I appoint my wife Nancy Riggins Executrix and Wm. H. Thomas Executor. Dated 4 Aug. 1886. Wit: John B. Stewart. Lewis E. Hunnicutt, John Eads. Signed: Allen Riggins. Filed 5 Oct. 1886.

Sion Riggins. Estate of Sion Riggins. Box 108 #1031. Probate Judge Office. Pickens, S. C. Winny Howard plaintiff against Emaline Riggins, Malinda Riggins, David Riggins, Lycena Riggins, Charlotte Riggins, Elizabeth Breazeale, Elizabeth Riggins of Pickens Co. and James O. H. Rigdon whose locality is unknown and James Forester, unknown. Are seized in fee as tennants in common of the following tract of land lying on waters of Crow Creek, adj. land of Jordan Rice, Daniel Alexander and others. Containing 144 acres having descended from her father Sion Riggins in common with his other chn., heirs and legatees. Elizabeth Riggins entitled to one third in right of her dower. Filed July 1875.

Allen Riggins. Estate of Allen Riggins. Box 117 #7. Probate Judge Office. Pickens, S. C. He died 1886. Heirs Rebecca Stewart nee Riggins, Clarinda Stewart who resides in Clarksville, Habersham Co., Ga. Nancy Crenshaw, Mary Hunter and Milly Spearman chn. of Wm. Riggins a predeceased son, Burris Riggins, Andrew Riggins chn. of Andrew Riggins his predeceased son and Nancy M. Elgin formerly his widow... 15 June 1887 M. E. Hunter states that Rebecca Stewart, Clarinda Stewart lives in Ga. and Calif. as she is informed. Wm. A. Hunter married Mary Riggin a granddaughter of Allen Riggins. Owned land in Huricane Township also the tract of land known as the Anthony Stewart Tract of 60 acres.

RITCHEY

John Ritchey. Estate of John Ritchey. Box 81 Pack 1978. Probate Judge Office. Abbeville, S. C. Est. admr. the 4 Nov. 1808 by Nancy Ritchey, Rev. Hugh Dickson, John Weatherall, Hugh Morrah and John Hodges Esq. in the sum of $10,000.00. We the under named the near kinsman of John Ritchey decd. so hereby certify that it is our desire that Hohn[?] Morrah and John Hodges Esq. in the sum of $10,000.00. We the under named the near kinsman of John Ritchey decd. do hereby certify that it is our desire that John Weatherall and Hugh Dickson be admitted as assistant administrators with Nancy Ritchey wife of the decd. In witness whereof we have hereunto set our hand this 3 Nov. 1808. Wit: William Norris, Signed: Joseph Richey, William Dunn, James Richey, John X Richey, Robert Richey. The sale was held on 24 Nov. 1808. Buyers; Joseph Richey, Mrs. Nancy Richey, Hugh Dickson, John Weatherall, William Dunn, Jordan Moseley, Benjamin Butler, Hugh B. Hairston, Charles Caldwell, Robert Martin, Peggy Nash, James Petty, James Richey, James Cobb, John Richey, Gabriel Long, Jr., John Goudy, Hugh Huston, Henry Johnson, Samuel McIlroy, Charles Cullins, William Hodges, Theophilus Martin, Archibald Hamilton, David Henderson, Bartholomew Mabry, James Grimes, George Shirley, Robert Richey, George Foreman, Hugh H. Wardlaw,

William Barmore, Lanta Maddox, Robert Hairston, James Hodges, Andrew
Agnew, William Richey, Edward Sharpe, William Norris, Jonadab Gaines,
James Baird, Peggy Richey, Ann Richey, Betsey Richey, John Russel, Jesse
Calvert, Edward Haggan, Eli Norris, Frances Calvert, William Long,
William Henderson, James Main, Robert Wardlaw, William Blain, Robert
Richey, Sr., Thomas Cunningham, John Burton. The negroes that was sold,
Harry, Hannah, Susan, Synthia, Moses, Thom, Peter, Aaron, Harriet,
Luce, Charlotte, Hampton, George.

William Richey. Box 32 Pack 712. Estate Records of Wm. J. Ellis.
Abbeville, S. C. Nandrana Ellis widow of William J. Ellis in 1844.
After her husband death, she married William L. Richey of Abbeville
Dist.

James Richey. Pack 646 #5. Clerk of Court Office. Pickens, S. C. On
14 March 1859 James Richey of Pickens Dist. makes oath that he has
a title claim and interest in the real and personal estate of David
Wiley decd. late of Arkansas in 50 acres of land on Whtstone Creek, adj.
land of Burnet Wilson and others.

Elizabeth Richey. Equity Rec. of Jas. McClinton. Pack 7. Clerk of
Court Office. Abbeville, S. C. Elizabeth Richey a minor in May 1856 of
Abbeville Dist. Was a niece of James R. McClinton decd. who died in
May 1856. Her uncle owned 400 acres of land near Due West. Jane
McClinton and Caroline McClinton were her aunts.

RISER

George Riser. Will of George Riser. Box 25 #896. Probate Judge
Office. Edgefield, S. C. I George Riser of Edgefield Dist. being very
low and weak of body, but of perfect mind and memory, etc. I give to
my son George Martin three negroes named Chesiah, Mason, Anny. I desire
my executors to sell so much of my estate either real or personal to
pay all my just debts. I give to my beloved wife Elizabeth one third
part of my resident of my estate, and the rest I give to my aforesaid
son George Martin Riser to aid him when he shall be of lawful age. I
appoint Capt. Jacob Long and Micheal Long executors. Dated 28 March
1821. Wit: Nathan Norris, William Austin, C. D. Lester. Signed:
George Riser. Recorded 21 Sept. 1821.

George Risor. Will of George Risor. Book A page 371. Probate Judge
Office. Edgefield, S. C. I George Risor of Edgefield Dist. being very
weak in body but in perfect mind and memory, etc. I give to my brothers
Jacob Riser, Jacob Demmick, Jacob Collins, John Lightse, John Lagrene
and Adam Koon the lad that I have raised, the sum of $1,887.00 to be
equal divided bwtween them, to be raised from debts that are due me.
Also I give Adam Koon a negro boy named London, one negro girl named
Hannah and two hundred acres of land lying on Cloud Creek called the
Bates tract, one horse, saddle and bridle, horse to be worth sixty
dollars, with plows and geers, sows and cows to be given to him when he
attains the age of twenty one years or marry. The other legacies to be
paid soon after my decd. I give to my beloved son George Riser all the
rest and residue of my est. both real and personal. I appoint Nathan
Norris, John Bates, William Norris my executors. Dated 16 May 1816.
Wit: Jacob Long, Jr., Jne A. Kinard, Elizabeth X Long. Signed: George
X Riser. Proven on oath of Jacob Long, Jr. the 13 Sept. 1816. Same
time qualified John Bated and William Norris executors.

H. H. Riser. Will of H. H. Riser. Will Book 1887-1905. Page 185.
Probate Judge Office. Edgefield, S. C. I H. H. Riser, being weak in
body and of sound mind, memory and understanding, etc. I appoint my
sons James H., E. Elbert and A. Pickens Riser to be executors. I
direct that all my debts and funeral expenses be paid as soon as
possible. I direct that all my personal property (also one note
against my son James H. Riser) shall be sold at public outcry. One
third of the proceeds of the sale to be given to my wife Keerrenhappuck

275

Riser, and the remaining two thirds ot be divided between my five children, viz; Matilda E. Wyse, James H. Riser, Sallie A. Etheredge, J. Elbert Riser and A. Pickens Riser or their heirs. Also I direct that all my real estate be left unsold and rent and proceeds to support my wife Keerrenhappuck during her life time, at her death all real estate must be sold and monies equally divided between my five chn. Dated 11 Feb. 1892. Wit: C. P. Boozer, S. J. Derrick, M. G. Bowles. Signed: H. H. Riser. Proven date not given.

John Rizer, Sr. Estate of John Rizer, Sr. Bundle 27 Pack 4. Probate Judge Office. Barnwell, S. C. Est. admr. 25 Oct. 1816 by Mary Ann Rizer, Christian Rizer, David Lightsey, Frederick Scheuberd who are bound unto O. D. Allen, Ord. in the sum of $14,000.00. On 4 Oct. John Rizer, Mary Ann Rizer made suit for letter of admr. Citation published at St. Barthelomew Church, 20 Oct. 1816. On 15 Oct. 1816 mentioned that John Rizer, Jr. had also died.

George W. Rizer. Estate of George W. Rizer. Bundle 113 Pack 9. Probate Judge Office. Barnwell, S. C. Est. admr. 15 Oct. 1852 by Sarah Rizer, John W. S. Tucker, Joseph H. Stokes who are bound unto R. C. Fowke, Ord. in the sum of $20,000.00. Died about the 16 Aug. 1852 leaving a widow Sarah Rizer and one child named William Rizer. On 23 March 1852 paid Wm. C. Rizer minor taxes $7.91.

William C. Rizer. A Minor. Bundle 115 Pack 12. Probate Judge Office. Barnwell, S. C. On 16 Apr. 1853 John W. S. Tucker, Sarah Rizer, Peter Stoke were bound unto Johnson Hagood, Ord. in the sum of $14,000.00. Whereas John W. S. Tucker made gdn. of William C. Rizer a minor under 21 years.

William C. Rizer. Estate of William C. Rizer. Bundle 217 Pack 1. Probate Judge Office. Barnwell, S. C. Est. admr. Jan. 1885 by Peter Stoke, Sarah Boyd, Annie E. Rizer who are bound unto B. T. Rice, Esq. Ord. in the sum of $600.00. Wm. C. Rizer died 19 Dec. 1884. Annie E. Rizer the widow.

ROGERS

Major James Rogers. Will of Major James Rogers. Box 15 #201. Probate Judge Office. Pickens, S. C. Will dated 18 Aug. 1847 in pickens Dist. No executor names. Wit: Nathan Boon, John Sharpe, Rachel McWhorter. Wife, Ann Rogers, Dtr. Margaret Rogers. Chn. mentioned but only one named.

William Rogers. Estate of William Rogers. Box 21 #257. Probate Judge Office. Pickens, S. C. Est. admr. Dec. ___ 1849 by Catharine Rogers widow, J. W. Norris, Jr. who are bound unto Wm. D. Steele, Ord. in the sum of $200.00. Died in Oct. Sett. ment. children no names given.

Maj. James Rogers, Sr. Estate of Maj. James Rogers, Sr. Box 43 #482. Probate Judge Office. Pickens, S. C. Est. admr. 1 March 1858 by James Rogers, Jr., James E. Hagood, W. N. Craig who are bound unto W. J. Parson, Ord. in the sum of $16,000.00. (Note: The will of Maj. James Roger in box 15 #201 same as this will that was found in this package.) Heirs: Temperance McWhorter, Hugh Rogers, Edward Rogers, Prudence Drenan, Elander Robinson, Margaret Rogers, A. D. Rogers, the heirs John Rogers decd. James Rogers, Jr. recd. property from his father. On 13 Oct. 1858 Hugh Rogers of Catoosa Co., Ga. recd. property from his father. On 15 Mar. 1859 Temperance McWhorter of Walker Co., Ga. states that she had property advanced by her father to her. On 14 March. 1859 Elender Robinson of Hall Co., Ga. had property advanced by her father to her... Sarah was the wife of John McWhorter of Pickens Co. and left ten. chn.

Wm. Dever Rogers. Estate of Wm. Dever Rogers. Box 71 #756. Probate
Judge Office. Pickens, S. C. Est. admr. 6 July 1863 by Adam D.
Rogers, James E. Hagood who are bound unto W. E. Holcombe, Ord. in the
sum of $400.00. Mrs. Sarah Rogers, etc. bought at sale.

William Amos Rogers. Estate of William Amos Rogers. Box 10 #134.
Probate Judge Office. Pickens, S. C. On 19 Aug.1875 E. F. Allgood,
Alexander Allgood, Hardy Gilstrap are bound to I. H. Philpot, Ord. in
the sum of $5,000.00. E. F. Allgood gdn. of Wm. Amos Rogers a minor
over 14 years. On 17 April 1875 his father Thos. A. Rogers died.
Wm. A. has no mother or brother to manage the est. and desires that his
brother-in-law Edward F. Allgood be his gdn. On 3 May 1882 Edward F.
Allgood gdn. of Wm. A. Rogers decd. is indebted to the following persons
viz; Lou F. Allgood, Elizabeth P. Allgood, Telitha E. Boggs, Margaret
A. Ford, Mary J. Hester, T. Emma King heirs of said Wm. A. Rogers decd.

Henry Rogers. Estate of Henry Rogers. Box 133 #9. Probate Judge
Office. Pickens, S. C. Est. admr. 4 Jan. 1900 by R. J. Rogers, J. D.
Rogers, W. E. Alexander, J. P. Alexander who are bound unto J. B.
Newberry, Ord. in the sum of $250.00. Died 9 Sept. 1899. R. J. and
J. D. Rogers his sons.

Thomas A. Rogers. Will of Thomas A. Rogers. Box 89 #1119. Probate
Judge Office. Pickens, S. C. I Thomas A. Rogers being of sound mind
and memory, etc. Having heretofor disposed of the greater portion of
my estate both real and personal. Now to each the sum of $2,207.14.
Leaving to myself a tract of 52 acres in Spartanburg Co. for my own
use. I desire my just debts shall be paid. I give to my son William
Amos Rogers in addition to his equal share with his six sisters,
articles of relics of the family, my secretary and book case, my
library of books, my gold watch, my rifle gun and clock. Having had a
disagreement with his son-in-law Thomas E. Boggs over some land known
as the Slab Town Place that gave his son Wm. A. Rogers an unfavorable
portion of said land, in order to give each child equal part according
to my own sense of justice. At his death both real and personal
property are to be divided into seven equal shares and son William S.
Rogers is to get two shares and his dtr. Talitha Ellen Boggs is hereby
excluded from a share. The other dtrs. are; Frances L. Allgood,
Elizabeth P. Allgood, Margaret A. Rogers, Mary J. Hester and Tersa E.
Rogers. I appoint Edward F. Allgood and Samuel J. Hester executors.
Dated 10 April 1875. Wit: W. S. Smith, T. Roper, C. L. Hollingsworth.
Signed: T. A. Rogers. Filed 19 April 1875. Heirs viz: Lou F. Allgood,
M. A. Ford, T. Emma King, M. J. Hester.

Hugh Rogers. Power of Attorney. Box 15 #201. Probate Judge Office.
Pickens, S. C. I Hugh Rogers of the county of Washington in the State
of Arkansas do hereby appoint John McWhorter of the County of Walker
in the State of Georgia. To use my name, to ask, demand, receive,
recover, receipt all money or property both real and personal due or
owing to me from the estate of the late James Rogers decd. of Pickens
Co., S. C. Dated 25 April 1859. Wit: Thos. M. Gunter, James W. Carny.
Signed: Hugh Rogers. This power of attorney was proven on oath of the
within named witnesses before Cyrus G. Gilbreath, J.P. Cyrus G. Gilbreath, J.P. was certifyed by P. R. Smith, Clerk of Court. Who was
certifyed on oath of John A. Wilson, Judge of the 4th Jud. circuit.

Notes on the Rogers Family. Box 10 #157. Probate Judge Office.
Pickens, S. C. On 26 April 1876 Mary Jane Hester wife of Samuel J.
Hester was a daughter of T. A. Rogers.

Andy Rogers. Warrant for Assault. Pack 220 #14. Clerk of Court
Office. Pickens, S. C. On 29 March 1880 Lidia Rogers took out a
warrant for Andy Rogers for assault and battery, by hitting her 3 or
4 times over the head with a bit of wood and with his fist.

Zelpha Rogers. Too out warrant. Pack 227 #10. Clerk of Court Office.
Pickens, S. C. On 16 Feb. 1860 Zelpha Rogers made oath that J. R. Neal,
John E., Saml. and Jesse Lowden and Hiram Scruggs did on the 2 Feb.

last assault her with firearms and clubs and threatening to shoot her
and also threatening to strike her with their clubs all done in a very
rude manner.

Sarah Rogers. Will of Sarah Rogers. Admr. Book F, Page 424. Anderson,
S. C. I Sarah Rogers, desirous to make disposition of my property do
make my will as follows. First I desire my just debts and funeral
expenses be paid. My black man Scott I give to my son James Rogers
upon him paying a debt due Albert Madden, due by me for corn. The
ballance of my property, I desire to be sold and equal divided between
my children share and share alike. The colt which my gray mare is in
foal I give to my son James. The share to which my daughter Tabitha will
be entitled I desire my executor to pay over to my son James S. Rogers
who I hereby constitute trustee to receive the same for this use of
herself and children. I appoint my friend R. F. Simpson my executor.
Before my property is sold my executor deliver one bed and furniture
to my grand daughter Memine Martin. Dated 1 June 1832. Wit: Samuel
Downs, C. W. Allen, Aonth Allen. Signed: Sarah X Rogers. The within
will was proven before me in open Court the 20 Aug. 1952[?]. [This
date must be 1832] on oath of C. W. Allen. Signed: D. Anderson Ord.

William L. Rogers. Tavern License. Pack 181 #29. Clerk of Court
Office. Pickens, S. C. To the Board of County Commissioners; The
undersign petition for a license to retail spiritous at his house now
occupied by him from the 1 Nov. 1868 to 1 May 1869. Signed Wm. L.
Rogers. Dated 19 Jan. 1869. We the under signed free holders do
recommend that Wm. L. Rogers as a proper and suitable person to retail
spiritous liquors and he will comply with the law. His house is near the
Court house. Signed: H. Philpot, Riley Ferguson, R. A. Bowen, Robert
Craig.

Major James Rogers. Land Grant. Grant Book L #8. Secretarys Office,
Columbia, S. C. That in pursuance of an act of the legislature,
entitled, An act for establishing the mode of granting the land now
vacant in this State, passed the 19 Feb. 1791. We have granted a
tract unto Major James Rogers a tract of 127 acres, surveyed for him
the 4 March 1818 in Pendleton Dist. on the waters of Little River and
Oconny Creek, adj. land of Rogers own land, McDows, Boyds and Wm.
Hammonda land. Dated 4 Jan. 1819.

John Rogers. Equity records #23. Clerk of Court Office. Pickens, S. C.
"This is to certify that we were acquainted with a trade made between
John Rogers and James Rogers Sr. decd. and that James Rogers sold to
John Rogers. A tract of land whereon John Rogers now lives, and that
the said John Rogers paid the said James Rogers decd. the full payment
for said tract of land lying in North Carolina whereon the said John
Rogers lived. Given under our hand and seal this 17 July 1861. Signed:
T. W. Calhoun, J. J. Calhoun, Isaac P. Pool, A. S. Rogers, A. D. Rogers,
John S. Sloan, L. Rogers, Joel Moody." (Under this)
Wife name, Carolina Rogers. Children name... Sarah A., Nathan Rogers.

ROPER

Rev. Tyre L. Roper. Will of Rev. Tyre L. Roper. Box 110 #1050.
Probate Judge Office. Pickens, S. C. I Tyre L. Roper being sound in
mind and memory, knowing that we all have to die, etc. I will that my
just debts and funeral expenses be paid. My entire estate be left to
Darcas Jane Roper and support of my three chn. viz; Margaret A. Roper,
Leander Roper and Thomas Walters for their support, clothing and
schooling for the period of sixteen years. After this time all my
estate both real and personal be sold and divided equally amongst all
my chn. With my wife Darcas Roper taking a child share, one share to
Rachel Gillespie, one share to Rebecca C. Lewis, one share to Jesse E.
Roper, one share to Samuel Roper, one share to Elijah Roper, one share
to Ann Madison Saterfield, one share to Amos Roper, one share to Mary O.
Sutherland, one share to Vashti A. Jones, one share to Margaret A.

Roper now a minor, one share to Leander Roper (minor) and one share to Thomas Walters Roper a minor. I appoint Stephen D. Keith Lynch and Matthew Hendricks my executors. Dated 24 March 1876. Wit: Ira T. Roper, Samuel Edens, N. J. Williams. Signed: Tyre L. Roper. He died 27 March 1876. Filed 30 March 1876. On 27 May 1892 David and Rebecca Lewis of Eastland County, Texas appointed John T. Lewis of Pickens Co., S. C. their atty. to receive their share of Tyre L. Roper Est.

Benjamin Roper. Estate of Benjamin Roper. Box 3 #26. Probate Judge Office. Pickens, S. C. Est. admr. 8 Aug. 1831 by Wm. Sutherland, Wm. L. Keith who are bound unto James H. Dendy, Ord. in the sum of $400.00. Left a widow and 12 chn. Heirs ment. on 21 Nov. 1831, John H., Jacob, Aaron, Sarah Roper, Rachel Ward, J. M. Keith, Keziah Roper, widow Nancy, Benjamin Roper decd. Susana Roper who married Moses Hendrick. On 18 Oct. 1836 Wm. Sutherland wanted Mr. Dendy Ord. to pay Benj. Roper the part due John Byrus the husband of Cazzy Roper.

Aaron Roper, Sr. Estate of Aaron Roper, Sr. Box 36 $406. Probate Judge Office. Pickens, S. C. Est. admr. 17 Sept. 1855 by Tyre L. Roper, Alexander Bryce, E. M. Keith who are bound unto W. J. Parson, Ord. in the sum of $3,000.00. Expend; John C. Roper, a son recd. property. Aaron Roper a son recd. property also during the lifetime of his father. Amount of property $136.50 rendered T. L. Roper for Hamilton Roper decd. Amount of Tilman Roper schedule made by Joab Langford according to what he was told by Ropers wife $141.75. On 5 Oct. 1857 Marena Burgess states that $35.40 was the schedule rendered to L. Roper. Joab Langford schedule of property from said est. was $37.05 Charles Roper schedule rendered by his widow Abigal N. Roper was $49.50. Schedule rendered by Joab Langford for Jane Hagood was $35.00. Left 11 heirs in 1859 viz; Simeon E. Burgess, Lemnel or Samuel Roper heirs, Marcus Roper, Aaron Roper Admr. of Hamilton Roper, Joab Langford, Wm. Jones guardian for Charles Roper heirs, B. Hagood part of Jane Hagood share and to Z. Hagood the bal. in full of her share, Abigal Roper, paid J. C. Ropers share to T. L. Roper, paid J. E. Hagood gdn. for Tilman Ropers children.

Tilman Roper. Estate of Tilman Roper. Box 36 #407. Probate Judge Office. Pickens, S. C. Est. admr. 17 Sept. 1855 by Tyre L. Roper, A. Bryce, E. A. Keith who are bound unto W. J. Parson, Ord. in the sum of $1,000.00. Left a widow and seven chn., no names given. J. E. Hagood was the guardian of the seven chn.

Charles Roper. Estate of Charles Roper. Box 37 #424. Probate Judge Office. Pickens, S. C. Est. admr. 13 Oct. 1855 by William Jones, W. L. Keith who are bound unto W. J. Parson, Ord. in the sum of $1,000.00. Left a widow and two chn. Viz; two minors Ira Thomas Roper and Sterling Roper of whom Wm. Jones was the gdn.

Joshua Roper. Estate of Joshua Roper. Box 41 #465. Probate Judge Office. Pickens, S. C. I Joshua Roper being in a low state of health yet having a sound and disposing mind and memory, etc. First, after all my just debts and funeral expenses are paid, I will to my wife Mary Roper all my household and kitchen furniture together with all my farming tools, stock, cattle, hogs that she may need during her natural life or widowhood. I give to my son Absalom Roper I give all the land on the East side of the well known Town Creek, he is to give to my wife his mother a good maintainance from the proceed of the same, and after her death he is to pay my executors one hundred dollars to be divided between the other heirs who have no part in the land. I will all land on the West side of said Creek to my two sons Charles and Samuel to be divided as follows; beginning at Absalom's footlog thence to a corner on Rockey Branch which I made to my son Joshua some time ago. the line up the hill continuing to the back line. Samuel havin the lower part which he now lives. Charles the upper part. Each to pay my executor one hundred dollars to be divided between others that have no land. All remaining property and money to be equal divided between viz; Alfred, William, Singleton and Joshua Roper and Rutha Crow, Eleanor Spearman, Syntha Crain and Mary Byers. I have given my son

Singleton Roper one horse worth twenty dollars, to be counted in their
share. I appoint my son in law James Spearman executor. Dated 7 Feb.
1853. Wit: J. G. Ferguson (Judge), James Major, John W. Major.
Signed: Joshua X Roper. Proven 3 March 1856. Expend: On 29 Aug. 1857
paid Jesse Crain his share $61.22, 17 March 1857 paid Henry Lawson and
wife $5.90, 1 Jan. 1860 paid Adaline Lawson $4.10, paid Tyre Roper his
share $12.50, paid 7 Oct. 1862 Rebecca Roper in full $13.23, paid Malind
Roper Newmans share in full $13.23, paid Elizabeth Duncan share $13.45.
On 6 Jan. 1868 paid three minor heirs of Wm. Byers each $13.45, on 1
Jan. 1862 paid Redin Byers $12.93.

Rachel Roper. Estate of Rachel Roper. Box 5 #1. In Equity, Clerk of
Court Office. Pickens, S. C. Est. admr. 15 Oct. 1855 by Tyre L. Roper,
James H. Ambler who are bound unto W. J. Parson, Ord. in the sum of
$800.00.

Ropers Minors. Box 4 #101. Probate Judge Office. Pickens, S. C. On
4 July 1859, Wm. Jones gdn. of Ira Thomas Roper and Starling Roper
minors under 12 years. Abigail Roper their mother. Wm. Jones their
uncle.

Absalom Roper. Estate of Absalom Roper. Box 138 #8. Probate Judge
Office. Pickens, S. C. Est. admr. 3 Oct. 1901 by John Roper, J. M.
Stewart, W. T. McFall, F. C. Parson who are bound unto J. B. Newberry,
Ord. in the sum of $200.00. Died 7 Sept. 1901. On 28 Nov. 1902 Mrs.
L.D. Spann recd. a share. 3 Nov. 1902 Mrs. Anna Davis recd. an
interest. 21 Nov. 1902 Nannie A. Norris recd. a share. 23 Oct. 1902
Nancy Roper the widow, John Roper, W. H. Roper heirs Wm. Roper, Ellen
Moor, John Roper, Nancy Norris, Mattie Spann, Anna McDavid recd. shares.

Ira T. Roper. Estate of Ira T. Roper. Box 123 #12. Probate Judge
Office. Pickens, S. C. Est. admr. 24 April 1895 by Mrs. M. J. Roper,
Alen K. Edens, E. C. Edens are bound unto J. B. Newberry, Ord. in the
sum of $1,000.00.

Gideon Roper. Will of Gideon Roper. Box 59 #640. Probate Judge Office
Pickens, S. C. I Gideon Roper being of sound mind and weak in body
calling to mind the uncertainty of life, etc. First I will my just
debts and funeral expenses be paid. I will to my beloved wife Elizabeth
Roper my whole estate both real and personal to manage as she sees
proper during her natural life time, and at her death to be equal divide
between my lawful heirs. I will that as any of my children come of
age or marry anything my wife can spare have it appraised and keep a
record of the same so all may be equal. Dated 3 Sept. 1861. Wit:
Amie L. Young, Jane Duke, Reese Bowen. Signed: Gideon X Roper.
Filed 21 Oct. 1861.

Charles Roper. Estate of Charles Roper. Box 90 #952. Probate Judge
Office. Pickens, S. C. Est. admr. 19 Oct. 1883 by Margaret L. Roper,
Thos. R. Price, H. J. Lewis, J. B. Stewart who are bound unto J. H.
Newton, Ord. in the sum of $1,000.00. Died 19 Aug. 1883. Heirs,
Margaret Roper, the widow, chn; Martha Tripp, Elizabeth Kay, Adeline
Davis, Mary Davis, Margaret Smith, A. Alonso Roper, Sarah E. Saterfield
Frances L. Kelley, Laura A. Kelly, Daily Roper, Susan Lawson decd.
John T. Roper decd., Martha Jarratt decd.

Aaron Roper. In Equity. Pack 79. Clerk of Court Office. Pickens,
S. C. Tyre L. Roper, Marcus Roper, Aaron Roper, Marena Roper who
married Simeon E. Burgess states that Aaron Roper, Sr. died in 1855.
Owned 300 acres lying on Saluda River adj. land of Samuel Earle and oth
His wife died about the same time he did, and was buried about the same
time. Left ten chn. viz; Lemuel Roper, John Roper, Matilda wife of
Joab Lankford, heirs of Jane Hagood who died some years before her
parents, Benjamin Hagood the name and number of the others unknown if
any, the heirs of Tilman Roper who died before his parents leaving the
following chn. viz; Catherine Roper a minor over the age of 12 years,
John, James, David and Tilman Roper each minors under 14 years. The
heirs of Charles Roper decd. who died in 1855, and the above Tyre L.

Roper, Marcus Roper, Marena Burgess. Hamilton Roper decd. Carinda
Roper was the widow of Hamilton Roper decd. Lemuel Roper died leaving
a widow and 4 chn., William Noble Roper, Bailey Roper under 14 years,
Martha Roper and Elmina Roper under 12 years all reside in Georgia.
Filed 27 March 1856. Hamilton Roper died leaving no chn. Clarinda
Roper admits it to be true that she did leave and live separate and
apart from her husband for a period of 18 months, prior to his death.
She states that they were married in Greenville Dist. in Jan. 1853 and
lived together until June 1854 and she had a male child by him, which
lived but a few weeks. Her husband was cruel and unkind and inflicted
blows upon her person, etc. and at length drove her from his house. She
went to the house of her father Benjamin Turner in Greenville Dist.
She claims a widow share of what he has.

Aaron Roper. Estate of Aaron Roper. File 24 #14. Probate Judge
Office. Greenville, S. C. On 9 Jan. 1873 Perry D. Roper states that
his father Aaron Roper died in Jan. 1866. That he owned land on waters
of Saluda River, adj. land of J. K. Bates, William Hunt and others
containing 337 acres. Heirs: Charles E. Roper, Isabella Roper,
Alonza L. Roper, William N. Roper, Aaron T. Roper, Nancy R. Roper.

SALMON

George Salmon. Deed from George Salmon. Pack 378 #1. Clerk of
Court Office. Pickens, S. C. This indenture made between George Salmon of Greenville Co. and John Fields of Pendleton Co. Dated 31 Jan.
1793. In the sum of five shillings sterling, Salmon hath granted,
bargained, sold and convey a tract of land containing 290 acres, being
part of a tract granted unto George Salmon 1 June 1787, lying in Pendleton Dist. on both sides of South Fork. Adj. lands of Camerons land.
Wit: Lewis Wimberly, Sarah Anderson. Signed: George Salmon. Deed
attested to by Sarah Anderson before Bayley Anderson, J.P. Dated 31
Jan. 1793. Recorded 5 Feb. 1793. Book B Page 131.

SATTERFIELD

Bidwell Satterfield. Land Platt. Pack 1-A #1. Clerk of Court Office.
Pickens, S. C. Purusant to a warrant from Thomas Garvin Comm. Dated
5 Oct. 1830. I have admeasured and laid out unto Bidwell Satterfield a
tract of land of thirty acres, lying on Colonel fork a branch of Coneross
Creek waters of Seneca River. Adj. lands of William Perkins decd.,
Samuel Maverick's and Philips, Dated 3 Nov. 1830. Signed: Thomas
Lamar, Dep. Sur.

SAXON

Susannah Saxon. Petition. No ref. Greenville Dist. By Spartan
Goodlet, Esq. Ord. Whereas Susannah Saxon hath petitioned me, setting
forth that Leurana, Noah, Mary, John and Altha Saxon are minors under
the age of 14 years. hath a sum of money coming to them from the U. S.
and no person authorized by law to receive and take care of same, and
requesting to be appointed guardian to them for that purpose. After
considering the same, etc. I hereby appoint you the said Susannah
Saxon gdn. of (chn. named) until they arrive to the age of 14 years you
are to sue, recover, receive the whole of the personal estate of said
minors according to law, and make due returns to the Ordinary Office of
your proceedings, etc. Dated 21 April 1817. (On the back of this
paper, written by Miss Young). Reports of Mrs. Pruitt of Abbeville,
concerning my third grandfather Jackson Saxon. They came to America
from Bellfast, Ireland. His sister Nancy, married A Mohare and remained
in Ireland. The following were his sisters and brothers. John P.
(Mrs. Pruitts grandfather), "Plug Saxon, Lewis Washington, and Betsy
who married a Bill Burnes. Mrs. Pruitts father was Adam Crane Saxon

who was the son of John P. Saxon. The following are the children of Adam Crane's family. Jane Knight, Foster Saxon, John, Juluis, and Martha who married a Buzhardt. She said Thompson Saxon was a brother to Jack also. Suggested that I would find Saxon graves at Harmony Church, in Laurens County. Also see Miss Ethel Winn of Laurens, S. C. for information.

James Saxon. Deed from James Saxon. Book A Page 268. Mense Covy. Greenville, S. C. This indenture made between James Saxon of Laurence (Laurens) Co. and William Austin of Greenville Co. Dated 10 June 1788. In consideration of two pds. sterling, hath bargain, sold, and relased all that tract of land containing 346 acres in Greenville Co. lying on both sides of Gilders Creek, being part of a patent unto said Saxon dated 1 Jan. 1787. Wit: Wm. Mitchison, Richard Collins. Signed: James Saxon. Proven in open Court on oath of William Mitchison in the Aug. term. Dated 18 Aug. 1788.

James Saxon. Land Warrant. Book B Page 25. Probate Judge Office. Abbeville, S. C. For 100 acres on a branch of Generostee Creek waters of Savannah River, adj. land of Harry Pierson, Josiah East, Samuel Saxon surveyed by Joshua Saxon, D.S. on the 12 June last. recorded 13 July 1785. R. Anderson, Clk.

William Saxon. Land Warrant. Book B Page 25. Probate Judge Office. Abbeville, S. C. for 184 acres on a branch of Generostee Creek, waters of Savannah River. Bounded on all sides by vacant land when surveyed by Joshua Saxon D.S. on the 12 June last. Recorded 13 July 1785 by R. Anderson Clk.

Samuel Saxon. Land Warrant. Book B, page 42. Probate Judge Office. Abbeville, S. C. For 640 acres lying above the line on the branches of Generostee Creek waters of Savannah River. Adj. land of David Anderson, surveyed by Joshua Saxon, D.S. on the 13 June last. Recorded 5 Aug. 1785. By R. Anderson, Clk.

James Saxon. Land Warrant. Book B Page 42. Probate Judge Office. Abbeville, S. C. For 287 acres above the ancient boundary line on a branch of six and twenty mile creek, waters of Savannah River. Adj. land of James Edmons, others sides owners not known, surveyed by Joshua Saxon D.S. on the 6 Aug. 1785.

James Saxon. Land Warrant. Book B Page 43. Probate Judge Office. Abbeville, S. C. 340 acres lying above the line on a branch of six and twenty mile Creek, waters of Savannah River. Adj. land of James Cannons, others sides owners name not known. Surveyed by Joshua Saxon D.S. on the 13 June last. Recorded the 6 day of Aug. 1785. R. Anderson, Clk.

Jesse Saxon. Land Warrant. Book B Page 45. Probate Judge Office. Abbeville, S. C. 200 acres lying above the line on the West side of Twenty Three Mile Creek, a branch of Keowee River bounded on all sides by vacant land. Surveyed by Joseph Whitner D.S. on the 3 June last. Recorded 16 Aug. 1785. R. Anderson.

Charles Saxon. Land Warrant. Book B page 58. Probate Judge Office. Abbeville, S. C. 200 acres lying above the line on the 23 Mile Creek, bounded by land of Thomas Wadesworth all other sides vacant. Surveyed 5 July last. Recorded 27 Aug. 1785. R. Anderson, clk.

Joshua Saxon. Land Warrant. Book B page 59. Probate Judge Office. Abbeville, S. C. 472 acres lying above the line on Generostee Creek, waters of Savannah River. Adj. land of Samuel Dalrymple all other sides vacant. When surveyed by Joshua Saxon D.S. on the 14 May last, Recorded 27 Aug. 1785.

SHANNON

Moses Shannon. Estate of Moses Shannon. Box 14 #178. Probate Judge
Office. Pickens, S. C. Est. admr. 4 Nov.1844 by Ebenezer P. Varner,
Thomas W. Harbin, Thomas Harbin who are bound unto Wm. D. Steele, Ord.
in the wum of $2,000.00. On 4 Nov. 1844 E. P. Varner states that Moses
Shannon has left this Dist. several years ago and has not been heard
of in some 8 or 10 years and is believed to be dead.

SHARP

Peter Sharp. Inquest. Pack 125. Probate Judge Office. Pickens, S. C.
An inquest was held 26 Nov. 1859 for Peter Sharp. The jury brought it
out that he to his death by comjestion of some vital cause by intem-
perance at the cross road near Harvy Smith old work shorp. Lewis C.
Smith sworn says that he found Mr. Sharp a few minutes before he died
lying in the road near Harvey Smith old shop. He was lying on his
right side, with the right leg crooked rather under him. His left leg
was straight and was lying on his right side. His eyes were open and
set in his head and were red. His face was dark purple. I spoke to
him three times, he made no answer. Jeremiah Hinton said that he saw
Mr. Sharp at the muster grounds some 150 yards from where he was found
dead. He left the muster grounds about 3 p.m. Think he was alone, he
was drinking some, was not complaining any as I heard of. . .

SHAW

Robert Shaw. Will of Robert Shaw. Vol. 11 Page 38. Probate Judge
Office. Charleston, S. C. I Robert Shaw of Prince George Parish,
Craven County. Being low and weak in body, but of perfect and sound
mind and memory, etc. First I will that all my personal estate be sold
at the discretion of my executors to the best advantage of my heirs.
I will that all my land lately bought of Col. Rothnahler lying in said
county being 250 acres be managed or disposed of in such a way as the
best advantage of my heirs. I will my just debts be paid. The remaining
part of my estate be divided between my wife Elizabeth Shaw and my two
sons, Robert and John Shaw each to have one third part. In case one
child dies, his share goes to the other, in case both dies before
marriage or of age then all to go to my wife. In case my wife dies
L.f re my sons become of age or marry, her share to go to her mother
Abigail Smith. I appoint my wife Elizabeth Shaw Executrix and Robert
Ervin and Hugh Ervin executors. Dated 22 March 1767. Wit: Jared
Neilson, Richard Shingleton, Mary Smith. Signed: Robert Shaw. Proved
27 May 1767 at same time qualified Elizabeth Shaw Executrix. On the 8
Dec. 1769 Qualified Robert Ervin, Executor. On 11 Dec. 1776 Qualified
Hugh Ervin Executor. Signed: Wm. Burrows.

Daniel Shaw. Will of Daniel Shaw. Vol. 5 Page 382. Probate Judge
Office. Charleston, S. C. I Daniel Shaw, in the parish of Prince
Frederick in Craven County. Being in perfect mind and memory, etc.
My will is that my slaves be keep together and not be either divided
or seperated until all my debts be paid, they shall be in possession
of my wife, the children to be cared from the income from est. until
they come of age and are able to care for themselves. I give to my son
Amos Shaw all my land that I can properly call my own at present, and
what I shall purchase or by warrant. Amos to let the land belonging to
me at Cyprus Creek be sold and money divided by my dtr. There is
also a warrant in the house, and those who have no land I desire Amos
to get a warrant for them. I give to my son eight negroes, viz;
Samson, Bristoe, Jeam, Agner, Jochie, young Jack, Prince and Maria.
I also give to my son Amos all cattle and stock of hogs at the cowpens
on the Pee Dee River, also all household furniture except one feather
bed to each of his sisters. I give to my dtr. Jannet four negroes

viz; Mandingo, Florea, Redas, Uda. I give to my dtr. Mary four negroes,
Glasgow, Amoral, Dina, Stenie. I give to my dtr. Isabel five negroes,
viz; long Hester, Sukie, Herclus, Keat, Nanie. I give to my dtr.
Sarah five negroes, viz; old Jack, old Hector, Filis, Cafsais, Hegar.
I give to my wife four slaves viz; Edinborough, Betie, Bambora, Ketoe.
I will if my wife remarry the aforesaid negroes to be taken from her
and given to my son Amos Shaw. I give to my wife and dtrs. all cattle
belonging to me on the South side of the Pee Dee and South side of
Lynches Creek. I will to my son Amos my working oxen and my riding
horse called spark. My will is that each of my dtrs. to have a riding
mare, with Amos to have the rest after his sisters has theirs. My will
that George Clark shall be bound out as apprentice to learn some trade,
when he come the age of 14 years, he is to have four cows and calves
of his own, without reclaim or challange whatsoever. I will fifty pds.
current money to be given the church of Prince Frederick Parish towards
repairing. It is my will fifty pds be spent at my burial in gloves, and
other necessarys. My dtr. Sarah shall have one more slave named Pemkake
and my son two more slaves named blind Casar and little Casar. I appoin
William Fleming, Francis Futhie, James McPharson, executors and my wife
executrix. Dated 8 Oct. 1742. Wit: Alexander Shand, Chas. Winham,
Whitle X Herenton. Signed: Daniel X Shaw. Proven 28 Feb. 1744.
Recorded 22 March 1744.

Launch Shaw. Will of Launch Shaw. Vol. 9 page 146. Probate Judge
Office. Charleston, S. C. I Launch Shaw of Prince William Parish,
Indian land, S. C. being sound in body and mind but going on service
against the Indians. It is my will that all my estate in Europe should
be equal divided between my son Lauchlan Shaw and my dtr. Bridget Shaw.
All my estate in America shall be equally divided my wife Mary Shaw and
the child shoe goes with, but that the whole shall go to the child at
the decd. of my wife Mary Shaw. But in case the money now in Lieut.
Gov. Bulls hand should not be paid for Capt. Demere Company, it shall
be divided between my wife Mary Shaw and the child now in her womb.
The est. in American shall go to the longest liver, viz; Mary Shaw or
the child. If they die the est. to be divided between Lauchlan and
Bridget Shaw. I appoint my wife Mary Shaw executrix and James Parson
Esq. Lawyer in Charleston and Francis Kinloch Esq. of Gilmerton executor
Dated 20 Feb. 1761. Wit: James McPherson, Isaac McPherson. Signed:
Launch Shaw. Proven before the Governor in the Court of Ordinary
and July 1761 and James Parson qualified as executor.

William D. Shaw. Will of William D. Shaw. Vol. 33 Page 1363. Probate
Judge Office. Charleston, S. C. I William Shaw, merchant of Charleston
S. C. Do make this my last will·and testament. It is my will that my
just and lawful debts be paid. I give to my wife Eliza all my negroes
slaves, except two herein after named. Also my gold watch, Roshel's
make $25533 and my library books, also all household and kitchen
furniture. I give to my father David Shaw of the village of Athens,
N. Y. the sum of two thousand dollars. I give to my mother Mary Shaw
my gold watch #3725. I give to my sister Mary Ann Black the sum of
two thousand dollars, and my negroes named Acey and her son Stephen
together with her increase born after date of this will. I give to my
brother Robert Shaw the sum of five hundred dollars. It is my will that
whatever money may be owning me by my father at my death on notes or
otherwise be applied towards the education of Martha Jane Palmer, sister
of my wife Eliza and the balance if any should be paid to her on her
arriving at the age of twenty one years. The rest and residue and
remainder of my estate shall be put on interest, in bank stock, or any
good security as my executors think best. With all interest, income,
profit shall go to my wife Eliza. during her life time, and should she
marry the monies is not to be subject to any debts, control or charges
that her future husband may have, all monies to be paid to her alone.
And at her death, the stock, bonds etc. shall be equally divided into
two equal parts, one part to my sister Mary Ann Black, if she be living
at the time, if not then I give to such child or children of hers, to
be equally divided between them if more than one. The other half is to
be subdivided into five equal shares, I give one part to Martha Jane
Palmer, sister of my wife Eliza. One other share to my brother Robert

Shaw, one other share to my brother Franklin Shaw, one other share to
my brother Alexander Shaw, and the other share to my brother Henry Shaw.
In case my sister Mary Ann Black die and leave no child or children, or
any other of the legatees, shall go to the remaining sons of my brother
David Shaw, to be equally divided between his sons, except his son John
the fourth eldest now living, who is hereby excluded from any part of
my estate. I appoint my wife Executrix during her widowhood and no
longer, and my friends Thomas Blackwood, Alexander Black and Timothy
Street, executors. Dated 31 Dec. 1817. Wit: P. Cohen, Andrew
McDowall, James Palmer. Signed: Wm. D. Shaw. Proven before James D.
Mitchell, Esq. O.C.T.D., Alexnader Black and Timothy Street, executors.

Alexander Shaw. Will of Alexander Shaw, Vol. 10 Page 687. Probate
Judge Office. Charleston, S. C. I Alexander Shaw of St. Bartholamews
Parish, Colleton Co., S. C. Being weak in body but of perfect sound
mind and memory, etc. First I will my just debts and funeral expenses
be paid. I will to my beloved wife Martha Shaw one full third part in
lieu of her dower. I will to my sister nee Ann Gray now Ann Atkins
and her issue by William Gray decd. viz; John, William, Alexander and
Martha Gray. Another full share of my personal est. to be equally
divided between the said John, William, Alexander and Martha Gray
or their survivors of them at the decd. of Ann Atkins. I will the
other part of my personal est. to my beloved sister Martha Newman during
her natural life and at her demise to her issue. John, George, Alexander,
Susannah Newman and Ann Newman now Filput... Martha Newman otherwise Smith
to be equally divided between them. I give to Thomas Filput one tract of
land containing 500 acres on Savannah River in Granville Co. If any
other land in this province prove my property... I give all such land
to my beloved wife Martha Shaw. I appoint my well beloved wife Martha
Shaw executrix and Wm. McTier, Thomas Filput, John Newman, John and
William Gray executors. Dated 16 April 1765. Wit: Thomas Holman,
Mary Holman, Wm. Day, Jno. Hugh's. Signed: Alexr. Shaw. Proved by
virtue of a didmus directed to George Johnston Esq. the 14 June 1765.

SELF

Mary Self. Land Mortgage. Pack 211 #24. Clerk of Court Office.
Pickens, S. C. I Mary Self of Greenville Dist. to John Couch of
Pickens Dist. Dated 21 Oct. 1831. In consideration of $500.00 have
granted, bargained, sold and released a certain lot of land in the
village of Greenville, S. C. Known in Vardy McBees plat by the number
of 18. Together with all rights, members, etc. Provided unto the said
John Couch his heirs and assigns, that if the said Mary Self shall well
and truly pay or cause to be paid unto Hohn Couch the full and just
sum of $570.35 as set forth in several notes. Wit: James Osborne,
J. G. Fleming. Signed: Mary Self.

SHEARER

Hugh Shearer. Will of Hugh Shearer. Book 4-12 Page 74. Probate Judge
Office. York Co., S. C. I Hugh Shearer being in health as ordinary,
etc. I will to my beloved wife Lydia Shearer during her natural life
the use and benefit of the fifty acres of land I now live on (which a
reserve by me of a tract of land given my son William in his life time)
the use of all household and kitchen furniture, farm tools, one bay
mare, and the use of as much stock, cattle for her maintenance during
her life, together with the work of a certain negro named Beth Rachel..
"At my death they are to be free from slavery, yet to live with and
under the care of my executors (she the 3rd. negro to have the benefit
of her own labor), my Nengroes Rachel, Tom, Solomon, Edie and Abel, to
serve my executors until they are twenty one years and my executors
shall learn or use a lawful endeavor to learn the said negroes to read
the Bible, admonish and council them in the way of truth, using all
necessary means for instructing them in the fear of the Lord." During
the life time of my wife, Lydia will attempt for the instruction and

living of my negroes children. I will to my grandson, Thomas Shearer,
two cows and to Hugh Shearer my grandson one cow. At the death of my
wife my will is that the remainder of my property be divided between
my grand children, negroes excepted. I will unto my trusty and beloved
friend James Fowler on bay horse known by the name of Gilbert. I
appoint my friends James Fowler and David Gordan. Dated 15 Oct. 1789.
Wit: Robert Fowler, Lucy Neal, Hezekiah Salmon. Signed: Hugh X
Shearer.

Hugh Sherer. Land Warrant. Original Platts in State House Colubmia,
S. C. Pursuant to a warrant directed by Edgerton Leigh Esq. Surv.
Gen. Dated 2 Dec. 1760. I have laid out unto Hugh Sherer a tract of
200 acres, in Craven Co. on both sides of Hanging Rock Creek. Bounded
on all sides by vacant land. Certified the 10 Dec. 1760.

William Shearer. Land Warrant. Original Platt in State House. Columbia, S. C. Pursuant to a precept from Egerton Leight, Esq. Surv. Gen.
Dated 4 Jan. 1763. I have laid out unto William Shearer a tract of
150 acres on a branch of Bullock's Creek, a branch of Broad River,
bounded on all sides by vacant land. Certified the 18 Jan. 1763.
Signed: John Lewis, D.S.

SHERRILL

John Sherrill. Note on John Sherrill. Pack 606 #1. Clerk of Court
Office. Pickens, S. C. On 21 June 1841, John Sherrill in right of his
wife were heirs of William Halbert, Sr. decd. of Anderson Dist.

SHOEMAKER

Landy G. Shoemaker. Estate of Landy G. Shoemaker. Pack 5174. Clerk
of Court Office. Abbeville, S. C. To the Honr. the Chancellors; Your
orator George J. Cannon sheweth that on the 10 Oct. 1845 Landy G.
Shoemaker departed this life intestate leaving a widow and four infant
children viz; Horatia Hamilton, Elizabeth, Nancy and Landy Greenberry
Shoemaker, who are minor under age of 14 years. and resides without the
limits of this State. Landy G. Shoemaker died seized of no real estate,
and a small personal est. Sale was held on the 10 Dec. 1845 on credit
of twelve months, the creditors numerous and unable to reconcile their
demands. Filed 14 June 1847.

SKELTON

Wm. F. Skelton. Will of Wm. F. Skelton. Box 117 #6. Probate Judge
Office. Pickens, S. C. I William Skelton, being of sound mind and
memory, etc. After my lawful debts are paid and discharged the
residue of my estate both real and personal, I give to my beloved wife
the land and appertainances situated thereon known as Arter place,
together with all hogs, cattle, household, kitchen furniture, farming
tools, also all due coming to me for my service in the Confederate
Army during her natural life or widowhood, then to be equal divided
between my bodily heirs. I appoint my wife Mary Jane Shelton to be
Executrix. Dated 17 Dec. 1863. Wit: Caroline M. Jones, Mary Jane
Jones, N. J. Trannium, All lived in Pickens Dist., S. C. Will proved
on oath of Caroline M. Jones before W. Hester, N.P. on the 27 June 1889.
Filed 8 July 1889.

Samuel E. Skelton. Minor. Box 137 #10. Probate Judge Office.
Pickens, S. C. On 20 Feb. 1901 S. C. Skelton, Job F. Smith, B. H.
Callaham are bound unto J. B. Newberry, Ord. in the sum of $110.00.
S. C. Skelton gdn. of Saml. E. Skelton a minor under 21 years. Son of
Maggie E. Skelton decd. Born 13 Sept. 1895. Father was S. C. Skelton.

Mary Jane Skelton. Estate of Mary Jane Skelton. Box 138 #7. Probate
Judge Office. Pickens, S. C. Est. admr. 3 Oct. 1901 by J. T. Skelton,
James Massingill, H. A. Richey, M. F. Hester who are bound unto J. B.
Newberry, Ord. in the sum of $200.00. M. A. Skelton, H. A. Skelton,
S. O. Skelton, M. Alice Jones, Emma Stanell, Lawrence Skelton, Mary
Massingill recd. shares. Miss H. A. Skelton was of Table Rock, S. C.

SIMS

James Sims. Will of James Sims. Box 2 Pack 24. Probate Judge Office.
Union Co., Union, S. C. I James Sims of Union County, S. C. being weak
in body but sound mind and memory, etc. I give to William Gilliam and
Nancey his wife all the negroes and other property now in their possession theirs forever. I give unto Jeter Brasellmann and Drusilla his
wife all the negroes and other property now in their possession forever.
I give unto my dtr. Anne G. Sims one negro woman Tabl and her five
children; Milley, Fanney, Dilcey, Robin and Jeter. In case my dtr.
should die without heirs, the said negroes and their increase shall be
divided between Drusilla, Matthew, John, Nathan and Reuben Sims.
The reaminder of my estate shall remain in possession of my wife
Elizabeth and under direction of my executor. After my just debts are
paid and during her widowhood, property may be delivered as a loan to
either of my five sons as they may need, but not beyond the limits of
this State. Ever debaring the delivery of a slave to my son James.
After the death or marriage of my wife negroes are to be put into four
equal lots, one for Matthew, one for John, one for Nathan, and one for
Reuben, they paying my son James one fifty part of the appraisement of
the salves, and one fifty part of my other est. I appoint my wife
Elizabeth Sims Executrix and my friend Jeter Brasellmann, and John
Sanders executros. Dated 20 Nov. 1794. Wit: Joshua Kenworthy, John
Kenworthy, Cornelus Willson. Signed: James X Sims. Recorded 1 Jan.
1795.

SIMPSON

John Simpson. Nationalization. No ref. Clerk of Court Office.
Chester, S. C. Personal appeared in open Court; and upon his solemn
affiramtion agreeable to his religious persuasion that it is his
bonafide intention to become a citizen of the United States and that
he does renounce for ever all alligence and fidility to any foreign
Prince, Potenage, State and soveringty whatsoever and particularly the
King of Great Britain. That he was born in Ireland, and has resided
in the United States for five years and within the State of South
Carolina for one year. He has behaved himself as a man of good moral
character attached to the principles of the constitution of the United
States. Signed: John Rosenborough and John McCrary Esqs. Dated 3 Nov.
1806.

SIMMONS

Enoch B. Simmons. Estate of Enoch B. Simmons. Pack 245. Clerk of
Court Office. Abbeville, S. C. To the Honr. the Chancellors; Your
oratrix Harriet S. Simmons the relict of Enoch B. Simmons decd. that at
the time of his death he was seized and pssessed with two tracts of
land containing 100 acres, lying on Hard Labor Creek, adj. land of
Laurens and H. W. Wardlaw and others. That Enoch B. Simmons departed
this life on the 23 Jan. 1854, leaving the widow your oratrix and
Margaret F. the wife of John H. Pinson, Anna Eliza the wife of Stephen
Elmore, Emily J. Simmons, Harriet O. Simmons, Almira H. Simmons and
Nancy Elizabeth Simmons are minor under the age of 21 years. That
John P. Barratt was admr. of the est. and your oratrix believes that

the personal property will fully pay all demands against the est. And
that she prays for a partition be made of the real estate. Dated 18
April 1854.

George Simmons. Estate of George Simmons. Box 18 #226. Probate Judge
Office. Pickens, S. C. Est. admr. 5 Feb. 1849 by James E. Hagood,
John Bowen who are bound unto W. D. Steele, Ord. in the sum of $100.00.
Sale held 20 Feb. 1849. Buyers A. R. Simmons.

Andrew R. Simmons. Estate of Andrew R. Simmons. Box 106 #1115.
Probate Judge Office. Pickens, S. C. Est. admr. 19 Nov. 1873 by Riley
Simmons, Elisha Skelton, T. A. Williams who are bound unto I. H.
Philpot, Ord. in the sum of $300.00. Elizabeth Simmons, Riley Simmons,
W. T. Simmons G. Simmons bought at sale.

Katron Simmons. Church Records. Oolenoy Church. Pickens, S. C. On
7 Oct. 1838 Katron Simmons was recd. by letter from the Silver Creek
Church in Burke Co., N.C.

Notes on the Simmons Family. (See Campbell Will 5) Probate Judge Office,
York, S. C. Mrs. M. C. Simmons recd. a bed from the will of a Rachel
Campbell decd. of York Co., S. C.

Martha & Mary Simmons. Book B, page 50. Probate Judge Office. Pickens,
S. C. Martha C. the wife of Jordan Simmons and Mary the wife of
Tully Simmons were heirs of William Grant decd. of Pickens Dist. Dated
11 Oct. 1860.

Moses Simmons. Moses Simmons married Harriet Harbin probably the dtr.
of Thos. W. Harbin. On 29 Aug. 1848 they were residing in Talledega
County, Ala. Ref. Pack 5. Clerk of Court Office. Pickens, S. C.

SINGLETON

William B. Singleton. Will of William B. Singleton. Box 130 #11.
Probate Judge Office. Pickens, S. C. I William Singleton being of
sound mind and disposing memory, etc. I desire after my death my
executor collect all moneys due, and pay all my just debts with my
funeral expenses. I desire my beloved wife Mary Ann shall have my
entire plantation for her maintainance during her natural life. I desire
that my dtr. Harriet C. Griffin, Nancy Dow(Dorr), Myra A. Miller, Malinda
E. Smith and my son Henry D. Singleton and Mary L. Singleton shall have
an equal part of all my personal property, after my death and the death
of my wife, and that my dtr, Elvira Dickson shall be entitled to a home
with me. And at the death of me and my wife she be entitled to a home
on my plantation during her natural life or widowhood if she chooses.
I desire that after my death and that of my wife, my son Henry D.
Singleton shall have my entire plantation, whereon I now live, provided
he complies with the following. That said Henry is to maintain me and
my wife during our natural life, seeing that each is supported with a
comfortable home and good holesome food, and see that either medical
attention is given each of us at his own expenses, and that we are decent
burial. If and dissatisfaction exist with any of my heirs and any
attempt is made to set aside this will, it shall be done at the expense
of the one raising the complaint, and any heirs willing to abide to
my will shall not be compelled to defray any expense. I appoint my son
Henry D. Singleton executor. Dated 6 Sept. 1889. Wit: J. H. Newton,
R. A. Bowen, A. M. Morris, J. M. Stewart. Signed: W. B. Singleton,
Filed 24 Sept. 1898. In 1907 Mary L. was a Jackson. Myra Singleton
married Miller in 1889.

SITTON

Philip Sitton. Estate of Philip Sitton. Pack 31 #3. In Equity. Clerk of Court Office. Pickens, S. C. To Richard Burdine, Robert H. Briggs, Abraham Burdine, William Jameson and Beverly Thurston. You or any three of you are hereby commanded and authorized within one month after the receipt hereof, according to the best of your judgement to fairly, justly and impartially to partition and divide a tract of land whereon Philip Sitton lived at the time of his death. Containing 650 acres. Lying on the West side of Saluda River, adj. land of Beverly Thurston, Richard Burdine and others. Between Elizabeth the widow who is to get one third part, Arranah the wife of John Mansell, Mary Jane Sitton, James Sitton, Nancy Sitton, John Sitton Jr., Anna Sitton. To each one sixth part of the other two thirds. Witness: Wm. L. Keith, Clk. of Court. Dated 2 Nov. 1829. On the 7 Jan. 1830 Elizabeth Sitton the widow hereby give her consent to sell the whole of the land. Wit: Samuel Looper. John Sitton, Jr. was the gdn. of the three minors children viz; Mary Jane, James and Nancy Sitton.

Sitton Minors. John B. Box 6 #6. In Equity. Clerk of Court Office. Pickens, S. C. On 20 June 1839 John Sitton formerly the gdn. of John B. Sitton, Arranah Sitton and Anna Sitton has removed to Miss. Chn. of Philip Sitton decd. On 2 June 1833 John Sitton gdn. states that John B. Sitton, Arranah Mancell are of age, Anna Sitton still not of age. John Sitton was at this time in Greenville, S. C. Paid 6 July 1829 Joshua Mancell $50.00. 20 June 1834 paid Anna Sitton now Anna Reid $8.62. 8 Oct. 1838 John B. Sitton, Miles M. Norton, are bound unto W. H. Harrison Comm. in Equity in the sum of $600.00. John B. Sitton gdn. of James Y. Sitton minor under 21 years. States that he is entitled to a small est. from his grandfather John Young. John B. Sitton his brother.

SLOAN

William D. Sloan. Deed from William D. Sloan. Pack 642 #7. Clerk of Court Office. Pickens, S. C. This indenture made between William D. Sloan sheriff of Pickens Dist. and Capt. David Sloan of the same dist. Dated 13 Oct. 1832. Whereas Oliver Clark and wife one of the heirs at law of Col. Obadiah Trimmier decd. exhibit their petition in the Court, against Lucy Trimmier widow of Col. Obadiah Trimmier, decd. and the others heirs for a division of the real estate of said decd. It being the judgement of the Court that it would be to the advantage of the parties in interest to sell the same. And that Samuel Reid then sheriff did give public notice of the sale, agreeable to the order, did on the first Monday in Dec. 1830. The same was exposed and was knocked off to said Capt. David Sloan for the sum of $850. I William D. Sloan successor of Samuel Reid. Wit: Pleasant Alexander, Robert F. Morgan. Signed: William D. Sloan. Attested on oath of Pleasant Alexander before William L. Keith, Clk. on the 4 April 1833.

Thomas Sloan. In Equity, Pack 254. Clerk of Court Office. Pickens, S. C. Thomas M. Sloan states that some time in the year 1822 David Sloan bought at sheriff sale a tract of land sold as the property of Isreal Gillison, in Pendleton Dist. now Pickens Dist. on Richland Creek. That at this time Isreal was regarded as sole proprietoer thereof. That sometime in the year 1824 David Sloan obtained a deed for a tract adj. the same from one John Green. That on 19 Nov. 1826 Sloan leased the premise to Isreal Gillison and his brother Elijah Gillison. David Sloan departed this life intestate on 29 Oct. 1834. That your orator, with the widow of said intestate. That Jane Gillison the mother is now regarded as the owner of the tract. May it please your Honors to grant a writ of subpoena to Jane Gillison, Jonathan Gillison, Elijah Gillison, also Nancy Sloan widow of David Sloan, John T. Sloan, William D. Sloan, G. W. Bowen, and Emily his wife. Robert Maxwell and Lucy his wife, Andrew Lewis and Susan his wife. The purpose to determine the true owner of the tract of land.

David Sloan. Estate of David Sloan. Box 5 #57. Probate Judge Office.
Pickens, S. C. Est. admr. 3 Nov. 1834 by Benjamin F., Nancy, John T.,
Thomas M. Sloan and Jesse Stribling who are bound unto James H. Dendy,
Ord. in the sum of $50,000. B. F. Sloan was gdn. of Susan, B. F. Sloan,
Thomas Sloan of Lucy & C. Thomas Sloan.

David Sloan. David Sloan Real Estate. Book A, page 15. Probate Judge
Office. Pickens, S. C. The heirs of David Sloan decd. is to appear at
the Court House and show cause if any why a tract of land at Fairplay,
S. C. should not be sold or divided. Dated 10 March 1835. Heirs;
Nancy, the widow, Benjamin F., Wm. D., John T., Susan, Lucy, Thomas,
and Benjamin F. Sloan Jr., John W. Blasingame, George W. Bomer. Land
adj. land of Larkin Brown, Jacob R. Cox. Contained 2 acres.

Thomas M. & John T. Sloan. Deed from Thomas M. and John T. Sloan. Book
C-1, page 236. Clerk of Court Office. Pickens, S. C. Whereas Thomas M
Sloan and John T. Sloan to Nancy Sloan, widow of David Sloan decd. all
of Pickens, Dist. Dated 8 Oct. 1836. In the sum of $1,500.00 have
sold, released unto Nancy Sloan a tract of land lying on Cain Creek,
being a part of the tract which David Sloan decd. was buried, and some
land on Crooked Creek, adj. land of E. Fitzgeralds land and on Moultries
corner. Containing about 1,200 acres. Wit: Wm. D. Sloan, J. W. Bomer.
Signed: Thomas M. Sloan, John T. Sloan.

Capt. David Sloan. Deed from Capt. David Sloan. Book C-1 Page 27.
Clerk of Court Office. Pickens, S. C. Capt. David Sloan to Wm. Peterson
both of Pickens Dist. Dated 10 Oct. 1834. In consideration of Thirty
dollars, have sold, and released all that tract of land containing
177 acres whereon Wm. Peterson now lives, composed to two tracts, one
tract of 130 acres deeded from Wm. Thompson to John Peterson dated
15 Dec. 1803. The other tract of 45 acres deeded to John Peterson by
Phebe Suttles on the 20 Nov. 1826. Both were deeded to me by John
Peterson on the 5 Jan. 1832. Wit: Wm. D. Sloan, W. L. Keith. Signed:
D. Sloan. Recorded 6 Dec. 1834.

Notes on Sloan Family. In Oct. 1830 David Sloans' wife Nancy ment. as
the dtr. of Col. Obadiah Trimmer decd. and his wife Lucy Trimmier. Ref.
Pack 31 #6 in Equity. In the heirs of David Sloan, Sarah Sloan married
John Blassingame and Emily C. married George Bomar.

                              SMART

John Smart. Writ of Habeas Corpus. Pack 409 #2. Clerk of Court Office
Pickens, S. C. To the Honr. J. N. Whitner one of the law Judges of
S. C. The petition of Mrs. Rebecca Pierce sheweth that her son John
Smart has been arrested and is in custody of Capt. J. J. Norton, enroll-
ing officer of Pickens Dist. Your petitioner is informed that her son
John Smart is a deserter from Furgison's Artillary. Your petitioner
alleges that John Smart is exempt from all military service in the army
of the Confederate States by reason of being a minor under the age of
eighteen years. Your petitioner prays that a Habeas Corpus directed to
Capt. J. J. Norton requiring him to bring John Smart before your honor
and be a judge. Wit: Robert A. Thompson. Signed: Rebecca X Pearce.
Personally appeared Rebecca Pearce and being sworn saiths that the matter
in her petition are true. That her son was born on the 4 March 1849
as she believes, that records of his age having been destroyed by fire
in her house about five years ago. That she is confident he is not yet
fifteen years old and having been born in the State of N.C. and that in
her present destitute condition she is unable to fortify her affidavit
by relatives, etc. Dated 9 Dec. 1863. J. N. Whitner, Law Judge.
Signed: Rebecca X Pearce. This day appeared John Smart in person and
made oath that he was persuaded to enlist, never had the consent of his
mother and never received bounty or wages.

SMITH

John Smith. Will of John Smith. Box 18 #641. Probate Judge Office.
Anderson, S. C. I, John Smith, of Pendleton Dist. being weak in body
but of sound mind and memory. First I give to my mother Rachel Smith
the plantation whereon she now lives, containing 100 acres to enjoy and
possess during her natural life, and after her death, I devise the same
to William Smith the son of my sister Mary Smith and his forever. I
also give to my mother one bay mare, the notes and book accounts. I
also give to William Smith son of Mary one young mare or filly. I ordain
my mother sole executrix. Dated 5 Dec. 1792. Wit: Joshua Saxon,
Elijah Herren, Mary X Smith. Signed: John Smith. Recorded 24 Jan.
1794.

John Smith. Will of John Smith. Box 18 #641. Probate Judge Office.
Anderson, S. C. I John Smith of Pendleton Dist. being very sick and
weak in body but of perfect mind and memory, etc. I give to Ruth my
beloved wife my land and the crop their upon, also my farm tools, with
all hogs, cattles, oxen, one feather bed and furniture. This property
to remain hers during widowhood but if she marry this property to be
divided between Ruth my wife and Elizabeth and Jane my two eldest
daughters, so long as they live upon it. If my wife remain a widow the
plantation shall not be distributed. I give to my son John Smith one
shilling. I also give to my dtr. Mary one shilling. Dated 12 Aug.
1803. Wit: Isaac H. Walters, John Adams, Andrew McElwriath. Signed
John Smith.

Joseph Smith. Inventory. Box 19 #661. Probate Judge Office. Anderson,
S. C. An inventory of all goods and chattels and personal estate of
Joseph Smith decd. of Pendleton, S. C. Total $554.87 1/2. Dated 18 June
1814. Signed: Joseph Reid Esq., Jno. Green, Wm. C. Baskin.

Samuel Smith. Estate of Samuel Smith. Box 19 #671. Probate Judge
Office. Anderson, S. C. I, Samuel Smith, of Pendleton Dist. being weak
and sick in body but of perfect mind and memory, etc. I give to my
beloved wife Martha during her life time my dwelling house and her living
and support from my plantation, and at her death be buried out of the
estate belonging to me. I have given to my dtr. Elenor Alexander two
cows and calves, one side saddle and other furniture, as much as I think
as her part. I have given to my dtr. Margaret Willson two cows and
calves and other furniture as much as I think her part is. Also I have
given to my dtr. Nancy White one horse, one cow and calf and other
furniture to amount of her part. Also to my dtr. Elizabeth McIntire,
I give unto her as much as make her part up equal with those above mentioned, together with what she already got. Also to my dtr. Martha I
give at the option of my son Robert to give which he chooses. Also to
my dtr. Polly I give unto her as much property or cash as will make her
part equal with the rest, to be the choice of my son Robert to give as
he pleases. Also to my dtr. Ann as much property or cash as will make
her part equal with the rest above mentioned to be the opion of my
son Robert to give as he chooses, the above portions is to be raised
out of my estate, with my son Robert paying each heir their as they
come of age. I give to my son Robert my plantation, stock cattle,
etc. after the decease of my wife... Robert to pay all lawful debts
and to maintain my wife during her life time. Dated 5 Oct. 1805. Wit:
John Moore, Luke X Spruell, Robert Telford. Signed: Samuel Smith.
Proven on oath of Robert Telford before John Harris O.P.D. on the 6
Jan. 1806. An inventory was made on 4 Feb. 1806 by Robert Telford,
David Brown, John Moore, Est. amount $558.53 1/4.

SNEAD

Phillip Snead. Land Warrant. #125. Clerk of Court Office. Pickens,
S. C. By Wm. L. Keith, Clerk, to any lawful surveyor you are authorized
to lay out unto Philip Snead, Sr. a tract of land not exceeding one
thousand acres. Dated 18 Jan. 1850. Executed for 99 acres on 19 Jan.

1850... Certified 18 Mar. 1850 by Tyre B. Mauldin, Dep. Sur.

SPENCE

<u>James Spence</u>. Estate of James Spence. Box 87 Pack 2118. Probate Judge
Office. Abbeville, S. C. Est. admr. 13 Feb. 1808 by Agness Spence,
Samuel Spence, James Hutcherson, John Robinson, who are bound unto
Andew Hamilton, Ord. in the sum of $5,000.00. Est. appraised on the
19 Feb. 1808 by William Gray, John Gray, James Hutcherson, John Robinson
Buyers at sale. Agness Spence, Benjamin Houstan, John Berry Sr., Arthur
McCrery, Roda Crawford, John Berry, Jr., Samuel Evans, John Young, James
Hutcherson, Simeon Berry, John Weems, Wm. Baldy, John Cullertian, John
Chavis, Samuel Tallauch, James Potter, John Robinson, Isaac Deal,
Alexander Spence, Robert Pethiven, John Stewart, Wm. McDonald, Robert
Margen, James Patton, Pollard Brawn, Sterling Dincan.

<u>Ann Spence</u>. Will of Ann Spence. Box 110 Pack 3164. Probate Judge
Office. Abbeville, S. C. I Ann Spence of Abbeville Dist. being sick
and weak of body, but of perfect mind and memory, etc. I will that any
outstanding debts be collected and if any debts I may owe to be paid.
I will to my dtr. Polly Spence two beds and furniture with my household
and kitchen furniture and all my stock of cows. I will to my son Samuel
Spence the tract of land I now live on containing ___ acres, also one
horse, and all my farm tools. I appoint John Wardlaw and my son Joseph
Spence executors. Dated 23 March 1808. Wit: John Martin, Mabel T.
English, Mary Ann Wardlaw. Signed: Ann X Spence.

<u>Alexander Spence</u>. Estate of Alexander Spence. Box 85 Pack 2075.
Probate Judge Office. Abbeville, S. C. Est. admr. on 11 Dec. 1815 by
Samuel Spence, Hugh McCormick, James Miller who are bound unto Talia-
ferro Livingston, Ord. in the sum of $5,000.00. The citation was
published at Smyrna Church the 3 Dec. 1815. An inventory was made the
29 Dec. 1815 by Robert Smyth, Hugh McCormick, Joseph McCrery. Heirs
Rosey (widow) Spence, Mary McCrery, Charles Spence, Alexander Spence,
Sarah Spence, Agnes Spence, Samuel Spence. Sale held the 29 Dec. 1815.
Buyers Rosey Spence, Wm. Glanton, Charles Spence, Samuel Spence, John
Cochron, Robt. Gipson, Wm. Morrow, James McCree, James Patton, John
Swelen, Mary McCrery, George Allen, Thomas Lion, Samuel Coleman,
Young Ragon, Selah Walker, William McCree, John Hearst, Henry Wyley,
Egnes Spence, Adena Griffin, Mary McCrery, Samuel McClinton, Philip Sned
William Thomas, George Hearst, Sary Spence, Alexander Gray.

<u>Samuel Spence</u>. Estate of Samuel Spence. Box 85 Pack 2073. Probate
Judge Office. Abbeville, S. C. I Samuel Spence being weak in body but
of sound and disposing mind and memory. First I will all my lawful debt
be paid. I will to my beloved wife Mary Spence during her natural life
all my personal property of every kind. Except to my son William Spence
I allow my gray horse at sixty dollars, and a saddle and blanket at
twenty dollars, with a cloke at twelve dollars, also to my dtr. Rosey
Spence, I allow her one saddle at eighteen dollars. If my wife Mary
Spence marry I allow her a child part of the whole estate, or at her
death I will all my estate both real and personal be sold and each child
receive an equal share with the ones that have received. I allow my
dtrs. Mary, Nancy, Jane, my son Alexander, my dtr. Anny Spence. I
appoint my wife Mary and my son William Spence executors. Dated 30 Jan.
1824. Wit: Joseph McCrery, Margret Wiley, Sarah X Wily. Signed:
Samuel X Spence. Will proven on oath of Joseph McCrery before Moses
Taggart, O.A.D. on the 17 March 1824. Sam day qualified Mary and Wm.
Spence Exors. Sale was held on the 7 April 1824. Buyers, James Miller,
James Gray, West Donald, Alexr. Wiley, Dr. Mat. Burt, Vandel Mantz, Wm.
Gaston, Robert Stewart, Hugh McCormick, James McClinton, John Furguson,
Wm. G. Spence, Abrm. Thompson, Robert Hill, Wm. Morrow, Allen Glover,
David McCrery, Arthur L. Morrow, John Morrow, Robert Steart, Alexander
Jordan, James McGree.

Mary Spence. Estate of Mary Spence. Box 89 Pack 2198. Probate Judge
Office. Abbeville, S. C. An inventory of the estate was had on 7 March
1826 by Wm. Dale, Alexander Wiley, David H. McCrery. Sale was held on
8 March 1826. Buyers, Wm. G. Spence, West Donald, William Dale, David
McCrery, Joseph McCrery, James Gray, James Donald, Wm. Morrow, James
Stewart, Francis Wilson, Wm. Gaston, John Gibson, Mary Spence, Rosannah
Spence, Andrew McGill, John Cary, John Stewart, James Richey, Nancy
Jackson, Wm. Pettifrew, Mathew Burt, Ira Griffin, Dr. Samuel Pressly,
Moody Wright, Young Reagin. This sale was signed by Wm. G. Spence.
No other inf.

James Spence. Estate of James Spence. Box 88 Pack 2163. Probate Judge
Office, Abbeville, S. C. I James Spence of Abbeville Dist. being of
sound mind and memory but weak in body. First I desire that my just
debts be paid as soon as possbile after my decd. I desire that all my
plantation whereon I now live be and remain in possession of and under
the control of and for the use and support of my wife Ann Spence during
her natural life. After the death of my wife, I desire my executors
shall cause to be laid out to my son James Spence all that tract of
land N.W. of Robbesons branch, adj. land of widow Peggy Robbeson, William
Robbeson, Samuel Zimmerman including the spring my son now uses. All
the remainder of my land shall be equal divided between my two sons
William and John Spence. I give to my dtrs. Nelly, Sarah, Ann Spence and
Jan Young widow of George Young each one feather bed and furniture with
all their bodily clothing. I give to my little grand daughter Sarah
Young one cow and calf or the value in money when she arrives at the
age of twenty one or marry. I give to my sons William and John Spence
my blacksmith tools forever. The remainder of my property to be divided
or sold and the money divided between James, William, John, Sarah, Ann,
Nelly Spence and Jane Young. I give to my two sons in law Joseph and
Thomas Criswell husbands of my dtrs. Peggy and Mary each one dollar to
be paid if demanded. I appoint my two sons James and John Spence
executors. Dated 26 April 1834. Wit: Patrick Gibson, Rice Mills,
Samuel Zimmerman. Signed: James X Spence. No recording date. Est.
was appraised on the 19 Dec. 1834 by Rice Mills, Samuel Zimmerman, John
Robbeson. (The following receipts were in the same pack with this James
Spence, but date 5 Aug. 1811 must belong to the James Spence of Box 87
Pack 2118.) Recd. of Alexander Spence (amount not given), Sail Money,
John Gray, William Baldee, John Young, Robert Patecrue, Sterling Dixon,
John Robeson, Robert Marga, Margret Cheves, David Fife, Simon Berry, John
Berry, Pollard Brown, John Stuart, Arthur McCrery, Rodey Croford, John
Weems, Samuel Tullock, James Patton, Benjamin Huston, Benjamin Glover,
John Chiles, James Shanks, William Huthison, Agnes Spence, Robert
Peticrew... Paid to, Andrew Miltcans, David McCrery, Samuel Young, John
Calhoun, Margret Cheves, Andrew Lord, George Kidd, Hugh Armstrong,
Henry Livingston, Robert Smyth, John Gray, Nath. Weed, John Cheves, James
Paton, John Colwel, George Boue, David Pressly, John McCaula, Joseph
Herst.

James Spence. Estate of James Spence. Box 90 Pack 2216. Probate
Judge Office. Abbeville, S. C. To the Ordinary of Abbeville Dist. The
petition of John Spence sheweth that his brother James Spence has departed
this life intestate, having no widow, but an infant child and has a
small est. etc. Your petitioner prays for a letter of admr. Dated 6
Jan. 1842. Estate was appriased on 21 Feb. 1842 by Wm. Robinson, A.
Wideman, Jr., Rice Mills. Items listed, total not given.

STEVENSON

Alexr. Stevenson. Deed from Alexr. Stevenson. Pack 358. Clerk of
Court Office. Abbeville, S. C. Alexander Stevenson and Emry Van to
Henry Atkins all of Abbeville Dist. Dated 22 Jan. 1841. In consid-
eration of $1200.00 have granted, sold, bargain and released unto Henry
Atkins all that plantation containing 120 acres, on a branch of Norrises
Creek, waters of Long Cain. Adj. land of John Adams and Hugh
Armstrong. Wit: Thos. Hinton, John Adams. Signed: Alex. Stevenson and

Hugh Armstrong. Wit: Thos. Hinton, John Adams. Signed Alex. Stevenson
and Emry Vann. Deed attested on oath of Thos. Hinton before Samuel L.
Hill, J.Q. Dated 22 Jan. 1841. I George J. Cannon, Mag. do hereby
certify that Edney Stevenson the wife of Alex. Stevenson and Fanny Vann
the wife of Emry Vann appeared before me and renounced, released, and
forever relinquish all interest in the above tract of land. Dated 23
April 1841. Signed: Edny X Stevenson and Frances Vann.

Stevenson Tombstone Inscriptions. Taken from Lindsay Cemetery two miles
South of Due West, Abbeville Dist., S. C. Mrs. Mary Jane Stevenson born
27 Nov. 1824, died 24 Dec. 1903; Sabelle Aveline Stevenson born 2 July
1831, died 16 June 1906; Wm. A. Stevenson the only child of John and
Rebecca Stevenson born 17 Feb. 1820, died 6 March 1862, age 42 years
19 days; Rebecca Stevenson wife of Capt. John Stevenson departed 5 July
1873, 83rd year of her life. Capt. John Stevenson died 20 Jan. 1850,
age 63 years. In memory of my grandfather James Stevenson, father of
Capt. John Stevenson died 12 May 1822. In memory of my grand mother
Elizabeth Thompson wife of James Stevenson. Three unmarked graves.
Infant son of Andrew and Margaret Stevenson B&D 4 Oct. 1843. On the back
of will of Mrs. Ann P. Staley was written Mary Stevenson formerly Mary
Jefcoat. Mrs. Staley died in Orangeburg in 1864. Ref. J. P. Office,
Orangeburg, S. C. Box 13 #8.

STEWART

Robert Stewart, Esq. Estate of Robert Stewart Esq. Box 4 #95. Probate
Judge Office. In Equity. Pickens, S. C. To the Honr. Chancellors.
The petition of William J. Parson sheweth that about the year 1853 your
petitioner bought from Robert Stewart Esq. late decd. a tract of land
on the waters of 12 mile river, containing 175 acres by resurvey, being
the same tract sold as the real estate of Powel Riggins by W. D. Steele,
Ord. of sd. dist. to Robert Stewart Esq. Your petitioner was to pay
$300.00 for said land. Which he did at divers times and places. To
wit; Twenty seven dollars and 83 cents to Sheriff Bryce in settlement
of a case of J. J. Howard vs Robert Stewart. $25.00 to settle a debt
with Silas Kirksey by Robert Stewart Esq. $122.00 on judgment John
McWhorter for Robt. Stewart and J. J. Parson. $5.00 paid Thomas D.
Garvin. $5.00 paid Isaac Anderson, $5.00 paid Wm. S. Williams, $56.00
paid F. E. Harrison, admr. of the est. of Joseph W. Ross decd. Other
payments exceeded the total of $300.00 for the land. In Sept. 1857
about a month after the last payment, Robert Stewart Esq. departed this
life without executing a deed to your petitioner. Robert Stewart Esq.
left a widow and seven children viz; the widow Isabella, James M.,
Mareb M., Nancy J., Naomi J., Mary, Rufus J., and Robert Stewart.
Isabella Stewart and Thomas Price are admr. and the children are all
minors. Your petitioner prays that your Honr. will require the admr.
to deliver up a title to the said land.

Jacob L. Stewart. Estate of Jacob L. Stewart. Book A, page 174.
Probate Judge Office. Pickens, S. C. To W. J. Parson, Ord. The undersigned humbly petition your Court for an order to sell the real estate
of her late husband Jacob L. Stewart decd. lying on branches of 12 mile
River. Adj. land of Robert Kirksey, Jacob Lewis and others. Containing
156 acres. The following are heirs at law Sarah E., Mary E., James
Madison, Jatharine E. Stewart all are minors living in this State.
Prays for distribution between herself and the heirs above named. Dated
17 Sept. 1856. Signed: Clarinda Stewart. Land to be sold on 2 Oct.
1856.

Robert Stewart. Deed of Robert Stewart. Book A-1, page 107. Clerk
of Court Office. Pickens, S. C. Deed from Robert Stewart to Isaac
Rice both of Pickens Dist. Dated 7 Nov. 1831. In consideration of
$10.00. Have granted, sold, bargain, and released unto Isaac Rice all
that tract of land containing 124 acres, lying on the S.E. side of Crow
Creek waters of Keowee River. Originally granted unto Robert Stewart
the 7 June 1830. Adj. land of Isaac Rice and vacant on others sides.

Wit: Peter Robertson, Tyre Boon. Signed: Robert Stewart. Deed attested on oath of Tyre Boon before Wm. A. Keith, Clk. on the 7 Nov. 1831. Recorded the same day.

John Stewart. Estate of John Stewart. Box 89 Pack 2188. Probate Judge Office. Abbeville, S. C. I John Stewart of Abbeville Dist. being of sound and disposing mind and memory, but weak in body, etc. First I allow my just debts and funeral expenses be paid. I allow my beloved wife Elizabeth Stewart one third of my personal property during her natural life, at her decease to be euqal divided between my three sons Joseph, William and Alexander Irvin Stewart, and to my Dtr. Mary Stewart. I desire my sons William and Alexander Stewart to get one horse each, and my dtr. Mary I allow one cow and calf, one bed and furniture and one wheel (spinning) and unto my three sons Joseph, William and Alexander Stewart, I allow my plantation where on I now live to be equal divided between them at the death of their mother. And unto my grand daughter Elizabeth Morrow I allow one bed and furniture, one wheel, one cow and calf, and to be learnt to read the Scripture if she remains with the family until she arrives of age or marry. The remaining part of my est. to be divided between the above named heirs. Unto my children not yet named that is to say, my sons John Stewart, Robert Stewart, James Stewart, Archibald D. Stewart and unto my dtrs. Elizabeth, Agnes, Jane, Ann, Fanny Stewart, I have given unto them and their children the part of my est. that I allow them. I appoint my son Joseph Stewart and friend Charles Drennan executors. Dated 4 Nov. 1826. Wit: James Wiley, Robert Drenna, John Caughran. Signed: John Stewart. Proven on oath of James Wiley before Moses Taggart, Ord. on the 1 Jan. 1827. The inventory was made the 12 Jan. 1827 by Alexander Wiley, Francis Wilson, West Donald.

Adam Stewart. Estate of Adam Stewart. Box 85 Pack 2078. Probate Judge Office. Abbeville, S. C. I Adam Stewart being sick and weak in body but strong in mind. I have already given to my six oldest sons, what land or value thereof which I allow them. To my wife Jane, I will all the clear land North of the dwelling house, during her natural life, then to go to my youngest son Thomas Clark forever. I also allow my wife, one sorrel mare with two cows during her natural life. I also allow my wife Nat during her natural life. But is she brings any of her first husband children to live on the plantation, then Nat must be hired to the highest bidder, and the avail thereof to go to Clark my youngest son. At the decased of my wife I allow my negro girl Doll to be sold and fifty dollars of her price I will to my oldest son James, and fifty dollars, thereof to my dtr. Mary and the balance be divided between my dtrs. Ann and Elizabeth and my son Thomas Clark. I will all the land South and East of the dwelling house to Thomas Clark, the cleared to be rented year by year and the money keep by my executors unto he become of age. If God remove Thomas Clark by death, in his minority, the property mentioned to him must be sold and money divided between my children. The balance of my est. not mentioned in this will to be sold, and after paying my just debts and funeral expenses, I will to my sons Adam, John, William, Isaac, and Andrew five dollars each, and the ballance to be divided between my grand children (torn)... Dated 14 Nov. 1822. I appoint my son Adam and Joseph and Joseph C. Mathew, my executors. Wit: Elizabeth X Stewart, Jos. C. Mathew, John Stewart. Signed: Adam Stuart. Will proven on oath of John Stewart Jr. before Mowes Taggart, Ord. on the 20 Dec. 1822. James M. Foster recd. a legacy in the est. Sale held on 10 Jan. 1823. Buyers, Andw. Stewart, James M. Foster, Robert Hill, John Foster, Nathaniel Camron, John Pressly, James Miller, Adam Stuart, Elias C. Morgan, Wm. Steuart, Dr. J. L. Cooper, Richard Hill, James Steuart, Andrew English, Robert Crawford, Isaac Steuart, Mary Steuart, Thomas Wallass, Thomas Foster, William Ravlin Sr., John Caldwell, Luke Mathis, Christian Ruff, Wm. Sanders, Andrew Weed. Sale signed by James Foster.

Nancy Stewart. Land Warrant. Pack 603 #1. Clerk of Court Office. Pickens, S. C. By J. E. Hagood, Clk. To any lawful surveyor you are authorized to lay out unto Nancy Stewart and her heirs a tract of land not exceeding two thousand acres for the special purpose of obtaining a new grant given her by her father. Dated 1 Dec. 1866. Executed for 497 acres, on 8 Dec. 1866. Signed: Thos. D. Garvin D.S.

Cyrus Stewart. Estate of Cyrus Stewart. Box 3 #33. Probate Judge
Office. Pickens, S. C. Est. admr. 2 July 1832 by Allen Powell, Jacob
Garvin who are bound unto James H. Dendy, Ord. in the sum of $60.00.
Signed in the presence of Thomas D. Garvin, Samuel Parson. (was late
of the State of Georgia) Allen Powell in acct. with est. of Cryus Stewart Dec. 1832 to amt. due him from his father est. sold by the Sheriff
amounting to $29.75.

Jacob L. Stewart. Estate of Jacob L. Stewart. Box 40 #449. Probate
Judge Office. Pickens, S. C. Est. admr. 14 Aug. 1856 by Robert Stewart,
William Stewart, Allen Riggins who are bound unto W. J. Parson, Ord.
in the sum of $1,000.00. Left a widow and four chn. no names given.
Expend; 3 Oct. 1859, paid John Rees and wife Clarinda her 1/3 in full
$114.00. Paid R. B. Baker guardian for James M., Elvira Stewart their
share $114.00. 1 Oct. 1860 paid Anthony Stewart guardian for Sarah E.
and Mary A. Stewart their share $114.00.

Robert Stewart, Jr. Estate of Robert Stewart Jr. Box 44 #488. Probate
Judge Office. Pickens, S. C. Est. admr. 9 Nov. 1857 by Abraham Stewart,
Thomas N. McKinney, James E. Hagood, Miles M. Norton who are bound unto
W. J. Parson, Ord. in the sum of $2,000.00. Left a widow and three chn.
no names given. Expend; 4 Feb. 1861 paid J. E. Hagood, gdn. for Roxana
C., Elizabeth T., R. McKinney Stewart in full $743.93.

Isaac Stewart. Estate of Isaac Stewart. Box 68 #726. Probate Judge
Office. Pickens, S. C. Est. admr. 19 Jan. 1863 by Hardin Price, Abra-
ham Stewart, Robert Stewart, Levi N. Robins who are bound unto W. E.
Holcomb Ord. in the sum of $2,500.00. widow, Abraham Stewart, Angeline
Alexander, Mary Hinkle, Lucinda Stewart, A. J. Stewart, Sarah Alexander,
Margaret Moore etc. bought at sale.

George W. Stewart. Will of George W. Stewart. Box 77 #823. Probate
Judge Office. Pickens, S. C. I, George W. Stewart, being of sound
mind and memory, etc. I give to my beloved wife Adaline M. Stewart my
negro girl named Lucey and my negro boy named Sam to be hers during her
natural life or widowhood, and at the end of that time the negro boy
I give to my son Anderson B. Stewart to be his. I give to my beloved
wife my black mare and all my stock of hogs, cattle, and sheep, with
my wagon and household and kitchen furniture, during her natural life or
widowhood, I will that my beloved dtr. Nancy A. Stewart shall have the
stock and kitchen furniture and beds and enough to make her equal with
my son. I will all my money to my wife during her lifetime or widowhood, then to become the property of my dtr. Nancy A. Stewart. I
appoint my wife Adaline M. Stewart executrix. Dated 12 Jan. 1864.
Wit: A. Stewart, Wm. Nimmons, C. H. Stancil. Signed: George W.
Stewart. Proven 15 Aug. 1864.

Roxanna Stewart. Minors. Box 4 #69. Probate Judge Office. Pickens,
S. C. On 8 April 1859 James E. Hagood, Robert A. Thompson, Elijah E.
Alexander are bound unto W. E. Holcombe, Ord. in the sum of $1500.00.
James E. Hagood made gdn. of Roxanna C., Elizabeth T., Robert McKinney
Stewart minors under 21 years. Hester Ann Stewart wanted James Hagood
to be gdn. of her chn. Elizabeth and Thomas McKinney Stewart of age in
1877. On 8 Jan. 1861 recd. of A Stewart, T. N. McKinney admr. of
Robert Stewart Jr. decd. $740.93.

Stewart Minors. Box 4 #74. Probate Judge Office. Pickens, S. C.
On 28 Jan. 1863 Thomas Stewart, James E. Hagood, are bound unto W. E.
Holcombe, Ord. in the sum of $222.00. Thomas Stewart made gdn. of Elnor
Stewart a minor under 21 years. 3 Oct. 1859 Richard B. Baker, E. H.
Griffin, Thomas Stewart are bound to W. J. Parson, Ord. in the sum of
$448.00. Richard B. Baker made gdn. of James M. and Elnora Stewart
minors under 21 years. Thomas Stewart was an uncle. 1888 Mary Baker
wid. of Richard B. Baker the gdn.

Stewart Minors. Box 5 #79. Probate Judge Office. Pickens, S. C.
On 2 Jan. 1860 Anthony Stewart, William H. Anderson, James E. Hagood
are bound unto W. E. Holcombe, Ord. in the sum of $550.00. Anthony
Stewart gdn. of Sarah Elizabeth Stewart, Mary Angeline Stewart infant

dtr. of Jacob L. Stewart decd. Gr. chn. of Anthony Stewart. 27 May 1871 paid Sarah E. wife of Andrew Jackson Hunter $27.50.

Elnora Stewart. Minor. Box 4 #73. Probate Judge Office. Pickens, S. C. On 22 April 1875 James H. Hutson, Micajah Hutson, Thomas Stewart, R. A. Stuart are bound unto I. H. Philpot, Ord. in the sum of $195.00. Jas. H. Hutson gdn. of Elnora Hutson formerly Stewart minor. 3 Oct. 1859 Richard B. Baker wanted to be gdn. of his grand children Elnora and James M. Stewart. Hutson also written Hudson.

Nancy Stewart. Estate of Nancy Stewart. Box 90 #956. Probate Judge Office. Pickens, S. C. Est. admr. 11 Dec. 1884 by A. Stewart, E. Gilstrap, J. F. Stewart who are bound unto J. H. Newton, Ord. in the sum of $500.00. Abram Stewart her husband. Died 10 Aug. 1884. Heirs. Abraham Stewart, Sarah A. Stewart, John F. Stewart, Huldy A. Satterfield, Nancy V. Gilstrap, Elizabeth Thomas, Robert Mc. Stewart, Anderson K. Stewart, Elizabeth Grant, Amry M. Stewart, Nancy E. Stewart. Mary Hinkle. Nancy Stewart decd. inherited from Polly Anderson est. Isaac Anderson est.

Watson Stewart. Estate of Watson Stewart. Box 94 #996. Probate Judge Office. Pickens, S. C. Est. admr. 3 Nov. 1884 by James A. Stewart, J. J. Herd, R. M. Stewart who are bound unto J. H. Newton, Ord. in the sum of $1,000.00. Mrs. Malinda Stewart, J. A. Stewart bought at sale.

Andrew Jackson Stewart. Box 112 #1077. Probate Judge Office. Pickens, S. C. Admr. granted to J. J. Lewis 20 March 1877. Mrs. N. Stewart, W. K. Stewart, John Stewart, W. R. Price bought at sale.

John F. Stewart. Estate of John F. Stewart. Box 119 #6. Probate Judge Office. Pickens, S. C. Est. admr. 3 Sept. 1891 by Gideon M. Lynch, James T. Burdine, John L. Gravely who are bound unto J. B. Newberry, Ord. in the sum of $2,000.00. Died 9 Aug. 1891. Heirs, Emma Bridges, Edward Stewart, Ernest Stewart, Nettie Stewart.

Stewart Minors. Box 11 #170. Probate Judge Office. Pickens, S. C. On 8 Dec. 1881 S. S. Stewart, J. A. Stewart, A. P. Stewart are bound to Olin L. Durant, Ord. in the sum of $100.00. S. S. Stewart gdn. of Mary Malissy, Stewart, Vandaly M. Stewart, Ferninand Columbus Stewart, Watson C. Stewart minors under 16 years. S. S. Stewart their father. Were great grand chn. of Richard B. Baker decd.

Stewart Minors. Box 126 #4. Probate Judge Office. Pickens, S. C. On 3 Dec. 1895 B. S. Lynch, John T. Lewis, M. F. Hester bound to J. B. Newberry, Ord. in the sum of $100.00. B. S. Lynch gdn. of W. C., Sarahe, Alice May, Freeman E., Ernest A., and Flora V. Stewart chn. of J. F. Stewart decd. W. C. and Sarah Stewart minors over 14 years. Alice May age 12 years. Freeman E. age 10 years. Ernest age 8 years. Flora Vinetta age 5 years. Paid 7 Dec. 1904. Edward Stewart $15.00. Paid Ernest Stewart $15.00. Paid Vinetta Stewart $15.00.

W. C. Stewart. Estate of W. C. Stewart. Box 131 #9. Probate Judge Office. Pickens, S. C. Est. admr. 6 Oct. 1898 by J. M. Stewart, J. J. Lewis, F. E. Cox are bound to J. B. Newberry, Ord. in the sum of $200.00.

Mrs. Isabella Stewart. Estate of Mrs. Isabella Stewart. Box 119 #14. Probate Judge Office. Pickens, S. C. She died 31 May 1890. Admr. granted to J. M. Stewart.

Thomas Stewart. Estate of Thomas Stewart. Box 126 #24. Probate Judge Office. Pickens, S. C. Died 20 Feb. 1893. Owned 31 acres on waters of Crow Creek adj. lands of B. P. Powell, Est. of R. C. Stewart and others. The following are minors under 21 years and have no gdn. viz; Thomas E. Stewart, Janie Stewart, Martha A. Stewart, R. B. Stewart, T. F. Stewart, N. W. Stewart, M. J. Stewart, Grover Cleveland Stewart, Coat Stewart. Others heirs Sarah A. Stewart, Mary E. Alexander, Stokes S. Stewart, Malissa Garrett, Myrtie Stewart, Ferdinand Stewart. Sarah A. Stewart the widow. His grand children were T. H. Stewart, M. A. Stewart, R. B.

Stewart, T. F. Stewart, M. N. Stewart, Jane Stewart, G. C. Stewart, Malissa Stewart, Myrtie Stewart, Ferninand Stewart, Coat Stewart. The first seven grandchildren are chn. of R. A. Stewart who died before his father. The last four grand children of Stoke Stewart now living who married Nancy Stewart a daughter of Thomas Stewart and who is now dead.

John Stewart. Estate of John Stewart. Box 129 #7. Probate Judge Office Pickens, S. C. Est. admr. 13 Mar. 1897 by Robert Stewart, W. E. Alexander, J. M. Nations, who are bound unto J. B. Newberry, Ord. in the sum of $100.00. Died 30 Jan. 1895. summons for relief. 2 Oct. 1898. Robert Stewart admr. against Susan Stewart, Elizabeth Stewart, Loney Moore, Julia Moore, Minnie Moore, J. P. Moore, F. H. Stewart, Elisha Stewart, Newton Stewart, Lony Moore, Abraham Stewart, John E. Stewart, Alfred Stewart and the non resident defendants Nancy Ferguson, Alice Stewart, James Stewart, Jacob Stewart, Paul Stewart.

John F. Stewart. Estate of John F. Stewart. Box 133 #3. Probate Judge Office. Pickens, S. C. He died 9 Aug. 1891. Gideon M. Lynch admr. Owned two lots in Pickens known as lot 8 and 10 on South side of Main St. 800 acres on both sides of Big Eastatoe described in deed from Harriet Bowie to John F. Stewart dated 3 Feb. 1890. 350 acres on Big Eastatoe Creek adj. land of Wm. K. Stewart, James Lewis. described in deed from W. R. Price dated 2 Jan. 1883. 90 acres on West side of Big Eastatoe Creek on both sides of Big Laurel described in deed from John Price dated 4 March 1884. 40 acres adj. land of Abe Stewart, John F. Stewart, described in deed from Abe Stewart dated 6 Dec. 1883. Another tract of 51 acres adj. it. Another tract of 150 acres adj. Sarah Alexander described in deed from Wm. K. Stewart dated 21 Mar. 1882. 1000 acres on Big Eastatoe Creek deeded from Henry J. Lewis and James M. Stewart dated 4 Sept. 1883. 1497 acres on Big and Little Eastatoe and Cane Creek deeded from J. J. Lewis, C.C.P. dated 7 Jan. 1886. 1350 acres on both sides Big Eastatoe Creek deeded from Abraham Stewart dated 21 Dec. 1889. Summons for relief. Gideon M. Lynch Admr. against Oscar Stewart, Emma Stewart, Mary Stewart, Edward Stewart, Ernest Stewart, Nettie Stewart.

Alfred Stewart. Minor. Box 132 #4. Probate Judge Office. Pickens, S. C. On 21 Jan. 1899 Robert Stewart, W. E. Alexander, W. P. Stewart are bound unto J. B. Newberry, Ord. in the sum of $63.00. Robert Stewart gdn. of Alfred and Abraham Stewart minors under 21 years. Abraham over 14 years. son of John D. Stewart decd. and Susan Stewart. Robert Stewart his brother.

John Stewart. Estate of John Stewart. Pack 31 #5. Clerk of Court Office. Pickens, S. C. (In equity) To Champ Taylor, Elisha Dean, Thomas Lively, Thomas Garvin, John Lively. You and each of you are commanded and authorized that you are any three of you do immediately on the receipt hereof according to the best of your judgment fairly justly and impartially to partition and divide a tract of land lying on 12 mile River, containing 1180 acres, being the land where John Stewart decd. possessed at the time of his death between Josiah Stuart, John Garden (this name torn) and Patsey his wife, Daniel Rigsby and Lidia his wife, Clem Emery and Ann his wife, Daniel Garret and Lavinia his wife, Joseph Stewart, Alpha Stuart, John Stuart heirs at law of John Stuart decd. and Polly Stuart widow and Allen Powel and (Janey or Jincey his wife, Green Stephen and Alpha his wife, the children of the said John Stuart decd. To them an equal portion. Dated 6 Oct. 1830. By W. L. Keith, C.C.P. Signed: F. Burt.

Stewart. Notes on Stewart Family. Tabitha M. Stewart was a niece of a James Campbell of Marion Co., S. C. whose will was made in 1816. See Campbell Will 4. On 8 Sept. 1858 Robert Stewart decd. of Pickens Dist. owned 700 acres on Little Eastatoe Waters of Keowee adj. land of William Gilstrap, Enoch Chapman, and others. Isabella Stewart his widow left 7 chn. viz; James Madison Stewart, Marab Malinda, Nancy Jane, Naomi Josephine, John Rufus, Mary and Robert Stewart. Ref Book A, Page 240. Probate Office. Pickens, S. C. On 9 Jan. 1860 A. J. Stewart and wife Lucinda were heirs of Mary Hinkle decd. who was an heir of

Henry Whitmire dec. of Pickens Dist. Ref. Probate Office Book B Page
35. Eliza Jenkins married a Stewart and was living out of state on 28
Nov. 1859. Heirs of Francis Jenkins decd. of Pickens Dist. Ref. Est.
of Francis Jenkins Probate Office. Book B page 42. On 28 April 1856
Robert Stewart ment. as the husband of Peggy Spence of Abbeville, S. C.
she was a dtr. of James Spence decd. Ref. Eq., Rec. of Wm. & John Spence
of Abbeville, S. C. Pack 9 Page #18. On 1 Nov. 1849 Sarah Stewart
was ment. as "dead" dtr. of Wm. Murphy decd. Her mother was Mary
Murphy. Ref #63 Basement Pickens, S. C.

Nimrod W. Stewart. Estate of Nimrod W. Stewart. Pack 332. Clerk of
Court Office. Abbeville, S. C. To the Honr. the Chancellors. Your
oratrix Rebecca Stewart and orator J. J. Cooper both of Abbeville Dist.
Sheweth that Nimrod W. Stewart now decd. was the husband of your oratrix departed this life in 186__ leaving a widow and three chn. namely
Emma J. Stewart, Lawrence Stewart, Rush Stewart. All minors under the
age of twenty one years. Recently Emma J. Stewart, intermarried with
James N. King. Nimrod W. Stewart was a merchant and at the time of his
death had considerable amount due him and uncollected, with two tracts
of land, one near the village of 96 containing 321 acres, adj. land of
John Saddler, John Goulden, Dr. John A. Stewart. Another a lot in the
village with house and blacksmith shop, adj. land of James Richardson,
J. F. Cason and others. The admr. of the est. was granted unto your
oratrix on the 14 Jan. 1865. Your oratrix found debts pressing and
money depreciating, the est. is unable to pay the debts without a sale
of the real estate. Your oratrix prays of a order for a sale. Filed
11 Feb. 1867.

Margaret Stewart. Estate of Margaret Stewart. Box 88 Pack 2183.
Probate Judge Office. Abbeville Dist., S. C. I, Margaret Stewart,
of Abbeville Dist. being in a low state of health but sound in mind etc.
I desire that my son have the tract of land I purchased from Eddy Caldwell of 23 acres, also the tract of land whereon I now live containing
229 acres, also the mare named Cate, with a saddle and bridle, one
bedstead and bed furniture. I will to my son John Stewart my Mary Ann
large chest and the largest and best bedstead and bed furniture. After
my just debts are paid and a note my son John gave me to the executor of
Halls est. for $18.75. The balance of my property be sold at public
outcry, the proceeds to be equally divided into four parts, one part to
Mary Ann Stuart, one part to John Stuart, one part of Sarah Buchanan,
the other part equally divided between Emely Turner, Louisa Sample,
Sarah Sample, Malissa Sample and John Sample my grand chn. the children
of my dtr. Susan Calhoun. I appoint my friend Dr. E. R. Calhoun and my
son John Stuart executors. Dated 20 Nov. 1838. Wit: William B. Beazly,
James F. Pinson, Philip Wait. Signed Margret Stuart. Proven on oath
of W. B. Beasly and qualified Dr. Calhoun Executor on the 15 Jan. 1839.
Inventory made on 2 Feb. 1839. Total amount $1733.50.

STONE

Notes on the Stone Family. Pack 14 Equity, Basement. Pickens C. H.
Pickens, S. C. In Nov. 1856 L. B. (Berry or Benj.) had married Mary
Jones a dtr. of Henry Johns decd. and his wife Martha Johns of Pickens
Dist. According to their Power of Attorney, dated 11 April 1859 they
were living in Canton, Cherokee Co., Ga.

Thomas Stone. Estate of Thomas Stone. Box 73 #781. Probate Judge
Office. Pickens, S. C. Est. admr. 16 Feb. 1864 by Nancy A. Stone,
widow, Silas Stone, Jacob H. Boroughs who are bound unto W. E.
Holcombe, Ord. in the sum of $1500.00.

Silas Stone. Estate of Silas Stone. Box 95 #1045. Probate Judge
Office. Pickens, S. C. Est. admr. 12 Jan. 1869 by Aaron P. Stone,
John Stewart, John Garrett who are bound unto I. H. Philpot, Ord. in
the sum of $600.00. Mary Stone the widow. On 4 Sept. 1875 Elizabeth
Carson says that she nursed Mrs. Silas Stone from March to middle of
Sept. her business is nursing the sick and that she was 56 years old.

The heirs of Silas Stone are: Rachel C. Durham, Wm. Stone, John Stone, Aaron Stone, Isaac Stone, J. P. Neighbors, Margaret Merck, John Stewart, Susan Stewart.

STRINGER

Reuben Stringer. Deed from Reuben Stringer. Book A Page 54. Mesne Conveyance. Greenville, S. C. This indenture made between Reuben Stringer and Richard Briant both of Greenville Dist. Dated 16 July 1787. In consideration of 100 pds. sterling, hath grant, bargain, sold and release all that tract of land lying North side of Saluda River containing 200 acres. Bounded on the South by the river and other sides vacant when run. Originally granted unto Reuben Stringer on 21 Jan. 1785. Wit: Ambrose Blackburn, Thompson Dickerson, James X Briant. Signed: Reuben Stringer and Elizabeth X Stringer. Proven in open Court at the August term 1788 and ordered to be recorded.

STYLES

Samuel Styles. Estate of Samuel Styles. No Ref. Greenville Dist, S. C. An inventory of the est. was made 25 Aug. 1843 by H. I. Gilbreath, Alfred Gilbreath, Co___ Bennett. Negroes named; Jim, Tom, Marlin, Charles Aaron, Andy, Bill, Lewis, Anthony, Hanband, Sarah, Maria, Lucinda, Martha, Lotty and Child, Nancy, Polly Ann, Della, Keziah. Gabriel B. Styles and Sion Bennett were executoe of the will. (Will not in notes.) In a petition to the Court on the 13 Jan. 1853 G. B. Styles and Z. Bennett are ready to make a final settlement with the heirs, viz; James Springfield and wife Nancy, Simeon Styles, Emily Styles, Andrew Jackson Styles, Elizabeth Styles who resides in Greenville Dist. and Lea and William Bennett and Hollyberry Bennett his wife, Claiborn Styles, John Coward and Jane his wife who resides out of State. In 1849 the executors paid Edmund Waddell and his wife Dicey Waddell (formerly Dicey Springfield) $105.00 in full satisfaction of the share going her as one of the children of Amy Springfield decd.

SWORDS

John Swords. Pension record of John Swords. W 8773. Copies as per Miss Youngs notes: John Swords of district of Pendleton in the western circuit of the state aforesaid who states in the spring of 1777 at the Cross Roads, in Chester County, S. C. He enlisted under Mr. Johnson, into Capt. George Varleys company of the 6th regiment of infantry of the South Carolina line of the Continental army for term of 3 years. He was first marched to Tawcaw Swamp from there to Charleston, S. C. where he remained in the new barracks about one year. He was then ordered on a tour of duty and marched to Augusta, St. Mary's, St. Tilley's and fort onion in Ga. and returned by water to Charleston again, and afterwards marched to Purensbury stono-Beufort, S. C. and then to Savannah, Ga. He was 9 weeks at the seige of Savannah under Capt. Boyce, who was slain in the battle. This deponent in assisting one of his fellow soldiers to carry off his Captain was taken prisoner by the British and kept 2 weeks in Savannah and would have starved but for charity of some Americans who divided their privision with him. The British gave him no vituals while he was a prisoner about 2 weeks. He made his excape from them and made his way up towards Augusta and thence home. He remained at home a while and Col. Bratton of the militia requested him to assist to turn the militia out which he did. As they were dilitary in going into service at that time. He this deponent went with the militia into service and was at Lauren's Ferry on Santee when the Va. regiments were ordered home and passed on after peace was made. He was 2 years and 8 months in the regular service before he was taken prisoner, that his father who was in service at the same time was made a prisoner at Charleston--States he reared a family by manual labor--

Affidavit by Elijah Brown of Pendleton Dist., S. C. 3 Sept. 1819 made
affidavit stating in 1777 General or Colo. noe Gen. Sumpter was
appointed to raise a command the sixth regiment of this state, the place
for the officers and soldiers to assemble was at the old X roads now a
part of Chester Dist. My father Wm. Browne lived in 2 miles and Major
of the regiment, this led me to resort to the place when and where I
first became acquainted with John Swords mustered as a soldier of the
regiment aforesaid, enlisted by Lt. John Montgomery and finally enrolled
in Capt. George Worley's company. In 1778 I again met John Swords leading a life of a common soldier, after this from reports he marched in
the noted Florida expedition and when the United attack was made by the
French and Americans on Savannah--Swords was among the besiegers and made
prisoner. Affadavit by Hamilton Brown. Pendleton Dist., S. C. States
that John Swords at the time he enlisted with Lt. Montgomery lived in
2 miles of me in a part of this state now called York Dist. and after
he joined the regiment at the Cross X Roads, I was him there doing his
duty as a soldier. Signed by Hamilton Brown. Application made 26/10/1847
in Anderson Dist., S. C. John Swords a resident of said Dist. and son
of John and Eleanor Swords decd. age 52, (mentions his father John
Swords and Eleanor Swancy his mother as appears by the family records
was married 24/4/1782 and lived together until death of said John
Swords 28 Sept. 1834, and his mother remained a widow until her death
3 May 1841 as appears from the family records. And the heirs at law of
his parents are William Swords, Isabella Pilgrim, Dorcas Elrod, Elizabeth Elrod, Ruth Newton, Esther Moore, Mary Morris having died 30/3/
1841 and Johnathan and Andrew Swords having removed to the far west,
he known but little about them and has small hopes of ever seeing them
again.

Family Records of John Swords Senior. He was born 19 March 1755.

Eleanor Swords born 9 June 1754
John Swancy born 21 Jan. 1766
Robert Swancy born 26 March 1775
Nathaniel Swancy born 1 Sept. 1777
William Swords born 19 March 1783
Isabella Swords born 10 April 1784
Dorcas Swords born 24 Oct. 1785
James Swancy Swords born 20 June 1787
Elizabeth Swords born 30 Jan. 1789
Ruthy Swords born 21 Nov. 1790
Esther Swords born 15 March 1792
Mary Swords born 21 Oct. 1793
John Swords born 13 May 1795
Johnathan Swords born 31 Dec. 1796
Andrew Swords born 28 July 1799

Rods was born 28 Feb. 1828
Biner was born 14 Feb. 1830
Saraan born 10 March 1832
Sopha born 19 Jan. 1841

John Swords and Eleanor Swancy were married 24 April 1792.

Robert Swancy died 7 Jan. 1791
William Swords died 30 Jan. 1794
James Swancy Swords died 16 June 1796
Elizabeth Swords died 15 June 1881, married 19 May 1824
James Moore died 9 Dec. 1823
John Swords, Senior, died 28 Sept. 1834
Mary Morris died 30 March 1841

John S. Swords a resident of Anderson Dist., S. C. made affidavit in
1849 that he was a resident of Anderson Dist., age 54, etc.

TAGGART

Moses Taggart. Estate of Moses Taggart. Pack 270 In Equity. Clerk of Court Office. Abbeville, S. C. To the Honr. Chancellors; Your orator William Patterson by Moses T. Owen his next friend. The great grand-father of your orator, Moses Taggart, Esq. late of Abbeville Dist. on the 10 April 1819 made and executed to his son a deed of trust, in favor of his daughter then Mary Perrin for life with certain limita-tions over negroes to wit: Rachel with her male child named George and her female child named Anika, to have and to hold said negroes with their increase unto the said son James Taggart trustee. By said trust Mary Parrin the wife of Thomas Perrin to enjoy the interest, increase, and profit during her lifetime, and at her death to be divided among such child or children as she may have the lawful heirs, when they arrive at the age of twenty one or marry. After the death of her first husband Thomas Perrin, she has intermarried with and now the wife of Arthur Murphy, she and her husband are still in possession of said negroes and their increase, sixteen in number to wit: Rachel, George, Anika, Ben, Joe, Hannah, Lewis, Jane, Alfred, Frank, Abram, Sally, Willie, Alexander and Adaline. The said Mary Murphy has no chn. by her last husband, by her first husband she had two chn. Elizabeth and Sarah Ann. Elizabeth intermarried with Dr. Thomas Mabry and had one child, but both mother and child died many years ago. Sarah Ann intermarried with Cary P. Patterson and left at her death (which occurred on the 14 Feb. 1852) four chn. Ann, Sarah, Eliza, and the complainant William Patterson. A question arose among the parties as to the fact whether negroes were not the property of said Mary before the execution of the deed of trust. By an agreement Mary Murphy and her husband relinquished all their rights during her life time to the following negroes, George, Ben, Anika, Joe, Hannah, Lewis, Jane and Matha, these were conveyed to John W. Hearst trustee for the use and profit of Sarah Ann the wife of Cary P. Patterson, during her natural life. (No more of this suit in Equity found in notes.)

TALLY

Curril Tally. Estate of Curril Tally. Box 94 #1003. Probate Judge Office. Pickens, S. C. On 27 Dec. 1884 Curril Tally owned three tracts of land each containing 100 acres on branchs of Oolenoy River adj. land of Mrs. Martin, H. M. Fortner. Heirs Joseph Tally, Angeline Williams, Thomas Blythe and Effie Furgerson are minors, the former two over 14 years, the latter two under that age. Dudley Tally, Abraham Tally, Seprona Whittenberger, John Tally, Emily Carr reside out of State. Abraham Tally, Emily Carr in Tenn. and Sephrona Whittenberger in Texas. Absalom B. Tally Executor of will.

Sarah Ann Tally. Will of Sarah Ann Tally. Box 119 #12. Probate Judge Office. Pickens, S. C. I Sarah Ann Tally of Easley Township, being of sound mind and memory, etc. First I desire my just and lawful debts be paid, likewise my funeral expenses. The remainder of my real and personal property, I give to my husband James D. Tally to be owned by him as his own property, in Equity and in law. I appoint John R. Gossett my executor. Dated 27 Aug. 1884. Wit: C. W. Moore, teacher, Easley, S. C., W. H. Kirton, Minister of the Gospel, Easley, S. C. Leila E. Gossett, Easley, S. C. Signed: Sarah Ann Tally. Filed 20 Aug. 1891.

TANNERY

Levi Tannery. Estate of Levi Tannery. Box 14 #182. Probate Judge Office. Pickens, S. C. Est. admr. 27 Nov. 1846 by Parthenia Tannery, widow, Joshua Perkins, Samuel R. Kanady who are bound unto Wm. D. Steele, Ord. in the sum of $1,000.00. He owned 380 acres lying on Choestee

Creek, adj. land of Major Cole, Coleman Fowler, John Anderson. Heirs
Parthenia Tanner, the widow, Narcissa the wife of B. B. Moon, Alfred
Tannery, William, John, Samuel, Eveline Tannery minors, with J. W.
Norris. Guardian ad litem for the minors.

TARRANT

Larkin Tarrant. Estate of Larkin Tarrant. Apt. 7 File 496. Probate
Judge Office. Greenville, S. C. I Larkin Tarrant being of sound mind
and memory, etc. First I desire my executor give my body a decent
burial and pay my just debts. I give to my son Thomas Tarrant a plantation by deed known as the Cross Road in this dist. containing 200 acres,
together with stock and furniture, in all the value of two thousand
dollars. At the death or intermarriage of my wife Mary Tarrant, I desire
my whole estate both real and personal be divided between my eight chn.
the then survivers or their heirs. To my dtr. Patsy Tarrant a tract of
land in Pendleton Dist. lying on the Saluda River, containing 540 acres,
one negro girl called Catty, 12 years old, one horse colt, worth one
hundred dollars. (some words torn) all which she is to receive at
her marriage. My other six chn. to receive the same amount when they
come of age or marry, provided it can be done without injury to the
support for my wife Mary during her life time or widowhood. Each of
the last six chn. to receive two thousand dollars worth of land and, or
personal property. I appoint my wife executrix and my son Thomas
executor. Dated ___ July 1804. No witness is given nor did he sign the
will. On the 2 Jan. 1805 William Robertson, Jesse Goodlett, John Archer
and Samuel A. Easley came before me and made oath that they do ___
verily believe from long acquaintance with the hand writing of Larkin
Tarrant decd. that the within will is the hand writing of said decd.
Given under my hand. J. Thomas, Jr. Ord. G. D. An inventory was made
of the estate totaling $4,003.76 3/4. No date given on the inventory.
Names that may be the other six chn. as given in the paid acct.
from 1806-1808. Note due L. Tarrant. Paid wood for title to R.
Tarrant land. Paid Richd. Tarrant acct.

Benjamin Tarrant. Estate of Benjamin Tarrant. Apt. 7 File 465. Probate Judge Office. Greenville, S. C. I Benjamin Tarrant being weak
in body but in perfect mind and memory. I give to my beloved wife
Marth Tarrant all my estate personal and real during her life time or
widowhood. After my just debts are paid and the death or marriage of
my wife Martha, the estate to be divided between my chn. as to my dtrs.
Milley Hollon, Betsey Snow, and the heirs of my dtr. Molley Wade decd.
and Benjamin Tarrant Jr. each have recd. five pds. sterling, with
twenty pds. to be paid by my executors. The remaining part of my est.
to be equally divided between my sons, Leonard, Wiatt, Robert, Samuel,
James and John Tarrant and I appoint my beloved wife Martha Tarrant, my
sons Leonard and Samuel Tarrant, Executors. Dated 15 Nov. 1808. Wit:
Henry Machen Jr., James Tarrant, Solomon Dalton. Signed: Benjamin
Tarrant. This day came Solomon Dalton who made oath that he saw Benjamin Tarrant sign the within will, etc. Dated 20 Aug. 1819 S.
Goodlett, Esq. Ord. G.D. Samuel Tarrant this day applied to me in this
Court to prove the last will and testament of Benjamin Tarrant decd.
Dated 2 Aug. 1819. An inventory was made on 7 Sept. 1819, with the
negroes listed as: Molly, Noble, Sinda, Absalom, Matilda and child
Elizabeth, Mary, Stephen, Malinda, Chany, Dinah. A sale of the per-
sonaly property was had on the 16 Dec. 1825. With the final settlement made the 7 June 1830.

John Tarrant. Estate of John Tarrant. Apt. 7 File 476. Probate Judge
Office. Greenville, S. C. I John Tarrant being of sound mind and
memory, do make this my last will and testament, etc. I desire my just
debts be paid. I have given to Sally McKenzieons a feather bed and
furniture and one mare colt. I have given to Samuel Tarrant one
feather bed and furniture and one young mare be all of my estate I
intend for him. I have given to Rowland Tarrant one young mare and
I have given one feather bed and furniture. I now give to Richard

Tarrant one young horse colt and one feather bed and furniture. I now
give to my three youngest children viz, Nancy, John and George Tarrant
each of them a twenty pound horse saddle and bridle, when they come of
age or marry, also each to get a feather bed and furniture. I now give
to Edward Hampton Tarrant son of Samuel Tarrant decd. one twenty pound
horse saddle and bridle when he come of age. I now give to my beloved
wife Tabitha Tarrant during her life time or widowhood all my estate both
personal and real, after the death or marriage of my wife Tabitha my
estate to be keep together till my youngest child come of age, then to
be equally divided between my six children viz; Sally McKenzie, Rowlan,
Richard, Nancy, John and George. I appoint my wife Tabitha and sons
Rowland and Richard executors. Dated 8 April 1799. Wit: James Tarrant,
Benjamin Tarrant, David X Crofford. Signed: John Tarrant. An
inventory of the estate was made 2 Dec. 1811. Negroes named, Jack,
Stephen, Dick, Silva and child.

James Tarrant. Deed from James Tarrant. Book 1 page 88 Mesne Conveyance
Greenville, S. C. James Tarrant to David Cotton both of Greenville Dist.
Dated 1 March 1819. In consideration of $120.00. Have granted, bar-
gained, sold, and released unto David Cotton all that tract of land
containing twenty acres, being part of a 640 tract granted unto John
Bowie and sold to me on the 14 April 1804. Being all that lies on the
East side of Golden Grove Creek. Wit: Robert Tarrant, John Tarrant.
Signed: James Tarrant. Deed proved on oath of Robt. Tarrant before
Lee Tarrant, QM. on the 23 Sept. 1891. Recorded 14 March 1820.

TATE

William Tate. Estate of William Tate. Box 20 Pack 21. Probate Judge
Office. Union, S. C. Est. admr. 17 Jan. 1832 by Elijah Dawkins, Joseph
Collins, Thomas N. Dawkins who are bound unto John J. Pratt, Ord. in the
sum of $10,000.00.

James Tate. Estate of James Tate. Box 28 Pack 5. Probate Judge Office.
Union, S. C. Will. I James Tate being weak in body but of sound mind
and memory, etc. I desire my just debts be paid, and all my estate both
real and personal be keep together and my wife be supported out of it
until my youngest child come of age. In case she marry I desire my
executors have my property all appraised and she have a child's part
and each have an equal share. I desire my friend Zachariah Tate and
Edmund Blanton my executors. Dated 27 Jan. 1842. Wit: Wm. Goudelock,
Stephen Pearson, Margaret Tate. Signed: James X Tate. Recorded 2
Feb. 1842. Union Dist., S. C. By J. J. Pratt, Esq. Ord. to Mrs.
Elizabeth Tate, John Pursley and wife Mary, Susan Tate, Fanny Tate,
William Tate, James Tate, David Tate, and Elizabeth Tate heirs at law
of James Tate decd. You are admonished to appear and show cause if any
why the last will and testament of James Tate decd. should not be
proven. Dated 10 Sept. 1846.

Elizabeth Tate. Estate of Elizabeth Tate. Box 38 Pack 22. Probate
Judge Office. Union, S. C. I Elizabeth Tate being low in health but
of sound mind and memory, etc. I wish my just debts be paid. I will
to the children of my decd. dtr. Emilem Brown two hundred dollars to
be equally divided between them. I will to the chn. of Mary Pursely,
those that she now has and those that she may have hereafter two
hundred dollars. To my dtr. Susan Pettel three hundred dollars cash.
I will to my dtr. Erephama Pettel three hundred dollars in cash. I
will to my dtr. Elizabeth one negro boy named Peter. I will all the
remainder of my est. both real and personal be equally divided between
them viz; James Tate, David Tate, and Elizabeth Tate. I appoint my
son-in-law John Pettel and William Pettel and my friend Dr. Samuel A.
Goodman executors. Dated 22 May 1854. Wit: Stephen Pearson, Elijah
Jenning, W. R. X Campbell. Signed: Elizabeth X Tate. Emilem Brown
the wife of Green B. Brown lived in Pickens Co., Ala.

James Tate. Estate of James Tate. No Ref. may be same. Box 20 Pack 21.
Probate Judge Office. Union Dist., Union, S. C. I James Tate being sick
and weak in body but of perfect mind and memory. I give to my wife Mary
Tate all my real and personal property during her life or widowhood.
I give to my dtr. Elizabeth Gregory one negro girl named Patsey and the
sum of fifty dollars. I give to my son Thomas Tate one negro boy named
Tom and one girl named Charlotte and fifty dollars. I give to my son
John O. Tate one negro named Ally and two boys named Warren and Jeff,
also two beds and bedding. I give to my son Joseph Tate one negro woman
named Sophy and her child Jane. I give unto my executors (John O. Tate
and John Gregory) one negro girl named Gilda for use and benefit of my
four grand children John O., James W., Francis E., and Mary C. Tate.
heirs of my son James Tate decd. Dated 12 July 1842. Wit: John
Gregory, James Thomson Gregory, Joseph McJunkin Jr. Signed: James X
Tate. Recorded 2 Sept. 1842.

Mary Tate. Estate of Mary Tate. Box 38 Pack 13. Probate Judge Office.
Union, S. C. Est. admr. 9 Feb. 1854 by Zachariah Tate, D. Goudelock,
B. H. Rice. who are bound unto B. Johnson, Ord. in the sum of eight
thousand dollars. Zachariah Tate applied for a letter of admr. on the
est. the 24 Jan. 1854. He stated that there were ten distributees.
(Note, that two James Tate died in 1842, with theirs wives dying in 1854,
some of the papers may be mixed. J.E.W.)

TATUM

Edward Tatum. Estate of Edward Tatum. Pack 725. Probate Judge Office.
Anderson, S. C. I Edward Tatum of Pendleton Dist. Do make this my
last will and testament. I will my just debts be paid. I will to my
son Luke Tatum three fourths of the land whereon I now live. I will to
my dtr. Martha Tatum the other fourth of the said land marked out by a
line including my dwelling house, also two negroes women Jude and Annasa,
also all my stock of all kinds, with household and kitchen furniture.
I will to my loving wife Martha Tatum (no items named). I will to my
dtr. Elizabeth Hendrick one negro named Hannah. I leave out the names
of my other children, having already given them their portion. I do
appoint my well beloved friend William ___ and Solomon Murphree my
executor. Dated 5 June 1804. Wit: Hamilton Reid, Charles X Durham,
Joseph X Stephen. Signed: Edward X Tatum. This day came Hamilton
Reid and Joseph Stephens and made oath that they was Edward Tatum
sign the within will. Dated 4 Feb. 1811. Before John Harris, O.P.D.
Same day qualifyed Solomon Murphrey executor.

John Tatum. Estate of John Tatum. Pack 711. Probate Judge Office.
Anderson, S. C. Est. admr. 24 Dec. 1824 by Hugh Tatum, William Tatum,
Edward Tatum who are bound unto John Harris, Ord. in the sum of two
thousand dollars. Citation published 19 Dec. 1824 at Fairview Meeting
House. Sale was held on 25 Jan. 1825. Buyers: Levi Burtz, Joseph
Young, Elijah Cannon, Rebecca Tatum, Edward Tatum, Perthany Tatum, Hugh
Tatum, William Tatum, Moese Hendrix, Jeremiah Field, John Humphreys,
John Prince, Mark Kirksey, William Barrett, John Gilstrap, Wiley
Gilstrap, John W. Tatum, Nathaniel Tatum, Sheriff Haynes.

John Tatom. Book B-1 Page 46. Clerk of Court Office. Pickens, S. C.
I John Tatom to Charles Durham both of Pendleton Dist. Dated 9 April
1819. In consideration of $100.00 paid by Charles Durham have granted,
bargained, sold and released all that tract of land on Wolf Creek waters
of 12 mile River. Adj. land of William Hunter and Charles Durham,
containing 34 acres. Wit: Levi Murphree, James Hunter. Signed: John
Tatom. Deed attested by Levi Murphree before John Clayton J.P. on the
4 Dec.1821.

William T. Tatom. Estate of William T. Tatom. Pack 404. Clerk of
Court Office. Abbeville, S. C. On 26 March a statement of the est.
of William T. Tatom in hands of his guardian Dr. William Tennant.
W. T. Tatom has now come of age.

Solomon Tatom. Deed to Solomon Tatom. Book B-1 Page 334. Clerk of
Court Office. Pickens, S. C. Deed from William Satterfield to Solomon
Tatom both of Pickens Dist. Dated 11 Dec. 1829. In consideration
$340.00 paid by Solomon Tatom have granted, bargained, sold and released,
one tract of land lying on waters of 12 Mile River adj. land of Lewis
Brown, Ropers Line, to Sandy Branch, Jenkins Line. Containing 150
acres. Wit: Samuel McCollu, Hugh Tatum. Signed: William Satterfield.
Personally appeared Samuel McCollum and made oath that he was William
Satterfield sign the within deed, before Nathl. Davis J.P. Dated
8 Jan. 1833. Recorded 28 May 1833.

James Tatum. Mortgage Deed. Deek Book B-1 page 43. Clerk of Court
Office. Pickens, S. C. Whereas I James Tatum stands justly indebted
to Samuel Westbrook in the sum of $175.00. In four notes, one per year,
for better securing said notes, have granted, bargained, sold and
released into Samuel Westbrook a tract of land being the same tract which
is this day conveyed to me by said Westbrook. Dated 4 Feb. 1831. Wit:
John Hunter, James Henderson. Signed James Tatum. Mortgage proven by
James Henderson before James Osborn J.Q. Dated 25 March 1831. Recorded
25 July 1831.

TAYLOR

Major Samuel Taylor. Estate of Major Samuel Taylor. Pack 727. Probate
Judge Office. Anderson, S. C. I Samuel Taylor of Pendleton Dist. being
in a weak and low state of body, but of sound mind and memory. To my
beloved wife Elenor Taylor, one negro man named Dave and one negro woman
named Vilet during her time, and at her death to be divided between the
legatees, also a decent support from the plantation whereon I now live
(on the East side of Seneca River). Also the use of the room in the
East end of the house I now live in, commonly called hers, during her
natural life or widowhood. One bed and kitchen furniture, a horse and
saddle and bridle. I give to my sons John and Samuel a tract of
land in Abbeville Dist. on the Savannah River. Adj. land of Joseph
Sanders to be equal divided between them. To John B. Earl, I bequeath
the land on the West side of Seneca River, above the mouth of Seneca
Creek. Prived he makes a title to my son William Taylor to the tract
granted to his wife and adj. the tract of land where i now live. I
give to my son William the tract of land where I now live on the East
side of Seneca River. I give to my son Joseph all that tract of land
on the West side of Seneca River below the mouth of Seneca Creek
opposite where I now live. To my son John I give one negro boy named
Henry with a bay horse called his... To my dtr. Dilly one negro wench
named Milly, one named Nance. To my dtr. Elizabeth I give one negro
wench named Molly, one named Tinah. The wagons, work horses, tools are
to be keep on the plantation for the use and support of the children
under age. To my grand daughter Hannah Earle I bequeath one negro girl
named Mariah. All other property not mentioned before to be sold and
after paying my just debts to be equally divided between my sons Samuel,
Joseph, and William and my dtrs. Dilley and Elizabeth. I appoint my
son John, Andrew Pickens, William Steele, George Reese executors. 20
April 1798. Wit: James Wood, Robert Glenn, Sarah Pickens. Signed:
Samuel Taylor. Proven in open Court the 27 June 1798 by James Wood and
Robert Glenn. Estate was appraised on the 21 Aug. 1798 by Wm. McGuffin,
Alexander Ramsey, Wm. McCaleb. Negroes named, Charles, Sampson, Pompey,
Frank, Little Charles, Moll, Violet, Dave, Mille, Lewis, Henry and
Nancy, a wench and family to wit, Patty, Peter, Esther, Isaac, London,
Marion, George, Tenah, John, Old Jack his wife Kate and 2 chn., Esther
and Lancaster, Nero his wife Dinah and two chn., Ransom and Frank.

Major Samuel Taylor. Land Plat of Major Samuel Taylor. Old Records
Book A, page 1. Probate Judge Office. Abbeville, S. C. To Major
Samuel Taylor on the bounty four hundred acres on the West side of
Keowee River. Bounded by the river and vacant land. Recorded 26 May
1784.

William Taylor. Deed to William Taylor. Deed Book E Page 188-189.
Mesne Conveyance, Greenville, S. C. This indenture made between Isaac
Preston and William Taylor both of Greenville County. Dated 12 Aug.
1798. In consideration of the sum of(___ amount not plain) hundred
dollars, paid by William Taylor have bargained, sold, released a tract
of land lying on branches of Enoree River, containing 500 acres.
Originally granted to Uriah Conner, beginning on a branch whereon the
old meeting house stands. Adj. lands of Isaac Preston, Henry Chambles
and Conner old line. Wit: Isaac X Low, Ezekrel X Preston, Abuham
McAfee. Signed: Isaac Preston.

Thomas Taylor. Estate of Thomas Taylor. Box 110 Pack 3203. Probate
Judge Office. Abbeville, S. C. I Thomas Taylor of the County of
Culpeper? Being infirm in body but in perfect health, etc. I
bequeath to Johnannah Taylor my dearly beloved wife two negroes girls
Lidda and Cats, and all other things of my estate so long as she is a
widow and after my just debts are paid, and after her death or widowhood
I desire it maybe divided equally amongst all my children (not named).
I appoint William Miles and John Taylor executors. Dated 2 Dec. 1787.
Wit: Micajah Stevens, Herod Freeman. Signed: Thomas Taylor. No
recording date.

John Taylor. Will of John Taylor. Will Book AA Page 473. Probate
Judge Office. Sumter, S. C. I John Taylor of Sumter Dist. being weak
in body tho of sound mind and memory, etc. I desire my Just debts to be
paid from my personal estate. I lend to my beloved wife the house
and out houses and plantation where I now live, with all my household
and kitchen furniture and plantation tools, with all stock during her
widowhood and no longer, my small children at the same time to be
supported out of it with her. I give to my oldest sons John and Hasten
Taylor all that plantation lying on dog funnel branch, commonly called
Norton tract of land to be euqally divided between them, with the stock
of hogs which they claim. I give to my sons Asa, Harvey, Leonard, Sion
and Tylor Taylor all the tract whereon I now live to be equally divided
between them at the death of my wife or her marriage. If my wife
Margret Taylor dies or marry the whole estate to be equally divided
between the following chn. Asa Taylor, Harvey Taylor, Tabitha Taylor,
Leonard Taylor, Sion Taylor, Milford Taylor, Tylor Taylor. I give to
my dtr. Rebeekah Bates one dollar to be paid to her fourteen years after
my death. I appoint my friends Jesse Nettles, Jr. and John Nettles my
executors. Dated 27 Feb. 1820. Wit: James Cantey, Mary McKellar.
Signed: John X Taylor.

Joseph Taylor. Deed to Joseph Taylor. Deed Book C-1 Page 551. Clerk
of Court Office. Pickens, S. C. Deed from Thornton D. Saterfield to
Joseph Taylor, both of Pickens Dist. Dated 5 April 1838. In consideration of $100.00 have granted, bargain, sold, and released unto Joseph
Taylor all that plantation containing 82 acres it being part of a grant
originally granted to John Stewart on marsh branch of 12 Mile River.
Wit: Charles Thompson, George W. Kilburn. Signed: T. D. Saterfield.
Proven on oath of Charles Thompson before F. N. Garvin J.P. on the
5 April 1838. Recorded 21 May 1838.

J. B. Taylor. Power of Attorney, Pack 650 #4. Clerk of Court Office.
Pickens, S. C. I, J. B. Taylor, of the County of Lee, state of
Arkansas. This day nominate L. N. Taylor of Pickens County, S. C. as
my lawful attorney to act in my name, place, stead and perform any act
with reference to the sale Loving tract of land in the County of
Pickens, S. C. Containing 58 acres. Dated 19 Sept. 1881.

William Taylor. Estate of William Taylor. No Ref. Probate Judge
Office. Kershaw Dist., S. C. I William Taylor, being of sound and
disposing mind and memory. I give to my son Simon Taylor one seventh
part of my whole estate both real and personal during his natural life
and no longer, not subject to his debrs, contracts, or disposal, after
his death to his widow if he has one, or to his child or children,
then to their heirs and so on. Subject to same limitations, I give to
my son John C. Taylor one seventh part of my whole estate. I give to my

son in law Jacob Bell his heirs, executors, assigns one seventh part of
my whole estate instrust for the sole use and benefit of my dtr. Sarah
M. Bell, not subject to any debts etc. to their heirs and so on. I
give to my son in law Peter A. M. Gregor, one seventh part of my estate
in trust for my dtr. Mary A. M. Gregor. I give to my son in law Robert
H. Edmonds in trust for my dtr. Martha E. Edmonds one seventh part of
my whole estate. I give to my son in law Robert H. Edmonds in trust,
a small negro girl named Maria about eight years old and the sum of
nineteen hundred dollars, also one seventh part of my whole estate in
trust for the sole and separate use and benefit of my dtr. Elizabeth C.
Taylor. Not subject to any debts or contract, after her death said shar
to her child or children and so on. I give to my grand son William
Smith $250.00. I give to my grand daughters Caroline E. Smith and Marth
J. Smith each the sum of $500.00, also one seventh part of my whole
estate, to their heirs and so on. I appoint my son Simon Taylor, my
son in law Jacob Bell and Robert H. Edmonds executors. Dated 10 Feb.
1857. Wit: R. G. Bryan, A. G. Baskin, W. H. Talley. Signed: Wm.
Taylor.

John Taylor. Will of John Taylor. Box 66 Pack 2365. Probate Judge
Office. Camden, S. C. I John Taylor in Caven County, being sick and
weak in body but of sound and perfect mind and memory. I lend to my
beloved wife Sarah Taylor during her natural life one third of my two
plantations on the Waterree that I bought from James and William
Harrison, with four negroes named Filles, Ned, Aprill, March, and one
third of my stock, hogs, cattle, household and kitchen furniture. I
give to my son John Taylor one tract of land containing 200 acres on the
Waterree that I bought from James Harrison. I give to my son Simon
200 acres on the Waterree which I bought from William Harrison. I give
to my son William Taylor two tracts of land on the 25 Mile Creek containing in the total 500 acres. I give to my dtr. Mary Taylor one tract
of land containing 300 acres, in the forks between Waterree and Ceder
Creek which land was given to me by my brother Thomas Taylor. The
remainder of my est. to be equal divided between my four above named
children. I appoint my beloved wife and brother Sarah and James Taylor
executors. Dated 16 March 1781. Wit: John Hirons, Jane Curry, Hannah
Grulk. Signed: John Taylor. Proven 2 Nov. 1782.

Samuel Taylor. Estate of Samuel Taylor. Box 93 Pack 3. Probate Judge
Office. Sumter, S. C. Est. admr. 25 Nov. 1833 by Margaret A. B. Taylor
and William Thaddeus Williams who are bound unto Wm. Potts, Ord. in the
sum of $100.00. Citation Pub. at Presbyterian Church, 24 Nov. 1833 at
Sumterville, S. C.

Samuel P. Taylor. Estate of Samuel P. Taylor. Box 93 Pack 15. Probate
Judge Office. Sumter, S. C. Est. admr. 5 Dec. 1842 by Thomas China,
John China Jr. and R. W. Harvin who are bound unto William Lewis, Ord.
in the sum of $10,000.00. Owned 6 negroes not named, Inventory made
17 Dec. 1842 by Joseph Montgomery, Robert R. Durant, Jared J. Nelson.
Est. admounted to $58.14.87 1/2.

John Taylor. Box 93 Pack 12. Probate Judge Office. Sumter, S. C.
Est. admr. 20 Nov. 1822 by Margret Taylor, Hastin Taylor, John Taylor,
Asa Taylor who are bound unto Wm. Potts, Ord. in the sum of $6,000.00.
Mrs. Mary McKeller, Mrs. Mary Garrett were ordered to appear in Court
3 Nov. 1822.

William Taylor. Estate of William Taylor Box 93 Pack 1. Probate Judge
Office. Sumter, S. C. Writ of partition mentioned Samuel P. Taylor,
Thomas China and Marie his wife, Mary Nelson Taylor, Susannah Elizabeth
Taylor children of Wm. Taylor. Also ment. Thomas J. Wilder, Samuel E.
Nelson, Samuel E. Plowden, Joseph Montgomery.

Isaac Taylor. Note on Isaac Taylor. Apt. 1 File 22. Probate Judge
Office. On 7 Aug. 1837, Isaac Taylor and his wife Mary were heirs of a
David Barnett, Sr. of Greenville Dist. who died in 1837. Isaac and
Mary Taylor were living at this time in S. C.

Benjamin Taylor. Estate of Benjamin Taylor. Box 66 Pack 2361. Probate Judge Office. Camden, S. C. Est. admr. 26 Oct. 1820 by Neil Smith, James Clark, John Smith who are bound unto the Ordinary in the sum of $500.00. Mrs. Taylor bought at the sale. Expend 29 March 1821 paid Zelpha Payne $4.00.

Jacob Taylor. Estate of Jacob Taylor. Box 66 Pack 2363. Probate Judge Office. Camden, S. C. Est. admr. 29 Nov. 1784 by William Taylor, Archibald Davy, John Crockett who are bound unto the Ordinary in the sum of ₺3,000. William Taylor next of kin. Owned a plantation near Winnsborough, S. C.

George Taylor. Abstract of George Taylor's Will. Box 66 Pack 2362. Probate Judge Office. Camden, S. C. Will dated 26 Aug. 1835. Recorded 31 Dec. 1838. Left estate to brother William I. or J.? Taylor. Wit: J. W. Cantey, James M. Taylor. A. Boykin.

Mrs. Ann Taylor. Abstract of Mrs. Ann Taylor, Will. Box 66 Pack 2360. Probate Judge Office. Camden, S. C. Will dated 17 Nov. 1843. Recorded 3 May 1844. Mentioned Nephew, Vincent Bell, Seignor. Died in 1844. Step son, William R. Taylor. Wit: B. F. Watkins, W. A. Ward, Mary B. Taylor.

James Taylor. Estate of James Taylor. Box 66 Pack 2364. Probate Judge Office. Camden, S. C. Est. admr. 10 Oct. 1782 by John Taylor, Francis Goodwyn, Sr., Francis Goodwyn, Jr. who are bound unto the Ordinary in the sum of ₺2,000. John Taylor was next of kin.

William Taylor. Estate of William Taylor. Box 66 Pack 2368. Probate Judge Office. Camden, S. C. Est. admr. 21 June 1783 by Mary Taylor, Benjamin Culp, Jr., Andrew Lockhart who are bound unto the Ordinary in the sum of ₺3,000.

Samuel S. Taylor. Estate of Samuel S. Taylor. Box 66 Pack 2367. Probate Judge Office. Camden, S. C. Est. admr. 13 Feb. 1845 by James P. Dickinson, Esq., J. B. Kershaw, W. B. Watkins who are bound unto the Ordinary in the sum of $3,000.00. Died 10 Sept. 1843.

TEMPLETON

John L. Templeton. Box 89 #937. Probate Judge Office. Pickens, S. C. I, John L. Templeton of Pickens Dist. being in sound mind and memory, etc. After my lawful debts are paid and discharged, the residue of my estate, I give in the following manner. I give to my mother my trunk, shoe tools, carpenter tools and lumber and my Bible and hymnbook, pocket knife and pocket book and contents. To my beloved sister Lutecia F. Templeton my gold watch and chain and gold buttons, gold locket and writing desk. My clothes and books to my two brothers David and Samuel Templeton and my hat to my brother Samuel. To my two nephews John Thomas and George Leland Boggs, I give on dollar each. To my nephew James Andrew Templeton I give one dollar. I appoint my sister Lutecia F. Templeton my executrix. Dated 14 May 1863. Wit: W. S. Williams, Elizabeth Hamilton, Elizabeth Gary. Signed: Jno. L. Templeton. Proven 10 Oct. 1866.

John Templeton. Estate of John Templeton. Box 10 #132. Probate Judge Office. Pickens, S. C. Est. admr. 9 Sept. 1841 by Samuel M. Fairbairn, John Godfrey, David Martin who are bound unto James H. Dendy, Ord. in the sum of $10,000.00. Est. admr. again 27 Sept. 1841 by Katherine Templeton, widow, Elijah Alexander, F. N. Garvin who are bound unto James H. Dendy, Ord. in the sum of $10,000.00. Citation published at Liberty Church mentioned that Samuel M. Fairbairn was of Laurens Dist. E. B. Benson was the guardian for W. A., Jane C., Letitia, D. H., Esther and D. T. Templeton. Left a widow and 8 chn. 15 Oct. 1844 paid James Templeton on note $38.78.

William A. Templeton. Estate of William A. Templeton. Box 25 #299.
Probate Judge Office. Pickens, S. C. Est. admr. 27 Aug. 1852 by
F. M. Glenn and H. M. Brown who are bound Wm. D. Steele, Ord. in the
sum of $1500.00. Mary Templeton the widow.

Martha E. Templeton. Estate of Martha E Templeton. Box 38 #427.
Probate Judge Office. Pickens, S. C. Est. admr. 5 Nov. 1855 by John
L. Templeton, Thomas H. Boggs who are bound unto W. J. Parson, Ord. in
the sum of $1,000.00. Est. divided between 8 heirs. No names given.
Had one note on Catharine Templeton for $265.00.

Templeton Minors. Box 1 #6. Probate Judge Office. Pickens, S. C.
On 6 Mar. 1848 E. B. Benson, James W. Crawford, John Maxwell are bound
to W. D. Steele, Ord. in the sum of $735.00. E. B. Benson gdn. of
Esther Chatherine, David Humphreys, Samuel Fairborn Templeton minors
under 12 years. Children of John Templeton decd. and Catherine Templeton their mother.

Samuel F. Templeton. Estate of Samuel F. Templeton. Box 3 #86. In
Equity. Clerk of Court Office, Pickens, S. C. On 15 Feb. 1861 Francis
M. Glenn, J. A. Boggs, of Anderson Dist. and T. J. Dickson, Thomas H.
Boggs of Pickens Dist. are bound unto Robert A. Thompson, Clk. of
Equity in the sum of $2400.00. Francis M. Glenn gdn. of Samuel F.
Templeton minor under 21 years.

James A. Templeton. Estate of James A. Templeton. Box 3 #83. In
Equity. Clerk of Court Office. Pickens, S. C. On 5 July 1858 Thomas
H. Boggs states that James A. Templeton his nephew is a minor under
12 years. A power of attorney with same Est.

Mariana A. Templeton. State of Georgia, Cobb County. I Mariana A.
Templeton widow of Andrew Templeton decd. late of Pickens Dist., S. C.
Have appointed Thomas H. Boggs of Pickens Dist. my lawful attorney to
demand, sue, etc. from Francis M. Glenn admr. of the est. of John
Templeton decd. late of Pickens Dist. I hereby waive my right to be
gdn. of my child James A. Templeton a minor under 12 years. Dated 11
Feb. 1857 in the presence of Marianna Templeton. Wit: James L. Hamil-
ton and R. A. Hamilton.

Luticia C. Templeton. Estate of Luticia C. Templeton. Box 1 #7.
Probate Judge Office. Pickens, S. C. In 1848 E. B. Benson was gdn.
for Luticia C. Templeton.

William Andrew Templeton. Estate of William Andrew Templeton. Box 1
#8. Probate Judge Office. Pickens, S. C. On 2 July 1847 E. B. Benson,
John B. Benson, John T. Sloan are bound unto W. D. Steele, Ord. in the
sum of $500.00. E. B. Benson gdn. of W. A. Templeton minor under 14
years. Son of John Templeton.

Samuel F. Templeton. Estate of Samuel F. Templeton. Box 1 #9. Probate
Judge Office. Pickens, S. C. On 6 March 1848 E. B. Benson, James W.
Crawford, John Maxwell are bound unto W. D. Steele, Ord. in the sum of
$735.00, E. B. Benson gdn. of Samuel F. Templeton a minor under 21 yrs.
Catherine Templeton wanted E. B. Benson to be gdn.

Templeton Minors. Box 6 #3. In Equity, Clerk of Court Office.
Pickens, S. C. On 4 Aug. 1856 E. B. Benson, W. H. D. Gaillard, John T.
Sloan of Anderson Dist. are bound unto Robert A. Thompson, Clk. of
Equity for $1200.00. On 30 June 1856, E. B. Benson gdn. of Catherine
Templeton, David Templeton, Samuel Templeton minors under 21 years.
Chn. of John Templeton decd.

F. E. Templeton. Will of F. E. Templeton, Box 41 #8. Probate Judge
Office. Pickens, S. C. I, F. E. Templeton, of the town of Liberty,
Pickens Co. being of sound mind and memory, etc. First pay my just
debts and funeral expenses. I give my personal est. as follows. To
L. L. Templeton my brother one share of Liberty Cotton Mill stock. To
my sisters Nora T. Perkins and Ida T. Sheldon each one share of Liberty

Cotton Mill stock. The remainder I give to my father D. H. Templeton and my mother S. E. Templeton. I appoint my father D. H. Templeton executor. Dated 31 Dec. 1902. Wit: Willie B. Glenn, N.P., W. C. O'Dell, N.P.C., S. D. Stewart. Signed: F. E. Templeton. Filed 4 Aug. 1903.

TERRELL

William H. Terrell. Deed from William H. Terrell. Pack 228 #1. Clerk of Court Office. Pickens, S. C. Deed from William H. Terrell to John Fields, Sr. Both of Pendleton Dist. Dated 1 April 1814. In consideration of $800.00 paid my John Fields Sr. have granted, bargained, sold and released a tract of land containing 500 acres, being part of two tracts, as shows from former deeds made from Charles Lay to G. W. Terrell and William H. Terrell on the waters of 12 mile creek. Wit: Bailey Barton, William R. Cochran. Signed: Wm. H. Terrell. On the 15 Jan. 1814. Cynthia Terrell the wife of William H. Terrell, relinquished all rights to dower on the above land. Before Joseph Davis, J.P. Deed proven on oath of Bailey Barton before JNO. Cochran. Dated 1 April 1814. Recorded 25 Oct. 1814.

Moses Terrell. Estate of Moses Terrell. Box 13 #171. Probate Judge Office. Pickens, S. C. Est. admr. 25 Nov. 1845 by Ebenezer P. Verner, Wm. C. Lee, Lemuel H., Samuel P. Verner, Andrew Jenkins who are bound unto Wm. D. Steele, Ord. in the sum of $25,000.00. Left widow Mary Terrell and 10 chn. viz; W. W. Mitchell and wife, Clark, Wm. G., John T., Solomon D., Julia Ann, Moses A., Lucy Ann Terrell, E. A. Mitchell and wife, John M. Coffee and wife. Julia Ann Terrell was dead, when settlement was made 1 Jan. 1847. Lucy Ann married a Dendy in 1867.

Terrell Minors. Box 3 #74. In Equity. Clerk of Court Office. Pickens, S. C. On 23 June 1852 Wm. L. Keith, James Robertson, Samuel Reid, are bound unto Miles M. Norton, Clk. of Equity. in the sum of $3,200.00. Wm. L. Keith gdn. for John T. Terrell, Solomon Terrell minors over 14 years. Chn. of Moses Terrell decd.

THACKER

Martin Thacker. Estate of Martin Thacker. Box 90 Pack 2233. Probate Judge Office. Abbeville, S. C. Where as William F. Baker has made suit to me for letter of admr. of the est. of Martin Thacker decd. dated 1 July 1835. Citation published at Cokeberry Camp Meeting. 2 Aug. 1835. Henry Bass M.G. Admr. bond was given 3 Aug. 1835 for William F. Baker, Joseph T. Baker, John C. Livingston, William F. Baker is admr. for the estate. An inventory was made 18 Aug. 1835 by Henry Brooks, Christian Barnes, Ezl. Gunnin. No heirs given.

Isaac Thacker. Estate of Isaac Thacker. Box 91 Pack 2239. Probate Judge Office. Abbeville, S. C. I Isaac Thacker of Abbeville Dist. being sick but of sound mind and memory do make this my last will and testament. I desire my just debts be paid. I give to my grand children the chn. of my dtr. Nancy one dollar to be equally divided between them. I give to my children viz; Betey, Cathin, Mary, Rachel, Peggy, Rosey Ann, Isaac, Sally, Jency, William Lesley and Jemimey one dollar each to be paid one year after my decd. The remainder of my property to be equally divided between my four youngest children. If my wife should die suddenly without making a will, it is my desire that my property be put into four equal lots and I give to my dtr. Sally two lots and my chn. viz; Jencey and Jemimey the other two lots. Dated 29 Dec. 1811. Wit: Wm. Lesly, Andrew McAlister, Joseph Johnston. Signed: Isaac Thacker. Will prove on oath of Joseph Johnston before Talo. Livingston, Ord. Dated 11 Feb. 1812. Inventory made on the 14 Feb. 1812. By Nathl. Bailey, Joseph Johnston, John X Perry.

THAYER

Daniel Thayer. On 8 July 1844 Daniel Thayer appointed a Constable of
Pickens Dist. Ref. Pack 634 #166. Clerk of Court Office. Pickens,
S. C.

THOMAS

John Thomas. Will of John Thomas. Book C Page 15-16. Probate Judge
Office. Greenville, S. C. I John Thomas being tho aged and infirm
in body, yet of sound understanding mind and memory. I will my just
debts be paid. I give to my son John Thomas Jr. thirty dollars as his
share. To the three daughters of my son Robert (who is dead) I give
twenty dollars each. To my dtr. Martha wife of Josiah Culbertson, I
give fifty dollars. To my dtr. Anne wife of Joseph McJinkins, I give
my negro woman Rose, to the children of my dtr. Lettice Lusk, I give one
hundred dollars equally divided. To my dtr. Jean wife of Joseph McCool,
I give fifty dollars. To my son William D. Thomas, I give my two negroes
men, viz; Sharper and March. To my dtr. Esther wife to Robert Carter,
I give twenty five dollars her full share. To John Thomas son of my
son Robert, I give one cow and calf over and above what he has received
already. To my grand daughters Anne Thomas and Lettice Lusk, I give
each one cow and calf and if the est. will admit of a small legacy to
them on a final settlement I am agreed and wish it. My negroe woman
Moll and her children viz; Frank, Seeboo, Ben, Edmond, Rose, Will,
Charles and Sinda. (If I gain the suit in the Court of Equity that is
about them) I give to my dtr. Anne McJunkin and my son Wm. D. Thomas
equally. I appoint my son Wm. D. Thomas and son in law Joseph McJunkin,
my executors. Dated 18 April 1811. Wit: Joel Graves, Thomas W. Mitchell, James Smith. Signed: John Thomas. A codicil was added on the
2 May 1811 that gives son Wm. D. Thomas my land not here to for conveyed
with all household and kitchen furniture. Will probated 7 April 1814.

Joshua Thomas. Deed from Joshua Thomas. Pack 382 #15. Clerk of Court
Office. Pickens, S. C. From Joshua Thomas to James E. Hagood both of
Pickens Dist. In consideration of $500.00. Have granted, bargained,
sold, released into James E. Hagood all that tract of land lying and
being on the waters of 12 Mile River and on both sides of the main road
leading from Col. B. Hagood to Mrs. Barton, agreeable to a plat made
by A. H. Archer for 215 acres. Adj. lands of James Lewis, Col. Benjamin
Hagood and Mary J. Barton. Dated 18 March 1860. Wit: James Hagood,
Joseph Masingill. Signed: Joshua Thomas. Proven on oath of Joseph
Masingill before J. E. Hagood, C.C.P. on the 18 March 1860.

Bryant Thomas. Will of Bryant Thomas. Box 24 #287. Probate Judge
Office. Pickens, S. C. I Bryant Thomas being of sound and disposing
mind and memory, but weak in body, etc. I desire my just debts be paid
from the first money come into the hands of my executor. I give to my
beloved wife Ritchel Thomas (items named) household, kitchen furniture,
and plantation tools and stock. No children ment. Dated 19 Dec. 1850.
Wit: Robert Stewart, Matthew Vickery, Richard X Dodson. Signed: Bryant
X Thomas. Proven 6 Jan. 1851. On another paper Expend; Paid Rachel and
Ann Thomas $15.10 1/2.

Isaac Thomas. Estate of Isaac Thomas. Box 8 #97. Probate Judge Office.
Pickens, S. C. Est. admr. 26 Feb. 1838 by Martha, Lemuel Thomas, Wm. K.
Alexander, W. L. Keith who are bound unto James H. Dendy, Ord. in the sum
of $6,000.00.

Martha Thomas. Estate of Martha Thomas. Box 75 #804. Probate Judge
Office. Pickens, S. C. Est. admr. 4 April 1864 by Lemuel Thomas,
John Price, Andrew J. Anderson who are bound unto W. E. Holcombe, Ord.
in the sum of $2,000.00.

Leander Thomas. Note on Leander Thomas. Pack 289 #3. Clerk of Court
Office. Pickens, S. C. Leander Thomas mentioned as the husband of

Sarah Thomas in 1861.

Mary Ann Thomas. Estate of Mary Ann Thomas. Pack 408. Clerk of Court Office. Abbeville, S. C. In 1857 Dr. F. G. Thomas was gdn. of his daughter Mary Ann Thomas. Expend. 1 June 1847 recd. from William Chiles exor of Richard White $59.15. 19 Nov. 1845 recd. from L. White admr. of Nancy Coleman personal estate $486.80. Recd. from Wm. Waller by L. White admr. of George White $557.20. Recd. from John White Admr. of Wm. Bullock, ward share of grandfather real estate $901.81. In 1848 Mary Ann Thomas had intermarried with John W. Suber.

George Thomas. Deed from George Thomas. Pack 382 #20. Clerk of Court Office. Pickens, S. C. Deed from George Thomas to John W. Bagwell both of Pickens Co., dated 24 Dec. 1855. In considerationof $90.00... have sold, granted, bargained and released unto John W. Bagwell all the one half of a certain tract of land whereon said George Thomas now lives and whereon Joshua Thomas also now lives, lying on the waters of 12 Mile River, adj. land of Mrs. Jane Barton, James Lewis, Col. E. Alexander, Col. Benjamin Hagood. Containing 215 acres, land known as the Jacob Guerin tract. Wit: J. E. Hagood, George Rewin. Signed: George Thomas.

Lemuel Thomas. Estate. Box 3 #143. Probate Judge Office. Pickens, S. C. On 1 July 1904 W. E. Herd recd. from D. A. Herd $26.05 his part of the estate of Lemuel Thomas decd.

Elizabeth Thomas. Note on Elizabeth Thomas. Will #28. Probate Judge Office. Edgefield, S. C. Elizabeth Thomas was a dtr. of Caroline McDaniel whose will was recorded in 1878 in Edgefield County, S. C.

James Thomas. Estate of James Thomas. Book A page 38. Probate Judge Office. Union, S. C. I James Thomas being sick and weak in body but of perfect mind and memory. My desire that my loving wife (not named) to enjoy the plantation and all my personal and moveable estate during her widowhood and to raise up my chn. and school them. If my wife marry my land to be equally divided between my chn. with my wife taking a child part. I appoint my friend William Thomas and Rubin Wilks executors. Dated 26 Sept. 1787. Wit: William Williams, James X Tate. Recorded 7 April 1795. An inventory was made 10 July 1795 by Wm. Sims, Wm. Johnson. Negores named, James, Patt and one child, Juda and three children, Lette and one child, Will.

THOMASSON

Jane Thomasson. Note on Jane Thomasson. Will #23. Probate Judge Office. York Dist., S. C. Jane Thmasson recd. $1.00 in 1841 from the will of Elizabeth Neely of York Dist. William P. Thomasson was a witness to will.

THOMBS

Samuel Thombs. Estate of Samuel Thombs. Box 7 #85. Probate Judge Office. Pickens, S. C. Est. admr. 27 Feb. 1836 by Alexander Bryce, Wm. Perkinson, Sterling Garner who are bound unto James H. Dendy, Ord. in the sum of $300.00. On bond Samuel Thombs was formerly of Pendleton Dist. who died in Texas. Sale held 14 March 1836. Buyers: Rebeckah, William Thombs, etc. Citation published at Perkins Creek Meeting House.

THOMPSON

Peggy Thompson. Estate of Peggy Thompson. Pack 397. Clerk of Court Office. Abbeville, S. C. On 8 June 1818 Elijah Foster, Esq., Robert Foster and Ebenzer Foster of Abbeville Dist. were bound unto John

McComb Esq. Comms. in Equity in the sum of $1,000. Wherefor Elijah
Foster was appointed guardian of Peggy Thompson a minor under 21 years of
age.

John Thompson. Will of John Thompson. Will Book 1791-1803. Page 31-
32. Ordinary's Office. Elbert Co., Georgia. I John Farly Thompson of
Elbert Co., State of Ga. Being in a low state of health and weak in
body but of perfect mind and memory, etc. I will all my just debts and
funeral expenses be paid out of my est. I desire that my negro wench
named Peg and my riding horse, and crop of tabocca be sold at Petersburgh at the highest bidder, profits arising from said sale be divided
between John, Isham, Peter, Sally, Mary, Mily and Tabby. I give to
my son William Thompson one hundred acres of land, whereon he now lives.
Also negroes, Frank, Ivey, Nancy. I give to my son Robert Thompson all
that tract of land whereon he now lives, containing 300 acres. Also the
negro boy now in his possession named James. I give to my dtr. Milly
Ragland a negro named Silas now in her possession. I give to my son
Farley Thompson that part of my land on Butrams Creek, lying West and
N. West of Harris Nunneler and William Thompson, Sr. Also one negro
named Isaac, one bay horse Buck, half of my stock of hogs, household
and kitchen furniture. I give to my son Lewis Bevel Thompson, all that
tract of land on Butrams Creek whereon John Norris now lives not already
given to son William, also one negro named Julias and half of my stock
of cattle, hogs and household and kitchen firniture. I give to my sons
Farley and Lewis Bevel Thompson all my debts due and open accounts,
and they shall pay all my just debts out of what I have given them. I
appoint my sons Farley Thompson and Lewis Bevel Thompson executors.
Dated 3 Sept. 1792. Wit: Robert Thompson, Sr., William Thompson, Sr.,
Stephen Ellington. Signed: John F. X Thompson. Recorded 5 Feb. 1793.

Robert Thompson, Duel. Pack 226 #9. Clerk of Court Office. Pickens,
S. C. On 26 April 1860 Placidia Adams made oath that Robert A. Thompson and Warren R. Mashall are engaged in or about to engage in a duel
to be fought on or about the 27 April 1860.

Joshua Thompson. Estate of Joshua Thompson. Book 1 #1 and Book 1 Page
8. Probate Judge Office. Pickens, S. C. Est. admr. 5 Oct. 1829. His
wife Mary and a son James Thompson was granted letter of admr. on 25
March 1829. But on 5 Oct. 1829 James Durham, Joel Morton and James
Thompson were the admr. Owned 212 acres on 12 Mile River, bounded by
land of Daniel Durham, Levi Murphrey, B. Barton. Left 10 chn. viz.
James Thompson, Winney wife of Samuel Smith, heirs of John Thompson
decd., Jane the wife of Jonathan Gregory, Elijah Thompson, Charlotte
Thompson, Mary Thompson, Louisa Thompson, Ethalind Thompson, William
Thompson. On 7 Feb. 1831 Elijah Thompson a minor son over 14 appointed
James H. Dendy his guardian. On 9 Oct. 1829 Jones Evatt and wife Mary
of Pickens Dist. in consideration of $50.00 paid by James Thompson, do
grant, sell, release unto James Thompson a tract of land living and being
on the waters of Wolf Creek waters of 12 Mile River, being part of the
land which fell to the widow of Joshua Thompson decd.

Charles Thompson. Estate of Charles Thompson. Box 105 #1102. Probate
Judge Office. Pickens, S. C. Charles Thompson estate was admr. on 6
Dec. 1873 in Pickens Dist.

Ranson Thompson. Estate of Ranson Thompson. Box 119 #8. Probate Judge
Office. Pickens, S. C. Est. admr. 29 Sept. 1891. By Robert A.
Thompson, James E. Hagood, R. A. Bowen. Summons for relief mentions
John W. F. Thompson, Rebecca M. Grant, R. A. Thompson, against George
McD. Thompson, S. Francis Hamilton, Charles Neal, Silas M. Neal, John
W. Neal, the heirs at law of Abbie Dean decd. names and resident unknown.
The hiers of Dempsey Thompson unknown, the heirs of Rebecca Evatt,
unknown. (from loose papers). On 20 Nov. 1838 James H. Dendy promised
to pay John L. Thompson (son of Fleming) $2.72 due him under the will
of his grandfather Eli Davis.

Adam Thompson. Estate of Adam Thompson. Box 30 #361. Probate Judge
Office. Pickens, S. C. Adam Thompson of Pickens Dist. owned 260 acres
lying on Gregory Creek. In Sept. 1844 Susan Sanders his daughter and

Adam Heath Thompson legal heirs of the said Adam Thompson were residing in Hall Co., Ga.

John Thompson. Estate of John Thompson. Pack 4057. Clerk of Court Office. Abbeville, S. C. In Equity, To the Honr. Chancellors: Your orator James Huey and Polly his wife complaining that in the year 18__ John Thompson departed this life, having first made and executed his last will and testament, who devised considerable real and personal property to his wife Sarah Thompson who has since intermarried with John Ramey of this Dist. and his children to wit: Polly Thompson who has married James Huey, Jane who has married Samuel S. Baker, William Thompson, Jason Thompson, Samuel Thompson, Elvira Thompson, which Jason, Samuel and Elvira Thompson are minors over the age of 14 years, and Julia Thompson a minor under the age of fourteen. In said will wife Sarah Executrix and William McMullin and William H. Caldwell his executors, and that William Caldwell is now the only acting executor. Leaving his wife Sarah the plantation where on he lived, with negroes, Molly and child named Miney, two horse, also other stock as she may choose with plantation tools and household and kitchen furniture, and as much from the present crop to maintain the family and use in schooling the children. If necessary to let the negroes out to rent, or sell some at public sale. If the wife remarry she is to get only a child share after sale of the whole estate. John Ramey and wife Sarah made a deed of gift on the 31 Dec. 1825 and recorded 6 Feb. 1826 for 300 acres lying on Little River, adj. land of James Huey and others, the said land is entirely insufficient to support the family. Filed 15 June 1829.

Robert Thompson. Estate of Robert Thompson. Pack 3584. Clerk of Court Office. Abbeville, S. C. Ninety Six Dist., S. C. In Equity. To the Honr. the Judge of Equity. Your Orator and Oratrix, Thomas T. Thompson, Robert Thompson, Elizabeth Thompson, Sarah Thompson, and Margaret Thompson, children and co heirs of Robert Thompson decd., infants under the age of twenty one years. By Elijah Foster their next friend. That Robert Thompson departed this life about the ___ 1806 leaving the widow Margret Thompson. That on ___ 1806 the widow Margret Thompson and a certain Samuel Thompson procured a letter of admr. of the personal estate, the sale of personal effects amounted to over three thousand dollars, of which your orator and oratrix are entitled to a two third part. Your orator sheweth that Margaret Thompson the widow intermarried with one Newell Scott, which after the marriage the widow is entitled to a child share. Your orator sheweth that Newell Scott has entered upon and possessed himself with the whole of the monies from the personal est. of their father and still threatens to dispose of and squander the balance. Filed 28 March 1818.

Thompson Chart. This chart is the line of a Robert Thompson, B. & M. in Ireland died in 1772 Abbeville Dist., S. C. Married Mary Doris B:N. Ireland, Died 1779 in Abbeville Dist. chn. William, Robert, Mary, Elizabeth, Archibald, Moses, James, John Porter, Millie. The son John Porter Thompson born 24 April 1767. Abbeville Dist. Married Mary Glasgow. She married a Gibson after the death of J. P. T. Their chn. were; James, Mary, Samuel Glasgow and Betsy. His brother Archibald and James moved to Illinois in 1804. Samuel Glasgow Thompson born 7 April 1799, married 23 Dec. 1819 in Ranndolph Co., Ill. to Mary Ann Crozier, she born 24 Aug. 1797, in Abbeville, S. C. died 5 May 1853 near Evansville, Ill. Chart in Miss Youngs notes.

THOMSON

Elizabeth Thomson. Pack 439 #4. Clerk of Court Office. Pickens, S. C. To any lawful Constable, Whereas Elizabeth Thomson a single woman hath on her examination taken in writing before me declareth that on the 1 Jan. last past (1829) at Flanders Thomsons in said Dist. was delivered of a female child, and that the said child is likely to become chargeable to the Dist. and hath charged Hiram Gibson of said Dist. with having gotten her with child. I do therefor command you to apprehend the said Hiram

Gibson and bring him before me or some other Justice of said Dist. to
find security for his appearance at the next general sessions of the
peace. There to abide and perform such orders as shall be made in
persuance of an act of Assembly entitled an act against bastardly.
Dated 4 Sept. 1829. Signed: James Looper.

THORNLEY

John L. Thornley. Estate of John L. Thornley. Box 135 #10. Probate
Judge Office. Pickens, S. C. Est. admr. 5 Nov. 1900 by L. C. Thornley,
J. McD. Bruce, Earnest Folger who are bound unto J. B. Newberry, Ord.
in the sum of $2,000.00. Heirs, Ernest Thornley, N. E. Thornley, John
L. Thornley, Bertram K. Thornley, Meline Thornley, Rachel Seabrook,
Elizabeth E. White, Oliva A. Oliver. Died 19 Sept. 1900.

THRIFT

Elizabeth Thrift. Estate of Elizabeth Thrift. Box 13 #171. Probate
Judge Office. Pickens, S. C. Est. admr. 1 April 1845 by Allen Thrift,
Samuel Moseley, Alexander Bryce who are bound unto Wm. D. Steele, Ord.
in the sum of $100.00. On 29 Nov. 1845 appeared Narcissa P. Thrift and
made oath that John Thrift and Elizabeth his wife decd. stands indebted
to her.

TIDWELL

Elizabeth Tidwell. Power of Attorney. Pack 228 #14. Clerk of Court
Office, Pickens, S. C. State of Arkansas, White County. We Elizabeth
Tidwell late (Elizabeth Caradine) with her husband James Tidwell, have
this day appointed Thomas W. White of the County of Desoto, State of
Miss. our true and lawful attorney in fact and in law for us in our room
and stead to have, demand, recover from Robert A. Thompson Commissioner
in Equity of Pickens Dist., S. C. Our share of the proceeds of the real
estate of Thomas Caradine grandfather (of said Elizabeth Tidwell) now
decd. To sign, seal and receipt etc. Dated 15 Feb. 1859. Wit: J. J.
Bailey, P. E. Tidwell. Signed: Elizabeth X Tidwell and James Tidwell.

TOLBERT

James Tolbert. Estate of James Tolbert. Pack 306. In Equity. Clerk
of Court Office. Abbeville, S. C. Abbeville Dist. To the Honr. the
Chancellors: Your oratirx the relict of James Tolbert decd. complained
that on 21 Aug. 1853 James Tolbert departed this life intestate, sezied
and possessed with tracts of land, one lying on the waters of Curltil
Creek containing 275 acres, adj. land of James Martin, Louisa Logan,
Ephraim Davis, on which tract said James Tolbert lived at the time of
his death. Leaving his widow, and chn. John H. Tolbert, Mary Isabella
wife of John F. H. Davis, Nancy Jane wife of James W. Buchanan, William
K. Tolbert and Joseph Marshall Tolbert, minor under the age of 21 years.
and Levi Strawhorn who married Martha Rebecca, dtr. of James Tolbert
decd. who died on the 2 Aug. 1853 leaving an only child named William
H. Strawhorn which child has died since the death of its grandfather
James Tolbert decd. Your oratrix believes that it would be in the
interest of all if the real estate be partition. Filed 17 Nov. 1853.

James P. Tolbert. Petition to be Released. Pack 186. Clerk of Court
Office. Abbeville, S. C. Abbeville Dist. To the Honr. the Chancellors
The petition of James P. Tolbert sheweth that s writ De Lunatic issued
from the Court of Common Pleas, that in pursuance of said writ Rachel
Tolbert was found to be an idiot, that your petitioner was appointed by

order of the Court of Equity Committee for said idiot in 1854. Your petitioner has in his hand $1,100.00 belonging to said idiot, and said Rachel Tolbert has another $1,100.00 left by her mother to William Tolbert in trust, the said William is now dead and his executors Thomas Riley and J.F. Tolbert still hold that portion left by her mother. By an order of the Chancellor Wardlaw to appropriate the interest accuring on both sums, as would give an annual amount of $140.00 enough for attention and board to said Rachel. Your petitioner expects to leave for the West soon, and has left said Rachel in charge of her sister Mary Riley who has consented to take charge of her. Therefore your petitioner prays to be released from charge. Filed 3 Nov. 1857.

<u>Daniel Talbert</u>. Estate of Daniel Talbert. Pack 3338. Clerk of Court Office. Abbeville, S. C. In Equity. To the Honr. Chancellors; Your orator and oratrixes, Mary Talbert, James Talbert, William Talbert, Andrew Riley and Mary his wife, nee Mary Talbert a str. of Dan Talbert, James P. Martin and Ellender his wife a dtr. of Dan, Vachel Hughey and Anna his wife a dtr. of Dan, and Rachel Talbert. That Dan Talbert late of Abbeville Dist. departed this life intestate on __ Oct. 1840 seized and possessed with two tracts of land on the head waters of Curltail Creek, one containing 300 acres, the other 210 acres, adj. land of James Y. Jones, Samuel Jenkins, Thomas Riley. Others heirs are John Talbert of Cowetee Co., Ga. and his children and Margaret Hall and Mary Hall of Newberry Dist. Chn. of Elizabeth Hall decd. grand children of said intestate and Nancy Livingston (formerly Nancy Wilson) who married John Livingston and Martha Wilson children of Jane Wilson decd. formerly Jane Talbert, and grandchn. of said intestate, also of Newberry Dist. Your orator and oratrixes desire partition of the said land. Filed 8 March 1843.

TRAMMELL

<u>Thomas Trammell</u>. Will of Thomas Trammell. Box 50 #551. Probate Judge Office. Pickens, S. C. I Thomas Trammell being of sound mind and memory, etc. I desire that after my decd. that my wife Racheal Trammel and my son B. E. W. Trammel shall pay my debts and funeral expenses, I desire that my son B. E. W. Trammel have fifty acres of land run off the West side of the tract whereon I now live, bounded by J. A. Ballengers line to Elender McCoy line. I desire that my wife Rachael have all remaining land whereon I now reside, with my chattle property, cattle hogs, horses, sheep, also my household and kitchen furniture, and farming tools, and that my wife remain unmolested on the premises that is to be her home during her life time. I also desire that my dtrs. M. C. and A. L. Trammel have a home on the premises while they remain single. I desire also that after my wife death that my youngest son Thomas Oliver Trammel shall heir all the above mentioned property, that was left to his mother. Also my son B. W. Trammel shall assist his mother in business and helpful to her in her efforts to make a comfortable support. I hereby appoint my wife Racheal Trammel executrix Dated 26 March 1859. Wit: J. A. Ballenger, T. A. Rogers, Gideon Ellis? Signed: Thomas Trammel X his mark. Proven 1 Aug. 1859.

TRIMMIER

<u>Col. Obadiah Trimmier</u>. Estate of Col. Obadiah Trimmier. Pack 31 #6. Clerk of Court Office. Pickens, S. C. Col. Obadiah Trimmier died in 1830. Owned a total 956 acres of land, 200 acres bought from P. Carpenter, 25 acres bought from James Doran, 431 acres bought from Henry Dodson, 300 acres bought from John Nichols. He resided on Toxaway Creek waters of Tugaloo River. Left a widow, Lucy Trimmier. Whereby the premises desended in right of their wives. Oliver Clarke and wife Elizabeth, Staret Dodson and wife Mary, James Blair and wife Arrina, George Blair and wife Maria, Jefferson Roland and wife Lucy, Thomas Trimmier, William Trimmier and Selena Trimmier, David Sloan and wife

Nancy and two minor chn. Obadiah Trimmier and Marcus T. Trimmier, minors over 14 years. Dated 4 Oct. 1830.

TRAINUM

Willis Trainum. Estate of Willis Trainum. Box 105 #1098. Probate Judge Office. Pickens, S. C. Est. admr. 12 Nov. 1873 by Jeremiah Trainum, B. F. Morgan who are bound unto I. H. Philpot, Ord. in the sum of $50.00. Jeremiah Trainum petitioner against John Trainum, Anne Bradley, Wm. Bradley, George W. Trainum, Mary Norris, Catharine Trainum. Died 24 Sept. 1873 owned 100 acres adj. land of Est. of Robert Latham decd., James McAdams, Sr. decd. Harvey C. Hunt decd. and others. Chn. of Jeremiah Trainum, Anne Bradley wife of Wm. Bradley of N. C., Mary wife of Absolum Norris decd., Geo. Trainum, John Trainum, Catharine Trainum of Pickens Dist. Miss Elvira Trainum lived with her uncle John Trainum 4 years and 9 months and dtr. of Mrs. Catharine Trainum.

John Trainum. Estate of John Trainum. Box 110 #1053. Probate Judge Office. Pickens, S. C. Est. admr. 28 Nov. 1876 by George McAdams, James McAdams who are bound unto I. H. Philpot, Ord. in the sum of $300.00. Catharine Trainum and Elvira Trainum bought at sale.

George Trainum. Estate of George Trainum. Box 94 #995. Probate Judge Office. Pickens, S. C. On 1 Oct. 1884, J. J. Lewis admr. Died more than 6 months ago.

Jeremiah Trainum. Will of Jeremiah Trainum. Box 127 #8. Probate Judge Office. Pickens, S. C. I Jeremiah Trainum being of sound mind and memory, etc. First I desire my lawful debts be paid and discharged. I give to my beloved wife M. J. Trainum one third of my real estate during her natural life, and after her death be sold by my executor and divided between my bodily heirs. I also give to my wife M. J. Trainum one third of my personal property. Also I devise that two thirds of my real estate to stand unsold and rented until James A. Trainum son of John M. Trainum decd. arrives to the age of twenty one years. I devise the two thirds of my real estate be sold after the said James A. Trainum is of age, or to be sold at his decd. if before he is full age, and after paying all expenses the remainder to be divided between my heirs. I appoint W. M. Trainum and William W. Roper executors. Dated 1 May 1889. W. N. Hughes, J. S. Williams, T. T. Hughes, all of Loopers in Pickens Dist. Signed: Jeremiah X Trainum. He added a codicill on the 6 June 1891. "I have revoked the appointment of W. M. Trainum as one of my executor and do now therefore appoint N. H. Jones to be one of my executor in his stead..." Wit: W. N. Hughes, John O. Sheck, T. T. Hughes. He died 6 Feb. 1897. Filed 22 Feb. 1897.

Catherine Trainum. Will of Catherine Trainum. Box 127 #3. Probate Judge Office. Pickens, S. C. I, Catherine Trainum, being of sound mind and memory, etc. I will my estate real and personal or mixed to my beloved daughter Elviry Trainum. I appoint my said dtr. Elvira Trainum to be my executrix. Dated 12 Sept. 1896. Wit: John W. Thomas, S. P. Hinton, B. O. or C. Jones. Signed: Catherine X Trainum. Filed 28 Oct. 1896.

THREADAWAY

John C. Treadaway. Deed from John C. Treadaway. Pack 211 #11. Probate Judge Office. Pickens, S. C. I, John Chapman of Cherokee Co., State of Ala. In consideration of $200.00 paid by Benjamin Chapman for the use and benefit of John C. Treadway and Rebecca his wife and William S. Post and Elizabeth his wife. Have granted, sold, bargain, and released unto Benjamin Chapman all the rights titles and interest the real estate of James Chapman decd. It being two ninths part after deducting the one third part of the tract of land James Chapman was seized and possessed containing 256 acres, land adj. Thomas Hallum, James Garner lying on 18 mile Creek. Dated 2 Feb. 1841. Wit: F. N. Garvin, Daniel J. Chapman. Signed by John Chapman atty for John C. Chapman and Rebecca his wife, William S. Post and Elizabeth is wife. Another deed made by James Chapman of Pickens Dist. for the sum of $100.00 paid by Benjamin Chapman have sold and transferred all rights, titles and interest in and to the real estate of James Chapman decd. It being one ninth part of the two third part. Dated 2 Feb. 1841. Wit: F. N. Garvin, Daniel J. Chapman. Signed: James Chapman. Proved 31 Aug. 1841.

TRIMBLE

James Trimble. Estate of James Trimble. Box 92 #2268. Probate Judge Office. Abbeville, S. C. Abbeville Dist. Admr. bond: We Esther Trimble (widow), John Hamilton of (Savannah), and Alexander Clarke, Jr. are bound unto the Judge of said Dist. in the sum of $2,000.00. Dated 27 March 1797. The condition of the above obligation is such that if the above bound Esther Trimble admor. of the goods and chattles of James Trimble.(her son) decd. do make a true and perfect inventory. etc. Wit: James Wardlaw. Signed: Esther X Trimble, Jno. Hamilton, Alexander Clarke. Recorded 27 March 1797.

Esther Trimble. Will of Esther Trimble. Box 92 Pack 2290. Probate Judge Office. Abbeville, S. C. I Esther Trimble of Abbeville Dist. widow being sick and weak in body, but of sound and disposing mind and memory, etc. I will my just debts and funeral expenses be paid. I give to my son John Trimble my tract of land containing 18 acres, on the following conditions, viz; that he pay to my dtr. Esther Smith five dollars for each acre of land, also ninety dollars for a horse he put to his own use, belonging to the estate. If he refuse to pay the above sum of money to my dtr. Then I give to my dtr. the above mentioned tract of land. I give to my dtrs. Sarah Shannon and Esther Smith my cupboard and furniture, bed and beding cloath to be equally divided between them. It is my will that my negro woman Suckey be sold and one hundred dollars of her price be given to my son Joseph Trimble. The residue of her price be given to my dtr. Sarah Shannon. My negro woman Nancey was given in deed of gift by my mother, to my son John and dtr. Esther to be equally divided between them at my death. I appoint my son John Trimble and son in law Robert Smith executors. Dated 13 Nov. 1818. Wit: Thos. Finley, Fras. Mitchel, William Clark. Signed: Esther X Trimble. Will proved on oath of Francis Mitchel before Moses Taggart, Ord. on the 26 April 1819.

TRIPP

Elizabeth Tripp. Pack 650 #7. Clerk of Court Office. Pickens, S. C. Sarah Elizabeth Tripp of Pickens Dist. charged George W. Davenport as being the father of a male bastard child that was born to her on 9 June 1855.

TODD

John Todd. Deed from John Todd. Deed Book C Page 382. Clerk of Court Office. Anderson, S. C. This deed made between John Todd and Adam Todd both of Pendleton Dist. Dated 13 March 1797. In consideration of thirty three pds. sterling, hath bargained, sold and released unto Adam Todd all that tract of land containing 100 acres, being part of a tract containing 200 acres granted unto Patrick Forbush the 15 March 1787. Lying on Hencoop Creek waters of Great Rockey Creek. Vacant land on all sides when surveyed. Wit: Elisha Bennett, Jenny Todd, Sarah Bennett. Signed: John Todd. Proved on oath of Elisha Bennett before William Hall, J.P. on the 25 July 1797.

Adam Todd. Deed to Adam Todd. Deed Book M Page 271. Clerk of Court
Office. Anderson, S. C. Deed from Arnsterd Carder to Adam Todd both
of Pendleton Dist. Dated 12 Nov. 1813. In consideration of $215.00
paid by Adam Todd have bargained, sold, and released all that tract of
land containing 206 acres on a branch of Hencoop Creek waters of Rockey
River. Originally granted to John Jackson on the 5 March 1787. Adj.
lands of Adam Todd, Hugh Wordlaw, Major Lewis, Austen Mayfield. Wit:
Stephen Bennett, Allen Dowdle. Signed: Armsterd X Carder. On the
26 Feb. 1814 Margret Carder wife of Arnsterd Carder did renounce,
release and relinquish all rights to her dower on the above land.
Before Hezekiah Rice, J.P.

Adam Todd. Deed to Adam Todd. Deed Book L, page 234. Clerk of Court
Office. Anderson, S. C. Deed from Joseph Thompson of Jackson Co., Ga.
to Adam Todd of Pendleton Dist. S. C. Dated 11 March 1811. In
consideration of $200.00 have granted, bargained, sold and released unto
Adam Todd all that tract of land containing 400 acres on the North Fork
of Cane Creek waters of Savannah River, being part of a tract containing
440 acres originally granted for Dudley Pruitt and granted to James
Hughes and conveyed by Sheriff title as the property to Thomas Collins,
conveyed from Collins to Joseph Thompson. Adj. lands of Philip Cox,
Solomon West, Isaac Gray, John Wright and Thomas Collins. Wit: W. Brown
Jonathan Reeves. Proven on oath of Jonathan Reeves on the 11 March
1811 before W. Brown. Recorded 10 Dec. 1811.

Archibald Todd. Deed to Archibald Todd. Deed Book U Page 218. Clerk
of Court Office. Anderson, S. C. I, James McKinney, Sheriff of
Anderson Dist. Whereas by virtue of Fieri Facias (an execution to be
levied on the goods of a detor) issued from the Court of Common Pleas
held in Anderson Dist. on the 15 March 1832 at the suit of Van A. Lawhon
to me. commanding that the goods and chattles of George R. Lewis to
levy the sum of twenty nine dollars and 75 cents, with interest from 3
Feb. 1832. I have taken the land and tenements of said George R. Lewis
a lot in the village of Anderson adj. land owned by John Archer, known
as lot #9 and #30 and has been exposed to public sale and purchased by
Archibald Todd of the Dist. of Anderson in the sum of $18.00 being the
highest bidder. Dated 15 Jan. 1834. Wit: John Bruce, George E. W.
Foster. Signed: James McKinney, S.A.D. Proven on oath of George E. W.
Foster, beofre Van A. Lawhorn Clk. as is Registered and recorded,
examined and certified for the 16 June 1834.

Archibald Todd. Deed from Archibald Todd. Deed Book X Page 335. Clerk
of Court Office. Anderson Dist., S. C. Deed from Archibald Todd to
William Gilliam Woodward both of Anderson Dist., S. C. Dated 2 Dec.
1839. In consideration of $75.00 have granted, sold and released unto
William Woodward two lots in the village of Anderson #9 and #30. Wit:
F. Rice, J. Warnock Jr. Signed: Archibald Todd. Proven on oath of
F. Rice before Elijah Webb Clk. on the 26 May 1842. Recorded same date.

Elizabeth Todd. Estate of Elizabeth Todd. Pack 374. Clerk of Court
Office. Abbeville, S. C. To the Honr. the Chancellors. In Equity.
Your orators and oratrixes, William Eddins, George W. Glenn and Eugenia
A. his wife, William B. Telford and Susan his wife, Winfield Scott and
Julia R. his wife, James Deaving and Mary C. his wife, Mrs. Eddins relict
of James B. Eddins decd., William A. S. Eddins, William E. Glenn, Mary
A. Eddins and James Bolivor Eddins, the last five minors by their gdn.
John G. Wilson all of whom live beyond the limits of this State. B the
will of Mrs. Elizabeth Todd decd., Mary Ann Eddins her dtr. was alive
at her mothers death but is now dead. She left a considerable pecuniary
legacy which at her death has fallen to your orators and oratrixes as
her heirs. They stand in the following relation. Your orator William
Eddins is her surviving husband, Eugenia A. Glenn, Susan F. Telford,
Julia R. Scott and Mary C. Deaving are her dtr. William A. Eddins is
her son, William E. Glenn her grandson the sole offspring of her decd.
dtr. Amanda L. Glenn, Mary A. Eddins and James B. Eddins are her grandchildren, the offspring of her decd. son James Bolivor Eddins. Your
orators and oratrixes sheweth that Mrs. Elizabeth Todd late, departed
this life in the early part of 1855 leaving in full force her last W & T,

which has been probated by William Hill Esq. Ord. of Abbeville, Dist.
Her executors are her son James McCracken and her sons Patrick H.
Eddins and Benjamin F. Eddins. The first two has undertaken the burden
of executing the paper. The Testatrix directed her executors to sell
her freal and personal property and after paying her debts to distribute
her est. among her dtrs. Mary Ann Eddins, Elizabeth Eddins, Harriet
Eddins, Rebecca McCracken, her son James McCracken and her grandson
William Child. The share of dtr. Mary Ann Eddins is vested James
Bolivor Eddins as trustee for her sole and separate use with power to
dispose of it as she may desire, which power Mary Ann Eddins never
exericsed. Your orators sheweth that on the 4 May 1855 came to a
special settlement of the est. with all the legatees, excepting the
minor William Child and paid to each over $3,000 by transferring to them
notes belonging to the estate, to be taken into account when final
settlement is made. Mary Ann Eddins and her trustee James Bolivar
Eddins have both died since the aforesaid partial settlement, and since
said settlement James McCracken on of the executor has become insolvent,
the other executor P. H. Eddins is however --- and has in his hand what
remains of testatrix est. P. H. Eddins and wife Harriet, Benjamin F.
Eddins and wife Elizabeth resides in Alabama. Filed 5 May 1858.

John Todd. Estate of John Todd. Box 54 #587. Probate Judge Office.
Pickens, S. C. Est. admr. 7 May 1860 by Elizabeth Todd, William C.
Todd, James George, James Todd who are bound unto W. E. Holcombe, Ord.
in the sum of $600.00. Buyers at sale, Elizabeth Todd, J. R. Hunnicut,
Samuel R. McFall, John Rankin, James Lee.

Robert Todd. Estate of Robert Todd. Box 66 #709. Probate Judge Office.
Pickens, S. C. Est. admr. 17 Nov. 1862 by Elizabeth Todd, John W. L.
Cary, Madison F. Mitchell who are bound unto W. E. Holcombe, Ord. in
the sum of $700.00. Left a widow and two chn. 21 Sept. 1866 paid
Elizabeth Todd gdn. for the 2 chn. $49.14.

William Todd. Estate of William Todd. Box 67 #725. Probate Judge
Office. Pickens, S. C. Est. admr. 16 Jan. 1863 by David Duncan, David
H. Kennemore, Madison F. Mitchell who are bound unto W. E. Holcombe,
Ord. in the sum of $800.00. Expend, 1 Jan. 1865 recd. for acct. on
Eliza Todd $47.00.

Todd Minors. Box 7 #110. Probate Judge Office. Pickens, S. C. On
6 Oct. 1866 Elizabeth Todd, Nathaniel M. Madden, Frederick N. Garvin
are bound unto W. E. Holcombe, Ord. in the sum of $100.00. Elizabeth
Todd gdn. of John J. and William J. Todd minors under 21 years and chn.
of said Elizabeth Todd. On 28 Dec. 1867 Elizabeth Freeman formerly Todd
the gdn.

Archibald Todd, Admr. Bond. No. 1681. Probate Judge Office. Anderson,
S. C. A petition of A. O. Norris for a letter of admr. on the goods
and chattels of the late Archibald Todd of Anderson Dist. Submitted
17 Dec. 1860. The bond: We A. O. Norris, C. L. Gaillard, J. W. Harrison are bound unto Herbert Hammond, Ord. to make a true and perfect
inventory of the goods and chattels of Archibald Todd. Dated 31 Jan.
1861.

TOWERS

Notes on Towers. Pack 213 #5. Pickens, S. C. On 1 April 1848 Daniel
Pruitt took out a warrant for H. R. Towers for assault for drawing a
knife on him the 18 March last.

Leonard Towers. Warrant. Pack 220 #9. Probate Judge Office. Pickens,
S. C. On 2 Ma7 1859 Leonard Towers took out a peace warrant for Albert
G. Kenady and Loranzo Kenady stating that he has reason to believe that
they will attempt to burn his house.

Henry Trotter. Will of Henry Trotter. Box 65 #698. Probate Judge
Office. Pickens, S. C. I Henry Trotter being of sound and disposing
mind and memory, etc. I desire my executor to pay must just debts and
funeral expenses out of the first money that come unto their hands. Or
sell such property as needed to pay all debts. I give to my wife Susan
Trotter all my property that remains both real and personal for her and
the children support and at her death to be divided among all my childre
I appoint my son Robert Trotter executor. Dated 16 Dec. 1861. Wit:
G. W. Keith, Mangum Compton, Mathew Gillaspie. Signed: Henry Trotter.
Filed 20 Oct. 1862.

John Reid Trotter. Will of John Reid Trotter. Box 83 #878. Probate
Judge Office. Pickens, S. C. I John Reid Trotter now expecting to be
called in the service of my country. After my just debts and funeral
expenses are paid. I will to my wife Sarah Trotter my negro girl Hannah
with all household and kitchen furniture and stock of all kinds. I
will the two tracts of land, one known as the home tract and the other
tract as the Duncan tract to my beloved wife Sarah during her life time
or widowhood, but in case she should see cause to marry or does marry,
I will the above land to my son Josiah Trotter forever. I will and
direct that my son be schooled in good English. I appoint my wife Sarah
executrix and son Josiah my executor. Dated 27 April 1863. Wit:
Anner Lathem, Hames M. Ferguson, J. G. Ferguson. Signed: John Reid
Trotter. Proven 17 May 1864.

Notes on Trotter Family. Box 38 #432. Probate Judge Office. Pickens,
S. C. Griffin Trotter and wife and Henry Trotter and wife recd. shares
from the estate of Moses Hendricks of Pickens Dist. whose est. was admr.
12 Nov. 1855.

Isaiah Trotter. Deed from Isaiah Trotter. Pack 124. Clerk of Court
Office. Pickens, S. C. Deed from Isaiah Trotter to Josiah Trotter
both of Pickens Dist. Dated 7 Oct. 1842. In consideration of $400.00
paid by Josiah Trotter have granted, sold, bargained and released, two
tracts of land, one of fifty acres, another of ten acres, adj. land of
James Ferguson, Binums Line on town creek and muddy branch. Wit:
A. S. Bird, Robert Norris. Signed: Isaiah Trotter. Deed proven on
oath of Robert Norris before William Smith, M.P.D. on the 10 Oct. 1842.
Recorded the same date.

James Trotter. Will of James Trotter, being in feeble health but of
sound mind and memory, etc. I will that all my just debts and funeral
expenses be paid as soon as possible I give to my loving wife Elizabeth
all my real estate, also all rent that is due or may be due from the
lease of my plantation which is leased to my two sons Robert and James
for a term of none years, and my executors are hereby impowered to see
that she receive the same yearly as per their written contract. I also
give to my wife all household and kitchen furniture and all my personal
property or as much as she may need or desire for her support. I also
give to my dtr. Elizabeth Mahaly after the death of my wife all the
household and kitchen furniture, and that she receive the same as the
other chn. as I consider it so much justly due her for service rendered
to myself and her mother. After the death of my wife, except as mentioned above, all real and personal property to be sold and equal
divided between my seven chn. viz; William, Griffin, Henry, Rebecca
Williams, Robert, James, Elizabeth Mahaly. I appoint my sons Griffin
and Robert Trotter executors. Dated 1 Dec. 1851. Wit: Bennett C.
Jones, Samuel Chapman, Joseph B. Reid. Signed: James X Trotter.
Proven 29 March 1852.

Susan Trotter. Estate of Susan Trotter. Box 127 #5. Probate Judge
Office. Pickens, S. C. Est. admr. 25 Feb. 1897 by J. A. Whitmire,
A. K. Edens, S. C. Sutherland are bound unto J. B. Newberry, Ord. in
the sum of $100.00. Died 27 Jan. 1897. J. A. Whitmire a grandson.
29 Oct. 1898 Elizabeth H. Trotter, Rebecca Whitmire, Leuiza E. Fortner,

J. L. Trotter, Rachel M. Howard, Sarah Trotter, J. Thomas Trotter and heirs of James Trotter each recd. share of $2.58 1/2. Paid Nancy Reece, R. G. Trotter, the heirs of Caroline Rogers each $2.58 1/2. Paid William Burgess, Mary Jane Fortner, Elizabeth Fortner, John L. Burgess, Lee Burgess, Mary J. Masters, W. H. Burgess. (loose papers) On 26 Jan. 1859 J. R. Trotter, B. J. Williams, J. E. Hagood, are bound unto Robert A. Tompson in the sum of $800.00. J. R. Trotter gdn. of Arminda Trotter minor under 21 years. John R. Trotter her brother.

G. C. Trotter. Petition of citizens asking lenniecy. State vs. G. C. Trotter. Pack 236 #3. Clerk of Court Office. Pickens, S. C. To Honr. W. F. Ansel: Solicitor of Eight Dist., S. C. We the undersigned citizen of Pickens Co., S. C., most respectfully ask that G. C. Trotter be dealt with as lightly as the law allow. All men err, and are at times liable to do acts for which they will afterward be truly sorry, and now as Mr. Trotter is a young man, and has a young wife to support, and hereby promises to be law abiding ever here after. We earnestly beg you to hear our entreaty. Signed No date or the crime given.

J. H. Miller	W. A. Duncken	McElroy Jamesson
N. Duncan	A. P. Robinson	Riel Barnett
B. H. Williams	W. W. Norris	T. J. Cisson
W. T. Bowen	S. A. Gary	A. J. Barnes
A. A. Simmons	M. Y. Curry	J. T. Hitt
J. Williams	E. T. Taylor	

Susan Trotter. Deed from Susan Trotter. Pack 379 #1. Clerk of Court Office. Pickens, S. C. Deed from Susan Trotter to James W. Friddle both of Pickens, S. C. Dated 29 Aug. 1887. In consideration of $88.00 paid by James W. Friddle have granted, bargained, sold and released a tract of land being part of the Rusk tract, containing 40 acres. No water ways given or adj. lands. Wit: W. U. Hunt, J. L. Trotter. Signed: Susan X Trotter. Proven on oath of J. L. Trotter before W. U. Hunt. Dated 29 Aug. 1887.

TUCKERS

Mrs. Tucker, the mother of Charles Tucker, recd. a legacy from the will of Hugh George Campbell of Charleston, S. C. in 1820. (Will 1)

TURNER

Starling Turner. Will of Starling Turner. Box 113 #1089. Probate Judge Office. Pickens, S. C. I Starling H. Turner, being of sound and disposing mind and memory, etc. I give to my grandson Turner Snoddy, a tract of land consisting of 40 acres bought by me from the est. of Tilman Miller decd. I give to my grandchildren the chn. of my son Silas Turner the sum of $1600.00 to be divided between them. To be paid as they come of age. I give to my grandchildren the chn. of my son William Turner the sum of $1400.00... to be divided between them as they come of age. The rest and residue of my property both real and personal to be divided between my sons, Thomas Turner, B. F. P. Turner, and my dtr. Emily Elizabeth Snoddy, Frances Ellen Latham share and share alike. I appoint my son Thomas J. Turner and son in law John S. Latham as executors. Dated 17 Feb. 1877. Signed: Starling H. X Turner. Wit: W. H. Perry, Wm. Beattie, John Jameson. Codicil added "My son B. F. P. Turner being dead I will and bequeath his share above devised to his son, but out of said share I wish $300 to be deducted which said B. F. P. Turner est. owes me." Dated 17 Jan. 1879. Signed: Starling H X Turner. Wit: B. F. Perry, N. P. Walton, W. H. Perry. Filed 2 Jan. 1883... (Loose papers) On 1 Nov. 1853 James E. Hagood, Robert A. Stewart are bound unto W. J. Parson, Ord. in the sum of $200.00. James E. Hagood gdn. of Emarilla Turner minor over 12 years.

William Turner. Estate of William Turner. In Equity #197. Clerk of Court Office. Abbeville, S. C. To the Honr. John Mathew and Hugh

Rutledge Esqs. Judges. The petition of Mercer Babb of Newberry County and Francis Devenport and Mary his wife the late Mary Turner, widow and executrix of the last will and testament of William Turner late of Newberry Co. Sheweth that William Turner on or about 30 Dec. 1789 did publish and declare his last will and testament. And appointed Mary Turner now Devenport, executrix and the said Mercer Babb executor. Your petitioners took on themselves the burden of execution. That the said Mary has married one Francis Devenport, and that before his death William Turner sold to one James Cooke a tract of land in Newberry Co. He made a note in writing called promissory note signed in his own hand and dated 5 Oct. 1785 in the sum of twenty five pds. sterling. On or about the 1 day of Feb. 1786 one John Satterwhite of Newberry Co. got in possession of said note when William Turner was in a state of intoxication by unfair and dishonest means. William Turner not having indorsed it to John Satterwhite, the said note was in personal estate of William Turner and after his decd. Satterwhite has demanded it of the executor. (The rest of this suit missing.)

TURNBULL

John Turnbull. Estate of John Turnbull. Pack 3202. Clerk of Court Office. Abbeville, S. C. To the Honr. the Judges of the Court of Equity. Your orator Herbert Darracot and oratrix Floride B. Darracot his wife. Your orator Elijah Turnbull and your oratrix Sarah Turnbull. That John Turnbull late of Abbeville Dist. being seized with a tract of land of about 400 acres, leaving one third to his wife and two thirds to his chn. Executrix his wife Jane and executor Elijah Turnbull. The said testator left his widow and the following chn. Floride B. Darracot the wife of Herbert Darracott, Elijah, Sarah S., John S., Jane, Nancy, James Theodore, Mary K. and Martha Turnbull the last six are under age of twenty one and the last four under 14 years. Your orator and oratrix prays for a division of the said real estate. Filed 18 April 1825.

TUSTIN

James H. Tustin. Estate of James H. Tustin. #33. Clerk of Court Office. Abbeville, S. C. In Equity; To the Chancellors; Your orator Samuel T. Tustin that on the 13 Sept. 1844 James H. Tustin the father of your orator departed this life, seized with a tract of land lying near the village of Abbeville containing 220 acres, adj. land of John A. Calhoun, Thomas Perrin, Robert Wardlaw. That James H. Tustin left a widow Mrs. E. M. Tustin who died on the 23 March 1855. Chn. viz; Sarah A. Allen the widow of John E. Allen decd. Hiram T. Tustin, John L. Tustin, a minor and your orator Samuel Tustin prays for a partition of the real estate. Filed 5 June 1855. Admr. of the estate of Edny Tustin was granted to Hiram Tustin on the 30 May 1855 by William Hill, Esq.

WADE

Nancy Wade. Estate of Nancy Wade. Box 17 #213. Probate Judge Office. Pickens, S. C. Admr. bond missing. On 5 Jan. 1849 P. J. Wade made suit for letter of admr. of estate of Nancy Wade decd. Of Pickens Dist. On 9 Oct. 1850 William Burgess stated that the estate of Nancy Wade was indebted to him.

David Wade. Estate of David Wade. Book 1 Page 45. Clerk of Court Office. Pickens, S. C. On 23 Jan. 1843 David Wade owned 100 acres on Saluda River, adj. land of Ligon, Easley and others. Heirs, Wm. T. Dacus, Simeon Wade vizt. Henry Wade out of State, Noah Wade out of State, Solomon Wade in State, Elijah Wade, Talitha Wade, Sarah Wade out of State. (Real estate release.)

Nancy Wade. Estate of Nancy Wade. Box 98 #1029. Probate Judge Office. Pickens, S. C. On 8 Aug. 1870. Owned 150 acres on waters of South Saluda. Adj. land of Reuben Talley decd. Joberry Rigdon and others. Heirs, Richard Wade and wife, Catharine Holder of Greenville Co., Stephen Rains and wife Phabba, Joseph Hardin and wife Eliza who resides in Greenville Co. Grandchildren of Nancy Wade decd. Burrell Pace and wife Hannah, Henry Norman and wife Harriett & Samuel Wade grand chn. of Nancy Wade who resides in Alabama and Hampton Wade of Greenville County. 14 Sept. 1870 the petition of Margaret Steele, Jane Dendy, Agness Ellison of Oconee Co. shews that Wm. D. Steele husband of Margaret Steele and father of Jane Dendy, Agness Ellison purchased at sheriff sale the undivided interest of Preston J. Wade in the real estate of Nancy Wade decd. (Loose papers) On 31 Oct. 1843 Simon Wade relinquished his claim of interest in the estate of David Wade for the payment of Wm. T. Dacus proven account. Viz; the estate of Mrs. Sarah Wade to Wm. T. Dacus... Nancy Wade was the widow of David Wade.

WAGGONER

Cathy Waggoner. Box 16 #205. Probate Judge Office. Pickens, S. C. Cathy Waggoner was a daughter of Henry Gaines, Sr. who died in Pickens Dist. His will proved in 1830.

WAKEFIELD

John Wakefield. Deed from John Wakefield. Mesne Conveyance. Book ___ Page 165. Greenville, S. C. This indenture between John Wakefield and Thomas Mayfield of Greenville Dist. Dated 15 Jan. 1788. In consideration of ten shillings sterling have bargained, sold, and released unto said Thomas Mayfield a tract of land containing 200 acres lying on the waters of Enoree River and the old Indian boundary line. Wit: William Willson, Henry Wood, Robert X Wood. Signed: John Wakefield.

WALDROP

Nancy Waldrop. Pack 611 #11. Clerk of Court Office. Pickens, S. C. On 20 July 1867 Nancy Waldrop took out a peace warrant for her husband Berry Waldrop of Pickens Dist.

Martha Waldrop. Pack 640 #3. Clerk of Court Office. Pickens, S. C. On 23 June 1878 Martha Waldrop states that she is a daughter of B. S. Porter of Pickens Dist. That he died about 5 years ago.

John Waldrop. Pension statement about Rev. service. Greenville Dist. Dated 10 Oct. 1832. Said John Waldrop a resident of the district of Greenville, S. C. age 79, states he entered service in the spring of the year in which the battle of Eutaw Springs was fought under Capt. Lusk, Col. Thomason, Gen. Sumpter called the state troops, served ten months, lived in N. C. when entering service, County called Sullivan now part of Tennessee. States he volunteered and was in the battle of Stono and Eutaw Springs. He was under Capt. Walters, Col. Thomas at Eutaw. Does not recollect any continental regiments, he knew Col. Washington, Col. Lee and Gen. Green. He marched from N. C. down to High Hills of Sante. Was stationed sometime at Orangeburg under Col. Henderson, he was wounded at the battle of Eutaw Springs, arm broken, he knows of no one except Abner Thompson who can testify to his service. He was born in Amelia County, Virginia in 1753, he has a record of his age at home in an old prayer book, was living in N.C. when called into service. Has lived in Greenville Dist. ever since the revolutionary war and now lives here. We Nathan Berry, clergyman resides in the district of Greenville, and William Blasingame residing in same, states they are well acquainted with John Waldrop.

Jeremiah Walker. Will of Jeremiah Walker. Will Book 1791-1803 Page 25-26. Ordinary's Office. Elbert County, Elberton, Ga. I Jeremiah Walker of the State of Georgia Elbert Co. being afflicted in body, but of sound mind and memory, etc. I give to my wife Milly a negro man named Peince, also a negro woman named Rinah with Tom with Gloss her chn Also a negro woman named Saffold with Rachel and Peg her chn. Her choice of a bed and furniture. Also a sorrel mare and saddle, a chest with drawers, a red trunk, also her dower of the third part of the land I bought of Hutson that part I devise to John Williams Walker in lew of all other dowry. Also Walkers Sermons, W Roes Exercises Creek Poams, and Pilgrims Progress, also two cows and a heffer. I lend to my dtr. Polly Coleman, the first female child that negro Easther, Sally or Prudance shall have during her natural life and then divided between her three dtrs., Elizabeth, Narcissa, Melinda to them forever, I also give to Polly my black walnut table, part of my crockery, and a part of my books. I give to my son Henry Graves Walker 400 acres of land, being part of the land I bought from Robert Chambers. (corners given). I give to my son Henry G. Walker a lot I bought in Petersburgh, also a negro girl named Agg, one feather bed and furniture, also a part of my books. I give to my son Memorable Walker 350 acres known as the Cabben land, which I have Coalsons bond for titles and my and desire that the titles be made to my son Memorable Walker. Also one negro boy named David and the first male child that either Sally or Prudance shall have, also one feather bed, and a part of the books. I give to my son Jeremia 150 acres on the South side of Savannah River, being part of the tract of 700 acres bought from Chambers. Also 100 acres on the upper part of the island, also a negro boy named Tom, also a horse colt, one feather bed and part of my books. I give to my son James Sanders Walker 150 acres, joining my son Jeremiah land at the mouth of Spring Branch, also a negro named Saffer, a small horse colt, one feather bed and furniture, a part of my books. I give to my son John William Walker 250 acres on the river below Sanders line, also 100 of the island, also one negro boy named Webster, one feather bed and furniture, also a part of my books. I give to my daughter Elizabeth what she has in possession already, and a share of my books, with what books she already has. I appoint my brother Sanders Walker and my friend James Tate Esq. the executors. I desire that the tract of land of 622 acres I have on Brushey creek, with negroes Tom, Sally and Prudance be hired out till my son John Williams Walker shall come of age. Whatever shall be left when John Williams Walker is of age shall be equally divided between my chn. viz; Polly Coleman, Elizabeth Marshall, Henry Graves Walker, Memorable Walker, Jeremiah Walker, James Sanders Walker, John Williams Walker. Dated 14 Sept. 1792. Wit: William Tate, Richard Harvy, John Avren. Signed: Jeremiah Walker. Recorded 17 Oct. 1792.

Henry S. Walker. File 30. Clerk of Court Office. Pickens, S. C. Henry S. Walker was the husband of Louisa Rohanna Benson dtr. of William P. Benson who died in Pickens Dist. in 1853 and his widow Nancy G. Benson.

John Walker. Will of John Walker. Case 94 File 4643. Probate Judge Office. York Co., S. C. I John Walker of York, S. C. being of sound mind and memory, etc. First I will my debts and funeral expences be paid from the first money that come into the estate. I give unto my two daughters, Jane B. Walker and Sarah E. Walker all the land whereon I now live forever. I give the above named dtr. all my stock of horses, cattle, hogs, sheep, theirs forever. I give to above named dtrs. my shop tools, household and kitchen furniture of every description, with all provision on hand at my death, also all money, notes and debts due to have and hold forever. In all things the two dtrs. to share and share alike. I appoint my friend Jane B. Walker my lawful executor. Dated 26 Dec. 1874. Wit: James A. Barnwell, Allen L. Robinson, Leroy Whites. Signed: John Walker. Probated 23 July 1887.

Walker-Weeks. Court of Equity, File 359. Clerk of Court Office. Abbe-
ville, S. C. Simeon Matthews vs. Solomon Walker. Bill for petition
and accounts and others. For division of Aaron Weeks decd. estate who
was the father of Nancy Weeks. Aaron Weeks home located on Turkey
Creek, containing 160 acres of land. Aaron Weeks died 1824 wife Nancy
Chn. of Aaron and Nancy Weeks;
Emily, m. Simeon Matthews   Isaac Weeks, m.
Nancy, m. Solomon Walker   Sampson Weeks m.
Duke Allen Weeks, m.   Eliza Weeks, m.
Aaron Weeks, m.

SOLOMON WALKERS FAMILY

Solomon Walker. B. 1775 S. C. d. abt. 1855, Abbeville, S. C. m.
Nancy Weeks b. 1790. Children: Sanders Walker, Admr. of his father
est. 12 Feb. 1858. Abbeville. Burton Walker. Margaret Walker, b.
June 1810 d. 1885, Clay Co., Ala. m. James F. Martin b. 1810, S. C. d.
1880 Clay Co., Ala. Lucinda Walker, m. Gallant Hardy. Elizabeth Walker
m. William Delashaw. Chesley Walker. Samuel Walker, b. 1808, d. 1880
m. Mary Ann Carmical, b. 1810, d. 1895. Samuel Walker was one of the
first grand jurors of Cowetta Co., Ga. Superior Court which was held
25 June 1827, about 2 1/2 miles from Newman, Ga. and the village in which
it was held was Bullsboro, Ga. and now a lost town but was the first
settlement in Cowetta Co., Ga. Samuel Walker was a pioneer of the Co.

Jane Walker. Estate of Jane Walker. Box 40 #447. Probate Judge Office.
Pickens, S. C. Est. admr. 7 Nov. 1856 by John S. Walker, D. K. Hamilton,
Thomas H. McCan, E. B. Benson who are bound unto W. J. Parson, Ord. in
the sum of $30,000.00. Expend. Paid Editor Central Presbyterian
Richmond, Va. $3.00. Left 7 heirs, no names given. On 15 Oct. 1860,
paid A. Fuller, James Walker, Thomas H. McCann, Martha Alexander,
Matilda Walker, John S. Walker, David K. Hamilton in full for rect. each
one recd. $3214.29.

John S. Walker. Will of John S. Walker. Box 84, #887. Probate Judge
Office. Pickens, S. C. I John S. Walker being of sound mind and
memory & understanding etc. First I will my just debts be paid out of
the rents. I give unto my beloved wife Eleanor J. Walker all the tract
I now live on, known as the 18 Mile tract, containing by resurvey by
T. V. Clayton 10 June 1874, 287 acres. Also all stock, tools to be
hers and at her disposal. I appoint my wife Eleanor J. Walker my
executrix. Dated 2 Aug. 1875. Wit: C. T. Pollard, Silas X Perry.
Proven 15 Jan. 1880.

Matilda Walker. Will of Matilda Walker. Box 105 #110. Probate Judge
Office. Pickens, S. C. I Matilda Walker being of sound mind and perfect memory. My body to be interred near my father and mother at the
Old Stone Church three miles from Pendleton. I direct that my debts
and funeral be paid as soon as possible. I direct that all my personal
property be sold and disposed of in like manner. I will and direct
that all my rights claims in the tract of land on which I now live,
lying in the fork of 18 & 15 mile Creeks, containing by the old survey
700 acres be the property of my much loved and esteemed niece Roseline
Hudson and in case of her death, to the heirs of her body. I appoint
my esteemed friend William A. Hudson executor. Dated 21 Feb. 1874.
Wit: John L. Nix, V. P. Hudson, Leathe Chapman. Signed: Matilda
Walker. Proven 2 June 1874.

Walker Minors. Box 108 #1030. Probate Judge Office. Pickens, S. C.
On 19 July 1875 G. W. Taylor appointed gdn. of Andrew J. Walker, Robert
M. Walker, Anderson B. Walker, James R. A. Walker, Daniel Walker,
Maxwell Walker minors. William N. Walker Plaintiff, C. L. Hollingsworth
his atty. shows that Wm. N. Walker, Rebecca L. Corbin, Wiley T. Walker,
Robert M. Walker, Andrew B. Walker, Charlotte Walker, Daniel Walker,
James R. A. Walker all of Pickens Co. Mary Ann Stancill of Georgia,
Susan Walker, Maxwell Walker of Missouri are tenants in common of 160

acres on waters of Estatoe Waters of Keowee River, adj. land of Alpha
Barton and others has descended to them from James Walker, John Walker
and Riley Walker all who are dead. William N. Walker, Rebecca L. Corbin
Mary Ann Stancill, Wiley T. Walker, Andrew J. Walker, Robert M. Walker,
Anderson B. Walker are descendants of James Walker decd. Charlotte
Walker the widow of Riley Walker decd. and James R. A. Walker, Daniel
Walker are sons of said Riley Walker decd. Susan Walker the widow of
John Walker decd. and Maxwell Walker the only child of John Walker.

William Walker. Estate of William Walker. Box 9 #124. Probate Judge
Office. Pickens, S. C. Est. admr. 22 Feb. 1841 by John S. Walker,
Thomas H. McCann, W. L. Keith, William Boggs, F. N. Garvin who are
bound unto James H. Dendy, Ord. in the sum of $50,000. John S. Walker,
Thomas H. McCann were of Anderson Dist. Citation published at Carmel
Church. Left 7 chn. and widow. Advanced to Col. D. K. Hamilton
$952.50, T. W. Alexander $1797.50, T. H. McCann $1760.00, James Walker
$975.00, Matilda $20.00, Eliza Walker $20.00, paid Jane Walker in full
$790.09 1/2.

John S. & Ellender Walker. Box 11 #156. Probate Judge Office.
Pickens, S. C. (Letter) Pendleton Factory, 12 Dec. 1876. To Judge
Philpot, Pickens, S. C. Dear Sir: I wrote last week W. G. Field
asking him to appoint a committee to manage the business of my uncle
Jno. S. Walker of your County. The facts are these, he is very old
indeed and his mind is entirely gone so far as business is concerned and
his wife is pretty much in the same condition, entirely incompetent to
manage their affairs. Their property being entirely used up except the
land which will soon be put on the block unless your court interfered an
have these old people provided for. They are helpless in many ways,
especially from the cold and for want of a fire and even water to drink
it being some distance to the spring and neither of them able to carry
water any distance, and no one hired to do the work, will not even for
large pay stay there and wait upon them, etc. I beg that you appoint
a jury of six respectable citizens in the neighborhood to appear before
your court or to take evidence as the law directs, I suggest the
following gentlemen, Warren Knight, T. V. Clayton, Leander Boggs, T. F.
Glenn, Warren Martin, T. C. Martin and dr. Silas Clayton. It is
actually necessary that something be done for them immediately, etc.
Signed: W. Walker Russell, Pendleton Factory, Anderson, S. C. P. S. I
neglected to say that they had no heirs. W. W. Russell states that
John S. Walker is 80 years, has 280 acres on 18 mile River known as
the Walker place. Has another tract on Double Branch. Deeded to Mr.
Knight 100 acres. Has no brothers, but has brothers chn. living in
State of Miss. Has but one living sister. Has many sisters chn.
family of Fullers, Alexander, McCann, Hamilton. No minors in family.
W. W. Russell on oath he was acquainted with E. (Ellender) J. Walker
have known her for 12 years. Has a lot and house in Charleston, S. C.
is about 65-70 years. Has no chn. Next of kin the Boyd family of
Charleston, corrected, it is her sister Miss Eliza McElroy. Grandchildren: Boyds and sister chn. Baileys or Bailes in Rhode Island her
father is dead.

James Walker. Estate of James Walker. No ref. Pickens, S. C. On
14 Oct. 1876, Rebecca L. Corbin states that James Walker is her father.
Wiley Reeves the admr. He left seven chn. Lucinda Corbin, William
Walker, Mary A. Stancil, Wiley T. Walker, all of age, Andrew J. Walker,
Robin Walker, Anderson B. Walker under age. Lucinda Corbin and husband
Tyrie Corbin in Pickens. William Walker 26 years in Pickens, Mary A. M.
Stancil and husband Eli in Lumpkins Co., Ga. 24 years. Wiley T. Walker
age 22 in Pickens, Andrew J. age 20 in Pickens, Robin M. age 18 years
in Ga., Andrew B. age 16 years in Pickens.

WALLACE

Joseph Wallace, Sr. Estate of Joseph Wallace, Sr. Box 64 #2950.
Probate Judge Office. York, S. C. Est. admr. 31 June 1807 by Jean

Wallace, Joseph Wallace, Francis Adams, John Miller who are bound unto Alexander Moore, Ord. in the sum of $500.00 Citation pub. at Beraheba Church.

Robert Wallace. Estate of Robert Wallace. Box 64 #2951. Probate Judge Office. York, S. C. Est. admr. 7 Aug. 1809 by Elizabeth Wallace, John Wallace, James Wallace, Jonathan Newman, Charles Bradley who are bound unto Alexander Moore, Ord. in the sum of $1500.00. Citation published at Beershaba Church. Rebecca Wallace, Elizabeth Wallace, James Wallace were legatees.

James Wallace. Estate of James Wallace. Box 6 #239. Probate Judge Office. York, S. C. Est. admr. 10 Dec. 1838 by Isaac M. Wallace, John T. Plexco, Allen Crosby, John J. Bratton who are bound unto Benjamin Chambers, Ord. in the sum of $10,000.00. Citation published at Bethasda Church. Est. divided between the widow, and 8 shares viz; E. Boggs, W. Wallace, John Wallace heirs, Mrs. Burris heirs, R. J. Wallace, Mrs. Robinsons heirs, Samuel W. Wallace, J. W. Wallace, Jane Robinson. Avaline Wallace, etc. bought at the sale of the estate.

James Wallace, Sr. Estate of James Wallace, Sr. Box 2 #64. Probate Judge Office. York, S..C. Dated 3 March 1835. Widow, Jane Wallace. Chn. Robert Wallace, James Wallace, Jr., Elizabeth Wallace the gdn. of 6 minor chn. of James Wallace, Jr. Decd. John S. Moore gdn. of 4 chn. of John Wallace decd. William Whiteside and wife Sarah, Joseph Caldwell in right of wife Rebecca, Elizabeth Wallace widow of James Wallace, Jr. decd., Polly Wallace the widow of John Wallace decd. Andrew Wallace in Tenn. On 23 Jan. 1834 Elizabeth Wallace the gdn. of Margaret Wallace, Andrew Wallace, William Caldwell Wallace, Weston Wallace, Parmela Wallace, and James Adams Wallace minors under 14 years. On 1 Feb. 1834 John S. Moore the gdn. of Sarah Emaline Wallace minor over 14 years of John Wallace decd. son of James Wallace decd.

E. R. Wallace. Will of E. R. Wallace. Box 81 Pack 20. Probate Judge Office. Union, S. C. I Adwin R. Wallace of the town of Union, do make and ordain this to be my last will and testament. I will to my wife Mary Jeanetta Wallace my whole estate, real, personal or mixed. In event of the remarriage of my wife in the life time of my children the estate thereby conveyed shall cease, and the whole of my estate shall be distributed, with my wife taking one third. It is my hope and expectation that my wife provide for and educate our chn. I will and direct that my wife have full power to manage my estate as she thinks proper, with full power to sell convey and dispose as she shall seem expedient. I appoint my wife Mary Jeanette Wallace executrix. Dated 26 Aug. 1879. Wit: David Johnson, Jr., Chas. C. Culp, James Munro. Signed: Edwin R. Wallace. Recorded 1 Feb. 1892 by James M. Gee, clk.

William Wallace. Will of William Wallace. Will Book B page 133. Probate Judge Office, Union, S. C. I William Wallace of Union Dist. do make this my last will and testament. I wish no sale of my estate be at public auction. I wish my executors to choose five disinterested free holders to assess and value the whole of my negroes, and make an equal division between my wife Jennet Wallace and my six children. I wish my executors to pay my just debts, from the crop of cotton and what cash is on hand. I give to my wife Jennet Wallace the following negroes, old Nanna, old Hall, old Sam, old Land and Captain to live with her during her natural life, and at her death the mentioned negroes may choose which of my children to live with. I give to my wife Jennet the whole of my stock, with every kind of my household and kitchen furniture. As one of my children become of age, I wish my wife to give them one horse of the value of one hundred dollars, I have already given to son Robert W. Wallace a horse of that value. I wish my estate to stay together to raise the chn. upon. I give to my son Robert W. Wallace one negro man Prince, blacksmith when he arrives to the age of twenty one. I give to my dtr. Mary Ann Wallace one negro woman named Catey at the age of twenty one. I give to my dtr. Caroline Wallace woman Judah when she arrives to twenty one or marry. I give to my son John P. Wallace one negro boy Edson at age twenty one or marry.

I give to my son James M. Wallace negro boy named James son of Linda when he arrives at twenty one or marry. I give to my son William M. Wallace negro boys Stephen & Edwin sons of Minder when he arrives to twenty onq or marry. The remainder of my negroes to be lotted into seven lots, with the wife having her choice, and the chn. to draw for their lot. I appoint my son Robert W. Wallace, Francis Parham and my wife Jennet Wallace as executors & executrix. Dated 13 Nov. 1825. Wit: John Gage, Jr., J. Rodgers, D. A. Mitchell. Signed: Wm. Wallace. Recorded 19 May 1828.

James Wallace. Will of James Wallace. Case 36 File 1538. Probate Judge Office. York, S. C. I James Wallace of York Dist. do make and declare this my last will and testament. I will unto John James McArter all my land lying on the East side of the creek and $100. I also bequeath unto Elisa Gimelin one third of the balance of my est. I also bequeath unto Rebacka Rhea of Pike County Missouri State one third of my est. I bequeath unto Margret Wallace of York Dist, S. C. one third of my est. I appoint James Caldwell my executor. Dated 14 Nov. 1856. Wit: Robert Neeland, Abram Neeland, John Whiteside. Signed: James Wallace. Recorded 19 Dec. 1856.

Joseph Wallace. Will of Joseph Wallace. Case 51 File 2237. Probate Judge Office. York Dist. I Joseph Wallace do make this my last will and testament. I will my just debts and funeral expenses be paid. I will to my wife Margaret G. my plantation whereon I now live, with household and kitchen furniture, farm tools, stock of all kinds, one note on Andrew Tate for fifty dollars dated 17 Dec. 1857. I will and direct that out of the cash and notes $50.00 be paid to each of my children. I appoint my son George F. Wallace executor. Dated 9 Aug. 1858. Wit: R. Allison, Andrew Tate, J. M. Ross. Signed: Jos. Wallace. On 10 Aug. 1861 a codicil was added "I hereby annul and revoke that portion of the third clause of my foregoing will which directs that out of the cash I may have on hand and notes and accounts then due me." Wit: J. M. Ross, L. L. Gardner, I. B. Jackson. Signed: Joseph Wallace. Probated: 7 March 1864.

James Wallace. Estate of James Wallace. Box 57A Pack 1491. Probate Judge Office. Chester, S. C. Est. admr. 15 Oct. 1852 by William Wallace, Samuel Hamilton, James N. Knox who are bound unto Peter Wilie, Ord. in the sum of $200.00

William Wallace. Estate of William Wallace. Box 68 Pack 1059. Probate Judge Office. Chester, S. C. Est. admr. 6 Feb. 1832 by Andrew Young, Dr. John Douglass who are bound unto Peter Wylie, Ord. in the sum of $200.00. Est. admr. again 24 Oct. 1831 by Andrew Young, Daniel McMillan who are bound unto the Ord. in the sum of $1,000.00. On 16 March 1832 Daniel McMillan recd. $10.00 on account of Robert Wallace. 18 Oct. 1832 paid Littleton Wallace $4.50. 7 Jan. 1832 Nancy Hughes made oath that the estate was justly indebted to her. Martha Wallis, Robert Wallis bought at sale.

S. Milinda Wallace. Estate of S. Milinda Wallace. Box 90 Pack 1426. Probate Judge Office. Chester, S. C. Est. admr. 29 April 1843 by James A. Lewis, who was bound unto the Ord. Peter Wylie in the sum of $1500.00 On 11 Dec. 1843 to Sarah M. Wallace share of her mother's (E. Wallace) estate $211.36. Amount of note on William L. Wallace $86.75. E. A. Wallace etc. bought at the sale.

Peter D. Wallace. Estate of Peter D. Wallace. Box 105 Pack 46. Probate Judge Office. Chester, S. C. Est. admr. 11 Oct. 1858 by Mary Wallace, Hugh B. Wallace, William E. Estes, William Dickey who are bound unto James McDaniel, Ord. in the sum of $2200.00. Peter Wallace died about 10 July 1858.

Mary Wallis. Will of Mary Wallis. Case 79 File 3860. Probate Judge Office. York, S. C. I Mary Wallis of York Dist. being of sound mind and disposing memory and understanding. I give to my son Robert Bratton $100 to be paid one year after my death. To my grand daughter

Betsey E. Bratton I give one negro girl named Dianna and the first child negro woman Caroline has., and if she marries to fix her with common furniture for house keeping, I allow her to live with my son Isaac M. Wallis as long as she is single. To my grand son James C. Bratton one bed and furniture. To my son Isaac M. Wallis the balance of my negroes and household and kitchen furniture. I appoint James B. Good and my son Isaac M. Wallis my executors. Dated 12 Sept. 1842. Wit: James A. Murphy, Zenas A. Walker, Henry Tipping. Signed: Mary X Wallis.

Joshua Wallis. Estate of Joshua Wallis. Pack 289. Clerk of Court Office. Abbeville, S. C. Vol. W. Traylor and wife vs. J. C. Willard, guardian. Joshua Willis by his will gave to his children viz; Julia F., Martha W. Mars, Milly Ann D., Thomas J., Mary E., and Sarah C. each their negroes by name and out furniture, a cow and calf, a horse and saddle valued at $100. Two tracts of land on Savannah River, adj. land of Isaac Moragne and Peter Smith, land to be sold and the money equally divided amongst my above named chn. If any should die without heirs the surviving heirs to get it share. After the death of the estator, Rachel his widow first died and after her Mary E. a dtr. under the age of 16, and Milly Ann D. another dtr. intermarried with Wistonn. Traylor and died without issue. Filed 6 Jan. 1838.

Mrs. Jennette Wallace. Estate of Mrs. Jennette Wallace. Box 50 #17. Probate Judge Office. Union, S. C. On 9 Feb. 1867 Letter of admr. was granted to Benjamin H. Rice on the estate of Mrs. Jennette Wallace decd. of Union Dist. Expend of Est. Paid to J. M. Wallace $2896.20. M. A. Wallace $666.25. R. W. Wallace $396.98. E. R. Wallace $215.83. J. C. Wallace $29.25.

Leila & Edwin R. Wallace. Estate of Leila & Edwin R. Wallace. Box 41 #14. Probate Judge Office. Union, S. C. On 27 May 1857 Daniel Wallace was bound unto B. Johnson Ord. of Union Dist. in the sum of $800.00. Daniel Wallace was appointed the guardian of Leila E. & Edwin R. Wallace minor. Your petitioner further sheweth that his late wife Sally W. Nance, now decd. was a sister of Alfred Nance and that she left at her death surviving and who still survives by her marriage with your peti- tioner, two chn. Leila E. and Edwin R. Wallace who are both infants under the age of choice and who are together entitled to a share of the est. of said Alfred Nance their uncle, as their mother would be entitled to if alive. Daniel Wallace the petitioner also states that Alfred Nance late of Dallas Co., State of Alabama died intestate about 3 or 4 years ago.

Mrs. Sarah W. Wallace. Estate of Mrs. Sarah W. Wallace. Box 36 #9. Probate Judge Office. Union, S. C. Est. of Mrs. Sarah W. Wallace was admr. 23 April 1851 by Daniel Wallace, W. H. Wallace who are bound unto B. Johnson, Ord. in the sum of $2,000.00. Sarah W. Wallace wife of the said Daniel Wallace died in Feb. 1849.

Harry Wallace. Will of Harry Wallace. No Ref. Spartanburg County, S. C. I Harry Wallace, feeling the uncertainty of life and the certainty of death. I give to my dtr. Moriah Wallace, my interest in the place I bought from R. K. Carson and G. W. Nichols, of which will be found recorded in deed EEE page 167. I give to my dtrs. Marilda Jenkins, Mary Wallace, Mattie Wallace the place I now live on during their natural life, and at their death among their chn. That is to say after the death of all of above named dtrs. The property to be sold and each dtr. chn. to have their mother share. I give to my son Hair Wallace one bedstead if he should see fit to claim it. I give to my dtrs. Mary and Hattie all my household and kitchen furniture. I give to my son William all my wearing clothes to be delivered to him at my death. I appoint my dtr. Moriah Wallace and my brother in law Douglass Wallace, executrix and executor. Dated 13 March 1896. Wit: S. T. McCravey, Douglas Wallace, P. L. Austin. Signed: Harry X Wallace.

Douglas Wallace. Will of Douglas Wallace. No ref. Spartanburg, S. C. I Douglas Wallace do make this my last will and testament. I will my just debts and funeral expenses be paid soon after my death. I will my

wife sell the mule and wagon and apply to the payment of my debts and
funeral expenses so far as necessary. I give the balance of my
property both real and personal to my wife Meoriah Wallace for her
natural life, and at her death, one half to go to my grand son Lewis
Wallace, with the other half to his wife, her heirs and assigned, to do
as she pleases with. I appoint my wife Moriah Wallace executrix.
Dated 19 June 1900. Wit: George W. Nicholes, John M. Nicholes, Andrew
Peak. Signed: Douglas X Wallace.

WARD

Ward Family. Notes on the Ward Family. Pack 611 #6. Clerk of Court
Office. Pickens, S. C. On 23 Sept. 1867 Garrison Timms took out a
peace warrant for James Ward and his wife Harriet Betty Ward of Pickens
Dist.

Rufus Ward. Book B Page 42, Probate Judge Office. Pickens, S. C. On
28 Nov. 1858 Rufus Ward and wife Belinda also called Linney were heirs
of Francis Jenkins decd. of Pickens Dist.

WARREN

Nancy Warren in 1841 the dtr. of Elizabeth Neely of York Dist. (will
23).

WASHINGTON

George Washington. Deed to George Washington and William Terrell.
Book I page 177. Clerk of Court Office. Anderson, S. C. I Charles
Lay to George Washington and William Terrell all of Anderson Dist.
Dated 2 Aug. 1805. In consideration of $900 paid by the said Geo.
Washington and William Terrell, have granted, sold, released all that
tract of land lying and being on the South fork of 12 Mile River, con-
taining 300 acres, adj. lands of Duncan Camerons, Earles White. Wit:
James Jett, Demony Pace, John Simmons. Signed: Charles N. Lay. On
the 4 Jan. 1806 Ann Lay the wife of Charles Lay appeared before John
Cochran, J. Q. and relinquish her rights to her dower.

WATSON

Leroy Watson. In Equity #5 Clerk of Court Office, Abbeville, S. C.
Abbeville Dist. To the Honr. the Chancellors; Your orator John W.
Watson sheweth that Leroy Watson the father of your orator departed
this life in the month of July 1844 leaving his will in full force.
Leroy Watson left eight chn, a dtr. Frances Mary the wife of James H.
Wideman and seven sons; Your orator John W. Watson, James Leonard
Watson, Leroy Watson, William H. Watson, Alfred H. Watson, Charles E.
Watson, Joseph B. Watson. Soon after the death of his father James
Leonard Watson volunteered in the Mexician War and died in Mexico, with-
out marring or leaving heirs, but brothers and sister. In the will of
Leroy Watson the executors to sell his whole estate except the
negroes, they to be hired out annually, and they belonged to the
estate privately. After paying his just debts, all money, notes due,
accounts together with real and personal property to be equally divided
between the named chn. When each son shall become twenty one years of
age, they are to receive their distributive share, and my dtr. Frances
Mary at time of marriage or when she arrives at twenty one years to
recd. her share. James F. Watson the brother of the decd. and an uncle
of your orator was named one of the executors. He delivered the
specific legacies, sold the property, hired out the negroes and settled

332

with Frances Mary who married James H. Wideman before his death, which
took place 6 Sept. 1851. Now Albert Waller, Esq. also named executor
has taken the execution of the will. Your orator is now of age, all
his brothers are still minors, and he is desirous of his share in the
estate. Which he is told is $5562.74 and a share of the negroes, An
agreement to let five gentlemen lot the said negroes for distribution,
viz; Larkin Reynolds, John McKeller, R. R. Tolbert, C. W. Sproull,
Staphen Elmore appraised and divided the negroes on 26 Dec. last with a
total appraisement of $35,500 being $5916.66 for the six chn. Your
orator drew lot #5 being 11 in number viz; Ben, Judy, Jane, Morial,
Margaret, George, Ananna, Gus, Abby, Willis and Martha Ann. All the
said negroes have been hired out this year. Your orator prays that the
Honr. Court to confirm this appraisment and partition. Filed 1 June
1855.

Richard Watson. Estate of Richard Watson. Box 97 Pack 2380. Probate
Judge Office. Abbeville, S. C. Est. admr. 23 Dec. 1824 by John Wesley
Brooks, James Dosier, Albert Waller who are bound unto Moses Taggart,
Ord. in the sum of $30,000.00. Sale was had on 6 Jan. 1825, with
Lavina Watson buying most of the items and slaves. The negroes she
bought are; Lewis, Rachaiel, Larkin, Mary and child, Zack, Queen and
child, Eliza, two small children, Mariah, Rhody and child, woman and
two children, Nathan, Mary, two small children, Milly, Joshua, Sally
and two chn. Willis, Mat, Daniel, Woman and child, Dick, Woman and
child, two small chn. Other who bought Abraham Light negro Boston, Ira
Griffin negro Jynin, John Wynns negro Dennis, Robert Turner negro
Charity and child, Bradley Lewis, Thomas Henderson, Isaac McCool,
Samuel Henderson, William Hacket, James Watson, William Watson, William
Hammon, William Prichard, Samuel Colwell, Wm. Hamon, Westley Brooks,
Samuel Cothran, Jesse Payne. Notes due the est. in 1825. Joseph
Griffin, Martin Bullocks, Beverly Burton, James Vaughn, Mathias Burt,
John L. Roberson, John Marsh, Maxililian Hutchison, James Sales.
Articles purchased for chn. which I have given Levina. Paid Mary E.
Watson, Sarah M. Watson, Elizabeth Watson, Edward Watson, Richard Watson.

Anne Rebecca Watson. Pack 48, Clerk of Court office. Abbeville, S. C.
Anne Rebecca Major in 1862 minor heir of Matilda L. Major her mother
and Samuel B. Major decd. of Abbeville Dist. On 12 Jan. 1877 she was
mentioned as Anne Rebecca Watson.

James Watson. Land Survey. Pack 516. Clerk of Court Office. Abbeville, S. C. At the request of James Richardson admr. of James B.
Foshee decd. I have resurveyed and laid out unto James Watson a tract
of 272 acres, on Coranaker Creek, waters of Saluda River. Formerly
owned by Charles B. Foshee decd. Dated 27 Aug. 1850 Chain carrier,
Pearce Little, Nathan Calhoun, Land adj. Nathan Calhoun, Watson &
Wardlaw, Thomas B. Byrd.

James F. Wallace. Estate of James F. Wallace. Pack 271. Clerk of
Court Office. Abbeville, S. C. Abbeville Dist. To the Honr. the
Chancellors: Your orator James Franklin Watson sheweth that on the
6 Sept. 1850 James F. Watson the father of your orator, departed this
life, leaving unrevoked and in full force his last will and testament.
After making specific provision for his wife Margaret Watson, bequeath
as follows, I will and desire that my chn. William Edward Watson, George
McDuffie Watson, James Franklin Watson, Thomas Anthony Watson, and
Dorothy Jane Watson, receive all my real and personal estate, with
money, notes, etc. after paying my just debts. To be divided by five
disinterested freeholders, when my sons become the age of twenty one,
and my dtr. marry or come the age of twenty one. That James H. Wideman
is the executor of said will, and that son William Edward Watson departed this life, intestate and never married. That since his death
the said Margaret Watson also died. That on the 2 June 1855 George
McDuffie Watson instituted in this Court to have his interest in his
father's estate set apart to him in severalty, he having attained the
age of twenty one years. By virtue of said proceeding, an accounting
by which the value and debts of the said James F. Watson decd. and the
share of sd. George McDuffie Watson were accertained. On the 14 June

1856 an order setting asise his share of the property without the payment
of the debts of the estate.   Filed 25 May 1859.

Thomas Watson. Estate of Thomas Watson. #43. Clerk of Court Office.
Pickens, S. C. In the will of Thomas Watson decd. that his just debts
be paid, to do this some land and negroes and other items to be sold.
Everything left to his wife to use to support and school the children.
Wife Malinda C. Watson and my dear friend and brother Joseph Grisham to
be executrix and executor. dated 19 Sept. 1842. Wit: Mary Grisham,
Daniel Wiseman, Robert A. A. Stelle. A codicil added the 8 Nov. 1842
gave the executor power to sell the farm whereon I now live to pay his
debts. Wit: Thomas Dickson, M. T. Miller, Delphia Herdeon. Signed
Thomas X Watson. Proven 21 Nov. 1842 before John Martin, Ord. In
Equity, Your orator Joseph Grisham and your Oratrix Malinda C. Watson,
sheweth that Thomas Watson late of Anderson Dist. died leaving a will
and testament. And left a widow and four chn. viz; John Watson
a minor over 14 years, Alfred Watson, Elizabeth Watson, Joseph Watson,
The males under the age of 14 and the female under 12 years. He owned
considerable property one tract entirely and an interest in ten other
tracts, of over 4,000 acres,and 11 slaves to wit; Mose and his wife
Rachel, both are old and unhealthy, Patterson and wife Eliza and their
five children, viz; Ann, Amanda, Andrew, Robert an infant, Jane and
Milly and her child Elias. The tract of land in Anderson Dist. has
been sold and the land in Pickens Dist. is unimproved, and most of it
mountain lands incapable of cultivation or of yielding any support to
the family, and that they are a constant tax to her. Your oratrix desire
that the land be sold, that she may purchase a small farm in this district to support the family. Filed 22 April 1851. On 27 Jan. 1853
states that John O. and Alfred H. were "bound out" and Joseph G. and
Elizabeth were at home. James Hunter guardian of John O. Watson.
John B. Sitton guardian of A. H. Watson.

Mary Pettus Watson. Estate of Mary Pettus Watson. Pack 337. Clerk of
Court Office. Abbeville, S. C. Abbeville Dist. To the Honr. the
Chancellors; The petiton of Benjamin S. Pulliam sheweth. By the will
of Mary P. Watson who lately died, a legacy is given to your petitioner
in trust as trustee for his aunt Belinda Cunningham wife of Charles
Cunningham which is in the hands of the executor of the said Mary P.
Watson and will probably amount to one thousand dollars. This legacy
is given for the sole and separate use during her life, and at her
death to be divided between your petitioner and Mary Ann Tharp a dtr.
of John J. Tharp, Mary Ann is about 15 years of age. Mrs. Belinda
Cunningham is very ppor and over fifty years old and need the use of a
negro man servant to do work about the house. She has applied to your
petitioner for the purchase of a certain negro man named Albert to be
paid for from the legacy. Your pettioner in order to blige his aunt,
has purchased the boy named Albert, who is about 21 years old, for a
reasonable price of $1,000. Your petitioner prays your honorable will
confirm the purchase. Filed 6 May 1859.

Mary P. Watson. Will of Mary P. Watson. Box 148. Pack 4205. Probate
Judge Office. Abbeville, S. C. I Mary Pettus Watson of Abbeville Dist.
Wishing to make a disposition before my death, etc. I will that Susan
and her four chn. Albert, Lucinda, Thomas and Betsy shall be sold after
my death and the payment of my debts, that the proceeds be divided as
follows, I will my son Jubal Watson shall have three fifths of the
proceeds. And one fifth of the proceeds to Benjamin S. Pulliam to hold
in trust for the use of my dtr. Belinda Cunningham wife of Charles N.
Dunningham, and at her death to be divided between my grand chn.
Benjamin S. Pulliam and Mary Ann Tharp. I will my dtr. Nancy the wife
of John J. Tharp to have the other fifth. I give to my grandson Moten
Watson (son of Jubal Watson) the house and lot whereon I now live. I
give to my dtrs. Matilda Strawhorn, Huldy Pulliam and my son John A.
Watson of the proceeds of the sale five dollars each. I appoint John
H. Munday and William J. Arnold executors. Dated 30 June 1851. Wit:
Wm. McNairy, Jno. Buchanan, O. J. Steele. Signed: Mary P. Watson.
Filed 6 May 1859.

WEATHERSPOON

John Weatherspoon. Pack 645 #11. Clerk of Court Office. Pickens, S.C. John Westherspoon died the 4 Jan. 1846 in the Poor House in Pickens Dist.

WEBB

William & Esther Webb. Deed of Trust. Pack 228 #3. Clerk of Court Office. Pickens, S. C. Whereas Elisha Laurence on the 12 Nov. 1842, execute and deliver to W. L. Keith & G. W. Liddell, trustees, a deed of trust for the only use and benefit and behoof of his wife Martha Laurence during her natural life and after her death to the only use and benefit of her heirs of her body. With a provison that the said trustee should have power and were authorized to sell any part of said property to pay any existing debts of Elisha Laurence. Now know all men that we William and Esther Webb his wife, who is an heir of the said Martha Laurence of the county of ___, State of Texas. That the remainder of the property so deeded in trust as above stated has not been sold to pay the debts of Elisha Laurence, or been given to the heirs of Mrs. Martha Laurence from this State. Have released and for ever discharged for ourselves and the said W. L. Keith and G. W. Liddell from all claim, demand or liability from either of us, etc. Dated 27 March 1853. Wit: J. W. Smith, John E. Smith. Signed: Esther C. Webb and William E. Webb.

WELLS

Sarah Wells. Equity Records. Pack 13. Clerk of Court Office. Abbeville, S. C. Sarah Wells was the wife of Josiah Wells. Their children were; William Wells, Lucretia Wells, Martha E. Wells, Catherine Wells who were minors under 21 years. Her father was John Clay of Abbeville Dist. who died in Jan. 1855 and of his wife Elizabeth Clay. She died before her father did.

WELLBORN

James and Aaron Wellborn, were living in Old 96 Dist. which was called Pendleton Dist. now Anderson Co. in 1790. Both were in the revolutionary war. Both had a land grant South of White Plains Church, between Williamston and Allen Shoals on Saluda River. James & Aaron married sisters Rebecca and Elizabeth Younger, daughters of James Younger who was born 1737. The old Wellborn home place in 1790 was East of Old West Pelzer School House. At this place Thomas Wellborn was born 1 Aug. 1790. He married Polly (Mary) Martin a daughter of Thomas Martin and Hester Roundtree born in 1770. They had 12 children, from this family are the Wellborns, Martins, Bennetts, Hoggs, Rogers, Elrods, Celeys, McWhorters, Pickens, Coxc, Poores, Richardsons, Manlys, Smiths, and others, some went to Missour and Texas. Most settled around Palestine, Fosterville, and Whiteboro, Texas. James Wellborn a "Deacon" is listed on the Old Big Creek Church records in the roll for 1801 as also his wife Rebecca. This Church was established by Moses Holland around 1788 who lies buried there in the old cemetery. James Wellborn left here in 1812 and went "West." His son William born 1798 remained here. He married Nancy Waddell. All the above family are buried in or near Due West, S. C.

Old Newton Cemetery, on the Liberty and Anderson Highway, S. C.

Ruth M. Welborn wife of
Larkin Newton
8 Nov. 1829 - 13 May 1908

Major L. Newton   Died
1 June 1890   age 68 yrs.

Lebabon Cemetery. Located on the Liberty and Anderson Highway, S. C.

Chesley Martin Ducworth
18 Mar. 1853
16 Aug. 1922

Sarah Guyton Ducworth
30 Sept. 1855
16 June 1925

Rosa Welborn wife of
B. F. McMurtrey
1873 - 1948

Baylus F. McMurtrey
1870 - 1920

Lemuel H. Welborn
27 Aug. 1825
15 Feb. 1898

Caroline Elizabeth wife of
L. H. Welborn
7 July 1829 - 10 Aug. 1908

Mary A. Welborn
18 June 1860
8 June 1879

D. K. N. Welborn
4 Mar. 1894 - 9 Nov. 1922
Co. M. 118th Infantry, 30th Division
Wounded at St. Quentin, France

Thomas M. Welborn
22 April 1855
14 Feb. 1936

Lizzie C. Harper
22 Dec. 1858
9 Dec. 1931

Elizabeth Millwee Hunnicutt
11 Aug. 1811
1 Dec. 1880

Cynthia Hunnicutt
1 Jan. 1801
15 March 1880

MARRIAGES - Lincolnton, Ga.

Book H, page 40
Issued license to marry Robert B. Wheeler to Miss Polanna S. Welborn.
2 Apr. 1834. I do hereby certify that Robert B. Wheeler and Polanna S.
Welborn were joined together in the Holy bond of matrimony by me the
3 April 1834.   Signed Richard J. Holleday, J.P.   Rec. 23 April 1834.

Issued license to marry Dr. Jno. A. Simmons and Ann Wellborn the 28
March 1844. I do certify that Jno. A. Simmons and Ann Wellborn were
joined together in the Holy bonds of matrimony by me on the 28 March
1844. Signed: J. West, M. G.   Recorded 31 May 1844.

MARRIAGES - Elberton, Ga.

James Clark, married Permelia T. Welburn, 25 Aug. 1828. Will Book
1825-1829, p. 415.

Burkit Welborn married Nancy Pace 16 Sept. 1808. Will Book 1816-1824,
page 261.

Newspaper clippings

Mr. Aaron Welborn died 24 July 1896 in his 70 year. He had moved from
Williamston, S. C. to Elberton, Ga. about three years ago. His body
was returned to Williamston, S. C. and buried in Spring Park Cemetery.
Mr. C. A. Welborn, age 65 years of Garvin township, died at his resident
Tuesday night of last week. He was a confederate Veteran. Buried at
Lebanon Church Cemetery. No date on this clipping.

*   *   *   *

Will of William S. Burch. Book M, page 203. Ordinary Office. Elber-
ton, Ga. "Bequeath to the children of Sarah Hardin wife of Henry
Hardin, sister to my wife Elizabeth." "Polly Welborn wife of Thomas
Welborn, sister to my wife Elizabet." "Rebeccah Upshaw wife of John

Upshaw, Jr. A sister to my wife Elizabeth." "Mary Ann Cook and William T. O. Cook, heirs of Wm. T. Cook, decd. The said William being a brother to my wife Elizabeth." Sister, Betty Cook. Brothers and sisters: Thomas Burch, Benjamin Burch, Moza Burch, John Burch, Cheadle Burch, Polly Johnson, Jinny Divine, Hannah C. Perkins, Sarah Kesee. Will dated 15 May 1817. Recorded 17 Jan. 1822.

Will of Barnabas Pace, Book 18, page 32. Ordinary Office. Elberton, Ga.
Wife, Mary Pace; son in law, John Cazy who married Elizabeth; grandson, Barnabas Pace; son, Dredzie Pace; son, Thomas Pace; daughter, Nancy, who married Burkit Welborn; son, Bazil Pace; son, Paris Pace; son, Noel Pace. Will dated 24 March 1827. Recorded 8 Sept. 1831.

Welborn Family from Anderson County Court Records. Pack 1640. Anderson, S. C. William W. Welborn died 12 Oct. 1859. Wife, Letty Welborn who died before her husband. Was a dtr. of John Murphey late of Cass County, Ga. Children William O. Welborn, a minor. John R. Welborn, a minor. Mentioned: Richardson Murphey decd. was a son of John Murphey decd.

#2442. William W. Welborn died in 1867. Wife Nancy Welborn. Children: C. A. Welborn, A. F. Welborn, W. J. Moore & wife, James C. Welborn, R. H. Welborn, W. W. Welborn, Mrs. Mary Thompson, N. H. Welborn, Mrs. M. A. Huff wife of Moses Huff, L. H. Welborn.

#1931. Nancy Welborn died before 7 Sept. 1868, the widow of Wm. W. Welborn decd. Son, A. F. Welborn was admr. Heirs; C. A. Welborn, Sarah Garrison, Willis Allen, Benjamin Johnson, J. M. Barr, Moses Huff, B. F. Mauldin, R. O. Elrod, J. D. King, T. M. Welborn, Thomas Crymes.

#2009. W. W. Welborn died between 1863-1864. Wife Zilpah Welborn. Chn. Mary E. Welborn, John A. Welborn, M. L. Welborn, Nancy Jane Welborn. Will dated 2 July 1863. Left property to William and John Welborn when they become of age. Fought in Confederate War.

#2717. Savilia Welborn Smith, died before 1858. Husband, Edward Smith went to Georgia. He was the son of Simeon Smith. Children: Edward Rial Smith, Mary Lucinda Smith, minors under 14 years before 20 June 1859.

#2821. Sarah Welborn owned 223 acres bounded by land of James M. Welborn, Mrs. Mary D. Anderson, Mrs. Martha Rogers and others. Children #1. Julia Welborn married. Pickens, who had, Welborn Pickens, Andrew Pickens, Halbert Pickens. #2. Elizabeth Welborn Pegg, who had, John M. Pegg who was living in Wachita Co., Arkansas by 20 May 1874. Martha J. married James A. Gaines, Samuel M. Pegg, John M. Pegg, Sarah C. married John B. Neal, Nancy E. married William W. T. Harrison.

Elias Welborn. Land warrants, Book B. Pages 204 and 205. Probate Judge Office, Abbeville, S. C. 146 acres on North side of Toogalow River, surveyed by John C. Kilpatrick D.S. dated 15 May 1787. Recorded 29 May 1787. 250 acres on a branch called Kelso or Kees Creek waters of Toogalow River surveyed by John C. Kilpatrick, D.S. on 14 May 1787. Recorded 21 May 1787.

WERNICKE

Lewis Wernicke. Estate of Lewis Wernicke. Box 130 #6. Probate Judge Office. Pickens, S. C. Est. admr. 25 Jan. 1898 by Julia Wernicke who is bound unto J. B. Newberry, Ord. in the sum of $1,000.00. Died 17 Dec. 1897. Julia Wernicke a daughter.

WERTZ

Wertz Minors. Box 124 #3. Probate Judge Office. Pickens, S. C. On 28 June 1894 R. M. Wertz, E. B. Richardson, J. H. Brown are bound unto J. B. Newberry, Ord. in the sum of $200.00. R. M. Wertz gdn. of James Claudius Wertz, Joseph Julian Wertz minors under 21 years. On 11 Jan. 1894 J. Addington Boggs died intestate and left as one of his divisees Adeb. Wertz. On 15 May 1894 Ada B. Wertz died leaving surviving her as heirs at law her husband R. M. Wertz, and Claudius, Joseph Julian Wertz her chn. under 14 years.

WEST

William West. Will of William West. Box 98 Pack 2406. Probate Judge Office. Abbeville, S. C. I William West, of 96 Dist. Weak in body but of sound mind and perfect understanding. I will and positively order my debts be paid. I leave to my wife Jane West one sixth part of my personal during her life or widowhood. I give to my son Thomas West the house and plantation of land. I give one fifth part of my personal estate to my dtr. Mary Chiles, then the remainder of my estate to be equally divided betwix my other four chn. viz; Thomas West, Jane West, Elizabeth West, and Patty West. I appoint my wife Jane West, Jacob Pope and Andrew Lea executors. Dated 14 Feb. 1785. Wit: John Wood, Nancy Wood, Elizabeth Marsh. Signed: William X West. Inventory of estate made 1786 by Nathan Melton, Daniel Parkins, Alexander McDougal.

WHERRY

William Wherry. Will of William Wherry. Case 14 File 611. Probate Judge Office. York, S. C. I William Wherry of York Dist. being of sound mind and memory. I desire my executor to sell all my personal property sufficient to pay my just debts and funeral expenses. After paying my debts, I give to my wife Elizabeth Wherry the whole of my estate, both real and personal during the term of her natural life, and after her death, I give to my daughter Elizabeth Wherry the plantation on which I now live. The balance or rest of my estate not before dispose of, I leave to be equally divided amongst my children. I appoint my son Andrew Sherry executor. Dated 23 Feb. 1850. Wit: Harvey H. Drennon, Archabald Steele, Mathew H. Williams. Signed: William Wherry. Probated the 12 March 1850.

WHISENANT

B. C. Whisenant. Book B, page 34. Probate Judge Office. Pickens, S. C. On 19 Oct. 1859 B. C. Whisenant and wife Milly H. were heirs of Joel Mason decd. of Pickens, Dist. and his widow Frances Mason.

Christopher Whisenant. Estate of Christopher Whisenant. Book B Page 86. Probate Judge Office. Pickens Dist., S. C. On 20 Nov. 1865 Christopher Whisenant died intestate lately owning 142 acres on Beaver Dam Branch, waters of Toxaway Creek, adj. land of S. E. Maxwell, Joseph Liles. Heirs, viz; Jane Whisenant widow with whom he lived several years and had no children. The following children by his former wives viz; 1. Heirs at law of Nicholas Whisenant decd. 2. Heirs at law of Robert Whisenant decd. 3. George Whisenant, Flemming Bates and wife Polly, 5. ___ Dickey and wife Sarah. 6. Salina Liles. Jeremiah H. Johns and wife Rebecca. 7. Heirs of Eliza Norris decd. viz; J. J. Hunnicut and wife Nancy, Barbary Alberson, T. R. Norris and Rebecca Norris. 9. Levi Phillips and wife Rachael. 10. Heirs of Letty A. Liles decd. viz; Jonah Liles, Arena Liles, Fanny Liles, Derby Ann Liles,

Rachel Liles, Nancy J. Liles, John Bell Liles. 11. Heirs of Bartholomew Whisenant decd. viz; Sarah F. Whisenant, William L. Whisenant, Mary
Ann Whisenant, Jefferson Davis Whisenant, Nancy Moore. The heirs at
law of Nicholas Whisenant. The heirs at law of Robert Whisenant
decd. Flemming Bates and wife Polly. ___ Dickey and wife Sarah,
Selina Liles, Jeremiah Johns and wife Rebecca resides without the
limits of this State.

WHITE

Andrew White. Estate of Andrew White. Box 98 Pack 2399. Probate
Judge Office. Abbeville, S. C. Est. admr. 11 June 1798 by Jane White,
widow. William White of Colhouns Creek, William Garrett, Alexander
White who are bound unto Andrew Hamilton, Adam Crain Jones, Hugh Ward-
law, Esqs. Judges of Abbeville Dist. in the sum of one thousand dollars.
Citation was published at Long Cane, Abbeville, 14 May 1798. Sale of
the estate held on second Tuesday in July 1798. Buyers. William
White, Jr., Jane White, William Fletcher, William Childres, Alexander
Gaminct, Samuel Coiel, James Nelson, Dudly Jones, James Holland, William
Garrett, Hugh Calhoone, John Post, Andrew Gelaspey, James Williams,
Francis Drinard, Christopher Brooks. In a return made for the years
1798-1799 it was made by John and Jane Strain. Was signed Jane X
Strain.

Margaret White. Bastardy, Pack 439 #25. Clerk of Court Office.
Pickens, S. C. The examination of Margaret M. White of Pickens Dist.
a single woman, taken upon oath before me John Adair one of the Justices
of the peace. This first day Feb. 1838. She saith that on the 19 April
now last past at the house of John Carter in the aforesaid Dist. she
was delivered of a male bastard child and that the said child is likely
to become chargeable to the said Dist. and that Edward Rogers, Esquire,
of the said dist. did get her with the said child. Signed: Margaret
M. White. Signed: John Adair, J.P.

Alexander White. Will of Alexander White. Box 30 #346. Probate
Judge Office. Pickens, S. C. I Alexander White of Pickens Dist. being
in sound mind and memory, I give to each of my sons namely, Wm. H.
White, R. M. White, A. S. White, A. R. White, J. B. White, R. J. White
and equal share of my est. after what I will to my dtrs. I will to
Martha Cox five dollars, to Jane Carter fifty dollars, to S. A. Hunecut
five dollars, to Nancy Moss fifty dollars, to Catrine Sharp that receipt
that John Sharp give for that land I let him have. Unto Meriah Randolf
two children that she had to Randolf namely Buford & S. Harvey six
dollars each to help school them. The notes of my sons, A. R. White,
J. B. White, A. P. White, to be void. I appoint my son Wm. H. White
and J. Diole executors. Dated 6 Oct. 1845. Wit: Charles H. White,
Sarah J. White, Wesley B. White. Signed: Alexr. White. Proven 10 June
1853.

H. N. White. Ref. Est. of J. Stribling. Book B, page 48. Probate
Judge Office, Pickens, S. C. On 6 Feb. 1860 H. N. White and wife Nancy
White were heirs of Jesse Stribling decd. of Pickens Dist.

Thomas A. White. Book B Page 78. Probate Judge Office. Pickens Dist.
On 30 Dec. 1865. Thomas A. White decd. of Pickens Dist. owned 50 acres
adj. land of Gideon Ellis, Jacob Boroughs. Left a widow Elizabeth
White who is his only heir.

Alexander White. Book B page 91. Probate Judge Office. Pickens, S. C.
On 23 Jan. 1866 Alexander White and his wife Milly White were heirs of
George Ross decd. of Pickens, S. C.

Andrew P. White. Pack 634. #179. Clerk of Court Office. Pickens, S.C.
On 1 April 1845 Andrew P. White was appointed a constable of Pickens
Dist.

Yancey White. Pack 646 #1. Clerk of Court Office. Pickens, S. C.
Mary M. Carver, a single woman states that on 4 Feb. 1851 at the house
of Yancey White in Pickens Dist. she was delivered of a female bastard
child with deep blue eyes and light colored hair and that Yancey White
a farmer did get her with child.

Elisha White. Apt. 1 File 22. Probate Judge Office. Greenville, S. C.
On 7 Aug. 1837 Elisha White and his wife Margaret White of Izard County,
Arkansas were heirs of a David Barnett,Sr. who died in 1837 in Green-
ville Dist.

                              WHITMIRE

Henry Whitmire. Estate of Henry Whitmire. Book B Page 35. Probate
Judge Office. Pickens, S. C. On 9 Jan. 1860 Henry Whitmire decd.
owned two tracts of land in Pickens Dist. #1. The home place, adj. land
of Daniel Whitmire, Isaac Crow on Jocasse and Toxaway Rivers, containing 566 acres. #2 on Toxaway River, adj. tract #1 and Isaac Anderson,
containing 134 acres. Heirs are William Whitmire, heirs of Mark Hinkle
decd. viz; Henry Hinkle, John Hinkle, Peter Butler and wife Eliza Beth,
William Hunter and wife Mary, Elijah Hinkle Jr., Carr Hinkle, Elias
Hinkle, A. J. Stewart and wife Lucinda, Silas Hinkle, Martha Hinkle,
Jeremiah Morton and wife Lucinda, Daniel Whitmire, John Whitmire,
Jonathan King and wife Nancy and Henry Whitmire.

Anna Whitmire, Eq. Records, of Allen Robertson. #654. Clerk of
Court Office. Pickens, S. C. On 7 April 1855 Anna Whitmire wife of
Jeremiah Whitmire were living in Pickens Dist. Dtr. of Allen Robertson
decd. of Pickens, S. C. who died in 1854 and of his widow Catherine
Robertson.

                              WHITNEY

Malcom Whitney. Box 48 #10. Probate Judge Office. Barnwell, S. C.
I Malcom Whitney of Barnwell Dist. being in perfect health of body and
of sound mind and memory. I give to my wife Rachel Whitney the whole
of my estate both real and personal, during her natural life, or widowhood. If she should marry after my death, I will and desire that the
whole of my estate, both real and personal be sold and equal division
take place between my wife and my children, she my wife taking a child
part only. I appoint my wife executrix. Dated 14 Oct. 1817. Wit:
Tolliver Martin, Rebekah Martin, Zachariah Martin. Signed: Malcom
Whitney. Proven on oath of Toliver Martin before Orsamus D. Allen, ord.
on the 31 Oct. 1827. Inventory was made by David Buckhalter, Jesse
Johnson, William Conway, John Bush. Sale of estate made 16 Oct. 1834,
Buyers were: William Walker, Jesse Youngblood, Rachel Youngblood,
Edmond Stringfield, Hardy Wall, Reason Woolley, Rachel Whitney.

Archibald Whitney. Will of Archibald Whitney. Box 40 #11. Probate
Judge Office. Charleston, S. C. I Archibald Whitney of Charleston
city being of sound mind and disposing memory. First I desire my just
debts be fully paid, after paying my debts and funeral expenses. I
then give all my estate real and personal of what nature or kind whatsoever, to my beloved wife Mary Whitney to her and her heirs, assignes,
executor, etc. I appoint my beloved wife Mary Whitney and my three
sons executrix and executors viz; Octavious Lebbeus Whitney, Theodore
Archibald Whitney, Cornelius Gardner Whitney. Dated 26 June 1846.
Wit: W. Loyd, Randal Robinson, T. A. Wilbur. Signed: A. Whitney.
Proven on oath of W. Loyd before M. T. Mendenhall Esq. on the 24 June
1847. On the 29 June 1847 qualified Theodore Archibald Whitney,
executor.

Aaron Whitten. Family of Aaron Whitten and his wife ___ Whitten who
was the dtr. of Jonathan Whitten. Children not in order of birth.
1. A dtr. ___ Whitten, who married David Caldwell. 2. Elizabeth
Whitten married Jonathan W. Rochester. 3. Margaret Whitten unmarried
in 1845. 4. John C. Whitten. 5. Austen Whitten. 6. Jackson Whitten,
probably the man who was called "Jack Whitten" in the 1850 census in
Pickens Co. He was age 42, his wife Margaret was ago 40 and his chn.
Margaret 15, Austin 11, Harriett 9, Julia 7, John 5, Mary 3, George 1.
All born in S. C. 7. Greenberry Whitten. He was called "Green B"
on his headstone at Pendleton it is "G. B." born 1818 died 19 Jan. 1896.
His wife Harriet M. was born 1824 and died 27 Mar. 1892. Their chn. in
1860 census were: John 16, Byrd 14, Edward 12, and Andrew 2.
8. Rachel F. Carson (late Whitten) dtr. of Aaron and G. dtr. of
Jonathan, she married a Carson. Rachel with her children were heirs of
Jonathan and together were entitled to one child share of 1/4 of 2/3
of Jonathan estate.

Jonathan Whitten. Rev. Soldier. Per his pension application, made in
Pickens Dist., 6 Oct. 1835. He was born at Munford Cove, Va. in 1762.
He was brought into S. C. when a child by his parents, they lived in
Newberry during the Rev. War then moved to Union Dist., then to Pendle-
ton Dist. for 10 years. (That part called Pickens). Jonathan Whitten
died some time before Jan. 1845. Being survived by his widow, Elizabeth
the chn. of Jonathan & Elizabeth were: 1. A dtr. ___, who married
Aaron Whitten. Both died before 1845. 2. Peggy Whitten married
William Phillips. 3. A dtr. ___ who married William Rochester.
4. Frances Whitten, possibly she was the Frances Whitten age 48, who
with Martha Whitten age 26 was found in the 1850 census living in Union
Co., S. C. (Most of the above records is found in Real Estate Book A,
page 60. Pickens Co.)

Peter Whitten. Will of Peter Whitten. Book C.C. Page 19. Probate
Judge Office. Sumter, S. C. I, Peter Whitten, of St. Matthews
in and by bond or obligation bearing date, stands held and firmly bound
unto Thomas Sumter, Jr. in the sum of $9,000.00. Conditions for the
full and just sum of $4500 with interest from date there of, on the 15
June 1810-1811-1812. And in the sum of one dollar, paid by Peter
Whitten, and signed a deed of trust for the land that Whitten was buying
from Thomas Sumter, Jr. containing 300 acres lying near Dey Swamp in
Sumter Dist. Adj. land of Edmond Roach, James and John Atkinson and
Thomas Sumter Jr. Dated 15 June 1809. Wit: Hastin Jennings, David
Thompson. Signed Peter Whitten. On the 15 June 1809 Mrs. Natalie
Sumter the wife of Thomas Sumter, Jr. did release, and forever relin-
quish unto Peter Whitten all her rights in the above land. Before John
Horan, J.Q. Peter Whitten of St. Mathews bought 300 acres of land
from Thomas Sumter, Jr. for $9,000 and paid half the price that day and
gave to Sumter a deed of trust on the same land for a three years to
pay off the remainder.

Lindsay Whitten. Estate of Lindsay Whitten. Book not given, page 246.
Probate Judge Office. Laurens, S. C. Settlement of the estate of
Lindsey Whitten decd. made before the Ord. on the 9 Jan. 1846. Heirs
the widow Nancy and three chn. viz; John Whitten, Alfred Whitten, the
wife of James Dillard. Alfred was a minor

William Whitten. Deed from William Whitten. Book T, page 109. Clerk
of Court Office. Anderson, S. C. This deed made 2 Aug. 1828. Between
William Whitten and Benjamin Smith both of Pendleton Dist. In the sum
of $417.50 paid by said Benjamin Smith for a tract of 167 acres, being
part of four tracts, 68 acres originally granted to Elizabeth Oliver,
15 acres granted to Samuel Norwood, 24 acres granted to John Whitten,
50 acres belonging to a tract that Jeremiah Williams Jr. now lives,
originally granted to Elizabeth Johnston, 10 acres granted to Thomas
Garvin, all on the waters of 23 mile creek, adj. land of Benjamin
Smith, Samuel Maverick, Jeramiah Williams, Jr., Hardy Fennell, James A.

Wilson. Wit: James McKinney, Aaron Nalley. Signed: William Whitten.
Recorded 22 May 1831.

Rebecca Whitten. Deed from Rebecca Whitten. Book T, page 159. Clerk
of Court Office. Anderson, S. C. Deed made 2 May 1836. Between
Rebecca Whitten of Anderson Dist. and D. K. Hamilton and T. H. McCann.
In the sum of $700 paid by D. K. Hamilton and T. H. McCann all that
tract of land being in Pickens Dist. on east side of Indian Branch,
West prong of 23 Miler River. Being part of a grant of Major John
Cannoway Smith, certified 14 July 1784 and granted 21 Jan. 1785. The
western part conveyed to Jacob Burriss, containing 300 acres, adj. lands
of Jacob Burriss, Hamilton and McCann, Dr. James Earle and Mrs. Wilson.
Also a grant of John Whitten of 14 Dec. 1826 of 74 acres and a grant
to Francis Bonneau. Wit: Joseph A. Whitner, Jacob Burriss. Signed:
Rebecca Whitten. Recorded 2 May 1836.

John C. Whitten. Bond from John C. Whitten. Book J-2 page 275. Clerk
of Court Office. Anderson, S. C. I John C. Whitten in and by my bond
dated 1 Dec. 1869 stand firmly bound unto John B. Sitton and William
H. D. Gaillard in the sum of $932.00 for the payment of the full and
just sum of $450.16. Do sell unto John B. Sitton and Wm. H. D. Gaillard
all that tract of land lying and being in Anderson Co. containing 204
acres. Land of the late Robert A. Maxwell, known in the division as
tract 7. Adj. land of John Whitten and Pickney. Dated 1 Dec. 1869.
Wit: M. W. Sitton, Joseph J. Smith. Signed: John C. Whitten.

Green B. Whitten. Deed from Green B. Whitten. Book T-2, page 532.
Clerk of Court Office. Anderson, S. C. I Green B. Whitten of Anderson
S. C. I Green B. Whitten of Anderson Co. for the sum of $700.00 paid to
me by William W. Smith of Anderson Co. have released unto said Smith
all that tract of land purchased by me from R. F. Simpson and Margaret
M. Simpson, lying on the South side of 23 Mile River. Containing 60
acres, adj. lands of R. F. Simpson, on the North by Warren Martin, on
the East by Thomas Dickson. Dated 4 Feb. 1881. Wit: R. W. Simpson,
M. A. Lanier. Signed: Green B. Whitten. On 19 Dec. 1881 Mrs. Harriet
Whitten wife of Green B. Whitten did appear and relinquish all her claim
right of dower. Harriet Whitten.

J. C. Whitten. Deed from J. C. Whitten. Book U-2, page 360. Probate
Judge Office. Anderson, S. C. Deed from J. C. Whitten of Oconee County
in consideration of the sum of $510.00 paid by O. H. P. Fant of Anderson
County have sold unto Fant all that land lying in Anderson Co. on waters
of Seneca River, being part of a tract conveyed to me by J. B. Sitton
and W. H. D. Gaillard assignees of R. A. Maxwell, containing 62 acres.
Adj. land of myself, O. H. D. Fant, J. C. Carson, John R. Zacherys.
Dated 10 Oct. 1881. Wit: L. G. Phillips, William Young. Signed:
J. C. Whitten. On 10 Oct. 1881 Mrs. Elmira Whitten wife of J. C.
Whitten did relinquish her right of dower.

Jonathan Whitten. Deed from Jonathan Whitten. Book A-1 page 236.
Probate Judge Office. Pickens, S. C. I Jonathan Whitten of Pendleton
Dist. in consideration of $300 paid by David Sloan of the same Dist.
have granted, bargained, sold and released all that tract of land where-
on I now live containing 413 acres, on a branch between Solomon West
and Philip Cox line, also on Todd line. Dated 16 Mar. 1829. Wit:
Johnathan Rochester, William D. Sloan. Signed: Jonathan X Whitten.
Recorded 10 Feb. 1830.

Marthy Whitten. Power of Attorney. No ref. Probate Judge Office.
Union, Dist., S. C. I Marthy Whitten have this day authorized and
appointed William Phillips my true and lawfull attorney to use my name
to receive any amount of money due me in the Ordinary Office in Pickens
Dist. as my part of the legacy coming to me from Jonathan Whitten decd.
Dated 6 Nov. 1845. Signed Marthy Whitten (seal) under this name is
Frances Whitten.

Albert Whitten. Inquisition of Albert Whitten. (Taken from basement
records.) Clerk of Court Office. Anderson, S. C. An inquisition
taken at the house of Capt. John P. Benson, in Pendleton Dist. Dated

7 Dec. 1825. Before Joseph Gresham Coroner upon view of the body of
Albert Whitten, being dead by the oath of John Miller Esq., foreman, Jury.
Jeremiah Winters, William Miller, John Archer, John P. Benson, William
Dennis, Samuel C. McCroskey, Elias Roberts, John Hoyt, Isabey B. Bull,
M. W. Bull and M. T. Miller being good and lawful men of the Dist.
The jury said that Albert Whitten came to his death by a sudden and
violent fall from a horse near the village of Pendleton on the evening
of Monday the 5th inst. By which he received one mortal wound on the
back of his head. He lanquished until between the hours of 5 & 6 p.m.
of this day when he died. The jury said he was killed or came to his
death by misfortune. Each juryman signed his own name.

WHORTON

William Whorton. Deed from William Whorton. Book C page 113. Mesne
Conveyance. Greenville, S. C. This indenture made 13 Sept. 1791
between William Whorton and Jean his wife and William Chandler both of
Greenville Dist. In consideration of ten pds. paid by said William
Chandler have granted, sold, released a tract of land containing 100
acres, being in Greenville Co. above the old Indian Boundary on the
North side of Saluda River on both sides of Mountain Creek, waters of
Enoree. Adj. lands of William Whorton, vacant land on other sides,
granted to Wadsworth and Turpin the 1 Jan. 1787. Wit: Mark Thompson,
Nis. Darby. Signed: William X Whorton and Jane X Whorton. Proven on
oath of Nicholas Derby before Robert McFee Esq. on the 1 Mar. 1792.

Benjamin Whorton. Deed from Benjamin Whorton. Book C, page 251.
Mesne Conveyance. Greenville, S. C. This indenture made 25 Aug. 1790
between Benjamin Whorton of Pendleton Dist. and Peter Sarter of Green-
ville Dist. In consideration of 100 pds. sterling paid by the said
Peter Sarter have granted, sold and released a tract of 202 acres in
Greenville Dist. being the same were on Peter Sarter now live, lying
on both sides of Bush Creek. Originally granted to Henry Hays on 15
Oct. 1784. Wit: Eli Norman, Aaron Kemp. Signed: Benjamin Whorton.
Recorded 4 June 1793 on oath of Aaron Kemp.

Benjamin Whorton. Deed from Benjamin Whorton. Book B page 342. Clerk
of Court Office. Anderson, S. C. This indenture made 4 July 1793
between Benjamin Whorton of Pendleton Dist. and Thomas Robertson of
Pendleton Dist. In consideration seventy pds. sterling paid by the said
Thomas Robertson have granted, sold, and released a tract of land
containing 383 acres on Occony Creek waters of Little River, a branch
of Keowee River. Wit: William McCaleb, James Hendrix. Signed: Benj.
Whorton. Proven on oath of Wm. McCaleb before J. Miller, J.P. on the
22 Jan. 1795.

Benjamin Whorton. Deed of Benjamin Whorton. Book I, page 170. Clerk
of Court Office, Anderson, S. C. This indenture made between Benjamin
Whorton of Pendleton Dist. and Solomon West of Jackson Co., Ga. In
consideration of $400 have granted, sold, bargained, and released all
that tract of land lying on a prong of Cain Creek waters of Keowee
River. Adj. land of Philip Cox. Dated 29 Oct. 1860. Wit: William
McFarland, Cleveland X Coffee. Signed: Benjamin Whorton. Proved 22
Dec. 1807.

Benjamin Whorton. Deed from Benjamin Whorton. Book G Page 160. Clerk
of Court Office. Anderson, S. C. This indenture between Benjamin
Whorton and Zachiriah Holcomb both of Pendleton Dist. Dated 14 Dec.
1801. In consideration of $100 paid by the Zachiriah Holcomb have
granted, sold, and released all that tract of land containing 200 acres
lying on the North Branch of Cane Creek, beginning at a stake on
Caleb Starr's corner, then to Prewett old line, then along a line
between Holcomb and James Hugheys lands. William Smith, Thomas Williams.
Signed: Benjamin Whorton. Proven on oath of William Smith before
Henry Burch, J.P. on the 19 Dec. 1801.

Benjamin Whorton. Deed from Benjamin Whorton. Book C page 330. Clerk
of Court Office, Anderson, S. C. This indenture made 4 Feb. 1797.
Between Benjamin Whorton and James Caddell both of Pendleton Dist.
In consideration of 40 pds. sterling hath bargained, sold, released a
tract of land lying and being in County aforesaid containing 200 acres.
Beginning on South side of Cain Creek on Calopsanes South line. Wit:
John Bezley and Oburn Buffington. Signed: Benjamin Whorton. Proven
on oath of Oburn Buffington before Joseph Reid, J.P. on the 22 Apr.
1797. Recorded 25 April 1797.

Samuel Wideman. Estate of Samuel Wideman. Pack 403. Clerk of Court
Office. Abbeville, S. C. To the Honr. the Chancellors; in Equity,
your oratrix Frances E. Zimmerman sheweth that in the year 1849 the late
Samuel Wideman, Jr. departed this life leaving a widow Margaret Wideman
and children as follows, Mary S. Wideman, Columbus A. Wideman, William
H. Wideman, James A. Wideman, also a decd. dtr. Emily Pennel, James A.
Pennel and William H. Pennel who represent their mother and whose father
is dead. Your oratrix further sheweth that all the hiers and distri-
buteees are minors under the age of twenty one. At the time of his
death the father of your oratrix was seized and possessed with three
tracts of land, one the home tract containing 497 acres, adj. land of
Joseph J. Lee, Thomas P. Dowtin, William W. Belcher. tract two, called
Long Cane Tract, of 354 acres, adj. land of Joshua Wideman, Vincent
McCelvey, Uel Wideman, tract three, the Glasgow tract on Bold Branch of
211 acres, adj. land of Thomas Thomson, William W. Belcher. The persona
property by estimation at $16,000 with no more than $100 in debts. The
mother of your oratrix has applied for letter of admr. upon the est.
Your oratrix prays that the land be allotted to the heirs and dis-
tributees in severalty. Filed 20 Nov. 1849. Samuel Wideman bought the
tract #3 from William D. Gallaugher. Tracts #1-2 he bought from James
Glasgow and his wife Mary Ann. They had a dtr. named Mary Ann
McClelland who they gave 72 1/2 acres on Long Cane Creek waters of
Little River. Originally granted to Sarah Crozier. Deed dated 16 Nov.
1839.

WILEY

David Wiley. Pack 646 #5. Clerk of Court Office. Pickens, S. C.
On 14 Mar. 1859 James Richey of Pickens Dist. made oath that he has
"a title claim and interest in the real and personal estate of David
Wiley decd. late of Arkansas, in 50 acres of land on Whetstone Creek
adj. lands of Burnet Wilson and others.

WILLARD

French P. Willard. Box 96 #1007. Probate Judge Office. Pickens, S. C.
Est. admr. 5 July 1869 by David F. Bradley, Joab Mauldin who are bound
unto I. H. Philpot, ord. in the sum of $238.00. In 1870 paid Thomas E.
Willard burial expenses $10.00.

WILLIAMS

John Williams. Estate of John Williams. Box 99 Pack 2438. Probate
Judge Office. Abbeville, S. C. Est. admr. 11 Dec. 1782 by Isreal
Pickens, William White, Alexander Noble who are bound unto John Ewing
Calhoun Ord. in the sum of fourteen thousand pounds. Whereas Isreal
Pickens of Little River hath applyed to me for letter of administration
of all the goods and chattles, rights and credits of John Williams
late of said Dist. as the highest creditor. A list of the notes due
the estate on 12 Mar. 1783 viz; John Verner, John McCurdy, William
Little, Alexander Denham, John Kennedy, Henry McMurdie, George Pettigrew
James Thompson, William White, Isreal Pickens, William Harris, Mary
Price, Phillip Mathew, Andrew Gillespie, William Elliot, Alexander Hall,

Joseph McCleskey Senr., Samuel Nelson, James Long, Samuel Foster, William Manson, William Baxter. A note at the end of an inventory states that a former inventory was made 30 April 1781. That to their knowledge there was not an Ordinary Office in 96 Dist. as the enemy being then in this District. The appraisement being made without legal authority but of necessity. Signed: Jno. Luckie, William White.

Jeremiah Williams. Estate of Jeremiah Williams. Pack 747. Probate Judge Office. Anderson, S. C. Est. admr. 21 Jan. 1831 by Jeremiah Williams, Ezekiel Murphey, Lewis Owen who are bound unto John Harris, Ord. in the sum of $4,000. On 25 Nov. 1831, I John Hughes and Francies my wife, give it as our opinions for to do equal Justice their ought to be twelve months credit on the sale of the land of Jeremiah Williams decd. Signed: John Hughes. On 26 Nov. 1831 we Hannah Williams, Lucy Williams and Patsey McAllister certify that we agree with John Hughes and Francies his wife as respects the term of payment for the above lands. Signed Test, Jerhm. Williams. Hannah Williams, Lucy X Williams, Patsey McAllister. On 25 Jan. 1831 before John T. Lewis C.C. & Qm. E., Jeremiah Williams of Pickens Dist. personally appeared before me and sworn in due form that the subjoined list does contain to the best of his knowledge the names and places of residence of every heir at law of Jeremiah Williams decd. viz; Hannah Williams, Lucy Williams, Patsey Williams (now Patsey McAllister, widow), Dorcas Williams (now Dorcas Owen), Nancy Williams (now Nancy Cason), Frances Williams (now Frances Hughs), Rosanna Fox (now Rosanna Elliot) being the dtr. of Elizabeth Williams who is said to have married Thomas Fox and by him to have had the said Rosanna, all of Anderson Dist. (Out of State heirs). David Williams, (Hall County, Ga.), Daniel Williams (Hall Co., Ga.), Benjamin Williams (Habersham Co., Ga.), Thomas Williams (Habersham Co., Ga.), Graham Williams (Habersham Co., Ga.), Rosanna Williams now Rosanna Johnson, in Alabama County not known., James Williams wife of Harard or Harvard last account in the State of Miss. County not known. The husband full name as given in another paper viz; Stephen Johnson, Charles Daily or Harvard?, Edward McAllister, Joseph Cason, Lewis Owen. The land of Jeremiah Williams was on Hurricane Creek waters of Saluda River, adj. land of John Simpson, Samuel Maverick, being the whole except what was given to chn. Hannah, Lucy and Benjamin, contains 132 acres.

Richard Williams. Estate of Richard Williams. Pack 791. Probate Judge Office. Anderson, S. C. Est. admr. 7 Sept. 1829 by Nathan Berry, Micajah Berry, Mary William, Ransom Cobb, William Copeland who are bound unto John Harris, Ord. in the sum of $2,000. Citation published at Big Creek Meeting House 6 Sept. 1829. He left a widow and five chn. (only the sale of the negroes is given.) Dated 16 Mar. 1833. Mary Williams bought, George and Easter his wife and Fany a little girl, and Moses a little boy. J. B. Gambrill, bought, Mary and child. M. B. Williams, bought, Baylus and Ben., M. B. Williams gdn. for Newton Williams, bought, Willis, M. B. Williams gdn. for Jasper Williams, bought, Seasor. M. Berry, gdn. for Sarah A. Williams, bought, Isaac.

Robert Williams. Estate of Robert Williams Box 94 pack 2334. Probate Judge Office. Abbeville, S. C. Est. admr. 9 Aug. 1823 by Joseph Williams, John Williams and Stephen Henderson who are bound unto Moses Taggart, Ord. in the sum of $700.00. Money due the est. of Robert Williams decd. in notes as of 4 Oct. 1823, viz; Charles and Willis Holmes, Henry Johnston Jr., Dudley Brooks, John Williams, Sr. Henry Johnston, Jr., Joseph Williams, John C. Williams, John R. Youngblood, John C. Williams, Jonathan Johnston, James Bradley. (Another Estate in this Pack) 96 Dist. by James Yancey Esq. Surogate to John Thomas, Jr. esq. Ord. to Van Swearingen, Ezekel McLendon, William Noble and Thomas Swearingen, freeholders you are authorized to repair to all places in the Dist as you may be directed by Leonard Nobles and Jno. Swearingen admr. upon the est of Robert Williams decd. and return a true inventory within forty days to this office. Dated 10 Oct. 1786. Edgefield Dist. This is to certify that I have qualified the within named Van Swearingen Jr., Ezekiel McLendon, Wm. Nobles, as appraisers, dated 10 Oct. 1786. John Purves, J.P.

Samuel Williams. Estate of Samuel Williams. Box 99 Pack 2433. Probate
Judge Office. Abbeville, S. C. Est. admr. 27 April 1782 by Benjamin
Tutt, William Moore, Joseph ___? who are bound unto John Ewing Calhoun
Ord. in the sum of fourteen thousand pounds. 96 Dist. You Benjamin
Tutt do swear that Samuel Williams and John Nobles, decds. made no last
will and testament as far as you know and believe, and that you will
show the appraisers that shall be appointed by the Ordinary, all the
goods and chattles of the deceased, in your hands or will come into
your hands. You will pay their debts and legacies as far as the estate
will extend. You will make a true and perfect inventory of goods
and chattles, ready money, noted etc. Dated 27 April 1782 Jno. Ewing
Calhoun. (Another estate admr. during the British control. In the same
Pack another Samuel Williams decd. est. dated 18 June 1801 to Joseph
Williams, only paper found is cash paid to viz; year 1802, William
Watson, cash lent to widow to buy tin ware, Mr. Lilly for preaching
funeral. Mrs. Grigsby for making negroes clothes, Wm. Owen, Richard
Williams proven acct. Jno. Monroe, Samuel Ramsey, T. Steele, Williamsons
Samuel Goode, Dr. Meriwether, S. Henderson, James McCracken, Jos.
Stallsworth. Abbeville Dist. Appeared before me James Caldwell Esq.
executor of Joseph Williams decd. and made oath that the foregoing is a
true copy of the expenditures (made by said decd.) of the est. of Samuel
Williams decds. as found amongst his papers. Sworn to 19 Dec. 1804
before A. Hamilton J.P. Signed: James Caldwell.

Simeon Williams. Estate of Simeon Williams. Box 99 Pack 2435. Probate
Judge Office. Abbeville, S. C. (Will) Abbeville Dist. I being at
this time in my perfect sences and right mind, I leave this as my last
will and testament with my wife Eaduf Williams and my brother Arthur
Williams as executors. First I will my debts be paid, my land in Greenville County shall be sold to pay off my debts also the debts due me
be paid for the better discharging my own debts. All the rest of my
estate to my wife Eaduf Williams during her widowhood or life, if she
remarry the estate to be sold and divided among my chn. and my wife son
Isaac Sherodine he is to have an equal part with my children. Dated
8 April 1801. Wit: Charles Dodson, John Williams. Signed: Simeon
Williams. Recorded 23 Sept. 1801. Sale held 23 Oct. 1802 Buyers:
Eduf Williams, Partain Hagewood, John Wilson, James Read, Can McGee,
Joseph Eassery, John Adams, John Williams, Terry Lomax, James Lomax,
William Brown, Larkin Cutter.

William A. Williams. Pack 107. Clerk of Court Office. Abbeville,
S. C. Abbeville Dist. To the Honr. Chancellors; your petitioner Samuel
S. Marshall sheweth that he is the uncle of the infant William A.
Williams, that the said minor under the age of nine years and is
entitled to a distributive share in the estate of his decd. father
William A. Williams, amounting to about $15,000. Your petitioner there-
fore prays that he may be appointed guardian of the said minor. To
the Honr. the Chancellors of the Court of Equity; I consent that my
brother Samuel S. Marshall be appointed guardian of the estate of my
son William A. Williams. Dated 13 June 1859. Katty F. Williams.

                              WILSON

Matthew H. Wilson. Estate of Matthew H. Wilson. Box 122 Pack 3601.
Probate Judge Office. Abbeville, S. C. The est. admr. 25 April 1849
by John H. Wilson, Samuel Reid, Lemuel Reid who are bound unto David
Lesly, Ord. in the sum of $2,000. To the Honr. David Lesly, Ord.
The humble petiton of John H. Wilson sheweth that Matthew Harvey Wilson
died intestate the 13 Dec. 1847. That he left personal estate and
effects in the Dist. That the decd. left as his next of kin, his mother
and brothers and sisters, namely, your petitioner, a brother prays for
a letter of admr. Dated 30 March 1849. The petiton of admr. of
M. H. Wilson decd. who died without wife or children, prays for a sale
of the personal effects. Dated 8 May 1849. Sale held 5 June 1849.
Elizabeth Wilson bought two negroes Linda at $350, Squire at $375, and

J. H. Wilson bought Andrew at $400. This is a true bill of the sale of the personal est. of M. H. Wilson decd. On 20 Dec. 1850 J. H. Wilson as admr. of Matthew Harvey Wilson decd. that he desires that the est. be settled, and that the usual notice be given to the parties out of State, etc. Signed: J. H. Wilson.

Atkinson, John 341
  Polley 30
  Timothy 30
Attaway, H.B. 30
  Mary Ann 30
Atwell, Joseph 88
Auguste, Holley 30
  Januy 30
  John 30
  Patcey 30
  Peggay 30
  Seasor 30
Auldrig, Benjamin 10
  Rebekah 10
Austin, Elender 31
  James 31
  James M. 30
  Jane 31
  John 31
  John P. 31
  Margaret H. 30
  Mary 23
  Mary Jane 31
  Nancy 30,31
  Nathaniel 31
  P.L. 331
  S. 23
  Sarah Ellen 30
  W.T. 31
  Walter 31
  William 275,282
  William M. 31
  William Thomas 31
Avren, John 326
Aycock, Patty 99
  William 99
Ayers, Daniel 110
  Susan A. 211
Babb, Mercer 324
Babbitt, Caleb 212
Baber, Mary 4
Bacon, Ludwell 169
  Mary 169
Badger, Nathaniel 71
Bagby, John 31
Bagget, Randle 255
Bagwell, John W. 313
Bailey 328
  Alen 241
  Caroline 54
  Charles 55,56
  Charles A. 32,55
  J.J. 316
  James M. 54
  Nathaniel 170,311
Baily, John 35
Baird, James 275
  John J. 270
Baker, Barsheba 76
  Elijah 76
  Elizabeth Elliott 45
  Frances 55
  Harriet 11
  Harriet M. 32
  Jane 315
  John W. 12
  Joseph 60
  Joseph T. 311
  Laura Toccoa 32
  Mary 296
  R.B. 296
  Richard B. 296,297
  Richard Bohum 45
  Robert 139
  Samuel S. 315
  William 241
  William F. 311
  William R. 32
Baldee, William 293
Baldwin, Drucilla 2,32
  Elisa Ann 32
  Elizabeth 32
  Elsy C. 32

Baldwin, George W. 32
  Isaac 1
  Levi G. 32
  Margaret 32
  Mary E. 32
  Nancy 32
  Peggy 32
  Samuel 32
  Sarah 32
  Stephen 32,129,241
  Thomas H. 32
Baldy, William 292
Balentine, Albert C. 33
  Andrew E. 33
  James A. 33
  Lucinda A. 33
  Mary A. 33
  Nancy 33
  Richard 33
  William A. 33
  William C. 33
Ball, B.W. 197
  Elizabeth 32,33,219
  George 33
  Jeremier 32,33
  Jinsay 33
  Lewis 33
  Lucay 33
  Nancy 33
  Peter 32,33
  Pollay 33
Ballard, Edward 83
  Rheuber 237
  Thomas 237
Ballenger, J.A. 2,317
  W.D. 9
Ballew, Robert 14,15
Ballinger 165
  E.L. 9
  James A. 2
  Marie E. 2
Balwin, George 269
  Nancy 269
Bandy, Bryant 143
  Phebe 143
Bankhead, Elizabeth 33
  Hannah 33
  James 33
  John 33
  Margaret 33
  Robert 33
  Samuel 33
  Thomas 33
Banks, Abram 34
  Baylis 34
  Dicy 171
  Elizabeth 34,148
  Emily 34
  Frances 34
  G.W. 34
  George 34
  Henry 34
  James 171
  James A. 34
  James M. 34
  Joab 34
  John 34
  John Henry 34
  M.M. 34
  Mary 217
  Mary C. 34
  Nancy 34
  Rachel 34
  Rachel J. 217
  Rachel Jane 34
  Ranson Allen 34
  Robert 148
  Roswell 34
  S.M. 38
  Sallie 34
  Sarah 34
  W.M. 34
  W.T. 34

Banks, Warren T. 33,148
  William 34
  William H. 34
Bankstone, Agnes 1
  Joseph 1
Barbor 159
Barkaloo, William F.D. 85
Barker, Charlotte 35
  Eli 35
  Elizabeth 35
  James 35
  Joshua 35
  Josiah 35,230
  Martha 35
  Mary 230
  Peggy 35
  Rebecca 35
  Richard R. 71
  Samuel G. 181
Barkley, Andrew 156
Barksdale, Daniel 220
  Delia Ann 35
  Fanney 35
  George T. 36
  Henry 35
  Higgason 35
  James T. 36
  John Lewis 36
  Patty 35
  Richard 35
  Sherod 36
  Steth 35
  Susannah 219,220
  Thomas 35
  William W. 36
Barlow, John 170
Barmore, Polly 234
  William 275
Barnard 137
  Timothy 137
Barnes, A.J. 323
  Christian 7,36,311
  J.F. 245,246
  James T. 36
  Jane 4
  John N. 36
Barnet, Mary 93
Barnett, Ann 70
  David 308,340
  Elijah 57,93
  Emilia 70
  John 216
  Riel 323
  Thomas 181
Barnhill, James 17
Barns, Elizabeth 157
  Gabriel 157
Barnwell, James A. 326
  John 263
  Mary 263
  Nathaniel 263
  Phebe 263
Barr, G.S. 220
  J.M. 337
  Malissa 192
  Rebecca 267
  W.H. 267
  William H. 77
Barram, Elizabeth 26
Barrett, Arthur 36,75
  Arthur I. 36
  Arthur J. 36
  Benjamin 37
  C.P. 184
  Caswell 36,115
  Coswell 36
  Charles P. 252
  David 36,37,86
  Elizabeth 36
  Frances 36
  Hannah 36
  James 34
  Jane 37

Casey, Joseph 19
Cashwell, Peter 145
Cason, Benjamin 217
  Elizabeth 76,247
  J.F. 299
  Joseph 345
  Nancy 345
  William Austin 247
Cass, James 12
  Catharine 76
  Ephraim 76
  Fanny 76
  Francis Marion 76
  Hamilton 76
  John 76
  Louisey 76
  Mary 76
  Meley 76
  Nancy 76
  Nathaniel Anderson 76
  Rosey Ann Jane 76
  Sarah 76
  Temperance 76
  William 76
  Zelia A. 76
Castle, John 17
  Milly 17
  Wyley Ann 17
Catlin, G.W.O. 59
Cauble, William A. 86
Caudle, Barsheba 76
  Elijah 76
  Richard 76
Caughran, John 295
Caulley, James F. 192
Cauly, Mary J. 192
Cazy, Elizabeth 337
  John 337
Ceeley, Henry 11
  Jane Caroline 11
Celey 335
Cethea, James 8
Chambers, Adam 77
  Alexander 77
  Arabella 77
  Benjamin 70,77
  Daniel 108
  James 77
  Jane 77
  Josiah 61,77
  Margaret 77
  Martha 77
  Mayfield 77
  Philip 78
  Polly 78
  Rachel 77
  Robert 326
  Ruth 77
  Samuel 77
  Stephen 77
  Thorowgood 112
  William 77,224
Chambles, Henry 307
Chamblin, D. 164
  Daniel 76
Chandler 87
  Batey 123
  Eliz abeth 163
  Frances 171
  Henry 171
  Henry F. 170
  Mordecai 111
  Polly 123
  R.A. 213
  Temperance 86
  William 343
  Willie 86
Chapman 163,233
  Amelia 79
  Ann G. 22
  Anna 79,318
  Benjamin 79,318
  Boro 79

Chapman, Caroline 113
  Caroline M. 78
  Catherine 79
  Cyntha J. 78
  Cyrus 78
  Daniel J. 113,153,319
  Eliza 79
  Elizabeth 78,103,113,
    140
  Enoch 78,298
  Essey 79
  Esther 78
  George J. 78,79
  Giles 78
  Green E. 79
  Harleston 78
  Hewelet 22
  Ida 79
  Isaac A. 78
  Isreal 78
  J. Harvey 79
  Jacob 78
  James 113,319
  James A. 78,79,80
  Joe 103
  Joel 78
  John 4,78,79,318,319
  John B. 79
  John F. 78
  John W. 79
  Josephine 207
  Joshua 78,140
  Julia 79
  Julius 78,79
  Leathe 327
  Luke 79
  M.T. 79
  Mack 79
  Margaret 78
  Martha E. 79
  Mary Ann M. 78
  Mary Jane 79
  Mary M.H. 241
  Matilda 78
  Miles 113
  Nancy 170
  Nancy S. 79
  Rachael 78,79,217
  Rebeckah 80
  Rosaline 79
  Roy 79
  Sam 170
  Samuel 78,79,140,241,
    252,322
  Sarah 78,114,207
  Sophia 4
  Susan C. 78
  Thomas D. 79
  Thomas H. 79
  William A. 79
  William B. 79
  William J.B. 78
Chappell, Amelia 80
  Caleb 80
  Caroline 80
  Charly 80
  Elizabeth Frances 80
  Henry 80
  Humphris 80
  Jane 80
  Jesse 80
  John 80
  Martha 80
  Mary 80
  Maryan 80
  Rebecca 80
  Robert 80
  Samuel 80,81
  Thomas 80
  William 80
Charles, Barksdale 31
  Mary 31
Chastain, Abner 17,101

Chastain, Edward 76,101
  J.F. 71
  Jacob 101
  James 27
  Matilda 192
  Maxwell 101
  Rebecca 101
  William 202
Chasteen, John 64
Chatham, Kate R. 40
  Robert 204
  Thomas 233
Chatwin, Joseph 219
Chavis, John 292
Cheatham, Patsey 122
  Robert 22,33
  Thomas 22
Cheeks, John L. 226
Chepman, Samuel 34
Cherry, David 143,174
  G.R. 129
  S.S. 252
  Thomas 174
Chestnut, James 270
  John 270
  John A. 228
Chevas, Margret 204
Cheves, Margret 293
  John 293
Chevis, Martha 273
Child, William 321
Childress, Emma 192
  John A. 139
  S.E. 192
  Sarah J. 192
  William 339
Childs, Benjamin 218
Chiled, James 155
Chiles, 232
  Benjamin 159
  David R. 175
  Garland 159,160,204
  Henry 159
  John 218,243,293
  Larkin 204
  Mary 338
  Mary G. 159
  Nimrod 155
  Robert 159
  W.M. 8
  William 257,313
Chilse, Thomas W. 8
China, John 308
  Marie 308
  Thomas 308
Chipley, William 160
Chisolm, Alfred 40
  C.A. 40
  Eliza 40
  Susan E. 39
  Valeria North 39
  William B. 40
Choice, William 97,172
Christian, Thomas 4
Christie, Alexander 181
  David Lamb 181
  Joan 180
  Jasper 181
Christiansen, Jasper 227
Christopher, Ephraim 182
  R.A. 167
Chumner, Dolly 123
  Sally 123
  William 123
Cisson, T.J. 323
Clardy, Benjamin 156
  John B. 94
  Mariah 134
Clark, Alexander 186
  Augustus 58
  B. 176
  Benjamin 104
  Cadaway 235

Doogan, James 69
  Margaret 69
Dooly, Hetha 109
Doran, James 212,317
Doris, Mary 315
Dorn, William B. 108
Dorr, Nancy 288
Dorrill, John 88
Dortch, Lydia 175
  S.D. 175
Dosier, James 333
Douglas, Donald 8
Douglass, Archibald 90,
  160
  Barbara 91
  Donald 90
  John 330
  Thomas 154
  William A. 91
Dothit, Benjamin 134
  J. 98,252
  S.J. 238
Dover 235
  William 160
Dow, Nancy 288
Dowdle, ALlen 320
  Jenny 42
  Robert 201
  Sarah 121
Dowis, John 1
  Sarah 1
Downey 255
Downing, Downey 103
Downs, Ann 55,236,278
Downy, John 8
Dowthit, Davis 202
  Robert 202
Dowtin, Thomas P. 344
Doyle, J.A. 162,178
  Sarah 3
  Susannah 105
  William 105
Dozier, Darcus D. 73
  Elizabeth 73
Drake, Mary 46
Drakeford, James 270
Drenan, Prudence 276
Drenna, Robert 295
Drennan, Billy Gilliland
  91
  Charles 295
  David 91,92
  James Wilson 91
  Mariah 92
  Mary Weems 91
  Samuel 92
  Thomas 92
  W.E. 107
  William 92
Drennon, Harvey H. 338
Drinard, Francis 339
Drinkard, Francis 63,148
  John 173
Drinkwater, John 173
Ducan, William 181
Duckworth, Benjamin 201
  Joseph 201
  Wilburn 201
Ducworth, Chesley Martin
  336
  Sarah Guyton 336
Duff, Adaline 92
  James 92,206
  Margaret B. 92
  Mary 92
  Merab 92
  Naomi L. 92
  William R. 92
Dugan, Park 168
Duke, Abraham 72
  Harriet 72
  Jane 280
  Joseph 270

Duke, Ransom 72,168
  Thomas 73
Dulin, John 224
Dunbar, James 12
  William 25
Duncan, David 321
  Elizabeth 186,280
  Henry 193
  J.V. 108
  N. 323
  Robert B. 16,98
Duncken, W.A. 323
Dunifins 136
Dunkin, Mary 193
Dunklin, Joseph 27
Dunlap, Benjamin 223
  James P. 223
  Rebecca 71
  William 64,148,161
Dunn, Calvin 71
  Joseph 97
  Mary 153
  Nehemiah 92
  William 199,274
Dunning, Peter F. 211
  R.W. 211
Dupee, Rachel 135,136,137
Dupre, Benjamin D. 25
Durant, O.L. 28,121,149
  Olin L. 57,58,113
  Robert R. 308
Durham 157
  A.J. 94
  A. Lucinda 93
  A.P. 94
  Ailmisa Narcissa Jane
    94
  Albert P. 94
  Allen 94
  Andrew 94
  Augustus 95
  B.C. 94
  Benjamin 92,95
  Berry 93,94,95
  Betsey 93
  Carter 12,93,94,95
  Charles 92,93,95,127,
    305
  Clary 95
  Daniel 57,92,93,94,95
    131,149,314
  David C. 94
  Delilah 93
  Elisar 93,94
  Eliza 93,94
  Elizabeth 12,93,94
  Ellen 93
  Emaly 95
  Ervin 94
  Eveline 94
  F.M. 10,95
  Fanny 94
  Gazille 93,94
  Hannah 12,95
  Harrison 95
  Isaac 93,94
  J.A. 95
  J.W. 93,94
  Jackson 95
  James 314
  Jane Elizabeth 95
  Jeremiah 92,93,149,176
  Jesse 95
  Joel 94
  John 93,94
  Joseph 12,92,93
  Julius 95
  L.A. 176
  Lenard 94
  Litha M. 94
  Lorenzo 95
  Lucinda 93
  Lucy 93

Durham, M.A. 94
  Malinda 13,94,95
  Mary 57,92,93
  Mary Ann 93,94
  Nancy 93,94,95
  Nancy Ellen 95
  Narcissa 93
  Nelly 94
  Patsey 93
  Perry 94
  Polley 92,93
  Rachel C. 300
  Rebecca 93,94
  Rhoda 93
  S.B. 94
  Sarah 94
  Sarah A. 176
  Sarah C. 10,95
  Sarah Ellender 94
  Sarah H. 93
  Stephen 93
  Thomas 93,95
  W.D. 93
  W.K. 94
  W. Riley 94
  William 13,93,94,95
  William O. 93
  William R. 95
Duthrie, Benjamin D. 135
Dyall, John 48
Dyass, Ann 95
  John 95
  Moses 95
Dyle, John 48
Dyres, John 98
Eads, John 274
Eakin, Joseph 21,23,168
  Benjamin 96
  Elizabeth 96
  Joseph 96
  Mary 96
  Sally 96
  Samuel 96
  Sarah 96
  Thomas 96
  William 96
Earl, B.J. 201
  J.R. 202
  John B. 306
Earle 118
  Andrew Pickens 96
  B.J. 172
  Baylis John 96
  Cecil 97
  Damaris Meriam 97
  Edward Hampton 96,97
  Edwin 97
  Elias 174
  Elias Theron 96,97
  Essie 97
  Eve 97
  George W. 97
  Hannah 306
  Harriet 97
  J.I. 273
  J.W. 1
  James 342
  James Harrison 96
  John B. 32
  Lucius L. 97
  Morgan Priestly 96
  Samuel 42,96,280
  Samuel Maxey 96,97
  Sarah Marie 97
  T.J. 88
Easkin, Thomas 237
Easley 324
  Catherine 98
  Elizabeth 98
  Huff 208
  John 98,143
  Mary 98
  Nancy 98

Hadden, Esther 158
  Jane 157
  Jean 158
  Mary 158
  Polly 105
  Robert 157
  William 158
  Zachariah 105
Haddon, Abram 158
  Hannah 158
  Permelia P. 158
  Thomas Luther 158
  Winube 158
Hagewood, Partain 346
Haggen, Edward 275
Hagood 118
  Adaline 158
  B. 16,140,253,279
  Benjamin 97,158,159,167,
    179,248,280,312,313
  Buck 159
  Eliza 158,159,160
  Elmina E. 158
  Elvira C. 158
  Fannie Miles 159
  George 116,160
  Gideon 158
  J. 121
  J.E. 206,258
  J.R. 159
  James E. 17,32,37,49,51,
    54,78,97,99,101,104,
    109,116,117,121,127,
    139,140,143,146,158,
    159,162,175,179,185,
    200,217,276,312,314
    323
  Jane 279,280
  Jerry 159
  John 255
  John H. 158,159
  Lucie Virginia 159
  Lydia 158
  Mary Elizabeth 159
  Randolph 159
  Rebecca 159,160
  Richard 159,160
  Susan 19,158
  Osborne 158
  W.M. 17,121,159
  W.W. 121
  William 158,159
  Z. 279
Hair, Job 71
Hairson, Agness 160
  James 160
  Jane 160
  John 160
  Peter 160
  Thomas 160
  William 160
Hairston, Hugh B. 274
  Robert 275
  William 63
Haise, Milly 121
Halbert, Arthur 161
  Enos 161
  James 161
  Joel 161
  John 161
  Joshua 161
  Martha 161
  Susannah 161
  William 157,160,161,286
Haley, W. 179
  Willis 179
Hall, Alexander 344
  Ann 162
  Benjamin 161
  Caroline 162
  Catherine 162
  Daniel 162
  David 161

Hall, Elizabeth 161,317
  Ezekiel 162,163
  F.H. 48
  F.S. 201
  Fenton 161,162,163,206
  Fleming 161
  Frances E. 162
  Francis M. 162
  G.W. 163
  George 162
  Henry 43,162
  Hugh 162
  J.D. 163
  James 162
  James S. 28
  Jesse 161
  John 161
  John E.M. 162
  Joseph 84
  Laurel V. 161
  M.A. 162
  Margaret 161,317
  Martin 201
  Mary 162,163,317
  Merry 43
  Nancy 162
  Nathaniel 161
  Robert 172
  Ruth 161,162
  Salena 162
  Samuel 127
  Sarah 161,162,163
  Thomas 162
  W.N. 163
  William 155,162,163
  Zach 162
  Zachariah 155,162
Hallum, A.C. 163
  Basil 70,163
  Eliza A. 163
  Elizabeth 163
  Isaac 141,163
  Jane 163
  John 163,195
  Julia A. 163
  Malissa 195
  Margaret B. 92,163
  Margaret Malinda 163
  Martha 67
  Martha Adeline 163
  Mary Ann 67,163
  Melinda Naomia 163
  Nero 163
  R.T. 35
  Richard 163
  Sary Emily 163
  Thomas 67,163,164,319
  William 163
Ham, John 145
Haman, S.A. 152
Hambleton, John 124
Hambright, L.B. 26
Hamby, Elizabeth 164
  James 164
  Sarah 164
Hamelton, Andrew 173
  C. Earl 51
  Margret A. 51
Hamilton 328
  A. 346
  A.C. 39
  A.M. 166,167
  A. McDuffie 117
  A.R. 57
  Alexander 8,20,70,168
  Alice Orean 167
  Andrew 37,53,61,63,77,
    91,124,128,156,164,
    166,167
  Ann A. 168
  Anna E. 167
  Archibald 274
  C.E. 166

Hamilton, Caroline 166,167
  Catherine 168
  Celia 166
  Chloe Jane 166
  Christiana 167,168
  Clemenia 166
  Cyrus E. 166
  D.K. 327,328,342
  David 164,166,167
  Effie C. 166
  Elizabeth 164,165,309
  Elizabeth Anne 165
  Ellen 167
  Emily 167
  Griffin 43,98,167
  Hampton 168
  Harriet A. 167
  Harriet E.D. 168
  Harrison 167
  Hester Ann 166
  Ira Griffin 168
  Isabella 165
  J.G. 43
  J.P. 167
  J.W. 166
  James 165,167
  James L. 310
  Jane 164,165,166,167
  Jean 166
  Jeremiah 168
  John 165,319
  Joseph A. 167,168
  L.G. 168
  L.J. 114
  Lemuel 166,167,168
  Leonard S. 164,166
  Leuvinia 149
  Luke 165
  McDuffie 167
  Mahala 167
  Margaret 119,164,165
  Mary 164,165,167
  Mary Anne 165
  Mary Malinda 167
  Mat 50
  Milton 166
  Nancy 168
  Nora J. 167
  Paul 168
  R.A. 310
  Rachel C. 167
  Richard A. 168
  S. Francis 314
  Samuel 330
  Samuel S. 168
  Sarah 165
  Sarah Jane 37,167
  Sarah Waddel 165
  Temperence 27
  Terrel 167
  Thomas 165,166
  Thomas Twining 165
  Waddy 166
  Warren 166,167
  Whitten A. 166
  William 61,63,149,165,
    166,167,168
Hammett, Jesse 84
  Nancy 84
Hammon, William 333
Hammond, Charles 219
  Frances 5
  Herbert 81,201
  William 278
  William J. 194
  William P. 196
Hampton, Charlotte 169
  Edward 169
  Gale 169
  Joanna 169
  Lucy 169
  Mary 169
  Richard 169

Hawthorne, J.L. 177
  Jane 176,234
  Jasper N. 149,176,177
  Joseph J. 176,177
  L.N. 177
  Luvinia 149,176
  Mary D. 176,177
  Orpha 177
  Polly 234
  Robert 177
  Sarah 176
  Sarah E. 177
  Sarah Jane 176
  Susannah M. 176,177
  William 234
Haynes 159,191
  Amry Adaline 178
  Andrew 178
  Anna M. 241
  Annie M. 178
  Dorcas A. 178
  G.W. 178
  George H. 178
  Harper 178
  Harrison 178
  Hiram 249
  Jesse 178
  John 178
  M.J.F. 178
  Mary 178
  Nancy A. 178
  Nancy J. 178
  Nathaniel 178
  Rebecca 178
  S.P. 178
  Sarah P. 178
  Sheriff 178,305
  Susannah 178
  Taylor 178
  William 234
Hayney, Charles 201
  Stephen 201
Hays, Abram 179
  Anderson 179
  Barbara 178
  Benjamin 179
  Charles H. 179
  Charlotte 179
  David 178,179
  Elijah 179,180
  Eliza 179
  Elizabeth 179
  Henry 343
  James 179
  John N. 179
  Malindy 180
  Malissa 179
  Margaret 179
  Mary 179
  Mary Elizabeth 179
  Milly 121
  Robert 179
  Sarah 180
  Solomon 179
  Thomas 179
  William Fields 180
Hayward, William 89
Hazle, Phill 80
Head, George 30,235
Heard, Armstrong 218
  James 218
  Richard 218
  Stephen 218
  Thomas 218
  William 218
Hearne, Joane 19
Hearse, John 77
Hearst, George 292
  John 77,108,241,257,292
  John W. 197,302
Hearston, James 219
Hembree, I.D. 2
  James 84

Hembree, Margaret 32
  William 32
Hemphill, Mary 195
Henderson, Brasher 46
  David 98,274
  Elbert 160
  Eli 160
  James 190,215,257,306
  Jessee 22
  John 206,216,251
  Ransom 76
  Robert 77
  S. 346
  Samuel 160,333
  Stephen 345
  Thomas 160,206,333
  William 21,98,190,255,
   275
Hendley, Mary 124,126
Hendrick, Abel 120
  Elizabeth 305
  F.E. 148
  John 113
  Julia Ann 113
  Mary C. 273
  Morning Jane 120
  William C. 51
Hendricks, Abel 130
  Barbara 178
  Cynthia Jane 167
  D.E. 132
  David 130,192
  Delar 192
  Elizabeth 67,130
  G.T. 258
  George 148,179,180
  George W. 220
  H.B. 263
  Henry 67
  J.S. 244
  John 51,267
  John M. 49,149
  Larkin 258
  Matthew 279
  Moses 130,178,186,267,
   279,322
  Mourning 130
  Rachel 110
  Rhoda 93
  Rosana 186
  Sephaniah A. 51
  Susan 178
  Susana 279
Hendrix, D.E. 180
  David 196
  James 343
  John M. 199
  Lawrence A. 67
  Mary 192
  Moses 126,305
  Rutha 199
  Sarah 196
Hennery, William 89
Henry, J.E. 81
  Jackson N. 222
  Jemima 42
  Peter 105
  Thomison 42
  William 221
Henson, Anny 87
  Ebenezer 87
  Frances 87
  James 87
  Lloyd 87
  Polly 87
  Rebecca 87
  Richard 87
Herd, D.A. 313
  J.J. 297
  John 16
  Letty 12
  W.E. 313
  William 12

Herdeon, Delphia 334
Herenton, Whitle 284
Herndon, E.L. 202
Heron, Thomas 172
Herren, Thomas 23
Herrin, Ephraim 201
  Fredrick O. 121
Herron, Elijah 291
Hers, John F. 16
Herst, Joseph 293
Hester, A. 18,261
  Alfred 150
  Carwell 196
  Elizabeth E. 74,75
  Henry 74
  James B. 206,207
  L.C. 120
  Loretta 206
  Lucetta 206
  M.F. 244,287,297
  Mary 273
  Mary J. 277
  Mattie A. 185
  Samuel J. 277
  Waddy T. 74
  William 171,258,273
Hicks, Tabitha 4
Hidden, Dave 124
Hide, Charles 46
  Elizabeth 46
  Jacob 46
  Jeremiah 46
  Reuben 46
  Sarah 46
Higginbotham, Joseph 145
Higginbottom, W. 195
Higgins, G.W. 117
  George 212
  John A. 142
  Samuel G. 122
  Samuel Gary 142
High, Nancy 82
  Sarah E. 82
Hightower, John F. 238
Hill, Asaph 97
  B.F. 6
  Caleb 201
  Ewal 76
  Hamilton 36,154
  James 241
  John 81
  Joshua 64,146
  Margaret 132
  Richard 295
  Robert 292,295
  Roswell 46,119,179
  Samuel L. 7,294
  W. 29
  William 174,324
Hillhouse, Elizabeth 89
  William 89,201
Hillian, Margaret 221
  Mary 221
Hillin, T.B.R. 217
Hinkle, Carr 340
  Elias 340
  Elijah 340
  Henry 340
  John 340
  Mark 340
  Martha 340
  Mary 296,297,298
  Silas 340
Hinten, Edney 7
  John 7
Hinton, Cynthia 79
  Elizabeth 114
  J.B. 166
  Jeremiah 283
  S.P. 318
  Thomas 7,114,293,294
Hirons, John 308
Hitt, Henry 33

ORDINARIES

Allen, Orsamus D.
Buist, George
Calhoun, John Ewing
Chambers, Benjamin
Dendy, James H.
Fowke, R.C.
Hagood, James E.
  Johnson
Hall, S.B.
Hamilton, Andrew
  John
Hammond, Herbert
Harris, John
Harvin, R.W.
Hill, William
Kay, Robert M.
Keith, W.L.
Lesly, David
Martin, John
Moore, Alexander
McBee, L.M.
McComb, John
McDaniel, James
Newberry, J.B.
Norton, Miles M.
Parson, W.J.
Philpot, I.H.
Potts, William
Pratt, J.J.
Rice, B.T.
Ross, John M.
Steel, William D.
Taggart, Moses
Taylor, William
Thompson, Henry
  Robert A.
Wardlaw, James
Wilie, Peter
Wilson, John L.

SLAVE INDEX

All are Negro slaves with
the exception of a few
Indian slaves which are
noted.

Aaron 56,70,189,275,300
Abby 333
Abbegale 198
Abel 285
Abin 70
Abner 210,240
Abraham 88,136,137
Abram 61,98,155,302
Absolem 90,303
Acey 284
Achlin 243
Adam 102,173,262
Adaline 237,302
Aenius 257
Affee 289
Affie 89,210
Agga 76,326
Agnis 56,60,243
Albert 219,334
Alcy 98,218
Aleck 96,218
Alexander 128,235,249,302
Alfred 81,249,266,302
Alice 221
Alick 174
Allen 249,252
Ally 305
Amanda 64,86,235,334
Amelia 64
Amoral 284
Amos 122
Amy 60,81,89,106,133,144,
  218
Anderson 60,165,252
Andrew 81,170,198,243
Andy 300
Angeline 235
Anger 283
Ann 56,62,72,82,86,90,129,
  163,217,218,219,275,333,
  334
Ann Mariah 163
Annely 90
Annica 189,217,302,305
Anthony 129,165,217,238,
  300
April 308
Arch 170
Armstead 189
Arrena 75
Asbury 235
Augustus 129,136,249
Auber 198
Austin 86,106
Balass 130,345
Bambora 284
Barbara 135,136,137
Basil 238
Bathsheba 86
Beck 70,76,84,198
Belton 221
Ben 56,72,84,96,98,116,
  122,184,232,249,302,
  312,333,345
Berry 88,165,243
Berry Carolina 158
Bess 135
Beth Rachel 285
Bethany 177
Betsey 122,135,136,137,
  198,228,334
Betty 64,95,99,135,152,
  189,210,241,262,284
Beverly 129

www.ingramcontent.com/pod-product-compliance
Lightning Source LLC
Chambersburg PA
CBHW021844020426
42334CB00013B/183